# RUSSIA
## *A History of the Soviet Period*
### Second Edition

**Woodford McClellan**
University of Virginia

PRENTICE HALL, Englewood Cliffs, New Jersey 07632

*Library of Congress Cataloging-in-Publication Data*

MCCLELLAN, WOODFORD.
   Russia: a history of the Soviet period / Woodford McClellan.—
   2nd ed.

    p. cm.
   Bibliography: p.
   Includes index.
   ISBN 0-13-784505-7
   1. Soviet Union—History—1917–   I. Title.
DK266.M357 1990       89-35144
                 CIP

Editorial/production supervision and
interior design: **KATHLEEN SCHIAPARELLI**
Manufacturing buyer: **CAROL BYSTROM**

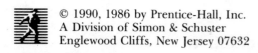

© 1990, 1986 by Prentice-Hall, Inc.
A Division of Simon & Schuster
Englewood Cliffs, New Jersey 07632

Printed in the United States of America

10 9 8 7 6 5 4 3 2 1

ISBN 0-13-784505-7

PRENTICE-HALL INTERNATIONAL (UK) LIMITED, *London*
PRENTICE-HALL OF AUSTRALIA PTY. LIMITED, *Sydney*
PRENTICE-HALL CANADA INC., *Toronto*
PRENTICE-HALL HISPANOAMERICANA, S.A., *Mexico*
PRENTICE-HALL OF INDIA PRIVATE LIMITED, *New Delhi*
PRENTICE-HALL OF JAPAN, INC., *Tokyo*
SIMON & SCHUSTER ASIA PTE. LTD., *Singapore*
EDITORA PRENTICE-HALL DO BRASIL, LTDA., *Rio de Janeiro*

# CONTENTS

# 3
## Civil War and Intervention    35

# 4
## The Bolshevization of Russia    52

# 5
## Economic Reform and Political Constriction, 1921–1927    65

# 6
## The Way They Were: Life in the 1920s    82

# 7
## Foreign Policy in the 1920s    100

# 8
## Stalin's Revolution, 1924–1932    114

# 9
# The Great Terror    129

# 10
# Russia in the 1930s    144

# 11
# Foreign Policy in the 1930s    158

# 12
# The Great Fatherland War    174

# 13
# The Cold War    194

# 14
# The Late Stalin Years    207

# 15
## The "Thaw"   223

# 16
## The Great Reform: Khrushchev and "De-Stalinization"   237

# 17
## Reform Era Foreign Policy   249

# 18
## Internal Affairs in the Reform Era   266

# 19
## Rule of the Troika, 1964–1971   282

# PREFACE
# TO THE SECOND EDITION

The Soviets have added whole new wings to their national memory palace, and have unceremoniously demolished others that stood useless over many decades, since the appearance of the first edition of this book in January 1986. Among the extraordinary developments of the Gorbachev era is an unprecedented explosion of uncensored information about Soviet history; this new edition seeks to incorporate and analyze the new material. In addition to a new introduction designed to ease the reader into the great flow of Russian and Soviet history, I have rewritten sections of all chapters. Readers who compare the two editions will note that the revelations that have come out of the USSR since 1985 have in most instances confirmed the arguments presented in the first.

Two new chapters appear here, on the Andropov-Chernenko interlude and the first few years of Gorbachev's administration. The economics of publishing, as Steve Dalphin, executive editor at Prentice Hall, explains them to me, demand that subtractions match additions; and so I have eliminated two chapters and portions of others.

The first edition listed dozens of Soviet works in English; because the Soviets are furiously rewriting their history, the second eliminates all but a handful of such references. I have revised and updated the bibliography of Western sources in English and have again tried to provide a comprehensive index.

Beyond expressing my deeply felt gratitude to Steve Dalphin, who has sponsored this book from the beginning, I wish to record my thanks to my production editor for the second edition, Kathleen Schiaparelli, and to the many colleagues and students in the United States and abroad who have used the first edition and have written to me with suggestions for improving the second. Special thanks to reviewers Jane E. Good of the U.S. Naval Academy and Neil Weissman of Dickinson College. I am grateful to Thomas T. Hammond, the *New York Times,* the *Washington Post,* AP/Wide World Photos, and Russica Publishers for permission to use illustrative materials. Finally, Irina McClellan helped gather information on *glasnost* including a major unpublished essay by Vladimir Soloukhin, carefully reviewed the new chapters, and gave her husband invaluable advice.

*W.M.*
*Alexandria, Virginia*

# RUSSIA
## *A History of the Soviet Period*

Map of the USSR. Russian Soviet Federative Socialist Republic (RSFSR): (1) Bashkir Autonomous Soviet Socialist Republic; (2) Daghestan ASSR; (3) Kabardin-Balkar ASSR; (4) Kalmyk ASSR; (5) Karellan ASSR; (6) Mari ASSR; (7) Mordovian ASSR; (8) North Ossetian ASSR (cap. Ordzhonikidze); (9) Tatar ASSR; (10) Tuva ASSR; (11) Udmurt ASSR; (12) Chechen-Ingush ASSR; (13) Chuvash ASSR; (14) Advgel Autonomous Region; (15) Gorno-Altai Autonomous Region; (16) Jewish Autonomous Region; (17) Karachal-Circassian Autonomous Region; (18) Khakass Autonomous Region; (19) Nenets Autonomous Area; (20) Komi-Permyak Autonomous Area; (21) Ust-Ordynsk Buryat Autonomous Area; (22) Aginski Buryat Autonomous Area; (23) Kaliningrad Region, I. Byelorussian Soviet Socialist Republic, II. Uzbek SSR; (24) Kara-Kalpak ASSR, III. Georgian SSR; (25) Abkhasian ASSR; (26) Adzhar ASSR; (27) South Ossetian Autonomous Region (cap. Tskhinvali), IV. Azerbaijan SSR; (28) Nakhichevan ASSR; (29) Nagorno-Karabakh Autonomous Region (cap. Stepanakert); V. Lithuanian SSR, VI. Moldavian SSR, VII. Latvian SSR, VIII. Kirghiz SSR, IX. Tajik SSR; (30) Gorno-Badakhshan Autonomous Region, X. Armenian SSR, XI. Estonian SSR.

# 1

# TOWARD OCTOBER

The West's relative unfamiliarity with Russian history stems in no small measure from its lack of knowledge of the Eastern Roman or Byzantine Empire, which survived more than a thousand years after the Visigoths sacked and burned Rome. Heir to the glories of ancient Greece as well as those of Rome, in terms of cultural level, wealth, size, and ethnic diversity, Byzantium had no rival in the West during the first nine centuries of its existence.

When the Byzantine capital, Constantinople, or New Rome, fell to the Ottoman Turks in 1453, a small East Slav principality assumed the dignity and burden of leadership of the Eastern Orthodox Christian community. In time, some of that state's leading clerics would advance the claim that God had designated its chief city, Moscow, to be the Third and Final Rome, its prince the Defender of the True Faith.

## THE ORIGINS OF RUSSIA

Toward the end of the 10th century, the pagan East Slavs from whom the Russians are descended accepted Christianity from Eastern Orthodox priests-missionaries under the authority of the Patriarch of Constantinople. Clergy from Rome were not in a competition that included—according to legend—Islamic mullahs (religious scholars) and rabbis. The mullahs came from the Middle East, the rabbis from the only state other than Israel ever to adopt Judaism as its official religion, Turkic Khazaria on the lower Volga. When the Eastern and Western branches of the Universal Catholic Church split in 1054, the newly Christianized East Slavs remained faithful to Eastern Orthodoxy. Rome and Constantinople exchanged excommunications, anathemas, denunciations. Nearly a millennium later, the wounds still fester.

Because of the church schism, the East Slavs—modern Russians, Ukrainians, and Byelorussians—and all other Eastern Orthodox communicants (modern Greeks, Bulgarians, Romanians, Serbs, and others) did not experience at firsthand the Renaissance, the Reformation, or the Counter-Reformation. They did not know the teachings of St. Thomas Aquinas, Blaise Pascal, Erasmus of Rotterdam. They benefitted only belatedly from the 17th-century scientific revolution and but imperfectly— through the prism of Byzantine-oriental experience—from the Enlightenment.

Founded by Scandinavian adventurers-traders and native Slav princelings, the first East Slav state, Rus, the fortified town of Kiev on the Dnepr River and its hinterland, grew from humble beginnings in the eighth and ninth centuries into a thriving principality. Byzantium accorded it full diplomatic recognition, Hungary and France contracted dynastic marriages with its rulers, and in the 11th century its religious institutions were fully integrated into those of Eastern Orthodoxy.

Then came the Mongol invasion of the early 13th century. Kiev Rus, already in decline because rivalry among various princes—and in some areas embryonic democratic institutions—had thwarted the rise of a powerful central monarchy, collapsed under the weight of these last, most powerful conquerors from inner Asia. Part of the population fled the southern steppes (prairies) to the forests of the northeast, to the "mesopotamia" of the triangle formed by the upper Volga and two smaller rivers, the Moscow and the Oka.

The refugees from Kiev Rus blended with indigenous Finnic peoples and others to forge the modern Great Russian ethnic group. Those who remained behind on the Dnepr and its tributaries became the modern Ukrainians, those west of the "mesopotamia" and east of medieval Poland became the Byelorussians or White Russians.

The peoples who moved to the northeast slowly built a principality whose capital took the name of the river on which it was located, Moscow. Toward the end of the 15th century that principality, known to the West as Muscovy, finally shook off the last vestiges of vassal status vis-à-vis the descendants of Genghis Khan. A succession of capable rulers warded off threats from various foreign enemies, including the powerful Polish-Lithuanian state, and in the second half of the 16th century the ruler known as Ivan the Terrible extended Muscovite territory beyond the east bank of the Volga. Muscovite explorers and a few settlers spread over vast Siberia.

By 1613, when a new dynasty began its reign in Muscovy, Europeans who lived west of the Oder, the Morava, and the upper Danube knew more about the Western Hemisphere than about the kingdom on the Moscow River. This had not changed when the Romanov dynasty fell 304 years later.

Social and economic relations in Kiev Rus differed from those of contemporary Western Christian principalities and kingdoms only in that they were more progressive. The hallmark of the citizen was freedom rather than serfdom, the capitalist market developed absolutely normally, and rulers vied for power with both an aristocracy descended from ancient princely retinues and—especially in the rich sub-principalities Novgorod and Pskov—unruly proto-democratic town councils.

The Mongol invasion and protracted rule over the East Slavs changed all this. Individually and ultimately collectively, the tiny successor principalities—Moscow was but one of a couple of dozen—were swept inexorably into the vortex of centralized power. From commoners and aristocrats alike, the central authorities collected tribute due the Great Khan. Commoners who could not otherwise pay their share of these and other, purely local, levies found themselves reduced from freeholders to serfs of the state or of private landlords. Aristocrats fallen on hard times attached themselves to a prince, agreeing to become his vassals in return for protection and recognition of their social standing vis-à-vis the free peasantry, minuscule free town population, and growing class of serfs.

As Mongol power stabilized, became complacent, and began to decline, the central authority in some principalities organized military operations aimed at establishing independence. A decisive victory came in 1380, the final rout of Mongol forces a century later; princes from Moscow led both campaigns. By the late 15th century Muscovy had brought most of Central Russia's principalities under its sway.

Mongol rule foreclosed continuation in Muscovy of the Kiev Rus tradition of limited princely power checked by aristocracy and free commoners. Nearly 260 years of submission to a foreign conqueror forged a new system born of the dual Byzantine-Mongol heritage: Byzantium knew no form of government other than autocracy, the Mongol Horde only the Great Khan's despotic rule. The Romanovs came to the Muscovite throne as personalistic rulers whose decisions outweighed all law and brooked no counterclaim. At a time when Western Europe hovered on the verge of intellectual developments that would topple divine-right monarchs from their thrones, Muscovy was putting the final touches on an autocracy based on the submission to the crown of a serf-owning aristocracy.

## MODERN RUSSIA

Russia entered the modern world an Eastern Catholic country driven by the quest for power more than the search for wealth. She would never know a genuine bourgeois-capitalist stage of history because she would not know Protestantism; the names Martin Luther and John Calvin mean no more to Russia than those of Nil Sorsky and Joseph of Volokolamsk to the West. A Byzantine-Mongol rather than a Protestant ethic would guide Russia.

This is not to say that Russia would not be part of the world capitalist economy. Kiev Rus had participated in that economy; after the collosal dislocations of the Mongol period, Muscovy resumed the process in the 16th century. But until the 20th century, Russia would not achieve a fully articulated capitalist mode of production.

The Muscovite tsar (or czar, deriving from "caesar") was First Landlord as well as ruler, and that made him First Capitalist, land being the chief form of capital. Peter the Great—under whose rule from the late 17th century until 1725 Muscovy became the Russian Empire—retained the political attributes of his predecessors but tried to revolutionize society and the economy. Russia could not compete on the world market, he realized, by exporting agricultural and forestry products and importing manufactured goods—i.e., by being a colony. But as he set out to develop manufacturing in Russia, Peter did not follow the European example of permitting native entrepreneurs free rein; he himself became First Businessman.

The state rather than private capital financed the establishment of about 90 factories during Peter's reign, at the end of which only 191 such enterprises existed in the country. Moreover, as the *glasnost*-era Soviet scholar Vasily Selyunin has pointed out, Peter created "something unprecedented in history: a serf working class." Previously, only the crown and private landlords had the right to own serfs. Along with credits, technical expertise in the form of hired foreign specialists, and extensive bureaucratic oversight, Peter extended that right to factory owners.

Peter's successors down to the end of the 19th century continued and extended the state's financial and bureaucratic interference in the economy. With an assured supply of labor and capital that normally guaranteed profits, manufacturers had no incentive to modernize, seek innovations, expand. Coddled and protected from the vagaries of domestic and world markets by the state, such entrepreneurs could no more carry out an industrial revolution than Russia's serf-owning landlords could duplicate the productivity of Western farmers. Matching British iron output ton for ton in the late 18th century, Russian producers doubled production in the next 50 years, but their British counterparts increased tonnage 2,900 percent. The heavy hand of bureaucracy stunted the growth of the economy as surely as it prevented the modernization of the machinery of state.

## RED HORIZONS

Paradoxically, class conflicts worsened in Russia after the formal emancipation of the serfs in 1861–1863. Juridically free, millions remained economically bound to the lands they worked, obligated to make "redemption" payments, i.e., to pay the state—which had compensated the landlords for the loss of serf labor—for their freedom. The peasants detested the payments and despised the government bureaucrats who took over police and fiscal functions from the landlords. Still loyal to the "good" tsar in St. Petersburg, the peasants coveted the vast lands of the crown and the Russian Orthodox Church.

A nation whose history was so marked by strife was almost certain one day to undergo a major social upheaval. As foreign invasions, more than any other single factor, had spawned the highly centralized, despotic rule of the tsars, so did the violence of the tsars and landlords against the peasantry generate periodic convulsions in the countryside. Peasant rebellions, however, produced more bloodshed than social reform, and it was not peasant violence but rather the threat of it that led to the Emancipation. The liberation of the serfs brought great changes, but in many important respects the peasants merely exchanged one set of masters, the landlords, for another, the bureaucratic state.

These historical patterns and the absence of industrial capitalism made Russia the despair of Western Marxists. Toward the end of his life Marx himself, pressed by his tiny handful of Russian disciples, toyed with the idea that agrarian Russia might somehow leap across the gulf that separated it from industrialized Europe and America and become the first nation to make a socialist revolution. He never worked out a coherent position on the issue, however, and he maintained that no matter what happened in Russia, no revolution there could survive unless there were simultaneous upheavals in the West. His insistence on Russia's dependence on Western developments was to color Bolshevik ideology well into the 1920s.

Russians who made an effort to reconcile Marxist theory with Russian reality had adopted a fundamentalist position, interpreting Marx literally: only a fully industrialized country, which would obviously have a large working class, could make a socialist (proletarian) revolution. It followed that revolution in Russia, a country just beginning to industrialize, was generations away.

The leader of the Russian Marxists, Vladimir Ilich Ulyanov, known to history by his revolutionary *nom de guerre*, Lenin, rejected this view. Basing his projections on an optimistic assessment of the strength and political consciousness of the Russian proletariat and a creative reading of Marx's random thoughts, he concluded that revolution could take place in Russia in the not-too-distant future. A strong revolutionary party could prepare the way through propaganda, education, agitation, and political leadership. History itself would supply the critical complex of events—economic depression, war, breakdown in government—that would force a crisis.

This man Lenin was born at Simbirsk on the middle Volga on April 10, 1870 (April 22 in the West—Russia used the Julian calendar until 1918), one of six children of a middle-level state bureaucrat. His mother was German and quite possibly German-Jewish on both sides of her family. His paternal grandmother came from the Mongol Kalmyk people; his paternal grandfather was either Kalmyk or Tatar. Lenin thus almost certainly had little or no Russian blood in him.

In May 1887 Lenin's older brother Aleksandr and four of his associates were hanged for plotting to assassinate Tsar Aleksandr III. Enrolling a few months later at Kazan University, Lenin read law, philosophy . . . and the works of Karl Marx. By 1890 he had become a Marxist determined to make a revolution. As a Marxist, he could not take his brother's execution into account as he shaped his view of history, which moves in majestically impartial ways indifferent to the fate of any individual. But as a human being he could hardly forget that scaffold in St. Petersburg. As some historians believe Genghis Khan's enormous conquests vengeance for the ill treatment of his family and clan, so several modern specialists see Lenin obsessed by a desire to avenge his brother's blood; no satisfactory biography of Lenin exists.

In 1892 Lenin took and passed the bar examination by correspondence. In September 1893 he arrived in St. Petersburg to begin a clerkship with an established attorney.

He practiced law, but most of his prodigious energy was expended on the study, discussion, and propagation of Marxism and revolution. He became convinced that the misery he saw all around him in tsarist Russia could be overcome not through peaceful reform but only by violent revolution. His interpretation of Marx's theories had convinced him that there would be war between the classes. He joined a Marxist circle composed of disciples of the leading Russian Marxist, G. V. Plekhanov, then in exile in the West, and tested his own ideas against those of the St. Petersburg intellectuals.

He had not yet solved the vexing problem of terror. Not surprisingly, given his own youth and his brother's fate, he clung to the illusion that the teachings and practical experience of The People's Will might be useful to a Marxist party. But nothing Marx ever said or wrote dovetailed with the kind of terror advocated and practiced by some of the revolutionary Russian populists: Lenin was confusing the style with the goal. The single-minded dedication to a cause, the secrecy, the tight organization, the irresistible élan of the People's Will—*these* were the qualities needed in a revolutionary party.

The party which Lenin forged over the years 1903–1917 would display these traits in full measure. Before he created it, however, he changed his position and expressly rejected individual acts of terror as useless from a practical standpoint and profoundly un-Marxist. If the removal of a few officials could overthrow a society, one could hardly maintain that that society had been produced and could be destroyed only by impersonal historic forces. But this majestic, implacable march of history was the quintessence of Marxist theory; Lenin had no choice but to reject terror directed against individuals.

After the 1905 Revolution, however, he would insist that "revolutionary class terror" was fully consonant with Marxism. He would also maintain that the peasants, millions of whom supported a party one of whose wings actively preached and practiced terror, the Socialist Revolutionaries or SRs, could play a revolutionary role in history. This did considerable violence to Marx, who never advocated any kind of terror and who considered the peasantry a hopelessly reactionary class from which nothing positive, and much that was negative, was to be expected.

It was neither the first nor the last time Lenin proved himself ideologically flexible, able to promote new and qualitatively different products under reliable old labels. He considered himself the most consistent of Marxists, yet his whole career after 1905 demonstrated his willingness to modify theory when tactical considerations demanded.

Arrested in 1895 for revolutionary and strike activity, two years later Lenin was exiled to a remote Siberian village. It is ironic that exile provided him with a peaceful, productive interlude. He married Nadezhda Krupskaya; carried on a wide political correspondence; wrote a major work, *The Development of Capitalism in Russia;* hiked, hunted, and fished; did some minor legal work for the locals; and took the name Lenin ("Lena River man") from the region where he lived.

By 1905 Lenin had worked out his strategy of revolution. He believed that the events of that year in Russia confirmed its correctness and helped produce a major new tactic, the formation of an alliance between the workers and the poorest stratum of the peasantry. Less than a decade later, millions of Russian peasants and workers would be in uniform, fighting and dying for a tsarist regime that could offer them no better fate. Ultimately they would in despair forge the alliance Lenin sought.

New and potentially more dangerous class antagonisms quickly developed when capitalism swooped down upon the Empire with a rush in the 1890s. Peasants fleeing the impoverished countryside flocked to the cities to find jobs, but they also encountered misery and degradation worse than that they had known in the "hungry village" eloquently depicted by Russian writers. The peasants who had tolerated landlord rule and privilege for centuries, only occasionally rising up in short-lived insurrections, became implacably angry men once they entered the ranks of the landless, rootless, industrial proletariat.

Unlike its counterpart in the industrialized West, the working class of the Russian Empire did not experience two generations of essentially leaderless development in which it was at the mercy of the entrepreneurs and the state. The Russian workers were from the beginning influenced by professional revolutionaries. This proletariat, the newest in the world, quickly won a reputation as a work force singularly disinclined to submit to management. The peasant transplanted to the city had become an aggressive rebel who regularly showed his distaste for the 11½ hour working day—a frequently ignored legal maximum established in 1897—by beating up foremen, wrecking machinery, and illegally going out on strike. The peasant's refusal to submit to capital and state the way his ancestors had submitted to the landlords was grist for the Socialist mill. In the Revolution of 1905, 93.2 percent of all enterprises were struck at least once. The proletariat had matured quickly; and there were those among the Socialists who correctly gauged its revolutionary potential.

The Marxists preached class struggle and revolution, exhorting workers to rise up against their masters and seize not just factories but control of the state. Hostile or indifferent to the peasantry, as most Marxist parties then were, the Russian Social-Democratic Labor party (RSDLP), founded in the period 1898–1903, concentrated its propaganda and organizational activities among the workers. The aggressive, impatient wing of that party broke with the more gradualist elements in 1903 to form the Bolshevik (Majoritarian) faction of the RSDLP; the cautious Russian Marxists formed the Menshevik (Minoritarian) wing.

The January 9(22) "Bloody Sunday" massacre of peaceful working-class demonstrators in St. Petersburg touched off the Revolution of 1905. In that great upheaval the two RSDLP factions together won the allegiance of the urban workers but had little impact on the countryside. Russia experienced enormous turmoil throughout the year, however, as the middle class, shocked by "Bloody Sunday," came forward with demands for reform. Urban elements in general, excepting the rich, voiced their discontent with the regime. Some factory owners, determined to secure state concessions to business and industry, continued to pay striking workers. Finally, in October, an 11-day general strike—the most massive such work stoppage in modern history—brought the regime to its knees.

Nicholas II was forced to establish a parliament, extend the franchise, guarantee civil liberties: his October Manifesto blunted the revolutionary impetus and split the opposition. The middle class, its revolutionism satisfied by the reforms, accepted the tsar's promises at face value and affirmed its loyalty to the crown. The entrepreneurs won the regime's assurance of an improved climate for capitalist development. But the workers, their illusions badly shaken, remained hostile to the regime and late in the year launched armed uprisings in several cities. The most serious conflict took place in Moscow in December and ended only after more than a thousand people had been killed.

A key element in the labor equation in 1905 was the emergence of workers' Soviets, or councils. Such organizations, spontaneous creations of working class despair that were quickly seized and shaped by Socialists, arose in many cities; the most famous and important was the St. Petersburg Soviet, which won immense authority in the capital and the country at large. For several weeks in the autumn of 1905 it was the only authority recognized by hundreds of thousands of workers. Its chief spokesman and later its chairman was a young Socialist using the name Yanovsky. His real name was Bronstein; he is best known as Leon Trotsky.

No less skeptical of the October Manifesto than the workers, the peasants were unorganized and accustomed to sinking back into a resigned torpor after a revolutionary outburst. After 1905 they were slowly reduced to submission by a regime which imprisoned or hanged troublemakers and assisted the most prosperous peasants to enrich themselves further.

The tsarist regime survived the Revolution and there was every indication, by 1914, that Nicholas's reforms—many drastically modified after the crisis passed—had succeeded in shoring up tsarism and capitalism against a repetition of the events of 1905. Marxist leaders despaired of seeing another great upheaval in their lifetimes. But should the time come when the great peasant masses (80 percent of the population) would act simultaneously with the workers, however, revolution in Russia might well have a different outcome.

## RUSSIA AND THE WAR

When Austria-Hungary resolved to avenge the June 1914 murder of Archduke Franz Ferdinand in Bosnia by invading Serbia, suspected of supporting the Bosnian Serb assassins, Nicholas II and his circle saw an unacceptable threat to Russian national interests. The Austrian attack upon Slavic Serbia, Russia's ally, could not be tolerated. The long series of humiliations had to end somewhere: the Crimean War, the Congress of Berlin, the 1908 Austrian annexation of Bosnia-Herzegovina—these and other defeats had tarnished Russia's honor, compromised her reputation as a great power. Nicholas and his advisers decided to go to war despite the certainty that Russia would have to fight not only the Habsburg Empire but also its ally, the mighty German Reich.

The outbreak of what was until 1939 called the Great War signalled the beginning of a new and uncertain era in Russian history. Despite the fervent prayers of thousands of people who knelt in Palace Square in August 1914 to pledge their lives to God and tsar, the important early victories went to the Germans. Russia could hold her own against Austria-Hungary, but she could not compete on equal terms with the armed might of industrialized Germany. After enormous losses in East Prussia in August and September, it was, as we can see in hindsight, all over. The Russians did not have commanders of the caliber of Hindenburg and Ludendorff, the German generals. Worse than that, they had nothing worth fighting

and dying for. The Romanovs and tsarism would not survive the war.

Military disasters followed each other in rapid succession and only the fact that her enemies were fighting on two fronts saved Russia from annihilation in 1914. In 1915 Britain and France, fearing that their Russian ally might pull out of the war, promised Nicholas Constantinople, control of which had long been a goal of Russian foreign policy. Just what he would do with it was not clear, but much more blood was shed, and the Russian earth soaked it up greedily. It would never be replenished, nor would the abolition of the monarchy or the demise of the aristocracy ever atone for it.

## THE FEBRUARY REVOLUTION

In 1917 there were antigovernment and antiwar demonstrations around the country on the anniversary of "Bloody Sunday," and the demonstrators also protested the critical food situation. The manifestation in Petrograd, as St. Petersburg was renamed in 1914, was the largest and most important, with nearly 150,000 workers on strike. Serious interruptions of production and street marches also took place in Moscow, Baku, Harkov, Nizhny Novgorod, and elsewhere. More demonstrations followed on February 23 (March 8), the day generally acknowledged as marking the formal beginning of the Russian Revolutions of 1917. The next day, more than 200,000 Petrograd workers went out on strike, and many marched down Nevsky Prospekt crying "Down with the war!" and "Down with the autocracy!" and singing revolutionary songs. They demanded food.

Nicholas II, Tsar of all the Russias and Autocrat, was at General Staff Headquarters at Mogilyov in White Russia. His beloved, empty-headed Alexandra wrote to him on February 25 (March 10) that all would be well if only the Duma, the parliament created by the 1905 Revolution, behaved itself. But by this time nothing depended upon the Duma. Demonstrations and strikes continued, people gathered around bonfires at intersections and listened to fiery political speakers. The police were strangely indifferent.

The tsar basically agreed with his wife's assessment of the situation. He ordered General S. S. Khabalov, commander of the Petrograd Military District, to put down the "inexcusable" disturbances. The autocrat had spoken. It might have been Ivan the Terrible expressing his will in Red Square in the 16th century.

The turmoil showed no sign of abating and for lack of any better policy Nicholas ordered the dismissal of the Duma. But the citizens of Petrograd, not the tsar, would decide the issue. They revived the Petrograd Soviet and entered the Tauride Palace *en masse* to demand that the deputies formally certify the existence of a new order. Naturally no one knew what the new order was, but hundreds of thousands of people knew beyond any doubt, by the afternoon of February 27 (March 12), 1917, that the *old* order was no more.

A Temporary Executive Committee of the Soviet of Workers' Deputies came into existence. It immediately issued an invitation to the workers and soldiers of the capital to elect deputies to the Petrograd Soviet, the first meeting of which was scheduled for that evening. The process of creating Soviets in the various military units was already under way. Conservative deputies formed a Provisional Committee of Members of the State Duma for the Restoration of Order in Petrograd and for [the Establishment of] Relations with Institutions and Functionaries.

With the revival of the Petrograd Soviet and the creation of the Provisional Committee of the Duma, the Revolution formally sanctioned its own existence. It was now impossible to reverse the flow of events. Frantically trying to do *something*, General Khabalov called on one unit after another to obey the tsar's order to crush the demonstrations; each unit in turn declined to recognize the tsar's authority. On the night of the 27th–28th (March 12–13), Khabalov and 2,000 or so loyal troops took refuge first in the Winter Palace, then the Admiralty, and finally just melted away into the early morning gloom.

In Moscow the Mensheviks, best-organized of the radical parties, spurred the formation on February 27 of a Provisional Revolutionary Committee. It was open to all who supported the Revolution; the next day, several Bolsheviks were co-opted onto it. Mass demonstrations and meetings took place all over the city, especially in working-class districts. On the 28th, armed workers and a few soldiers seized the prisons and released the political prisoners. A Workers' and Soldiers' Soviet quickly came into existence.

Spontaneous creations of the working class and the soldiery, Soviets appeared all over the country: by late spring there were 600. In the beginning they were invariably controlled by some combination of Mensheviks, Trudoviks, and SRs. The Mensheviks projected a calm, reasoned, and progressive message to the workers, while the SRs and Trudoviks were agrarian socialist parties which appealed to peasants. The Bolsheviks ran fourth, but in the cities they already had strong positions in many of the factory committees—one of the major sources of delegates to the Soviets.

The rest of Russia followed the lead of revolutionary Petrograd. In many areas the pent-up pressures of nationalism blended with and helped shape political and class trends; this was especially true in Finland, the Baltic region, and the Ukraine. The Muslim peoples of Central Asia began to stir, and the ancient Christian civilizations in Georgia and Armenia found new hope for deliverance from colonial status.

All afternoon on March 2(15) telegrams poured into the imperial train's communications center. Military commanders who had tirelessly proclaimed loyalty to the tsar now unanimously advised abdication. Late in the evening, two deputies from the old Duma arrived to plead with Nicholas to step down. After an exhausting conversation the tsar agreed.

The news was published the next day: after 304 years, the Romanov dynasty had come to an end. The tsar proceeded to Tsarskoe Selo near Petrograd and rejoined his family, which was placed under gentle house arrest for its own protection. Nicholas was back home where he was happiest, and life went on pretty much as before, albeit with less pomp and ceremony.

## PROVISIONAL GOVERNMENT

On the recommendation of its Menshevik-SR leadership, the Soviet's Executive Committee approved the formation on March 2(15) of a Provisional government controlled by the middle-class Kadet and Octobrist parties. Prince G. E. Lvov was to be prime minister. Several members of his cabinet were big landowners or industrialists; the lone Socialist was Aleksandr Kerensky, minister of justice.

History has judged the Provisional government harshly. It changed over the spring and summer as more Socialists entered it, however, and was never merely the servant of the upper classes. Anxious to please all sectors of society, it tried to reconcile peasant and landowner, worker and capitalist,

soldier and officer, rich and poor. This was impossible, but freedom confused everyone in Russia in 1917. Those who had power sometimes did not recognize it. No one knew where power came from, how long it would last, whether it bore any resemblance to power as Russia had known it for a thousand years. Democracy was a concept alien to the Russian experience: was it people shouting in the streets, decorous debate in the Duma, committees of workers and soldiers, or something else?

In the first few months after the February Revolution all sectors of Russian society supported the Provisional government. All Socialist parties and most Soviets backed the new regime; before Lenin's return from exile even the Bolsheviks gave it their support. The crucial, overriding issue on which the government would come to grief was the war. Had it carried out a land reform and acceded to all labor's demands it would surely have fallen anyway because it refused to abandon the war effort, unable to understand that Russia could no longer fight.

## ORDER NO. 1

No one in the Provisional government knew what the Petrograd Soviet was beyond the fact that no official decision was valid unless the Soviet approved it: this was "dual power." The government represented a link with the tradition of more or less orderly administration of the nation's affairs, while the Soviet embodied the spontaneous, elemental popular forces that had overthrown the old order. Establishing itself as a kind of inspectorate-general of political and social policy, the Soviet pursued an ambivalent line that now demanded democratic reforms, now meekly went along with policies manifestly not in the best interests of labor or the soldiers.

The most urgent problem facing the Petrograd Soviet was the proper care of the masses of soldiers roaming the streets. The Provisional Committee of the Duma had ordered the troops to return to their barracks and obey their officers. Many soldiers took this as a move to restore the old order; they wanted no part of that. The Executive Committee of the Soviet discussed the matter at length and produced a document stating its position.

The Petrograd Soviet's Order No. 1, the old army's death warrant, was distributed throughout the city in leaflet form on the night of March 1–2(14–15). It provided for the election of soldiers' committees in all units; for the election of soldiers' representatives to the Petrograd Soviet; for soldiers' control of weapons; and for full civil rights for soldiers including civilized treatment by officers. It also specified that the soldiers would obey the Military Commission of the government only when its orders did not conflict with those of the Petrograd Soviet.

Order No. 1 made it all but impossible for any authority other than the Soviet to control the soldiers. Nothing in existing law or tradition gave it the slightest legality, but it spoke with the clarity and force of the Revolution itself and was received by the troops with something akin to reverence. The officers, on the other hand, were horrified. And when a few days later the new government announced its firm intention to continue the "vigorous" prosecution of the war, the confusion knew no bounds. The army had been democratized; would there now be voting in each unit on the wisdom of attacking the enemy? The logic of the order indicated that this was not such a far-fetched possibility. Not only were soldiers to control the weapons and quartermaster functions of their units, they were also to have the right to dismiss "undesirable" officers.

This was no longer an army; but then,

Russia had just about ceased to be a nation. It was now a question of sorting out the strongest waves in the revolutionary tide. In the first week of March, the clear winner was the Petrograd Soviet.

## BOLSHEVIKS

According to their own figures, which seem greatly to exaggerate their strength, the Bolsheviks had only 24,000 members at the beginning of March. But the core party was composed of professional revolutionaries who could put many times their own number into the streets in a peaceful or—if the need arose—a violent demonstration. This discipline was one factor that made the Bolsheviks stronger than numbers indicate. Another was their revolutionary audacity, which would increase dramatically after Lenin's return to Russia. In an incredible period when hundreds of thousands of people went into Petrograd's streets every day just to see what was going on; when political speeches and harangues were heard on every street corner for the first time in Russian history; when nearly everybody addressed everybody else as "comrade"; when the hated "Pharaohs" (policemen) disappeared from the streets, giving way to joyful young men and women with red armbands; when democracy and equality were in the air and the war seemed distant and surely soon to end—when all this was going on, it was a good time to be a Bolshevik. Thousands of workers and soldiers and sailors rushed to join what was known to be an élite party. In an atmosphere of radical change, this was the most radical organization of all. By the second week in May, Bolshevik membership passed the 100,000 mark.

Lenin was in Zürich when the news came. He immediately conceived the idea of traveling to Russia via neutral Sweden, but at first the Germans would not let him cross their territory. Protracted negotiations, however, led to the organization of a journey in a "sealed" train across Germany to Sweden. Lenin, Krupskaya, Grigory Zinoviev, Karl Radek and several others left late in March for Petrograd. It was clearly in Germany's interest to have an antiwar politician of Lenin's caliber on the scene in Russia, but historians have been unable to determine whether Lenin did in fact, as his enemies have charged, accept far greater assistance from Berlin than a mere train ride.

At 11:10 p.m. on April 3(16), 1917, Lenin and his colleagues stepped off the train at the Finland Station in Petrograd. In a speech he greeted the "victorious Russian Revolution," which he called the first shock of the great social earthquake that would soon strike all capitalist countries. World revolution, he declared, was at hand.

The speech prefigured the one he gave a couple of hours later at Bolshevik headquarters. Members of the party's Central Committee had assembled to welcome him; he proceeded to castigate them severely. It was time, he said, to stop congratulating themselves on making a revolution and get on with the work of transforming the bourgeois-democratic revolution into a Socialist one. Like everyone else, the Bolsheviks were still drunk with freedoms never experienced by Russians; their leader's words were like jets of ice-water.

Three days after his arrival Lenin published his "April Theses" in which he declared that Russia must simply stop fighting. An imperialist war remained just that, no matter what the Provisional government called it. A "revolutionary war" to defend Russian territory would be permissible on condition that political power first pass to the Soviets, and that annexations and indemnities were renounced. From this it followed that workers, peasants, and soldiers must withdraw their support from the government and transfer all power to the Soviets. Further, Lenin called not for a parliamentary republic but for a "republic of Soviets." He would abolish police, army, bureaucracy. A popular militia would replace the army; it was not clear what, if anything, would fulfill the functions of police and bureaucracy. He would immediately nationalize all land, permitting local Soviets to distribute it to the peasants. He urged his followers to rename themselves Communists.

Many Bolsheviks were stunned by this harsh political line, and the government branded Lenin insane, a traitor, an enemy of freedom. Worse, the sympathies of the Petrograd mob were clearly not with him in the spring of 1917: his call for the overthrow of the government outraged untold thousands of people.

The Bolshevik Central Committee had already angered Lenin by supporting the Provisional government, even to the extent of accepting its war policy. Now it challenged him again by initially rejecting his "April Theses." But membership in the party continued to grow, and Lenin was confident that it, and the public, would come around to his side.

## THE "KERENSKY" OFFENSIVE

The Provisional government reorganized in April following a crisis over war aims. Four more Socialists joined Aleksandr Kerensky in the cabinet. Defenders of the government, including its Menshevik and SR ministers, insisted that the Revolution was over. Any attempt to continue it constituted aid and comfort to Russia's enemies.

The First All-Russian Congress of Soviets of Workers' and Soldiers' Deputies, which had a Menshevik-SR majority, convened in Petrograd on June 3(16) and debated the issue of relations with the government. It approved a resolution backing the regime's foreign policy and gave carte blanche for a military offensive "if strategic considerations warrant."

Although the overwhelming majority of the Congress supported the resolution, a substantial minority led by the Bolsheviks vehemently opposed it. The Bolsheviks had planned to take their campaign to the streets on June 10(23), but the Congress forbade this and the party backed off. The Mensheviks and SRs scheduled a pro-government demonstration for June 18 (July 1). The sanctioned affair took place on schedule, but scores of pro-Bolshevik marchers infiltrated carrying banners and placards reading "All Power to the Soviets!" and "Down with the 10 Capitalist Ministers!" This was not what the government's friends had in mind, and they clashed frequently with the Bolsheviks.

The "Kerensky" offensive in early July saw the Russian forces not only repulsed but thrown back to the lines they had started from in 1914, suffering 58,000 casualties including more than 7,000 killed. The Germans were forced to withdraw 11 divisions from France to deal with the offensive; the Austro-Hungarian command pulled three divisions out of Italy for the same purpose. No one can say how many British, French, and Italian lives were spared because of Russia's sacrifices.

The 58,000 battle casualties in the nine-day offensive (22,000 *per month* was the average in 1916) flooded the villages and towns of Russia with yet another wave of unbearable sorrow. Widows, orphans, and parents who had to perform that most unnatural human act, burial of the young, looked to the capital and fixed their hatred on those responsible for their agony.

The ill-fated offensive sealed the fate of the Russian Revolution. By approving it, the Petrograd Soviet lost its original character as the spontaneous, elemental expression of Revolution and became an adjunct of the Provisional government. The revolutionary, democratic instincts of the masses, expressed in the Soviet in the late winter and spring, were sacrificed to the same old political game that tsarism had played and lost. This tragic development confirmed Lenin's analysis of the revolutionary situation and paved his way to power. The Menshevik- and SR-dominated Soviet proved unable to comprehend the rapidly changing events or to manage the Revolution. A tougher, uncompromising party would have to assume command. Lenin had been building that party for nearly 20 years.

## JULY DAYS

The failure of the "Kerensky" offensive helped produce the greatest crisis yet to confront the Provisional government. Before its close on June 24 (July 7) the All-Russian Congress of Soviets elected a Central Executive Committee of 320: 123 Mensheviks, 119 SRs, 58 Bolsheviks, the rest from splinter factions. Like the Petrograd Soviet, this CEC became an ally of the government, which was now so strong that there was no chance the Bolsheviks could overthrow it.

On July 3(16), however, soldiers from one of the machine-gun regiments organized a demonstration against the government and summoned the workers to join them. The soldiers demanded the overthrow of the government and the seizure of power by the Central Executive Committee.

Incessant Bolshevik propaganda had succeeded beyond Lenin's expectations. He had repeatedly warned the party against getting too far ahead of the masses; now that was happening. The translation into reality of the old slogan "All Power to the Soviets!"

Lenin in disguise, summer of 1917. (Bolshevik party photo)

failed. Lenin himself went to the Finland Station in midmorning on July 4(17) and saw a sea of banners proclaiming "Down with the Provisional Government!" and "All Power to the Soviet of Workers' and Soldiers' Deputies!" When he met a group of supporters at Bolshevik headquarters he was uncharacteristically subdued, and no wonder: half a million people were in the streets of Petrograd offering him what he had been asking for since the day he returned to Russia. Speaking to some of the most zealous Bolsheviks, the Kronstadt sailors, Lenin declared that the slogan "All Power to the Soviets!" was a correct one and that "it must win and will win despite all the zigzags along the historical way." If this was an exhortation to seize power, it was well disguised.

Unable to cancel the July 4(17) demonstration, Lenin went to the Tauride Palace, where the bulk of the demonstrators had gathered to call for the Soviet's accession to their demands. The Central Executive Committee stalled for time, waiting for reliable troops to reach the capital. The mood of the demonstrators, however, oscillated dangerously. The possibility of a major insurrection hung heavily in the air and was not dampened by a fierce thundershower.

Finally, loyal troops arrived and dispersed the mobs with gunpower. There was panic as people ran for cover. The appearance of troops should not have come as the surprise it did: they had been summoned by the Soviet, obedience to which they had pledged in accepting Order No. 1. On July 4(17), this loyalty led to the death of about 400 people. The July Days produced both the greatest political confusion and the most bloodshed yet in the revolutionary year.

The Central Executive Committee had supported the government; under the circumstances that was tantamount to surrendering to it. The Menshevik-SR coalition, its

would greatly benefit his chief enemies, the SRs and Mensheviks, who still controlled these organizations and the CEC. Furthermore, in July the Soviets themselves were different. No longer quite the spontaneous revolutionary organisms of the spring, they had become more conventional political bodies: the Provisional government had co-opted them into the management of political power. Recuperating from a minor ailment in the Finnish countryside not far from Petrograd, Lenin considered the machinegunners' revolt a case of mistaking the fourth month of pregnancy for the ninth.

February had belonged to Petrograd, but not July: the rest of the country had not caught up with the politics of the soldiers and workers in the capital. Lenin's colleagues worked through the night of July 3–4 (16–17) trying to calm things down; they

July victory notwithstanding, had foreclosed its options. It was now an agency of a regime determined to halt the Revolution.

The government closed down the Bolshevik press and issued an order for the arrest of the party's leaders. Lenin was forced underground in Petrograd. His situation exceedingly precarious, on July 10(23) he fled to a hideout in Finland.

The rest of Russia was confused by the news from Petrograd. It was not clear who was fighting whom, or for what reason. But because of the almost unanimous acceptance of the February Revolution, appeals to support the government spawned by that Revolution fell on receptive ears. The citizenry approved the suppression of the Bolsheviks despite having little understanding of the case against the party. It was enough for the ministers and the leaders of the Soviet to identify the Bolsheviks as enemies of democracy. The mood of Russia favored the government, but it was fickle. What held in July might not prevail in August.

## KERENSKY AND KORNILOV

Replacing Lvov as head of the Provisional government on July 7(20), Kerensky supervised the suppression of the Bolsheviks and put the capital under martial law. He ordered the dissolution of political organizations in the Petrograd garrison, restored the death penalty and courts-martial at the front, and withdrew recognition of Finland's right to autonomy. To sweeten this bitter medicine he offered anew what his predecessor had promised early in March: the summoning of a Constituent Assembly that would determine Russia's permanent form of government, decide the land question, formulate new labor legislation, and draft a constitution. He declared that elections to the assembly would take place as scheduled in mid-

September; later he would postpone the date until November. Finally, on July 24 (August 6) Kerensky announced his new cabinet. He would continue as prime minister and minister of war and navy. The government gave him full powers to deal with "counterrevolution" and empowered him to use such measures as arrest without warrant, exile from the country, and suspension of civil rights. The government also forbade unsanctioned meetings and assemblies.

Kerensky appointed General Lavr Kornilov commander of the armed forces and gave vague general instructions about keeping troops ready to fight the enemy "wherever he might appear." That referred to "counterrevolutionary" elements in Petrograd, and *that* meant the Bolsheviks. Kornilov drew up contingency plans for placing the capital under military rule.

With the fall of Riga to the Germans on August 21 (September 3) the moment arrived: Kornilov decided to march on the capital, crush the Bolsheviks and other opponents of the war, and oversee the formation of a new regime, presumably with himself at the head. Telegrams of support poured into his headquarters. The Union of the Russian People and the Black Hundreds, right-wing, violently anti-Semitic organizations, pledged their backing to the general, as did many industrialists and landlords.

A dumbfounded Kerensky received the news that troops were marching on Petrograd and wired Kornilov for an explanation. Back came a reply indicating that the purpose of the action was to "restore order." Kerensky ordered the general to rescind his commands. Kornilov refused. Kerensky relieved him of his post; Kornilov declined to comply.

At this point the prime minister believed he had no choice but to make temporary peace with the Left, including the Bolsheviks. He emptied the jails of all but a few of those arrested in July and appealed for the "defense of the revolution" against Kornilov. Within 48 hours the Bolsheviks had put 25,000 Red Guards armed with weapons supplied by the government on duty across the southern approaches to the city. From his hiding place Lenin wrote, "We are going to fight against Kornilov. We are not supporting Kerensky but exposing his weakness." The Bolsheviks never returned those weapons.

What followed was anticlimax. The Red Guards, soldiers, Baltic Fleet sailors, and railway workers had established a strong defense perimeter which was not needed. The commander of the advance column of Kornilov forces lost control of his troops, who were unenthusiastic about attacking their comrades in Petrograd, and committed suicide. Other units rebelled and refused to continue their march. Officers loyal to the government arrested Kornilov, whose putsch had failed.

Lenin declared that his party's position was unchanged after the Kornilov affair. The Bolsheviks demanded anew what they had sought in April, namely, the transfer of all power to the Soviets and a government of SRs and Mensheviks responsible to the Soviets. If these demands were met, Lenin said, the Revolution could proceed in a peaceful manner.

The Bolshevik leader's position was much more secure after the events of late August. The Kornilov affair exposed the Provisional government as unscrupulous, antidemocratic, and—worst of all—incompetent. The Bolsheviks were regarded as the saviors of Petrograd. The new, favorable image of the party was promptly reflected in the political arena: on August 31 (September 13) the Petrograd Soviet went over to the Bolshevik side. Five days later the Moscow Soviet followed suit. Now "All Power to the Soviets!" took on a new meaning.

## TWILIGHT OF THE PROVISIONAL GOVERNMENT

That workers began to flock in great numbers to the Bolsheviks was not surprising: this was a party that professed to speak on their behalf. But in a new development, the peasants were also beginning to support Lenin's party. For months the peasant party, the SRs, had been in a powerful position not only in the Soviets but also in the Provisional government itself. The lot of the peasant had not improved. In the countryside people continued to ask, "When will we get the land?" The government urged them to wait for the Constituent Assembly. The peasants, no longer in a mood to wait, began to take seriously the Bolshevik exhortations to seize the land and worry about legality later. Their impatience became all the greater when the peasant soldiers, bombarded by Bolshevik propaganda for months, came back to the villages demanding land. Instances of land seizure were so numerous that the authorities lost count. Peasant Russia would wait no longer for land and justice. The simple, straightforward Bolshevik program of peace, land, and bread won over millions of peasants.

The centrifugal forces that would sweep away the Kerensky regime included strong breakaway movements among some of the minority peoples. The Provisional government had resigned itself to the loss of Russian Poland, but that was the extent of its concessions. It insisted that Finland remain under Russian control, warned the Romanian government that it would not tolerate the seizure of Bessarabia, and denounced nationalists who were calling for Ukrainian independence. The demands of the Baltic populations for independence were rejected. Separatist movements took shape only slowly in the Caucasus and Central Asia, but warning signals abounded and the government loudly proclaimed its determination not to cede one meter of its territory.

The Provisional government rejected compromise with national-independence movements and declined to consider an accommodation with the Bolsheviks. This ensured the hostility of many non-Russian minorities and forced Lenin's party to concentrate its efforts, from the middle of September, on the preparation of an armed uprising.

Kerensky believed he could outflank the Bolsheviks with gestures. Taking his cue from the French Revolution, he established a "Directory" (Council of Five) that "ruled" Russia for the first three and a half weeks of September. This body proclaimed a republic; announced the dissolution of the Duma; promised that elections to the Constituent Assembly would take place as scheduled; and called a "Democratic Conference" to discuss national issues and create a new coalition government.

The Bolsheviks would not be in the coalition and indeed their participation in the "Democratic Conference" was restricted by their enemies. Kerensky, the Kadets, the Menshevik-SR "compromisers," and most middle- and upper-class citizens in Russia were determined to keep the Bolsheviks isolated. This policy succeeded, the only one that did. It could not stave off disaster.

## SUGGESTED ADDITIONAL READING

**Agursky, Mikhail,** *The Third Rome: National Bolshevism in the USSR,* New York: Cambridge University Press, 1987

**Ascher, Abraham,** *The Revolution of 1905,* Stanford, Calif.: Stanford University Press, 1988

**Browder, Robert P., and Alexander F. Kerensky,** *The Provisional Government, 1917: Documents,* 3 vols., Stanford, Calif.: Stanford University Press, 1961

**Burdzhalov, E. N.,** *Russia's Second Revolution: The February 1917 Uprising in Petrograd,* Bloomington: Indiana University Press, 1987

**Chernov, Victor,** *The Great Russian Revolution,* New Haven, Conn.: Yale University Press, 1936

**Deutscher, Isaac,** *The Prophet Armed: Trotsky, 1879–1921,* New York: Oxford University Press, 1954

**Hasegawa, Tsuyoshu,** *The February Revolution: Petrograd 1917,* Seattle: University of Washington Press, 1981

**Kingston-Mann, Esther,** *Lenin and the Problem of Marxist Peasant Revolution,* New York: Oxford University Press, 1983

**McClellan, Woodford,** *Revolutionary Exiles: The Russians in the First International and the Paris Commune,* London: Frank Cass, 1979

**[Pasternak, Alexander],** *A Vanished Present: The Memoirs of Alexander Pasternak,* San Diego and New York: Harcourt Brace Jovanovich, 1985

**Pipes, Richard,** *Russia under the Old Regime,* New York: Scribner's, 1974

**Rabinowitch, Alexander,** *Prelude to Revolution: The Petrograd Bolsheviks and the July 1917 Uprising,* Bloomington: Indiana University Press, 1968

**Saul, Norman,** *Sailors in Revolt,* Lawrence: Regents Press of Kansas, 1978

**Tirado, Isabel A.,** *Young Guard: The Communist Youth League, Petrograd 1917–1920,* Westport, Conn.: Greenwood Press, 1988

**Wildman, Alan K.,** *The End of the Imperial Russian Army,* vol. 1, Princeton, N.J.: Princeton University Press, 1980

——, *The Road to Soviet Peace and Power,* vol. 2, Princeton, N.J.: Princeton University Press, 1987

**Wilson, Edmund,** *To the Finland Station,* Garden City, N.Y.: Doubleday, 1953

# 2

# THE OCTOBER REVOLUTION

In the autumn of 1917 the Provisional government still had no plan for feeding the cities, providing fuel for the winter, provisioning the army. It had no scheme for making peace or resuscitating the economy. Industrial production was off 36.5 percent in comparison with 1916, which had not been a good year. Inflation ran out of control: 1917 prices stood 248 percent above those of 1913 and real wages had fallen 57.4 percent in the same period. Virtually the only people who still supported the government were those little affected by this inflation. Though few in number, the fact that they existed at all means that the real burden upon the poor was even worse than the figures indicate.

The summer and early autumn of 1917 was a time of overwhelming social anxiety in Russia. The country raced—everyone sensed it—toward an abyss: humiliating defeat and German rule? restoration of the tsarist-landlord-capitalist regime? military dictatorship? unrelieved anarchy? The February Revolution that had begun with such promise, briefly making Russia, as many people said proudly at the time, the "freest country in the world," had somehow failed to bring forth the promised millenarian harvest.

The Sixth Congress of the Bolshevik party, which had not yet adopted Lenin's demand that it rename itself Communist, met in Petrograd from July 26 to August 3 (August 8–16) and shelved the slogan "All Power to the Soviets!" on the grounds that those bodies had capitulated to the government. Nevertheless, the party increased its efforts to win control of the Soviets; and because since the spring it had controlled the factory committees that staffed them it was in a strong position to accomplish that goal. Directing the work of the Congress from his hideout, Lenin advised the 267 delegates to work for the "complete liquidation of the counterrevolutionary bourgeoisie."

The Congress reaffirmed the party's long-standing call for the nationalization of industry, "workers' control"—by workers loyal to the Bolsheviks—of production and distribution, and the distribution of all the land to the peasants. Some party members, notably Nikolai Bukharin and E. A. Preobrazhensky, demanded that the party slow its revolutionary activity, arguing—as Lenin always had—that a socialist revolution could not succeed in Russia in the absence of others in Western Europe. After fierce debates the Congress rejected this view.

Enforced isolation in Finland had the advantage of freeing Lenin from the day-to-day cares of running the party to which he had always devoted too much attention. He had time to reflect on the events of spring and summer and ponder the future of the Revolution. In early September he concluded that the crisis was rapidly maturing, and that the Bolsheviks should prepare for an armed insurrection. Quite independently of anything his party did or did not do, he realized, public opinion in Petrograd, Moscow, and other large cities was clearly moving rapidly in a leftward, more radical direction. This was also true of the masses of soldiers and sailors. Lenin understood that the working class, the men under arms, and the preponderance of the urban population, aware of their power, were more willing than ever to use it. New military units were coming over to the Soviets daily as pacifist sentiment at the front soared in the wake of the infamous "Kerensky" offensive. In the countryside, the peasant movement had

taken on the character of a land war. The Provisional government daily proved its incompetence and the "compromisers"—as the Bolsheviks derisively called them— among the Mensheviks and SRs, with no program of their own, supported it.

The handful of Bolsheviks of February had become more than 100,000 by the end of April, and the delegates to the Sixth Congress that summer represented about 200,000 party members. There were trimmers and bandwagon-jumpers in abundance among the new recruits, but in the summer and autumn of 1917 that mattered relatively little. Whatever their motives, many of these individuals were enthusiastic and energetic people who would distribute leaflets, bring crowds into the streets, monitor demonstrations, form noisy claques for Bolshevik orators, jeer and whistle at speakers from other parties, and finally, use weapons when the time came.

There was wide disagreement in the party on this last issue. Many Bolsheviks possessed what Lenin sarcastically called a "Menshevik mentality," opposing an armed uprising on a variety of grounds. In their view, "All Power to the Soviets" meant precisely that. The Bolsheviks were not a wholly united party; substantial opposition to Lenin existed.

When the Petrograd and Moscow Soviets came over to the Bolsheviks, Lenin believed he could take control of the country. The Kornilov affair, the government's inept handling of the aftermath, and the Menshevik-SR refusal to back the Bolshevik demand for transfer of power to the Soviets, convinced him to begin the end-game.

Lenin churned out articles for the Bolshevik press and for Socialist newspapers all over the country on the deepening crisis, arging that the revolutionary consciousness and ardor of the working class had matured to the point where its seizure of power was entirely possible. Again many party members—both leaders and rank and file—opposed him. No less devoted to Marxism than he, they thought that he was confusing it with insurrectionism. They saw his insistence upon an armed uprising simply as his pet theory, a weakness, a chink in his armor. Infuriated, Lenin threatened at one point to quit the Central Committee if the opposition did not capitulate.

## THE BOLSHEVIKS PREPARE

The Petrograd and Moscow Soviets had adopted Bolshevik resolutions on the war, land, and worker control of industry. But those first votes were close; a more meaningful test took place in the Petrograd Soviet on September 9(22). On that day, Trotsky engineered a test of strength that amounted to a no-confidence vote against Kerensky: the Bolsheviks won 519 to 414, with 67 abstentions. The margin of victory came from the military deputies, who had lost confidence in the prime minister and would henceforth follow only their own leaders and the Soviet, as Order No. 1 had urged months earlier.

The soldiers had become especially fond of the dynamic Trotsky, who since his release from prison had established himself as a leader of the Petrograd Soviet. On September 25 (October 8) he was elected chairman, a position he had held in the Revolution of 1905. In his first official speech he recalled how the Ismailov Regiment had suppressed the Soviet shortly after his election in 1905. "But now," he continued, "the Ismailov . . . is quite different."

Events favored the Bolsheviks in Moscow, too. The party won 350 of 710 seats in the October municipal elections. The change in party fortunes in the old capital between July and October was dramatic:

| *Change in Total Vote, July–October* | | | *Percentage Change* |
|---|---|---|---|
| SRs | down | 320,511 | SRs | −85.5 |
| Mensheviks | down | 60,520 | Mensheviks | −79.2 |
| Bolsheviks | up | 122,911 | Bolsheviks | +263 |
| Kadets | down | 7,675 | Kadets | −7.0 |

The total vote dropped precipitately, but not nearly at the rate of decline of SR support; and Kerensky was an associate of the SRs. The Mensheviks had thrown in their lot with him. The Kadet vote in Moscow stayed about the same between July and October. No new Kadet votes had appeared and some people who had earlier supported the party had left the city.

The Bolsheviks offered a haven not only for the hungry, poorly housed, underpaid, inflation-gouged workers but indeed for every malcontent and bearer of real or imagined personal grievances in Russia. Beyond that, many lower middle class individuals—foremen and straw bosses, white-collar workers, retail clerks, young professional people, intellectuals—found Lenin's party attractive. In such numbers did people flock to his banner in Moscow that Lenin came to believe the insurrection should take place there rather than in Petrograd, where he had to contend with a fractious organization.

The Moscow party organization, however, was less insurrectionist than its Petrograd counterpart; its relatively moderate image accounted in part for its success at the polls. The Moscow workers were a different kind of proletariat. Unlike the heavy-industry working class of Petrograd, they labored in textiles, manufacturing, food processing. Their history differed from that of the Petrograd workers, who were historically better paid because of chronic labor shortages. Moscow workers were better housed, and—the massive uprising of December 1905 notwithstanding—their strike record was less impressive than that of their brothers in the capital.

In March the Bolsheviks had created a special party military organization to spread propaganda, recruit and organize, win over the Petrograd garrison and Baltic Fleet. The success of this outfit led to the July Days. That fiasco proved only a temporary reverse; the military organization resumed its work. Now, in early October, the Bolshevik-dominated Petrograd Soviet decided, at *Menshevik* initiative, to create its own Military Revolutionary Committee (MRC).

The first chairman of the MRC was a young Left SR whose chief function was to "serve as a 'front' for the Bolsheviks." Trotsky actually directed the work but it was as chairman of the Soviet, not as a Bolshevik leader. The MRC had a highly "organic" character in that it was extremely flexible and could "adapt itself to every change in the mood of the revolutionary masses." Programmed action and bureaucratic discipline were alien to it; that is why it could lead a revolution. The original body had 66 members: 48 Bolsheviks, 14 Left SRs, and four Anarchists. The leading Bolsheviks were Vladimir Antonov-Ovseyenko, A.D. Sadovsky, N.I. Podvoisky, K.A. Mekhonoshin, and M.M. Lashevich.

The moderate Socialists in the Soviet refused to cooperate with the MRC, whose main task was to coordinate the politics and revolutionary activity of the Petrograd Soviet with that of the garrison and the Baltic Fleet. It also acted as a liaison between the Bolshevik Red Guards, whose numbers in Petrograd stood at about 40,000, and the Soviet. The MRC quickly emerged as the unchallenged directorate of the 150,000-man garrison and the 80,000 sailors. It also had at its disposal several thousand working-class irregulars.

No one has ever explained why Lenin remained in hiding across the frontier in Finland after the government, under siege in the Kornilov affair, amnestied the Bolsheviks and other leftists arrested in the July Days. He cannot have been in much personal danger. Morever, it was awkward for him to communicate by letter with his lieutenants, many of whom strongly disagreed with his assessment of the strategic situation. Couriers took his notes into the capital several times a day. Always he demanded that the party prepare for the immediate armed seizure of power; rarely did he receive a satisfactory reply.

At last, fear of losing the moment overcame prudence and he returned secretly to Petrograd. Shortly thereafter, the Bolshevik Central Committee voted on October 10 (23) to make "an armed insurrection the order of the day." Only Grigory Zinoviev and Lev Kamenev opposed him in the 10 to 2 vote, but 10 members of the full Central Committee were absent. As their public comments at the time indicated, three absentees—Viktor Nogin, A.I. Rykov, and Vladimir Milyutin— would have voted against an uprising. Further, several speakers expressed grave reservations about the wisdom of an insurrection in general and the timing in particular.

When the Central Committee vote was communicated to party activists, opposition immediately surfaced. The MRC denounced the plan; these were the Bolsheviks most concerned with the practical problems of mounting an insurrection. Even those who sided with Lenin had little inkling that the party leader would push them into an immediate uprising: they heard his words but declined to take them at face value. It was one thing to place an insurrection on the agenda, another to issue marching orders. Zinoviev and Kamenev, haunted the rest of their uneasy lives by their votes, expressed what many party leaders and rank-and-file members thought.

Many Bolsheviks wanted to wait for the

convening of the Second All-Russian Congress of Soviets, scheduled for October 25 (November 7), before making plans for the future. The Congress would presumably be the most democratic and truly representative body yet elected in 1917, and the overwhelming majority of workers, soldiers, sailors, and socialists in Petrograd looked to it for direction. But Lenin could not wait; and in Leon Trotsky, formerly a Menshevik leader and until July 1917 the most influential critic of the Leninist political line, he found a brilliant field commander who could translate his strategy into victory.

## TROTSKY IN OCTOBER

Until *glasnost,* Communist accounts usually did not mention Trotsky's contribution to the October Revolution. Right after the Revolution, however, Joseph Stalin said this about his colleague's role:

The entire labor of the practical organization of the insurrection was placed under the immediate direction of the president of the Petrograd Soviet, Comrade Trotsky. It can be stated with certainty that the party owes the rapid coming over of the garrison into the camp of the Soviets and the skillful work of the Military Revolutionary Committee above all and essentially to Comrade Trotsky.

Taken from the party newspaper *Pravda,* these remarks were to be omitted from Stalin's *Collected Works.*

Trotsky supported Lenin's call for an immediate armed uprising when—that 10 to 2 vote notwithstanding—it was difficult to find another member of the Central Committee who truly believed in this course of action. Most Bolsheviks wanted the party to be in power someday; that was why they were in politics. Nevertheless, few wanted to risk everything on one roll of the dice.

Trotsky, a newcomer to Bolshevik ranks and frequently Lenin's opponent before July 1917, now backed the party leader without reservation. He directed the MRC and the Bolshevik military organization and formulated the tactical plan for the uprising. As chairman of the Petrograd Soviet he directed the flow of debate and made at least some of the members believe Lenin's claim that Kerensky was about to overthrow it.

On October 21 (November 3), after hearing Trotsky speak, the regimental committees of the garrison passed a resolution stating that the "All-Russian Congress of Soviets must take power into its own hands and guarantee the people peace, bread, and land." This was Lenin's program in all its ultimately persuasive simplicity.

The same day the commander of the Petrograd Military District refused the MRC's demand for the right to countersign orders to the garrison. The next day Trotsky appealed to the soldiers: "The General Staff has broken with the revolutionary garrison and the Petrograd Soviet [this was an exaggeration] . . . thus making itself the tool of counterrevolutionary forces. . . . The Revolution is in danger!"

The Provisional government no longer controlled any significant part of the garrison. The units stationed in the suburbs vied with one another to sign oaths of loyalty to the Soviet. Attempts to bring troops from the front to Petrograd were frustrated both by the refusal of the men to move against their brothers in the capital and by the warning of Vikzhel (railwaymen's union) that it would block any such movement by rail.

The soldiers of the Peter-Paul Fortress, mostly older veterans and reservists, refused to recognize the authority of the MRC. Antonov-Ovseyenko wanted to storm the fortress, but Trotsky went there, made a speech, and swung the troops around. The

Leon Trotsky. (National Archives)

MRC took command of the fortress without firing a shot and seized 100,000 rifles.

## THE CROSSROADS

On October 18(31), unable to dissuade the Central Committee from following what he considered Lenin's reckless course, Lev Kamenev revealed Bolshevik intentions to a Petrograd newspaper controlled by the writer Maksim Gorky. This could only be interpreted as an act of disloyalty. Outraged, Lenin demanded that the party oust Kamenev and Zinoviev, who had associated himself with the letter. The other party leaders refused, content to accept Kamenev's resignation from the Central Committee and order him and Zinoviev to refrain from quarreling publicly with party decisions.

Lenin thought that publicity given his plans would thwart them; in reality it helped ensure victory by forcing the party's hand. The Bolsheviks could not have survived another crisis like the July Days, when they lagged behind the workers and lost control of street demonstrations. Lenin was probably correct in regarding July as a false opportunity, but the situation had changed drastically by October, when a stronger Bolshevik party faced weaker opponents.

Since early September, i.e., when the party legally obtained arms to fight Kornilov, there had been talk in the streets of a Bolshevik plot to seize power. Kerensky took note of the rumors when he spoke to the Pre-Parliament on October 20 (November 2):

I must inform you that a part of the Petrograd population is in a state of open insurgency . . . I have proposed that judicial investigations be started immediately and I have also ordered arrests [protests from the left]. Yes, yes, because at the moment, when the state is imperiled by deliberate or unwitting betrayal and is on the brink of ruin, the Provisional government, myself included, prefers to be killed and destroyed rather than betray the life, the honor and the independence of the state [ovation from all but the left]. All those elements of Russian society, all those groups and parties which have dared raise a hand against the free will of the Russian people . . . are subject to immediate, final and definite liquidation.

The right-wing delegates cheered and gave him a standing ovation, but it was Kerensky's swan song. Facing an armed insurrection at any moment, the government had at its certain disposal only the cadets of the military academy, a battalion of women, and a few Cossacks.

So pitifully small were Kerensky's forces that it is still a mystery why many garrison soldiers believed Lenin's claim that the government was about to launch a massive attack and wipe out all the gains of the Revolution. It was a matter of crisis feeding on rumor and rumor on crisis, and of effective Bolshevik propaganda.

Desperately afraid that his own party and the Petrograd Soviet it controlled would procrastinate and miss the crest of the wave, Lenin kept up a barrage of warnings to his colleagues not to delay, not even for the Congress of Soviets. A political sixth sense told him to seize the moment; there would be no second chance.

## OCTOBER 24–25, 1917

Lenin's warnings and exhortations had not gone unheeded despite the party's lack of enthusiasm for an uprising. Trotsky mapped out the tactical situation, the Bolshevik and Bolshevized soldiers and sailors prepared for action, the Petrograd Soviet hourly moved further to the left. The Red Guards, disciplined squads of energetic, excited young men and women (most under 25) checked weapons, adjusted red armbands, gulped tasteless "victory tea," wolfed down bread and sausage of uncertain provenance, slept only an hour or two in 24, waited impatiently for the order to take up positions. All units were ready; but they could not maintain such a state indefinitely.

Knowing that the revolutionary fervor of the Bolshevik rank and file was unstable, Lenin redoubled his frantic efforts to force the party into action. The revolutionary convulsions approached the moment of destiny.

Late in the evening on October 24 (November 6), the day before the convening of the Congress of Soviets, Bolshevik detachments moved quietly to their assigned positions around Petrograd. Few shots were fired; occasional scuffles attracted little attention. The city went about routine night-time business. Few citizens dared object to showing identification papers to stern-faced, brusque irregulars with red armbands. The regular police simply melted away at the approach of the Bolsheviks. No one challenged the uniformed servicemen.

Around midnight, bursting with the agonizing tension that afflicts people who normally contain their emotions tightly, Lenin put on a workman's cap and scarf and walked across the city to Bolshevik headquarters, now at the Smolny Institute, formerly a finishing school for daughters of the rich. He had difficulty getting past the guards: he was in disguise, did not know the password, and at first there was no one to vouch for his identity. The guard did not know whether he was a spy, panhandler, or a simpleton trying to pass as Lenin, but they finally recognized him and let him in. As the news began to come in from the city he surely permitted himself a smile. His instincts had not betrayed him. The proletarian revolution had come to pass.

At about 2:00 in the morning of October 27 (November 7) the Central Committee received confirmation that Bolshevik units had seized the central telephone exchange, the central telegraph office, the main post office, and the railway stations. Soldiers, sailors, Red Guards, and deputized workingmen had taken up positions at the bridges across the Neva, key intersections, power stations, the State Bank. They had encountered little resistance. Remaining in government hands at daybreak were only the Winter Palace, where Kerensky had foolishly (given the symbolic significance of the building) transferred his own headquarters, the general staff building, and a few other offices.

At 10:00 a.m., the Military Revolutionary Committee of the Petrograd Soviet issued Lenin's hastily-drafted proclamation:

### TO THE CITIZENS OF RUSSIA!

The Provisional government has been overthrown. State power has passed into the hands of the organ of the Petrograd Soviet of Workers' and Soldiers' Deputies, the Military Revolutionary Committee, whch stands at the head of the Petrograd proletariat and garrison.

The cause for which the people have struggled—the immediate proposal of a democratic peace, the elimination of landlord estates, workers' control over production, the creation of a Soviet government—the triumph of this cause has been assured.

Long live the workers' and peasants' revolution!

By coincidence the scheduled opening of the Congress of Soviets was only hours away when Lenin wrote this proclamation and had it telegraphed all over Russia. It was necessary to present the Congress, to which even many of Lenin's own supporters looked for leadership, with a *fait accompli*.

It was an eerily unrevolutionary revolution. Trams continued to run, cafés and restaurants were open, and although the bustle in the streets seemed greater than ever there was no general atmosphere of momentous events. At 2:35 p.m. Trotsky addressed an emergency meeting of the Petrograd Soviet and gave an account of events to date. Lenin arrived to an enthusiastic welcome and said, "Comrades, the workers' and peasants' revolution has come to pass, the revolution which the Bolsheviks have long shown to be necessary." He com-

mented upon the significance of the seizure of power, stressed the critical link between Russian workers and the "world labor movement," and concluded, "In Russia, we must now devote ourselves to the construction of a proletarian socialist state. Long live the socialist world revolution!"

There was an odd calm to all this, one of history's decisive moments. After Lenin spoke, nothing would be the same. People would not live their lives in the same way. The course of history was changing; Lenin and the party he dragged along with him gave it direction. The other elements in the October equation hesitated, debated, waited—a cautious posture that many, perhaps a majority, of Bolsheviks preferred. But for one brief moment a single iron-willed, brilliant political strategist united a quarrelsome party behind him and forced it to seize a unique opportunity.

Meanwhile the government tried to summon loyal troops but found none who would respond. The ministers won a few extra hours in office because the sailors from Kronstadt who had been assigned to arrest them failed to arrive on time. The action scheduled for 2 p.m. was postponed several times. The sailors finally showed up late in the evening—the delay has never been explained—and delivered an ultimatum. From its moorings across the river, the cruiser *Aurora* fired some blank shells to soften up resistance. A little after midnight a Winter Palace telephone operator contacted Konovalov, who was now in charge. The operator told Konovalov that a "delegation" was approaching the palace. Kerensky had slipped out earlier, fleeing in an automobile supplied by the American legation.

This procession was led by Vladimir Antonov-Ovseyenko, who simply walked up to the gates and pushed past the guards and servitors. *There was no storming of the Winter Palace*, decades of both Soviet and Western myth-building notwithstanding. There did not have to be: Antonov-Ovseyenko's detachment was knocking at an open door. Russia's middle class went down to defeat without a real struggle.

The Red Guards found the ministers in darkness in an interior room. Antonov-Ovseyenko read out the MRC order for their arrest. Konovalov: "The members of the Provisional government yield to force, and surrender to prevent bloodshed." Nothing became them in office so much as the leaving of it. The ministers were escorted to cells in the Peter-Paul Fortress. Along the way Antonov-Ovseyenko's Red Guards held back the sailors and workers who wanted to lynch them.

There were no lynchings, no real fighting. Only a handful of casualties were recorded for the night of October 25–26; some say as few as five. Whatever the numbers, there were more than one would expect in a mere changing of the guard, too few to indicate an epochal convulsion. Contrary to Marx's prediction, violence was not the "midwife" of *this* new society.

## SECOND ALL-RUSSIAN CONGRESS OF SOVIETS

At 10:40 p.m. on October 25 (November 7) the Second All-Russian Congress of Soviets convened in Smolny Institute, central headquarters of the Soviet since early August and of the Bolshevik Central Committee since September. The members were significantly younger than those of the First, and there were more soldiers. The new Congress, which would be asked to sanction and legitimize the insurrection, was dominated by the Bolsheviks—300 of the 670 delegates present. Supported by the Left SRs, the Bolsheviks prevailed on all questions. Fourteen Bolsheviks, including

Lenin, Trotsky, Antonov-Ovseyenko, Aleksandra Kollontai, and the erstwhile renegades Kamenev and Zinoviev, were elected to the presidium. Seven Left SRs and one Ukrainian Socialist were also elected.

At this stage the Mensheviks, Martov's Menshevik Internationalists, the regular SRs, and the members of two small Jewish parties, declaring their opposition to the "military plot and the seizure of power," walked out of the Congress. This was a significant political gesture. These people would later argue that they had had no choice: they had to leave or be tainted by complicity with Bolshevism. They also pleaded, after the fact, that they had assumed their walkout would lead to the collapse of the Bolshevik regime before it could legitimize itself.

The action cast the anti-Bolsheviks in an awkward role. They naturally opposed the establishment of a Leninist regime which many believed would not last through the night. Even if the Bolsheviks had fallen shortly after the exit of their opponents, however, so long as they controlled the speaker's rostrum they were Russia's only government. By rebelling against this regime at the moment of its birth, the anti-Bolsheviks cast their lot with counterrevolution.

At 3:10 a.m. (October 26 [November 8]) the Congress received a telegram from Antonov-Ovseyenko: the Winter Palace had fallen. All the ministers save Kerensky were in custody. Cheers and applause, no wild demonstration: the details of the mopping up were a little concern at this hour.

Around 4:00 a.m. the Bolshevik floor leader, Anatoli Lunacharsky, read Lenin's manifesto "To All Workers, Soldiers and Peasants" and asked for its immediate adoption. As one scholar has noted, this manifesto was "ultimately the source of Soviet political authority." It announced the passing of political power into the hands of the Congress and

Lenin and his colleagues, Petrograd, late 1917. (National Archives)

of local Soviets all over the country and declared the old regime defunct. It provided again for the transfer of all land to "peasant committees" and for workers' control in industry. It declared that the Soviet would "at once" propose a "democratic peace to all nations and an armistice on all fronts." The manifesto provided for the care of the "revolutionary army," which would be supplied through "requisitions from and taxation of the propertied classes." Soldiers' families would be provided for; no previous regime had lifted a finger for them. Finally, the document called on the Congress and the people to resist the counterrevolutionary forces already being formed.

The delegates sensed that they were listening to history's statement of what had just been accomplished in Petrograd and repeatedly interrupted Lunacharsky with shouts and cheers. The Left SRs announced they would support the adoption of the manifesto, which was approved around 5:00

a.m. with 2 votes against and 12 abstentions. A new era had begun.

## LENIN TAKES COMMAND

On October 26 (November 8) the MRC took control of police functions and calmly began to organize the life of the city. The shops were open; public transportation ran more or less on schedule; there was no interruption in water, electricity, or gas service. That evening music lovers went to the theatre to hear the great basso Fyodor Chalyapin. Fashionable cafés and restaurants on the Nevsky had delicacies and expensive French champagne for customers who could afford them; long lines indicated many could.

Over at Smolny, hectic activity. The Bolsheviks were trying to organize a government. First question: what to call the heads of government departments? The Bolsheviks ruled out "minister" because of its "capitalist" connotations, whatever those were. Somebody called out "comissar?" At once all agreed: that was it. Comissars in charge of comissariats. The new government would be called "Council [Soviet] of People's Comissars." It had, Lenin observed, a nice revolutionary ring.

Lenin became chairman of the new government, Trotsky, comissar of foreign affairs. Military affairs went to the *troika* of Vladimir Antonov-Ovseyenko, Nikolai Krylenko, and Pavel Dybenko, leaders of the MRC. The relatively minor post of comissar of nationalities was reserved for a non-Russian; Stalin (Dzhugashvili), an Ossete from Georgia, received it. Sub-cabinet slots were assigned in haphazard fashion. The job of running the state bank went to a man whose qualifications consisted of attendance at a couple of lectures at the London School of Economics.

A little before 9:00 a.m. on October 26, Lenin arrived at Smolny to preside over the Congress of Soviets and introduce his government. Kamenev, who saw no reason to remind anyone of his opposition to the insurrection that now catapulted him into a prominent position, was in the chair. A couple of minor items—including abolition of the death penalty at the front, a step Lenin firmly opposed—being disposed of quickly, the Congress turned to the first of the three main items on the agenda, the question of peace. Lenin rose and read his "Decree on Peace," composed earlier in the day after only the briefest of naps; this may account for the uncharacteristically weak argument. He merely repeated what he had said in the general manifesto early that morning. When he finished, there was an enormous cheer. Speaker after speaker rose to praise the Bolshevik proposal for an immediate 90-day armistice and for the summoning of a general peace conference.

One or two delegates mumbled something about the need to have a government composed of all Socialist parties; they were shouted down. Kamenev asked for a show of voting cards: the lone dissenter was put in fear of his life. Russia became the first belligerent to demand an end to the war.

Lenin's "Decree on Land" addressed the second major issue before the Congress. Delegates listened in surprise as he read it; they had heard these words before, in the SR program. The first article declared that private land holdings were abolished immediately without compensation. The right to use the land belonged to all citizens as long as they worked it themselves; it was forbidden to hire labor. The land was to be divided among those who worked it and periodically redivided—an ancient custom in many areas of Russia—to reflect population changes and new agricultural methods. The last point of Lenin's Decree declared that "the land of ordinary peasants and Cossacks shall not be confiscated." This contradicted the first article, but no one paid any attention. The Decree and its SR supplement did provide for the final solution of the land problem by the Constituent Assembly, which would shortly be elected.

The final item on the agenda involved the formation of a government. Trotsky called for an exclusively Bolshevik regime; other speakers, among them several Bolsheviks, insisted that all parties be represented. A delegate from the railwaymen's union declared that it was not about to become a Bolshevik puppet and warned of reprisals if Lenin tried to become a dictator. The debate became ragged as the hour grew late. The Bolsheviks offered posts in the cabinet to the Left SRs, who had by now declared themselves an independent party, only to be rebuffed. Finally, shortly before 5:00 a.m., the Congress approved the all-Bolshevik list. The Council of People's Commissars, or

Sovnarkom (an acronym), now became the legal government of Russia.

## OUTSIDE PETROGRAD

The essentially peaceful Bolshevik seizure of power in Petrograd stood in marked contrast to events elsewhere. A major problem was sheer confusion: few people in the hinterland knew exactly what had happened in the capital. Most evidently believed that the Petrograd Soviet had seized power and that several parties were battling to form a new government. Many people believed that the SRs would emerge victorious; the prospect emboldened members of that party around the country.

In Moscow, 20,000 well-armed men were poised to suppress a leftist uprising, and the city fathers had every reason to expect reinforcements from the Southwestern Front and from Cossack units in southern Russia and the Ukraine. The local garrison of 30,000 men was not wholly reliable but was less infected with the virus of revolution than its Petrograd counterpart. Beyond that, the officers had locked away the garrison's weapons, issuing them only to friendly units. The Moscow City Duma formed a Committee of Public Safety and prepared to do battle.

The central industrial region around Moscow was crucial to Bolshevik hopes for success. Nearly half the country's 3 million workers were here; if they linked up with revolutionary Petrograd, the heartland would be secure.

The local Bolsheviks, Lenin's assessment of their revolutionary zeal notwithstanding, were not anxious to fight in the streets. The Bolshevik chairman of the Moscow Soviet, Viktor Nogin, had opposed the insurrection. Now he appealed for support for the Petrograd uprising but stressed its defensive nature against the counterrevolutionary Provisional government. The Mensheviks and SRs in the Soviet opposed Nogin's motion; when the vote was taken, the Bolsheviks won. The Moscow Soviet thereupon formed a Military Revolutionary Committee which had at its disposal 6,000 Red Guards and a large number of workers. Opposition within Moscow Bolshevik ranks to a seizure of power remained strong, however, and in the beginning the Left in that city was unable to present a unified front against the forces loyal to the Provisional government.

The outcome of the fighting that began in Moscow on October 27 (November 9) remained in doubt for several days. Loyalist military academy cadets seized control of the Kremlin and dealt savagely with the guard, which had gone over to the Bolshevik-dominated Soviet. The Committee of Public Safety secured the central districts and awaited reinforcements. The Soviet received help first, however, in the form of Red Guard detachments from other cities, notably Petrograd. The arrival of a contingent of pro-Bolshevik soldiers and sailors from the capital tipped the balance. A cease-fire took effect on the morning of November 2(15); the Soviet seized control of the city. Approximately a thousand people died in the process of bringing the old capital into the Bolshevik camp. Anticipating the possibility of Lenin's government moving to Moscow, the local Bolsheviks lost no time in launching efforts to root out hostile elements.

Elsewhere in the central industrial region fighting continued until the spring of 1918. It was especially fierce in the arms manufacturing city of Tula, the Volga city of Nizhny Novgorod, and Kaluga. By June, however, most of the region was under Bolshevik control.

Second only to the Petrograd-Moscow axis and the industrial center to Bolshevik hopes was the Ukraine. There were about a million workers, a third of the empire total, in the Ukraine, and two-thirds of them were concentrated in the Donbas and in Harkov and Yekaterinoslav provinces. About 30,000 Bolsheviks had been agitating for months in the Donbas, and that heavily industrialized sector came under Bolshevik control soon after the October Revolution in Petrograd. Elsewhere in the Ukraine there were only 15,000 Bolsheviks, who were no match for the separatists, not to mention other contenders for power—anarchists, bandit gangs, and private Cossack armies. Not until February 1918 was the red flag of Bolshevism to fly over Kiev, capital of the Ukraine, and even then it did not fly long: A short-lived independent Ukrainian regime (Central Rada) succeeded in establishing control over the city, only to yield in turn to a puppet "government" under German control.

Kiev changed hands frequently in this chaotic period and not until after the end of the Russo-Polish War in 1920 did the Bolsheviks establish firm control over the city. Fighting continued in many areas of the Ukraine throughout the Civil War and indeed the political situation did not stabilize until the mid-1920s.

The war with Poland complicated the situation not only in the Ukraine but also in Byelorussia, Lithuania, and Russian Poland. The new Polish state incorporated some of the western Ukraine and Byelorussia as well as formerly tsarist Polish territories. Lithuania, Latvia, and Estonia all won independence and became hotbeds of anticommunism.

In the southwest, the province of Bessarabia, which Alexander I had seized from the Ottoman Empire in the war of 1806–1812, first declared its independence, then sought and achieved incorporation into Romania. Although about two-thirds of the Bessarabian population was Romanian, the Bolsheviks refused to recognize the loss of the province and swore to retake it.

The agricultural areas of the Northern Caucasus only slowly came under Bolshevik control. Comprising dozens of different nationalities, the population was by and large indifferent to politics save when politics intruded upon their normally peaceful lives. To the south, in Georgia, Armenia, and Transcaucasia, a no less heterogeneous population was far more active politically, with the Mensheviks the strongest party on the Left. The Bolsheviks did not succeed in taking Georgia and Armenia, both of which established independent regimes which would only be brought under Soviet control a few years later. The Turkic Azerbaijanis (Azeris), not politically progressive, were under the control of feudal landlords and the Muslim religious scholars. Because of the oilfields at Baku, however, Azerbaijan had many Russian and Ukrainian as well as Azerbaijani workers. Altogether they numbered about 57,000, and there was a large local Bolshevik organization that sought to control this work force. Power did pass to the Bolshevik-controlled local Soviet in Baku in the spring of 1918, but later in the year the anti-Bolshevik forces (notably the SRs), with the aid of British interventionists, would overthrow this regime.

In Central Asia, economically and politically one of the most backward areas of the old empire, the Muslim populations (Turkmen, Uzbeks, Kirgiz, and others) had traditionally submitted to the rule of the feudal landlords, religious leaders, and Russian conquerors. The Bolsheviks were at a double disadvantage in this and all Muslim areas in that they were not only Russian but atheists. The only real revolutionary center in Central Asia was Tashkent, capital of Uzbekistan, where a few thousand Russian workers—most employed on the railroads—came under Bolshevik influence. Some fighting took place in Tashkent between workers and the local garrison; by November 15(28) the city and its environs had come under shaky Soviet control. The cities of Samarkand, Ashkhabad, Krasnovodsk, Merv, Pishpek, Kushka, and Skobelev were nominally in the Bolshevik camp by February 1918. Only the Khanate of Khiva and the Emirate of Bukhara remained actively hostile; they were incorporated into the new Soviet state in 1920. Much of Central Asia, however, would long be bedeviled by anti-Soviet armed gangs. The members of these units described themselves as Islamic warriors fighting the atheistic Communists. The Soviet regime insisted they were *basmachi*—bandits.

The vast, thinly populated Kazakh steppe was likewise inhabited by a Muslim people, the Turkic Kazakhs. Nomads whose social and political life was dominated by the Islamic religious leaders and feudal barons, they had opposed Russian colonial rule for generations and, aided by another Turkic people, the Bashkirs, had frequently rebelled. In 1917 a nationalist party, Alash, challenged the Bolshevik claim to Kazakh lands and tried to establish an independent state. Fighting between Alash and Bolshevik forces continued until January 1919, when the Red Army finally conquered the area.

In Siberia and the Far East, an area almost twice the size of the United States, there were only about 9.5 million people, of whom about 325,000 were workers. The overwhelming majority of the population was composed of peasants. Most workers and some peasants were sympathetic to the Bolsheviks, but over the vast distances concerted action was difficult. Attempting to seize power in several key towns and cities along the route of the Trans-Siberian Railroad, the Bolsheviks encountered strong resistance from various tsarist and SR forces. In the Far East the Japanese and Americans intervened in force in 1918. Soviet control was not fully established in Siberia and the Far East until the mid-1920s.

Finally, the 6 million men still technically on active duty in the Imperial Army were crucial to Bolshevik plans. Should a substantial number side with anti-Bolshevik forces, Lenin's Revolution was doomed. There were about 21,000 Bolshevik agitators and propagandists among the 1.1 million men stationed at the Western Front; 13,000 on the Northern Front, where there were a million soldiers and sailors; about 7,000 on the Southwestern Front among 1.8 million troops; and about 7,000 among the 1.5 million men on the Romanian front. Another 2,000 or so Bolshevik agitators were assigned to military forces in the Caucasus and elsewhere in the interior.

The SRs and Mensheviks also had agitators and propagandists among the troops, and the SRs outstripped the Bolsheviks in popularity. The disastrous "Kerensky" offensive of the summer of 1917, which the SRs supported, began to reduce that party's influence in the army to the benefit of the Bolsheviks, however, and Lenin's party virtually controlled the Baltic Fleet. The sailors had formed a revolutionary organization, Centrobalt, that dominated the Petrograd garrison and played a key role in the October Revolution.

As the Provisional government continued to drift into late summer and early autumn, disillusioned soldiers increasingly looked to the Bolsheviks to deliver them from a hopeless situation. There was no possibility of victory at the front, and no government worth defending in the rear. Not all soldiers came over to the Bolsheviks, but in autumn 1917 few still in uniform actively opposed them.

## LENINIST OCTOBER

On the morrow of the Provisional government's fall it would have been difficult to find anyone outside the party speaking of the Bolshevik victory, and even many of Lenin's followers were confused by the events of October. It was clear who and what had fallen; but few people knew who had *won* what. The people of Russia regarded the Bolsheviks as agents of the Soviets, the Germans, the international proletariat, freemasonry, international Jewry, Satan, or various combinations of all these.

Any attempt to freeze the action at the moment the new regime came into existence distorts the momentum of the organic process of revolution; it is the uncertainty principle at work in the observation of history. In the autumn of 1917 it was by no means clear the Bolsheviks would survive. The Jacobins of the Russian Revolution, their seizure of control in Petrograd was certain to inspire their enemies. It seemed unlikely that they would be able to translate their program into action, and an attempt to do so would unquestionably alienate broad sectors of the population. If few people spoke of their victory, the Bolsheviks were at least at the center of political attention; their program and personnel would be scrutinized as never before. Those who knew—or thought they knew—them best, the sophisticated Petrograd politicians, smugly assured each other that this party of radical crackpots would never withstand such scrutiny.

The real optimists in 1917–1918—Woodrow Wilson is the best example—hoped that once in power the Bolsheviks would ameliorate their harsh political line, mute the call for class warfare, cease agitating for world revolution. Accustomed to meaningless campaign promises, some Western politicians wrote off Bolshevik rhetoric as mere bombast. Having confounded the world by seizing power in Russia, however, the Bolsheviks would soon prove that they did not speak in metaphors. They were not middle-class reformers who were content to develop capitalism slowly and wait genera-

tions for the proletariat to mature. They had every intention of instituting a communist program as quickly as they could.

They had a fanatically single-minded leader who had capable lieutenants, and despite internal differences they were less disunited than any other party. Their organizational structure, with its detailed hierarchy leading up to the supreme authority of the Congress, was superior to that of any other party. The other Marxist party, the Mensheviks, excelled at theory; but the Bolsheviks knew how to organize a demonstration, distribute propaganda, plan an armed uprising. The Kadets understood parliamentary democracy, but the Bolsheviks had agitators who could transform an audience into a revolutionary combat arm.

The Bolsheviks claimed to represent the wave of the future. They had a simple program from which they did not deviate. On the great questions of the war, land, labor, class relations, and organization of state and society, their position was unambiguous and capable of being understood by peasant and worker masses. They called for radical surgery to remove the painful excrescences of tsarism and capitalism; the other parties denied the pain or prescribed nostrums.

Despite their adherence to a foreign ideology, the Bolsheviks stood squarely in Russia's Byzantine-Mongol-Muscovite tradition and spoke of a world of black-and-white certainties. The people should overthrow the state, not try to reform it. Workers should rise up against capitalists, not try to reach an accommodation. The peasants should take *all* land.

Bolshevik opponents spoke either for the past (Octobrists and other parties on the Right), for middle-class democracy (Kadets), or for glacially slow change (Mensheviks and SRs). Those parties were weak, uncertain, pessimistic. They had had the opportunity to take power or at least share in it, and they had failed to bring Russia out of chaos. Now it was the turn of Lenin's Bolsheviks.

The Bolsheviks came to power promising an inescapably painful transition to a better future. Russia would have to get out of the war. Under existing circumstances, that could only mean admitting defeat and paying a heavy price for it. Crown, gentry, and church would have to give up lands and privileges. The capitalists would have to yield to the dictatorship of the proletariat. All this would take time and would not be accomplished peacefully. The propertied elements were certain to resist ferociously. If history were any guide, foreign defenders of the old tsarist-capitalist order could be expected to try to overthrow the new regime. The question was not whether there would be opposition but only what form it would take, and how the Bolsheviks would respond.

The moderate and conservative wings of Russian politics refused to accept the Bolsheviks as a legitimate party and excluded them from the political mainstream that had burst forth in February 1917. They denied Lenin's party a share in power despite the fact that its basic program—that simple "peace, bread, and land"—embodied the general aspirations of millions of citizens. This reinforced not only the Byzantine exclusionist tendency in Bolshevism-Leninism but also Lenin's personal desire for apocalyptic vengeance. Themselves ostracized, the Bolsheviks would never compromise with those who had cast them out, nor would they merely neutralize their enemies: they would annihilate them.

The Bolsheviks had made a revolution in the name of the poor, the oppressed, the weak, the hungry, the people without hope. They claimed, and hundreds of millions of people around the world eventually came to believe, that the downtrodden of the earth had at last found a champion. The possessing classes, the "haves," in all countries proclaimed this messianic movement false, branded it anathema, and declared the destruction of Bolshevism the sacred mission of Christian civilization.

Most of the people of the former Russian Empire, whatever their attitude toward Bolshevism, did not welcome this imperious crusade. And because they did not, Bolshevism, deformed at birth by foreign intervention and civil war, would survive, a modern dictatorship that grew out of the ruins of a traditional autocracy.

## SUGGESTED ADDITIONAL READING

**Bettelheim, Charles,** *Class Struggles in the U.S.S.R. First Period: 1917–1923,* New York: Monthly Review Press, 1976

**Carr, E.H.,** *The Bolshevik Revolution,* 3 vols., New York: Macmillan, 1951

**Chamberlin, W.H.,** *The Russian Revolution, 1917–1921,* vol. I, Princeton, N.J.: Princeton University Press, 1987

**Clements, Barbara,** *Bolshevik Feminist: The Life of Aleksandra Kollontai,* Bloomington: Indiana University Press, 1979

**Daniels, Robert V.,** *Red October,* New York: Scribner's, 1967

**Ferro, Marc,** *October 1917,* London: Routledge & Kegan Paul, 1980

**Kaiser, Daniel H., ed.,** *The Workers' Revolution in Russia, 1917: The View from Below,* New York: Cambridge University Press, 1987

**Koenker, Diane,** *Moscow Workers and the 1917 Revolution,* Princeton, N.J.: Princeton University Press, 1981

**Krupskaya, Nadezhda,** *Memories of Lenin,* New York: International Publishers, 1970

**Mstislavskii, Sergei,** *Five Days Which Transformed Russia,* Bloomington: Indiana University Press, 1988

**Rabinowitch, Alexander,** *The Bolsheviks Come to Power,* New York: W.W. Norton, 1978

**Raleigh, Donald J.,** *Revolution on the Volga: 1917 in Saratov,* Ithaca, N.Y.: Cornell University Press, 1986

**Schapiro, Leonard, and Peter Reddaway, eds.,** *Lenin,* Boulder, Colo.: Westview Press, 1987

**Slusser, Robert M.,** *Stalin in October: The Man Who Missed the Revolution,* Baltimore: The Johns Hopkins University Press, 1987

**Smith, S.A.,** *Red Petrograd: Revolution in the Factories, 1917–1918,* New York: Cambridge University Press, 1983

**Snow, Russell E.,** *The Bolsheviks in Siberia, 1917–1918,* Cranbury, N.J.: Associated University Presses, 1977

**Sukhanov, N.N. [Himmer],** *The Russian Revolution, 1917,* Princeton, N.J.: Princeton University Press, 1983

**Suny, Ronald G.,** *The Baku Commune, 1917–1918,* Princeton, N.J.: Princeton University Press, 1972

**Trotsky, Leon,** *The History of the Russian Revolution,* Ann Arbor: University of Michigan Press, 1974

**Tucker, Robert C.,** *Stalin as Revolutionary, 1879–1929,* New York: W.W. Norton, 1974

**Wade, Rex A.,** *Red Guards and Workers' Militias in the Russian Revolution,* Stanford, Calif.: Stanford University Press, 1984

# 3

# CIVIL WAR AND INTERVENTION

In the spring of 1918, the task of constructing a stable political regime and bringing order to the country seemed beyond the capabilities of Lenin's party. Bolshevik rule was recognized only in the new seat of government, Moscow, and in Petrograd and some other cities of central and northern Russia. Almost everywhere else in European Russia, in Trans-Caucasia, and along the route of the Trans-Siberian Railway, there was fierce fighting as foreign and domestic groups challenged the new regime. Foreign powers intervened.

The Octobrists, Kadets, SRs, Mensheviks, and other parties mounted violent attacks upon the Soviet regime ranging from assassination of Bolshevik officials to massive foreign-supported military campaigns involving large armies deployed across vast fronts. The domestic opposition and the foreign threat loomed all the more menacing after the Bolsheviks concluded a disastrous peace treaty with the Central Powers which severed much of the industrial and agricultural heartland of the old empire from the new Soviet state.

## TREATY OF BREST-LITOVSK

The day after the Revolution, Trotsky asked the Allied ambassadors to inform their governments of the Sovnarkom's proposal to accept Lenin's "Decree on Peace" as the basis for an armistice and peace negotiations. The diplomats ignored him—confirming the Bolshevik conviction that the Allies had no interest in peace. A few days later the British government announced that it would not recognize the new regime; other powers followed suit.

If the Allies would not join them, the Bolsheviks would have to act alone. On November 13(26) Russian emissaries crossed over to the German lines under a flag of truce and arranged for peace negotiations to begin six days later at the town of Brest-Litovsk, near where Byelorussia, Lithuania, and Poland meet.

The Germans and their allies presented an ultimatum: 150,000 km$^2$ of territory, a large indemnity, and the right to station troops on Russian soil. In Petrograd the stunned Bolsheviks split into two camps. Left Communists around Nikolai Bukharin wanted to wage a revolutionary war, counting upon the German, Austrian, and Polish workers to rise up in support of that war. A peace group around Lenin was convinced that Russia had to get out of the war immediately. This was no mere honoring of a campaign slogan: it was a matter, Lenin argued, of the life and death of the regime.

Trotsky took charge of the Bolshevik negotiating team after the New Year. He did not wish to surrender on German terms but he knew that Russia was incapable of fighting any longer. Like all Bolsheviks he sincerely believed that German workers were on the verge of launching their own revolution. Seeking to gain time, he adopted a stance novel in the annals of diplomacy: "neither peace nor war." He declared that the Sovnarkom was disbanding its army and thus not only would not but could not fight. Neither would it sign a peace treaty.

The Germans pondered this unusual position briefly, then resumed their offensive. The renewed drive threatened Petrograd and forced the issue. It was necessary to choose between capitulation and annihilation; while the Bolsheviks debated, the Germans increased their demands.

Lenin told the Central Committee that failure to accept the latest ultimatum would mean the prompt overthrow of the Soviet regime. Seven Central Committee members voted with him, but four abstained and four voted against him. Under party rules the majority of those voting carried the day. In symbolic protest Trotsky resigned and was replaced by Grigory Sokolnikov, who signed the treaty of Brest-Litovsk on March 3, 1918. An Extraordinary (Fourth) Congress of Soviets ratified the treaty 12 days later.

The Versailles settlement imposed upon Germany in 1919 was magnanimous compared to Brest-Litovsk. Russia lost a million square kilometers of territory, 34 percent of her population, 32 percent of her farmland, 89 percent of her coal fields, and 54 percent of her heavy industry. She had to accept the installation of a German puppet regime in the Ukraine. The Latvian, Estonian, and Lithuanian territories, Russian Poland, and part of Byelorussia were lost.

Savaged by this treaty, the Russian state was weaker than it had been since the accession of the Romanovs. Nevertheless it had gained a breathing-space without which it could not have survived, and it was in the hands of a regime not tied to old traditions and practices and norms. Just four days after the humiliating capitulation Lenin told his dispirited colleagues, many of whom were wondering whether the Left Communists who called for a revolutionary war might not have been right, that the Sovnarkom had neither illusions about nor respect for the treaty and would violate it at every opportunity. That had already begun: the Bolsheviks were supplying the Finnish Communists with weapons, ammunition, and propaganda materials.

Aside from mocking the agreement, Lenin's party could only wait for an uprising of the proletariat in the West or for Germany's defeat to recapture the lost territo-

Lenin speaking at the unveiling of the temporary Marx-Engels monument, Moscow, November 7, 1918. (Sovnarkom photo)

ries. To the surprise of almost everyone in Russia, military defeat came first, and the worker uprising never came at all. When the Armistice in the West went into effect on November 11, 1918, the Sovnarkom moved quickly to annul the Treaty of Brest-Litovsk.

## ALLIED INTERVENTION

The Bolshevik Revolution engendered violent hostility in the West. No Allied ambassador in Petrograd had taken Lenin's party seriously until it came to power; therefore the shock in Western capitals was all the greater. When it became clear that the Bolsheviks were indeed the revolutionaries they said they were, Allied governments launched a propaganda campaign against them. Paris, London, and Washington solemnly announced that the Bolsheviks were German agents; less formally they claimed that most of the party's leaders were Jews. If the Bolsheviks were allowed to survive in Russia, Allied propagandists warned, they would soon be in the West to "communize" women, sequester private property, and stable their mules in churches.

More to the point was the justifiable Allied fear that, with Russia out of war and her resources now apparently at Germany's disposal, the tide of battle would shift. It was a measure of the war-weariness in the Allied nations that this rational argument initially took second place to talk of a Bolshevik threat to sexual conventions and property rights. No one knew how many German divisions would now be withdrawn from the Eastern Front and sent to France, but the force would perhaps be sufficient to offset the increasing flow of aid from the United States. The Allies had been determined to keep Russia in the war; they did not abandon that hope now. At the very least they wanted to keep as many German divisions as possible pinned down in the East. They also sought to retain control of Caspian Sea oil and to protect munitions depôts at Murmansk and Archangel.

The Bolshevik repudiation of the tsarist debt, confiscation of private property (foreign property was particularly vulnerable), and shrill advocacy of world revolution struck fear into the hearts of the middle class everywhere. With a wary eye on their own working classes, Western industrialists, businessmen, and financiers put great pressure on their governments to intervene in Russia. Under the influence of these circles the British and French regimes entered into a secret agreement in December 1917 to partition Russia into spheres of influence.

Ironically, Trotsky and others in the new government including Lenin had some hopes for *aid* from the West; they were particularly sanguine about the prospects for American assistance, for President Wilson seemed less hostile to Bolshevism than French and British leaders. The sixth of his famous Fourteen Points called for evacuation of all foreign military personnel from Russian soil and an international guarantee of Russia's right to determine her own destiny.

This proposal collided with the brutal reality of power politics. The Allies were being pushed in the opposite direction by many politicians who called for intervention in Russia. Winston Churchill, minister of supply in Lloyd George's cabinet, emerged as the most vociferous advocate of this policy. Churchill was to prevail over Wilson in the dispute, though not to the extent he wished.

As it happened, Prime Minister David Lloyd George did not share the views of his minister of supply. He cared nothing for Russian aristocrats and refused to sanction the "big" intervention Churchill demanded because of his certain knowledge that the British public would not stand for it: there were no more generations to sacrifice to restore the old order in Russia. Had the prime minister not been so preoccupied, he might well have directed a more far-sighted Allied policy toward the Bolshevik regime.

As it happened Lloyd George authorized a series of operations neither fish nor fowl. In 1918–1919 the British spent more than £100,000,000 in a futile attempt to protect the flow of Caspian oil and to find a leader to rule Russia in London's best interests. The oil flowed for a while after a British force helped local anticommunists overthrow the Baku Commune, as the new Soviet regime in the city was called, but the execution of 26 Bolshevik leaders in September 1918 inflicted a wound upon British-Soviet relations that festered for decades. And after the Communist victory in the Civil War Britain had to find oil elsewhere.

The French government shared Churchill's hostility toward Bolshevism. Raymond Poincaré, president of the republic, and Georges Clemenceau, premier and war minister as of November 1917, were determined to protect huge French investments in mining and manufacturing in Russia. The difficulty was, however, that the French public had no stomach for yet another war, this one against an "enemy" who a few short weeks earlier had been a valiant friend. Bled white at Verdun, on the Marne, and on the Somme, and beset by terrible morale in the army, France simply could not undertake a campaign in Russia. The government could send only small forces to the southern part of the country, where French investments were greatest, support various anti-Bolshevik commanders and movements, and hope for the best.

The Japanese proved to be the biggest interventionists. Overcrowded in their home islands, they wanted to seize Manchuria, the Russian Maritime Provinces, and a large area of eastern Siberia. To Japanese imperialists, expansion on the Asian mainland was simply a matter of survival. They knew they would never have a free hand in China, where the West had first claim. A disintegrating Russia was therefore the perfect victim. Japan intervened in force and remained on Soviet territory for several years.

President Wilson, who saw a strictly limited purpose for intervening in the stricken country, opposed Japan's actions. Unlike European and Japanese leaders he genuinely believed in the right of nations to determine their own destinies. He certainly did not approve of Bolshevism, but he regarded its propaganda as a species of campaign rhetoric and did not share Churchill's visceral hatred of Lenin's regime. Wilson sent American forces to protect the munitions depôts and to keep an eye on the Japanese.

In addition to the Western Allies and

Intervention and civil war, 1918–1920.

Japan, Germany inflicted enormous damage upon Russia. The Germans systematically looted the Ukraine; it would be years before the region would recover. Berlin sought to make the Ukraine a breadbasket and source of cheap labor.

In all, 15 countries intervened in Russia. The Turks moved into Trans-Caucasia. The Romanians took Bessarabia, an ethnically mixed area between the Prut and Dnester Rivers. Even the Greeks and Persians intervened, and the Czechoslovak Legion, a force of prisoners of war, became involved. Most of the intervening powers supported one or several of the domestic opposition groups during the Russian Civil War which raged simultaneously with the intervention. This outside interference made a terrible situation worse and led to the hardening of Bolshevik attitudes toward the nations which participated.

The Russian Civil War of 1918–1920 pitted the "Reds" (Bolsheviks) and their supporters against the "Whites" or "White Guards"—loosely, all domestic anti-Bolshevik forces. The White movements, which took shape in the spring and early summer of 1918, were scattered over the territory of the former empire. The Bolsheviks at that time controlled only an area shaped like a huge irregular oval: Petrograd and Voronezh at opposite poles of the long axis, Smolensk and Yarolavl opposite each other on the short. Bolshevik-dominated Soviets existed in other areas, but these were isolated enclaves and many were easily overrun by hostile forces.

## BREAKAWAY NATIONALIST MOVEMENTS

Among the first to declare independence of the Bolshevik regime, and indeed of Russia in general, were some minority peoples on the periphery of the old empire. Because the Bolsheviks had both advocated the right of national self-determination and insisted that the working class and the poor in any country would, given the choice, choose a communist regime, they were in an awkward position with regard to the national liberation movements. Few of the empire's national minorities demonstrated any interest in communism.

The Finns were the first to go. Long an autonomous Grand Duchy, Finland had become restive as a result of the Russification policies of the last two tsars. The first Provisional government had acknowledged Finland's right to independence; the Bolsheviks had no choice but to follow suit. A new government in Helsinki proclaimed Finnish independence. Finland would not be under Russian Communist rule.

The Estonians, Latvians, and Lithuanians likewise established independent states. Literate and industrious, these peoples were few in numbers but quite capable of establishing and maintaining viable political entities. Many of the poor peasants in Latvia and Lithuania supported the Bolsheviks, but by and large the populations of all three countries detested both Bolshevism and Russia.

The German puppet regime in the Ukraine fell right after the Armistice of November 11, 1918. The victorious Western Allies asked the Germans to keep troops in the Ukraine as a bulwark against Bolshevism, but the general staff refused, knowing that the army might be needed to control the rebellious working class at home. The German withdrawal was followed by a nightmarish period when control of the Central Ukraine changed hands 10 times in 23 months. Simon Petlyura, last leader of the independent Central Rada before the German occupation, now rejoined the struggle for power in the Ukraine at the head of a motley, anti-Semitic group of Cossacks, deserters, brigands, and nationalists.

A major contender for power in the Ukraine in 1918 was Nestor Makhno. Unfurling the black flag of anarchism, Makhno quickly proved himself a capable and popular guerrilla leader. He fought Germans, Petlyura, Bolsheviks, and anyone else who needed fighting. In 1919 he joined the Communists, left them, rejoined them, and was then attacked by them.

Still another Ukrainian leader with a swashbuckling apolitical approach to politics was Nikifor Hryhoriv (Grigoriev). Hryhoriv had an army of 15,000 partisans in the field by early 1919; his forces terrorized vast areas. Then an ally of the Bolsheviks, by summer he had changed his mind. He was killed by Makhno himself in July 1919.

In Bessarabia, an agricultural province southwest of the Ukraine, ethnic Romanians formed the largest single population group. They proclaimed their independence early in 1918, then opted for union with Romania. The Bolsheviks, declaring that the Romanian army had invaded the province and annexed it by force, refused to accept the loss of Bessarabia.

Armenia and Georgia, two culturally advanced areas of the old empire, declared their independence early in 1918. There were then relatively few Armenians in the Bolshevik party, but there were many Georgians, including the new commissar of nationalities, Stalin—a Georgianized Ossete. The loss of Georgia to the anti-Bolshevik camp, galling to Stalin personally, outraged the Bolsheviks because Mensheviks were instrumental in organizing the independent Georgian state.

The Muslims in Trans-Caucasia and Central Asia also sought to break away from Russian domination. Most of these peoples remained politically less sophisticated than the European minorities, however, and

their attempts to win national independence were badly defined and poorly led. It would be some time before the example of their ethnic kin and co-religionists across the frontiers, notably in Turkey and Iran, would inspire a more progressive approach to politics.

## TSARIST AND PROVISIONAL GOVERNMENT FORCES

Disbanded soon after the October Revolution, the tsarist general staff remained a potent source of anti-Bolshevik plots and machinations. Kerensky and General Krasnov commanded a comic-opera operation on the outskirts of Petrograd which was easily suppressed. General Kaledin, the Don Cossack commander, took the field against the Bolsheviks immediately on learning of the Revolution. In November 1917 he tried and failed to take the key southern city of Rostov-on-Don. Disgraced, he committed suicide. Kerensky's erstwhile comrade-in-arms, General Krasnov, was then elected chief of the Don Cossacks. He put together an army and attacked the Bolsheviks on two fronts in the summer of 1918. Tsarist officials were instrumental in forming various "governments" and "commissions" around the country, which they offered to the Russian people as alternatives to the Bolshevik regime, concealing the foreign strings.

Tsarist commanders were instrumental in bringing the Czechoslovak Legion into the battle against the Bolsheviks in May 1918. The 40,000 former prisoners of war were spread across Siberia in 60 troop trains. The Bolsheviks had permitted them to leave through Vladivostok, but at the instigation of tsarist officers the Legion—maintaining internal contact by telegraph—rebelled against its Soviet escorts and began assembling in western Siberia. It encountered little opposition from the Bolsheviks, whose rule in Irkutsk, Omsk, Tomsk, and other Siberian cities had been overthrown by White forces in the spring of 1918.

The Legion helped to establish the Committee of Members of the Constituent Assembly (KOMUCH) in Samara in June 1918 and the Provisional Siberian government in Omsk the same month. In August the Legion captured Kazan and seized that portion— about half—of the Imperial Russian gold reserve in temporary storage there.

Pressure from the Czechoslovak Legion on Bolshevik positions led to the massacre of the tsar and his family. The Romanovs and their entourage had been moved for their safety to Yekaterinburg (now Sverdlovsk) in May 1918, pending the trial of Nicholas. That there would be a trial no one doubted. The Bolsheviks intended to emulate the French revolutionaries who tried and executed Louis XVI; Trotsky had asked for the role of Bertrand Barère de Vieuzac, prosecutor of the French king.

The Urals quickly proved not a sanctuary (Lenin had intended to move the Sovnarkom there if Moscow fell) but a combat zone. In mid-July the Communist authorities in Yekaterinburg warned that the city was in imminent danger of falling to the Whites and Czechoslovaks. A Cheka (secret police) officer, Yakov Yurovsky, was in charge of the guard over the royal family.

On the night of July 16–17, Nicholas and the others were awakened after midnight and told to dress quickly. The guard informed them that the city was about to be attacked; they must go to the cellar for their safety. No doubt too sleepy and frightened to understand their predicament, the family quickly made its way downstairs. A dozen or so Chekists burst in, revolvers in hand. Yurovsky hastily read an order from the *local* Communist authorities: the Romanovs were to be executed. The Chekists opened

fire instantly, each man having received his assigned target in advance.

The detachment took the bodies to an abandoned mine, dismembered them, drenched them with sulfuric acid, and burned them. The executioners later scattered the ashes in a nearby forest.

In April 1989 Yakov Yurovsky's son, Vice Admiral Aleksandr Yurovsky, and a detective writer, Geli Ryabov, revealed their discovery of what appeared to be the remains of the royal family, including the skull of the tsar. The collaboration of the ministry of the interior bolstered the claim and lent authority to Ryabov's published inference that Lenin and the Sovnarkom ordered the slayings. The dramatic find, yet another manifestation of *glasnost,* struck at the long-standing Communist assertion that the SR party had massacred the royal family to discredit Lenin's regime.

The SRs, who had made common cause with the Provisional government in the summer of 1917, joined the active opposition to the Bolshevik regime after the October Revolution. In the spring and summer of 1918 they organized and led major anti-Bolshevik uprisings in several cities, notably Moscow and Yaroslavl. Although their uprisings were put down, the SRs retained wide support in the country, especially in the Volga valley.

It was after an SR-sponsored revolt in Penza in August that Lenin ordered all individuals suspected of treason put in concentration camps. There was no basis in law for the measure, which stands as an ominous landmark of a period when the Communists ruled by executive fiat. Legal authorization for the camps came with the decrees of May 17 and September 5, 1919. Rule by decree was hardly an improvement.

At the end of summer 1918, three-quarters of the old empire's territory was in Allied, White, or other anti-Bolshevik hands.

It is difficult to imagine a bleaker situation than that which now confronted Lenin.

## FIRST ANTI-BOLSHEVIK COALITION: KOLCHAK

By the latter part of 1918 the Allies had achieved a certain amount of harmony in the matter of Russian policy; they recognized Admiral A.V. Kolchak as leader of the White movements against Bolshevism. Washington, London, and Paris had been deeply distressed over the failure of those movements to coalesce on their own. In expressing preference for Kolchak, they hoped to effect an agreement among the anti-Bolshevik Russians.

Sir Samuel Hoare, the British military attaché, advised London that a military dictatorship would be the best solution for Russia and called Admiral Kolchak "the nearest thing to an English gentleman in Russia," an ideal candidate for the post of dictator. Part of Kolchak's attractiveness stemmed from his willingness to acknowledge the tsarist debt as binding upon the government he proposed to form, and part lay in his control of that half of the Imperial gold reserves— 651.5 million rubles worth—the Czechoslovak Legion had seized at Kazan.

With massive aid from the Allies paid for with the tsar's gold, Kolchak put an army of 250,000 in the field in late 1918. But that force was spread across enormous distances. Essentially Kolchak controlled a thin line along the Trans-Siberian Railway.

In the beginning the Red Army fought Kolchak on a guerrilla basis, and the Kolchak regulars treated captured partisans savagely. Monstrous reprisals at Omsk and in Yekaterinburg province, where the tsar had been killed, horrified all Russia.

For Kolchak, everything depended upon the support of the local population and continued assistance from the Allies. The admiral alienated the Siberian peasantry, however, by attempting to introduce the old landlord system, which had never been fully operative in Siberia. Further, Kolchak missed his opportunity to keep Wilson from turning against him when he spurned the American president's call for peace talks between the various factions. Lenin was skeptical but accepted the proposal in principle; Kolchak and other White leaders rejected it. Their refusal did not end allied aid, but it did strengthen Wilson's growing conviction that intervention had been a mistake.

In January 1918 Lenin's government established the Workers' and Peasants' Red Army (RKKA), and in February the Red Fleet was created. The Red Guards of 1917 provided the nucleus of the new proletarian armed forces. Trotsky, commissar of army and navy (war comissar), insisted there be at least one Communist in all army units down to platoon level. Thus began the politicization of the armed forces.

Early in September 1918 Soviet authorities established the Revolutionary Military Council of the Republic (RMCR) and gave it responsibility for military operations. Chaired by Trotsky, the RMCR did on the battlefield what the Defense Council did in the civilian war effort. The formation of this body followed immediately on the Sovnarkom's decree placing the entire country under martial law. That decree was issued on September 2, three days after an attempt on Lenin's life.

At the outset of the war Soviet authorities announced their intention to raise an army of three million men. This proved impossible. Men might have been found, but there were not enough officers to train them, nor were there enough weapons or food. Over the objections of many Communists Trotsky pressed thousands of ex-Imperial Army officers into service to the Soviet regime, assigning political commissars to all units to keep the officers in line and, as added insurance, held their families hostage. By early 1919, 29,000 officers and about 166,000 sergeants and corporals of the old army were in the Red Army. In the ranks there were about 1.2 million men, many in noncombat units. The Communists could put only about 450,000 men in the field to face the spring 1919 White offensive. The size of the White force, however, was approximately the same, perhaps slightly smaller.

The multipronged but poorly coordinated offensive began on March 4, when Kolchak, having withdrawn from the river to regroup over the winter, sent a large force westward toward the Volga. At the same time, General Anton Denikin marched his French-supported army northward against Harkov, Kiev, Voronezh, and Oryol. Those cities fell one after the other, although the Communists soon retook Oryol. A more or less simultaneous attack was launched by General E.K. Miller—a Russian despite his name—at Archangel. Miller had the support of the British and American troops and more supplies than he knew what to do with. In Estonia, General N.N. Yudenich was still building an army and could not mount a major attack until October. In the spring and summer, however, he harassed the new regime with hit-and-run raids, seizing and briefly holding several Russian towns.

The White attacks on so many fronts dwarfed Napoleon's 1812 invasion and in geographical scale, if not results, put Genghis Khan's 13th-century expedition to shame. The Mongols and the Grande Armée destroyed everything in their paths—which constituted only narrow lines across the Russian expanses. The White fronts now stretched from Archangel to the Aral Sea; from the Caspian to the Don; and from the Sea of Azov to Riga and Tallinn. In Siberia, there was heavy fighting along the Trans-

Lenin in Red Square, Moscow, May 1, 1919. (Sovnarkom photo)

Siberian Railway and on the coast near Vladivostok. Surrounded, without friends, its industry and agriculture in ruins and its population demoralized, the Russian Republic should have fallen. But the vast distance again worked to the greater disadvantage of the attacker, and Russia's immensity favored those who held the heartland.

There were many days in 1919 when the regime seemed on the verge of collapse. The Whites made impressive advances on all fronts. Kolchak's forces crossed the Urals and swooped down on European Russia but could not establish a position on the Volga. White forces under Denikin swept everything before them in the Ukraine, but they made the mistake of leaving nothing behind but devastation and an embittered population. In Petrograd a nervous party organization under Zinoviev panicked and called for reinforcements when the Whites advanced on the city. The RMCR sent Stalin; a recent Soviet source drily notes that "his arrival didn't change things." The Whites took Pskov on May 25. The garrisons of two forts that formed part of the western defenses of Petrograd rebelled against the Communists.

At that point Trotsky and Lenin intervened, rushing reserves to the Petrograd sector and directing suppression of the revolts. The situation stabilized for a few months. Then in September 1919 General Yudenich launched a new strike, using six British tanks to support his infantry, that took him to the gates of Petrograd by mid-October. Once again the RMCR sent reinforcements. Yudenich halted, then withdrew to Estonia.

In the south, General Denikin had several able commanders and ample equipment supplied by the Allies. He ordered an offensive in the direction of Moscow in July 1919. Lenin declared that the "most critical moment" in the war had arrived. At the cost of enormous casualties, the Red Army beat back the attack and saved the capital. Denikin regrouped and moved north once again in September. His forces competed for the million-ruble prize offered by Ukrainian businessmen to the first regiment to fight its way into Moscow.

The prize went unclaimed. Their lines stretched taut across increasingly hostile territory, the Whites failed to advance north from Oryol. The RMCR threw every force at its disposal against Denikin and again turned him back. The First Cavalry—it took that name only after the battle—of S.M. Budyonny played an important role in the successful Communist counterattack, as did

Red Army parade, Moscow, 1919. (National Archives)

the 8th Army of the RKKA. Harkov came back under Soviet control on December 12, Kiev on December 16. Early in January 1920 the Red Army recaptured Tsaritsyn and Rostov-on-Don.

Contemplating the defeats suffered by Kolchak's forces, the Western Allies concluded that their protégé had not lived up to expectations. British support began to waver. The French had serious morale problems with the forces they sent to Russia despite the fact that those troops saw almost no combat. Facing increasingly negative public opinion at home, Britain and France began withdrawing their forces from Russia.

The admiral knew a sinking ship when he saw one. Kolchak resigned his grandiose title (Supreme Ruler of All Russia) on January 4, 1920, but he might as well have kept it. He was captured by his erstwhile friends, the Czechoslovaks, who handed him over to a newly installed Bolshevik regime in the Siberian city of Irkutsk. They executed him on February 7.

## WAR WITH POLAND

Kolchak was gone, Yudenich was gone, Miller had fallen back to the White Sea, Denikin was on the run. Knowing that and nothing more, one might conclude that the Communists had victory in hand. Enter the Poles.

The Poland that was restored to life in 1918 naturally had enormous grievances against the three powers—Austria, Russia, Prussia—which had partitioned the country out of existence in the 18th century. Austria and Prussia-Germany had just gone down to defeat; Russia had simply disintegrated. The time seemed ripe for Poland to regain her historic frontiers.

The difficulty was that the Ukrainians, White Russians, Russians, Lithuanians, Germans, and Czechs who surrounded the Poles

did not accept Polish historical or ethnic cartography, to say nothing of Polish political aspirations. There was little for the Germans or Czechs to fear, for the Allies would not permit any armed aggression against them. Those same Allies, however, welcomed Poland's assault on the territory of the former Russian Empire. Nationalistic Poles dreamed of "reestablishing" a Poland that stretched from the Baltic to the Black Sea, from Smolensk to Berlin's eastern approaches. Such a Poland had never existed, although Polish arms did conquer the territories involved at one time or another, and Poles had ruled in Moscow briefly in the 17th century.

Polish attacks to the south and east began early in 1919 as hit-and-run raids. When Polish forces took Minsk in White Russia, however, the war began in earnest. By late 1919 the Poles had put together a large, well-equipped army. France supplied 350 airplanes, 2,800 machine-guns, more than 300,000 rifles, and a corps of military advisers—including the young Charles de Gaulle—under General Maxime Weygand. With all this aid the Poles had no difficulty raising an army of 200,000 men. With nearly 80,000 of those troops, General Joseph Pilsudski struck southward on April 25, 1920. His forces drove 200km into the Ukraine in six weeks and seized Kiev on May 6. Pilsudski proclaimed Polish sovereignty over the entire right-bank west of the Dnepr River—Ukraine.

Trotsky and the RCMR worked out a counterattack that had Budyonny's First Cavalry driving southwest toward Kiev and other units under G.D. Gai and M.N. Tukhachevsky moving west on Brest-Litovsk. In the time-honored manner of Russo-Polish conflicts, pro-Russian Polish Communists formed a Temporary Revolutionary Committee at Bialystok and "invited" the Red Army into Poland to "liberate" the country. The Soviet plan was initially successful.

Kiev was retaken on June 12. Tukhachevsky ripped through the Polish forces in White Russia and moved on into Poland proper. By the middle of August his forces were approaching Warsaw and Lwow. Among those in Warsaw anxiously watching the Soviet advance was the papal envoy, Achille Ratti, the future Pope Pius XI.

At this point the RMCR representative on the Southwestern Front, Stalin, made a series of crucial mistakes. He underestimated the threat from the south, where the last important White commander, Wrangel, menaced the Soviet forces trying to push the Poles back across the Dnepr. Having assured the RMCR in Moscow that everything was under control, Stalin prepared to detach three units including the First Cavalry and send them to the aid of Tukhachevsky, who seemed on the verge of taking Warsaw.

Trotsky and Lenin assumed that this repositioning of forces was militarily sound. Budyonny and the First Cavalry were thrown back by the Wrangel forces, however, before they could disengage and move west. Stalin's plan collapsed. The Tukhachevsky forces poised to install a red flag atop Warsaw City Hall now scurried ignominiously back toward Moscow.

The British government had failed to find a Russian who could defeat the Bolsheviks; now it would try a Pole. On July 21, 1920, Lloyd George announced that Great Britain and France would render all necessary aid to help Pilsudski build up his armed forces. The Poles soon had half a million men under arms.

## SECOND ANTI-BOLSHEVIK COALITION

It was not difficult to arouse Lloyd George's sympathy for the Poles. Poland, to be sure, had attacked Soviet Russia, and not the other way around, but somehow that fact got lost. Too, Churchill and others had sold the prime minister a shoddy bill of goods about making the Crimea a new Gibraltar or Hong Kong, and they offered him one last White general, Baron Peter N. Wrangel.

Wrangel had served as one of Denikin's commanders in the Great War, and after the Bolshevik Revolution he commanded an anticommunist Volunteer Army in the Caucasus. When he transferred his operations to the Ukraine, he quickly came into conflict with Denikin over both military strategy and politics. Denikin eventually exiled him to Constantinople for plotting to take command of the army.

With Denikin's defeat early in 1920 the remnants of his forces, plus some anticommunist units that had been defeated in Trans-Caucasia, gathered in the Crimea to wait for evacuation by the Allies. The leaders of these troops deposed Denikin and with Allied approval appointed Wrangel to replace him. A British warship promptly brought the general from Constantinople and deposited him at Sevastopol on April 2. Two days later the "Black Baron"—he designed his own exotic dark uniforms—took command.

Wrangel differed from previous White commanders in that he had something he called a political and social program. Where his predecessors never really went beyond anticommunism and anti-Semitism, Wrangel addressed himself to the land question. He proposed to nationalize landholdings above 600 desyatins; permit the peasants to buy this land over a 25-year period; and establish agencies of rural self-government (zemstvos). Finally, he promised to defend the interests of the workers.

All the White leaders wanted to turn back the clock; Wrangel was no exception. He had no more popular support than any of his predecessors, and neither he nor any other White commander ever consolidated a battlefield position long enough to establish a smooth-running political administration.

Wrangel rebuilt his forces and equipped them with British and French arms. In the spring of 1920 he moved out of the Crimea into the Ukraine and northwest Trans-Caucasia. Once again the White advance was aided by Stalin's blunders. Not until the Khrushchev era did Soviet historians begin to acknowledge that Stalin had repeatedly defied orders in the Civil War, and that his disobedience and incompetence led to costly defeats.

In August 1920 the RMCR decided to establish a new front in order to bring all available forces to bear against Wrangel. For reasons that are not clear the bungling Stalin was entrusted with the task of coordinating the creation of this new front. He failed; the Red Army sustained heavy losses. The Southern Front was created in September without Stalin, who was recalled to Moscow. Under the direction of M.V. Frunze, assisted by S.I. Gusev and the Hungarian Communist Béla Kun, the RKKA forces on the new front gradually pushed Wrangel's army back.

The final, decisive battles were fought November 7–17, 1920, on the Perekop and Chongar isthmuses that link the Crimean Peninsula to the mainland. At a cost of 10,000 casualties Frunze's troops routed Wrangel. French and British warships evacuated 80,000 White troops, camp followers, and anti-Communist civilians to Turkey, Bulgaria, and Yugoslavia.

## END OF WAR AND INTERVENTION

A few weeks before the final battles in the Crimea, the Poles agreed to a truce. Once again there were Soviet zealots who wanted to keep fighting to establish a Communist regime in Poland, but Lenin declared that he and his party had "overestimated the revolutionary readiness" of the Polish workers and peasants. A treaty was signed at Riga, Latvia, on March 18, 1921.

The border between Poland and Soviet Russia was fixed east of a line recommended earlier by the British foreign secretary, Lord Curzon, who had little sympathy for Russia. It deprived Poland of some Lithuanian territory she coveted but gave her sizable areas in White Russia and the Ukraine. Poland would later pay the price of placing faith in lines on maps.

With the collapse of Wrangel's army, the signing of the Russo-Polish armistice, and the withdrawal of the Allied forces, the worst of the Civil War was over. The Japanese remained on the mainland for another year, but the Americans kept a close watch on them and they did little harm.

Still ahead lay the fierce uprisings at Tambov and Kronstadt, both of which the Red Army would have to suppress. So-called bandit gangs kept the Ukraine, part of the Volga Valley, and much of the strip along the Trans-Siberian Railway in turmoil, but dealing with them involved mere mopping-up operations. The *basmachi*—both Islamic guerrillas and ordinary bandits—in Central Asia posed some threat to the Soviet regime, but they were far removed from the heartland, and when the Communists devoted their full attention to them they were quickly subdued.

The Red Army had won a victory inadequately described as astonishing. How did this happen? Why were Britain, France, the United States, and a dozen other nations, plus hordes of anticommunist Russians, unable to defeat the infant revolutionary regime?

The Communists had a number of practical advantages, notably control of the Central Russian heartland. Operating under martial discipline, for once they contained their internal frictions, and they commanded the allegiance of the proletariat. Having secured communications and supply lines, they found excellent field commanders to lead the war against the foreigners and counterrevolutionaries. To a remarkable degree they proved able to exploit the infrastructure of the tsarist war effort—war industry committees, supply committees, civilian auxiliary organizations, zemstvos, and so forth. Above all, the Communists had a cause: Russia freed, independent, and socialist. No opponent produced a remotely acceptable alternative.

The peoples of the Western nations, as distinct from some megalomaniac politicians (none of whom cared to shed his own blood), had little stomach for intervention. The Great War had so drained Britain and France of blood and treasure and spirit that there was little left over to fight a country that had been an ally until October 1917. As for the United States, there was little point in intervening at all, let alone on the side of a White movement that was not going to help Wilson make the world safe for democracy.

The Whites themselves had no unity and no program, and theirs was a woefully inadequate military force. Most of their leaders, like the French aristocracy after 1789 who had learned nothing and forgotten nothing, favored the restoration of landlordism. Further, the behavior of most White commanders indicated that they wanted either a military dictatorship or the restoration in some form of the monarchy. They could not make up their minds, and this was another index of their lack of unity. Kolchak claimed to unite all anti-Bolshevik forces but could not sustain that posture and ended a lonely, isolated figure.

The Whites never won the support of the Russian and Ukrainian people. With the sole exception of Wrangel's brief public-relations campaign of 1920, they did not even try. The peasants were certainly not wildly enthusiastic about the Communists, but they were exhausted, and above all they wanted the peace that only the Bolsheviks had promised them back in 1917. That peace had not come was not, most people came to believe, the fault of the Bolsheviks; the treaty of Brest-Litovsk surely proved that. The war had continued and had been transformed into a civil war because opponents of the Bolsheviks did not accept their seizure of power.

The Allied attempt to crush Bolshevism came to nothing. Winston Churchill and those who shared his views tried to convince political leaders in the West that Lenin's regime had vast potential for future mischief; they had some success with the leaders, almost none with the public. Anticommunism was not a cause to inspire the Western masses, at least not right after the Great War.

## IMPACT OF CIVIL WAR ON SOCIETY AND PARTY

Beginning as an armed contest for political supremacy, the Russian Civil War developed into a great class conflict. To a considerable extent this was foreshadowed in the treatment the soldiers and sailors of 1917 accorded their former officers—most of whom were from the middle and upper classes—in the wake of Order No. 1. As institutions disintegrated in the months after the October Revolution, social relations degenerated to the level of an elementary struggle for survival. The "war communism" of 1918–1920 was in part a cause, in part a result, of this process. The state—such as it was—itself became a bandit, stealing the food it required to feed its soldiers, workers, and bureaucrats.

There was no protection from the marauding state in areas where the Red Army enforced its will, and still less was there any defense against the White forces where they held sway. As usually happens in civil wars, people were forced to choose between two terrible alternatives, recognizing that, whatever the choice, the most likely outcome was disaster. Many families were torn asunder as members clashed less over ideology—the struggle was too primitive for that—than over violent differences of opinion concerning the survival of the family and the clan.

As the Whites learned to their sorrow, the social conflict quickly reached the point where peasants could no longer be persuaded, let alone coerced, to fight for the interests of the upper classes. The *muzhiks* of 1918–1920, whose ancestors had periodically burned and slaughtered in great rebellions, were utterly indifferent to the death agony of the Russian landlords and aristocrats. And the workers, those peasants transplanted into the misery of the industrializing cities, fought the forces of counterrevolution and intervention with a passion that far transcended ideology.

In the course of the war the Bolshevik-Communist party itself underwent a profound transformation, becoming militarized as no political party in history up to that time. To be a Communist in 1918–1920 was literally to be a front-line soldier. To *become* a Communist in that period meant that one accepted the death sentence decreed by the Whites and many Interventionist commanders, who publicized their intention to massacre party members. As the ferocity of the anti-Bolshevik regimes in various parts of Russia clearly demonstrated, a White-Interventionist victory would unquestionably have been followed by a monumental bloodbath.

A party membership forged in civil war was unlikely to be magnanimous toward its external enemies or tolerant of internal dissent. The democratic traditions of Bolshevism were inescapably compromised as the party fought for its own, and Russia's, existence. Nor would the coming of peace dilute this war experience. Of all party members in 1927, fully a third had joined in the 1917–1920 period, only one percent before 1917. Militant Bolshevism was not born in the Civil War, but that conflict shaped the party's future as much and in some respects more than its revolutionary tradition.

At the birth of the Bolshevik regime, the West presented Russia's new rulers with an immensely important psychological weapon. Every Communist leader since 1917 has been able to rally popular support for an aggressively defensive (!) foreign policy and for the suppression of internal dissent by raising the spectre of "capitalist encirclement." The siege mentality of Soviet leaders was born in 1917, and it is part and parcel of the emotional baggage of most party members.

Against overwhelming odds the Workers' and Peasants' Red Army defeated all Soviet enemies. When the Perekop and Chonkar battles ended in victory on November 17, 1920, Russia knew peace for the first time since July 31, 1914. She had been at war for 2,301 consecutive days.

## SUGGESTED ADDITIONAL READING

[Babine, Alexis], *A Russian Civil War Diary: Alexis Babine in Saratov, 1917–1922*, Donald J. Raleigh, ed., Durham, N.C.: Duke University Press, 1988

Benvenuti, Francesco, *The Bolsheviks and the Red Army, 1918–1922*, New York: Cambridge University Press, 1988

Borys, Jurij, *The Sovietization of the Ukraine, 1917–1923*, Downsview: University of Ontario Press, 1980

Bradley, John, *Allied Intervention in Russia*, New York: St. Martin's, 1968

**Brovkin, Vladimir N.,** *The Mensheviks after October,* Ithaca, N.Y.: Cornell University Press, 1987

**Carley, Michael J.,** *Revolution and Intervention: The French Government and the Russian Civil War, 1917–1919,* Kingston and Montreal: McGill-Queens University Press, 1983

**Chamberlin, W.H.,** *The Russian Revolution, 1917–1921,* vol. II, Princeton, N.J.: Princeton University Press, 1987

**Getzler, Israel,** *Kronstadt 1917–1921,* New York: Cambridge University Press, 1983

**Kenez, Peter,** *Civil War in South Russia, 1919–1920,* Berkeley and Los Angeles: University of California Press, 1977

**Koenker, Diane, W.G. Rosenberg, and R.G. Suny,** eds., *Party, State, and Society in the Russian Civil War,* Bloomington: Indiana University Press, 1989

**Mawdsley, Evan,** *The Russian Civil War,* Winchester, Mass.: Allen & Unwin, 1987

**Radkey, Oliver H.,** *The Unknown Civil War in Soviet Russia: A Study of the Green Movement in the Tambov Region, 1920–1922,* Seattle: University of Washington Press, 1975

**Sakwa, Richard,** *Soviet Communists in Power: A Study of Moscow During the Civil War, 1918–1921,* New York: St. Martin's, 1988

**Swietochowski, Tadeusz,** *Russian Azerbaijan, 1905–1920,* New York: Cambridge University Press, 1985

**Ullman, R.H.,** *Britain and the Russian Civil War,* Princeton, N.J.: Princeton University Press, 1968

**Wandycz, Piotr S.,** *Soviet-Polish Relations, 1917–1921,* Cambridge: Harvard University Press, 1969

**Wheeler-Bennett, J.W.,** *The Forgotten Peace: Brest-Litovsk, March 1918,* New York: Morrow, 1939

**Wrangel, Piotr,** *The Memoirs of General Wrangel,* New York: Duffield, 1930

# 4

# THE BOLSHEVIZATION
# OF RUSSIA

Tsarism had fallen with scarcely a whimper and the overthrow of the Provisional government proceeded almost as smoothly. These victories confirmed thousands of Bolsheviks in the belief that the natural instincts of the proletariat would produce, now that the "dictatorship" of that class was in place, a just and equitable society almost overnight.

## CONSTITUENT ASSEMBLY

The institution that was supposed to define and shape the new society was, so millions of citizens thought, the Constituent Assembly. The left wing of the intelligentsia had called for its summoning since the 1860s, and one of the Provisional government's first acts was to set up a board to prepare elections.

After several postponements the date was fixed for November 12(25), 1917.

Although in 1903 they had favored a Constituent Assembly, the Bolsheviks now opposed it on several grounds. It smacked of peasant-oriented populist socialism, and the Assembly seemed likely to become a vehicle for middle-class parliamentary democracy. In the "April Theses" Lenin had defined a "republic of Soviets" as the state form of the dictatorship of the proletariat. Clearly there was no room for a Constituent Assembly.

Wary Bolsheviks suspected the country would return a strong SR majority. Whatever its weaknesses in the cities, the SR party retained enormous popularity in the countryside. The *muzhiks*—and their womenfolk now—would unquestionably vote for the party that promised to look after their interests.

As it happened the Bolshevik Revolution occurred just 18 days before the balloting. Because the parties had already published lists of candidates and had begun the electoral campaign, Lenin did not dare dispense with the elections.

Once again the voting took place in unsettled conditions, but it could not have been otherwise: the Civil War had already begun. In only 39 of 79 electoral districts did the election take place on the day scheduled. Other districts voted in December and January. In all, the returns showed that 45 million (of 90 million eligible) had voted, with these results:

| | |
|---|---|
| SR | 40.0% |
| Bolshevik | 24.0% |
| Kadet | 4.7% |
| Menshevik | 2.6% |

The remainder of the voters cast ballots for religious and national parties—Muslim, Polish, etc.—or for small splinter groups.

The Bolsheviks never ceased to claim that the vote did not reflect the mood of the country, but on a "one citizen, one vote" basis, the elections—the freest in Russian history—unquestionably indicated the will of the people. What actually happened was that the rural areas dominated the urban. Bolshevik strength was overwhelmingly concentrated in the cities. In Petrograd, for example, they received 45 percent of the vote, compared with 16.7 percent for the SRs; in the surrounding rural areas the Bolsheviks won 49 percent, the SRs 25 percent. In the city of Moscow the Bolshevik margin of victory over the SRs was 50 percent to 8 percent, and in Moscow province, 50 percent to 26 percent. Further, the Bolsheviks received large majorities from the soldiers on the Western and Northern Fronts and from the Baltic Fleet sailors. In the army as a whole, however, the SRs outpolled them.

What was the Bolshevik regime to do, now that the voters had returned the expected SR plurality, really a decisive majority when SR allies were counted? Lenin's enemies helped make the decision. The regular SRs, the Popular Socialists, and some Mensheviks and Kadets formed a Union for the Defense of the Constituent Assembly in December 1917. Active in Petrograd, Moscow, Odessa, Samara, and other cities, this organization called for the immediate summoning of the Constituent Assembly. Borrowing a page from Lenin, it proclaimed "All Power to the Constituent Assembly!" It organized conferences around the country, published broadsides and proclamations, and ceaselessly agitated for the overthrow of the Bolsheviks.

Lenin's response to the Union was to outlaw the Kadet party, which had taken control of the organization, on November 28 (December 11), and to serve notice that he would not long tolerate the Constituent Assembly. He argued: The majority has voted for other parties and against the Bolsheviks. But the Bolsheviks represent the working class and the Army plus the "poorest stratum of the peasantry," that is, the productive classes, the soldiers merely being peasants in uniform. These classes have given the Bolsheviks clear majorities in the Soviets, which represent a new, "higher" form of democracy. The Constituent Assembly represents discredited bourgeois parliamentary democracy. The will of those who have given the Bolsheviks a majority in the Soviets must therefore prevail.

The Assembly convened on schedule on January 5(18), 1918, in the Tauride Palace in Petrograd. Only 410 of the 715 elected deputies appeared. They had difficulty entering the building through the ranks of the secret police, the guard, and a Bolshevik crowd.

Once the proceedings got under way the SR majority elected its leader, Viktor Chernov, as chairman. The Bolsheviks and their Left SR allies constituted a noisy opposition block of 155. Chernov read an opening speech, and then Yakov Sverdlov, the Bolshevik chairman of the Central Executive Committee (of the Congress of Soviets) spoke on behalf not of the CEC but of the Sovnarkom, a body that most of the deputies refused to recognize. Sverdlov proposed the adoption of the "Declaration of the Rights of Toiling and Exploited Peoples," an updated version of the French Declaration of the Rights of Man. This document spelled out in detail the promises of Lenin's manifesto "To All Workers, Soldiers and Peasants" and constituted the basis of the first Soviet Constitution, which would be introduced later in the year. The "Declaration" had been unanimously adopted by the CEC on January 3(16); now, however, the Assembly deputies refused (237–146) to approve it. The majority held that the CEC was usurping the job the Constituent Assembly had been elected to perform.

There was a little more politicking; then, on a prearranged signal, the Bolsheviks walked out. The Left SRs remained a while longer to debate the regular SRs on the questions of peace and land, and then they too departed. In the galleries, armed sailors pointed their weapons at speakers who displeased them, jeered, whistled, and generally disrupted the proceedings. Finally, shortly before 5:00 a.m. on January 6(19), the session ended when the sailors, who ostensibly constituted a guard, refused to stay on duty any longer and ordered the delegates to quit the building.

The Constituent Assembly was never to meet again. Russia, it must be said, seemed largely indifferent to the fate of what was until the spring of 1989 the only freely elected deliberative body in her history.

## FIRST STEPS OF THE NEW REGIME

In the process of laying the foundations of the new society the Bolsheviks had to contend not only with the hostility of most other political parties but also with still more dissension within their own ranks. On November 17(30), 1917, five members—almost a quarter—of the Central Committee resigned to protest the "exclusion" from the Sovnarkom of members of other parties. This was a political miscalculation. Lenin had tried to include the Left SRs and was still negotiating with them; they actually entered the government in December. No other party accepted the Bolshevik stand on the war, and so it would have been impossible to include anyone but the Left SRs. All the resignees save Zinoviev soon realized their mistake and asked reinstatement.

As in any new administration, decrees, orders, directives, proclamations, and guidelines emanated from the Sovnarkom with bewildering rapidity in the early days. With regard to civil status, a decree of November 10(23) abolished estate distinctions and civil ranks. No more gentry, peasants, merchants, townsmen, and so forth: now all were simply citizens of the Russian Soviet Republic, as the new state was then called. An earlier decree had declared all citizens equal before the law regardless of ethnic origin.

Women received equal rights under the law. A November 1920 Sovnarkom resolution abolished penalties for performing or undergoing abortions; Russia thus became the first nation to legalize the practice. There was, however, strong resistance to the emancipation of women, and men continued to enjoy preferred status in politics and in most sectors of the economy. Aleksandra

Kollontai was the only woman on the Central Committee in this period; her influence there was limited. The wives of party leaders—including Nadezhda Krupskaya, Lenin's wife—were largely relegated, no matter what their abilities, to positions considered suitable for women, e.g., cultural and educational activities.

Marriage and divorce procedures were established early in 1918. Marriages could now be dissolved at the request of one party; this would change several times over the years, as would family law in general. Church marriage became a matter of private preference having no force in law; only a civil ceremony was legally binding. In the freewheeling atmosphere of those early years wedlock lost its role as a social regulator: common-law (unregistered) marriage, long practiced among the radical intelligentsia and people in the arts, lost the wicked Bohemian stigma it always had and became quite popular. Children born outside registered marriages had the same rights as those of registered unions and could not legally be discriminated against.

On January 20 (February 2), 1918, the Sovnarkom proclaimed the separation of church and state. Church land had earlier been nationalized, and now most other church property was seized by the state. Churches could continue to hold religious services, but the comissariat of justice, which was responsible for church affairs until 1924, ordered them to make their buildings available for secular purposes as well. The party converted some churches into antireligious museums; the most notorious example was Kazan Cathedral on Nevsky Prospekt in Petrograd. Parochial schools were abolished and the teaching of religion in schools forbidden. The Constitution of July 1918 stripped the clergy of most civil rights. As disfranchised persons they either received no food-ration cards or cards of the lowest category. The highest categories, permitting purchase of the largest amount—about 2,700 calories worth—were reserved for workers, the Red Army, and party officials. The children of the clergy could not attend state schools above the elementary level, and clerics had to pay higher taxes and rents.

On the chaotic economic front the new regime moved at first through the Central Executive Committee of the Soviet. On November 14(27), this body adopted "Rules of Workers' Control" which were transmitted to all enterprises employing hired labor. The Rules declared that workers were to exercise an undefined "control" over a given enterprise through trade unions, councils of elders, and other worker-elected groups.

A Supreme Economic Council was formed on December 2(15) to direct economic planning. Actual nationalization, which this council was supposed to oversee, proceeded initially on an *ad hoc* basis. Foreign trade became a state monopoly, and the banks were nationalized in December 1917.

Nationalization of the land was accomplished in the first hours of the Revolution: Lenin's "Decree on Land" had turned the land over to those who worked it, but it had specified that the actual transfer was to take place under the supervision of local Soviet authorities. Early in 1918 the city councils, zemstvos, and other agencies and institutions of tsarist times gave way—on paper—to a hierarchical network of Soviets. In practice the setting up of Soviets would take years; in 1918 the process of land transfer was ragged and irregular.

On the last day of January 1918 the vexing problem of the calendar was solved in the only possible way, adoption of the Gregorian calendar. Russia went to bed on January 31 and woke up on February 14.

In March 1918 the Sovnarkom moved the capital back to Moscow, from which Peter the Great had removed it more than 200 years earlier. The dangerously exposed location of Petrograd lay behind this, but the move also made sound psychological sense. Peter's "window on the West" always had too much of the West about it for old Muscovy's taste. Better to retreat into the heartland, back to Russia's roots, away from the corrupting influence of foreigners.

## CREATION OF A NEW GOVERNMENT

The inefficiency, sloth, and corruption of old Russia were more native than foreign and had no greater enemy than Lenin, proponent of a foreign ideology. Lenin's hostility to those deeply ingrained attitudes can only be compared to that of Tsar Peter, who also tried to remake Russia in a Western image. Lenin was determined, once in power, to introduce "precision, discipline and accountability in government."

The tactical organization that had actually made the Revolution, the Military Revolutionary Committee, could not serve as the administrative vehicle to achieve these goals. The MRC's "organic" character was indispensable in October 1917 but inappropriate to the making of a state. In the urgent matter of supplying food to Petrograd, for instance, the 20 to 25 members of the MRC present for duty at any given moment would simply organize "flying food-supply squads"—in effect, gangs of legal thieves—to go into the countryside and take food from peasants and merchants, sometimes against a worthless receipt. This could work only briefly. To ensure the orderly provisioning of the cities and the military forces it was necessary to create a bureaucracy, a formal body with a fixed mandate, established procedures, and legal responsibilities. In other words, it was necessary to replace the "organic" MRC with a body of bureaucrats.

To a certain extent the All-Russian Central Executive Committee (CEC) of the Congress of Soviets served, in the beginning, as an alternative to the MRC. Lenin called the Congress the "highest type of democracy," and its representatives on the CEC spoke, he maintained, for the revolutionary people, for "Soviet democracy." The CEC was an important organ in the power structure for the first half of 1918, but after June of that year it met only every few weeks and in 1919 ceased to meet altogether. Chiefly responsible was the decline of the Soviets themselves. Under Civil War conditions, those bodies, so indispensable in the Revolution, proved incapable of making quick, coordinated decisions. The Civil War did not create the unity that the struggle against tsarism did. The dream of Soviet democracy died as Lenin's regime moved rapidly toward a system of centralized decision-making that involved a minimum of consultation with democratic institutions.

The Sovnarkom filled the breach created by the demise of the MRC and the CEC. Some scholars trace the origin of Stalin's despotism to Lenin's destruction of the MRC, the one body that had responded to the pulse of a nation in revolution. Lenin's defenders argue that there was no choice; a state cannot depend on "flying food-supply squads" to feed its population. It was also true, however, that Lenin had promised something new and radically different. In power he began to copy the old system.

The Bolshevik party bureaucracy took over the old institutional structures and both transformed them and was remade by them. At the top there was little, in the beginning, to distinguish the Sovnarkom from any modern European cabinet save the name. Lenin remained the unchallenged head of the government and the leader, but in no sense the dictator, of the party that dominated it. After he finally put together a stable group of commissars in mid-1918, the Sovnarkom began to function reasonably well.

Achieving that stability proved difficult. There were frequent resignations of Bolsheviks who opposed this or that policy, and the six Left SRs who were briefly in the government left in protest against the Treaty of Brest-Litovsk. People with administrative skills who were willing to work for the Bolsheviks were in critically short supply. In the circumstances it was only natural that Lenin would work through the old administrative apparatus. His party had, however, come to power promising to destroy that apparatus, not assume control of it, and Lenin's pragmatic approach to the problems of governing introduced considerable tension into the emerging system.

Two bodies within the Sovnarkom acted as specialized arms of the executive power. The first was the Defense Council (in 1920 renamed the Labor and Defense Council), entrusted with the mobilization of the "human and material resources of the country in the interests of defense." During the Civil War it had unlimited powers; its decisions "had the immediate and unqualified force of law." It was composed of five men, including Lenin, Trotsky, and Stalin.

The second sub-agency of the Sovnarkom was the Little Sovnarkom. Unlike the Defense Council, from whose decisions there was no appeal, this body was subordinate to the Sovnarkom. It dealt not with grand questions of defense but rather with the routine, inescapable administrative problems that demand bureaucratic intervention in all modern societies in normal times. Lenin called the Little Sovnarkom his "chief assistant" and delighted in supervising its handling of minutiae.

Through the Defense Council the party-appointed Sovnarkom quickly became the true government. It was not merely the executive agency; it had all power. The Civil War was the main cause of the withering-away not of the state but of the Soviets.

After the Civil War, the Central Committee of the Communist party and ultimately its Politburo replaced the Sovnarkom as the sole repository of power. Lenin realized too late what was taking place. He tried from the spring of 1922 until his final, incapacitating stroke to strengthen the state and thwart the growth of the party machine. It had been difficult to create the monster; it would prove impossible to destroy it.

From the beginning the new state apparatus and the party structure existed side by side, something like the parallel religious and secular institutions of medieval Europe. In the first few years of Communist rule almost all leading party officials held state offices more or less corresponding to their party rank. Because of the nature and philosophy of the ruling party, any tension between party and state interests, or between party and state obligations of office-holders, was invariably resolved in favor of the party. The state structure was open to public scrutiny, and, initially, office-holders to public accountability. The party, however, was responsible only to itself.

## FIRST CONSTITUTION

As Petrograd could not long be fed with forcibly requisitioned supplies, so Russia could not long be governed by decrees, resolutions, declarations, and revolutionary rhetoric. The Bolsheviks recognized the modern state's need for a coherent set of general principles expressing the sources of its legitimacy and its aspirations. The Third

Congress of Soviets (January 1918) had directed the establishment of a constitutional commission, but because of the international situation that body was not formally created until April by the Fourth Congress. On the commission were the Communists—the Bolsheviks having adopted the name—Sverdlov, Stalin, Bukharin, M.N. Pokrovsky, and several Left SRs.

The commission produced a draft that proved unacceptable. Bukharin and Pokrovsky, both Left Communists, took the old revolutionary slogans seriously, and some fellow members on the commission agreed with them. They genuinely believed in the possibility of creating a revolutionary "commune state" which would have no need of coercive bodies such as police, army, or bureaucracy. Lenin had argued precisely this point in his *State and Revolution*. Bukharin and his allies regarded communism "less as a commitment to actual policies than to a vision of the new order as the antithesis of the old."

Times had changed, however, and Lenin himself was no longer so wary of Leviathan. Now, wielding the club of power, he thought it too small and fragile. He pressed the constitutional commission to accept his revised view of the state and won a substantial victory. On July 10, 1918, the Fifth All-Russian Congress of Soviets confirmed the new constitution, which received some last-minute editing from the CEC before publication on July 19, five days after the exclusion of regular SRs and all Mensheviks from all Soviets, two days after the execution of the Romanov family.

The Constitution of the Russian Soviet Federated Socialist Republic (RSFSR), as the state was now called, consisted of 17 chapters and 90 articles. Part I was a "Declaration of the Rights of Toiling and Exploited Peoples" which proclaimed world revolution, the overthrow of capitalism and imperialism, and a dictatorship of the Soviets in Russia. It also stated that "he who does not work does not eat." Supreme authority was vested in the All-Russian Congress of Workers', Peasants', Cossacks' and Red Army Soviets, a body of more than 1,100 deputies that was to meet twice a year (yearly from 1921). Day-to-day business was to be carried on by a 200-member Central Executive Committee of the Congress. Actual power, however, resided in the Sovnarkom, which had the authority to legislate by decree, a weapon its Defense Council used repeatedly; those decrees were in theory subject to review by the CEC. Village, town, city, district, and provincial Soviets, through their own executive committees, exercised local authority and served as liaison agencies with the central power. Because Communists dominated the Soviets at all levels, outlawing some parties and placing severe restrictions on *all* other parties, "Soviet democracy" meant confirmation of the Communist monopoly on political power. The 1918 constitution thus marked out the road toward the one-party state even if it did not create it.

With an eye on the Constituent Assembly elections, the framers of the constitution made one urban elector—any citizen 18 or over not disfranchised under other provisions of the document—equal to *five* rural electors. The principle of "one citizen, one vote" was unacceptable to the makers of a proletarian revolution in a state where the peasantry had an overwhelming majority.

The constitution specifically disfranchised certain categories of people: those who hired labor or who lived on interest, rents, or dividends (i.e., "exploiters"); private businessmen; the clergy; ex-policemen; the Romanovs; the mentally unfit; convicted criminals; and "enemies of the people" as the state defined the term. The number of the disfranchised seems not to have exceeded 3 percent of the adult population.

## CHEKA

Early in November 1917 the Military Revolutionary Committee in Petrograd posted a guard of "forty sober men" over the tsar's Winter Palace wine cellar. Drunkenness, disorder, and street violence had reached almost unmanageable proportions and the new regime was forced to introduce severe discipline. The tsar's wine was poured into the Neva, great batches of drunks and "hooligans" were arrested, and Lenin, blaming the Kadets for much of the lawlessness as well as for "counterrevolutionary" agitation for the Constituent Assembly, outlawed that party.

These measures proved insufficient. Early in December the MRC, which initially had responsibilty for keeping order, went out of existence, and the Sovnarkom created an All-Russian Extraordinary Commission for Combating Counterrevolution and Sabotage. The name of this organization was to undergo several changes over the years, and its mandate was soon extended to cover everything that impinged, however remotely, on state security. The name was shortened to Cheka, an acronym; a member of the commission was a Chekist.

The first director was Felix Dzerzhinsky, a Polish revolutionary of upper-class origins. Widely known as an incorruptible Bolshevik, Dzerzhinsky was a revolutionary fanatic. A few days before the Bolshevik seizure of power, the MRC had appointed him commandant of Smolny, and in that position he quickly became an expert on security. It will be recalled that the CEC of the Congress of Soviets and the Bolshevik Central Committee both met in Smolny; the Sovnarkom met there after the Revolution. Dzerzhinsky was thus the logical choice to head the organization which would become, under his leadership, the "shield and sword of the revolution."

In an administrative decision with fateful consequences for the future, the Cheka was attached not to the Central Executive Committee of the Congress of Soviets, the body that had the most democratic mandate, but rather to the Sovnarkom, the executive agency. As the Sovnarkom's power gave way to that of the party's Politburo, the security forces would be left in a murky zone beyond the government, somewhere in the vicinity of the party, utterly removed from the people.

The Cheka was originally charged to suppress counterrevolution and sabotage. Later the mandate would include speculation and malfeasance in office. The Sovnarkom directed the Cheka to pay special attention to the press, the Kadet and SR parties (not Left SR), and strikers.

In the beginning the Cheka was authorized to employ only "soft measures"—as the Communists would later refer to them: confiscation of property, expulsion from domicile, deprivation of ration card, and publication of lists of "enemies of the people." This quickly changed.

Interpreting party instructions liberally, Dzerzhinsky promptly ordered the shooting without trial or investigation of "enemy agents, counterrevolutionary agitators, speculators, organizers of uprisings" and other undesirables. In the climate of the times that not infrequently meant that innocent citizens were accused of being "enemies of the people" and were shot.

Dzerzhinsky and his revolutionary vigilantes went with the rest of the government to Moscow in March 1918, leaving behind a detachment to deal with Petrograd problems. Units of the Cheka were established all over Bolshevik-controlled territory.

The Bolsheviks had many enemies, most of whom were willing to use violence to overthrow them. There was widespread political and economic sabotage. Speculation in all kinds of valuables had assumed colossal dimensions. Some new office-holders misused their positions, bringing discredit upon the regime and fueling hostility toward it. The frontiers were unstable; anti-Bolshevik agents of many nationalities were constantly infiltrating, committing acts of sabotage. A prominent Petrograd Bolshevik, Moses Volodarsky, was murdered by an SR agent on June 20, 1918. In July, the Left SRs in Moscow assassinated the new German ambassador, Count Wilhelm von Mirbach-Harff, hoping to provoke a renewal of the war with Germany and thus topple Lenin's government. The Left SR plotters, many of them Cheka agents, managed to kidnap Dzerzhinsky and a couple of his associates, and they bombarded the Kremlin with artillery. On that same day, a Left SR uprising began in the north Volga city of Yaroslavl; it continued until July 21 and inspired similar revolts in Murom, Rybinsk, and Arzamas. On August 30, Moses Uritsky, Petrograd director of the Cheka, was assassinated. In an unrelated incident on the same day, Lenin was shot and severely wounded in Moscow by a woman named Fanya Kaplan. Although an SR, Kaplan had acted strictly on her own initiative.

The Civil War was raging out of control. To combat all this, the Cheka swung into action.

The Left SR uprising in Moscow was put down by Latvian riflemen, one of the few military units in the city that did not waver in its allegiance to the Communists in that crucial period. The Cheka freed its chief from his kidnappers and proceeded to execute 13 leaders of the plot. The Communist regime blamed the whole affair on the British, who allegedly hired the SRs and who did indeed have an active secret agent, Bruce Lockhart, in Moscow. To this day the circumstances of the plot remain obscure.

It was not until after the assassination of Uritsky and the attack on Lenin that the regime finally unleashed the "Red Terror." Nationwide martial law was declared on September 2. On September 4, the Sovnarkom newspaper *Izvestiya* (The News) published the text of a telegram from the commissar of internal affairs to all Soviets around the country demanding the taking of hostages and "mass shootings."

The Communists responded to violent opposition by declaring war not only on the oppositionists but also on the social groups from which they came, notably the middle class. The secret police became the agency entrusted with the dragooning of the population into total submission to the will of the party. From the beginning the principle was established: better to condemn any number of innocents than risk the escape of a single guilty one. At Lenin's direction, the Cheka initiated a savage tradition that was ultimately to cost millions of innocent lives.

Abstract theory as well as politics lay behind Lenin's thinking. As the *glasnost*-era writer Vasily Selyunin pointed out in a May 1988 article pinning a major share of responsibility for the Civil War's savagery on Lenin, the party leader believed that, unless it destroyed both market-oriented production and the market itself, the Bolshevik triumph might degenerate to the level of a mere bourgeois revolution. In February 1918 Lenin signed a decree authorizing the shooting on sight of all speculators. At the time, *anyone* who sold food could be called a speculator.

## WAR COMMUNISM

Russia was in a state of unbelievable chaos in the months after the Bolshevik Revolution. To understand why Lenin's party now embarked upon the policy known as war communism, however, we need to examine three sets of figures:

| *Industrial Production* | *Area under Cultivation* | |
|---|---|---|
| (1913 = 100) | | |
| | average 1909–1913: | 83 million desyatins |
| 1917: 74.8 | 1920: | 63 million desyatins |
| 1918: 33.8 | 1921: | 58.3 million desyatins |
| 1919: 14.9 | | |
| 1920: 12.8 | | |
| | *Gross Yield of Crops* | |
| | pre-1914 average: | 3,850,000,000 poods |
| | 1920: | 2,082,000,000 poods |
| | 1921: | 1,689,000,000 poods |

The figures for industrial production would seem to bear out the contention of some historians that what happened to Russia was the most severe depression ever to strike an industrialized or semi-industrialized country. Much of the blame for the situation can obviously be laid to war, foreign intervention, and Civil War, but the Communists brought a great deal of it upon themselves in declaring war upon the productive elements of society.

Life in the cities, increasingly difficult since August 1914, became under Bolshevik rule a grim daily struggle for survival. Moscow and Petrograd lost between one-third and one-half their populations; people could not find work and only rarely food. In Moscow's Sukharevka Market, for centuries a social crossroads, one paid 500 rubles for a lump of sugar in 1918. Milk cost 1,800 rubles a mug, and 50 cigarettes cost 6,000 rubles. "We lived," the writer Ilya Ehrenberg recalled, "on hope and rations." And on *psha* (millet gruel). They burned furniture, shade trees, interior and exterior wood molding, doors—anything combustible in the attempt to keep warm. People dressed in fantastic getups: old uniforms, draperies, tablecloths, canvas, gunnysacks, even newspapers. And the newspapers in Moscow in 1919 were printed on blue paper made from sawdust; the pressure of the eye on the page, people said, made it disintegrate.

Everyone ate and dressed and warmed himself, or tried to, in this way. The shortages, they joked, were divided equally among all the comrades.

In the villages, to which millions of urban dwellers flocked in search of food and warmth and escape from the violence of the cities, life was horrible, and it would get worse before it got still worse than that. The peasants had supported revolution in general in 1917 but the majority of them had voted against the Bolsheviks. When they saw early in 1918 that the Lenin reform brought most of them only about a desyatin (2.7 acres) or so of new land, they sank back into their accustomed distrust of all authority. Any surplus food they grew they tried to sell at a good price; failing that, they stored it away, waiting for better conditions, or kept it for their own needs. Currency had largely lost its value, and anyway the cities were no longer producing anything the peasants could use. The peasants increasingly refused to supply the cities with the goods they needed for survival. The deadly downward spiral terrified all who were trapped in it.

To combat this trend, beginning in May 1918 the authorities introduced the policy that came to be known as "war communism." Historians in the Soviet Union and the West still debate whether Lenin and his party intended this policy as a temporary expedient or as a deliberate leap into pure communism. There is no scholarly consensus. The exigencies of the moment, however, unquestionably obliged the Bolsheviks of 1918 to move more quickly than they had foreseen to translate rather vague and imprecise theory into practice. The state was to take over the means of production and reduce the sphere of private ownership to the narrowest possible dimensions. The principle of universal labor service was introduced, wages were equalized. Because money was practically worthless, however, the Communists attempted to "naturalize economic relations" by introducing that most primitive method of exchange, barter. They instituted the direct exchange of goods between town and countryside. In theory they took grain from the peasant and gave him matches and kerosene in return. In practice there were no matches and kerosene, but this did not save the peasant's grain from confiscation. Further, war communism was marked by the extreme centralization of the economy.

In the first few months of Bolshevik rule, only 72 large factories and plants were nationalized by the government; another 449 were taken over by Red Guards or by their own workers. A decree of June 1918 expanded this program and nationalized all large-scale enterprises. Labor conscription was imposed for some categories of production in January 1919 and for all categories a year later. This was Trotsky's "militarization" of labor: the country's economic problems were the enemy, and he would organize the working class into an army to fight and overcome them.

The decree nationalizing *all* industries was issued in November 1920, when the Civil War had already been won. In actual practice, most small-scale enterprises remained in private hands. Next, two decrees promulgated in December 1920 authorized free distribution of food to workers and officials and free provision of "objects of wide use" (fuel, clothing) to all "productive citizens." Finally, in January 1921 the authorities eliminated rents and utility charges for workers and the poor. It appeared now that communism, for better or for worse, had arrived.

War communism not only did not induce an increase in production: It nearly destroyed production altogether. This was not due solely to Communist mismanagement, of which there was a superabundance. The working class, large sectors of which were already marked by anti-Bolshevik tendencies that would soon find political expression in the "Workers' Opposition," responded to the attempt to introduce communism by simply staying off the job, or by showing up and not working. Nearly two-thirds of the possible working-days in 1919 were lost to such job actions.

The factories and small enterprises that did remain in production managed to supply the Red Army, but on the whole war communism was a disaster in industry. Its record in agriculture was even worse. In May 1918 the Sovnarkom gave the food comissariat dictatorial control over the food supply. This measure proved inadequate; the cities and the Red Army were threatened with starvation. On January 11, 1919, the Sovnarkom decreed the requisitioning of foodstuffs. So-called food requisition detachments went into the countryside and seized all grain held by the peasants in excess of official norms, which were sometimes insufficient to sustain human life. Peasants who held back grain were branded with the hot iron marked "enemy of the people."

The food requisition detachments, composed largely of armed workers from the cities, encountered fierce resistance. The peasants rightly regarded receipts for the seized grain as worthless, and as time went on the detachments did not even bother with these pieces of paper. The peasants resisted with fists, axes, clubs, anything they could find. The detachments were authorized to use deadly force against this resistance and did. In this uneven combat, there could be only one winner—in the short run.

A popular ditty of the time went like this:

I'm sittin' on a barrel,
A barrel of flour.
Don't think, you sonofabitch,
That Russia's in *your* power!

But if the detachments could find the barrel of flour, they took it, and often they shot the peasant who had hidden it.

The peasants did not totally lack means of retaliation and resistance. They concealed their grain or, failing that, burned it to keep it out of the hands of the state. This was war, instigated by the Bolsheviks, and in the beginning the peasants held their own: 7,300 men out of 36,000 in the food requisition detachments were killed by October 1918.

The authorities created "Poor Peasants' Committees" in June 1918 in a deliberate attempt to fan the flames of this war. This added the horrors of intra-class war to the conflict that already existed between the regime and the peasants. The committees had the task of helping the food requisition detachments; in other words, the poorest peasants, who staffed the committees, had license to plunder their neighborhoods. This amounted to an incentive to denounce and ruin the more prosperous elements in the countryside, the so-called kulaks (better-off farmers); the poor peasant considered almost *everyone* a kulak. The opportunities for everything from malicious mischief to murder were limitless, and under war communism many people took advantage of them.

As Trotsky had tried to "militarize" labor, so would the party deal with the peasants.

The Communists tried to rule by decree, always a hallmark of dictatorships, and tried to enforce their decrees through the Cheka. The old tsarist bureaucracy had intruded into the lives of citizens, but the new Communist administrative apparatus threatened to smother the population with rules, regulations, ordinances, decrees, and directives. In the period of war communism people quoted this quatrain:

I'll be in trouble, that I know,
Goin' to the privy, no pass to show.
I'd gladly get one, but, alas,
There's no one around, to issue a pass.

People greeted each other with, "Nothin' to eat, but life's a treat!" And as always in the Russian village, they said that there was plenty of everyone for food.

## SUGGESTED ADDITIONAL READING

**Bukharin, Nikolai, and Evgenii Preobrazhensky,** *The ABC of Communism,* Baltimore: Penguin Books, 1969

**Ehrenberg, Ilya,** *People and Life, 1891–1921,* New York: Knopf, 1962

**Fitzpatrick, Sheila,** *The Commissariat of Enlightenment,* New York: Cambridge University Press, 1970

**Gerson, Lennard D.,** *The Secret Police in Lenin's Russia,* Philadelphia: Temple University Press, 1976

**Gleason, Abbot, Peter Kenez, and Richard Stites, eds.,** *Bolshevik Culture,* Bloomington: Indiana University Press, 1985

**Jansen, Marc,** *A Show Trial Under Lenin: The Trial of the Socialist Revolutionaries, Moscow 1922,* The Hague: Martinus Nijhoff, 1982

**Leggett, George,** *The Cheka,* New York: Oxford University Press, 1981

**Lewin, Moshe,** *The Making of the Soviet System,* New York: Pantheon, 1985

**Malle, Silvana,** *The Economic Organization of War Communism,* New York: Cambridge University Press, 1985

**Pipes, Richard,** *The Formation of the Soviet Union,* Cambridge, Mass.: Harvard University Press, 1964

**Rigby, T. H.,** *Lenin's Government: Sovnarkom 1917–1922,* New York: Cambridge University Press, 1979

**Rosenberg, William G.,** *Liberals in the Russian Revolution: The Constitutional Democratic Party,* *1917–1921,* Princeton, N.J.: Princeton University Press, 1974

**Schapiro, Leonard,** *The Origins of the Communist Autocracy,* Cambridge, Mass.: Harvard University Press, 1977

**Suny, Ronald G.,** *The Making of the Georgian Nation,* Bloomington: Indiana University Press, 1988

# 5

# ECONOMIC REFORM
# AND POLITICAL CONSTRICTION,
# 1921–1927

As the conflict with the Whites and the foreigners wound down, serious challenges to the new regime emerged among the sectors of the population that should in theory have been most sympathetic. Peasant discontent erupted in Tambov province in the summer of 1920. An obscure artisan named A.S. Antonov put together an anti-communist army that eventually numbered 40,000 men; not until August 1921 were the rebel units defeated. In March 1921 the Baltic Fleet sailors based at Kronstadt, formerly the staunchest defenders of the Bolsheviks, rebelled against Communist rule. They saw themselves as the vanguard of a revolution that would recapture the gains of 1917 taken away by Lenin. The striking Petrograd workers on whom they had counted for aid, however, had been beaten into submission by the party and the Cheka; no one joined the mutineers. Red Army troops under M.N. Tukhachevsky attacked on March 16 and crushed the rebellion.

Lenin telegraphed congratulations to Tukhachevsky and his superior, Trotsky, but he knew the victory was a hollow one. He used the Kronstadt and Tambov uprisings to persuade the 10th Party Congress, then in session in Moscow, to accept his new program. To the peasants and to petty entrepreneurs in the cities he would make concessions so broad that many Communists considered them a repudiation of party history.

## DIMINISHING RETURNS OF TERROR

Most of the Kronstadt sailors who had not been killed in action and who had not managed to escape to Finland were executed. This barbaric act of vengeance was directed by Trotsky and Tukhachevsky, themselves future victims of the Revolution. Bolshevik retaliation against the rebellious peasants of Tambov was no less severe: an unknown number went before firing squads; thousands were sent to concentration camps.

The chief advocate of terror began to have doubts. In March 1921 Lenin denounced "scandal and gossip" about the excesses of the food requisition detachments, but his attack of scruples came too late to save the victims. Russia seemed on the verge of another great peasant rebellion; this nightmare frightened him as much as it had the tsars. It was necessary somehow to placate the peasants, to soothe their anger and reestablish their alliance with the workers which Lenin's opponents swore had never existed. The tension between town and countryside had to end. Industrial production was virtually at a standstill, and unless the peasants agreed to supply food the entire economy and with it the regime would collapse. The peasants needed a fair price for their grain, but they could not be paid in currency so worthless that the equivalent of 100 U.S. dollars in 100,000-ruble notes weighed a kilogram (2.2 pounds).

Trotsky had called for a retreat from war communism in 1920, for an accommodation with the peasants. Now briefly allied with Bukharin and the Left Communists, Lenin rejected this proposal. Civil War victory seemed to confirm his judgment.

The Left Communists were prepared to accept continuation of the terror to hold and consolidate what the party had gained. Lenin, however, saw the necessity for change: terror could make Russia submit, but it could not, in the 1920s, make Russia produce. Lenin never swerved from his goal of creating a communist society, but he accepted the necessity for flexible means to achieve that goal.

Before he could get a new policy functioning, however, a disaster of terrifying dimensions supervened. Debates within the party ceased as Russia gazed in horror on the suffering along the Volga.

## FAMINE

By the time the 10th Party Congress approved Lenin's demand for an "economic breathing-space" the meteorological and man-made conditions necessary to produce a catastrophe were in place. The peasants throughout European Russia were just winding down their war against the authorities; grain and seed stocks were dangerously depleted; hundreds of thousands of peasant-soldiers had not yet returned to the villages. And in the spring and summer of 1921 the rains did not come to the Volga Valley.

Late in spring American officials in Constantinople intercepted Sovnarkom radio messages warning of the dangers to public health and order posed by the famine in the middle Volga region. In some localities people were already eating grass, leaves, bark, and clay. Tree bark was selling for 40,000 rubles a *pood* (36 lbs., or about a bushel), bitter dock (horse sorrel) for 50,000. The Volga was so low that men and animals—the few animals that had not been eaten—could wade it at Green Island near Saratov. From May into September temperatures stayed well above normal. The heat baked the soil and seared the bodies and minds of the millions of starving people who wandered about aimlessly, looking for the food that was nowhere to be found. There exist nauseating photographs of traffic in human flesh.

Vladimir Mayakovsky wrote in his poem, "My Speech at the Genoa Conference,"

Cast your gaze upon the Volga:
Isn't this starving inferno,
This peasant desolation,
The ass-end of your wars and blockades?*

It was easier to blame the West, which unquestionably bore a share of the guilt, than Communist rule.

No one knows how many people were affected. The official Soviet famine relief agency, Pomgol, put the figure at well above 25 million; the head of the British trade mission then in Russia estimated 35 million. No fewer than 3 million and perhaps as many as 5 million people starved to death.

The wounds of the Intervention were too fresh for the Sovnarkom to appeal directly to the international community. Lenin asked the writer Maksim Gorky, who then opposed the Communists but accepted the legitimacy of their rule, to make the plea. Gorky issued a dramatic cry for help, "To All Honest People," and the West responded. Anatole France donated the money from his 1921 Nobel Prize for Literature. George Bernard Shaw, Albert Einstein, Theodore Dreiser, and others prominent in science and the arts raised funds. Fridtjof Nansen, the Norwegian polar explorer, organized a massive relief campaign in Western Europe. President Harding's secretary of commerce, Herbert Hoover, who had organized assistance to Belgium during World War I, headed the American rescue effort.

The fiercely anticommunist Hoover may have had the base motives that the Communists and many of his critics in the United States claimed he had. Senator Thomas Watson of Georgia charged that he used American relief funds to pay off General Yudenich; Senator James Reed of Missouri declared that he had financed the Poles in their war against Russia. The Soviet government expelled the American Relief Administration (ARA) in 1922. By that time, however, the organization had managed to distribute more than $20,000,000 worth of food and seed.

There was little the Sovnarkom could do on its own. Pomgol tried to organize relief measures, and a special "agit-prop" (agitational-propaganda) train called "Red October" toured the stricken districts. Equipped with loudspeakers, films, printed matter, agitators—everything but food—the train rolled through the Volga Valley. As the crisis worsened Pomgol was obliged to concentrate its efforts upon helping local authorities control the millions of refugees who fled the area seeking food.

The weather improved, aid poured in from the West, the spring and autumn 1922 harvests were good. The crisis passed.

## NEW ECONOMIC POLICY

In March 1921 Lenin told the delegates to the 10th Congress of his party that some drastic changes were in order:

In this backward country, the workers, who have made unprecedented sacrifices, and the mass of peasants, are in a state of utter exhaustion after seven years of war. This condition borders on complete loss of working capacity. What is needed now is an economic breathing-space.

He was describing conditions *before* the famine.

Lenin proposed a compromise with the peasantry. Admitting privately in March and publicly in July that the food requisition

---

*Vladimir Mayakovsky, "Moya rech na Genuezskoi konferentsii," in *Polnoe sobranie sochinenii*, vol. 4, Moscow: Gos. izdat. Khudozhestvennoi literatury, 1957. English translation by W.M. On the Genoa Conference, which Mayakovsky did not attend, see Chapter 7.

policy was "bad and primitive," he proposed a tax in kind to replace it. Despite opposition from the Left Communists, this plan, similar to the one Trotsky had proposed a year earlier, was adopted. The amount of the new tax was fixed at 60 percent of the tonnage forcibly collected in 1920.

This was the cornerstone of Lenin's new economic policy, or NEP, for which he received overwhelming approval at the 10th Congress. An American scholar has written that NEP "originated as an ignoble retreat." Although more than a few party members— perhaps including a majority of those who had joined since the October Revolution— refused to acknowledge the fact, war communism was a failure. There was no viable alternative to a change of course.

Soviet historians have maintained that Lenin conceived both the new economic policy and its discredited predecessor as mere tactical moves with limited life expectancies. Western scholars, however, have demonstrated conclusively that Lenin and his followers, especially Bukharin, regarded the new economic policy as a reform program that would have a long tenure. They had not abandoned communism, nor had they become Menshevik gradualists. They had however learned—as Lenin was fond of saying—from life itself, and they accepted the necessity of taking a different route to their goal. With varying degrees of grace all party leaders accepted NEP; Bukharin and Trotsky became its chief spokesmen. Stalin likewise went along with the party majority.

The peasants were permitted to own land, and private ownership of small shops and plants was legalized. Worst of all, from the standpoint of Communist true believers, rural and urban entrepreneurs were permitted to hire labor. Lenin's opponents complained that NEP meant "new exploitation of the proletariat."

Lenin pressed on and put forth another slogan: "Learn to trade!" Condemned by generations of Marxists, the marketplace now offered a way out of the country's economic difficulties. Supervised but essentially free trade in grain was allowed. Peasants were encouraged but not forced to join producer cooperatives; attempts to herd them into collective and state farms were abandoned.

The state retained control over the "commanding heights" of the economy: heavy industry (mining, metals, heavy machinery, etc.), financial and credit institutions, transportation, and foreign trade. The state also kept its monopoly on political power, communications, and education. State enterprises were organized into vertical or horizontal "trusts" and ordered to make a profit. Communist apologists explained that the profit, extracted from labor's hide, went to benefit the proletarian state, not an individual or group of individuals.

Gone was the attempt to equalize wages, to pay the lowliest hod-carrier the same as the manager of the largest plant. The formula "to each according to his work" replaced the utopian "to each according to his needs." Engineers and other specialists were well paid. The salaries of party and state bureaucrats remained low, but a system of special perquisites allowed those at the top to live relatively well.

All this added up to a mixed public-private economy. The public or state sector predominated in industry, the private in agriculture. Because free trade was now permitted, the peasants had an incentive to sell; at least in theory they could get a fair price for their products. A steady supply of food would feed the cities and enable the workers to get production rolling again. That, in turn, would provide the manufactured goods the peasants needed and could purchase with profits from the sale of their own products. A money economy was reintroduced, the currency stabilized.

Three agencies directed the NEP. The Supreme Economic Council had overall responsibility for the economy, and two new planning bodies were established, the State Commission for the Electrification of Russia (Goelro) and the State Planning Commission (Gosplan). Neither agency provided the data that would have made it possible to check the regime's startling declaration in 1925 that it had balanced its budget.

Like many economic schemes the NEP was tidy on paper. In practice a crisis soon developed.

Agriculture recovered quickly. With a sufficient supply of grain by the end of 1922, free market prices declined. Industry, however, did not rebound rapidly, and production remained inadequate to meet demand. Further, the state's monopolistic practices enabled industrial managers to set artificially high prices. The purchasing power of agricultural products thus declined: the peasants had to supply more grain to obtain a steel plow or other agricultural implement. The manager of the plant that produced the plow, however, now needed to sell fewer of them because the price was so high.

This situation spawned what Trotsky called the "scissors" crisis. Plotted on a graph, the downward curve bisected the upward one in September 1922. At that point, on an index of 1913 = 100, the price of farm produce was 89, that of industrial goods, 276. The gap between the blades of the "scissors" continued to widen for another 13 months. After October 1923 the crisis began to ease; the state improved the peasant's position by intervening in the marketplace with agricultural subsidies. The authorities also reduced prices of manufactured goods.

Recovery now began in earnest. Industrial production reached 35 percent of the 1913 level in 1922, 73 percent in 1925. Thus, in the latter year Russia still produced only three-fourths of what she had manufactured prior to the Great War, but this was an *increase* of more than 500 percent over 1920 levels. The record in agriculture was even more spectacular despite poor harvests in 1921 and 1925. Grain production returned to prewar levels; meat lagged behind.

Lenin sought to learn from and make use of the capitalists. His regime granted wide concessions to foreign entrepreneurs; the capricious American businessman Armand Hammer received the first, to mine asbestos in the Urals and organize foreign trade. Royal Dutch Shell obtained the concession to exploit Caspian Sea oil. Swedish Nobel interests obtained mining rights in the Ukraine and the Urals. Henry Ford supplied 300 million gold rubles' worth of motor vehicles over four years, technical assistance and invention-use rights over nine years. By the end of 1928, 49 foreign individuals and firms had come to do business, everyone conveniently overlooking the Bolshevik promise to wipe the capitalists off the face of the earth. Lenin even invited foreign governments to invest on favorable terms.

## NEW GOVERNMENTAL SYSTEM

As a member of the minorities, Joseph Stalin was a reasonable choice for the relatively minor post of comissar of nationalities in the first Sovnarkom. An Old Bolshevik—that is, party member since 1903—he had long served as Lenin's expert on the nationality question. Following the Civil War he was charged with revising the Constitution to integrate the regained territories—the Ukraine, Byelorussia, Trans-Caucasia, Siberia—into the new state.

Along with many other Communists, Stalin favored a highly centralized state, with no concessions to the minorities. At Lenin's insistence, however, the 1918 Constitution had provided for a federal structure consistent with the Bolshevik championing of national self-determination. In Lenin's view, the minorities should have rights surpassing those of the states in the United States. He argued that the larger minorities should have their own political-administrative entities with the right to conduct foreign policy.

The intense Russophobia encountered during the Civil War forced both centralizers and federalists in the Communist party to rethink their positions. Stalin wanted to make all non-Russians submit to Moscow's domination. Lenin had abandoned his utopian view of a free association of sovereign and independent states, but for tactical reasons demanded that this fiction be incorporated into the new Constitution. He did insist, however, on some concessions to the non-Russian population in order to bring peace and stability and ease introduction of the Soviet system. He hoped that, by allowing a wide degree of cultural autonomy in the non-Russian areas, the regime would encounter less resistance to social and economic innovations.

The language of the new Constitution, worked out while Lenin lay dying and adopted on January 31, 1924, shortly after his death, reflected his wishes. On paper, each constituent republic was sovereign, independent, and equal. Each joined the union freely and could leave freely. Freedom of speech was guaranteed. Citizenship was not in one of the constituent republics but in the union. The union had control over defense, foreign relations, the general economic system and plan, the national budget, the monetary and credit systems, transportation, and communications. The republics had control over "everything else."

Under the amended Constitution sovereign power resided in the people through the All-Union Congress of Soviets. There was no change in the favored status granted

workers in the election of this body: one worker's vote equalled five peasant votes. Even so, direct elections took place only at the local level. Each next higher Soviet (district, province, republic, union) was elected by the body directly beneath it; this was in effect a system of electoral colleges. There was no provision for a secret ballot. The Central Executive Committee of the Congress and its presidium were in continuous session to govern the country. In practice, power remained concentrated in the party Politburo, which formally exercised it through the Sovnarkom. It was clear from the beginning that, in a conflict between the party wishes and the provisions of the Constitution, the party would win.

An October 1922 plenum of the party Central Committee approved a plan to create a new state organization. On December 30 of the same year the Union of Soviet Socialist Republics (USSR) came into existence as a merger of the Russian, Ukrainian, Byelorussian, and Transcaucasian republics of the original Communist state.

## THE PARTY

The Bolshevik faction of the Russian Social-Democratic Labor party had changed its name to Russian Communist Party (b) in March 1918, the lower-case "b" in parentheses standing for "Bolsheviks." The RKP (b) made another change in December 1925, when the 14th Congress renamed it the All-Union Communist Party (b), or VKP (b).

In 1921 the Communists enjoyed enormous prestige as the victors of October, conquerors of Whites and foreign Interventionists, vanguard—so their propaganda claimed—of the international working-class. The hostility demonstrated in Tambov province and at Kronstadt could not be ignored, but party leaders and thousands of rank-

and-file members remained unshaken in their sense of themselves as agents of history. They were creating a new society; victory would be theirs.

In theory anyone not a member of the "exploiting classes" or other "hostile element" could become a party member. Admission required the sponsorship of three members who had known the candidate for a year or more at her or his workplace, enterprise, or military unit. Upon passing the scrutiny of a review board, which in the 1920s looked chiefly for purity of class origin and ideological reliability, the applicant became a candidate member (nonvoting probationer) for one year. At the end of the year, assuming he or she had demonstrated satisfactory ideological, political, and personal behavior, and had proved herself or himself a good worker or member of the armed forces, full party membership was bestowed in a ceremony conducted by local dignitaries.

Not many people were admitted to the party in the first four years of the decade. In 1921 Lenin had ordered the purge of "rascals, bureaucrats, dishonest or wavering Communists, and of Mensheviks who had repainted their 'façade' but have remained Mensheviks at heart." The people said he was attacking "radish" Communists—Red outside, White inside. The purge rendered the number of full members from 567,000 in 1921 to 350,000 in 1924. If all the 165,000 candidates in 1921 had become full members, this represented a decrease of more than 382,000.

On the leader's death the party announced a "Lenin Enrollment" aimed at rebuilding its depleted forces. Within two years membership more than doubled, to just over one million. The recruiting drive concentrated on industrial workers, peasants, and members of the Red Army and the Red Fleet. At the beginning of the drive

only 18.8 percent of the party membership was of working class origin; by January 1927, the percentage had risen to 39.4. There are no figures for peasant membership in 1924, but by 1927, 13.7 percent of party members and candidate members were peasants. These were impressive gains. Nevertheless, in January 1927 only 8.4 percent of all industrial workers, and only 0.6 of the peasants, were party members. In the Red Army, 13.9 percent were Communists.

The proportion of working-class and peasant members continued to rise, however; the figures do not reflect the considerable success of this policy. By 1927 more than a quarter of a million people who had entered the party as workers had been promoted to white-collar jobs or to other positions—the military, college studies—that technically removed them from the proletariat. In the same year, only 0.8 percent of party members had a college degree, and only another 7.9 percent had finished secondary school.

The party structure had as its basic unit the primary party organization, or cell. Composed of as few as three members, it might number hundreds, as for example in a large mill or factory, where there would be several large cells. Those with 300 or more members had their own bureaus and secretariats.

The next higher organization, the city or county conference, amalgamated local primary party organizations. The conference established its own committees and had its own secretariat. All cells were subordinate to it. The local conference was in turn subordinate to the provincial conference, which had its own central committee and secretariat. While full-time, salaried party workers were found at all levels (but only in large cells), it was at the provincial level that they began to dominate party work.

Above the province was the republican party congress, which elected a central committee and a secretariat. Originally elected locally, as were all lower bodies in the party structure, the republican officials were increasingly appointed by Moscow. The inexorable trend toward centralization affected the party organization no less than governmental agencies.

At the top of the pyramidal structure, the All-Union Congress was the supreme authority during Lenin's lifetime and on paper has remained so. The Congress met annually through 1925. After that year, party rules were suspended or ignored as the Congress met at the pleasure of the Stalinist faction. In the 1920s the Congress elected a tenth of its members to a Central Committee entrusted with the day-to-day work of the party. In the summer of 1917 there were 21 members of the Committee, plus 18 candidate members. This number grew to 40 members and 17 candidates in 1923, and to 53 members and 34 candidates in 1924.

Even in the beginning the Central Committee was too large a body for effective decision-making. In March 1919 the Eighth Congress instructed that body to create three new organs: (1) a Political Bureau (Politburo) of five Central Committee members; (2) an Organizational Bureau (Orgburo), also composed of five CC members; and (3) a Secretariat consisting of one general secretary, who had to be a member of the Politburo, and five technical secretaries chosen from among party officials.

Always in session, the Politburo dealt with matters requiring immediate action. It became not only the chief executive arm of the party but also the main policy-making body. Lenin, Trotsky, Stalin, Kamenev, and Krestinsky were the original members; Bukharin, Zinoviev, and Kalinin were soon added as candidates. This was the inner circle which set policy and decided questions requiring intervention of the highest authority.

Charged with "all party organizational

work," the Orgburo met three times a week and like the Politburo had to make biweekly reports to the Central Committee. Stalin and Krestinsky, both Politburo members, were appointed to the Orgburo, which Stalin was to transform into the foundation of his own personal party organization. Krestinsky was soon removed from both bodies, leaving Stalin as the sole Orgburo link to the Politburo.

By 1921 Stalin, widely acknowledged as the party's leading authority on organizational and personnel questions, had come to dominate the Orgburo. His power was all the greater because of his control of the Secretariat, the third new agency created in 1919. The ill-defined mission of this body, which functioned as a high-level secretarial agency in the first three years of its existence, took on a real clarity only after the appointment of Stalin as general secretary on April 4, 1922. He made the Secretariat an adjunct of the Orgburo.

The Secretariat was divided into departments, of which the single most important was Records and Assignments, a personnel department. Through it, using the authority that was his through his positions on the Secretariat, the Orgburo, and the Politburo, Stalin regularly reviewed the qualifications of party officials. A second important department of the Secretariat was Organization-Instruction, which transmitted the decisions and orders of the Central Committee and its agencies to all lower party organizations. Organization-Instruction also had investigatory functions and was empowered to determine compliance or noncompliance with party directives.

The process by which the Communist party was transformed into a coercive bureaucratic agency is still not fully understood. A major factor was the contradictory nature of certain key party rules, one of which provided for free discussion until a decision was made; then there had to be compliance. This was "democratic centralism." Not only was there to be no dissent: all members were required to give active support to party decisions. Members and party agencies were charged to ensure the strictest discipline.

All this presupposed infallible majority decisions. The "either-or" certainties that had always characterized Russian religious and political thinking surfaced again in the rules of the Communist party: there was truth and error, right and wrong, black and white, no compromise.

The rendering of Central Committee and by extension Politburo decisions sacrosanct had profound implications. At each level of the hierarchy party members elected representatives to the next higher level. In theory this organization should have made the top officials responsive to the rank and file, but in practice this was not the case. Old Muscovy's despotic, centralizing traditions surfaced again as the party established the principle that the lower must be slavishly responsible to the higher. Key local party officials were appointed directly by the Central Committee of the VKP (b).

The emerging state structure paralleled the Communist party organization at all levels, and officials held governmental positions corresponding to their party rank: in his governmental capacity Lenin was chairman of the Sovnarkom, or prime minister. The other members of the Politburo also held high positions in the government. By the mid-1920s the top positions in union and republic governmental bodies were held exclusively by Communists. There were elections, but after 1920 there was only one candidate for each post, and he or she was invariably a Communist selected by party authorities or—rarely, and only at the lower levels—a docile "nonparty" individual. Voters could show their disapproval by

declining to vote, but abstention came to be equated with disloyalty.

At the 10th Congress in 1921, an exasperated Lenin pushed through a resolution banning factions and factionalism within the party. Having grown accustomed to military-administrative procedures in the Civil War, the membership by and large did not oppose this savaging of its political traditions.

Seeking to defend Lenin against the charge of having prepared the way for Stalin's dictatorship, some scholars in the USSR and the West have insisted that the party leader intended only a temporary ban on factionalism in order to smooth the transition from war communism to the NEP. There is no evidence that Lenin calculated this particular move so carefully. The many thousands of members who had joined the party during the Civil War were largely indifferent to and even ignorant of its pre-October traditions, and they had little patience with the infighting and bickering that had *always* characterized Bolshevism. Accustomed to settling differences with gunpowder and steel, the new Communists demanded unity and order.

Even before the 10th Congress, central party authorities had indicated how they would deal with dissent. A Communist group calling itself Democratic Centralists seized control of the Ukrainian party organization in 1920; it was committed to upholding the democratic traditions of Bolshevism. The VKP (b) Central Committee promptly dismissed the Ukrainian Central Committee and appointed a new one. In 1921 the Workers' Opposition, party members who urged that a freely elected "Congress of Producers" take over the economy, seized control of the Samara provincial party organization. The Central Committee again threw out the dissidents and appointed its own people.

By 1922 Lenin realized that the Central

Committee was becoming the nucleus of a powerful dictatorial tendency. He sought to curb the process by restoring the power of the Sovnarkom. It was too late.

## THE STRUGGLE FOR POWER

Lenin suffered a stroke in May 1922. After an initial period of recovery in Moscow, he was obliged to spend several months at a *dacha* (country home) in the village of Gorki. He seemed to improve over the summer; the prognosis was guardedly optimistic. In October he returned to the Kremlin and a full work load despite the pleas of his physicians and his wife. A second stroke in December removed him from active politics.

It was axiomatic that no one individual could succeed the leader. Lenin's legacy could only be parcelled out among his closest colleagues. The question was not who would succeed him but rather which group; nevertheless there was speculation as to which of the lieutenants would emerge as first among equals. In terms of political power the chief contenders were Kamenev, Zinoviev, Bukharin, Stalin, and Trotsky.

Lev Kamenev was head of the Moscow party organization, member of the Politburo and deputy chairman of the Sovnarkom, Old Bolshevik. In October 1917, however, he betrayed the plans for the armed uprising. He passed as an intellectual, but his learning had little substance; he was shallow and insecure. In a country with a long history of anti-Semitism, his Jewishness and marriage to Trotsky's sister were liabilities. His own sister would later be linked romantically to Stalin, but that would not save Kamenev.

Grigory Zinoviev, also Jewish, headed the Leningrad party organization, was president of the Communist International, and sat on the Politburo. He too was an Old Bolshevik. He was a bombastic public speaker; this had served him well earlier but the demand for fiery speeches lessened after the Civil War. He was widely known as the other man who betrayed the plans for the October Revolution. Until that monumental error he had been closer to Lenin, in the strictly political sense, than anyone in the party. That, however, was a mixed blessing: he inevitably aroused jealousy.

Zinoviev had ruthlessly suppressed the Petrograd strikes of 1920–1921 and the blood of Kronstadt was on his hands. Nevertheless he had consistently supported labor in the period of war communism and never ceased to remind Leningrad workers that they had bread on their tables only because he had made the party squeeze the peasants. In addition to his labor support he enjoyed some popularity among students.

Nikolai Bukharin, youngest of Lenin's lieutenants and one of the youngest Old Bolsheviks, had a reputation as a Marxist theorist. Lenin once charged that he had never fully understood the dialectic, but he also called "Bukharchik" the "favorite of the whole party." Bukharin was editor of *Pravda* and a member of the Politburo. He frequently opposed Lenin, however, and the rapid adjustment of his views after a defeat indicated a certain ideological instability. He fought the Treaty of Brest-Litovsk, but that was not fatal: thousands of party members shared his concerns. More serious, despite the fact that he had support on this issue too, was his hostility toward the new economic policy. He argued for continuing war communism after it became clear that it had brought disaster.

Bukharin reversed himself and became one of the strongest supporters of the new line. The centrist faction, which never allowed itself to be seduced by Left or Right, welcomed his conversion, but again he had not enhanced his standing. His political and philosophical disquisitions, championing of the arts, urbane manner and civilized personal conduct—all this won him friends who were attracted to him in no small measure because he *lacked* the cold-blooded skills of the political infighter.

Joseph Vissarionovich Stalin, the Russified (by 1917) Ossete from Georgia, was not the favorite of any first-rank leader other than himself, but he was the candidate of many Communists at lower levels of command—the *komitetchiki* (committeemen) who were in their jobs because he had put them there. In addition to this personal organization within the party, which he had quietly been constructing since 1919, Stalin's chief asset was longevity of service. He was not unshakably loyal to Lenin: witness his support for the Provisional government early in 1917, his disobedience during the Civil War, and his stand on the centralism-federalism issue.

By 1923 Stalin had made mistakes serious enough to cost a dozen men their careers, maybe their heads. The Bolsheviks, however, had an "old boy" network that protected even the most wayward from the wages of sin. At every turn Stalin was shielded, often by men who detested him and whom *he* could hardly wait to destroy.

Stalin had the ability to spot and exploit weakness in an adversary. He saw Kamenev and Zinoviev for the puny politicians they were but defended them against Lenin's wrath in 1917; he was to call in this debt in 1923–1924. He urged leniency for those who opposed the Treaty of Brest-Litovsk, asked for understanding of comrades hostile to war communism and counseled patience in the case of opponents of the new economic policy.

Not only officials but also many of the rank and file were indebted to Stalin. He was given the post of general secretary, which at the time had no conventional

power. The general secretary was to coordinate the work of party commissions, committees, agencies, and departments, and present reports on their activities to the Central Committee. Bent as most of them were on strengthening their own more glamorous fiefdoms, Lenin's other lieutenants failed to see that the general secretary's control over the flow of information to the Central Committee and its Politburo gave him enormous power. Stalin sat on the Politburo and the Orgburo, directed the Workers' and Peasants' Inspectorate or Rabkrin (Lenin had been especially critical of his work here, and he soon lost the job), and remained commissar of nationalities. Beyond all this, his timing was impeccable: he was consolidating his position while Lenin was ill and absent from Moscow much of the time.

In short, Joseph Stalin was a clever and ambitious politician, the ideal committeeman who performed routine work behind the scenes to make the party function. His various responsibilities allowed him to insinuate himself into control of party personnel at all levels. As his power grew, so did his arrogance.

Leon Trotsky had come late to the Bolshevik camp with a modest dowry, the tiny Interdistrictite faction of Socialists. The public record was filled with his vituperative attacks on Lenin, especially from 1903 to 1912. All was forgiven, however, in the heady days of 1917 when more than any other single individual he translated Lenin's will into action.

Trotsky clashed with Lenin over the Treaty of Brest-Litovsk but seemed to atone for that with a brilliant record in the Civil War. Once again Lenin was the master strategist, Trotsky his indispensable tactician. Trotsky's building of the Red Army out of the ruins of 1914–1918 stands as one of the most remarkable episodes in military annals. At the end of the Civil War, before the

Lenin and Stalin at Gorky, late summer 1922. Some specialists believe this is a fake photo, made to suggest a closer relationship than actually existed. (Sovnarkom photo)

suppression of the Kronstadt Rebellion, he was unquestionably the second most respected and popular figure in the country.

A challenge to Trotsky materialized simply because he was there. After Zinoviev's fall from grace, someone had to be ranked next to Lenin, and anyone in that position attracted envy and opposition. Trotsky however was particularly vulnerable to the three Old Bolsheviks, Kamenev, Zinoviev, and Stalin, who resented him as a parvenu who had reaped rewards they coveted.

Lenin wrote in December 1922 that Trotsky was distinguished by "exceptional ability" and that he was "the most able man in the present Central Committee." He also spoke of Trotsky's "too far-reaching self-confidence," his love of the "purely administrative side of affairs."

It would seem at first glance that this comment more accurately described Stalin, the administrator-bureaucrat par excellence, but Lenin apparently referred to Trotsky's readiness to use military administrative methods and coercion rather than political manipulation. In December 1920 Lenin prevailed on the Central Committee to pass a resolution criticizing Trotsky.

## 12TH PARTY CONGRESS

Lenin finally grasped the direction of the succession struggle and tried in the winter of 1922–1923 to stop Stalin. In a memorandum dictated in December 1922 and amended slightly in January 1923 he wrote,

Comrade Stalin, having become General Secretary, has concentrated enormous power in his hands, and I am not sure he always knows how to use that power with sufficient caution. . . . Stalin is too rude, and this fault, acceptable among us Communists, is intolerable in the office of General Secretary. Therefore I propose to the comrades to find a way to remove Stalin from that position and appoint to it a man who is . . . more patient, more loyal, more polite, and more attentive to comrades, less capricious. . . .

It is not clear whether, at the time he wrote this, Lenin knew of Stalin's mistreatment of Krupskaya. The Central Committee had entrusted its general secretary with responsibility for overseeing Lenin's medical treatment. In December 1922 Stalin berated Krupskaya for conveying messages from her husband to various party members, notably Trotsky. Stalin already knew of Lenin's hostility toward him; possibly he knew too of Lenin's desire to remove him as general secretary.

Lenin was paralyzed and could barely speak. Nevertheless he recovered sufficiently to issue instructions for the forthcoming 12th Party Congress. He urged Trotsky to press for a motion of censure against Stalin for sending the Red Army into Georgia in defiance of Politburo orders, and he wanted him ousted as general secretary. On the eve of the Congress Lenin dictated a note to Stalin, sending copies to Kamenev and Zinoviev, demanding an apology to Krupskaya. He declared that he would consider Stalin's refusal an indication that he wished to break relations with him (Lenin).

The 12th Congress, the first without Lenin in attendance, came and went in April 1923. Trotsky did not make use of the weapon Lenin had given him. His reluctance has been explained by his followers as the product of his fear of being seen as a Bonaparte, a man on horseback riding in to steal political victory after battlefield triumph. Those supporters also point to Stalin's taunting of Trotsky for refusing to accept the deputy chairmanship of the party: was he too arrogant to serve as Lenin's deputy?

Lenin's "testament" was not the crucial document of Trotskyite and post-1956 anti-

From right: Lenin, Krupskaya; Lenin's nephew, Viktor; Lenin's sister, Anna Yelizarova-Ulyanova; unidentified child, Gorky, August 1922. (Sovnarkom photo)

Stalinist myth. When he was healthy Lenin used far stronger language against associates with whom he had fundamental differences. All things considered, his attack on Stalin was relatively mild. He had merely suggested the party find a way to reduce the man's power. As a guide to political maneuver the "testament" had little value. Lenin did not claim that the party's fate hinged on Stalin's removal, nor did he give any clearcut guidelines, still less express a preference, concerning his successor or successors. This is why Trotsky declined to use the document at the 12th Congress.

A secondary reason was the composition of the meeting: Stalin's supporters occupied all key leadership roles. There were many delegates who supported Trotsky or were friendly toward him, but they were heavily outnumbered. Nevertheless, had the hero of October and the Civil War acted as Lenin requested, the Congress could not have ignored him. Stalin would surely have suffered a public rebuke, perhaps a demotion. A silent Trotsky, however, stood on the fringes and watched the general secretary direct his first Congress flawlessly.

## "PERMANENT REVOLUTION" VS. "SOCIALISM IN ONE COUNTRY"

Engrossed in developing his theme of "permanent revolution," in peacetime Trotsky showed little interest in the routine affairs of the commissariat of war. Disinclined to believe in the ebb of the Western revolutionary tide and the grasping at every street fight in Germany as the harbinger of cataclysmic upheaval, Trotsky held that socialism could not succeed in Russia in the absence of proletarian revolutions in the West. A socialist island such as Soviet Russia could not long exist, he maintained, in a capitalist sea: sooner or later the capitalists would unite to

destroy it. The isolated socialist state would lose its identity. The necessity of maintaining a large national defense and of coercing the population would create a state-capitalist society. It was therefore the international class duty of the Soviet workers to subordinate their own immediate interests to those of the world proletariat, to foster and support revolutionary movements in the industrialized countries.

Stalin counterpoised Bukharin's theory of "socialism in one country": Russia *could* go it alone. The Marxist-Leninist historical timetable, never very precise, would simply be adjusted. If revolution did not come in the West it was the duty of the Soviet Communists to build up Russia as the bastion of socialism, a beacon to the oppressed and downtrodden peoples of the world. Stalin agreed that Russia was threatened by the capitalist states but disagreed concerning the proper response. Trotsky argued that the best defense lay in providing ideological and political cadres and, when necessary, arms to revolutionary and working-class movements in the West. Employing Bukharin's arguments, Stalin insisted that Soviet Communists had first to build their own military might; that meant building a powerful Soviet state.

Stalin quickly got into step behind Lenin concerning Brest-Litovsk, while Trotsky clung to illusions concerning the imminence of revolution in the West. Stalin approved war communism from the beginning; Trotsky had to be won over. When it was time to recognize the failure of that policy and turn to NEP, Stalin supported Lenin. Trotsky, having earlier proposed his own new economic policy, declared that Communists should not abandon war communism. Temporarily allied with the Right, Stalin would steadfastly champion the new economic policy to the very end, while Trotsky and the Left would call for an "unequal exchange" between town and country, that is, for the exploitation of the peasantry to finance industrialization.

After the 12th Congress Trotsky realized the magnitude of his mistake in failing to oppose Stalin and tried to put together a broad attack upon the bureaucratization of party and state. But even Lenin had come to his senses too late. Trotsky did not stand a chance.

Several second-level leaders attacked Stalin in an October 1923 "Letter of the 46," expressing alarm over the direction party and country were taking and calling for reforms. Trotsky did not sign the letter, but the Stalin faction that now dominated the Central Committee condemned him anyway, warning that he and the signers were violating the 1921 ban on factions. The Central Committee suppressed the letter and stepped up the whispering campaign against Trotsky. Proclaiming the infallibility of the Politburo, where they had a majority, the Stalinists claimed that he was preparing to stage a military *coup d'état* the moment Lenin died. There was no truth to the charge, but Trotsky was on the defensive.

Rumors and innuendos swirled about in ever-widening circles. Having neglected to build a personal political organization, Trotsky was obliged to fall back on the old socialist tactic of appealing directly to the proletariat. He toured factories and workshops in Moscow and Leningrad, attempting to explain his criticism of the party and bureaucracy. He had to walk a thin line: at what point did disagreement become factionalism, thus a violation of the 1921 ban?

He who had so recently used naked power to such advantage now made the mistake of appealing to reason. In trying to explain, to justify, and to persuade, Trotsky appeared weak and vulnerable.

## DEATH OF LENIN

In March 1923 the attending physicians, including German and Swedish specialists, declared Lenin's recovery entirely possible. The Sovnarkom intended the statement to reassure the public. In fact, whole sections of his brain ossified from calcification of the blood vessels, Lenin was dying. All anyone could do was to try to make him as comfortable as possible.

The end came on Monday, January 21, 1924. Lenin was dead. Attendants placed the body on a bier in the *dacha;* flowers and fir branches were laid around it. The Central Committee, Stalin in the chair as its general secretary, met the next day and decided to embalm the body and put it on permanent display in a mausoleum to be erected in Red Square.

This decision outraged Krupskaya and most of the Old Bolsheviks, who rigorously opposed glorification of individuals. For an atheistic party to display the mummified corpse of its leader seemed grotesque.

And yet Stalin and his friends on the Central Committee knew their Russians and other Christian peoples, millions of whom continued to profess their faith. Stalin shrewdly calculated that a people who *had* nothing needed to *believe* in something. In this difficult period, the Central Committee majority reasoned, a cult of Lenin would provide the spiritual sustenance peasant and worker ached for. It would also serve as a unifying force, a system of basic, unchallengeable beliefs. A cult would also demand a priesthood of interpreters and keepers of the mysteries. One was already in place.

In the midst of a winter which even Muscovites considered severe, for three days hundreds of thousands of citizens queued patiently, 24 hours a day, to pass the open coffin in Union House on Hunters' Row, a main street in the center of the city. It seemed that the whole city was sobbing; medical personnel were swamped by cases of hysteria, shock, frostbite. Bonfires burned at corners all over Moscow as people congregated to share their grief and their fear. On January 26 Petrograd was renamed Leningrad.

On the morning of January 27 Stalin, Zinoviev, and six workers carried the open coffin the two city blocks from Union House to Red Square. There, the next contingent of pallbearers took over and bore it across the square to a temporary wooden crypt. At four in the afternoon, the leaders disappeared from public view as they followed the coffin into the crypt. At that moment every siren, factory whistle, ship's horn, motor vehicle horn, and other noise-making device in the country sounded in a deafening cacaphony heard from Vladivostok to the Polish border. Thousands of artillery guns fired salvo after salvo.

Stalin had delivered the main funeral oration the previous evening. It was couched in the cadences and rhythms and to a certain extent the language of the Russian Orthodox Church. The speech grated on the nerves of party members, but to the Soviet people by and large it gave some comfort and reassurance.

## STALIN'S EMERGING VICTORY

The grief of Russia was real. As the peasants had for centuries believed in a "good tsar" who did not know of their distress and so bore no responsibility, so "Ilich"—the patronymic by which Lenin was affectionately known—seemed remote from the harsh conditions and commissars of war communism. Too, the country had begun to recover under NEP, and that was Lenin's doing. Life was easier; it was possible to hope again. One could improve one's position through hard work, sharp practices, thrift.

When Lenin died, Trotsky was in the southern part of the country recuperating from an illness. He was informed only when it was too late to rush back to Moscow and thus could not participate in the awesomely symbolic funeral. The "most able man in the present Central Committee" did not serve as a pallbearer, nor did he speak. His absence had less political significance than his followers claimed, but the party certainly noticed it.

On the eve of the 13th Congress in May 1924, Krupskaya gave the Central Committee Lenin's December 1922–January 1923 memorandum and noted his wish that the first Congress after his death review it. The "testament," a weaker document than myth has it, would have compromised Stalin, who had many supporters on the Central Committee—Molotov, Voroshilov, Mikoyan, Kirov, Ordzhonikidze—but did not control it. He still needed the backing of Kamenev and Zinoviev, and of the party committeemen around the country.

No reliable account of the debate in the Central Committee has surfaced; and the members decided not to publish the "testament." The man whom Lenin wanted to remove as general secretary escaped with nothing worse than hurt pride.

The embarrassed Stalin remained in office, and Trotsky remained on the Central Committee. Grown pudgy in power and called "baba au rhum" to his face, Zinoviev once again proved himself a fool in asking Trotsky to "recant" his views. The Congress applauded Krupskaya's attack on the absurd demand.

Lenin has manifestly become irrelevant as the Communist party entered the crucial stage of the struggle for power. The Soviet citizens huddled around streetcorner bonfires that cold Moscow January never suspected that the outcome would doom them to three decades of horror.

## SUGGESTED ADDITIONAL READING

**Atkinson, Dorothy,** *The End of the Russian Land Commune, 1905–1930,* Stanford, Calif.: Stanford University Press, 1983

**Ball, Alan M.,** *Russia's Last Capitalists: The Nepmen, 1921–1929,* Berkeley and Los Angeles: University of California Press, 1987

**Carr, E.H.,** *The Interregnum, 1923–1924,* New York: Macmillan, 1954

**Carr, E.H., and R.W. Davies,** *Foundations of a Planned Economy,* 3 vols., New York: Macmillan, 1969–1979

**Chase, William J.,** *Workers, Society, and the Soviet State: Labor and Life in Moscow, 1918–1929,* Urbana: University of Illinois Press, 1987

**Cohen, Stephen F.,** *Bukharin and the Bolshevik Revolution,* New York: Oxford University Press, 1980

**Danilov, Viktor,** *Rural Russia under the New Regime,* Bloomington: Indiana University Press, 1988

**Erlich, Alexander,** *The Soviet Industrialization Debate, 1924–1928,* Cambridge, Mass.: Harvard University Press, 1960

**Fisher, H.H.,** *The Famine in Soviet Russia, 1919–1923,* Stanford, Calif.: Stanford University Press, 1935

**Lewin, Moshe,** *Political Undercurrents in Soviet Economic Debates,* Princeton, N.J.: Princeton University Press, 1974

**Narkiewicz, Olga A.,** *The Making of the Soviet State Apparatus,* Manchester, England: Manchester University Press, 1970

**Rees, E.A.,** *State Control in Soviet Russia: The Rise and Fall of the Workers' and Peasants' Inspectorate, 1920–1934,* New York: St. Martin's, 1987

**Reiman, Michal,** *The Birth of Stalinism: The USSR on the Eve of the "Second Revolution,"* Bloomington: Indiana University Press, 1987

**Sutton, Antony C.,** *Western Technology and Soviet Economic Development, 1917 to 1930,* Stanford, Calif.: Hoover Institution Press, 1968

**Tumarkin, Nina,** *Lenin Lives! The Lenin Cult in Soviet Russia,* Cambridge, Mass.: Harvard University Press, 1983

**Weissman, Benjamin,** *Herbert Hoover and Famine Relief to Soviet Russia,* Stanford, Calif.: Stanford University Press, 1974

# 6

# THE WAY THEY WERE
## Life in the 1920s

In 1921 the great Soviet economic experiment was seriously—many distressed Communists believed fatally—modified when a dramatic policy reversal ushered in the golden reform age of NEP, the period of "Communists but no communism." The capitalists were gone but petty entrepreneurs rose up to resume the capitalist tradition. The peasants could own land, sell their produce on the free market, hire labor. There were at least one million unemployed workers—all too often a hallmark of free enterprise. The heady revolutionary communism of 1917–1921 disappeared. In September 1921 cinemas and theatres, admission to which had been free, began to charge for tickets. October saw the end of free newspapers and magazines.

Old Bolsheviks and new Communists were shocked by the party's betrayal, as they saw it, of their ideals. They had given their lives to communism, fought and suffered for it, made one of history's greatest revolutions. Had it all been in vain? So enormous was Lenin's prestige that few outside the highest councils dared criticize the new economic policy, but there was great dissatisfaction among the rank and file and more importantly among the committeemen who were beginning to regard Stalin as the most likely post-Lenin leader.

Because their party retained a monopoly on politics, Communists had little reason to fear that Lenin would permit the return of old opposition parties or the creation of new ones. Their fears were concentrated on the economic and social sectors, where they had anticipated changes as sweeping as those in politics. The Communists had always insisted that they would revolutionize not only politics but the whole of society. A new social order would transform egotistical, selfish people into altruists; each would learn to identify his or her welfare with the welfare of society. With the end of exploitation and the establishment of a Communist social order, people would attain hitherto undreamed-of spiritual and material levels. Communist culture would be accessible to all.

It quickly became obvious that the social and cultural revolution was not going to take place under NEP. The Communists were in control but also in retreat. To some party members and to optimists among their enemies it seemed another case of "plus ça change, plus c'est la même chose."

## URBAN LIFE

Nothing could ever be the same, however, if only because of the demographic disaster that had struck Russia: in 1926 the population was about 30 million fewer than it should have been. The losses included approximately 4 million victims of wars and revolutions; about 1.5 million deaths in the worldwide influenza epidemic of 1918–1919; at least 5 million deaths in the famine of 1921; roughly 12 million inhabitants of areas of the old Empire who were now citizens of other countries and 7 to 8 million children not born because of these developments.

The work force and the Red Army, to say nothing of science, education, and the arts, suffered irreparable harm. And the grim statistics do not tell the whole story. It is impossible to determine how many people were lost to society because of psychological wounds associated with war, revolution, and other calamities. Emotional disorders, alcoholism, domestic violence, indifference to social norms including work, and crime all

rose dramatically in the 1914–1921 era. Attempting to deal with this phenomenon, in 1919 Professor P.B. Gannushkin laid the groundwork for what became a system of regional neuropsychiatric clinics. This was a progressive step, but the state had few funds for mental health and need far outstripped resources.

Moscow lost half its population in this period and more than ever resembled, as the humorists Ilf and Petrov wrote, a "large, badly planned village." No one would ever mistake regal Petrograd for a village, but that city had lost two-thirds of its inhabitants, and hunger and fear stalked its streets.

The new economic policy quickly turned the situation around. People came out of hiding, returned to the cities, and life improved. A key element in the urban recovery was the *nepman*, the petty entrepreneur spawned by NEP. He was a wheeler-dealer, a fixer, an intermediary. He could bring buyer and seller together at a satisfactory price, and he learned more quickly than anyone the limits of Communist toleration. He knew which laws and regulations were rigidly enforced, which were flexible. He knew who could be bribed and who was incorruptible; who was an alcoholic or drug addict; who wanted sex enough to cut a deal; who had a personal grudge against whom; who had skeletons in the closet. Everyone had his price and the *nepman* knew how to discover it.

The *nepman* was not a capitalist but he was indispensable in an economy which was neither capitalist nor socialist but an odd blend of the two. He could oversee the grain market, ensure that the cities were fed, help get factories back into production.

There were about 75,600 *nepmen* in 1926/1927; with their families they numbered about 209,000. (There were in the same period 339,000 "servants," another social category incompatible with communism.)

Communists who had revolutionized society's political superstructure detested those who were restoring the economic base.

The *nepmen* hardly constituted an élite, yet their highly visible contribution to economic recovery, for which they were amply rewarded, made them the premier urban element. After them came party officials and government bureaucrats, the new political and administrative masters. Like bureaucrats everywhere they tried to create empires and often succeeded. At the top, the staff of the party Secretariat—one of Stalin's organizations—increased from 30 to 602 between 1919 and 1921; by 1926 it had grown to 767. At that level officials naturally insisted that they needed a large body of underlings, but lower-ranking bureaucrats and officials, too, demanded sizable staffs. By 1927 there were 3.65 million governmental and party employees.

The bureaucrats of the 1920s probably earned their keep. The idealism of the early years had by no means died, NEP's compromise with capitalism notwithstanding, and most officials labored tirelessly to build the new state. They were paid only at the level of skilled workers, 250–300 rubles per year. Inevitably there were opportunities for graft and corruption and some bureaucrats succumbed, but the problem was not serious.

The creation of a new state system was a monumental task, and few overworked bureaucrats had any technical skills. The regime was obliged to employ specialists (*spetsy*) from tsarist institutions. Tensions arose between these "former people" and the new masters; violence was not uncommon. In April 1922 four Communist zealots were convicted of hounding the director of the Moscow waterworks, a distinguished engineer and university professor, to suicide. They had harrassed him because they did not want noncommunists in responsible positions. The four were convicted by the Supreme Revolutionary Tribunal and sent to prison. When a Communist who could take charge of Moscow's water supply could be found, Lenin declared, he would be employed. Until then the *spetsy* would serve the state and receive its full protection.

The social class in whose name the Bolsheviks had made their revolution did not attain the exalted status the party had promised, but it fared reasonably well in the 1920s. By 1927 the number of workers had grown to 4.5 million, up from 3 million in 1917. Industrial workers, the core proletariat, numbered 2.56 million, of whom 215,500—about 8.4 percent—were members of the Communist party.

Huge billboards proclaimed GLORY TO LABOR! and other Communist slogans. Poets such as Vladimir Mayakovsky and Demyan Bedny glorified work in their verse; artists produced posters and paintings of workers in heroic poses; songwriters extolled the proletariat. All this may have been good for morale but it did not raise labor's standard of living, which remained unacceptably low from the viewpoint of both workers and party.

The nationalization of private property had put thousands of urban dwellings at the disposal of the state, which apportioned them among party and governmental officials, new and old specialists, and the workers—in approximately that order. Many mansions were converted into office buildings. As people streamed back into the cities after the Civil War, and as demobilized soldiers returned in search of work and excitement and a place to live, officials redivided and repartitioned housing space repeatedly. Communal apartments, in which two or more families shared cooking, bath, and toilet facilities, became the accepted norm. As the urban population grew, people were often forced to divide a room simply by hanging a sheet or blanket from the ceiling.

Crowded living conditions remained the bane of urban life for decades, sapping morale and adversely affecting production. For many workers, however, a cramped communal apartment was an improvement over the filthy doss houses—converted in the 1930s into apartment dwellings—in which they had lived before the Revolution. (It is instructive to note that Russian, like Chinese, has no word for "privacy"; but French has no word for "home," English no equivalent of the Russian "sobornost," sometimes misleadingly translated as "togetherness.") Still more serious was the problem of food: workers who did not eat could not produce. In the difficult years of Civil War and war communism the party assigned the workers first priority after the Red Army. That priority remained unchanged after the recovery got under way, and the state provided subsidies to hold down the cost of staples. Sometimes the subsidies were by-products of inadequate planning, as in the "scissors crisis," but more often there was deliberate state intervention.

In the educational and cultural sphere, the party moved rapidly to bring workers out of the morass of illiteracy in which the old regime had kept them. A successful innovation was the concept of *rabfaks* or workers' schools, special institutions for adult workers with little or no education—the overwhelming majority. The first was opened in an impressive ceremony in February 1919. Anyone wishing to enroll had to present evidence from a factory political committee, by now a ubiquitous institution, or party cell stating that the applicant (1) belonged to the worker or peasant class and had never exploited the labor of others, and (2) supported the Soviet regime.

Usually attached to existing institutions (e.g., Moscow University), the *rabfaks* educated several million workers prior to World War II, among them Nikita Khrushchev.

They began to decline in 1933, however, and the last was closed in October 1941.

The *rabfaks* served workers and state well, but as late as 1939 only 8.2 percent of the proletariat had seven or more years of education. This was, however, comparable to the situation in the United States. The Bolsheviks had been the party of the illiterate masses; two decades after the Revolution, the Communists were the party of the undereducated masses.

Because NEP unofficially operated under the slogan "From each according to his ability, to each according to his work," and not "to each according to his need," the Communist ideal, skilled workers were paid more than the semi-skilled and unskilled. Technicians, engineers, and specialists of all kind were paid at a higher rate than skilled workers; foreign specialists in Soviet service were paid more than anyone.

Wage differentials meant that favored groups could compete with free-spending nepmen for tables at expensive restaurants and for luxuries at a Moscow food shop unambiguously called "The Stomach." Workers did not frequent such restaurants and shops. After 1921 they had enough to eat, but their diet was limited to the traditional fare of bread, cabbage, and potatoes; they rarely ate meat.

Workers were the social group most affected by the imposition of charges for newspapers, theatres, concerts, and other cultural events. Once again the Bolshoi Theatre was the province of the privileged.

Worst of all, from the Communist point of view, was the existence of privately-hired labor and unemployment. From an ideological standpoint this was not only unacceptable but unthinkable. With an undetermined number of workers employed by small—five or fewer employees—private enterprises and at least one million workers unable to find jobs (1926–1927), the Communist utopia

Rehabilitation of prostitutes, Moscow, late 1920s. (National Archives)

seemed more remote than ever. A primitive welfare system provided the unemployed with a marginal existence, but the spectacle of some workers laboring for private employers and others depending on the dole was bitter gall for party members.

Communists could scarcely contain their hatred of the *nepmen* who danced the tango, shimmy, and black bottom—more imports from the capitalist West—at expensive clubs and restaurants. The women with the *nepmen* were sometimes prostitutes, whose numbers had dropped from about 28,000 in 1916 to 3,000 in 1928. The existence of *any* amount of prostitution, however, was incompatible with Soviet ideals.

It was in Odessa that this lament was first heard:

Comrade, comrade, my wounds hurt,
Comrade, comrade, what did we fight for,

Why did we shed our blood.
The bourgeoisie are feasting, the bourgeoisie
Are gloating.*

And once again the war ditty resounded:

Eat pine-apple,
Gorge on grouse.
Your last day is coming,
Bourgeois louse!

There was a substantial criminal element in the cities in the 1920s. It was a time when, as one writer said, the laws were unsettled and it was easy to find the road to jail. For the criminals, social instability meant not increased danger but greater opportunity. There are no figures indicating how many

*From Ilya Ehrenburg (Erenburg), *Sobranie sochinenii*, vol. 8, Moscow: Izdat. "Khudozhestvennaia literatura," 1966. English translation by W. M.

normally law-abiding people were driven by desperation to crime, but the number must have been considerable. Newspapers and the literature of the time indicate a great deal of crime in the first decade after the Revolution. The most common offenses were robbery, assault, drug trafficking, breaking and entering, pilfering, and "banditry."

Not a little of the crime was the work of roughly 6 million orphaned, homeless children or *besprizorniki* who wandered around European Russia and the Ukraine for a decade after the Revolution. Aged from five or six to the late teens and organized into gangs, these children terrorized the cities, committing crimes ranging from petty thievery to drug—cocaine, hashish, opium—dealing, prostitution (girls as young as eight were involved), and murder. The children were frequently the object of vigilante retribution. Only toward the end of the decade did the state succeed in bringing this tragic problem under control.

In January 1919 Lenin himself was held up and robbed while on a drive in the Moscow suburbs. The highwaymen knew who he was, for they took his wallet containing his identification card with a photograph. They also lifted and no doubt treasured the small Browning automatic he always carried outside the Kremlin. The robbers permitted Lenin, his companions, and his chauffeur (who related this story) to go free but took the Rolls-Royce. When the vehicle was found the next day, a policeman and a Red Army soldier who had apparently stopped it lay murdered nearby. The criminals were never apprehended.

## MANNERS AND AMUSEMENTS

The party attempted to organize the leisure time of workers, but it tended to influence primarily the few who were party members.

Although workers were joining the party in increasing numbers, the majority were apolitical, interested in resting and having a good time after work, not in political rallies. Too, their spare time was often spent in trying to make life a little more comfortable. Such mundane problems as finding a decent mattress occupied them. Most prerevolutionary mattress factories had closed, and it was extremely difficult to locate something to sleep on. Several writers produced short stories and plays on this theme.

After hours the workers sometimes went to soccer matches, but in the 1920s mass spectator sports had not yet developed to a very substantial level. A crowd of 15,000 was considered large at games of even the most popular teams, one of which was Dinamo, formed in 1923 to represent the secret police. Organized gymnastics, cross-country skiing, ice-skating, swimming, and hiking were likewise only in an embryonic stage.

After hours the workers gathered in their clubs and in beer halls to eat black (rye) bread, dried *vobla* (Caspian roach, a fish), and drink Volga Hawk, Zhiguli, or Tip-Top beer. Much to the distress of Communist officials they perpetuated the old custom of "wetting" a young worker's first pay packet with alcohol. They smoked Kavkaz (Caucasus) *papirosy*, a kind of cigarette with a long hollow mouthpiece and a short tobacco end, and Cannon, Sappho, Our Mark, Beach, and Boxing cigarettes. When they could not afford cigarettes they smoked *mahorka*, a cheap, coarse tobacco rolled in newspaper.

They celebrated "red weddings" at factories, bride and groom standing before a piece of machinery and pledging their loyalty first to the Communist state, then to each other. A party official performed the frequently raucous ceremony. The workers discussed everything but politics, which was reserved for Communists, but popular wit produced some intriguing commentary:

Chicken roasted, chicken steamed,
Just to live, the chicken dreamed.
Ain't no Kadet, ain't no Red Star,
I'm just a chicken com-iss-ar!
Didn't cheat, didn't shoot,
Just pecked a little grain,
With my snoot.*

That one poked fun at nepmen and bureaucrats, and this popular ditty summed up the whole era:

My dad's a drunk, for the shot-glass he pines,
He lies, he blusters, he whines.
My brother's a crook, sister's a whore,
Ma took up smoking—I can't take any more!*

The workers could always get *samogon* (home brew) if they looked hard enough, but it was illegal and sometimes, if improperly made, fatal. At the very least, the peasant suppliers said, it would remove all your doubts. To combat the abuses connected with the sale of home-distilled liquor, and to obtain the enormous revenues from the liquor monopoly, the government ended the 10-year prohibition on "hard" liquor in 1924 and put 30 percent (60 "proof") vodka on the market. This "children's drink" did not satisfy Soviet thirsts, especially in the Russian and Ukrainian Republics, and in the summer of 1925 the manufacture and sale of 40 percent vodka was permitted. The state treasury and the thirsty public rejoiced; the stronger drink, which sold at a higher price, produced greater euphoria in both. But Russia again became the victim of increased alcoholism rates, lost production, domestic violence, crime, and accidents. The All-Union Council of Anti-Alcohol Societies, established early in the Soviet period, promoted the cause of temperance through public education campaigns and in its

monthly magazine *Sobriety and Culture*, but it had limited influence in the cities and virtually none in the countryside. The ineffective organization was disbanded in 1930.

The workers went to public baths, washed themselves with Hammer & Plow soap, and even after reimposition of a charge for tickets sometimes went to the Bolshoi Theatre, Tchaikovsky Conservatory, and the Moscow Art Theatre. Much more often they went to the cinema, especially when a Douglas Fairbanks, Rudolph Valentino, or Charlie Chaplin film was playing. They attended cultural events dressed in the only clothes—other than work-clothes—they had. An aggressive slovenliness replaced fashion even among white-collar workers and bureaucrats as ambitious young party members tried to dress like "hegemon," the worker.

From the standpoint of purists who exalted the literary language of the 19th century, the Russian language suffered under the impact of the Revolution. It was not merely that upper-class accents and vocabularies were shunned; the situation was worse than that. The new regime had its own cant. Communists were especially fond of acronyms: Sovnarkom, Cheka, Goelro, NEP, rabfak, sovhoz, kolhoz, Piatiletka (Five-Year-Plan), and so on. To a certain extent this was inevitable, but bringing so many poorly educated Communists into responsible positions in government, industry, and other fields meant that insecure newcomers would go overboard in adopting what they believed to be the proper revolutionary terminology. One satirist summed up this phenomenon in a story about a bureaucrat who began to talk in the acronyms that surrounded him in his work: *Privzhendet*, which in "English" might be "Helwichi," was Sovietese for "Say hello to your wife and children." Foreigners derisively referred to the Soviet Union as "Sovdepia" (Soviet of Deputies) after an acronym then in wide use. Even worse was the intro-

---

*From Ilya Ehrenburg (Erenburg), *Sobranie sochinenii*, vol. 8, Moscow: Izdat. "Khudozhestvennaia literatura," 1966. English translations by W. M.

duction into everyday speech of Communist terminology such as "diamat" from dialectical materialism, awkward enough to begin with. Other unenlightening coinages were "hegemony of the proletariat," and so on.

The coarser language reflected the atmosphere of the times, as did manners and customs in general. Because polite conduct was considered as much the province of middle class and aristocracy as stylized table manners, people were terribly rude to each other. Many shops displayed the sign FINISH YOUR BUSINESS AND GET OUT. On the walls of bureaucrats' offices hung the admonition, BY YOUR VISIT YOU ARE DISTURBING A BUSY MAN. Few said "thank you," and "please" was out of style. The satirist team of Ilf and Petrov and the comic writers Mikhail Zoshchenko and Mikhail Bulgakov went to the heart of these unhappy developments in short stories and articles for the popular press.

Even some of the most intelligent Communists were perplexed by the failure of an egalitarian society to emerge overnight from the ashes of the old regime. The capitalists had departed, but arrogant *nepmen* and bureaucrats rose up to lord it over the masses and ensure that everyone knew his place and kept to it. Ilya Ehrenburg recorded this scene: In 1921 an old peasant woman boarded a train and by mistake entered a first-class (sic!) compartment. The conductor yelled at her, "Where d'you think you're going?! Get out! This isn't 1917!" And one of Zoshchenko's characters says to someone unsuitably clad at the Bolshoi Theatre, "It's not 1919 now. You can't sit in a theatre in your overcoat." It was all right to go to the Bolshoi without a tie, *nekulturny* (uncouth) to keep one's overcoat on. It was all quite arbitrary, of course, and that was what Communists lamented. Life under communism was supposed to be rational and predictable, patriotic revolutionism always fashionable.

## RURAL LIFE

In the countryside no less than in the cities the impact of millions of lives lost during 1914–1921 was severe, but there remained more than 120 million rural dwellers in 1917. The overwhelming majority lived in roughly 25 million households. About 70,000 village Soviets, representing on average 1,750 members of 350 families, acted as primary administrative agencies in the countryside.

The country folk were divided into kulaks or well-to-do, average (called middle in Russia), poor, and landless. In 1927 there were about 750,000 kulak households embracing roughly 5.25 million people. These kulaks, whom the Communists detested as exploiters, employed about a million landless peasants as farmhands. There were all told about 2.3 million without land; those who did not work for the kulaks were employed by state or peasant associations or existed on charity.

The kulaks produced 15 percent of the grain on about 4 percent of the land. A 1927 survey showed that each kulak had two or three cows, up to 10 hectares for sowing, and an annual income of about 240 rubles per family member. He was thus better off than a rural official, who was paid 297 rubles, and earned about twice as much as a middle peasant in the grain-growing districts of European Russia. The kulak owned about one-third of the agricultural machinery and draft animals.

The overwhelming majority of peasants belonged to the middle and poor categories, within which there were many gradations. A technically poor peasant who lived in a part of the country blessed with mild climate and good soil—the North Caucasus, for example—was sometimes better off than middle peasants in the center and north. Middle and poor peasants produced 83 percent of the country's grain.

The kolhozes (collective farms) and sov-hoses (state farms, in effect agricultural factories) still in existence from the war communism period produced 2 percent of the grain. These enterprises, on which the state had bestowed its blessings, were widely regarded as failures, but for ideological reasons the party kept them afloat.

Life in the villages under NEP tended to resume patterns interrupted in 1914 by World War, Civil War, and war communism, and by the 1921 famine in the Volga valley. After 1921 the peasants resumed their historic task of feeding the country; in the NEP years that was all anyone asked of them. Perhaps the most revolutionary change to come to the village in the 1920s was the introduction of electricity. Lenin had declared that "Communism is Soviet power plus electrification of the whole country," confounding even his most devoted followers, but the project moved forward and in the 1920s consumed a large portion of state allocations for development. By the end of the decade about 15 percent of farms in European Russia and the Ukraine, 6 percent nationwide, had electric power.

The Communist party created *rabfaks* for the illiterate and undereducated workers, and in the countryside, where the problem was worse, it established "circles for the liquidation of illiteracy" or *likbezy*. The success of these organizations may be measured by the rise in the aggregate literacy rate from 30 percent in 1897, the year of the last tsarist census, to 51 percent in 1926. The increase was especially striking in rural areas, where illiteracy had been the rule. Female literacy more than doubled, to 37 percent; male literacy rose from 43 to 66 percent. Much of the teaching in the countryside was done by young idealists from the cities, modern counterparts of the students who had participated in the "to the people" movement of the 1870s.

Because the Communists represented an urban constituency it was to be expected that the countryside would get short shrift. Marxists had always despised the peasants; Marx himself made a famous comment about the "idiocy of rural life." The villages began to participate in the modernization process only slowly. Medical care reached them long after electricity; consumer goods only slowly made their way to the countryside; educational-cultural facilities for less populated areas developed at a glacial pace.

In the 1920s the peasants continued to go to mass on Sundays, tip the priest at holidays, and get married in church. The state tried to discourage these practices. The authorities insisted, for example, that peasants go through the same procedure as city dwellers with regard to marriage, i.e., present themselves at a registry office (ZAGS) to have the union legitimized. Millions ignored the regulation.

Marx and Lenin had denounced religion as the "opium of the masses," but the peasants did not read their works. In the cities the sophisticates might teach their children to taunt priests with "What's the price of opium today?" but in the villages the clergy retained a certain status and authority.

The Orthodox village priest, like his parishioners, was all too frequently a victim of alcoholism, at once a tragic Russian tradition and a reflection upon the pointlessness and ennui of rural life. Another problem was sexual promiscuity. Aside from the question of morality, carefree attitudes and practices in this realm kept the rate of venereal disease high. The problem also existed in the cities, of course, but medical care was readily available there, and by the end of the decade the urban problem had been reduced to manageable proportions.

The village remained terribly isolated. Only slowly did the state begin to supply electric power and with it, beginning in 1924, radio broadcasts. It would however be three decades before mass communications brought the majority of the peasants into regular contact with the outside world. In the years down to World War II the appearance of a portable film projector in the village caused a sensation, and even Communist agitators could draw sizable audiences without necessarily resorting to coercion; the peasants simply wanted to be entertained.

## EDUCATION

There was more to education under the Communist regime than *rabfaks* and *likbezy*. The party set two major goals: (1) universal literacy, (2) elimination of the class character of education, sometimes contradictorily called the "proletarianization" of education.

The task of revamping the educational system was not made easier by the hostility of the teachers toward the new regime. But like the middle class in general, teachers had few options. They could leave the country, find jobs as common laborers, or make their peace with the Communists and return to the classroom. Most chose the third course.

The standardized ideals proclaimed by the Politburo penetrated the educational system at all levels from kindergarten to university. Students of all ages were taught to regard Lenin and the party as the ultimate sources of truth, happiness, and material blessings.

The Soviets established "unified labor schools" designed to give students an "active, mobile, creative acquaintance with all that is most useful in life." In a society which exalted labor, schools were at first heavily oriented toward vocational training. The social sciences and humanities were treated with suspicion by the Communists, who were determined to impose Marxist-Leninist interpretations.

Higher education witnessed some striking excesses in the early years. Party officials declared in 1918 that "purely formal" obstacles such as lack of preparation would not impede workers who wished to attend a university. A Sovnarkom decree gave every citizen "not belonging to the exploiting classes" the right to enroll in any university regardless of whether he or she had completed high school. This was motivated not by reason but by anger and a sense of righteous retribution; before the Revolution the universities had been instruments of class rule. The Communists soon came to realize, however, that destroying them was not the best way to reform them.

The authorities abolished tenure for university faculty in October 1918, did away with the "bourgeois" practice of examining students, and prohibited the "bourgeois" lecture method of teaching. All classes became "laboratories"; in practice that usually meant political discussion groups.

Dozens of universities, not counting the "Communist universities" which had an avowedly political mission, sprang up around the country. Moscow had a Proletarian University, Sverdlov Communist University, Evening Communist University, Komsomol University, Extension Communist University, Julian Marchlewski Communist University of the National Minorities of the West (western districts of the state), and a host of institutes and advanced schools. Foreign students were enrolled at the Communist University for the Toilers of China and the Communist University for the Toilers of the East.

As early as 1922 the party saw that some educational experiments were not worth continuing. As revolutionary passions cooled, officials pondered the consequences of allowing people ostensibly trained, for example, as physicians and civil engineers to practice without first passing examinations. Further, the policy of open admissions had created enormous problems; the universities and institutes were deluged with hordes of un-qualified students who disrupted the educational process. In 1922 the government ordered the registration of all students; those who did not have a high school diploma could not register anywhere but in the *rabfaks*. A rigorous examination system was reintroduced in all fields; diplomas were awarded to graduates. Many of the new universities quietly closed down.

## THE YOUNG GENERATION

The combination of disasters which struck Russia in the period 1914–1921 placed an immense burden on children and young adults. The young could never live as their parents had; class roles were turned upside down, traditional values anathematized. Norms vanished and no new ones were immediately available.

As part of its approach to the youth problem in general, and in connection with its long-range goals, the party established organizations which were to become important sociopolitical agencies. Children to age 10 were enrolled in the Octobrists, where they learned nursery rhymes, games, and songs. Most of these were traditional but as in any country some inculcated patriotic attitudes and behavior.

A more highly structured mass organization for children 10 to 14 formally came into existence in May 1922. Originally called "Spartacus Young Pioneers," it became Leninist Young Pioneers in 1924. It had the task of training children in good citizenship, proper personal and public manners, and reverence for Lenin and, after 1927, Stalin.

The children also learned rudiments of close-order military drill.

The Russian Communist Youth League was created in October 1918 as an organization for young people 14 to 28. About 25,000 members fought in the Civil War, and later the League participated in reconstruction of the country. It was from this organization, according to Communist legend, that Lenin took the idea of "subbotnik," voluntary work on occasional Saturdays for the benefit of the state. The League became the All-Union Leninist Youth League, or Komsomol, in 1926, when it had 1.25 million members. This figure indicates that the Komsomol, like the party, was originally an élite organization. This changed as the Stalinist dictatorship took hold. For all practical purposes membership became mandatory; by 1941 there were 10.3 million members.

These organizations had the task of indoctrinating and guiding the youth along party-approved lines. The Komsomol was also charged with developing cadres for the Communist party, entrance into which was increasingly limited to people from its ranks. Membership in the Komsomol gave a sense of shared identity and loyalty and of participation in a grand cause. The organization was also a major source of practical guidance for the individual's progress toward the projected Communist future.

## THE REVOLUTION AND WOMEN

The Bolsheviks had come to power under the flag of complete social equality for all citizens, certainly including women. Women had been active in the 19th-century revolutionary movement and some had suffered varying degrees of martyrdom for it. Several women had occupied prominent roles in one or another of the revolutionary parties and proto-parties. Among the Bolsheviks, Nadezhda Krupskaya and Aleksandra Kollontai were the most conspicuous women officials, but their power and influence were limited.

The ease with which women moved in revolutionary circles was atypical. In Russian Empire society they were at best second-class citizens, and in the Russian and Ukrainian villages and the Muslim areas they were often treated little better than beasts of burden. Among the Uzbek, Kazakh, Kirgiz, Tajik, Turkmen, Azerbaijanian, and other Muslim peoples, no women other than the wives or concubines of rulers or famous outlaws had any historical existence at all. It is all but impossible to find the names of Muslim women in official records. In Estonia, Latvia, and Armenia, the lot of women in the pre-revolutionary period was easier than elsewhere in the empire.

The rights of women were guaranteed in the first Soviet Constitution, which outlawed discrimination on the basis of sex. In practice this meant that women had new opportunities for education and work; millions began to take advantage of them. The party created special women's sections (*zhenotdely*) within its ranks to advance the cause of women's rights. The organizations were dissolved in 1921, but by the mid-1920s there were as many women as men in most institutions of higher education. In such fields as medicine, not a particularly prestigious occupation either before or after the Revolution, women predominated. Women also constituted a substantial majority of the students in the pedagogical institutes, but teaching was likewise not a highly respected profession. The socially glamorous and rewarding fields were engineering and the sciences, where women only slowly began to chip away at traditional male dominance.

In politics, few women outside the closed circle of Old Bolsheviks attained positions of real power. No women sat in the highest councils of party or state. Increasing numbers of women participated in the work of the Soviets, especially at the local and district levels, but at the republic and union levels pure tokenism prevailed. In the bureaucracy women won such positions as directors of registry offices, post offices, and the like, but power eluded them. There were few women heads of factories or other state enterprises. On the private farms of the NEP period women continued to perform heavy physical labor. As the cities grew, increasing numbers of women were employed in construction as hod carriers, laborers, or apprentices. Women took up such occupations as driving trolleys and buses, and they predominated in the low-paid, socially despised retail trade sector.

In terms of its impact on daily life the October Revolution did less to improve the lot of women than its makers had intended. Wife-beating remained one of the most common crimes, periodic official campaigns against it notwithstanding. Few men saw any reason to overturn traditional roles, which saw women burdened with all household chores, including the enervating task of queuing for almost every purchase, and child rearing. Those who had no moral objections saw the legalization of abortion as a major step in the emancipation of women. This extreme form of birth control, however, was an urban phenomenon that had little impact on peasant women.

Finally, the Revolution brought women rough equality in one unexpected area: many thousands went to prison. In the first decade of Soviet rule most victims were upper-class women who fell afoul of the authorities one way or another; often their only crime was their class origin. In succeeding years women would be charged with various crimes against the state on a more or less equal basis with men and would help populate the Gulag Archipelago.

## RELIGION

Marx considered religion both a delusion and a device to maintain class rule. Lenin shared that view and argued that, in the modern European world, the bourgeoisie utilized the main sects in the cause of the exploitation of the proletariat. Religion preached submission to the secular authorities controlled by the bourgeoisie and to economic and social injustice. The coming of communism would end what he considered religion's cooperation with tyranny.

Its control established over the entire country, the Communist party moved against the church. In spring 1922 several Russian Orthodox leaders were convicted in Moscow on charges of refusing to turn over valuables to Pomgol, the famine relief agency. The Patriarch himself, Tikhon, was called as a witness; later he was arrested and held without trial for more than a year. Five of the convicted churchmen were shot, and the remaining 12 received prison sentences.

A month after the Moscow trial a similar process began in Petrograd. Several dozen people were in the dock; the verdict was the same. Ten people were sentenced to death; four were actually shot. Among those executed was Benjamin, Metropolitan of Petrograd.

The trials of the Orthodox clergymen marked the first battles of a campaign—in which the Komsomol was deeply involved—that was to proceed at varying tempos over the next 20 years. There were no more mass trials and executions, but individual clerics and nuns were persecuted. Many priests were denied the right to minister to their congregations, and thousands of churches and chapels were destroyed, converted to secular use (often as taverns or dance halls), or simply padlocked. The famous monastery on the Solovetsky Islands in the White Sea became one of the most notorious concentration camps for political prisoners.

In 1925 the party founded the League of the Godless, a nationwide organization of propagandists with the mission of educating the masses in the ways of "scientific atheism." The society sponsored lectures and antireligious films, of which two of the more sensational were *Judas* and *Opium*. It staged "debates" in which the religious side was upheld by Communist stooges. The League issued a number of publications, among them *Revolution and Church* (1919–1924), *Science and Religion* (continuous since 1922), *Atheist* (newspaper 1922–1941, journal 1925–1941), *Workbench Atheist* (1923–1931), *Antireligionist* (1926–1941), *Atheism* (1922–1930), and *Militant Atheism* (1931).

All this activity failed to produce the results the Communists wanted. Millions of people continued to worship in defiance of the regime. As an indication of the party's determination to step up the campaign against religion, in 1929 the antireligious association was renamed the League of the Militant Godless.

Other faiths did not initially suffer quite the degree of persecution that befell the dominant Russian Orthodox. While the churches of Baptists, Mennonites, Lutherans, Uniates, Roman Catholics, and other Christian sects, and Jewish synagogues, did suffer vandalism, by and large the clergy were left alone. In the 1920s, the Communists permitted the existence of a Baptist Youth Union (Bapsomol), a Baptist organization infelicitously called Christ-o-Youth (Khristomol), and a Mennonite Youth Union (Mensomol).

In the Caucasus and Central Asia, far removed from the Slav heartland, the Muslim peoples suffered severe persecution on religious grounds. The Red Army and local Communist officials destroyed nearly all the mosques and arrested the mullahs (religious

Honor guard at funeral of Viktor Nogin, Moscow, May 1924. (National Archives)

scholars). As religion and nationalism began to coalesce in the Muslim lands, the local peoples came into ever more serious conflict with the new regime. Especially bloody clashes involved the *basmachi* in the Uzbek, Kazakh, Kirgiz, Turkmen, and Tajik regions. The last important rebel leader, Ibrahim Beg, was captured near Dushanbe in 1931.

## CULTURAL LIFE

The October Revolution promised total liberation in the realm of culture. For a brief period the Communists assumed the role of liberators and innovators and universalized access to the arts. The elimination of admission charges to cultural events symbolized this new policy, but those charges were reinstituted in 1921. The Revolution had promised more than it could deliver, but it nevertheless brought substantial, often positive, change. In overall charge of cultural policy was Anatoli Lunacharsky, the commissar of enlightenment whose contribution to the flourishing of the arts in the NEP period was of enormous importance.

Some talented writers supported the October Revolution. The symbolist poet Aleksandr Blok produced two of the greatest poems of the revolutionary era, *The Twelve* and *The Scythians*. In the first, 12 Red Guards patrol Petrograd in October 1917, ruthlessly destroying everything and everyone in their path that does not serve the Revolution. Although they do not recognize him, they are led by Jesus Christ. Russia was fulfilling her destiny, bringing a new world into existence. In *The Scythians*, Blok warned the West to accept not merely the fact of the Revolution but its spiritual importance or be condemned to damnation.

Vladimir Mayakovsky, who joined the Bolsheviks in 1908 at the age of 15, was a founder of the futurist movement, which sought radical innovation in poetry. Mayakovsky often used crude, unpoetic language in order to shock, stimulate, and outrage: "I love to watch children die." Uncertain where the future would lead, he nevertheless demanded to be its herald. After 1917 he wrote panegyrics to the Revolution which have not stood the test of time. His more lyrical poems such as *I Love* and *At the Top of My Voice*, however, won him lasting popularity. Toward the end of the 1920s Mayakovsky became disenchanted with Communist rule. In the spring of 1930 he was attacked by the Russian Association of Proletarian Writers (RAPP) for "betraying" communism; he committed suicide later in the year at the age of 37.

Sergei Yesenin, one of the most popular of the 20th-century poets, was born into a peasant family. His first important published work (*Radunitsa*, 1915) revealed a major lyric talent; his poems were love songs dedicated to the Russian village. After the Revolution, which he welcomed, Yesenin moved to Moscow and tried to fashion a public image befitting the peasant-poet of the new era. His efforts to lead a bohemian life included a disastrous marriage to the American dancer Isadora Duncan. In such collections as *Tavern Moscow* he revealed his bitter disappointment with the regime. On the eve of his death he tried to make peace with the party, but the insincerity of his verse was transparent. In 1925 he wrote a last poem in his own blood and committed suicide. He was 32.

Four enormously talented poets perplexed by the collapse of the old regime were Osip Mandelstam, Anna Akhmatova, Boris Pasternak, and Marina Tsvetayeva. Prior to the Revolution they had adhered to one or another of the various avant-garde tendencies in the arts: futurism, acmeism, symbolism. Pasternak became famous with a collection of poems entitled *My Sister, Life*, in which he conveyed the excitement of 1917. With good reason, Akhmatova quickly came to fear the Bolsheviks. They shot her husband, the poet Nikolai Gumilyov, in 1921 as a "White Guardist." Tsvetayeva sided with the Whites and emigrated in 1921; she would return on the eve of World War II, only to commit suicide. Mandelstam, perhaps the greatest poetic talent of the century in Russia, published two major collections in 1922, *The Stone* and *Tristia*, then ceased writing for more than a decade.

Some brilliant poetry was produced in the midst of the great upheavals, but it would be several years before any artistically significant prose appeared. A novelist who had cooperated with the Bolsheviks in the prerevolutionary period was Maksim Gorky, whose fame was then exceeded only by that of Leo Tolstoi. Gorky had written several novels dealing with the seamy underside of life in the late tsarist period, notably the trilogy *Childhood, Among People*, and *My Universities* (the last published in 1923). His play *The Lower Depths*, set in a doss house, enjoyed great success.

The first of the major novelists to call attention to the dictatorial tendencies of the Communist regime was Yevgeni Zamyatin, who wrote in *The Cave* about Petrograd under war communism as an outpost of a dying civilization being overtaken by a new ice age. His masterpiece, *We* (1929), attacked "primitive, spiritually empty 'barracks' socialism." George Orwell (*1984*) and Aldous Huxley (*Brave New World*) were deeply in Zamyatin's debt and received much of the acclaim that should have been his. Harassed unmercifully in Soviet Russia, Zamyatin finally emigrated.

Another writer who identified the one-party dictatorship in its infancy was Mikhail Bulgakov, whose *Heart of a Dog* skewered the new Communist masters who used weighty vocabularies they did not understand to express views they often did not believe. Bulgakov's most important work, *The Master and Margarita*, has as its central theme the clash between the sacred and the profane: Christ on the cross, a writer persecuted by the rigidly authoritarian state. Ribald comedy does not obscure the theme.

Several comic geniuses emerged in this period, perhaps because only through laughter could one make sense of a world that often seemed to have gone mad. The Soviet public loved the team of Ilf and Petrov (I.A. Fainzilberg and E.P. Katayev), writers who poked fun at NEP in *Twelve Chairs* and *The Golden Calf*. An equally popular humorist was Mikhail Zoshchenko, whose short stories and vignettes were all the more powerful for their brevity and realistic language.

Not all writers opposed the party. One who embraced it wholeheartedly was Mikhail Sholokhov, whose *Quiet Flows the Don* is the classic novel of the Civil War. Other writers who supported Lenin's party were Dmitri Furmanov, Fyodor Gladkov (whose *Cement* was called the first proletarian novel), and Aleksandr Fadeyev.

Writers were an important force in shaping social attitudes, and if the Communists did not have their support they took measures to ensure their silence. The task of bringing the artists into line was much easier in the case of the cinema, a new art form. An outstanding cinematographic talent was Sergei Eisenstein, whose *Strike* (1925), *Battleship Potemkin* (1926), and *October* (1927) are film classics. Portraying the masses as a collective hero, Eisenstein pioneered such techniques as montage, overhead shots, moving cameras, dramatic lighting. Another eminent Soviet director, Dziga Vertov (Denis Kaufman), produced *Forward, Soviet!* and *A Sixth Part of the World* in 1926. Although not on a par with Eisenstein's best work, these films won wide acclaim, as did V.I. Pudovkin's *Mother* (1926) and *The End of St. Petersburg* (1927). Grigory Kozintsev and Leonid Trauberg collaborated on *New Babylon* (1929), a classic of expressionist cinema for which Dmitri Shostakovich later composed a score.

Lenin said that "the cinema is for us the most important of the arts." The party was dismayed to find that Eisenstein's *Battleship Potemkin*, which portrays an episode in the Revolution of 1905, drew only a fraction of the audience that crowded Soviet theatres to see the American production, *Robin Hood*. The great Soviet films of 1925–1930, which had an enormous impact in Europe and America, enjoyed less popularity at home.

Like the cinema, the legitimate stage prospered in the early years of Soviet rule. The renowned director Konstantin Stanislavsky (real name Alekseyev), who was born in 1863, put his talent at the service of the Revolution and created "method acting." Another genius was the director-producer Vsevolod Meyerhold, who also developed his art prior to 1917. Meyerhold specialized in staging the works of Gogol (notably *The Inspector General*) and Aleksandr Ostrovsky; later he produced Mayakovsky's *The Bedbug*, *Mystery-Bouffe*, and *The Bathhouse*.

In the field of classical music, Nikolai Rimsky-Korsakov's most talented pupil, Igor Stravinsky, left Russia before the Great War. For political reasons not related to his emigration, Stravinsky's music represented anathema to the Communists for more than half a century. It was perhaps a step down in talent to another Rimsky-Korsakov student, Sergei Prokofiev, composer of extremely popular works. Prokofiev left Russia in 1918 but returned in 1932. A giant among Soviet composers was Dmitri Shostakovich, pupil of Aleksandr Glazunov. Shostakovich's immense talent was first revealed to a wide audience with the 1925 première of his First Symphony. Two years later he was commissioned to write a work celebrating the 10th anniversary of the October Revolution. The result, his Second Symphony, was also an artistic success despite—and a political success because of—his incorporation of a factory whistle into the score. A brilliant Armenian composer, Aram Khachaturyan, began to attract the attention of music lovers.

As in literature and art, the 1920s were a decade of exciting experimentation in music. The attack on Stravinsky and other avant-garde composers would come later. The works of innovative foreign composers were regularly performed: Alban Berg's opera *Wozzek* was staged in Leningrad in 1927, the composer in attendance. The works of Arnold Schoenberg, Maurice Ravel, Ernst Krenek, and Paul Hindemith were frequently heard in Soviet concert halls. A Soviet engineer, Lev Termen, invented the theremin, the first new musical instrument since the saxophone. The electronic device was extensively employed by several Soviet composers in the 1920s but was banned by the Communist party in 1932 as "decadent." (The saxophone was to be outlawed briefly in 1949 on the same grounds.) In the West, however, the theremin enjoyed great success, especially in film scores; Alfred Hitchcock was particularly fond of the eerie, ethereal sound quality of Termen's invention.

So far as popular music is concerned, the decade was officially dominated by songs celebrating the October Revolution and the Communist victory in the Civil War. Few had any lasting popularity; most of the great tunes and marches exalting—for example—Budyonny's horse cavalry appeared later, in the 1930s. Some of the poems of Mayakovsky ("Left, March!") and Sergei Yesenin ("I'm

not sorry . . .") were set to music and enjoyed continuing favor. Less enduring were Pavel Gherman's "Song of the Brick Factory," "Mine No. 3," and Ivan Molchanov's "Give us a ride on the tractor, Pete!" Such odes to revolutionary patriotism caressed Communist ears gently, however, and the party encouraged and rewarded the composers. Fortunately, in the villages and in the less fashionable cafés and taverns of the towns, Russian, Ukrainian, and other folk music survived.

Avant-garde art flourished in the new state for the first few years after 1917. Under the patronage of Lunacharsky, such artists as El Lissitsky, Kazimir Malevich, Vasily Kandinsky, Aleksandr Rodchenko, Vladimir Tatlin, Marc Chagall, Ivan Puni (Jean Pougny), and others set off on an exciting search for new forms. Most artists soon became disillusioned, however, as the party denounced their projects as decadent, obscene, incomprehensible, or worst of all, antisocialist.

Chagall had returned from France, as had Kandinsky, to participate in building the new society. He founded and briefly directed the famous Vitebsk school in Byelorussia. Unable to tolerate the restrictions imposed on him, he went back to France in 1922. His successor at Vitebsk, Malevich, was one of the creators of the supremacist school, which sought to go beyond cubism and futurism to depict nonvisible reality. Ultimately the party declared the works of the supremacists, and indeed of all avant-garde artists, inaccessible—because they were abstract—to the masses and therefore decadent and unworthy of support or even toleration. By 1932 free expression in art no longer existed.

## THE WAY THEY WERE

Before the claws and tentacles of extreme authoritarian rule seized Russia in a deadly grip, there were a few brief years when life was pretty good for most people—"like cheese in butter" is the Russian saying. Ideology was shelved in pursuit of a respite from seven years of hell. People were exhausted and needed a rest. The party eased up, and people half-wondered whether a capitalist restoration was at hand.

The authorities closed down the old thieves' markets, but by 1922 no one missed them because the *nepmen* could provide almost anything. In the cities and even in some provincial towns one could buy French champagne and Western clothes. Singer sewing machines, which had been manufactured in Russia before the war, were again available, as were Ford vehicles for the few who could afford them. Westinghouse was again installing elevators and air brakes (and inspiring a Zoshchenko feuilleton); Royal Dutch Shell provided technical expertise in the Caspian oil fields; American geologists and mining engineers helped extract the mineral wealth of Siberia; Swedish experts advised the Soviets how to exploit their vast forests. Café life flourished in the cities. It was not Paris, people said of Moscow, but neither was it the miserable Russian village.

It was an unstable period. *Nepmen* or no, capitalism was not going to make a complete recovery. But how long could the new economic policy continue, and what would succeed it?

In their pursuit of happiness and the good life, few people gave much thought to these questions. Serious Communists understood however that under NEP, politics—merely a part of society's superstructure in the Marxist scheme—rested on a dangerously inappropriate base. A party dedicated to a planned economy based upon heavy industry could not long maintain its hold on power by sacrificing principle to peasant prosperity. Communists made poor managers of a quasi-capitalist economy. Something would have to give.

The committeemen and hundreds of thousands of rank and file members looked to the post-Lenin leadership to end this apotheosis of the peasant proprietor and restore the Revolution to its rightful course. Those Communists were counting heavily upon Joseph Stalin to show the *nepmen*, prostitutes, *spetsy*, and foreigners the broad open road leading to doom.

## SUGGESTED ADDITIONAL READING

**Barron, Stephanie, and Maurice Tuchman, eds.,** *The Avant-Garde in Russia, 1910–1930*, Cambridge, Mass.: MIT Press, 1980

**Bridger, Susan,** *Women in the Soviet Countryside*, New York: Cambridge University Press, 1987

**Brown, Edward J.,** *Russian Literature since the Revolution*, Cambridge, Mass.: Harvard University Press, 1982

**Ehrenberg, Ilya,** *Memoirs: 1921–1941*, Cleveland: World Publishing, 1964

**Fitzpatrick, Sheila,** *Education and Social Mobility in the Soviet Union, 1921–1934*, New York: Cambridge University Press, 1979

**Gibian, George, and H.W Tjalsma, eds.,** *Russian Modernism: Culture and the Avant-Garde, 1900–1930*, Ithaca, N.Y.: Cornell University Press, 1976

**Kenez, Peter,** *The Birth of the Propaganda State: Soviet Methods of Mass Mobilization, 1917–1929*, New York: Cambridge University Press, 1987

**Leyda, Jay,** *Kino: A History of Russian and Soviet Film*, Princeton, N.J.: Princeton University Press, 1983

**Maguire, Robert A.,** *Red Virgin Soil: Soviet Literature in the 1920s*, Ithaca, N.Y.: Cornell University Press, 1987

**Pethybridge, Roger,** *The Social Prelude to Stalinism*, New York: St. Martin's, 1974

**Taylor, Richard,** *The Politics of the Soviet Cinema, 1917–1929*, Cambridge, England: Cambridge University Press, 1979

**Taylor, Richard, and Ian Christie,** eds., *The Film Factory: Russian and Soviet Cinema in Documents, 1896–1939*, Cambridge, Mass.: Harvard University Press, 1988

**Willett, John,** *Art and Politics in the Weimar Period*, New York: Pantheon, 1978

# 7

# FOREIGN POLICY
# IN THE 1920s

The new regime sought in the beginning not so much to export its own revolution as to make the proletariat of other countries, above all Germany, aware that the time had come to rise up and overthrow capitalism. Only a small part of the world proletariat, however, shared Lenin's reading of history. There were relatively few revolutionary uprisings, and those that did erupt were quickly put down. This necessitated reorientation of Soviet plans. Communist excesses, especially in Germany and Hungary, had alienated many governments and alarmed whole populations; establishing normal diplomatic relations was not an easy task. The post-Lenin leadership, acknowledging that the capitalist system had stabilized, modified the strategy of world revolution and began constructing a nationalist foreign policy.

## SOVIET INTERNATIONAL ORGANIZATIONS

In the first few years of Soviet rule Lenin's party founded a number of organizations designed both to keep an ideological commitment and to advance the national interests of the fledgling state. The most prominent was the Third or Communist International (Comintern), founded early in 1919. The organization actually came to life only at its Second Congress in Moscow in July–August 1920. Peace had been restored to most of the world—Russia was an exception—and conditions appeared more favorable to the Communist movement. Some 217 delegates from 37 countries attended; they represented 67 leftist organizations, including 27 functioning Communist parties.

The Second Congress established 21 Conditions for membership that constituted a politico-ideological litmus test: parties, groups, associations, and individuals wishing to join the Comintern had to accept them. Chief among the requirements was the commitment to purge anyone deviating from the Leninist political line defined by the Russian-controlled Executive Committee. Member parties were to maintain strict internal discipline, give unconditional support to Soviet Russia, and create parallel illegal organizations within existing legal party structures. The remaining rules elaborated these crucial ones and dealt with housekeeping matters. There was nothing about any material improvement in the lives of the workers, nothing about their political and social emancipation.

The precarious situation of Communist parties had the effect of making them dependent upon Moscow, which was what the Soviet leaders intended. The centralizing, despotic tendencies that had characterized Russian politics for centuries were reflected in the Comintern.

By the latter part of 1921 communism seemed a failure everywhere, including Russia, where the only regime ever to introduce a communist system had been forced to restore a substantial degree of free enterprise. Two basic assumptions had proved erroneous, namely, that the collapse of capitalism was imminent and that the proletariat in other countries would rise up in revolution.

The Soviets insisted the theory was correct and that only their timing needed adjustment. They had however to deal with reality, and they put forward the concept of a "united front": under certain conditions Communists would unite with other leftist parties. Sometimes this would be "from above," for example, merely an agreement with leaders of Socialist parties. Sometimes the united front would be "from below," an alliance between Communist and Socialist rank and file. This awkward, risky game was to result in disaster.

On the initiative of the Comintern's Executive Committee and the Soviet federation of trade unions, the International Council of Professional and Industrial Unions was founded in Moscow in July 1920. A year later it was succeeded by the Red International of Trade Unions, or Profintern. The Profintern condemned various Western trade union organizations and rejected their attempts to promote class harmony. It had some success in infiltrating labor unions in several countries, notably Germany and France, but proved an unsatisfactory weapon in the great struggle against Nazism and fascism. Stalin disbanded it in 1937.

A working-class party, Communists were always slow to take up the cause of the peasantry and were never comfortable with that class. Thus, the Peasant International, or Krestintern, did not come into existence until October 1923, when the founding congress took place in Moscow. Delegates from Soviet Russia, Poland, Denmark, France, Czechoslovakia, Bulgaria, the United States, Mexico, Norway, Sweden, Finland, Indochina, and Japan met under Soviet auspices to work out a program dedicated to the advancement of peasant interests around the globe.

As the Comintern was originally a "counter-intervention" and the Profintern a response to the formation of anticommunist labor organizations, so the Krestintern was designed to counter the International Agrarian Bureau, often called the Green International. Never recognized anywhere as an authentically peasant organization, the Krestintern was almost forgotten by the Communists themselves as the collectivization of Soviet agriculture got under way at the end of the decade. It ceased to exist in 1933.

The organizing congress of the Communist Youth International took place in Berlin November 20–26, 1919. Only 29 delegates attended; they claimed to represent 219,000 members of youth organizations in 13 countries. In reality they spoke only for the Soviet Communists and a few of their friends around Europe. Only at the second congress, held in Moscow in July 1921, did KIM (the Russian initials) assume a real identity.

By 1921 Lenin's hopes for proletarian revolutions in the West were fading; and KIM, like the other offshoots of the Comintern, was dedicated to the advancement of Soviet Russia's national interests. It was committed to promote harmony and solidarity among the youth of member nations, agitate against militarism, and above all preserve and protect the mother country of socialism, Soviet Russia.

In the 1930s KIM served as an important Communist agency in the fight against fascism. A measure of its effectiveness was its survival until 1943, the year in which Stalin liquidated both it and the parent Comintern.

The leaders of the new Soviet state believed that they were history's advance guard whose international class duty it was to mobilize "progressive" forces in other countries for the decisive clash with capital. The Comintern and its subsidiaries Profintern, Krestintern, and KIM, were instruments for that mobilization; there were many others.

In 1921 the Soviets created the Communist University for the Toilers of the East (KUTV) in Moscow to train cadres for party and government service in the eastern republics and provinces of the country. The institution's mission quickly expanded, however, to embrace the schooling of revolutionaries from East and Southeast Asia. In the early years about half the students came from the Soviet east and about half from Japan, China, Indonesia, Indochina, and the Arab lands. By 1927 KUTV had students of 74 different nationalities. The most prominent graduate was Hô Chi Minh, one of the founders of the Vietnamese Communist party. Hô studied at the school in 1924 and—calling himself "Comrade Linov"—at one of its affiliated institutions in 1934–1938. Its faculty caught up in the purges, KUTV ceased to exist in 1936.

Acting through the Comintern, in 1925 the Soviet government established Sun Yatsen University for the Toilers of China, in 1927 renamed Communist University for the Toilers of China or KUTK. About 600 students were enrolled. In 1927 the first rector, Karl Radek, lost his job to Stalin's China expert, vice-rector Pavel Mif (Mikhail Aleksandrovich Fortus). Mif remained in the position only two years, during which time he created a nucleus of 28 Chinese students who were consistent supporters of Stalin in his struggle against Trotsky, Zinoviev, and Bukharin. They were known as "Stalin's China Section" and later as the "28 Bolsheviks." The Soviets intended to create ties between the Chinese students at KUTK and those at Whampoa Military Academy in China, but after the massacre of the Chinese Communists in 1927 that proved impossible.

Still another Soviet creation was the International Organization for Aid to Fighters for Revolution (MOPR). A kind of Red Cross for leftists, MOPR provided funds and legal assistance to imprisoned revolutionaries around the world. It tried unsuccessfully to intervene in the famous Sacco-Vanzetti case in the United States in the 1920s.

Several international organizations sponsored by the Soviet Communists came into existence in the early 1920s. Some were openly Communist, others ostensibly nonpolitical agencies. The Anti-Imperialist League, for example, was heavily influenced by the Soviets although it was technically not under their control. The League held two congresses, one at Brussels in 1927, which the prominent Asian Communists Hô Chi Minh and Sen Katayama attended, and one at Frankfurt-am-Main in 1929.

## THE MUSLIM EAST

On July 3, 1920, Soviet newspapers published a Comintern summons "To the Enslaved Peoples of Persia, Armenia, and Turkey" to attend a congress in Baku dedicated to the "liberation of the Near East." Comintern representatives fanned out in search of likely candidates to attend the conclave on the shores of the Caspian.

Nearly 1,900 delegates assembled in Baku in September 1920 to spend a week listening to speeches in languages which no one other than the speaker and his compatriots understood; translation posed an enormous problem. Somehow they managed to agree on two issues. They opposed colonialism, and they wanted a holy war, a *jihad,* against the infidel. The Communist delegates, however, lumped the mullahs together with feudal exploiters and urged Muslims to extend the proposed holy war to an attack on their own faith. The posturing of Zinoviev, Radek, and others of Lenin's men compromised the Communist cause in the Near East before it took to the field.

A few weeks after the fiasco in Baku, a less spectacular but more successful meeting was held in the foothills of the Caucasus. This was the Extraordinary Congress of the Peoples of Dagestan, directed by Stalin and Ordzhonikidze. The Muslim minorities of the Caucasus figured prominently in Soviet political calculations because the Communists were determined to spread the revolution to the Islamic lands. Most of the peoples of Dagestan were Sunni Muslims, and it would obviously be difficult for an atheistic party to win their allegiance. Stalin, however, evidently persuaded his colleagues that he could persuade the Dagestani Muslims to refrain from joining the anti-Soviet movements in Trans-Caucasia. In the longer term he would try to educate the young generation away from the religion of their fathers. He was to take an active role in the founding of a special university in Moscow for students from Muslim areas in Soviet Russia and abroad.

On November 13, 1920, Stalin proclaimed the creation of the Autonomous Soviet Socialist Republic of Dagestan to 300 delegates assembled in the market town of Temir-Khan-Shura (Buinaksk). He vigorously denied the rumor that the government would ban the *shariat,* the canonical law of Islam which governed not only religious but also secular life in Dagestan. The Kremlin would not shrink from a head-on collision with Russian Orthodoxy, but it would proceed cautiously with the Muslim peoples of the mountains. Stalin went on to assure his listeners that the Kremlin would grant them the same autonomy already enjoyed by the "Turkestan, Kirgiz, and Tatar republics." He urged the delegates to recognize Moscow's authority.

Ordzhonikidze gave a short speech praising the mountaineers for not joining Imam Gotsinsky (Nazhmutdin of Gotzo) or Colonel Alikhanov, anticommunist military leaders supported by the Georgian Menshevik state. Several of the delegates interrogated Stalin and Ordzhonikidze about Communist intentions with regard to religion. The congress ended with organizers and delegates proclaiming the unbreakable union of the peoples of Dagestan and workers all over the Soviet state. Dagestan was incorporated into the RSFSR on January 20, 1921.

## TREATY OF RAPALLO

The matter of the Imperial Russian debt, calculated in 1918 at 18.496 billion gold rubles, complicated the Communist regime's relations with the West. Europe had failed to restore a smooth-functioning economic system after the war, and some politicians believed that repayment of the tsarist debt could finance reconstruction.

France and Great Britain desperately sought ways to shore up their faltering economies. Politicians in those countries even began to consider the wisdom of excluding the two largest and most populous continental states, Germany and Russia, from the European economic system. Both countries had been good customers, and Russia had been a reliable supplier of raw materials.

In January 1922 French and British officials issued invitations to Germany and Russia to attend a general economic and financial conference in Genoa in April. The Soviet government immediately accepted, regarding the invitation as tantamount to diplomatic recognition. It was not that, but it was a sign that a break in the West's efforts to isolate Russia was in the offing.

The Soviets sent a delegation headed by Comissar of Foreign Affairs Georgi Chicherin. They were still not willing, however, to abandon the pranks that had cost them credibility at Brest-Litovsk, where Radek had distributed revolutionary leaflets to the German honor guard. Moscow announced that James Larkin, an Irishman serving a sentence for "criminal anarchy" in Sing-Sing prison (New York), would be a member of its proletarian internationalist delegation. He had been elected, the Soviet press reported, by the workers of a textile mill outside Moscow, many of whom were immigrants from the United States. The foreign commissariat demanded that the prisoner be re-

leased and given a new suit, pocket money, passage to Italy, and full diplomatic honors. Larkin remained in Sing-Sing.

On their way to Genoa the Soviet delegates stopped off in Berlin. In secret negotiations with the German government, they agreed on almost all points of a diplomatic bombshell to be hurled a few days later.

At the first session in Genoa Chicherin declared that, before there could be any talk of economic recovery, the conference should determine how to bring about disarmament. The French foreign minister, Louis Barthou, objected strenuously to this attempt to introduce a subject not on the official agenda, and at Lloyd George's urging Chicherin abandoned his efforts.

The conference settled into a battle of claim and counterclaim. The Allies demanded that the Communists settle past accounts; only then could they expect the normalization of relations. Chicherin replied that the Soviet government would indeed acknowledge the tsarist debt and pay compensation for nationalized foreign property. First, however, it would be necessary for the West to pay the bill, which the Soviets reckoned at 39 billion gold rubles, for the blockade and Intervention.

For a week the conference was bogged down. Then, on April 16, Easter Sunday, the German and Soviet delegations announced they had concluded a treaty at Rapallo, a nearby resort town. Under the terms of the agreement, diplomatic and consular relations were to be restored immediately. Germany renounced all claims on the Soviet government, and the most favored nation principle was to rule in all commerical relations. The two countries were to give each other "mutual assistance for the alleviation of their economic difficulties."

The Treaty of Rapallo, which constituted definitive cancellation of the Treaty of Brest-Litovsk, surprised and divided the Western

Allies. Barthou signed a note condemning Germany but refused to go along with a virtually identical note to Russia. His accounting if not his logic was impeccable: France and her ally, Belgium, were tsarist Russia's two biggest creditors. France had tried and failed to recoup her losses through force of arms; now she would try diplomacy. After a week of bickering the Allies finally agreed that the new treaty was acceptable insofar as it did not violate existing agreements.

Having come together at Genoa to try to get another pound of flesh from Russia, the Western Allies were outmaneuvered by the German and Russian delegations. The only sensible comment from the Allied camp was Lloyd George's warning of the danger posed by a "hungry Russia equipped by an angry Germany." Military collaboration between the two countries, however, did not figure in the Treaty of Rapallo, although the agreement did lay the groundwork for German-Soviet cooperation in many fields, and the Germans would soon obtain Soviet assistance in surreptitiously building up their armed forces. In the 1920s the Germans both developed and tested on Soviet territory weapons forbidden them by the Versailles settlement, and they trained military cadres in Russia.

## RECOGNITION

Rapallo ended the isolation of Germany and Russia and made potential enemies, especially France, think twice about attacking either nation. When the French occupied the Ruhr in 1923, they were forced to prepare contingency plans in case the Soviets sent troops to assist Germany. There was never any possibility of Moscow doing that, but Paris could not take chances. The French alliance system was anchored in the East by the *cordon sanitaire* around Commu-

nist Russia's western frontiers; the Quai d'Orsay now moved to bolster its Polish, Czechoslovak, and Romanian allies.

One crisis followed another in 1923. There were Communist uprisings in Hamburg, Berlin, and other cities as the Germans struggled and failed to cope with an inflation of incredible dimensions. It was widely suspected that the Comintern had a hand in the affairs, which were quickly suppressed. There was indeed some such involvement, but Moscow was keeping the Comintern on a fairly short leash in this period. With Lenin weakening and the fight to succeed him intensifying, there was little enthusiasm for extensive foreign adventures. And the Kremlin was not willing to put its recently restored relations with Germany at too great a risk.

Chicherin had negotiated a commercial agreement with the British in 1921, but that did not involve formal recognition of the Soviet regime. In 1924 the first Labour government in British history took that step. Mussolini's Italy followed London's lead on February 7; France held out until the end of October. Japan recognized the Soviet Union in January 1925 and agreed to withdraw its forces from the northern half of Sakhalin Island. Of the major countries, only the United States refused to establish normal diplomatic ties.

The curbing of the Comintern after 1921 made it easier for European nations to recognize Moscow. In the early 1920s Soviet leaders concluded that the extreme right-wing parties such as the Italian Fascists and the German National Socialists (Nazis) were less dangerous than the Marxist Social Democrats, Mussolini's success in Italy notwithstanding. Watching a German government dominated by the Social-Democratic party crush Communist uprisings with great ferocity, the Soviets decided that they would deal with that government because they had no choice, but would fight the ruling party to the death.

In the wake of a scandal, diplomatic relations between the USSR and Great Britain collapsed within months of their birth. Four days before the October 29, 1924, British elections, the Conservative (Tory) party published what it claimed were instructions from Zinoviev and the Comintern to the British Communist party. Zinoviev allegedly directed that party to step up its revolutionary activity and to infiltrate the British Army. There was no time for the Labour government, which had been severely criticized for recognizing the USSR, to mount a defense against this sensational "disclosure." The Conservatives won by a large margin.

The "Zinoviev Letter" was a forgery concocted by officials of the British foreign office with ties to the Conservative party; they were aided by Russian émigrés. Evidently Britain's master spy Sidney Reilly, in reality a Russian Jew named Sigmund Georgievich Rozenblum (one of the models for Ian Fleming's James Bond), acted as agent for the émigrés. In 1928 Sir Eyre Crowe of the foreign office collected £5,000 "on behalf of X" (Reilly-Rozenblum) from the Conservative party. The Conservatives had earlier financed the spy's scheme to overthrow the Bolsheviks by humiliating Lenin and Trotsky, whom he proposed to parade through the streets of Moscow without their trousers. Although it was not clear how he would organize such a procession, the Tories paid him handsomely for the idea.

Two weeks after taking office the Conservative government denounced the diplomatic and commercial treaties which its Labour predecessor had negotiated with Moscow. Relations remained suspended for several years; there was even a mild war scare in 1927 when Stalin's government overreacted to some bombast from London concerning Soviet interference in British internal affairs. Labour returned to office in 1929 and reestablished ties.

## DISARMAMENT AND COLLECTIVE SECURITY

The Versailles settlement had not ushered in an era of harmony in Europe. There was enormous tension between France and Germany, almost every state feared and hated Soviet Russia, and the successor states of Eastern Europe all had grievances with one or more of their neighbors. The Genoa Conference recognized that economic recovery had not come. No nation was prepared to lay down its arms, but none could afford to maintain its forces at existing levels, let alone increase them.

In 1922 the Soviets began an effort to negotiate arms control agreements. On its way to Italy, the Soviet delegation to the Genoa Conference visited Riga, where Chicherin obtained the signatures of Latvian, Estonian, and Polish officials to the Riga Protocol, a rather innocuous document which simply called upon all nations to agree to arms reductions. Chicherin referred to the protocol at Genoa in his unsuccessful attempt to discuss disarmament.

The Kremlin next tried to obtain a disarmament agreement at the Moscow Conference of December 1922. Representatives of Latvia, Estonia, Finland, and Poland joined Soviet diplomats in a search for a formula for negotiations. The Baltic states were deeply suspicious of their gigantic neighbor, however, and both Poles and Finns had claims on Soviet territory. The Poles, especially, were not interested in an arms control agreement that would require them to reduce the large military forces they kept poised on their eastern borders.

The Moscow Conference thus ended in failure, with Warsaw charging that the Soviets had convened it merely as a propaganda exercise. There was some truth to that accusation: Lenin and his colleagues knew that the Poles would not disarm. Nevertheless the Soviets strengthened their moral position in some quarters by presenting themselves as the only nation sincerely interested in disarmament.

Europe's search for collective security involved lengthy talks in Paris, Berlin, and London in 1925. The negotiations seemed to bear fruit at the Locarno Conference held October 5–16. France, Germany, Great Britain, Belgium, Poland, and Czechoslovakia signed a series of agreements in the Swiss resort town which effectively guaranteed Germany's western frontiers and gave Poland and Czechoslovakia assurances that France would come to their aid if either were attacked by Germany.

The press promptly gave birth to a "spirit of Locarno" that seduced public opinion in Central and Western Europe and for a few years sustained the illusion that goodwill would henceforth rule relations between states. So desperate was the desire for peace that millions of people believed in a paper guarantee that Germany could not again march westward. It did not matter, their politicians said, what happened in the faraway East.

Excluded from the Locarno Conference, the Soviet Union denounced the agreements. Moscow pointed out that the failure to declare Germany's *eastern* frontiers fixed and inviolable indicated the indifference of France and Great Britain toward German aggression in the East. In the Kremlin's view, the Locarno accords represented an attempt to create a united anti-Soviet front, to contain Germany in the West and offer her a free hand against the USSR.

Although Germany became a member in 1926, Soviet Russia was not permitted to join the League of Nations or allowed to participate on the Preparatory Commission for a Disarmament Conference, the first meeting of which took place in May 1926. Established by the League, the Commission included even the United States, which had previously rejected cooperation with League agencies. The United States joined Britain and France in opposing Soviet participation.

That opposition finally softened in November 1927 and Maksim Litvinov, Chicherin's deputy, came to Geneva to represent the Soviet Union on the Commission and act as an observer at the League. In his first speech in the Palace of Nations Litvinov called on the member delegations to declare their governments in favor of complete and immediate disarmament. The Western diplomats dismissed this proposal as a Communist trick. Litvinov pointed in vain to the Soviet record in this area: the Riga Protocol, the Moscow Conference, the treaties of nonaggression and neutrality with Turkey (1925) and Iran (1927).

France and Great Britain had no interest in any disarmament proposals which threatened either their hegemony in Europe or their overseas possessions, and they declined to be instructed by Communists in the ways of peace. Litvinov's proposal, the Western diplomats charged, was absurd: no nation could simply lay down its arms against the unverifiable assurance that all other nations would do likewise.

The Westerners knew little of Marxist-Leninist political philosophy and could not conceive that the Soviets might be sincere. Believing that time and history were on their side, the Communists calculated that they had nothing to lose from disarmament. The development of capitalism would, in their view, inexorably deepen class contradictions and eventually produce proletarian revolution. Disarmament was thus ultimately irrelevant, but the Soviets would work for it in the short term.

The West rejected the Soviet proposals but could not ignore the clamor for peace. In the summer of 1928 Secretary of State Frank Kellogg of the United States and Foreign Minister Aristide Briand of France negotiated the Pact of Paris Concerning the Renunciation of War as an Instrument of National Policy (Kellogg-Briand Pact). Representatives of 15 nations affixed their signatures on August 27, 1928; the USSR was not invited. The agreement simply called upon nations to renounce war; it had no provision for sanctions.

The Kremlin first denounced the pact as an attempt to isolate the Soviet Union, but two days after the document was signed in Paris the Soviet Union ratified it. The formulators had invited all nations to accept the pact as national policy; the Soviets were the first to respond positively.

The original agreement would not become operative until ratified by a majority of the original signatories, but again the Soviets tried to seize the initiative in the search for peace and security. The Moscow or Litvinov Protocol of February 9, 1929, saw the Soviet Union, Poland, Romania, Estonia, and Latvia agree to put the Kellogg-Briand Pact into force immediately. Turkey adhered to the Protocol on February 27, Iran on April 3, Lithuania on April 5. At the League of Nations later in the year, Litvinov's proposal to implement the Kellogg-Briand Pact by providing for conciliation and arbitration was accepted by a majority of member nations.

## CHINA

Shortly after the Communists seized power in Russia they renounced tsarist concessions in China, declared their implacable hostility toward imperialism, and pledged support of Chinese independence. They hinted willingness to renegotiate the treaties through which the tsars had seized enormous tracts of territory historically part of the Chinese Empire. The Soviet gestures were warmly welcomed in China, especially by the educated urban youth who bitterly resented the West's arrogant treatment of their country. The Western allies had announced at Versailles that Germany's colonial holdings in Shandong (Shantung) would not be returned to China but would be given to Japan.

In January 1922 the Comintern sponsored the First Congress of the Toilers of the Far East in Moscow. (English-language accounts referred to the meeting as the Congress of Oppressed Far Eastern Peoples; German sources called it the First Congress of Communist and Revolutionary Organizations of the Far East.) There were about 150 delegates, including a 16-member Japanese contingent consisting of nine Communists, four anarchists, and three without specific party affiliation. More than 80 Chinese and Korean delegates attended, as did several Mongolians and some Yakuts and Kalmyks from Soviet Russia.

As president of the Comintern, Zinoviev delivered the opening address. Mikhail Kalinin, titular head of the Soviet state, also spoke, as did Sen Katayama, leader of the Japanese delegation. All three insisted on the need for peoples of the Far East to overthrow Western and Japanese imperialism. Zinoviev and Kalinin proclaimed Comintern and Soviet government support of all national independence movements, even bourgeois ones, throughout Asia.

The attempt to reconcile proletarian internationalism with nationalism made sense to some Soviet Communists but seemed preposterous to others. In any event it became official Comintern policy. This was the chief result of the Moscow meeting, which also led to the formation a few months later of the Japanese Communist party.

A.A. Joffe, a negotiator at Brest-Litovsk and one of the ablest Soviet diplomats, went to Beijing (Peking) in August 1922 to establish relations with the Chinese government. The difficulty was, however, that Beijing's writ did not run very far, and nothing substantive came from his efforts in the old capital. A secessionist regime in Guangzhou (Canton) had a broader if still limited mandate; Joffe journeyed south to meet its leader, Sun Yatsen. The Soviet diplomat had some success, and Sun sent a delegation to Moscow a year later. It was still not possible, however, to conclude a meaningful accord.

In September 1923 the Soviet government and the Comintern sent one of the best Communist political organizers, Michael Borodin (Gruzenberg), to Guangzhou to help Sun prepare a political-military offensive aimed at seizing control of all China. Early the following year General Vasili Blücher (called Galin [Kaling] in China) of the Red Army was sent to head the Soviet military mission. Borodin—who had lived in Chicago for several years—and Blücher reorganized both the Chinese Communist party and the Nationalist party, the Guomindang (Kuomintang). They also helped raise and train an army. The Soviet military mission established the famous Whampoa Military Academy, headed by Jiang Jieshi (Chiang Kaishek). The deputy head of the Academy's political department was a brilliant young Communist, Zhou Enlai.

After long negotiations with Joffe, in January 1924 Sun urged the Guomindang to unite with the infant Chinese Communist party. This was an example of the Comintern's "united front" policy in action. The merger was based on Sun's Three Principles of the People: nationalism, livelihood, and democracy. This meant essentially that the two parties would fight for the national liberation and unification of China, for the independence of the country, and for the

raising of China's economic and educational level. Sun also advocated the reorganization and revitalization of rural life to end the timeless misery of the Chinese peasant.

The China policy of the Soviet government and the Comintern reflected the quarrel between Stalin and his rivals. Stalin knew little about foreign affairs and next to nothing about China; his chief source of information about the country was the self-taught Sinologist Pavel Mif. Nevertheless, basing his views on Lenin's oft-repeated observation that China was on the verge of a bourgeois revolution, Stalin declared that it was necessary to support a "united front" policy in China, allying the Chinese Communists with the bourgeois Guomindang. Such a policy seemed to make sense for the Guomindang, which at its first All-China congress in January 1924 accepted Sun's proposal for an alliance with the Chinese Communist party and proclaimed itself in favor of close ties with Soviet Russia.

Trotsky was skeptical of a Communist-bourgeois alliance. In his view, cooperation with the Guomindang would lead to disaster. Further, he insisted that China in 1924 was where Russia had been in 1917. The time was ripe for a proletarian revolution.

Stalin won on this issue as on all others where he faced Trotsky. As Sun's health declined in late 1924, Stalin and the man who was then his ally, Nikolai Bukharin, backed Jiang Jieshi as the new Guomindang leader. Opposing cooperation with Jiang, Trotsky urged the establishment of a Soviet political system in China.

On May 31, 1924, the Soviet plenipotentiary in Beijing, L.M. Karakhan, signed an agreement "On the General Principles for the Regulation of Questions between the USSR and the Chinese Republic." The accord provided for the establishment of diplomatic and consular relations on a new basis, all "conventions, agreements, accords, contracts and so forth" between tsarist Russia and China being annulled (Art. 3). The Soviets declared "null and void and without force" all agreements infringing on the rights and sovereignty of China concluded by the tsarist regime with any third party or parties (Art. 4). The Kremlin recognized Outer Mongolia as part of China. The Soviets and Chinese agreed not to interfere in each other's internal affairs and to regulate navigation on waterways constituting part of the international frontier. The complicated matter of the Chinese Eastern Railway, in which the tsarist government had part ownership, was to be the subject of further negotiation. The Soviets renounced the right of extraterritoriality, the Russian share of the Boxer Rebellion indemnity, and "all special rights and privileges" won by the tsarist regime through unequal treaties.

Articles 3 and 4 of the agreement seemed to annul the unequal treaties, and Article 7 provided for the "examination" of the frontiers between the two countries, pending which were to remain valid. Did this mean that the Soviets would renegotiate the treaties, and restore to China the territories seized by the tsars? When the Sino-Soviet accord was signed a few months after Lenin's death this was vaguely the intention of some Soviet officials. The situation in China was unstable, however, and Soviet Russian nationalism had already begun to assert itself after the failure of communist revolutions in Europe. The frontier dispute was to continue for decades.

Karakhan also signed a series of bilateral declarations on May 31 that further defined the basic accord, provided for the disposition of tsarist and Russian Orthodox church property in China, and regulated the position of Soviet citizens on Chinese soil. On the same day, a separate agreement established a 10-member board (five Soviet and five Chinese) to oversee the joint operation of the Chinese Eastern Railway until the dispute over ownership was resolved.

In July 1929 the Chinese authorities seized control of the railway and imprisoned thousands of Soviet citizens who were its employees. The Soviet Union broke diplomatic relations. Late in July a Soviet-Chinese protocol signed at Khabarovsk restored joint ownership of the railway and reaffirmed the international frontiers; but diplomatic relations were not restored until December 1932.

Sun died early in 1925 and Jiang succeeded him. The following year Jiang confounded Borodin, then on some secret mission to Beijing, by swooping down on Chinese Communist headquarters in Guangzhou and arresting party leaders. Isolated and denied access to the highest councils of the Guomindang, Borodin went back to Moscow for consultations. General Blücher, however, remained the Guomindang's chief military adviser. Jiang needed his expertise for the Northern Expedition, the July–October 1926 military campaign in which Guomindang forces conquered and united most of China south of the Chang Jiang (Yangtze) River.

Developments in China stunned Moscow, and there were those in Stalin's own entourage who shared Trotsky's distrust of Jiang. Stalin did not, however, change his mind, and the united front policy remained in effect. Moreover, he sent Borodin back to China to ensure that the Chinese Communists followed Comintern orders.

By the spring of 1927 Jiang Jieshi had extended his control still farther north. He established a capital at Nanjiang (Nanking), defeated some of the most powerful warlords, and with Soviet assistance created one of the largest armies in Chinese history. Having made use of the Communists, Jiang turned on them. At his order Guomindang street fighters—the Blue Shirts—struck in the Communist stronghold of Shanghai on April 12, 1927, slaughtering every Communist they could find. At least 300 and perhaps as many as 1,000 were killed in one day. According to Soviet sources about 337,000 Chinese revolutionaries, including 18,000 of the 58,000 members of the Chinese Communist party, were massacred between April 1927 and June 1928.

Stalin's response to the Shanghai Massacre was to radio some bizarre instructions to Borodin, who was to arm and equip 20,000 members of the Chinese Communist party; create a 50,000-man army in Hunan and Hupeh provinces; confiscate all landlord land in those provinces; pack the Guomindang central committee; and put "reactionary" officers of Jiang's army on trial. Stalin might as well have ordered the construction of a new Great Wall by the end of the month. His commands bore no relation to reality and indeed he did not intend them to. He was speaking to his own party, which knew that he had erred disastrously in his China policy and that Trotsky had been a better judge of Jiang and the Guomindang.

Soviet policy in China was in shambles. The Soviet composer Reinhold Glière's *Red Poppy* ballet celebrating Soviet-Chinese friendship opened at the Bolshoi Theatre in June 1927, at once a modest artistic success and a bad political joke.

In China itself the decimated Communists struck back in three unsuccessful attempts in 1927 to challenge the growing might of the Guomindang. Zhou Enlai and Zhu Deh were among the leaders of the Nanchang Uprising in August and September. Mao Zedong was one of the commanders in the Autumn Harvest Uprising in September in the Hunan-Jiangxi border area which saw the birth of the first division of the Chinese Workers' and Peasants' Revolutionary Army. A minor Communist revolt took place in Guangzhou in December.

The Communist-Guomindang alliance had been a "right" (conservative) policy from the Comintern point of view and it reflected the temporary cooperation between Stalin and Bukharin. After the 1927 disasters the Chinese Communists moved toward the "left," that is, they began to lay the groundwork for the seizure of political power by the revolutionary peasantry. A meeting of the party's Central Committee on August 7, 1927, decided upon this policy.

The 6th Congress of the Chinese Communist party met in Moscow in June-July 1928 and reaffirmed the leftward reorientation. Increasingly preoccupied with domestic Soviet policy, Stalin had even less time to devote to Chinese affairs, but he seems to have accepted the practical necessity of protracted guerrilla warfare.

## A DECADE OF PROLETARIAN DIPLOMACY

The new leaders of the Soviet Union had not learned to distinguish between an ideological and a pragmatic foreign policy. They saw no contradiction between supporting Communist parties dedicated to the overthrow of governments and conducting more or less normal diplomatic relations with the same governments. Soviet leaders clung to the fiction that the Comintern was a wholly independent agency with headquarters in Moscow and, by sheer coincidence, several Soviet leaders among its top officers.

Soviet foreign policy remained officially predicated on world revolution throughout most of the decade after 1917, and no real change could take place until Stalin elaborated the theory of "socialism in one country." He had first hinted at it in 1917 but no one took him seriously; he was not regarded as one of the party's thinkers. By December 1924, however, enormous changes in Soviet politics and Stalin's personal fortunes had taken place. Lenin was dead and Stalin, allied with Kamenev and Zinoviev, had defeated Trotsky in the first round of the struggle for power. Trotsky was still a threat, however, and Stalin kept up his attack, shifting the battle to the realm of theory and temporarily allying himself with Bukharin and the Right.

In an essay entitled "The October Revolution and the Tactics of the Russian Communists," Stalin struck at Trotsky's "permanent revolution" as theoretically flawed and politically seditious. Why had Trotsky so little faith in the ability of the Soviet Communists to construct a socialist society in Russia without the help of the proletariat of other countries? Relying upon arguments developed by Bukharin, Stalin had earlier begun to argue that capitalism had stabilized, and that revolution could no longer be considered imminent. To preserve and eventually expand the gains of October throughout the world, he now argued, it was necessary to build "socialism in one country." A portion of the world proletariat was already committed to the defense of the Soviet Union through the Comintern. It was the duty of Soviet Communists, Stalin declared, temporarily to shelve their hopes for world revolution and concentrate on strengthening their own country.

These arguments prevailed in the party and helped bury Trotsky. Even people who detested Stalin admitted that he had made excellent use of Bukharin's theories and in so doing had bested his adversary in the very area where he—Trotsky—had always excelled. Vindication in China could not redeem Trotsky.

The great fear of Soviet leaders in the 1920s was that the USSR would be attacked by a capitalist power or group of powers before the country had had time to build a strong industrial and military base. Because the state was so weak, Soviet foreign policy after 1924 was by and large conciliatory and defensive. The Soviets supported the concept of collective security and adhered to pacts aimed at establishing it. From 1927 they acted as spokesmen for immediate, universal, and complete disarmament. This was Moscow's policy. It would be wrong to dismiss it as mere propaganda even though the Soviets knew that there was no chance it would be accepted.

The Soviet stance on disarmament and impassioned defense of collective security made a favorable impression on millions of people around the world. In the titanic clash between communism and fascism that loomed on the European horizon, the Soviets would have friends among the populations of many countries—but not a single ally among states.

## SUGGESTED ADDITIONAL READING

**Adler, Alan, ed.,** *Theses, Resolutions and Manifestos of the First Four Congresses of the Third International,* Atlantic Highlands, N.J.: Humanities Press, 1980

**Borkenau, Franz,** *World Communism,* Ann Arbor: University of Michigan Press, 1962

**Brandt, Conrad,** *Stalin's Failure in China, 1924–1927,* Cambridge: Harvard University Press, 1958

**Chester, Lewis, Stephen Fay, and Hugo Young, eds.,** *The Zinoviev Letter,* Philadelphia: Lippincott, 1968

**Eudin, Xenia, and H.H. Fisher, eds.,** *Soviet Russia and the West, 1920–1927,* Stanford, Calif.: Stanford University Press, 1957

**Eudin, Xenia, and R.C. North, eds.,** *Soviet Russia and the East, 1920–1927,* Stanford, Calif.: Stanford University Press, 1957

**Feigon, Lee,** *Chen Duxiu, Founder of the Chinese Communist Party,* Princeton, N.J.: Princeton University Press, 1983

**Fink, Carole,** *The Genoa Conference,* Chapel Hill: University of North Carolina Press, 1984

**Fischer, Ruth,** *Stalin and German Communism,* Cambridge: Harvard University Press, 1948

**Haigh, R.H.,** *German-Soviet Relations in the Weimar Era,* Totowa, N.J.: Rowman and Littlefield, 1985

**Kennan, George,** *Russia and the West under Lenin and Stalin,* Boston: Little, Brown, 1961

————, *Soviet Foreign Policy 1917–1941,* Westport, Conn.: Greenwood Press, 1978

**McKenzie, Kermit,** *Comintern and World Revolution,* New York: Columbia University Press, 1964

**Mosely, Philip E., ed.,** *The Soviet Union, 1922–1962: A Foreign Affairs Reader,* New York: Praeger, 1963

**North, Robert C.,** *Moscow and the Chinese Communists,* Stanford, Calif.: Stanford University Press, 1956

**O'Connor, Timothy E.,** *G.V. Chicherin and Soviet Foreign Affairs, 1918–1930,* Ames: Iowa State University Press, 1987

**Rosenbaum, Kurt,** *Community of Fate: German-Soviet Diplomatic Relations, 1922–1928,* Syracuse, N.Y.: Syracuse University Press, 1965

**Roy, Samaren,** *The Twice-Born Heretic: M.N. Roy and Comintern,* Calcutta: Firma KLM Private Limited, 1986

**Ulam, Adam,** *Expansion and Coexistence,* New York: Praeger, 1968

**White, Stephen,** *The Origins of Détente: The Genoa Conference and Soviet-Western Relations, 1921–1922,* New York: Cambridge University Press, 1987

**Wilbur, C. Martin, and Julie Lien-ying How,** *Missionaries of Revolution: Soviet Advisers and Nationalist China, 1920–1927,* Cambridge, Mass.: Harvard University Press, 1989

# 8

# STALIN'S REVOLUTION, 1924–1932

Along a unique road to power, Joseph Vissarionovich Stalin carved a dictatorship out of a bureaucracy. His intelligence was well above average, but as dictator he became "mankind's greatest genius," a fairly restrained encomium employed by his army of sycophants. He had proved himself incompetent on the battlefield. His widely revered predecessor had suggested that he be removed from his key post in the party. Many high party officials considered him unfit to lead.

We have the testimony of Lenin that Stalin was rude, and from a variety of sources we know that his humor was coarse, unsophisticated, frequently scatological. He smiled little, laughed less, took offense easily, is not known ever to have forgiven a real or imagined slight. He was physically unimposing, standing only 1m 62cm (about 5′ 4″); but he was taller than Napoleon, Attila the Hun, and Julius Caesar. He had a slightly withered left arm. According to Anton Antonov-Ovseyenko and other well-connected sources, he treated women brutally. Acne or perhaps chicken pox had scarred his face in adolescence. Among his favorite music was a recording of a coloratura singing against a background of howling dogs.

Moody, surly, forever on the defensive, Stalin did not make friends easily. Few people liked him, but he loved himself enough, party members said, to make up the difference. He was personally close only to Vyacheslav Molotov and Kliment Voroshilov among the Old Bolsheviks. These two men were the prototypes of hundreds of humorless, amoral, blindly loyal mediocrities at the heart of the bureaucratic machine.

## CONSOLIDATION OF THE STALIN DICTATORSHIP

When Trotsky ignored Lenin's instructions to move against Stalin at the 12th Party Congress, for all practical purposes the struggle for succession ended. This blunder meant that the existing bureaucratic structure under Stalin's control took on an unassailable legitimacy. It would be too late to raise Lenin's attack on Stalin after Lenin was dead.

In the summer of 1924 Stalin moved against his erstwhile fellow triumvirs, Kamenev and Zinoviev, purging their supporters in Moscow and Leningrad. He seemed to draw close to the right wing of the party in this period. An August 1924 uprising in Georgia was, he declared, sparked by dissatisfaction among the peasants and urged the party to conciliate them; this translated into a call for the extension of the new economic policy. This was the position of Bukharin (promoted to Lenin's seat on the Politburo), Rykov, Tomsky and their followers on the Right.

Trotsky returned to the attack in the autumn of 1924 only to stumble anew. He published a collection of essays entitled *1917*; one, "Lessons of October," assailed Kamenev and Zinoviev for wavering during the revolutionary year. He was correct, but there was no point in raising the matter now. His attack drove the two men back into Stalin's arms.

Stalin mobilized his forces, accepted help from Kamenev, Zinoviev, and Bukharin, and isolated his opponent. Early in 1925 Trotsky lost his posts as comissar of military and naval affairs. Again he submitted meekly, believing he would no longer face the charge of "Bonapartism." Ever the opportunists, Kamenev and Zinoviev proposed in January 1925 to expel Trotsky from the party. The champion of reason and modera-tion, Stalin, objected that this would set a dangerous precedent: today Trotsky's head, tomorrow whose?

In the winter of 1924–1925 a suddenly alarmed Zinoviev decided to make his own move against Stalin. He had a strong base in Leningrad, directed the Comintern, and could often manipulate Kamenev. Perhaps— he apparently thought—he could sway Trotsky and Krupskaya as well. He made a series of speeches advocating a Left position, attacking the new economic policy's concessions to the peasantry. This made sense in proletarian Leningrad. It was madness in the rest of the country, where the economic recovery had blunted desires for further radical experimentation on the model of war communism.

Stalin moved quickly. He removed some of Zinoviev's key aides in the Leningrad party and Komsomol organizations and undercut his power in the Comintern. Stalin's friends of the moment, the Rightists Bukharin and Rykov, vigorously defended NEP against Zinoviev. Most party members believed that this defense was also Stalin's position; but Stalin generally let Bukharin and Rykov do the talking.

As a British authority on the history of the CPSU observed, the 14th Party Congress, postponed several times and finally held in December 1925, "marked the lowest ebb of political morality . . . the party had yet reached." Stalin and his allies had selected all the delegates save those from Leningrad. Jeers and catcalls greeted Zinoviev every time he spoke. Knowing he would be defeated, he pleaded to be heard. Anastas Mikoyan, an astute Armenian Stalinist, mocked him: "When Zinoviev is in the majority, he is for iron discipline; when he is in the minority, he is against it."

The Stalinists shouted Zinoviev down and insulted Krupskaya. Trotsky did not even try to speak. Kamenev behaved with courage: "I have come," he said, "to the conclusion that Comrade Stalin cannot fulfill the role of unifier . . . . We are against the doctrine of one-man rule, we are against the creation of a leader." The Congress erupted into a cacophony of shouts, curses, whistling, and general disorder orchestrated by Stalin's henchmen, who set up the chant, "Stal–in! Stal–in! Stal–in!"

When the ovation died down Stalin spoke reassuringly. Of course we must have collective leadership, he said. The party could not possibly do without leaders of the stature of Rykov, Bukharin, Tomsky, Kalinin, Molotov. "It is impossible," he declared, "to lead the party other than collectively. It is stupid to think of any other way after Lenin." But he added that "antiparty" activities and positions could not be tolerated: Kamenev and Zinoviev lost most—but not all—their major posts.

Trotsky, Zinoviev, and Kamenev patched up their quarrels in 1926. Trotsky invoked the precedent of the French Revolution and argued that the forces of "Thermidor," represented by the Stalinist bureaucracy, were leading the truly revolutionary forces, the masses, to defeat. For fear of being charged with violating the ban on factionalism he did not assert that "Thermidor" already existed, nor did he call upon the masses to revolt.

This was fine theory, ridiculous politics. By 1926 Stalin was firmly in control of the bureaucracy, and to attack him and his support system at their strongest point was folly. To counterattack, he had only to quote Trotsky, Kamenev, and Zinoviev against each other and indeed against Lenin. The three men had made enough mistakes to fill a large textbook on how *not* to play politics. As for Lenin's "testament," which some Oppositionists now began to mention, Stalin pointed out that both Krupskaya and Trotsky had denounced it as a "malicious invention."

In October 1926 Trotsky and Zinoviev sponsored a series of street demonstrations and meetings in which they demanded restoration of democracy in the party. The bureaucracy responded with a counterattack aimed at isolating and destroying them. They were forbidden to address workers in the factories and shops and were denied access to the media, which subjected them to vicious assault. Suddenly aware of the danger, Trotsky, Zinoviev, and Kamenev made the astonishing gesture of publicly denouncing their own activities. They admitted violating the ban on factionalsim and swore to refrain from such behavior. This was an empty, even cowardly gesture. The leaders could not save themselves, and their statement deprived their followers of all hope of protection. The OGPU, as the secret police was now called, could now move against those followers with impunity.

The upshot of all this was Trotsky's ouster from the Politburo. Zinoviev lost the presidency of the Comintern, Kamenev was removed as a candidate member of the Politburo. A few months later the Central Committee expelled both Trotsky and Zinoviev. Around the time of the 10th anniversary of the Bolshevik Revolution, Trotsky and his followers tried to take their case against Stalin and the bureaucracy to the workers in a series of illegal factory meetings and street demonstrations. To their dismay, Soviet labor did not respond. The workers in Moscow and Leningrad looked on with indifference as the Trotskyites put forward this last feeble challenge to the Stalinist bureaucratic machine.

In November 1927 Trotsky, Kamenev, and Zinoviev were expelled from the party. The latter two swallowed their pride and begged for reinstatement. Trotsky was exiled to Alma Ata in Soviet Central Asia early in 1928; a year later the OGPU threw him across the border into Turkey. Kamenev and

Zinoviev, formally readmitted to the party in 1928 on the basis of humiliating confessions of error, vigorously applauded his fate.

## THE SITUATION IN AGRICULTURE

The party struggles directly involved only the few score top officials who held the reins of power. The only spectators who really cared, the rank-and-file party members, numbered 1,236,190 (including 348,957 candidates) in December 1927. In a population of about 148 million, only they had anything at all to do with politics, and most of them merely tried to interpret and carry out orders from Moscow. The vast majority of the population was more concerned about the looming crisis in agriculture.

The Communists had not abandoned their dream of creating a planned, crisis-free economic system. They acknowledged that the free market in agriculture under NEP was largely responsible for the restoration of economic health but insisted that the "tyranny" of the market—the "boom or bust" cycles—could not be tolerated.

There were serious problems in agriculture in the 1920s despite the outward signs of good health. First, the historic backwardness of Russian farming remained unremedied. Second, even though production had regained pre-1914 levels, the peasants were not participating in the market as much as they had prior to the Great War; more food was remaining in the countryside. Food supplies in the cities, though adequate, were precarious; there were no substantial reserves. Third, there were wide variations in "patterns of peasant agriculture" around the huge country. The Muslim areas were prime for development, while the major grain-producing regions—middle Volga valley, North Caucasus, Ukraine—had not recovered as fully as other areas. Fourth,

the restoration of agriculture had taken place on a capitalistic basis; this threatened to undermine the regime.

The survival of communal land tenure and the strip system had a negative effect on food production. The village commune periodically redistributed the land among the peasants, determined which crops to sow on which parcels, and set the dates for plowing, sowing, and harvesting. The strip system involved granting each peasant a strip of good land here, a strip of mediocre land there; the ancient custom took different forms in different regions. After the Revolution, however, it was more or less standardized throughout European Russia. Terribly inefficient, it demonstrated that attempts to establish economic equality can sometimes impoverish all concerned.

A further problem was the lack of animal power, not to speak of machinery. In the Russian Republic of the USSR, 28.3 percent of peasant households had no draft animals in 1927; 31.6 percent *had no plows*. Only about 15.2 percent had horse-drawn agricultural implements.

The statistics get worse. Kulak farms constituted only four to five percent of the total in 1927, but their owners had about a third of all agricultural machinery in the country. As the leading British expert on Soviet agricultural policy in the 1920s has pointed out, perhaps the most startling statistic was this: the yields of wheat and rye per hectare in Russia (7 to 9 centners, where one c. = 100 kg) were lower than those of 14th-century French estates, only marginally greater than those of 14th-century English estates. Russian yields in the 1920s were less than half those of Germany. Millions of peasants could not subsist on their own plots and had to hire themselves out. This was anathema to Communists.

The problems did not stop there. Between 1928 and 1939 the urban population increased by 18.5 million; much of the increase came as peasants left the farms and came to the cities to work in the factories. Thus fewer peasant producers had to feed more mouths. Barring drastic changes, a major crisis seemed certain to develop.

## INDUSTRIALIZATION DEBATE

The short-range problem involved the feeding of the Red Army and the cities. The long-range one concerned the transformation of agricultural Russia into a modern industrial society. How was that to be accomplished? How was Russia to solve the problem that confronts all modernizing societies, the one Marx wrestled with in the last 200 pages of *Capital:* the accumulation of capital?

Factories could not be built nor foreign machinery purchased with copies of Lenin's tracts. Where was the money to come from? How was the rate of economic growth to be increased to the point where Russia could catch up with the capitalist states? How could the Soviet population, living reasonably well only because it spent everything and saved nothing, be made to accept the tightening of its belts as the state undertook a massive savings campaign to finance industrialization?

These were the problems that confronted Soviet planners and party officials in the mid-1920s. Several solutions were advanced by the old bourgeois economists employed by the State Planning Commission (Gosplan) and the Supreme Economic Council. With more revolutionary zeal than economic expertise, Communist theoreticians likewise offered a variety of opinions.

The only concensus that emerged was that Russia would have to squeeze agriculture to finance industrialization. The peasants would have to produce as much food as possible, and the people would have to

consume less in order for the state to sell the agricultural surplus on the world market. In that market, Soviet grain would be competing with the more efficiently produced, therefore cheaper, American, Canadian, and other foreign grain.

The Soviet Union might be obliged to sell at a loss because it desperately needed Western ("hard") currency to finance the purchase of machines, certain raw materials, and technical expertise abroad; the Communist ruble was never a convertible currency and had no value outside the USSR. Who would absorb the loss? Domestic producers and consumers. The peasants would not get a fair reward for their labor, there would be less food for consumers, and food would cost more because of the artificially created shortages.

These bleak prospects created a division in Communist ranks. Bukharin, Rykov, Tomsky and the Right argued in favor of maintaining NEP, and Stalin sided with them. They believed that the free agricultural market, which they accepted as a distasteful long-term necessity, could eventually produce the surplus needed to finance industrialization. That industrialization, and the collectivization of agriculture, would have to be postponed; this was the price the country had to pay for its historic lag behind advanced capitalist societies. Trotsky and the Left had insisted that the Soviet Union could not postpone industrialization if it was to survive. The only way to control the peasantry, the Left argued, was to collectivize private farms.

But even Trotsky, Preobrazhensky, and their followers shrank from forcing the peasants into collectives. Despite their differences both Left and Right supported NEP and neither anticipated its early demise. The 15th Party Congress (December 2–19, 1927) adopted a Bukharinist scheme for the first Five-Year Plan; it called for the collectivization of agriculture on a partial, voluntary basis. This "represented a kind of amalgam of Bukharinist-Trotskyist thinking as it had evolved in the debates of the 1920s." It was moreover an amalgam that enjoyed the full support of Joseph Stalin. The party leader's sudden reversal of the Bukharinist-Trotskyist program would produce the great Stalin revolution.

## 1928 CRISIS

The Communist party's most formidable foe was the backward economy. In the mid-1920s the majority of the proletariat was fully employed, well-fed, and largely—so long as it did not meddle in politics—left alone by the authorities. If it was not wholly on the party's side it was not against it. The proletariat cared only about bread and the good life under NEP.

That life was suddenly jeopardized in the autumn of 1927, when for a variety of reasons—including a minor war scare and rumors of the government's intention to resume forced requisitions—the peasants sold the state only about half as much grain as they had during the same period in 1926, the year of the best harvest of the decade. This happened again in 1928, when weather conditions that occur only once in 30–40 years drastically reduced the harvest; the state was indeed obliged to step in to force deliveries in many districts. Beyond that the peasants were planting more industrial crops and less grain because the state kept grain prices artificially low. This produced a major crisis: there would not be enough bread to feed the cities at pre-1927 levels.

Early in 1929 the government introduced bread rationing in Leningrad and Moscow, then in all cities. Inferior grains were mixed with wheat and rye to make flour, and the milling standard was lowered.

What else was Stalin to do? He had repeatedly said that the very idea of forced collectivization was so absurd as to be beneath discussion. The small private farm, he declared publicly in April 1929, would continue as the mainstay of agriculture for an indefinite period. But in a startling reversal, he privately attacked the "Right opportunist" Bukharin-Rykov-Tomsky group, which was demanding that the party maintain NEP and stick to strictly voluntary collectivization.

In April 1929 the 16th party conference approved the Five-Year Plan drawn up by Gosplan. The optimum variant called for collectivization of 20 percent of all peasant households by 1933. Approving this variant, the party swung into action. By the summer of 1929 there were about 57,000 collective farms; they had been formed by amalgamating more than a million private farms, 3.9 percent of the total. By and large this was accomplished peacefully.

These first few kolhozes—a handful was left over from war communism—were put together out of marginal farmsteads and lands that already belonged to the state. A great deal of money was expended in this period to make them attractive to the poorest peasants; this effort was more successful than Western critics have allowed. The Communists cosseted people on the lowest rungs of the economic and social ladders.

After the 1929 harvest, again an inferior one, Stalin and his associates made the decision that was to cost millions of people their lives: they would launch a drive for "all-out" collectivization. Made in October, the decision was not publicly announced. The leadership would use party cadres, the Red Army, and, where necessary, OGPU troops to force the remainder of the peasantry into collective farms.

The decision was predicated upon the belief that the acute grain shortage was artificial, the work of peasants infected with a "kulak mentality." These peasants, the Stalinists suspected, were deliberately withholding grain to force the regime to raise prices.

On November 7, 1929, *Pravda* carried Stalin's article, "The Year of the Great Change," which claimed that socialism had made a "great breakthrough" in the countryside. He called collectivization a huge success; the grain deliveries would solve the problem of accumulating capital. All this had come about, he claimed, because millions of middle peasants were flocking enthusiastically into collective farms. These claims bore little relation to reality. They were intended not to inform but to warn that collectivization would succeed—or else.

Five days later Bukharin, Rykov, and Tomsky publicly accepted Stalin's figures and admitted that collectivization had been successful. With his opponents taking this stand, Stalin was more convinced than ever of the validity of his policies. The November 1929 Central Committee plenum noted the Right's capitulation but nevertheless expelled Bukharin from the Politburo. It endorsed some fairly modest goals concerning the rate at which collectivization was to be achieved.

The published resolutions of this plenum were not intended as guides for local officials. Those officials took their cues from Molotov's speeches, which were, as a British expert has noted, "undoubtedly designed to persuade local party officials to press ahead with collectivization at breakneck speed." Soviet historians of the post-Stalin period have occasionally tried to shift blame for the terrible excesses of the winter of 1929–1930 to Molotov, but this will not do: Molotov did not open his umbrella, contemporaries said, until Stalin confirmed rain. Officials around the country read his speeches and interpreted them as Stalin's instructions.

This "great change" constituted a "radical act of revolution from above." It marked the beginning of the Stalinist nightmare. There was no warning, and despite the experience of war communism no real precedent: Stalin undertook a military-police campaign against the Soviet people. There was no one left in the party leadership capable of standing up to him.

## PUSH FOR TOTAL COLLECTIVIZATION

A nightmare ensued. The party moved against the peasants with brutal, overwhelming force, herding them like cattle into the kolhozes. Any peasant so identified by the party was a kulak. His property was seized and he was thrown into an unheated, overcrowded railroad freight car destined eventually for the forced-labor camps of the Arctic or Eastern Siberia.

There was panic, disorder, armed resistance. The peasants attacked the collectivizers with pitchforks, axes, clubs, rocks. The officials called in the Red Army. Composed of a cross section of peasants and workers, the Army was effective only up to a point, and that point was reached fairly quickly. When the party deemed it necessary to use violence against women and children, OGPU troops were called in.

In the last weeks of 1929 and the first two and a half months of 1930, resistance took on extreme forms. In the USSR (excluding the Ukraine) there were 1,678 armed attacks on collectivization in the first 10 weeks of 1930. The peasants buried their grain when they thought they had a chance to preserve it, burned it when they did not. In February and March 1930 they slaughtered 14 million head of cattle, and in the Russian Republic alone they killed 4 million horses. The slaughtered animals were left to rot in the barns and fields. Stalin published these figures in January 1934:

| Millions of Live Animals | | |
|---|---|---|
| | *1929* | *1933* |
| Hor | 34.0 | 16.6 |
| Cattl | 68.1 | 38.6 |
| Shee & Goats | 147.2 | 50.6 |
| Swin | 20.9 | 12.2 |

Tl s unprecedented killing had a ripple effect In 1929 about 85 percent of the land was plowed with animal power. With a substantial reduction in the amount of that power available, the fields were left untilled. Moreover, the slaughter reduced drastically the amount of organic fertilizer available, and that spelled still more trouble.

Were they not documented by Soviet authorities themselves, the excesses would be unbelievable. Squads of "dekulakizers" swarmed into villages in the Smolensk region west of Moscow and took clothing off the backs of wearers. Alcohol was "nationalized" on the spot; drunken orgies were commonplace. Food was confiscated, of course, and not just grain stocks. The expropriators frequently took the kasha off the stove and ate it or smeared it on the family's icons. Eyeglasses were no safer from confiscation than homes or cows.

Peasants who survived the initial swoop were herded to the railroad, where cattle-cars awaited. In bitterly cold January–February 1930, the trains frequently remained on sidings for days or even weeks at a time. The authorities had failed to foresee, let alone plan for, the problems of transporting millions of people to distant, uninhabitable regions. Families were separated, and uncounted numbers of helpless peasants perished in the trains, often within sight of their villages.

The Moscow authorities had never spelled out a precise definition of "kulak"; each local boss could define the term as he liked. As the pressure from the Central Committee to speed up collectivization became more intense, the definition became broader and more inclusive. An official who failed to produce his quota was himself liable to arrest, expropriation, and deportation. This process continued, as Stalin admitted, for four years, with only a brief respite in 1930.

Those cattle-trains on the sidings full of screaming, freezing, starving, fear-crazed people left no doubt in anyone's mind about the fate of "enemies of the people." As early as 1928 the better-off peasants began to sell their grain surpluses, agriculture implements, livestock, and other movable property. This "self-dekulakization" became a legal offense; people were to wait for the state to destroy them.

Agriculture was on the brink of disaster. Stalin's war against the peasantry produced the result achieved by Lenin's war communism, catastrophe. In the absence of some surcease, the country would collapse.

## "DIZZY WITH SUCCESS"

A break came with the publication in *Pravda* on March 2, 1930, of Stalin's article "Dizzy with Success: Problems of the Kolhoz Movement." To the consternation of local party officials Stalin blamed *them* for the excesses. What kind of lunatics, he asked, began collectivizing agriculture by removing the bells from a village church? Collectivization had to be voluntary. He roundly condemned the zealots and declared that their shenanigans were "grist for the mill of Right opportunism." No one dared remind him that Bukharin and the Right, and for that matter Trotsky, Preobrazhensky, and the Left, had always insisted upon *voluntary* collectivization. Forcing the peasants into the kolhozes was a uniquely Stalinist phenomenon.

In the countryside people regarded Stalin's article as commutation of a death sentence. Peasants paid high prices for that issue of *Pravda*, gathering in the rutted village streets to read it aloud and getting drunk to celebrate the reprieve. One peasant told a foreigner that his generation greeted the article as its forefathers had welcomed Alexander II's Emancipation Edict.

Again the timing was no accident. It was already the optimum period for the spring plowing in the southernmost grain districts, and plowing would have to commence immediately in the Ukraine and the Volga Valley if there were to be any crop at all in 1930.

There ensued a mass exodus from the collective farms. Of 14 million households—70 million people—forced into the kolhozes by March 1930, only 5 million remained in May. To save face the party declared that the farms that had been established on a "healthy" basis—those formed by the poorest peasants—had survived. By the summer of 1930, only 24.6 percent of all peasant farms remained collectivized. This obviously represented, however, a great increase over the 4 percent of June 1929.

Party cadres were in an awkward situation. They had carried out the Central Committee's orders only to be denounced. Moreover, top party officials came from Moscow to investigate and set things right; in the spring of 1930 there were hundreds of trials of "Left deviationists" and wholesale dismissals and demotions of local officials. Party members and reliable workers from the cities were sent to the countryside in 1930 to help clean up the mess. The press paid special attention to a contingent of 25,000 workers (two-thirds of them Communists, and about 7.5 percent women), but that group was only the vanguard. The number of party workers temporarily assigned to the villages nearly tripled to around 700,000 between 1927 and 1930; most of the increase came in the spring and summer of 1930.

The spring plowing took place a little behind schedule, but as events proved no harm had been done. Peasants rejoiced in the restoration of their farms. The 16th Party Congress (June–July 1930) noted the tranquillity in the countryside, blamed the winter excesses on local cadres, and called for increased state aid to kolhozes. It was at about this time that the last article critical of Stalin and the Central Committee appeared in *Pravda*. Its very publication constituted a measure of the collectivization disaster.

## RESUMPTION OF COLLECTIVIZATION

Incredibly, the harvest of 1930 was a good one, and it produced record deliveries of grain to the state, 22 million tons. This was 6 million tons more than the previous year, more than double the 1928 deliveries. This was something of a miracle and should have been so regarded. The dislocations and turmoil of the early collectivization drive had threatened to ruin agriculture. The farms recovered more quickly than anyone could have foreseen, and the spring weather in 1930 was unusually good throughout the major grain-producing areas.

The party regarded the harvest as indicative of what the peasants could do *every* year. Party leaders were more convinced than ever that the withholding of grain by kulaks had created the dangerous shortages of 1927–1929 and that collectivization would ultimately be successful.

In the autumn of 1930 the Central Committee ordered the resumption of collectivization on a massive if less frantic scale. The spring and summer respite was no longer considered a retreat but merely a temporary consolidation. The new drive marched forward at a steady pace: 26.1 percent of all peasant households were collectivized by

January 1931; 42.0 percent by April; 52.7 percent by June, when 13 million peasant households (65 million people) lived on 211,000 collective farms.

Class warfare resumed as doomed peasants fought Red Army and OGPU troops ferociously. Again the villages were aflame. Like the *muzhiks* who burned their homes in 1812 to deny them to Napoleon, peasants set fire to fields, grain stores, and even homes to keep them out of Stalin's hands. They poisoned wells, slit their animals' throats, and lynched officials when they caught them alone and unprotected. The Communists had not foreseen resistance on this scale.

The party overpowered the kulaks, forced the peasants into collective farms, and surveyed the damage. It spoke bravely of building tractors and mechanizing agriculture to make up for the loss of animals, but by 1933 it still could put only about 200,000 tractors with an aggregate horse-power of 3.1 million into the countryside. This was only a small fraction of the power provided by horses and oxen before the slaughter.

The 1931 harvest produced nearly 17 percent less grain than that of 1930. The shortfall outraged the party; more grain was needed for sale abroad. And export the Soviet Union did: 2.6 million centners in 1929; 48.4 million in 1930; 51.8 million in 1931. These grain deliveries to foreign countries, at the cost of reducing the amount of food available for domestic consumption, enabled the state to purchase a considerable amount of heavy machinery. They also led to starvation in some areas.

It seems not to have occurred to Stalin and his colleagues to enquire whether the quotas were unrealistically high, or whether unfavorable weather conditions in 1931 might have had anything to do with the shortfall. They again blamed the kulaks for sabotaging the harvest, and party officials fanned out into the countryside to seize

reserves (including seed grain), reorganize local party organizations, purge official cadres, and direct "mass repressions" against "enemies of the people."

Agricultural output declined throughout the first Five-Year Plan. Where 1928 equals 100, production stood at 81.5 in 1933. Nevertheless, the state made money, for example by charging Soviet consumers up to 40 times the procurement price for a kilogram of wheat flour. Similar mark-ups were applied to other foodstuffs.

By the end of the first Plan, 61.5 percent of all peasant households representing 70 percent of the crop area had been collectivized. In the major grain-producing areas the percentage of collectivized households was greater, ranging from 68 to 90 percent. Private farming in Russia had come to an end. In this manner the Bolshevik Revolution came at last to the Russian village.

Attempts to measure the human cost of collectivization have foundered less on Soviet secrecy than on the mind's inability to grasp the magnitude of the iniquity. In the spring of 1988 a member of the Soviet Academy of Agricultural Sciences published official statistics that indicated the "repression" of 10 million peasants. The figure is clearly too low; accepting it for the sake of illustration, however, we note that, if foreign invaders had killed the entire 1935 populations of Norway, Denmark, and Finland, they would have shed less blood than the Communists did in Russia during the collectivization of agriculture. And when Stalin and his henchmen had finished off the "kulaks," they began the killing in earnest.

In October 1988 the Soviet press reported the discovery of mass graves at a place called Kuropaty, near Minsk in Byelorussia. An archaeologist estimated that at *least* 102,000 people, mostly peasants, were murdered there in 1937–1941. This was only one of many "killing fields."

## FIVE-YEAR PLAN IN INDUSTRY

The Stalinists could to some extent conceal their political bankruptcy behind strident propaganda, and military weakness behind the façade of a large standing army, but there could be no denying industrial and technological backwardness. Not only did Russia lag behind the United States, Britain, and Germany: she was also inferior to France, Belgium, and even Holland in many important areas. In 1926 Russia had no machine-tool industry, only a very small chemical industry, no turbine or generator factories, no high-grade steel, no ferrous alloys, no aircraft-manufacturing plants—the list goes on.

Much of this stemmed from tsarist times, but the past could not be changed, and the Communists were now in charge. Russia had to industrialize or perish; the 20th century offered no alternative.

Where was the money to come from? Foreign credits and loans were out of the question. Russia's only friend, Weimar Germany, had more than enough problems of its own, and other capitalist states were not about to help the Communists. Russia had no colonies, no war booty; and Marxism-Leninism forbade the plundering of the Soviet people. The only conceivable solution was to abandon Marxism-Leninism.

Gosplan produced both a baseline and an optimum variant of the Five-Year Plan, and the party opted for the optimum. The first Five-Year Plan provided for the investment of 24.8 billion rubles in industry. Of that amount, 21.3 billion was to go to *heavy* industry. Prospects seemed favorable at the outset, but the sudden push for complete collectivization of agriculture disrupted both countryside and city by putting ever greater pressure on the food supply and taking workers out of the factories to enforce collectivization.

There was another factor. The Great Depression that began in 1929 and struck one capitalist country after another inevitably had repercussions in the world's only socialist state. The Depression debased the price of raw materials the Soviets sold on world markets, and Soviet grain was already selling below the cost of production. In the post-1929 market, it was necessary to export more of a given commodity to bring the same returns; but the world market could not absorb a significant increase in the chief Soviet export, grain. The fact that imported machinery and other goods now cost less did not offset the reduction in income from the sale of grain and raw materials.

About 45 percent of the budget for industry was expended on 60 giant projects. The Soviets declared that they would build gigantic hydroelectric complexes, huge automotive factories, enormous new cities. The grandiose nature of these undertakings ensured that they could not be completed on time, or, if completed, would cost so much that they could never be economical. A notorious example was the White Sea–Baltic Canal, which stretched 227 kilometers from the northern end of Lake Onega to the White Sea. Swamps, bogs, marshes, creeks, rivers, lakes, and forests constituted tremendous obstacles. The task was awesome; what better agency to carry it out than the OGPU, which had a vast reservoir of cheap labor? This labor came from concentration camps, and it was better than cheap: it was free and inexhaustible. They had only to arrest more people. Because there was almost no machinery available for the job, the government called in the OGPU with its human resources.

The canal was literally built by hand. It opened with great fanfare in 1933, Stalin and some of his associates cruising along it like a pharaoh and his court on the Nile. They only went part of the way, however, in a shallow-draft vessel; the waterway was neither deep nor wide enough for commercial craft. Economically practically useless, it

"Greetings to the factory's shock-workers from us, the little children!"
Young Pioneer demonstration, 1931. (National Archives)

would be rebuilt in the 1960s. Not one word was ever published in the Soviet press about the 300,000 OGPU prisoners, 15 percent of them women, who died building Stalin's folly with their bare hands in the northern cold.

The Soviet regime built the Turksib Railway to link Central Asia with Siberia. The gigantic Lenin hydroelectric complex on the Dnepr at Zaporozhe was a successful project despite its incredibly high cost. The metallurgical complexes at Magnitorgorsk and Kuznetsk were crucial in the drive to industrialize, as were the tractor factories at Stalingrad, Harkov, and Cheliabinsk. The list could be expanded a hundredfold.

There was to be no "Dizzy with Success" calling for easing the tempo of industrialization. On the contrary, at the 16th Party Congress Stalin proposed to *raise* the optimum goals of the Plan: 17 million tons of pig iron instead of 10 million; 170,000 tractors instead of 55,000; a 100 percent increase in agricultural machinery other than tractors; and so on.

In practical terms these new goals were simply unachievable. Not only that: a party hack dreamed up a new slogan, "Let's fulfill the Five-Year Plan in four years!" The exhortation, shortened to "Five in four!" in party propaganda, "came from the masses" in the same manner as did the welcome accorded food shortages. There is no doubt, however, that the country—particularly the younger generation—was gripped by an exhilarating sense of participation in a grand cause.

There were few volunteers to help the OGPU build the White Sea–Baltic Canal, but young people by the hundreds of thousands flocked to the industrial centers. They lived in shacks or tents while they built new dormitories in the old cities, and they lived outdoors while they built new cities such as Magnitogorsk. Their pay was as meager as their diet. From 1928 to 1930, the nominal wages of workers in industry rose 18 percent, but in the same period the cost of food rose 89 percent. They worked overtime without extra pay, worked Saturdays (the "subbotniks") for no pay, suffered deprivations. They grumbled when the government moved the clocks ahead permanently one hour ("decree time") in 1930, but there were no overt protests. Stalin's attempt to emulate the French Revolution and introduce a new 10-day week, however, encountered near-unanimous public opposition, and the project was dropped.

In 1929 the government introduced rationing for all basic foods and for many industrial goods. There were, to be sure, "commercial" stores where one could buy scarce goods at high prices, but these were available only to the privileged few. The decline in real wages for both blue and white-collar workers was not reversed during the first Five-Year Plan. They rose only during the second Plan, stood at about 60 percent of the 1928 level in 1940, and regained the 1928 level only in 1955—or, according to some Western specialists, in 1963.

All the shortcomings, blunders, and brutality notwithstanding, the Soviet people by and large achieved the goals of the first Plan. The claimed growth rate of about 18 percent does not stand up under investigation, but there can be no doubt that impressive results were achieved. The "shock-brigade" tactics—throwing large numbers of workers into a project on a round-the-clock basis—helped in some instances, proved a hindrance in others, but labor productivity did increase.

## RESULTS OF THE FIRST PLAN

The Supreme Economic Council and Gosplan had foreseen a 280 percent increase in gross industrial output between 1928 and 1933. As it happened, output had just about doubled by the end of 1932; but heavy industry increased by 270 percent. The overall performance of the economy was good, if short of the planner's goals. The following Soviet figures reflect the performance of the economy during the first Plan:

|  | 1928 | 1932 | [planned] |
|---|---|---|---|
| pig iron | 3.3 million tons | 6.2 | [10] |
| steel | 4.3 million tons | 5.9 | [10.4] |
| rolled metal | 3.4 million tons | 4.4 | [8.0] |
| tractors (units) | 1,300 | 50,600 | [170,000] |
| cement (barrels) | 11 million | 22.4 | [41] |
| superphosphates (tons) | 182,000 | 612,000 | [8–8.5 million] |
| cotton cloth (meters) | 2.678 billion | 2.694 | [4,588] |
| woolen cloth (meters) | 86.8 billion | 88.7 | [270–300] |
| electricity (kwh) | 5.0 billion | 13.5 | [22] |
| automobiles (units) | 800 | 23,900 | — |
| leather shoes (pairs) | 58 million | 86.9 | — |

May Day in Red Square, 1932. (National Archives)

There was a net decline in agricultural production. Moreover, this decline came at a time when the Soviet urban population was growing (17.9 percent of total population in 1928; 24 percent in 1932), and when the state was exporting large amounts of grain. All this clearly added up to the imposition by the state of immense hardships upon a population whose standard of living was already the lowest of any industrialized nation.

In January 1933 Stalin announced that the Plan had been fulfilled after four years and three months. His declaration bore no resemblance to the facts, but there had to be some dramatic marking of the stages of that extraordinary journey upon which the country had embarked. What had begun as an overly ambitious Plan became in 1930–1931 a crash program in which the rational allocation of scarce resources—a hallmark of

planning—was totally ignored. Nevertheless, the Soviet Union had created a powerful industrial-technological base, and Stalin's announcement embodied a significant general truth.

For a brief moment it appeared that the Communist leader, now master of the largest country in the world, would not be around to broadcast this announcement. A domestic crisis provided an opportunity for a no-confidence vote in his leadership.

On November 9, 1932, at a private dinner in Stalin's apartment in the Kremlin, Nadezhda Alliluyeva, the dictator's wife, brought up the forbidden subject of the awful famine then raging across the Ukraine and South Russia. She spoke, too, of the terror that was tightening its grip on the country. This was not the first time Alliluyeva had embarrassed her husband in front of his guests, but her bitter comments provoked him to a violent outburst that caused her to flee the room.

What happened next is unclear. The rumor immediately circulated that Stalin had strangled his wife. Avel Yenukidze, a longtime associate who was present at that fateful dinner, allegedly found Nadezhda's body with the marks of Stalin's fingers still on her throat. This naturally was not the version given out by the party, which informed the public that she had committed suicide while of unsound mind.

Whatever the circumstances, Stalin was shaken. He offered his resignation to the Central Committee. There was a moment of uncomfortable silence, and then the chief lackey, Molotov, assured him that he still had the confidence of the party. Stalin continued in office. He had Avel Yenukidze shot in 1937.

## SUGGESTED ADDITIONAL READING

**Antonov-Ovseyenko, Anton,** *The Time of Stalin,* New York: Harper & Row, 1981

**Bettelheim, Charles,** *Class Struggles in the USSR. Second Period: 1923–1930,* New York: Monthly Review Press, 1978

**Campeanu, Pavel,** *The Origins of Stalinism,* Armonk, N.Y.: M.E. Sharpe, 1986

**Chamberlin, W.H.,** *Russia's Iron Age,* Boston: Little, Brown, 1934

**Daniels, Robert V.,** *The Conscience of the Revolution,* New York: Simon & Schuster, 1969

**Davies, R.W.,** *The Socialist Offensive: The Collectivization of Soviet Agriculture, 1929–1930,* Cambridge, Mass.: Harvard University Press, 1980

——, *The Soviet Collective Farm, 1919–1930,* Cambridge, Mass.: Harvard University Press, 1980

**Filtzer, Donald,** *Soviet Workers and Stalinist Industrialization,* Armonk, N.Y.: M.E. Sharpe, 1986

**Fitzpatrick, Sheila, ed.,** *Cultural Revolution in Russia, 1928–1931,* Bloomington: Indiana University Press, 1978

**Hindus, Maurice,** *Red Bread: Collectivization in a Russian Village,* Bloomington: Indiana University Press, 1988

**Kuromiya, Hiroaki,** *Stalin's Industrial Revolution: Politics and Workers, 1928–1932,* New York: Cambridge University Press, 1988

**Lewin, Moshe,** *Russian Peasants and Soviet Power,* New York: W.W. Norton, 1975

**McNeal, Robert H.,** *Stalin: Man and Ruler,* New York: New York University Press, 1988

**Miller, Robert F.,** *One Hundred Thousand Tractors: The MTS and the Development of Soviet Agriculture,* Cambridge, Mass.: Harvard University Press, 1970

**Rancour-Lafferiere, Daniel,** *The Mind of Stalin,* Ann Arbor, Mich.: Ardis, 1988

**Rassweiler, Anne D.,** *The Generation of Power: The History of Dneprostroi,* New York: Oxford University Press, 1988

**Smith, Edward Ellis,** *The Young Stalin,* New York: Farrar, Straus, and Giroux, 1967

**Souvarine, Boris,** *Stalin,* New York: Alliance Book Corp., 1972

**Ulam, Adam,** *Stalin,* New York: Viking, 1974

**Viola, Lynne,** *The Best Sons of the Fatherland: Workers in the Vanguard of Soviet Collectivization,* New York: Oxford University Press, 1987

# 9

# THE GREAT TERROR

Late in December 1917 Feliks Dzerzhinsky, head of the newly established Cheka, asked the Sovnarkom to establish concentration camps to hold "violators of labor discipline, parasites, and people we suspect of counter-revolutionary activity but against whom we do not have sufficient evidence to punish through the legal process and whom even the strictest court would almost certainly acquit." Lenin wholeheartedly backed this proposal; the Sovnarkom routinely approved it. Coupled with the outlawing of the Kadet party the same month, the dissolution of the democratically elected Constituent Assembly in January 1918, and the formation of the savage food requisition detachments to steal food from the peasantry, this marked the beginning of Soviet Communist terror.

Lenin ordered the terror and rejoiced in its success. The blood of Russia's innocent millions is on his hands.

Lenin ordered the first "show" or public trial of Bolshevik political opponents; in June and July 1922 several members of the SR party stood trial on charges of counter-revolution. European Socialists came to Moscow to assist in the defense, and Western public opinion pressured the Kremlin to acquit, but a kangaroo court returned a guilty verdict and sentenced 15 defendants to death. The Cheka arrested their families, charging them with "being related to enemies of the people."

The grotesque farce took place shortly after Soviet Russia's bid for respectability at the Genoa Conference; this perhaps explains the state's failure to execute the sentences promptly. The doomed men sat in Moscow's Butyrka Prison until 1925, when they were shot on Stalin's personal order. So far as is known, their families never emerged from the Gulag Archipelago.

The trial of the SRs represented the first of a series of public spectacles. Several highly publicized affairs in the 1920s and early 1930s included the 1928 Shakhty Trial of alleged "wreckers" in the mines, the 1929 case of purported saboteurs in the transportation system, the 1930 trial of "members" of the nonexistent Industrial Party, and the 1933 case of the Metro-Vickers engineers, British subjects working in the USSR.

## 17TH PARTY CONGRESS

The 17th Party Congress met in Moscow January 26–February 10, 1934, billed as the Congress of Victors. Stalin declared in his report on the Central Committee's work that there was no one left to fight. Two of his closest collaborators, Molotov and Valeri Kuibyshev, gave glowing accounts of the first Five-Year Plan and presented recommendations for the second, covering the years 1933–1937. The new Plan was approved unanimously. No one spoke publicly of the mass starvation in the Ukraine in 1932–1933.*

The fact that Hitler had been in power in Germany for a year disturbed these Communists no more than did the famine. Stalin reigned in the Kremlin and all seemed right with the world. But it was not, and Stalin knew it, for there was talk of replacing him as general secretary. The human cost of collectivization and of the famine, both of which were his doing, had been enormous; many of the delegates knew the truth behind the lies. In quiet conversations in the

_____
*See Chapter 10.

corridors, delegates spoke of replacing Stalin with Sergei Kirov, Leningrad party leader. With Kirov they would call a halt to the disastrous policies of the preceding six years and initiate sweeping reforms, perhaps even return to something like NEP.

There was more to this than idle talk. At a meeting at Ordzhonikidze's apartment several top Communists urged Kirov to put forward his candidacy for the post of general secretary. Kirov not only refused but at the next session moved to accept Stalin's report as a resolution. The delegates agreed unanimously.

All was not lost for Stalin's opponents. When the votes for the new Central Committee were counted, 292 delegates had voted against the general secretary. This was slightly less than a quarter of the total 1,225, and it meant that Stalin had received fewer positive votes than any other member of the Committee.

The 41 nervous members of the electoral commission consulted Molotov and Lazar Kaganovich, secretaries of the Central Committee. Kaganovich burned all the negative ballots save three. There had been three votes against Kirov; it was unthinkable that there should be more against Stalin.

There was, however, another problem. The destruction of 289 ballots made it impossible to announce a total of 1,225. The credentials committee and the electoral commission simply reported that 936 delegates had voted.

Because nearly 300 Communists had voted against Stalin, and because at least 43 of them (the electoral commission, plus Molotov and Kaganovich) knew the extent of the protest, it was impossible to keep the secret. Stalin quickly learned what had happened. He could not, at that time, hold a trial and find the 292 guilty of treason; still less could he shoot all the delegates. But he could lay his plans.

Of the 1,961 delegates (736 nonvoting), 1,108 perished in the purges of 1936–1938. Nearly all electoral commission members were executed. By early 1939, 110 of the 139 members and candidate members of the Central Committee elected at this Congress had been arrested, and about 70 percent of them had been or would shortly be shot. Many more would never emerge alive from the Gulag. Among the victims were Nikolai Krylenko, G.K. Ordzhonikidze, Valeri Kuibyshev, V.A. Antonov-Ovseyenko, A.I. Rykov (Lenin's successor as head of the Sovnarkom) and the military commanders Yan Gamarnik, M.N. Tukhachevsky, and V.K. Blücher. Nikolai Bukharin was a member of this doomed "Class of 1934," and Mikhail Tomsky committed suicide on the eve of his arrest. Two infamous chiefs of the secret police, Genrikh Yagoda and Nikolai Yezhov, would also go to their graves with the distinction of having served on the Central Committee elected at the 1934 Congress.

## THE KIROV MURDER

The first and most famous victim was Sergei Kirov, by now the clear choice of the party as heir to Stalin. Rightly or wrongly, many members saw him as a potential reformer through whom they would call a halt to the terrible excesses of Stalin's rule. Born in 1886, Kirov was orphaned in infancy. He joined the Bolsheviks in 1904 and quickly established a reputation as a labor organizer. Handsome, cocky, and flamboyant, he was the kind of individual on whom the Bolshevik leadership of the day pinned its hopes for the future.

Kirov participated in the October Revolution and fought in the Civil War. Made a full member of the Central Committee in 1923,

he succeeded Zinoviev as Leningrad party leader in 1926. He owed his rapid rise to power chiefly to Joseph Stalin.

Kirov was not intellectually gifted, but the orphan's cynicism had honed his innate peasant shrewdness to a fine point. He knew how to make the best of his talents and understood that his workingman's approach to politics was the key to his popularity: he associated with working-class people even after he rose to power. The workingmen said of him, "On nash" ("He's one of us"), and they were right. He drank vodka with the uncomplicated enthusiasm of the *muzhik;* liked women and did not care who knew it; loved to be around machines and workers. He was also a Russian (his real name was Kostrikov) and that counted for much in a party chafing under the yoke of the Ossete, Stalin.

Kirov was a Communist's Communist, the prototype of the man the Five-Year Plan was built by and for. But he had the misfortune to have only three delegates vote against him at the 17th Congress, 289 fewer than voted against Stalin, and to have become identified—quite possibly erroneously—as a reformer. He was doomed.

Arranging the murder of the second most powerful man in the country was no easy task, even for Stalin. Kirov resisted persistent entreaties to move to Moscow; he was happy in his job in Leningrad. The first known attempt on his life came in the spring of 1934, not long after the Congress. Two criminals were taken from prison, driven by OGPU agents to Kirov's apartment building, and told that their freedom depended upon their murdering the party leader. They failed and were executed—a fate that would also have awaited them had they succeeded. A second attempt likewise miscarried. Stalin began to lose patience.

Apparently without consulting the man in

question, the Gensek—the acronym by which General Secretary Stalin was now known in the party—announced that Kirov's move to Moscow would take place early in December 1934. It seemed Kirov would have to submit and come to the capital.

The move never took place: on December 1, 1934, a disgruntled Communist party member shot and killed Kirov. The assassin, Leonid Nikolayev, had publicly expressed grievances against the party and was known to the police. Moreover, he had been apprehended near Kirov with a loaded revolver in his briefcase twice in the two months preceding the assassination. On both occasions he went free.

No country had stricter firearms-control laws or guarded its top officials more closely. Kirov never went anywhere without at least two bodyguards, but he was unguarded at the time he was murdered. Contrary to standard procedure there were no guards above the ground floor of party headquarters; the murder took place on the third floor. These lapses indicated that higher authority had ordered the removal of the guards; only one man outranked Kirov.

At the 20th Party Congress in 1956, Nikita Khrushchev declared that the Kirov murder needed a full investigation, and at the 22nd Congress (1961) he indicated that an enquiry was under way. Khrushchev fell in 1964. Nothing more was heard of the investigation until August 1988, when a Politburo member informed *Pravda* that it had been reopened.

A great deal of evidence demonstrating Stalin's complicity in the "crime of the century" is, however, in the public domain. Stalin planned the murder and used it to launch the Great Terror. Politically sophisticated contemporaries never had any doubts. A famous *chastushka*—humorous verse—of the day went like this:

Oh my cukes,
And tomatoes evermore,
Stalin nipped Kirov
Down by the cor-ri-dor.*

## GREAT TERROR: FIRST PHASE

Informed within minutes of Kirov's death, Stalin, accompanied by Molotov, Voroshilov, and the newest member of the inner circle, A.A. Zhdanov, immediately left for Leningrad to conduct the investigation. Before his departure from Moscow he announced a decree instituting a new procedure for the "adjudication" and disposition of "political" crimes. The timing indicates that it was in place and ready before Kirov's death. It ordered the speeding-up of the investigation of persons accused of preparing or perpetrating terrorist acts and declared that the Central Executive Committee Presidium would not consider petitions to pardon individuals sentenced to death for political terrorism. Finally, the decree directed the secret police (now called the NKVD) to carry out death sentences in cases of this type immediately after the verdict.

This decree had no constitutional validity, no standing in law. It was Stalin's personal order, and he held no governmental position. Nevertheless, a leading authority on the Great Terror has correctly called the decree a "Charter of Terror." Only later did the party and the government both to "approve" it.

Within hours of Kirov's murder the chief of his bodyguard was beaten to death by NKVD agents. It was officially reported that the man died in a traffic accident, but in 1956 pathologists who had assisted at the autopsy indicated that he had been beaten

---

*From *Nepodtsenzurnaia russkaia chastushka*, New York: Russica Publishers, 1978. Used with the permission of Russica Publishers. English translation by W.M.

on the head with a blunt metallic object. Khrushchev released this news at the 22nd Congress and also revealed that the men who had killed the chief of the guard were shot a few months later.

The interrogation of Nikolayev, the assassin, was perfunctory and according to some accounts even gentle. Stalin allegedly asked, "Why did you kill such a nice man?" Nikolayev, and 13 NKVD agents who had allegedly failed to protect Kirov, were tried *in camera* on December 28, convicted, and shot the next day.

Even before the execution of Nikolayev, the NKVD shot 37 "White Guards" in Leningrad, 33 in Moscow, 28 in Kiev. Mass deportations to Arctic camps and to Kolyma in the far northeast began almost as quickly. Within a few months 30,000 to 40,000 inhabitants of Leningrad had been sent to their doom, accused only of some vague connection with Kirov's murder. The press reported that they were "Trotskyites" and "rotten liberals." This was the "Kirov [or Leningrad] wave," the mighty swell that deposited hundreds of thousands of Leningraders in the Gulag.

The time had come for Stalin to settle old accounts. In January 1935 Zinoviev, Kamenev, and other "members" of what the NKVD styled the "Moscow Center" were tried in Leningrad on charges of complicity in the Kirov murder. The proceedings were conducted in secret. Led by former Menshevik Andrei Vyshinsky, who orchestrated the judicial persecution of Mensheviks and others in the 1920s, and who as a Kerensky regime official ordered the Moscow police to "arrest and bring to trial the German spy, Vladimir Ilich Ulyanov," the prosecution could not prove its case. Kamenev declared on the witness stand that he had never heard of a "Moscow Center" but agreed that, insofar as it might have existed, he was responsible for it.

The press carried only a truncated version of the trial record; the mild sentences proved to everyone that the state's case was made of whole cloth. Zinoviev received a 10-year sentence, Kamenev five years. Similar punishment befell the other defendants.

## THE OMINOUS LULL OF 1935–1936

The execution of Nikolayev and the Leningrad NKVD agents, the shooting of the "White Guards" in the three largest cities, the mass deportations, the trial of the "Moscow Center"—all this brought to an end the first phase of the Great Terror. It was not planned that way. There would have been no respite had Vyshinsky and Vasili Ulrikh, who later presided at the Kamenev-Zinoviev trial, been able to make a better case for the existence of "Moscow Center." Their failure necessitated a reevaluation of NKVD procedures.

Some sort of rationale had to be constructed for what Stalin had in mind. It was not yet possible to deport millions of people to the slave labor camps without explanation. The wave of public revulsion over Kirov's murder that Stalin had anticipated did not materialize. Kirov was popular, but he was not Lenin. There was no public demand for a gigantic purge; it would have to be manufactured.

The foreign situation complicated matters. Initially contemptuous of Hitler and the Nazis, the Soviet Communists had actually welcomed their accession to power in Germany in the belief that Germany would soon turn away from such gangsters in the direction of the Communists: "After Hitler, Us!" the German Communists predicted. That did not happen, and German domestic and foreign policy had taken an increasingly menacing direction. This too had to be taken into account when preparing the next stage of the Terror.

Finally, the economic miracle that was the industrialization of Russia was proceeding satisfactorily under the second Five-Year Plan, and according to official propaganda it was all due to Stalin's genius. He basked in the adulation and decided he could wait a little longer to settle accounts with enemies. Behind the scenes a special security commission he had established in May 1935 was writing the next act of the drama.

## TRIAL OF THE "TROTSKYITE-ZINOVIEVITE UNITED CENTER"

The commission consisted of Stalin, Zhdanov, Vyshinsky, Nikolai Yezhov (who would become head of the NKVD in September 1936), and Matvei Shkiryatov. These men did their work neither thoroughly nor well, but the prisoners they intended to put on trial had been held incommunicado for months or even years and denied access to legal counsel. And Stalin and his men controlled the courts and the secret police.

Zinoviev, Kamenev, and 14 others went on trial in Moscow on August 19, 1936, charged with complicity in the Kirov murder; plotting to kill Stalin and other Soviet leaders; conspiring with foreign powers against the Soviet Union; and other crimes. The trial was open in the sense that some independent foreign observers were present; the Soviet spectators were NKVD employees. Denied the right to have counsel or cross-examine witnesses, the defendants were badgered and humiliated by prosecutor and judge. They could communicate only with interrogators and jailors.

The "evidence" consisted of the defendants' pretrial depositions and their confessions in open court; hence, there were only minor obstacles in Vyshinsky's smooth progress toward convictions. I.N. Smirnov, a former Trotskyite, did put up some semblance of a defense, denying membership in an organization that did not exist. The other defendants quickly contradicted him.

Except for the prosecution and the defendants everyone who followed the course of events in that Moscow courtroom was shocked by the apparently uncoerced admissions of guilt. Most Soviet citizens and many gullible foreigners believed the confessions genuine. Millions more suspected that although the facts were not quite in accordance with the testimony, the defendants were probably guilty of *something* and were confessing to grave crimes in order to earn lighter sentences. A third, perhaps excessively sophisticated, view was that the confessions constituted the last service of dedicated Communists to the party.

In reality, various forms of torture obtained the desired results. Khrushchev admitted in 1956 that NKVD interrogators had deprived the defendants of sleep for days, even weeks. This treatment was invariably effective and left no visible marks; the jailers were not to blame if the prisoners refused to sleep. Other psychological torture involved threats against families; this almost always produced the desired results.

Finally, the secret police had perfected their own special techniques in the field of pharmacology and used drugs to break the victims. Will suppressants came into use in 1936, when Zinoviev, Kamenev, and their co-defendants jumped through Vyshinsky's hoops with robotlike obedience. Better confessions through chemistry.

The trial ended on August 24. Guilty verdicts were returned against all defendants. Within hours, the 16 condemned men had been shot in the back of the head—an NKVD trademark—in the cellars of the Lubyanka. A ghoulish chorus of approval greeted the news of the convictions and executions; many foreign apologists for Stalin joined in.

## STALIN AND IVAN THE TERRIBLE

A month after the trial Stalin and Zhdanov informed the Politburo that Yagoda and the NKVD were four years behind in the work of rooting out conspiracies and terrorism. That seemed to mean that the unholy work had lapsed in 1932, the year of Nadezhda Alliluyeva's death. Would Stalin now claim that Trotskyites murdered his wife? People began to wonder whether a new Ivan the Terrible brooded over the Kremlin.

Tsar Ivan IV's first wife, Anastasia, died in 1560 under mysterious circumstances. Shattered by her death, the tsar became increasingly paranoid and withdrew into a narrow circle of sinister companions. Some years earlier, the boyars (aristocrats) had refused to swear allegiance to Ivan's son when the tsar lay on what he thought was his deathbed. They would settle the succession without reference to his wishes.

Ivan recovered and neither forgot nor forgave. He suspected that some of the boyars had poisoned Anastasia. Moreover, Muscovy faced foreign enemies at the time; a few of the tsar's closest advisers defected to them and he suspected that others were planning to follow. Four years after his wife's death he launched a bloody purge of the upper classes that resulted in the extinction of all but a tiny handful of the old boyar families.

While he carried out this massive campaign of terror Ivan was technically not the tsar; he had gone through the legal motions of appointing an obscure Mongol prince to that post. He himself merely ruled an *oprichnina* (separate part) carved out of the estates of the destroyed aristocrats for his personal domain. He descended ever deeper into madness and in the end killed his own son.

The striking parallels license no extravagant claims but may offer some clues into the psychopathology of Stalin, an attentive student of Russian history who commissioned biographies and a film about Ivan the Terrible. Biographies and film depicted the tsar as a wise, perceptive ruler who, surrounded by treason, took severe measures for the good of the state.

The bloodiest phase of Stalin's Terror began four years after his wife's death, for which he bore at least a moral responsibility. He seemed to have convinced himself that he was puzzled by her death; the self-induced perplexity made it possible to deny his guilt. The Terror of the 1930s did not embody an attempt to avenge Nadezhda Alliluyeva's death, but something about that death apparently helped ignite it.

Like Ivan, Stalin was neither head of state nor leader of the government; those posts were held by Kalinin and Molotov, respectively. Stalin was merely commander-in-chief, though not technically the head of his own *oprichnina*, the NKVD. Trotsky had not *fled* abroad the way some of Ivan's opponents had, but he *was* abroad, and Stalin believed that he was conspiring with potential Soviet enemies. Many Communists had voted against their general secretary at the 17th Congress, hoping to replace him with Kirov. No Communists had been asked to swear allegiance to Stalin's son, and unlike the tsar Stalin did not kill either of his two sons. He did however refuse even to consider bargaining for the release of one of them, Yakov, who was captured and eventually executed by the Germans in World War II.

## TRIAL OF THE "PARALLEL CENTER"

The second of the three great "show" trials saw 17 "members" of a "Parallel Center" (also called Anti-Soviet Trotskyite Center) in the prisoners' dock in January 1937. From the state's point of view this was the least significant of the trials, designed to maintain momentum rather than to cover any new ground.

The best-known figure among the accused, Karl Radek, had published a denunciation of Zinoviev and Kamenev during their trial, and at his own he implicated everyone he could in an attempt to save himself. After Radek came Grigory Sokolnikov, a Trotskyite who had accepted Trotsky's defeat and had gone on to serve in a number of posts. The third chief defendant was Grigory Pyatakov, director of the State Bank, who had also sided with Trotsky and been expelled from the party. He had recanted and was readmitted in 1928. Another defendant, Leonid Serebryakov, once a secretary of the Central Committee, was likewise a former Trotskyite.

The defendants were charged with the usual crimes: sabotage, "wrecking," conspiracy to assassinate Soviet leaders, plotting with foreign governments, and so on. The prominent four had no defense counsel but the 13 others did. It was understood that all would testify against themselves. The star witness-defendant in January 1937, Radek, had been promised lenient treatment in return for his cooperation. He confessed to all charges and added new details, not one of which was true. He thus strengthened the case against himself and the other defendants, not to mention people still at liberty.

With the eager cooperation of Radek and Pyatakov, Vyshinsky claimed the existence of a "link" between Trotsky and Rudolf Hess, a high-ranking Nazi. This was supposed to prove that the two men had conspired to divide the USSR among Germany, Japan, and other powers. Vyshinsky demonstrated to the satisfaction of the court that the defendants had organized acts of "wrecking" and sabotage; after all, they had confessed. He introduced into "evidence" a letter to the editor from a young female railway switch operator published in *Pravda* on January 28, the next to last day of the trial. The young woman said that at 20 she had lost both legs averting a train wreck organized by the defendants.

At 7:15 p.m. on the evening of January 29, the judges retired to "deliberate." They returned to the October Hall at 3:00 the next morning.

Pyatakov, Serebryakov, and 11 "junior" defendants were sentenced to death. Sokolnikov, Radek, and one other received 10-year sentences, while the last of the small fry was given eight years. On hearing the verdict, Radek glanced at his fellow defendants, grinned foolishly, and shrugged his shoulders as if to say, "You never know!" He did know. His testimony helped Stalin justify the execution of scores, perhaps hundreds, of human beings.

Radek's feelings concerning the arrest of his daughter shortly before his trial began remain unknown. She was sent to the camps as a "ChSR," a member of the family of a "repressed" person; that was her crime. Radek's own term in an Arctic camp ended in 1939 when he died in unexplained circumstances.

## DESTRUCTION OF THE MILITARY

On June 1, 1937, the Red Army reported the suicide the previous day of one of its most distinguished officers, Yan Gamarnik, member of the party's Central Committee, head of the army political administration, editor of the army newspaper *Red Star*. He had been ousted on May 11, 1937, however, as first deputy commissar of defense, and *Pravda* claimed he killed himself because he had become "entangled . . . with anti-Soviet elements and evidently feared that he would be arrested."

On June 11 the Kremlin announced that

eight senior commanders had been arrested on charges of treason. The next day, the press published the news that they had been tried, convicted, and shot.

These unprecedented actions foreshadowed what was to come. In the purge of the military, the secret police decimated the officer corps. The dimensions of the massacre gradually became clear with the revelation that 55 percent of the officers in the uniformed services were imprisoned during the terror and that many were killed in 1937 and 1938. The purges slacked off after that, but the killing did not end until June 1941, the month Germany invaded the USSR.

It had been one thing for Stalin to settle accounts with former rivals. It appeared that he had gone mad when he tore the heart out of the Soviet military at a time when the world was toppling into a conflict in which the Soviet Union was certain to become involved.

The dictator believed himself threatened by the senior officers, especially Marshal M. N. Tukhachevsky. The military leaders who fell in the 1937 purge had distinguished Civil War records that stood in stark contrast to Stalin's blunders and insubordination. The commanders were popular in the Red Army, the country at large, and the party; Stalin was feared and respected but never popular. Further, some of them were brilliant military thinkers. Finally, the man at the center of the purge, Tukhachevsky, tall, handsome, unusually personable—was everything that Stalin was not.

The official rationale for gutting the military was that the officers had conspired with the Wehrmacht to sell the Soviet Union to Germany. Documents forged in Berlin with the complicity of Stalin's agents were passed through the culpably naive Czechoslovak government to Moscow. Stalin had them by early May 1937 and moved at once to de-

Marshal Tukhachevsky and his wife, Nina. (Soviet photo from Tukhachevsky family archives mote and isolate Gamarnik and Tukhachevsky. The documents "proved" the existence of a plot in which Soviet commanders had conspired with Trotsky to weaken the defenses of the USSR to pave the way for a German invasion.

There was no vast conspiracy, not even a half-vast one, at least not one involving Tukhachevsky and the Soviet military command. The real plot centered on Stalin, who had been conducting secret negotiations with the Germans since the autumn of 1936. He had belatedly seen that Hitler would not fall under the weight of his own bizarre policies, and he now realized that every day that Hitler remained in power increased the risk of an armed conflict between the USSR and Germany. How could this be avoided? Stalin resolved to negotiate a peaceful agreement and to this end sent a personal envoy to Berlin in December 1936.

The Soviet military commanders objected to Stalin's plan to reach an accord with Germany on what they considered a dangerously unsound basis. Stalin was proposing a high-risk game that would see the Soviet Union (1) supply Germany with raw materials at low cost, further strengthening a nation that was both rearming and becoming ominously aggressive, and (2) refrain from undertaking any defense measures that might appear to threaten Germany. That meant that the USSR could not build up its western defenses sufficiently to halt or even slow down a German invasion. Two commanders shot on June 11, Iona Yakir and I. P. Uborevich, were horrified by Stalin's plans. Yakir commanded the Kiev military district, Uborevich the Byelorussian—the two largest and most important districts, through which an invader would come.

The Red Army officers opposed Stalin's policy, which could only have disastrous consequences. The dictator saw only one foolproof way to overcome their objections:

fabricate a conspiracy and execute the "conspirators." In so doing he very nearly destroyed not only the Red Army, Fleet, and Air Force, but also the country.

## TRIAL OF THE "RIGHT TROTSKYITE CENTER"

The last great "show" trial took place March 2–13, 1938. The first had featured the pathetic ex-leaders Zinoviev and Kamenev, the second, the buffoon Radek. The third offered up stars of the greatest magnitude: Nikolai Bukharin, Aleksei Rykov, and Nikolai Krestinsky, all of whom had served on the Politburo with Lenin. Also in the prisoners' dock was Yagoda, the former head of the NKVD. Christian Rakovsky, a Communist of Bulgarian-Romanian origin who had served the Soviet Union as a diplomat, was also among the defendants. Eight obscure senior officials were included in the trial, as were five minor functionaries. Three civilian physicians rounded out the group of 21.

The trial saw Stalin and his henchmen jam together the last major pieces of their great puzzle. Bukharin and Rykov, synonymous with the former Right opposition, at one time had made common cause with Trotsky and the Left. They were also tainted with the brush of the Tukhachevsky-Nazi "plot" by the public testimony of Radek and others. Two of the senior officials were Uzbeks, leaders of the Uzbek republic. This was the first time non-Europeans had been tried publicly. One of the minor defendants who worked for the commissariat of agriculture was charged with "wrecking" in the food industry. The three physicians, who alone had defense counsel, had allegedly murdered several top officials as well as Maksim Gorky and his son.

When it was disclosed that Yagoda was among the defendants, people recalled Stalin's remark about the secret police being four years behind in its work. Yagoda had been in office at the time of Kirov's assassination and was responsible for carrying out the mass reprisals of 1935. Now he was in the dock.

One after another the accused faced the judges of the military collegium and pleaded guilty. When Krestinsky's turn came, however, he startled everyone with "I plead not guilty." This was not according to the text that Vyshinsky and Chief Judge Ulrikh had written, quite possibly with the direct assistance of Stalin. Asked about his earlier confession, Krestinsky admitted that he had made it; he was now withdrawing it. Prosecutor and judges agreed that a recess was in order.

When the proceedings resumed 20 minutes later Vyshinsky turned to one of the minor defendants and elicited testimony incriminating Krestinsky, who promptly reaffirmed his innocence. His admission that he had lied during the interrogation damaged the prosecution: "I simply considered that if I were to say what I am saying today—that . . . [my confession] was not in accordance with the facts—my declaration would not reach the leaders of the party and the government." Vyshinsky turned to another defendant.

On the second day of the trial, March 3, Vyshinsky altered the schedule to postpone Krestinsky's testimony until evening. When the proceedings resumed after an afternoon break, Krestinsky was again subjected to cross-examination. Would he now, the prosecutor asked, cease to play games and tell the truth, reaffirm the confession he made during the pretrial investigation? He would, and he did. Why had he lied in court? He had "mechanically" declared his innocence, he now said, because he was so ashamed of his guilt. He had seen the error of his ways and was ready to proclaim his "treason and treachery."

Krestinsky seemed unmarked when he returned to the October Hall on March 3, although the Westerners who observed the trial thought him listless. He had probably been warned that he had placed his family in grave jeopardy, and he may have been drugged. In any event he was now tame.

Rykov confessed to most charges against him, lulling Prosecutor Vyshinsky into a false sense of security. By accident or design, however, Lenin's successor as head of the Sovnarkom began to confuse a number of details, throwing the prosecution off stride. Rykov denied, for example, knowing anything about "wrecking" in the livestock industry and refused to admit to specific acts of espionage or sabotage.

Bukharin faced Vyshinsky on March 5. The man whom Lenin had once called the "favorite of the whole party" was physically unmarked. Here was an actor in the great drama who did not need physical inducement to cooperate. He believed that he had understood the madness.

Bukharin had lost control of the government newspaper *Izvestiya* in January 1937 and his liberty a month later. Just before his arrest he wrote a letter asking his comrades to remember that a drop of his blood would be on the banner they would carry on the victorious march toward communism. He said nothing about his own role in creating the martyrs who had already been sacrificed to the Soviet power he had helped build. As Stalinism took hold, he had tried valiantly, futilely, to halt the plunge into the abyss he and the other Old Bolsheviks had dug.

Before the trial Bukharin had agreed to plead guilty to all charges, but he changed his mind when he saw the script. He would not admit to having plotted to assassinate Lenin or having committed sabotage and espionage. Like Rykov he would accept general responsibility for the opposition to Stalin, opposition which his own political record seemed to justify and encourage. In effect, he agreed to say that by failing to commit himself totally and without reservation to Stalin, he had encouraged various opposition movements and lent them respectability.

Like Rykov, Bukharin sparred with the prosecution and scored a few telling blows. He denied any knowledge of Kirov's assassination. A confused Vyshinsky turned to Yagoda, former head of the NKVD, hoping to implicate Bukharin. That was a major blunder. Yagoda admitted that he had given "instructions" about the Kirov affair. To whom? To a high-ranking NKVD official in Leningrad. Had this anything to do with the Bukharin-Rykov "bloc"? Yagoda asked that he be permitted not to answer. This whole line of questioning had not been rehearsed; Vyshinsky dropped it.

It was too late. Yagoda had shed the first light on the Kirov murder. He had indeed given "instructions," and he could not have done so without Stalin's orders.

The prosecution tried to resurrect the charges against Bukharin of plotting to kill Lenin. Vyshinsky brought in two witnesses, members of the SR party; they proved unreliable. Not everyone could master the techniques of these farces, and non-Communists were at a greater disadvantage because they had never been subject to Communist party discipline. The two SRs kept stumbling over the truth as they remembered it; there had indeed been a Left SR plot to kill Lenin, but no one ever mentioned Bukharin's name.

The Bukharin-Rykov-Krestinsky trial involved so many alleged crimes and defendants that Solomon himself would have been hard pressed to sort them out. Espionage, "wrecking," treason, plots to murder officials, and other fantastic allegations were mixed in with murder charges. The three physicians were charged with the murders of Kuibyshev, Menzhinsky (head of the OGPU until his death in 1934), Gorky and his son, all on the orders of Yagoda.

The world watched the spectacle of two ordinary citizens being forced to acknowledge crimes and perversions of medical science such as only the most disturbed minds could even conceive. One of the physicians, I.N. Kazakov, was a quack who had been Menzhinsky's personal doctor, but Dmitri Pletnev and Lev Levin—the physician of Boris Pasternak's family—were highly respected in the medical profession. They had never met any of their co-defendants, never violated Soviet law. The state, however, was determined to prove the "medical murder" of officials.

There was much more to this satanic circus that passed for a trial, but the difficulty with flinging sensational disclosures at the public is that the public is quickly numbed. The trial came to a close. Vyshinsky called for the defendants (two minor ones excepted) to be "shot like dirty dogs!" This concluded the state's case.

Knowing they were doomed, Rykov and Bukharin used their concluding speeches to appeal to history. But it was not enough, the satirists Ilf and Petrov wrote, to love Soviet power. *It* had to love *you.*

Stalin was in the habit of working at night; that explains why the verdicts were announced at ungodly hours. At 4:00 a.m. on March 13, 1938, the judges returned to the October Hall. All 21 defendants were found guilty on all counts. Eighteen, including Lenin's old comrades-in-arms Bukharin, Rykov, and Krestinsky, were sentenced to death. Dr. Pletnev and Dr. Levin were let off with 25-year terms in the camps. Rakovsky got 20 years, a minor defendant 15. *Pravda* announced on March 15 that the death sentences had been carried out. The party of Lenin was dead.

## THE GREAT TERROR IN RETROSPECT

Wrapped in his carapace of insecurity, Stalin took bits and pieces of reality and fashioned them into a distorted image that ultimately only he understood. To him and to those who catered to his every whim, anything less than fawning servility was treason; and when Stalin became suspicious of servility that too became evidence of disloyalty.

Stalin did not surround himself with psychologically healthy people. He sought out individuals whose own pathology enabled them to humor him, to bear his own excesses and take pleasure in them. It was a risky business. Stalin arrested his own daughter's lover, Mikoyan's sons, Molotov's wife, Kalinin's wife, Poskrebyshev's wife, and other relatives of his closest associates. No member of the Politburo could be sure, when he was being driven to his Kremlin office, that his driver would not take that fatal left turn up Hunter's Row, past the Bolshoi Theatre and the Metropole Hotel, on to Dzerzhinsky Square and the Lubyanka.

Communist party sources including Nikita Khrushchev and officials of the Gorbachev regime have admitted there were at least 8 million victims of Stalin's Terror. Marshal Tito of Yugoslavia claimed there were 15 million, and some of the survivors insist that 20 million people died.

The innocent people who were shot or dispatched to the forced labor camps of Siberia, the far north, and Central Asia were taken out of a labor force already too small to fulfill the tasks of the Five-Year Plans, and their labor in the camps was to be as sterile and unproductive as that of the Egyptian slaves who built the magnificent, useless pyramids. The cost of maintaining the Gulag far exceeded the profits to the state from timber cut, gold mined, roads and canals built.

## A CASE HISTORY: THE TULIKOVS

No mere figures can tell the story, but a case history can perhaps be instructive. Boris Tulikov* was a lieutenant colonel in the Red Army. He fought with Zhukov at Khalkhin Gol and was decorated for bravery. In the Winter War against Finland he commanded an infantry battalion and again received a medal. But in January 1940 he criticized "higher-ups," whom he did not name, for the disasters of the early weeks of the war. In June this indiscreet remark caught up with him. He was arrested, tried on charges of spying for the British, and executed.

Vera Tulikova, Boris's wife, was arrested on July 2, 1940. After three weeks in NKVD captivity she broke down and confessed, falsely, to having worked with her husband for the British. She was sent to a labor camp on the White Sea, near the town of Kem; her sentence was eight years. Assigned to fell timber, Vera's health failed. She died in the spring of 1941.

A daughter, Zoya, 20, a student of biology, was arrested along with her mother and subjected to repeated interrogation. She became hysterical, was given injections of some unknown substance, and lost her mind. Placed in an insane asylum, Zoya committed suicide by jumping out a fifth-story window in January 1942.

A son, Andrei, 21, was studying medieval history at Leningrad University when his father was arrested. He had been active in the Komsomol; unlike the other members of the family, he was a Marxist. He was arrested on June 29, 1940, and interrogated at NKVD headquarters in Leningrad. He admitted nothing; there was nothing to admit. He was treated, all things considered, relatively leniently, and received a sentence of only five years in the Gulag. Some of his

---

*I have disguised the family's identity.

fellow prisoners were to regard him with suspicion. Such a "child's sentence" was often proof of collusion with the authorities.

Andrei Tulikov spent two years at a camp near Norilsk, in Siberia. Late in 1942, at the height of the Battle of Stalingrad, he and several thousand other "zeks" ("cons") imprisoned on political grounds were given the opportunity to atone for their crimes against the state by serving in punishment battalions of the Red Army; these battalions were cannon fodder and everyone knew it. Andrei, who at the age of 23 had lost his teeth to scurvy, accepted. He was given three days of training—those who served in punishment battalions usually got none at all—and then sent into action against the retreating Germans. Promoted to corporal after the Battle of Kursk, he fought on toward Warsaw and was wounded in Poland in August 1944 when a sniper's bullet shattered his jaw. Removed to a military hospital near Smolensk, he recuperated and was honorably discharged in June 1945.

Andrei went first to Harkov to visit relatives. He found none. Everyone had been killed in the war or had simply disappeared. He was shown his sister's death certificate but the authorities claimed to be unable to locate her grave. He learned for the first time of his mother's death in the form of a three-sentence letter from the NKVD; her grave was likewise unknown.

On July 18, 1945, someone recognized Andrei Tulikov on the street in Voronezh, where he had gone to visit an old friend, and reported him to the NKVD. The "someone" was apparently a former guard, or perhaps an inmate, of the camp near Norilsk; Andrei was charged with having escaped. He produced his discharge papers and various medical certificates, and asked that his former commanding officers be contacted. After he had spent six weeks in prison the mistake was sorted out and Tulikov was freed with as

graceful an apology as the NKVD was capable of making. They told him never to come back to Voronezh.

Andrei went to Leningrad and with the aid of his former professors resumed his studies. He obtained a baccalaureate degree in 1947 and continued at the university, intending to take a *kandidat* (doctoral) degree. His dissertation was to be a study of the migration of the Slavs from the middle Dnepr basin to the northeast in the early part of the 13th century, when the Mongol invasion finished off what was left of the Kievan Russian state.

In 1949 Tulikov was again arrested and this time charged with "anti-Soviet activity." His real crime, he soon realized, was his friendship with some minor officials caught up in the "Leningrad Affair," a major postwar purge. He was sent to the Gulag again, to serve 15 years. He worked in a lumber gang in the forests south of Archangel until his health collapsed in 1951. In such cases "goners" were generally left to die. But Tulikov was sent to a camp near the Aral Sea, 2,500 kilometers to the south. In the new camp, the regimen was less strict, the food was better, and of course the weather was much milder. He recovered.

Stalin died in March 1953. Andrei Tulikov was released in July. Most political "zeks" had to wait until 1956 and even later for their freedom.

Returning to Leningrad University in time for the autumn semester of 1953, he completed his dissertation a few years later. After receiving his degree he became an assistant professor of history at a university in Central Asia. He published a revised version of his dissertation and several articles that brought him favorable attention. In 1966 he was appointed to the faculty of one of the best universities in the RSFSR. In 1981 he became a full professor.

Andrei Tulikov has since published three

well-received books and more than a dozen articles. He lives in a comfortable three-room apartment with his wife, who writes popular children's stories. His two daughters have married and moved away; his son is a petroleum engineer in Novosibirsk. Andrei drives his own car, has a *dacha* on Lake Ladoga, and he and his wife have traveled to Romania and Bulgaria. They are not allowed to travel to the West, or to Poland or Hungary.

Tulikov is bitter about what he regards as the terrible perversion of socialism that took place under Stalin. He maintains, however, that the Terror which consumed his family has gone for good and cannot return. Both the Communist party and the people are different, he says, and neither would tolerate it. He believes that the post-1953 Soviet leaders have not been bloodthirsty men. Cautiously optimistic about the prospects for long-term reform under Gorbachev, Tulikov believes that only a firm bond between a reform-minded government and the military can preserve *glasnost* and *perestroika* against the determined assault of Communist party cadres and the bureaucracy.

There are photographs in Andrei Tulikov's apartment of his father in his Red Army uniform, decorations for valor on the tunic. A photo of his mother, a delicate, pretty woman dressed in the style of the late 1930s, stands in a silver frame on his desk alongside one of Andrei's sister, Zoya, a blonde synthesis of her handsome father and mother. Only when he speaks of Zoya does he struggle to control his emotions.

Andrei Tulikov has never returned to Voronezh.

## SUGGESTED ADDITIONAL READING

**Butson, Thomas G.,** *The Tsar's Lieutenant: The Soviet Marshal,* New York: Praeger, 1984

**Conquest, Robert,** *The Great Terror,* New York: Collier Books, 1973

———, *Kolyma,* New York: Viking, 1979

———, *Stalin and the Kirov Murder,* New York: Oxford University Press, 1988

**Dallin, David J., and Boris Nicolaevsky,** *Forced Labor in the Soviet Union,* New Haven, Conn.: Yale University Press, 1955

**Dyadkin, Iosif G.,** *Unnatural Deaths in the U.S.S.R., 1928–1954,* New Brunswick, N.J.: Rutgers University Press, 1983

**Getty, J. Arch,** *Origins of the Great Purges,* New York: Cambridge University Press, 1985

**Ginzburg, Eugenia,** *Journey into the Whirlwind,* New York: Harcourt Brace Jovanovich, 1967

———, *Within the Whirlwind,* New York: Harcourt Brace Jovanovich 1981

**Gorbatov, Aleksandr V.,** *Years Off My Life,* New York: W.W. Norton, 1965

**Lerner, Warren,** *Karl Radek,* Stanford, Calif.: Stanford University Press, 1970

**Medvedev, Roy,** *Let History Judge,* New York: Vintage Books, 1973

———, *Nikolai Bukharin: The Last Years,* New York: W.W. Norton, 1980

**Shalamov, Varlam,** *Graphite,* New York: W.W. Norton, 1981

———, *Kolyma Tales,* New York: W.W. Norton, 1980

**Solzhenitsyn, Aleksandr I.,** *The Gulag Archipelago, 1918–1956,* 3 vols., New York: Harper & Row, 1973–1978

**Štajner, Karlo,** *Seven Thousand Days in Siberia,* New York: Farrar Straus Giroux, 1988

**Tuck, Jim,** *Engine of Mischief: An Analytical Biography of Karl Radek,* Westport, Conn.: Greenwood Press, 1988

**Vyshinsky, Andrei,** *The Law of the Soviet State,* New York: Macmillan, 1954

# 10

# RUSSIA IN THE 1930s

According to a quip of the time, there were three categories of Soviet citizens in the 1930s: those who had been in prison, those currently in prison, and those who would soon go to prison. It was a time of terror that struck both the worker who did his job and kept his doubts to himself and the peasant who went docilely into the kolhoz. These were the people in whose name the Bolsheviks had made their Revolution, the people who were building the new society. They were not immune from "repression," but they were a little less insecure than other citizens if only because there were so many of them. They were exalted by the propaganda of their new masters, the Communists, who also forced them to work long hours for low wages. People whispered that the initials VKP (Vsesoyuznaya Kommunisti-

cheskaya Partiya, All-Union Communist Party) really stood for Vtoroye Krepostnoye Pravo—"second serfdom." No one said this out loud. It was a time, Anna Akhmatova wrote, when they would interrogate your shadow.

## FAMINE OF 1932–1933

There were no jokes about the second famine in 11 years. It struck in 1932, and weather conditions were only partly responsible. The summer harvest of 1931 had been inadequate, that of spring 1932 still worse. In the summer of 1932 the situation in parts of the country—the Ukraine, North Caucasus, parts of the Volga Valley—approached catastrophe. Once again there was hunger; but prompt intervention could have prevented mass starvation. Some grain-producing areas were affected only slightly or not at all by the drought, and state reserves could have compensated for the shortfall.

Stalin and the party refused to intervene. Far from reducing the quotas for the affected areas, they *increased* them and refused to send aid to the worst-hit sections.

Failure to meet the quotas was called "wrecking" and sabotage. Molotov, Kaganovich, and other high-ranking officials conducted punitive expeditions into the affected regions; scores of local party bosses and kolhoz managers were summarily executed by the OGPU. Peasants singled out by informers and local secret police agents as troublemakers were also shot.

The rationale for increasing quotas in a time of famine involved the problem of foreign exchange. The government had contracted to supply foreign purchasers with grain. Failure to deliver would mean loss of substantial hard-currency revenues, and that would slow the drive for industrialization.

Stalin and his associates made a conscious decision to let the people starve. They undertood the dimensions of the problem and could forecast its duration. Had this threatened to become a disaster on the 1921 scale, Stalin would have realized he could not keep it secret. Once the news got out, foreign markets for Soviet grain would surely have softened.

The regime saw to it that no foreigners learned anything concrete until the worst of the crisis had passed. The OGPU clamped restrictions on travel into the famine-stricken areas; only Soviet citizens who had legitimate business were allowed in. There was virtually nothing in the foreign press about the catastrophe. An American correspondent who visited the Ukraine shortly after the travel restrictions were eased in October 1933 estimated the death toll from starvation at five to six million.

Foreigners began to ask questions; Kalinin vigorously denied there had been a famine. The lie was repeated by all official spokesmen, but a famine there was, especially in the Ukraine, and millions died.

Stalin bet on a recovery in 1934 and won. The first spring vegetables eased the crisis, and there was a good harvest that summer. Once gain the Gensek had been proved right; his reputation for infallibility soared higher. No one dared pay tribute to the memory of those who had died in the first man-made famine in recorded history.

## SECOND FIVE-YEAR PLAN

The 17th party conference (January–February 1932) laid down the fundamental political principle which was to guide Gosplan and other agencies as they put together the second Five-Year Plan: the planners were to administer the *coup de grâce* to the last vestiges of capitalism. This meant that collectivization of agriculture was to be completed. The basic economic tasks of the plan involved the continuation of the technological revolution and the further development of industry, particularly heavy industry. The plan, which was to cover the years 1933–1937, was approved by the 17th Congress early in 1934.

The building of new industries and the reconstruction of old constituted a monumental assignment for both management and labor. By and large it was carried out successfully; by 1937, more than 80 percent of industrial production came from factories and enterprises that were either totally new or had been completely overhauled during the first two plans. Investment in capital projects of all types jumped from 50.5 billion rubles in the first plan to 137.5 billion in the second. The figures are even more impressive when we consider investment only in industry: 25 billion rubles in the first Plan, 65.8 billion in the second. Refining the data still further, we note that in the second Five-Year Plan the state invested 53.4 billion rubles in heavy industry; approximately 4,500 new factories went into production. According to Soviet statistics, massive investment brought impressive results:

|  | 1932 | 1937 | percentage increase 1932–1937 |
|---|---|---|---|
| pig iron (millions of tons) | 6.2 | 14.5 | 235 |
| steel (millions of tons) | 5.9 | 17.7 | 300 |
| rolled metal (millions of tons) | 4.4 | 13.0 | 295 |
| coal (millions of tons) | 64.4 | 128.0 | 199 |
| hydroelectric energy (billions of kwh) | 13.5 | 36.2 | 270 |

There was, people said, all the steel you could eat. The consumer-goods sector received short shrift in both first and second Five-Year Plans. The government insisted that the international situation dictated this order of priorities, and to a considerable extent this explanation was valid. The Soviet Union had undertaken the plans in order to industrialize; it was literally necessary to begin from scratch. Usable resources were scarce, capital limited. Skilled labor was in short supply, technology inferior to that of the West.

In order to compete, the USSR had to concentrate on heavy industry. The country had to produce steel and other metals; build machine-tool, armaments, chemical, and automotive industries and manufacture agricultural implements. Until all this was done there would be little left over for food-processing, textiles, or housing. All that would have to wait. Russia might go hungry, clothe her people in rags, and live in terribly crowded cities, but she would produce steel or die.

Collectivization proceeded apace and was 93 percent complete by 1937. This was called a great victory although the gross annual yields of crops were substantially lower than those obtained during the first plan and were far below 1913 yields. Grain production declined, meat production remained at low levels, and it was difficult to find vegetables and fruits in the cities.

On April 1, 1937, Stalin declared the second plan fulfilled. Despite all the hardships, Russia had in most important respects fulfilled the goals and tasks laid down by the party. The country was well on its way to becoming a great industrial power.

## STAKHANOVISM

During a five-hour, 45-minute work shift at a Donbas coal mine on the night of August 30–31, 1935, a miner named Aleksei Stakhanov allegedly mined 102 tons of coal, 14 times the standard output. Because the Soviet Union was in the middle of the second Five-Year Plan, the success of which was predicated on a dramatic increase in labor productivity, government and party seized on Stakhanov's feat as proof that the quotas were realistic.

There were widespread rumors that the record was rigged. Stakhanov used the new OM-5 pneumatic drill, he had several helpers, and party officials and the press were present to witness and record his feat. But no matter what the circumstances, Stalin used the publicity to launch a campaign to increase labor productivity. A "Stakhanovite movement" took shape overnight (one indication that there was less to Stakhanov's exploits than met the eye) and a conference of "Stakhanovite workers" was held in Moscow in November 1935. Addressing the participants, Stalin ordered Soviet workers to raise production levels. He accused "bureaucrats" of stifling worker initiative—a terribly ominous comment in 1935—and the planning agencies of setting industrial goals too low. Gosplan revised its quotas upward.

The party's aggressive support of Stakhanovism gave further proof that the Revolution was dead. The Bolsheviks had come to power on a wave of leveling and egalitarianism; that was abandoned as competition and rewards came back into vogue. Stakhanovite collective farmers raised more crops, locomotive engineers increased the average speed of their trains, steelworkers produced more steel, teachers taught more students better, fishermen caught more fish—at least, that was the way it appeared in the media, which exhorted the work force to emulate the superachievers. Now there were material incentives; the press publicized the shopping sprees of the Stakhanovites, who received cash awards for their prodigious feats.

The propaganda machine claimed that these enthusiastic workers were the examples of the "new Soviet man," that unselfish, herioc worker in the service of socialism. Soon, *Pravda* and the other newspapers declared, all Soviet workers would be like them. In actual fact many industrial zealots were beaten up and even killed by their fellow workers. A famous joke involved an awards ceremony at a kolhoz. For her exemplary service a milkmaid wins a trip to Moscow. Polite applause from the assembled kolhozniks. A tractor-driver gets a new suit for working a series of 102-hour workweeks during the harvest. More applause.

The kolhoz manager who directed these efforts receives an autographed set of Stalin's works. Silence. Then a voice calls out, "Serves the sonofabitch right!"

There were real and bogus Stakhanovites, and there were "shock workers" who "stormed" jobs and accomplished them at superhuman speed. One of Zoshchenko's characters demands, "Sleep quickly—somebody else needs the pillow!"

Some sham in the Stakhanovite movement notwithstanding, labor productivity increased significantly during the second plan. To be sure, the figures were juggled to show that, over the four years and three months of the plan, productivity increased by 82 percent instead of the projected 63 percent. Western experts have established that the projected increase, far from being surpassed, was not even achieved, and that the true annual growth rate was probably between 8 and 10 percent. This was itself an impressive figure, one not matched in the capitalist economies of the day.

## THIRD FIVE-YEAR PLAN

In March 1939 the 18th Party Congress approved the third Five-Year Plan for 1938–1942. Party propaganda claimed that the foundations of a socialist economy had been fully laid. The world would soon learn what Stalin meant when he declared, "Life has become better, comrades, life has become merrier."

Communists lost no opportunity to contrast the situation in the Soviet Union with that in the West, where the Great Depression had seized capitalist economies in a savage grip that was to be broken only by war. The Soviet government advertised in the West for technicians, engineers, skilled and even unskilled workers. A special effort was made to reach American blacks, a few hundred of whom actually went to the Soviet Union to settle. Of their number, several score went to Abkhazia in the Caucasus to join small communities of descendants of African slaves brought to Russia in the 18th century. There was no unemployment in the land of communism, the advertisements declared, no bread lines. There was no plowing under of crops or slaughtering of animals to raise farm prices as in the United States. That was true. The advertisements said nothing about the famine of 1932 to 1933.

The 18th Congress promised that the new plan would invest more heavily in the consumer-goods sector. The achievements of the first two plans had made this possible, the party declared; the people deserved some rewards. Special attention would be paid to housing. The plan provided for construction of 35 million square meters of living space. That figure was impressive; but even if it had been achieved and doubled, the Soviet people would have remained the worst-housed of any industrialized nation. Osip Mandelstam's wife, Nadezhda, recalled how people would commit crimes for those "wonderful, precious twelve and a half square meters of living space." That was the minimum Lenin had decreed. In Moscow in the 1930s people had less than half that.

The population of the capital almost doubled between 1926 and 1939, to 4,542,000. It was overcrowded at the start of the period, and by the end half of Moscow was sleeping in shifts in dormitories. Between January 1933 and January 1939 the number of inhabitants increased by 878,000. According to official statistics, 1.8 million square meters of living space were constructed in the period 1935–1940. No one has ever claimed that 1933–1934 witnessed the construction of housing on a massive scale; thus, only fractionally more than *two* square meters of living space were provided for

each new inhabitant 1935–1940. What this did to existing conditions is obvious. Moscow was far and away the most favored of all Soviet cities.

The third Five-Year Plan provided for a modest increase in funds allocated to the consumer-goods sector, but the overwhelming emphasis continued to be on heavy industry. The production of pig iron and steel once again increased dramatically as new plants were brought into production. The mining operations which produced raw ores likewise registered substantial gains. The chemical and automotive industries developed in a series of great leaps, but because they had started at nearly zero the country remained undersupplied in these areas.

The armaments industry took precedence over all others; although accurate statistics are not available, a sizable increase in production occurred during the first two plans. Even in this vitally important sector, however, the Terror undermined Soviet achievements. Key engineers, designers, production managers, technicians, and others were frequently imprisoned and sometimes executed. A few prominent prisoners, among them the aircraft designer Andrei Tupolev, managed to continue their work in special places of confinement ("sharashkas").

The increasingly menacing international situation diverted funds and resources from the civilian to the military sector of the economy from 1936 onward. It was surprising, all things considered, that this did not take place on a larger scale. The coming of war in 1941 interrupted the third plan.

## 1936 CONSTITUTION

By the middle of the 1930s the public sector had almost totally replaced the private. The number of private farms still in operation was statistically insignificant. Nonagricultural private enterprise had almost ceased to exist: one would have been hard pressed to find anyone who did not work for the state.

Because the public sector now enjoyed a near-total monopoly of production, and because the "exploiting classes" had been liquidated, the rulers of the country decided to replace the existing Constitution with one that would reflect the victory of socialism. A 31-member Constitutional Commission was appointed in February 1935. Stalin was a nominal director; the document the commission produced is known as the "Stalin Constitution." Bukharin, already under unpublished sentence of death, wrote the section on civil rights. The commission prepared a draft and presented it to party officials in the spring of 1936. After some changes, public discussion was invited. An enormous charade was played out as more than 55 percent—according to party propaganda—of the adult population debated the project.

The Eighth (Extraordinary) Congress of Soviets unanimously approved the new Constitution on December 5, 1936. In the midst of the Great Terror, the Communists announced the promulgation of the "most democratic Constitution in the world."

The bicameral legislature remained. The Supreme Soviet of the USSR was divided into co-equal houses, the Soviet of the Union and the Soviet of Nationalities. The Supreme Soviet alone had legislative powers; it was elected directly, by secret ballot.

A socialist bill of rights guaranteed employment, vacations, education, and support in old age, sickness, and disability. Communist spokesmen have long maintained that these guarantees prove the superiority of their system over "bourgeois democracy."

Among the 146 Articles was one (Art. 133) proclaiming defense of the country the "holy obligation of every citizen." Universal military service became the law of the land.

In 1936 there were 11 Union republics: the Russian, Ukrainian, Uzbek, Byelorussian, Tajik, Kazakh, Georgian, Armenian, Turkmenian, Kirgiz, Azerbaijanian. Five new ones were added in 1940–1941, reflecting Soviet conquests: the Karelo-Finnish, Latvian, Lithuanian, Estonian, and Moldavian. The new Constitution guaranteed all the right to secede from the Union.

Finally, the 1936 Constitution spelled out (Art. 126) the "leading role" of the Communist party. That organization was of course the sole political group permitted. Any attempt to create or advocate creation of another party was a criminal act.

On paper the Stalin Constitution was the most democratic in the world. In practice the Communist party continued to exercise its dictatorship over a dragooned population. Any attempt to assert constitutionally guaranteed freedoms constituted anti-Soviet agitation and treason.

## MISSING CENSUS OF 1937

The first Soviet census was taken in 1920 as the Civil War was winding down; the figures were unreliable. In 1926 a second count showed a population of 147,028,000. According to the estimates of Soviet demographers, the January 1937 census should have shown a population in excess of 180 million. In fact, it fell about 30 million short of that.

No juggling of the figures could conceal this. No one had questioned the 1926 census, but if the 1937 figures were released everyone would know that the rumors of millions of deaths during collectivization, the famine of 1932–1933, and the Great Terror, were true. Stalin could not have survived such a disclosure. Had he fallen, the Stalinist party would have fallen with him.

The easiest way out of the dilemma was to suppress the census results and arrest the census directors. On September 26, 1937, *Pravda* charged that "extremely crude violations of the most elementary principles of statistical science" invalidated the January headcount. The highest officials of the Central Statistical Bureau disappeared into the Gulag.

A new census conducted in 1939 reported that the population stood at 182.4 million, but an increase of 30–32 million in two years was not, in the normal course of events, possible. Not even Stalin could orchestrate that kind of activity. The real count, never released, was apparently on the order of 162–165 million. The published figures had far more to do with the dictates of foreign policy and national defense than the actual number of people. The Germans and Japanese had to be shown that a mighty nation had a large and rapidly growing population.

It was by no means certain that Stalin and his men could make the world believe their statistics. It was within their power, however, to take steps to counter the low birth rate.

The state had legalized abortion in 1920; no one had then thought of the effect on industrialization and national defense. An analysis of the 1926 census data, however, showed that trouble lay ahead, and this was before anyone had any inkling of the horrors of 1929–1938. Certain annoying but not insurmountable restrictions were imposed. Women had to fill out a more detailed and meddlesome questionnaire and pay a small fee for the abortion. The birth rate did not rise.

In May 1936 *Pravda* published the draft text of a law banning all save therapeutic abortions and called for a nationwide discussion. Letters came in criticizing women who regarded "the issue of child-bearing as a personal matter." There were other objections of both a political and moral nature. Many women, however, called attention to the difficulties of raising children in the pioneering days of the Five-Year Plans: housing was almost impossible to find; there were only a few day-care centers; and the mobility of the urban population made it easy for husbands and fathers who tired of a relationship to skip town.

The party had not anticipated objections. The discussion was therefore terminated and the law promulgated on June 9, 1936. The birth rate soared in 1937 and remained high until the war came. As a Soviet newspaper admitted in 1968, however, there was also a sharp increase in illegal abortions, which in turn led to a dangerous rise in the number of women suffering from chronic diseases and secondary sterility.

## EDUCATION AND SCIENCE

In the realm of education, including special efforts to liquidate illiteracy, the Communists made great progress. The aggregate literacy rate stood at 81 percent in 1939, up from 51 percent in 1926. The increase in literacy among females was particularly striking; it reflected the special attention paid to the Muslim lands, where women were traditionally kept in servitude, and to rural Russia and the Ukraine.

By the mid-1930s the teachers' colleges had produced thousands of young teachers. The professors who taught them were often graduates (inelegantly known as "Ikapisty") of the Institute of the Red Professoriat; the most famous was party theoretician Mikhail Suslov. Students in the teachers' colleges were thoroughly indoctrinated in Marxism-Leninism. In the natural and physical sciences and mathematics this generally involved no more than a perfunctory nod toward official ideology. In the humanities and social sciences, however, textbooks were rewritten to reflect party policy, teachers were closely observed, and the strictest hiring procedures were followed.

There was a shortage of teachers which the colleges only slowly reduced. Primary and secondary education was not a glamorous field, and only a small minority of graduates from the universities, which enjoyed much greater prestige than the teachers' colleges, entered it. For example, 55 percent of Moscow University graduates in the 1934–1938 period went into industry; 10 percent into the commissariat of agriculture and other agencies in that field; and 17 percent went into primary and secondary education. The remainder went elsewhere in the bureaucracy, higher education, and research.

The Great Terror struck the universities and institutes with terrible force. A commission to review higher education was established under A. A. Zhdanov in May 1935; it supervised a massive purge which swept thousands of people into the Gulag. Many institutes and laboratories were closed; and in 1936 both the Communist University of the Toilers of the East (KUTV) and the Communist University of the Toilers of China (KUTK) ceased to exist.

The year 1935 marked a turning point in scientific research in the Soviet Union. Until that year the government had given far more support to genuine scientists than to the impostors distinguished only for their obedience to Stalin. The Academy of Sciences, one of the most prestigious institutions in the world and the least "bolshevized" professional group in the USSR, won a 676 percent increase in its budget in the second Five-Year Plan. These funds, 63.765 million rubles, were allocated to genuine research. In 1935, however, when the "Kirov wave" caught up many scientists and scholars, the purgers began to apply an ideological test not only to individuals but to their disciplines as well.

The most notorious and devastating attacks of the pseudoscientists and their backers in the party came in biology, the agricultural sciences, and genetics. The attacks caused enormous damage in the first two fields and destroyed Soviet genetics for a generation. Many prominent scientists, some of world caliber, disappeared into the Gulag.

The main culprit—never forgetting, however, who captained the ship—was Trofim Lysenko, a Ukrainian crackpot with a spotty education, surpassing ignorance in the fields in which he claimed expertise, and the good fortune to be available when the Communist party needed someone to argue for lunatic theories. Lysenko came to stand in the same relationship to science that Vyshinsky did to justice.

Lysenko argued that acquired characteristics are heritable. If the environment produces a change, the offspring of the species in question will reproduce that change. For example, properly controlled vernalization could turn winter wheat into spring wheat. Lysenko declared that he could turn a baser grain such as rye into wheat, a pine into a spruce.

The genetic theories of heredity worked out by Gregor Mendel, August Weismann, and T.H. Morgan were jettisoned in a return to the theories of J.-B. Lamarck, who had insisted that changes undergone by an individual—the result of its habits or its environment—could be passed on to that individual's offspring over time. Lamarckism claims, for example, that the giraffe's long neck and forelegs come from ancestors who stretched to feed on the leaves of trees.

Although most scientists had long since abandoned this position, Lysenko, backed by a party which needed to demonstrate communism's ability to create an environment that could change mankind, enshrined it in the Soviet Union in the 1930s and 1940s. Soviet scientists either accepted it or left science. If they resisted, or if their prestige and expertise seemed to threaten Lysenko, they went to the Gulag. Such was the fate of Nikolai Vavilov, director of the Genetics Institute and a scientist with an international reputation. Lysenko engineered the ouster of this man of learning from his institute, which was soon closed down (along with genetics as a field), then prevailed on the NKVD to arrest him. Vavilov died in a forced-labor camp in 1943.

## THE ARTS

At the height of the Great Terror, in 1937 Dmitri Shostakovich composed his somber Fifth Symphony. The first performance took place the same year in Leningrad, the city that had suffered more than any other from Stalin's purges. Many people in the audience openly wept. A few were perhaps thinking of Kafka's words, "There is infinite hope, but not for us."

The most gifted of the 20th-century Russian composers (excluding from consideration the émigré genius Stravinsky), Shostakovich was fortunate to be alive to compose that musical tribute—as he later acknowledged—to the victims of the Great Terror. Early in 1936, Stalin attended a performance of his new opera, *Lady Macbeth of the Mtsensk District,* and did not like what he heard. On January 28 a *Pravda* editorial called "Muddle Instead of Music" attacked the opera and branded Shostakovich an "enemy of the people."

In those days people so labeled disappeared. Fortunately Shostakovich survived, even after his close friend Marshal Tukhachevsky was condemned and shot. The party inquisitors hurled the charge of "bourgeois formalism" at Shostakovich and other composers, and accused them of "insincerity." These terms had no meaning.

In literature, the party called for "socialist realism." This seemed to mean that literature had to glorify socialism. It had to tell not the literal truth—people were shot for that—but Stalinist-communist truth. All heroes had to be Communists or occasionally nonparty people who owed their good qualities and good fortune to "Soviet power." Unacceptable behavior had to be depicted as the relic of tsarist times or evidence of the penetration of foreign ideas.

Few novels of lasting merit appeared in the USSR in the 1930s, and the situation was worse in poetry. Boris Pasternak was silent, Anna Akhmatova could not write, and Marina Tsvetayeva was starving in Paris. Osip Mandelstam went to prison in 1934 for writing a poem savagely critical of Stalin.

It is necessary to stress the point that Mandelstam did not *publish* the poem; that would have occasioned as much consternation as an offer from Stalin to abdicate in Trotsky's favor. He read it at a private gathering of friends, and it quickly made its way around Moscow and Leningrad in typescript. Mandelstam was arrested, then on Bukharin's intervention released under surveillance. He and his wife spent the next few years in exile in Voronezh, forbidden to go anywhere without police permission. On May 1, 1938, they arrested him again.

The man most critics consider the greatest Russian poet of the century was swallowed up by the Gulag. He died in eastern Siberia on December 27, 1938. Nadezhda Mandelstam eventually received his death certificate. So far as she knew, no other prisoner's spouse ever received such a document.

The party demanded conformity and many people loosely called writers obeyed. The most popular was Nikolai Ostrovsky, a personally decent fellow of modest talent. His *The Tempering of the Steel* (1932–1934) sold 5 million copies. Confined to bed with polyarthritis, Ostrovsky created a hero,

Pavel Korchagin, who overcame wounds and illness to play a socially useful role in the creation of Soviet society. As his native Ukrainian town fights the ravages of war, foreign invasion, civil war, and the banditry of nationalist gangs, so Korchagin triumphs over the forces that threaten to destroy him. Korchagin's exploits were designed not to feather his own nest but to contribute to the betterment of society.

One of the best novels dealing with the collectivization of agriculture was Mikhail Sholokhov's *Virgin Soil Upturned,* originally called *With Blood and Sweat.* Although not on an artistic par with *Quiet Flows the Don,* the new work caught the spirit of the coming of the Revolution to the countryside. Other popular novels about collectivization were Fyodor Panferov's *Whetstone* and Vladimir Stavsky's *Running Start.*

A novel dealing with the Five-Year Plans was Leonid Leonov's *Soviet River.* The story revolves around attempts to construct lumber camps and paper mills on the banks of a pristine northern river. Struggling against the hostility and obscurantism of the local inhabitants and against the elements, idealistic young Communists emerge victorious over considerable odds.

A capable writer was Valentin Katayev, whose *Time Forward* tried to integrate technology into fiction in the way "rural" prose sought to make the land a major element in the story line. An under-equipped, badly housed, wretchedly fed labor brigade trying to build a steel plant in the Urals undertakes a crash program to set a new construction record. The race is ostensibly against a Harkov brigade, but readers did not fail to grasp the real message: Russia must catch up with potential enemies.

Few artistically commendable films appeared in the USSR between 1930 and 1957. An art form which had flourished in the 1920s found itself forced to produce works that generally amounted to little more than *Pravda* on film. One of the first films with sound was Nikolai Ekk's *Road to Life* (1931), which dealt in a technically interesting but excessively sentimental manner with the homeless waifs (*besprizorniki*) of the postwar era. The first real commercial success of the Soviet cinema was *Chapayev* (1934), a fictionalized biography of a minor Civil War hero. The film treatment of Vasili Ivanovich Chapayev, incidentally, spawned the "Vasili Ivanovich" genre of simple-soldier jokes that has lost little of its vigor.

Each of the three major state film companies produced one better than average propaganda film in this period. Moscow Film released *We Are From Kronstadt* in 1936, Leningrad Film did *Baltic Deputy* in 1937, and Kiev Studio produced *Shchors* in 1939. Moscow Film did the major work for the 20th anniversary of the Revolution, *Lenin in October,* which represented a quantum leap backward in comparison with Sergei Eisenstein's classic *October* (1927). Stalin was nowhere to be seen in the Eisenstein film, while in the 1937 work his role loomed larger than that of Lenin.

In no small measure because of Stalin's personal interference, the two-part *Peter the First* (1937, 1939) was merely an interesting failure. But in 1938 Eisenstein produced *Aleksandr Nevsky,* the story of the 13th-century Russian triumph over the invading Teutonic knights. Like *Professor Mamlock* of the same year, it was meant as a warning to the Germans. *Nevsky,* however, for which Sergei Prokofiev wrote a fine score, went beyond propaganda to win recognition as a film classic.

Sergei Eisenstein's *Bezhin Meadow* was surely an interesting film from a political standpoint, but we know almost nothing about it. Someone in authority, probably Stalin himself, ordered it destroyed. The film was a blend of a Turgenev short story and the saga of one of the Communist party's favorite children, Pavlik Morozov. Young Morozov had denounced his father for plotting to sabotage the harvest. The father was arrested and disappeared. In September 1932 Pavlik and his younger brother were lynched by outraged local peasants, friends of the elder Morozov.

This was a time when the drive for complete collectivization was approaching its final stages; the party jumped into the affair and commissioned a film. Eisenstein depicted Pavlik Morozov as a Christ-like figure. No doubt because party leaders realized that the public would find this unacceptable, the film was destroyed. A "première" consisting of stills and montages was held in Moscow in January 1968, but it is evidently impossible to find any prints of the real film. Not until 1987 did the Communist party strip Pavlik Morozov of his martyrdom.

This was not the decade of the artist, or perhaps in a perverted sense, it was. We have recorded the tragic fate of Osip Mandelstam, the most talented of the poets. Maksim Gorky died in 1936 undergoing "medical treatment" at Communist party orders. Anna Akhmatova's son, Lev Gumilyov, whose father was shot as a White Guard in 1921, was arrested several times and finally sent to the Gulag. His only crime was to be the son of poets the Communists detested. Akhmatova wrote the first poem in the cycle *Requiem* on her son's first arrest in 1935; these poems expressed the agony of the millions of Soviet women whose sons, husbands, and fathers disappeared into the Gulag. The writer Lidiya Chukovskaya's husband was arrested and shot, apparently because he had the same surname (Bronstein) as Trotsky. Vsevolod Meyerhold saw his theatre closed down in 1938 and his world collapse around him. He was tried in 1940, convicted and shot as an agent of Japan. His wife was murdered by the NKVD.

## LIFE IN THE 1930s

The huge granite and marble Lenin Mausoleum on Red Square was opened to the public in 1930. The dead founder's embalmed corpse, under glass and bathed in an odd orange-blue light, would be seen by scores of millions of people over the next half-century. It is communism's holiest shrine.

In 1931 the Communists dynamited the Cathedral of Christ the Savior near the Kremlin, destroying the view from the apartment of Boris Pasternak's parents. Built a century earlier to commemorate the victory over Napoleon, it was leveled to make way for a proposed Palace of Soviets, a gigantic, 320-meter tall structure atop which a 100-meter statue of Lenin was to perch. Fortunately for the city's skyline the structure was never built. A swimming pool now occupies the site.

Plans materialized in 1931 for the Moscow Metropolitan, or subway. Because there was only one interest group, the party, whose views had to be taken into account, municipal officials had no difficulty in agreeing on underground transportation as the best way to move a huge population from one point to another.

Work began in 1932; one of the directors was Nikita Khrushchev. In May 1935 the initial 11.5 kilometer-line opened to the public. The Soviets trumpeted this achievement as a great victory and proof of the superiority of socialism. The 11-kilometer Berlin subway had been six years in the building; 20 kilometers in New York took seven years; and the four-kilometer Tokyo subway—four years. The Metro was indeed a splendid accomplishment. The people of the capital were badly housed and fed in the 1930s, but after the subway was built they went about the city in comfort and style.

The subway was originally named after

Kaganovich, one of Stalin's closest associates. Private citizens could show love for the leaders who gave them the subway and all good things in life by naming their children after them, and millions did. It became the fashion to name girls Oktyabrina (from October) and Stalinka, boys Vladlen and Vilen (acronyms), sometimes Vil (Lenin's initials), and sometimes Ninel (Lenin backward). This fad began right after the Revolution but seemed to grow in direct proportion to the development of Stalin's dictatorship after 1924. No one knows how many male infants were named Melsor: Marx, Engels, Lenin, Stalin, October Revolution. When Khrushchev demythologized Stalin this name became Melor. One colorful coinage was Parlikder, an acronym for a Communist slogan, "The party face-to-face with the countryside," and Redema stood for "Revolutionary Youth Day." In the period of the Five-Year Plans, many parents named their children Traktor, Turbina, and Renat, for Revolutsiya, Nauka, Trud—Revolution, Science, Labor. Some children were saddled with the name Five-Year-Plan-in-Four. The situation got further out of hand in Armenia, where some parents, evidently uneducated people who misunderstood Communist party slogans, called children by such names as Embrion (Embryo), Vinegret (Vinaigrette), and even in one case Dizenteriya (Dysentery).

This mania extended to the towns. Municipalities were renamed Stalinabad, Stalingrad, Stalingradsky, Staliniri, Stalinka, Stalino (seven of these), Stalinsk, Stalinsky, Stalinskoye, Stalinogorsk. There were others: Zinovievsk proved to be an embarrassment and had to revert to the original Yelizavetgrad, only to be renamed Kirovgrad to demonstrate Stalin's love for his late deputy. Kamenevsk and Yezhovsk had to go, as did the names of many other towns. Ordzhonikidze, Frunze, Kuibyshev, and other municipalities kept their new names

even after Stalin engineered the murders of his former friends. All 16 cities named after Stalin, along with those called Molotov and Voroshilovgrad, would bear their names until the last, Stalingrad, became Volgograd in 1961.

An internal passport system went into effect in December 1932. Urban dwellers had to obtain a passport, an identification document valid only for domestic purposes, at the age of 16 and renew it at five-year intervals. It was mandatory for interurban travel and had to be presented on the demand of the authorities, the management of a workplace, and in certain other situations. Each time a citizen went to the militia (regular police) to obtain the five-year stamp, he or she was subject to scrutiny. Nadezhda Mandelstam renewed her passport in 1938 and lost the right to live in Moscow; the militia simply refused to validate the document for residence in the city. She waited 28 years for a new stamp for Moscow.

The largest and most important category of people exempt from passport regulations was the peasantry. That meant that peasants could not leave the kolhozes or sovhozes without special permission. To ensure a stable agricultural labor force, that permission was rarely granted. Only in 1974 did the government consent to give peasants passports and thus the right to travel freely and change their place of residence. The issuance of new passports actually began in 1976 and was completed early in 1982.

The Romanov doubled-headed eagles did not come down from the Kremlin spires until 1937. On the 20th anniversary of the Bolshevik Revolution, they gave way to heavy glass, illuminated red stars. The changing of public symbols was accompanied by innovations in private homes. Devout Communists, and people who hoped to stay out of trouble, replaced the ancient icon corner with the Lenin or red corner. A photograph of Lenin, in the 1930s often replaced by one of Stalin, stood in place of the icons on a small table covered by a red cloth. A candle was lit near the photograph when guests were expected, or feared. A volume of the works of one or the other of the leaders was also on the table, passages underlined to demonstrate close attention to the text. It is inconceivable that the NKVD was ever deterred by these displays of piety.

The Soviet people withdrew into themselves in the 1930s. One could not trust one's neighbors; they might be plotting a denunciation to the secret police in the hope of obtaining one's apartment. That happened to hundreds of thousands of people. Nor could one always trust one's children, who were taught in the schools and Young Pioneer meetings to sing songs of praise to Lenin and Stalin, and to recite every day, "Thank you, dear Stalin, for our happy childhood."

People protected themselves from listening devices and against the possibility that there was an informer in the group by offering the first toast at parties "To those who have given us such a happy life!" It was almost the only joke that could be told in public.

The wonder is that there were any jokes at all; life was so very grim. One was assailed on all sides by fear—thick, sticky fear that never went away. The party's motto was "Persuade by propaganda, coerce by terror." What hope could there be for a regime that taught schoolchildren hate ditties?

A bad kulak, *he's* our foe,
A good kulak?—The *same*, don'cha know!

Hope was for others. Only fear and work were left to the citizens of the USSR. Above the gates of some of the Gulag's camps were the words, "Work is honorable, glorious, valiant, and heroic." This had the same ring as the inscription over the gates of Nazi concentration camps: *"Arbeit macht frei!"* (Work liberates!). A German Communist poet, Erich Mühsam, who was in one of Hitler's camps at the same time that his wife was in the Gulag, observed that Stalin was just "Hitler plus Asia."

## SUGGESTED ADDITIONAL READING

**Badash, Lawrence,** *Kapitza, Rutherford, and the Kremlin,* New Haven, Conn.: Yale University Press, 1985

**Bailes, Kendall E.,** *Technology and Society under Lenin and Stalin,* Princeton, N.J.: Princeton University Press, 1978

**Benet, Sula, ed.,** *The Village of Viriatino,* Garden City, N.Y.: Anchor Books, 1970

**Ciliga, Anton,** *The Russian Enigma,* London: Labour Book Service, 1940

**Conquest, Robert,** *The Harvest of Sorrow: Soviet Collectivization and the Terror-Famine,* New York: Oxford University Press, 1986

**Dolot, Miron,** *Execution by Hunger: The Hidden Holocaust,* New York: W.W. Norton, 1985

**Fainsod, Merle,** *Smolensk under Soviet Rule,* New York: Vintage Books, 1963

**Graham, Loren R.,** *The Soviet Academy of Sciences and the Communist Party, 1927–1932,* Princeton, N.J.: Princeton University Press, 1967

**Huskey, Eugene,** *Russian Lawyers and the Soviet State: The Origins and Development of the Soviet Bar, 1917–1939,* Princeton, N.J.: Princeton University Press, 1986

**Makarenko, A.S.,** *The Collective Family: A Handbook for Soviet Parents,* Garden City, N.Y.: Anchor Books, 1967

**Mandelstam, Nadezhda,** *Hope Against Hope,* New York: Atheneum, 1970

**Oleskin, Stephen,** *The Agony of a Nation: The Great Man-Made Famine in Ukraine, 1932–1933,* London: Ukrainian Publishers, 1983

**Rigby, T.H., ed.,** *Stalin,* Englewood Cliffs, N.J.: Prentice-Hall, 1966

**Robinson, Robert,** *Black on Red: My 44 Years Inside the Soviet Union,* Washington: Acropolis Books, 1988

**Scott, John,** *Behind the Urals,* Bloomington: Indiana University Press, 1973

**Siegelbaum, Lewis H.,** *Stakhanovism and the Politics of Productivity in the USSR, 1935–1941,* New York: Cambridge University Press, 1988

**Starr, S. Frederick,** *Red and Hot: The Fate of Jazz in the Soviet Union, 1917–1980,* New York: Oxford University Press, 1983

**Sutton, Antony C.,** *Western Technology and Soviet Economic Development, 1930–1945,* Stanford, Calif.: Hoover Institution Press, 1971

# 11

# FOREIGN POLICY
# IN THE 1930s

A conservative foreign policy accompanied the revolutionary social and economic upheaval of the Five-Year Plans. The Bolshevik dream of a world-wide proletarian revolution was shelved indefinitely as the Soviet Union proceeded along the path of constructing "socialism in one country," the great issue on which Stalin had defeated Trotsky. The Stalinists declared "proletarian internationalism" still valid but devoid of practical significance until the socialist mother country built an invulnerable military and industrial base.

When the Great Depression struck the industrialized countries in 1929, stock markets collapsed, governments fell, factories closed, unemployment reached unprecedented levels. Predictions of capitalism's collapse suddenly appeared frighteningly accurate. Countries which had weathered the

revolutionary uprisings—aftershocks of the October Revolution—of the post–World War I period now braced for a new onslaught of demands for radical economic and social change, change which could only come after the transfer by whatever means of power to a party offering radical alternatives.

Only in Germany did this happen. Great Britain weathered the crisis with its political institutions intact; France's Third Republic managed to get through the 1930s in relatively good health; Italy had been Fascist since 1922 and remained the poorest of the major nations. The United States undertook a series of economic and social innovations radical only when measured against the unbridled capitalism of the past.

Their predictions notwithstanding, the 1929 collapse caught the Communists by surprise. Preoccupied with internal problems, notably the great economic experiment, the Soviet Union was unable to exploit capitalism's most severe crisis. This could not be helped, but no amount of rationalizing could conceal the fact that the most propitious moment in history for the Communist cause had passed Stalin's party by.

## SIXTH COMINTERN CONGRESS

After the 1927 fiasco in China the Soviet Union was obliged to undertake a thorough review of its foreign policy. The premises on which that policy was based proved false. There would be no worldwide uprising of the proletariat. Cooperation with bourgeois parties such as the Chinese Guomindang represented an exceedingly dangerous gamble. The USSR had no reliable friends.

The fruits of the reevaluation were revealed at the Sixth Congress of the Communist International in Moscow in July 1928. Present were 515 delegates from 57 countries representing 50 active Communist parties and 15 unofficial Communist groups and organizations. It is difficult to estimate the number of party members and sympathizers these delegates represented; excluding the Soviet party the total cannot have been more than a few hundred thousand.

This was the first Comintern Congress since 1924, thus the first since the settling of the Soviet succession question. It came soon after the disaster in China produced by Stalin's insistence on cooperation with the Guomindang, a policy Trotsky condemned. But as Stalin had defeated Trotsky only to reverse himself and adopt a super-industrialization policy, so he now turned the Comintern sharply to the left, declaring that there would be no more cooperation with bourgeois parties.

The new Comintern policy called for a "united front from below." Communists would ally with the rank and file of other leftist parties but would not cooperate with the leadership. The policy was adopted because, the Kremlin insisted, there was no significant difference between Fascist dictatorship and bourgeois democracy. No democratic regime was worth defending, even against the threat of a Fascist takeover.

In 1928 there seemed little likelihood that any major country would be threatened by fascism. Some smaller nations were headed in that direction, but no one sensed a general threat. The Comintern virtually ignored the German National Socialist Workers' Party (Nazis) of Adolf Hitler, which then held only 12 of the nearly 500 seats in the Reichstag. The main enemy of the German working class, the Comintern declared, was the German Social Democrats, the world's oldest Marxist party.

## GERMANY

From 1930 on, Soviet propaganda insisted that "the road to a Soviet Germany lay through Hitler." The Soviets were convinced that the crisis of capitalism had finally spewed forth the dregs of that system, the Nazis. Once Hitler and his thugs and street fighters came to power, the universal disgust they would inspire would leave Germany no one to turn to but the Communists.

This naive reading of German politics arose from the same assumption that had already produced disaster in China, namely, that every nation's history followed Russian patterns. Believing that one pervert was pretty much like another, Stalin saw Hitler as a kind of German Rasputin, his party as the analogue of the jaded Russian gentry. He fatally underestimated the revolutionary nature of nazism.

Stalin and his associates needed a year to

come to their senses about Hitler; the process took considerably longer for many Western politicians. In the interim the Soviet leader was not as concerned about the Nazis as about the Japanese menace in the Far East, and to a lesser extent about winning diplomatic recognition from the new Roosevelt administration. These two apparently unrelated phenomena were in fact closely linked; the United States was also concerned about Japanese expansion in Asia.

The German-Polish nonaggression pact of January 1934 made reexamination of Moscow's Germany policy imperative. (The agreement also stunned France, whose Eastern alliance system began to collapse.) The Soviets themselves had signed a similar pact with Poland in 1932, but their fears were genuine.

The agreement between Germany and Poland raised the distinct possibility that the bitter dispute over the Polish Corridor, a strip through German territory giving Poland access to the Baltic, would be resolved peacefully. That, in turn, raised the specter of German-Polish cooperation aimed against the USSR. Poland was then governed by a military junta about as anti-Soviet and anti-Semitic as Hitler's Nazis. No nonaggression pact between Poland and the Soviet Union would stand in the way of a joint Warsaw-Berlin decision to settle old scores with the Communists.

The Soviet Union's leaders now labelled Germany the major threat. Great Britain no longer held that position and was indeed a potential ally. The Soviets redoubled their efforts to achieve collective security.

## THE LEAGUE AND THE APPEASERS

The new Soviet state had been excluded from the League of Nations at its founding, and later, when the organization offered admission in return for concessions, Moscow spurned the overture. In the 1920s the Soviets called the League merely another capitalist alliance, the goal of which was the overthrow of the Soviet regime. Hitler's accession to power changed both Soviet and League attitudes.

Japan withdrew from the League of Nations after being branded an aggressor for the 1931 invasion of the Chinese province of Manchuria. Hitler took Germany out of the organization in the autumn of 1933. The Soviet Union became a member in September 1934.

The League was then in the midst of an International Disarmament Conference. Initially, 63 nations participated; nine, including the Soviet Union and the United States, were not League members. When he pulled out of the international organization in 1933, Hitler also left the Disarmament Conference, ensuring its failure.

Represented by Comissar of Foreign Affairs (since 1930) Litvinov, the Soviet Union called upon the Conference and the League to persuade nations to undertake immediate and total disarmament. The other delegations rejected this proposal out of hand. Litvinov then proposed that the League at least define the term "aggression" in order to expedite measures to halt it. That proposal too failed; but in October 1935 the other delegations joined the Soviets in denouncing the Italian attack on defenseless Ethiopia. The Western nations, however, refused to impose an oil embargo against Italy and successfully emasculated other sanctions voted by the League. Italy proclaimed the annexation of Ethiopia in May 1936 and two months later the League abandoned any pretense of indignation.

An organization powerless to stop Mussolini was paralyzed when confronted with the necessity of disciplining Germany. In March 1936 Hitler took his greatest gamble in sending troops into the demilitarized Rhineland. His excuse was that Germany's security was threatened by the 1935 mutual assistance treaty which the USSR and France had just negotiated.

The League of Nations and the world in general looked on with indifference as Hitler's soldiers trampled the Versailles settlement into the dust. Many people argued that Germany had been dealt with harshly at Versailles—no one mentioned the Treaty of Brest-Litovsk—and that she had legitimate security needs. Who could reasonably expect Germany not to post armed forces along the great river that was her main economic artery?

Alone among the leaders of major nations, Stalin regarded the reoccupation of the Rhineland as a grave threat to peace. He knew that this action was indeed Hitler's last demand geographically and psychologically centered in the West. The Nazi dictator's remaining objectives lay in Central and Eastern Europe, in the direction of the USSR.

The idea of striking a deal with Hitler had apparently been germinating in the Gensek's mind for some time, and now it began to take definite shape. The West had not responded to the Soviet calls for disarmament and collective security; Stalin would have to try something else.

Passively accepting the reoccupation of the Rhineland, Western politicians passed the point of no return on the road to appeasement. Moreover, the appeasers did not admit, to the public or even to themselves, that the policy was a gamble. British Prime Minister Neville Chamberlain, and the French leaders Pierre Laval and Edouard Daladier, made the mistake of banking everything on appeasement; they had no alternative to offer. If this course failed, disaster loomed.

The Soviets have always claimed that the appeasers wanted Hitler to satisfy his appetite at the expense of the USSR. Some Western observers have scoffed at this, arguing that the West was contemptuous of Soviet power in the 1930s and had no reason to work for its destruction. That presumably means that the West was no more interested in overthrowing the Soviet regime than it had been in 1918–1920.

Few conservatives—Churchill was the major exception—saw any Nazi danger even after the Rhineland episode. Hitler had coped with the Depression more successfully than anyone else. He had restored Germany's dignity and brutally suppressed the Communist party. No amount of second thoughts generated by World War II can conceal the fact that Hitler was almost as popular in the West as he was in Germany 1933–1939.

The European Left detested Hitler and the Nazis, but it was disunited. The Soviet Union was partly to blame; the myopic Comintern policy toward the German Social Democrats helped pave the way for Hitler's accession to power as surely as did the considerable support—just how much is a matter of intense historical debate—the German industrialists gave the Nazi party. When the Soviets finally recognized the dimensions of the Nazi threat, they called for an alliance of all anti-Nazi and anti-Fascist parties. The union of the Left that resulted became known as the Popular Front.

## THE SPANISH CIVIL WAR

The Spanish Popular Front of Socialists, Syndicalists, Republicans, and Communists came to power in the February 1936 elections. This was the first Popular Front government; the French version appeared four months later. The conservative Spanish parties, the military, and the Catholic Church united against the Leftist alliance in Madrid. A number of army commanders rebelled in

July; their revolt quickly spread, and a Junta of National Defense was established at Burgos.

Spain quickly became the testing-ground for the rival dictatorial systems. In October-November 1936 the German, Italian, and Japanese governments concluded a series of bilateral agreements known collectively as the Anti-Comintern Pact. The three "Axis" powers pledged themselves to combat communism at home and abroad; to Germany and Italy, that meant sending aid to the Spanish Falange (Fascists). Hitler and Mussolini despatched thousands of "volunteers" to fight for insurgents led by Generals Francisco Franco and Emilio Mola.

Britain and France banned the shipment of war matériel to Spain's democratically elected government on the grounds that they wished to limit the conflict—which had already spread as far as Berlin, Rome, and Moscow. Whitehall and the Quai d'Orsay seemed to signal preference for the Fascists.

Beset with domestic problems, the Soviets would have preferred to stay out of Spain, but the actions of Germany and Italy and the prejudicial inaction of France and Britain gave them little choice. The Soviet Union did not permit its citizens to fight in Spain, but it did send arms, ammunition, and several thousand military-political advisers.

Such key operations as counterintelligence, censorship, and communications quickly came under Soviet control. Arms and ammunition poured in by ship from Odessa; the Spanish gold reserve was sent to the USSR for safekeeping and to pay for the aid. In the beginning all this was in good faith. In 1936 and early 1937 Soviet intervention saved Madrid. It also cost the Spanish Republic all 500 tons of its gold.

Soviet aid to the Spanish Loyalists tapered off toward the end of February 1937; Stalin evidently changed his policy chiefly because of overwhelming problems at home. It was in this period that Bukharin was arrested and the decision made to try him at an appropriate time.

All the prominent victims of the Terror and uncounted others were linked by the secret police to Trotsky and "foreign imperialism." Many Western Trotskyites fought in Spain in the volunteer brigades that came from several countries; the Abraham Lincoln Brigade was largely composed of American supporters of Trotsky. Stalin could not be sure that the virus had not infected Soviet advisers. The NKVD conducted a savage purge on Spanish soil and in the USSR after the men were recalled; thousands were shot. The Spanish Republic was powerless to halt the bloody process.

Some observers have maintained that Stalin backed away from the Loyalist cause because he saw as early as the winter of 1936–1937 that it was doomed. Whether the Soviet dictator was indeed so prescient is open to question; the dictates of the purge were probably foremost in his calculations. Nearly all the advisers who served in Spain perished at the hands of the NKVD.

Stalin backed off, Hitler and Mussolini pressed forward. Democracy and socialism disappeared from Spain for more than three decades when Franco and the Falange triumphed in the spring of 1939.

## MUNICH

In part because he had begun to construct an alliance system in the West, Stalin believed he could afford to let the Spanish Republic fall and not suffer irreparable harm. In 1936 the French parliament ratified the Franco-Soviet mutual assistance pact of May 5, 1935, encouraged because the Soviets had signed a similar one with Czechoslovakia. That pact had one special provision: Moscow would come to Prague's aid only jointly with France.

There seemed no doubt in 1936 that France would honor her commitment in Eastern Europe; the Popular Front government was solidly anti-Nazi and anti-Fascist. France might have acquiesced in the reoccupation of the Rhineland, but she would not let Czechoslovakia, a democratic island in Eastern Europe, go under without a fight.

Czechoslovakia was menaced by Germany on several fronts. Publicly, Hitler spoke loudest about the need to unite all Germans into the new Reich; nearly 3 million ethnic Germans lived in the western part of Czechoslovakia. Those Germans had been included in the Czechoslovak state established in 1919 to give the country a defensible frontier along the ridge of the Sudeten Mountains (hence "Sudeten Germans"). This also had the intended effect of weakening Germany. But now Hitler was in power.

Hitler knew that because of her alliances with France and the Soviet Union, Czechoslovakia would have to be handled with care. Austria was less of a problem. After years of Nazi subversion, propaganda, and violence, Germany annexed that country on March 13, 1938. In an April 10 plebiscite, 99.75 percent of the Austrian voters approved *Anschluss* (annexation).

Hitler seemed invincible, having repeatedly violated solemn treaty obligations without penalty. European politicians were mesmerized by his moves; the more recklessly he acted, the louder the applause. In the summer of 1938 he demanded the dismemberment of Czechoslovakia. There was little doubt that he would get it. The only question was, What will Stalin do?

At the time of the *Anschluss* Stalin had been preoccupied; the last great "show" trial ended on March 15, 1938. Of course, he would not have intervened in the Austrian situation anyway. Russia had been excluded from the Versailles accords that established Austria, and beyond that, Stalin believed

that Hitler had a right to unite all German-speaking people.

Czechoslovakia was another matter. Neville Chamberlain and Edouard Daladier (French premier from April 1938) actually believed that the proposed annexation of the Sudetenland would be Hitler's "last territorial demand in Europe," but Stalin knew better. There were many ethnic Germans in Poland or surrounded by Polish territory (e.g. in the Free City of Danzig and the Corridor); the Nazis had railed about this injustice for years. Hitler was certain to turn to Poland after he settled his quarrel with Czechoslovakia. And after Poland? There were approximately 2.3 million ethnic Germans in the USSR, descendants of colonists invited to Russia in the 18th century by Peter the Great and Catherine the Great.

Neither Stalin nor anyone else expected Hitler to declare war on the Soviet Union for the sake of these Volga Germans. Hitler would attack because the Reich needed room for expansion, food and raw materials, cheap labor. The Volga Germans would merely serve as a pretext.

Preoccupied with the Terror and with reorganization of party, government, military, and economic cadres, Stalin could not devote his full attention to the Nazi menace. He could only hope that the Western democracies would deal more forcefully with Hitler. This did not happen. In the spring of 1938 Hitler told the Sudeten Germans to increase their demands.

Mindful of their treaty obligations but fearful of having to fight alone, the French asked the British to extend a guarantee of aid to Prague. Neville Chamberlain declared that his government neither knew nor wanted to know anything about Czechoslovakia, and that in any event it did not have enough aircraft to intervene.

Great Britain's pro-Nazi ambassador in Berlin, Neville Henderson, urged his government to pressure the Czechoslovaks into accepting Hitler's demands. A British mediator went to Prague in August to convey that message to Prime Minister Eduard Beneš. Beneš continued to hope for support from Paris and Moscow but received only expressions of concern.

The French government did call up about a million reservists in September 1938 in response to large-scale German maneuvers west of the Rhine, and the British admirality prepared a massive display of naval power. Stalin bided his time, faced with the necessity of rebuilding the officer corps he had decimated.

Under orders from Berlin the Sudeten Germans broke off negotiations with Beneš early in September. In a speech at Nürnberg on September 12 Hitler demanded that those Germans be given the right of self-determination. Immediately after he spoke Nazi-orchestrated street violence erupted all over Czechoslovakia. The moment of decision was at hand.

The risk of a general war in Europe was greater than it had been since 1918. Hitler had made it clear that he would fight if his demands were not met. Beneš's government, knowing that Czechoslovakia's strong western defense line could hold the Germans long enough to give France and the USSR time to enter the conflict, was not inclined to cooperate in the liquidation of the country. The Czechoslovaks found it hard to believe that if the survival of their state were in question, the French and British would still insist on appeasing Hitler. And if France and Britain stood up to the Nazi dictator, the USSR was treaty-bound to follow suit.

On September 29 Chamberlain and Daladier flew to Munich to meet with Hitler and his foreign minister, Joachim von Ribbentrop. Mussolini was also present. Czechoslovakia was not represented.

The politicians met at Munich to hear Hitler pronounce sentence; the Reichskanzler was both judge and jury. He knew that the British and French would not fight, and he was aware that French refusal to honor treaty commitments allowed the USSR to stay out of the whole affair. The agreement was signed shortly after midnight. Germany's demands were satisfied in full, and Poland and Hungary were to receive most of the Czech territory they coveted. Rump Czechoslovakia's frontiers would be indefensible; what was left of the state could not survive.

Back in London, Chamberlain informed the world that the Munich agreement spelled "peace in our time." Let Czechoslovakia go under, he said; the rest of us will remain at peace. By an overwhelming margin the British public agreed with him. The voters in the London suburb of Woodford very nearly recalled their MP, Winston Churchill, for opposing the agreement. Public opinion in France was no less enthusiastic about the success of the appeasers.

Stalin was less impressed. To him, "Munich" (the word became a synonym for appeasement) meant that the Western democracies were relentlessly pursuing their policy of giving Hitler carte blanche where the Soviet Union was concerned. Contemptuous of Western weakness, Stalin pointed to the USSR's own staunch willingness to come to the aid of a small country in danger. He implied that he would have sent troops to Czechoslovakia despite France's refusal to honor her own treaty obligations had it not been for the refusal of the Polish and Romanian governments to permit the passage of Soviet troops across their countries.

Historians who insist that Stalin was not sincere, that this was mere grandstanding, miss the point. The West, no less than Germany, Poland, Hungary, and Romania, denied the USSR even the possibility of defending Czechoslovakia. Stalin knew that, in the short run at least, the Soviet Union had more to lose from Nazi aggression than any Western nation. It seems clear that, had France honored her obligations to Czechoslovakia, and had Stalin obtained permission for his troops to cross Romania or Poland, he would have sent them. But the French defaulted, Britain rejoiced that the Nazi tiger would prowl the streets of Prague rather than those of London, and the myopic Polish and Romanian governments believed that Hitler could provide them with some insurance against the detested Soviets. Stalin would not forget this.

## JAPAN

Soviet foreign policy in the 1930s largely concentrated on developments in Europe. Given the fact that most of the Soviet population and the majority of Soviet industry were located in the Cisuralian part of the state territory, this was inevitable. By far the larger part of the territory itself, however, was in Asia, not Europe. And in Asia, the Soviets faced an aggressive, militaristic Japan.

Along with the Western powers, Russia, and the United States, Japan had won wide concessions in China at the end of the 19th and the beginning of the 20th century and had annexed Korea in 1910. The Japanese intervened with large forces in the Soviet Maritime Provinces after the Bolshevik Revolution; they evacuated Vladivostok only late in October 1922 under American pressure. Japan extended diplomatic recognition to the Soviet Union in January 1925; ten weeks later, the last Japanese forces on Soviet soil left the northern half of Sakhalin Island.

The apparently peaceful resolution of the conflict between Tokyo and Moscow could not mask Japanese determination to carve out an empire on the Asian mainland. Manchuria, rich in minerals and possessing the largest concentration of industry in China, was the first objective; any move against the province would lead to conflict with the USSR.

The tsarist government had built the Chinese Eastern Railway across Manchuria in the period 1897–1903; it gave the Russians direct access to the port of Vladivostok and saved greatly in time and distance. After the Intervention the European powers and the United States attempted to force Moscow and Beijing to internationalize the railway. The Soviets and Chinese successfully resisted this pressure and agreed to operate the line jointly. The Beijing government that signed the agreement, however, was only nominally in control of Manchuria, where a constantly shifting coalition of warlords actually held power.

In October 1929 the warlords attacked the Chinese Eastern Railway in force, hoping to seize control of the line from the Russians. They had about 300,000 troops augmented by a White Guard force of Russian émigrés estimated at 70,000 men.

In anticipation of trouble the Soviets had created a Special Far Eastern Army in August 1929 under General Blücher, who had helped Jiang Jieshi build the Chinese army. Blücher had only about 100,000 men to send into Manchuria, but he was far better equipped than were the warlords. Moreover, his trained and disciplined soldiers faced not a regular army but a rabble that excelled chiefly at plunder and rapine. Soviet forces routed the Manchurian-White Guard force by November 20 and reestablished security along the more than 1,000 km of the railway.

What the warlords could not accomplish, the Japanese could. Japan attacked Manchuria in September 1931, and by the following February her forces were in control of the huge province. The Japanese proclaimed the independence of Manchuria and renamed it Manchukuo.

The Japanese at first permitted the Soviet Union, theoretically still in partnership with

China, to continue to operate the Chinese Eastern Railway. Negotiations for the transfer of the line were begun in May 1933; in March 1935 the Soviet government sold its interest to Japan.

Three serious Soviet-Japanese clashes occurred toward the end of the decade. The first two took place in July-August 1938 at Lake Khasan and at Changkufeng Hill in the Soviet Maritime Provinces south of

Lake Khasan.

Khalkhin Gol.

Vladivostok, at the point where the frontiers of Manchuria, Korea, and the USSR meet on the Tumen River. Apparently testing Soviet frontier defenses, the Japanese attacked with a small force toward the end of July. The Special Far Eastern Army under Blücher, now a Marshal of the Soviet Union, repulsed the attacks; the fighting ended on August 11. Blücher was arrested by the NKVD three months later, charged with being an "agent of Japanese imperialism," and shot on November 9, 1938. This did not strengthen the Soviet defense posture.

The third major conflict took place in Mongolia: Japanese forces stormed across the Khalkha River on May 28, 1939. Once again the objective seems to have been to test Soviet reactions. Mongolia had been virtually a Soviet protectorate since the mid-1920s, and Soviet troops were stationed in the country under the terms of a 1936 mutual defense treaty.

The Japanese drove deep into Mongolia without encountering much resistance. Had their supply lines not been overextended, they might well have reached the capital of Ulan-Bator. Late in July the Soviets placed Georgi Zhukov, then a corps commander, in charge of the two Red Army groups rushed to Mongolia. At Zhukov's disposal were 35 rifle battalions, 500 tanks, about 500 aircraft, 350 armored cars, and heavy artillery. Almost the entire Mongolian army was thrown into the battle against the Japanese, but it was small, badly equipped, and untrained for modern warfare.

The Japanese attack centered on the tiny settlement of Nomon-Khan-Burd-Obo on the Khalkhin Gol (Khalkha River), which marked the Mongolian-Manchurian frontier in the area. It involved substantial forces. The Japanese struck along a 70-kilometer front with 182 tanks, 500 heavy artillery guns, 300–350 airplanes, and about 12 infantry divisions. This was, as an Ameri-

can specialist has written, "one of the major undeclared wars of recent times."

The battle of Khalkhin Gol lasted from August 20 to August 31, 1939. Zhukov's forces routed the Japanese, driving them back across the Khalkha into Manchuria. The invaders suffered enormous casualties. According to Soviet figures, 25,000 Japanese and Manchurian (i.e., Chinese) troops were killed in action in 1939, and another 27,000 to 30,000 were wounded. The Soviet-Mongolian casualty rate was only one-fifth that of the enemy.

An armistice was signed in Moscow on September 16, 1939. In June 1940, a joint Soviet-Mongolian-Japanese commission fixed the frontier between Manchuria and Mongolia.

## CHINA

After the 1927 Shanghai Massacre the small Chinese Communist party split into two camps. One was oriented toward Moscow; the other advocated a uniquely Chinese approach to revolution. The former was led by Wang Ming and Po Ku, two members of "Stalin's China Section," the group of 28 Communists loyal to the Soviet General Secretary which Pavel Mif had created at KUTV. In 1930 these two men and several associates secretly returned to the safety of the International Settlement in Shanghai, where Jiang Jieshi's men could not touch them. Under Comintern orders, they worked to prepare an uprising of the urban proletariat. Such a strategy was sheer folly in peasant China, but Stalin insisted that the Chinese revolution follow the Russian pattern.

A Soviet Republic of Ruijin was established in Jiangxi province in 1931. The first Congress of Soviets of Workers' and Peasants' Deputies took place there on November 7; it was a self-conscious attempt to emulate the Russians. Mao Zedong and other "peasantists" among the Communist leadership, however, insisted that the Chinese revolution would be decided in the countryside. In the bitter quarrels within the party Mao began to prevail over Wang Ming and others later described as "left adventurists," advocates of urban insurrection—the Stalin line.

The Jiang Jieshi regime undertook a series of "encirclement and suppression" campaigns against the Communists in Jiangxi. The fifth campaign in 1933–1934 succeeded in dislodging the Soviet Republic at Ruijin, and the Communists began the famous Long March to the northwest, which covered 10,000 kilometers and lasted 368 days. The marchers crossed 18 mountain ranges and 24 rivers in 12 provinces before reaching sanctuary in Shaanxi.

The experience of the Soviet Republic and the Long March convinced the Chinese Communists that agrarian revolution was the correct line. An enlarged conference of the party Politburo in January 1935 recognized Mao's leadership. The eclipse of the Stalinists ensured that the Chinese revolution would come from the countryside and not from the cities; China would follow its own path without reference to Moscow.

The "years of confrontation" between the Chinese Communists and the Guomindang that began with the 1927 Shanghai Massacre came to a temporary halt in 1937, when the two parties shifted their attention to the struggle against the Japanese. Imperial Japan had suspended military operations after the 1931–1932 conquest of Manchuria, but in 1937 the drive to conquer all China resumed. The Chinese Communist Army undertook a protracted guerrilla campaign in north China which saw the emergence of the Communists as the most likely heirs to postwar political power in Beijing.

## PRELUDE TO THE DIPLOMATIC REVOLUTION

The Japanese did not break off their August 1939 incursion into Soviet-supported Mongolia because of the heavy losses they suffered. Japan would normally have been willing to fight to the last citizen of puppet Manchukuo, and Japanese commanders had never displayed excessive concern over casualties among their own troops. Japan terminated the Mongolian conflict because of startling news that came from Moscow on August 24, 1939.

The Munich agreement safely tucked away, Hitler declared that he was satisfied. The Nazi dictator and the Western appeasers who fed his appetite had apparently preserved the peace over the corpse of Czechoslovakia. There was a great deal of goodwill and cooperation; Great Britain entered into negotiations aimed at granting a huge loan to Hitler.

Only two clouds dimmed the horizon. Mussolini decided that he too needed some territory in Europe, his Ethiopian conquest having proved less of an economic and theatrical success than he had hoped. The question of where he would strike obscured the diplomatic landscape. That artificially peaceful landscape was also marred by the pen and tongue of Winston Churchill. Then merely a member of parliament, Churchill had good press contacts and a gift for making people wonder whether the appeasers had been quite so clever after all. He had earlier expressed admiration for Hitler's economic performance, but after the 1936 Rhineland episode he had consistently warned that the Nazi dictator was not to be trusted.

In March 1939 Hitler suddenly marched into and occupied what was left of Czechoslovakia. Thus, less than six months after Munich he flagrantly broke his pledge to refrain from further expansion, and he showed that the German drive to acquire new territories would not be limited to lands inhabited by Germans. A few Westerners began to take Churchill's warnings seriously.

Later the same month the Spanish Civil War came to an end. It had cost approximately a million lives, a toll to which Nazi, Fascist, and Soviet intervention had contributed mightily. Francisco Franco and his Falange movement emerged victorious. A delighted Hitler offered his warmest congratulations, and Spain joined the Anti-Comintern alliance.

Mussolini annexed Albania on Good Friday, April 7, 1939. Albania had been an Italian satellite for some time; the move did not have much practical significance. In a world where internationally sanctioned violence bred still more violence, however, the action added fuel to the flames.

As Hitler made final preparations to invade the rump Czechoslovak state, the 18th Congress of the Soviet Communist party met in Moscow March 10–21. Stalin and Voroshilov asked the more than 2,000 delegates to believe that the massive purge of the military had strengthened the Soviet Union; the delegates roared agreement. The two leaders declared to thunderous applause that the judicial murder of Tukhachevsky, Blücher, Yakir, Uborevich, Kork, Putna, and others had been good for Army morale.

Given the way the Gensek and his men thought and operated, these comments were fairly predictable. Both Soviet and foreign observers were startled, however, by Stalin's jeers and taunts in a March 10 speech warning that the Soviet Union would not be drawn into a conflict with Germany in order to "pull Western chestnuts out of the fire." These comments were directed at those politicians like Churchill who had begun to hint that perhaps a pact with Stalin was the best way to stop Hitler and Mussolini.

At the time Stalin spoke there seemed no danger that those who were rather tentatively advocating alliance with the Soviet Union would be in a position to make policy. Neville Chamberlain, still firmly ensconced at No. 10 Downing Street, had often declared that he would resign before seeking an alliance with the Soviets.

Hitler sent his troops into Bohemia (Czechia) and Moravia on March 15, 1939. Native Fascists friendly to Germany took control of Slovakia. A week later, Hitler brazenly took the Baltic port of Klaipeda (Memel) from Lithuania.

On March 31, 1939, Chamberlain told a hushed House of Commons that the British government was extending a unilateral guarantee of aid to Poland. Should that country be attacked by Germany, Britain would go to her aid. A similar guarantee was given to Romania. After assisting in the liquidation of democratic Czechoslovakia, Britain suddenly found it expedient to make sweeping commitments to the reactionary military junta in Poland and to monarchic Romania.

All this was of immense potential importance to the Soviet Union. If Germany were to attack Poland, Great Britain would go to war against Germany. The British commitment thus constituted an assurance to the Soviets that if Germany attacked Poland *and* the USSR she would face the nightmare Bismarck had warned against, a two-front war.

Although the convoluted diplomatic ramifications of Chamberlain's March 31 declaration were immediately apparent, Stalin remained suspicious. What about the January 1934 German-Polish nonaggression pact? Was it not entirely possible, in view of the cozy relationship between the Polish junta and the Nazis, that the Poles might permit German forces to cross their territory to attack the Soviet Union? Stalin knew that German-Polish amicability was rapidly cooling, but hatred of the USSR had a way of reconciling differences between Central European nations.

On April 28, 1939, Hitler unilaterally abrogated the German-Polish nonaggression treaty. Moreover, announcing the decision, he departed from custom and did not refer to the Bolshevik menace.

Chamberlain had asked Stalin to extend his own unilateral guarantee to Poland. The Soviets, however, demanded a two-way pact; if they were attacked by Germany they wanted Poland to come in on their side. The Poles and later the Romanians rejected this proposal. Warsaw and Bucarest would welcome a Soviet declaration of war on Germany should that country attack either of them, but that was as far as they would go. Later in 1939, when the Soviet government asked whether Warsaw would permit the Red Army to cross Polish territory to fight Germany, the answer was again negative. The Poles refused to make any commitment and would promise only to examine the question of troop passage *after war came*. The Soviets broke off negotiations.

The chief of the German High Command issued a secret order on April 3, 1939, calling for an attack on Poland to begin September 1. The British guarantee to Poland *preceded* this order by three days. Any doubt the Germans had as to whether their attack on Poland would lead to war with Britain arose from a faulty reading of information available to them. Some Western historians have charged the USSR with precipitating the Second World War by signing a nonaggression pact with Germany, but war was certain no matter what the Soviets did or did not do.

## NAZI-SOVIET PACT

The ouster of Litvinov as a comissar of foreign affairs on May 3, 1939, constituted Stalin's most unsubtle signal that he was ready to deal with Hitler. A talented diplomat who had served with distinction for nearly two decades, Litvinov fell because he was Jewish. Short of publicly beheading the man in Red Square, Stalin could not have sent a clearer message to the Führer, who understood and applauded. Molotov, chairman of the Sovnarkom and a Russian, took over foreign affairs.

Other signals flashed back and forth between Berlin and Moscow. Hitler was anxious to sabotage the Anglo-French-Soviet negotiations; he did not know that Chamberlain was already doing a splendid job. He had plans that could be compromised by an alliance among those three states, and he had to assume—as Chamberlain refused to do—that Stalin was negotiating with the French and British in good faith. Hitler, however, genuinely detested the Communists and resisted the temptation to deal with them. He was confident that he could bring about his next great *coup*, the conquest of Poland, without reference to Moscow. But the persistence of Soviet signals and the machinations of Foreign Minister Ribbentrop brought him around to accepting the idea of an agreement with Stalin.

August 1939 was a tense month in an anxious year. The Soviet Union and Japan were fighting a major battle in Mongolia. Already in control of vast areas of China, the Japanese were extending their domination south and west. Great Britain and France were frantically rebuilding their arsenals.

The Soviets had asked for transit rights across Poland; no one could blame the Poles for not wanting the Red Army on their territory. But the colonels who governed Poland were guilty of criminally irresponsible judgment in believing that they could hold out against a German attack long enough for the British to enter the conflict and tip the balance in their favor. They should have known what the rest of the world knew: Britain had nothing with which to enter. The Poles kept the Red Army out, ensuring that the Wehrmacht and the SS would come in. The regime's hatred of the Communists blinded it to the Nazi threat.

On April 17, 1939, Soviet diplomats proposed a tripartite treaty among the USSR, Great Britain, and France. The contracting parties would provide aid, including military assistance, to any of their number attacked by Germany. Two months later the Soviets proposed to extend this agreement to Belgium, Poland, Latvia, Estonia, Finland, Greece, Romania, and Turkey.

After pondering this initiative for some time, Neville Chamberlain dispatched a low-ranking mission on a slow boat to Leningrad. These junior diplomats and officers were at sea for nearly three weeks. When they finally arrived in the USSR, they lined up with a nervous group of Red Army colonels for some photographs. One can read the apprehension in the faces of the Soviet officers: what better evidence of collaboration with foreign agents than these photographs?

The British officials, none of whom knew exactly what he was doing in the Soviet Union, did not receive a cordial welcome. It was too late. There was another delegation in town.

On August 20 there were three crucial developments. The battle at Khalkhin-Gol got under way. The Soviet Union and Germany announced a trade and credit agreement. The Nazi leader of Danzig declared that the city's hour of deliverance from the Polish oppressor was at hand.

Rumors that Germany and the USSR were about to conclude a nonaggression treaty spread around the world the next day. Someone in the German government leaked the news that Berlin had accepted in principle a Soviet draft of an agreement. Ribbentrop would fly to Moscow for important talks.

Ribbentrop and his aides met with Stalin and Molotov for three hours late in the afternoon of August 23 and negotiated a compromise. They took a recess around 7 p.m. and returned to the German embassy. Before returning to the Kremlin, Ribbentrop cabled Hitler for final instructions.

At dinner on the night of August 23–24, 1939, the pact was sealed. Ribbentrop declared that the Anti-Comintern Pact was directed not at the Soviet Union but at the Western democracies (sic). Stalin agreed that this was so and noted that it had frightened The City, London's "Wall Street," more than anyone else. Ribbentrop told his hosts a current Berlin joke: "Stalin will yet *join* the Anti-Comintern Pact!" Stalin responded with a toast: "I know how much the German nation loves its Führer. I should therefore like to drink his health." Molotov complimented the German guests on their keen understanding of Stalin's March 10 "no chestnuts" speech.

The terms of the pact were published on August 24. The six-article Treaty of Non-Aggression was to remain in effect for ten years. The two High Contracting Parties would not attack each other nor "participate in any grouping of powers whatsoever that is directly or indirectly aimed at the other party." Should either state be attacked by a third, the other would "in no manner lend its support to this third power."

The astonishment with which this news was greeted around the world would have been all the greater had the Secret Additional Protocol leaked out: Germany and the USSR had agreed to divide up Eastern Europe. The Soviets would take Estonia, Latvia, and Bessarabia; the pact was subsequently altered to permit them to seize Lithuania as well. The two parties would divide Poland along the line described by the rivers Narew, Vistula, and San. Whether there would be any Polish state at all after this new partition was left for later discussion.

Thus did Hitler and Stalin contrive to partition Poland and Eastern Europe. Hitler could now carry out his own solution to the Polish question, certain Russia would not interfere because Stalin was going to take a huge chunk of Polish territory for himself. The Soviets could strengthen their position on the Baltic, push the Finnish frontier back from Leningrad, and take Bessarabia from Romania. Nor was this all. Stalin's "no chestnuts" speech and the history of the relations between the USSR and the Western democracies in 1938/1939 made it clear that the Soviet dictator would raise no objections to whatever Hitler did in Western Europe. Hitler could rest assured that his eastern flank was not threatened.

Bent as they were on giving Hitler everything he wanted, the Western appeasers had arrogantly excluded the USSR from their calculations. The cry of anguish that rose from London and Paris on August 24, 1939, rang false.

Western politicians faced a cruel dilemma, a choice between evil and evil. They regarded Stalin as likely to reduce the world to barbarism. Hitler, on the other hand, was—whether one liked it or not—a son of the Western world. He believed in capitalism and at least tolerated Christianity, hated "non-Aryans," and pledged to wipe "Jewish Bolshevism" off the face of the earth.

At Munich in 1938, the West chose Hitler, and revisionist historians' attack on Stalin's alleged "insincerity" in pursuit of collective security comes to grief on that indisputable fact. The Western powers ignored the overtures of the Soviet dictator, who desperately sought to shore up his own country's security, and with little subtlety they suggested that Hitler look to the East for future conquests.

Stalin himself ordered the mass murder of the Soviet officer corps, and he alone bears responsibility for the resulting catastrophic state of Soviet defenses. In a frantic attempt to buy time, he entered into the surpassingly cynical agreement of August 23, 1939, propelled not only by his own monstrous crimes but also by the actions of the Western appeasers.

## SUGGESTED ADDITIONAL READING

**Beloff, Max,** *The Foreign Policy of the Soviet Union, 1929–1941,* 2 vols., New York: Oxford University Press, 1947–1949

**Brenan, Gerald,** *The Spanish Labyrinth,* New York: Macmillan, 1943

**Carr, E.H.,** *Twilight of the Comintern, 1930–1935,* New York: Pantheon, 1982

**Cattell, D.T.,** *Communism and the Spanish Civil War,* Berkeley and Los Angeles: University of California Press, 1955

**Churchill, Winston S.,** *The Gathering Storm,* Boston: Houghton Mifflin, 1948

**Haigh, R.H., D.S. Morris, and A.R. Peters, eds.,** *Soviet Foreign Policy, the League of Nations, and Europe, 1917–1939,* Totowa, N.J.: Rowman and Littlefield, 1986

**Hochman, Jiri,** *The Soviet Union and the Failure of Collective Security, 1934–1938,* Ithaca, N.Y.: Cornell University Press, 1984

**Kennan, George,** *Soviet Foreign Policy, 1917–1941,* Westport, Conn.: Greenwood Press, 1978

**Orwell, George,** *Homage to Catalonia,* New York: Harcourt, Brace, and World, 1952

**Read, Anthony, and David Fisher,** *The Deadly Embrace: Hitler, Stalin, and the Nazi-Soviet Pact, 1939–1941,* New York: W.W. Norton, 1988

**Seton-Watson, Hugh,** *From Lenin to Khrushchev,* New York: Praeger, 1960

**Sontag, Raymond J.,** *A Broken World, 1919–1939,* New York: Harper & Row, 1971

**———, and James S. Beddie, eds.,** *Nazi-Soviet Relations, 1939–1941: Documents from the Archives of the German Foreign Office,* Washington: Department of State, 1948

**Spriano, Paolo,** *Stalin and the European Communists,* London: Verso, 1988

**Thomas, Hugh,** *The Spanish Civil War,* New York: Harper & Row, 1977

# 12

# THE GREAT FATHERLAND WAR

Twenty-one years after Imperial Germany forced the infant Soviet state to accept the humiliating Treaty of Brest-Litovsk, Stalin and Molotov received Nazi Foreign Minister Ribbentrop in the Kremlin. So far as the world knew, it was a meeting of equals; in fact the Soviets were desperate supplicants.

The most urgent problem facing the USSR in the late summer of 1939 was the weak state of its defenses. The third Five-Year Plan (1938–1942) took that into account by doubling defense spending. Factories, smelters, refineries, mills, and shops in European Russia were obviously vulnerable to attack from the West; the new Plan provided for the relocation of a substantial portion of the industrial plant to the Ural Mountains and Siberia. The strengthening of the western military defense system, how-ever, had a relatively low priority, for Stalin did not wish to offend Germany.

## THE WAR BEGINS

German troops crossed into Poland all along the frontier at dawn on September 1, 1939: the European phase of World War II had begun after only 21 years of peace. Poland fell in less than a month, and Germany and the USSR partitioned the country. Moving quickly to implement the Secret Additional Protocol to the Non-Aggression Pact, the Kremlin made puppet states of Estonia, Latvia, and Lithuania.

Finland, the next Soviet objective, would side with Germany in any Soviet-German conflict; and in 1939 the Finnish frontier

Molotov signing documents incorporating Finnish territory into the USSR, December 1939. Standing from left: Zhdanov, Voroshilov, Stalin, Otto Kuusinen. (National Archives)

was only 32 kilometers from Leningrad. The Soviet government asked Helsinki to exchange some territory on the Karelian Isthmus for a much larger territory in the north; this would have pushed the frontier 20–30 kilometers farther away from Leningrad. The Finnish government refused even to consider this, and the talks collapsed. On November 30, 1939, 15 divisions of the Red Army attacked Finnish positions along the 1,500-kilometer frontier.

The Finns resisted valiantly and denied Soviet generals the quick victory they had promised Stalin. Overwhelming Red Army numerical superiority, however, wore down the defenders. A peace treaty was signed on March 12, 1940. Finland lost more

territory than it would have had it accepted Moscow's October proposals. Nevertheless, many Finns believed the blood of their soldiers had not been shed in vain.

Then came Romania's turn. On June 26, 1940, Molotov summoned that country's ambassador and presented an ultimatum: Bucarest would have to cede the province of Bessarabia and the northern part of the Bukovina. An answer would be expected the following day. Because the British could not possibly honor their commitment to come to their aid, the Romanians capitulated. Molotov said on August 1 that Bessarabia and the Bukovina had "obtained the opportunity" to become part of the Soviet Union, and he declared that "We now know with what tremendous joy the population . . . joined the ranks of Soviet citizens."

The Soviet government moved to increase production and tighten labor discipline. Factories operated 24 hours a day, seven days a week; the Red Army frantically trained officers and enlisted men; fear hung in the air. Stalin was obviously hoping for a miracle. He continued to send raw materials and food to Germany and refused to strengthen the western defense line.

Japan appeared to be removed as an immediate threat by the Neutrality Pact, which Foreign Ministers Matsuoka and Molotov signed in Moscow on April 13, 1941. Tokyo was pressing ahead with the conquest of China and Southeast Asia in order to construct a "Great East Asia Co-Prosperity Sphere." The USSR presented no obstacle to those plans. Imperial Japanese forces kept the Soviets off balance, however, by repeatedly mounting raids and feints (more than 100 in 1942 alone) into Soviet territory, and Stalin was forced to keep sizable military units in the Far East. Between June 1941 and the end of 1944 the Japanese navy sank or detained more than 170 Soviet merchant vessels.

In February 1941 British intelligence learned that the Germans would invade the USSR in the spring. The Americans obtained the same information; both Washington and London passed it along to Moscow. Stalin's chief spy in Japan, Richard Sorge, pried the details of the invasion plans out of the German ambassador and relayed them to Moscow in March and April. From the middle of March, ominous troop movements occurred in German-occupied Poland and in the Nazi satellite states of Slovakia, Romania, Hungary, and Bulgaria. Between April 10 and June 21 German reconnaissance aircraft violated Soviet airspace along the German-Soviet frontier at least 180 times, often to a depth of 150 kilometers.

On May 6, 1941, Stalin replaced Molotov—who remained comissar of foreign affairs—as chairman of the Sovnarkom. This was the first time in many years that he had held a government post.

A communiqué issued by the Soviet news agency on June 14 sought to calm fears. TASS denounced rumors of an impending German attack on the USSR and stated that the Germans were adhering to the pact between the two countries. Certain German troop movements in the vicinity of the Soviet frontier were, "one must suppose, prompted by motives which have no bearing on Soviet-German relations." The Soviet Union itself was not preparing for war, the statement concluded, and Red Army training maneuvers then under way reflected no hostility toward Germany. Stalin personally edited this statement.

At 5:30 a.m. on June 22, 1941, the German ambassador, having requested an urgent meeting with Molotov, came to the commissariat of foreign affairs and read a statement from Hitler accusing the Soviet Union of gross and repeated violations of the German-Soviet Non-Aggression Pact. It was a declaration of war, and it was late. The war was already 90 minutes old.

## JUNE 22, 1941

At 0400 hours Moscow time on June 22, 1941, Germany attacked the Soviet Union. The two largest and most powerful armies ever assembled confronted each other along a 3,000-kilometer line from the Barents Sea to the Black Sea. Hitler threw 183 divisions into the assault. Facing them were 170 divisions, 54 percent of the Red Army's total strength. The outnumbered Soviet forces had quantitative superiority in tanks and aircraft, but much of their equipment was

**European and Mediterranean Theaters, in World War II, 1939-1945**

European Theater of World War II.

177

inferior to that of the Germans. The tanks were old and insufficiently armored; only 27 percent were in working order. Many tank crews had only 90 to 120 minutes of actual experience inside the vehicles. The Soviet Union's military aircraft were outmoded, pilots sometimes had as few as four hours training in the air (the Luftwaffe and the RAF required 135 to 150 hours), and maintenance was badly organized. The airfields near the German frontier lay virtually unprotected. Within three days the Germans had almost complete control of the skies, having obliterated three fourths of the Soviet Air Force on the ground.

When Soviet officers radioed that they were under attack their superiors accused them of hallucinating and demanded to know why they had not transmitted in code. Stalin's wishful thinking extended all the way down the chain of command. It was however quickly established that an invasion was indeed taking place. At 6:00 a.m., Radio Moscow's chief announcer, Yuri Levitan, read the brief official announcement of the outbreak of hostilities.

The Soviet people were startled to hear not Stalin but Molotov broadcast a more detailed statement at noon. Stalin was not publicly heard from for 11 days: he had simply lost his nerve. No one knew better than he the price now to be paid for what he had done to the Red Army, the Red Fleet, and the Soviet Air Force. The Germans pushed more than 150 kilometers inside Soviet territory in the first 11 days.

Stalin finally addressed the nation on July 3. His opening words differed strikingly from his customary style: "Comrades! Citizens! Brothers and sisters! Warriors of our army and navy! I turn to you, my friends!" The enemy was advancing, he said, and Soviet losses had been severe. Although the Red Army was putting up an heroic resistance, the country was in mortal danger—

but Stalin reminded his listeners of the fate of Napoleon and Kaiser Wilhelm.

He justified the pact with the Germans on the grounds that it had given the country time to build its defenses, saying nothing of how those defenses had collapsed. He ordered the destruction of everything of potential use to the enemy in all sectors where Soviet forces were forced to retreat and called for the creation of partisan (guerrilla) units behind enemy lines. A State Defense Council with himself at the head had been established to manage the war effort. Stalin noted the offers of aid from Great Britain and the United States and exhorted the nation to give its all: "All the strength of the people must be used to destroy the enemy! Forward, to our victory!"

Stalin's words provided a measure of comfort at a time when there was little comfort to be had. By the end of July the Germans controlled an area of Soviet territory more than twice the size of France.

## BATTLE OF MOSCOW

The Germans mounted a three-pronged offensive. Field Marshal von Leeb's Army Group North marched on Leningrad. Army Group Center, under Field Marshal von Bock, had Moscow as its primary objective. Field Marshal von Rundstedt's Army Group South pushed initially toward Kiev, then toward the Crimea and the North Caucasus. Romania struck northward in the direction of Odessa; Finland retook the territory lost in 1939–1940; Hungarian, Slovak, and Hungarian units fought with Bock and Rundstedt. Franco Spain later sent a division.

German planes bombed Moscow early in the summer, but Muscovites did not hear artillery fire until October. Some of the capital's factories had already been moved by rail to various locations east of the Volga, and about half—more than 2 million—of the city's inhabitants had been evacuated. The government ordered the removal of many defense laboratories and institutes in October and transferred most government offices to Kuibyshev.

The flight of the bureaucrats weakened civilian morale. Something approaching panic ensued and lasted for three or four days, peaking on October 16. This was the only occasion during the entire war when a sizable segment of the population lost its nerve.

The authorities went to extraordinary lengths to reassure the Muscovites, pointing out that the State Defense Council, the *Stavka* (General Headquarters) of the Supreme Command, and a core cadre of officials remained in the capital. Stalin was there; he would not abandon them again. Red Army reinforcements rushed to the city. Air Force pilots performed as heroically as their RAF counterparts a year earlier, often simply ramming enemy planes when out of ammunition.

The Germans almost took Moscow, striking to within 50 kilometers of the western outskirts by late October before halting to regroup. The Wehrmacht invested the city along a semi-circular, 300-kilometer front from the city of Kalinin on the Volga north of Moscow to the headwaters of the Don River in the south. Reinforcements detached from Army Group North (Leeb) permitted Bock to resume his advance; by November 23, 1941, Nazi forces were poised within 23 kilometers of the Kremlin.

On December 6, 1941, 100 Soviet divisions under General Georgi Zhukov counterattacked. Hitler had not known of the existence of this force, which was equipped with far better tanks than the ones that had failed to hold the western frontiers in June. Thrown off stride, the Germans never fully recovered.

Having succeeded Marshal Semyon Timoshenko as commander of the central front only six weeks earlier, Zhukov built a force of regular units rushed from the Far East and reserves from European Russia and Central Asia; he was aided by unusually cold weather. Armed with weapons designed to function in the cold, Soviet troops were outfitted with heavy coats, mittens, felt boots. German equipment frequently malfunctioned at low temperatures; lengthy supply lines were vulnerable to partisan attack; and the troops were dressed for the West European climate.

The Soviets had regrouped psychologically as well as physically. On the anniversary of the Bolshevik Revolution Stalin had spoken to army units in Red Square, invoking the great military heroes of Russia's past—Nevsky, Donskoy, Suvorov, Kutuzov—and calling on the soldiers to be worthy of their great heritage. In a speech the previous evening he had referred to Pushkin, Tolstoi, Tchaikovsky, Glinka, Chekhov. His appeal to Russian national pride was a new departure; he called on the people to defend not communism but Russia. Coupled with his easing of restrictions on the Orthodox Church, this appeal embodied a glorification of the old values: Russian nationalism and patriotism, Orthodoxy, *sobornost* (sense of community). No one was asked to die for communism.

From this time forward the Red Army went into battle with the cry, "For the motherland and Stalin!" Stalin was the chief defender, indeed the embodiment, of the nation. He made his peace with the church and thus became—this required an additional leap of the imagination—the chief defender of the faith. Asking the church to support the war effort by rallying the people to defend the Orthodox homeland, he temporarily ended the harassment of religion.

## SIEGE OF LENINGRAD

On August 28, 1941, Nazi forces severed the rail line to Mga, 40 kilometers *east* of Leningrad, now virtually cut off from the outside world. Zhukov's arrival on September 11 saved the city from annihilation. He took over from the blundering Voroshilov, reorganized the defenses, shored up morale. There would be no panic in Leningrad.

The first air raid came on September 9 and destroyed the food warehouses; the Luftwaffe pilots thus struck a heavier blow to the city than they would have by knocking out a hundred anti-aircraft guns. Hitler now had Leningrad in a stranglehold.

Hundreds of thousands of people, including almost all the children, were evacuated in the autumn of 1941 and more followed later. About 2 million of the 1939 population of 3.85 million remained, however, and soon began to feel the effects of the bombing. Rationing was instituted at the start of the siege, in late August. On November 20, the daily bread ration was reduced to 250 grams for people in the highest category (manual workers), 125 grams for the lowest (white-collar workers).

By Christmas, supplies dropped by air made it possible to increase this to 350 and 200 grams—but still people starved. There were no vegetables or fruit. A foreign journalist who was there mentions a jelly made from 2,000 tons of sheep intestines; when the food supplies were at their lowest in winter, this was issued instead of meat.

From November 1941 to October 1942, about 630,000 people in Leningrad starved to death. This was equivalent to the entire population of San Francisco. People died in the streets, at their jobs, in darkened, unheated apartments. Often survivors lacked the strength to put the corpse on a sled and tow it to a collecting station. And as the ordeal deepened, often there were no survivors. Toward the end of the winter the authorities ordered a meticulous search to collect unburied corpses.

When the ice on Lake Ladoga east of the city froze to a thickness of about two meters the Red Army and the civil defense authorities built a "road to life" across to the eastern shore. This road was always under artillery fire and German aircraft bombed it whenever weather permitted. Trucks made two round trips across the ice every day; many were destroyed. There would be an explosion and a gaping black hole would open up. Military police marked the spot quickly with flags on long poles, then rerouted traffic. The "road to life"—actually three separate routes—came to resemble a 37-kilometer slalom course. Civilians who made the run described how drivers would dodge the holes and try to stay between the flags. They would curse Hitler and erupt into maniacal laughter when a shell or bomb burst nearby and showered their vehicles with ice but did not impede their progress toward the starving Leningrad shore. The last convoy before the spring thaw made it safely across on April 8, 1942.

A million people died in the siege of Leningrad, which lasted nearly 900 days. More than a million survived, and their collective heroism has no equal in the annals of warfare. Never in history had a city of that size been under siege for so long, or paid such a terrible price for its refusal to capitulate.

The siege and blockade officially did not end until January 27, 1944. The lovely city had seen the last of the Nazis, if not of Stalin.

## BATTLE OF STALINGRAD

Despite their failure to take either Moscow or Leningrad, in the spring of 1942 German forces appeared to be in command of the

Eastern Front. They had established fortified positions 135 kilometers east of Leningrad; they controlled the northern, western, and southern approaches to Moscow; and they held the entire Ukraine. The Crimea would fall in July. These vast territories had given the Soviet Union about two-thirds of its coal and pig iron before the war, nearly 60 percent of its steel and aluminum.

In reality, the war had not gone the way the Führer had anticipated. The promised *Blitzkrieg* had degenerated into a protracted campaign. The problem of supply was becoming increasingly critical as Soviet partisans blew up train after train and harassed truck convoys. Industries in the occupied territories were working at about 10 percent of capacity. The food grown in the Ukrainian "breadbasket" was used to feed German forces on the Eastern Front; very little got to Germany.

Soviet defenses along the Leningrad-Moscow line had not broken, but south of Moscow the line was less secure. After liquidating the last remnants of resistance in the Crimea in July 1942, the Germans made final preparations for an assault on Stalingrad. Code-named "Kremlin," the plan contained a "disinformation" scheme designed to convince the Soviet leadership that the chief German thrust in 1942 would involve a renewed assault on Moscow. Several Soviet generals expressed great skepticism about reports of an offensive against the capital, but Stalin overruled them and transferred men and matériel to the Moscow region.

The Wehrmacht struck at Stalingrad, as Zhukov, Chuikov, and several other Soviet commanders had warned it would. Not until 1987 did the Kremlin admit that the dictator had made yet another colossal blunder.

Stalingrad is situated on the west bank of the Volga where the great river is closest to the Don, which flows into the Sea of Azov.

Originally Tsaritsyn, it was renamed in 1925. The Soviet government began to develop Stalingrad during the Five-Year Plans. The gigantic Stalin Tractor Works, largest in the world, was located there, and on the eve of the war it converted to tank production. The 1939 population was almost half a million.

The Germans attacked on June 28, 1942, aiming to drive the Soviets out of the territory west of the Don inside that river's huge loop. In four weeks the Germans advanced 150–400 kilometers; by August 23 they were approaching the Volga north of Stalingrad. That same day the Luftwaffe bombed the city, causing thousands of casualties. By September 4 there was fighting in the suburbs, and nine days later the battle inside the city began.

The Soviet authorities had proclaimed a state of siege in Stalingrad on August 25. All nonessential personnel were evacuated across the Volga. On September 12 the 62nd Army under General V.I. Chuikov and the 64th Army under General M.S. Shumilov were assigned to defend the city. Stalin had given orders that the city named for him was to be held at all costs; Hitler had told his commanders to take it.

Stalingrad in 1942 stretched about 28 kilometers along the Volga along the north-south axis, but was only about five kilometers wide on the east-west axis. The peculiar layout presented special problems for both attacker and defender, but the Soviets were able to position their artillery on the eastern bank of the river, thus affording themselves an enormous advantage. The guns were protected, as was the rear; the Nazis could not encircle the city.

On September 13 the greatest battle ever fought inside a major city began. The Germans dictated the course of the fighting for nine weeks, but on November 19 the tide of battle suddenly changed. The Soviets mounted an offensive as troops under Generals Nikolai Vatutin and Konstantin Rokossovsky broke through German lines northwest of the city. On November 20 another army under General Andrei Yeremenko tore a hole in the German lines south of Stalingrad. The jaws of the pincers began to close. Several encircled Romanian divisions surrendered; but the commander of the doomed German Sixth Army, Field Marshal Friedrich von Paulus, was forbidden by Hitler even to consider negotiating with the Soviets. There were fortified German positions only about 40 kilometers west of Stalingrad, but Paulus did not try to break out.

The Soviets kept up an incessant artillery and aerial bombardment. After the battle ended, the center of the city lay in rubble. Fresh troops under some of the best Soviet generals bore down relentlessly upon the Germans. On the shortwave frequencies used by the Nazi forces the Soviets broadcast a monotonous, terrifying message in German: "Stalingrad—[tick, tock, tick, tock]—Massengrab!" ("Stalingrad—is a mass grave!—Stalingrad—"). The ticking of a clock added a dimension that helped destroy whatever German morale was left.

The battle ended on February 2, 1943. Paulus and 24 generals, plus 91,000 of their troops, were taken prisoner. Nearly

German soldiers surprised by a survivor, South Russia, 1942.
(National Archives)

50,000 wounded—and some Romanians who had lost their taste for battle—had been evacuated earlier. The Soviets buried 147,000 enemy dead. Red Army and civilian casualties slightly exceeded the German total.

## BATTLE OF KURSK

After Stalingrad the Red Army raced westward and seized the industrial center of Harkov, capital of Soviet Ukraine until 1934. Aware that his prestige had suffered a calamitous blow on the Volga, Hitler ordered the city retaken. The Germans dislodged the Soviet forces on March 15, 1943, a hollow victory. There was no sound military reason to hold the city if the Germans wanted it badly enough to stake everything on its recapture, for it had been devastated by repeated attacks and like Stalingrad was in ruins.

Because Harkov represented so little compensation for Stalingrad, Hitler searched for another theatre in which to stage one of his grand spectaculars. He settled on Kursk.

Kursk lies 330 kilometers south and slightly west of Moscow. An important rail center on the Moscow-Simferopol line, the city had about 120,000 inhabitants in 1939; its major industry was food-processing. It had little intrinsic strategic importance; the railway could easily have been cut at some other point. The Soviets had reoccupied the city during their post-Stalingrad counteroffensive. Expecting the Germans to attack in the summer, Soviet commanders Zhukov and Vasilevsky prepared strong, partially disguised defensive positions in the area.

Hitler knew that the defenses were strong at Kursk and reasoned that the Soviets would not expect him to strike there. He decided to do just that and snip off the Kursk salient. Powerful new Tiger and Panther tanks, Focke-Wulf 190 and Henschel 129 fighters, and the huge "Ferdinand" mobile gun would pound the Red Army to dust. Operation Citadel would be under two of his new field marshals, Kluge and Manstein. The old aristocratic officers had failed him; now Hitler would show the world what real Nazi commanders could do.

What they could do was lose. One of the largest engagements of the war began on July 5 with a massive Nazi assault on the Soviet defense line, now converted into a gigantic trap. At the start of the battle the balance of forces favored the Soviets, who had ample reserves. The Germans broke through the defenses but could not penetrate the salient deeply on any side. The Soviet lines held, and reserves were not needed.

Kursk was the scene of the largest tank battle ever fought: 2,700 German, 3,598 Soviet. On the evening of the first day of fighting, Yuri Levitan announced on Radio Moscow that the Red Army had destroyed 586 tanks. The destruction of so many in one day convinced the Soviet people as nothing before, not even the victory at Stalingrad, they they could not lose the war. The Soviet T-34 medium tank was as good as the Soviet generals said it was, and with it the Slavs had beaten the Germans at their own technological game. The T-34 took its place alongside the *katyusha* (multi-rail rocket projector) as one of the two most feared Soviet weapons.

The Battle of Kursk ended on August 23. Once again German losses were staggering. The Red Army also paid a high price, but the battle shattered the myth that the Germans were invincible in the summer. This proved to be Hitler's last major attempt to recapture the initiative in the East.

Soviet Women's Land Army, 1943. (National Archives)

## WARTIME DIPLOMACY

The Soviets pressed the British and Americans for a second front at every opportunity. Stalin did not care that the British had fought alone from the fall of France to the Nazi invasion of the USSR, was unimpressed by the Allied campaigns in North Africa and Italy, and had no interest in American problems in the Pacific. He knew only that the Soviet Union was bearing the brunt of the war against Hitler.

There were many high-level discussions on this issue in 1942 and 1943. Roosevelt and Churchill informed Stalin that it was physi-

cally impossible to mount a successful invasion of the European continent until they had had time to build up an enormous force in Great Britain. The agony of Moscow, Leningrad, Kiev, Stalingrad, and thousands of Soviet villages and towns, however, did not inspire a sober Soviet appreciation of the technical difficulties of invading the continent. It seemed to Stalin and his advisers, and to millions of Soviet citizens, that the West hoped to let Hitler bleed the USSR to death.

Stalin, Churchill, and Roosevelt met at Tehran from November 28 to December 1, 1943, to discuss the proposed Allied landing in France and problems of postwar cooperation. The invasion was scheduled for May 1944; it actually began on June 6. Stalin expressed satisfaction that a second front would at last take shape. The leaders took the measure of each other; Stalin concluded that he liked Roosevelt better than Churchill. For his part Roosevelt conceived a certain admiration for the Soviet dictator, who was now styling himself Marshal of the Soviet Union. He and Stalin agreed in principle that Germany should be divided into occupation zones after the war to ensure against future aggression on her part. Churchill preferred to isolate Prussia and to allow the South German states to join with Austria and even Hungary in a "peaceful confederation." Such a confederation would certainly have been hostile to the Soviet Union—as would, of course, an "isolated" and independent Prussia.

The Tehran conferees also discussed aid to the USSR. The Western Allies had provided huge amounts of military supplies in 1942 and 1943, unquestionably contributing in a major way to the Soviet victories. By the end of 1943 the American Lend-Lease program had shipped more than 7,000 airplanes, approximately 215,000 motor vehicles, and huge quantities of steel, machinery, and food.

## KATYN

Because the interwar Polish government had so resolutely opposed any sort of decent *modus vivendi* with the USSR, and because Soviet security depended heavily on developments in Poland, it was clear from the first day of World War II that some sort of showdown between Moscow and the Poles would follow the conclusion of hostilities.

In April 1943 the Germans reported finding the graves of 4,143 murdered Polish officers near Smolensk. They claimed that documents found on the corpses proved that the men had been murdered in 1940, when the Soviets controlled the part of Poland where the officers had been stationed. A team of forensic scientists assembled by the International Red Cross examined the bodies and confirmed the German account.

Eleven thousand soldiers were also missing; the Free Poles in London had long been trying to learn their fate. The officers and enlisted men had simply disappeared when the Soviets invaded in 1939, but the Kremlin had ignored all requests for information. When news of the mass murder was published in April 1943, Moscow declared that the *Germans* had committed the atrocity when they invaded in 1941. The Polish officers had been interned at Katyn, near Smolensk; the area had fallen to the Germans in September 1941. The attempt to blame the atrocity on the Soviet Union two years later, TASS said, was an attempt to split the wartime Allies.

Smolensk was retaken by the Red Army in September 1943 and a Soviet enquiry was initiated. Four months later, Soviet forensic specialists claimed that the Germans were guilty. Moscow did not allow independent experts to view the evidence.

The evidence now in the public domain allows only one conclusion: the NKVD murdered the Polish officers. When the Red Army seized Eastern Poland in 1939 the officers were first interned in Poland, then moved several hundred kilometers east, to Katyn Forest near Smolensk sometime early in 1940. In the summer of 1940, special NKVD death squads personally directed by the psychopathic Lavrenti Beria, comissar of state security, executed the officers one by one with a bullet in the back of the head.

When in April 1943 the Nazis broadcast news of finding the mass grave at Katyn, the West assumed another Hitler trick. On direct orders from Churchill and Roosevelt, however, the military authorities refused to discuss the matter with the press. Neither leader knew what to make of the atrocity; neither would permit anything to interfere with the war effort.

Stalin seized on the controversy as an excuse to break relations with the London Poles, the conservative government-in-exile. His own candidates for postwar Polish leadership, the Lublin group, included many Communists and pro-Soviet Socialists. The martyrs of Katyn slept in their uneasy graves, and the ancient hostility between Russia and Poland grew ever more intractable.

The Kremlin's lies about Katyn, which the Polish Communists slavishly repeated, survived the ouster and execution of Beria, the shattering of the Stalin myth, and naturally the neo-Stalinist Troika-Brezhnev period. But with Mikhail Gorbachev and *glasnost* hope sprang to life. In April 1985 the Polish government, having four years earlier destroyed a Solidarity memorial to the victims of Katyn, erected a monument in Warsaw. The inscription reads, TO THE POLISH SOLDIERS-VICTIMS OF HITLERITE FASCISM ON THE SOIL OF KATYN. No date appears; but all Poland knows that the Soviets controlled the area at the time of the atrocity.

Poland's Communists, having defended the Soviet version of the massacre for more than four decades, finally reversed themselves in February 1989 and publicly admitted that the Soviet secret police murdered 4,443 Polish officers whose bodies were found at Katyn. This came more than a year after the establishment of a bilateral commission to investigate what Gorbachev called "blank spots" in Soviet-Polish relations; as of the spring of 1989, the Soviets had published nothing on Katyn, and no one had accounted for the 11,000 Poles Warsaw still officially listed as "missing." Posthumous justice continued to elude most of the martyrs of Katyn.

## BABI YAR

When the Red Army retook Kiev on November 6, 1943, it discovered still another wartime outrage, one the Kremlin did not publicize the find for nearly 18 years. Most of the victims were Jews.

Kiev had fallen to the Germans on September 19, 1941. The conquerors had virtually completed their organization of the new municipal administration when delayed-action mines and bombs went off on September 25, destroying the central district. The day after the explosions, *Einsatzgruppe* (special-duty troops) *C*, elements of which had been arriving for two or three days, reached full strength. The commander, after conferring with the German military governor, blamed Kiev's Jews for the destruction.

Placards went up all over the city ordering the 100,000 remaining Jews—75,000 had fled—to assemble near the Jewish cemetery at 8:00 a.m. on September 29, 1941, bringing personal documents, money, valuables, warm clothing. Those who did not obey would be shot. The rumor went around that the Nazis were sending all Jews to Palestine.

The cemetery lay near a gash in the earth known as Babi Yar, Old Woman Ravine. Kiev's Jews assembled there as ordered. Troops of *Sonderkommando* (special commando) *4A*, a division of *Einsatzgruppe C*, herded the women, children, and elderly men into several narrow lanes. At a place where the lanes turned, the soldiers ordered the people to strip and place their clothes and belongings on one pile, the food they had brought for their journey on another. Those who balked were savagely beaten and stripped by the *Sonderkommando*'s Ukrainian helpers. As the naked, bleeding, terrified people were shoved rapidly into ever narrower lines, many went into shock and began screaming, laughing, jumping up and down, befouling themselves. The behavior of the doomed people, the shouts of the guards and their helpers, the barking of the police dogs, the sound of wooden truncheons and rifle butts striking human flesh—pandemonium.

Soldiers despatched small groups up a slope and around to the other side of the hill, where a ledge overlooked Babi Yar. People were shoved onto the ledge until there was no more room. Then the machine guns opened fire from across the narrow ravine. The murdered people fell, and at regular intervals the Germans and their helpers would descend into the ravine to make sure that no one survived. In two days *Einsatzgruppe C* killed 33,771 Jews. That set a record. Even at Auschwitz the Germans could only kill 6,000 people a day. The murders at Babi Yar continued throughout the Nazi occupation. In all, more than 100,000 people were murdered there during the 750 days that the swastika flew over Kiev.

There are war memorials all over the Soviet Union, but not until 1976 was one erected at Babi Yar. The inscription on the bronze tablet at the foot of the monument reads, "Here in 1941–43 the German fascist invaders executed more than 100,000 citizens of the city of Kiev and Soviet prisoners of war." There is no mention of the fact that the overwhelming majority were Jews.

## CAMPAIGNS OF 1944/1945

Every piece of liberated Soviet territory was a monument to the Red Army. Novgorod was recaptured in January 1944, and by the end of February the Soviets stood at the prewar Polish frontier. In early spring the Red Army reached the Romanian border. Those units halted operations while the reconquest of the Black Sea coast and the

Crimea was completed. Odessa was liberated on April 10; a month later the entire Crimea and all the Ukraine were again in Soviet hands.

By August 1 the Red Army had cut through Byelorussia and the eastern part of interwar Poland and came to a halt about 60 kilometers east of Warsaw; some small advance parties had moved to a position much closer to the Polish capital. The Polish underground and the Western Allies believed the Soviets in a position to take Warsaw.

The Polish underground had long planned an uprising against the German occupiers, wanting to liberate as much Polish territory as possible on their own and thus win the right to deal with the Soviets as equals in the postwar period. (Tito and the Yugoslav Partisans were to do precisely that.) The Poles launched the uprising on August 1, 1944.

If the Polish underground leaders genuinely believed they could overthrow the Nazis on their own, they were suffering from a tragic delusion. The Germans had five divisions in Warsaw, and their supply lines from the west were intact. Although the Poles claimed to have several divisions of their own, in fact they could only assemble about 2,000 armed men when the uprising began. The Germans launched a systematic slaughter.

The Red Army did not move, and Stalin refused to let British and American planes use Soviet airfields to make supply drops to the Poles. Denied those supplies and the support of the Red Army, the uprising collapsed after 63 days. On October 11, 1944, Hitler ordered Warsaw razed to the ground. That part of the city which had not been destroyed during the great Jewish uprising in the Warsaw ghetto in 1943 was now reduced to rubble.

The Poles have never ceased to blame the Red Army for this tragedy, which cost about

Red Army capturing a ruined Ukrainian town, 1942. (National Archives)

200,000 Polish lives, mostly civilian. Once again the unhappy Polish nation poured new rivers of blood into the already sodden soil.

The Soviets saw the Warsaw uprising differently. The Red Army had advanced 600–700 kilometers in the 40 days preceding August 1. It needed to rest, regroup, and resupply. It anticipated a German counterattack. Further, the Polish underground had not made a serious effort to coordinate with the Soviets; the implication that the Red Army either was not needed or would simply come without being called did not win friends in Moscow. Moreover, the Katyn story had broken the previous year. The anticommunist Poles had used that terrible stick to beat the Russians at every opportunity; Churchill was obliged to restrain them. This was another instance when the Poles were right, at the wrong time. Nothing would bring the Katyn dead back; only the Red Army could drive the Germans out of Poland. Too late did the Poles realize that the Soviets, who had earlier suggested that

an uprising might be in order, never had any intention of coming to their assistance.

The anticommunist Poles miscalculated badly. There was not the remotest chance that the Soviets would agree to the restoration of the interwar Polish-Soviet frontier or to the establishment of a truly independent government in Warsaw. If Stalin were to do nothing else in this war, he would make sure that postwar Poland was no threat to the USSR.

The Red Army finally marched through the ruins of Warsaw on January 17, 1945. The fact that liberation did not come until five and a half months after the beginning of the uprising indicates that those who thought the Soviets could have waltzed into the city in August 1944 erred.

## YALTA AND THE END OF THE WAR

The Polish question was settled, for better or for worse, at the Yalta Conference held February 4–11, 1945, among Stalin, Roose-

Molotov and Soviet officers greeting President Roosevelt upon his arrival in the Crimea, February 1945. (Department of Defense)

velt, and Churchill. The controversy of the Yalta "sellout" was to poison American domestic politics for more than a decade; repercussions are still felt in the 1980s.

The end of the war within sight, Stalin knew that his position was strong. He demanded and received the consent of Roosevelt and Churchill to what amounted to the shifting of Poland 200–300 kilometers to the west. The postwar Soviet-Polish frontier would closely follow the old Curzon Line, which had more or less followed the linguistic line. Those to the west spoke Polish, those to the east Ukrainian, Byelorussian, Lithuanian, Russian, or Yiddish. The Poles had rejected that line and had fought the Soviet state in 1920 to push it east. Now the Soviets pushed back. Poland would be compensated with German territory in the west.

The idea of shifting Poland to the west did not originate with Stalin. One of the Polish leaders, General Wladyslaw Sikorski,

foresaw early in the war that in the event of a Soviet victory Poland would be called upon to pay a price for its hostility toward Moscow. Sikorski therefore proposed substantially what Stalin demanded in 1945, reconstitution of the Curzon Line. He received little support from his compatriots.

So far as the postwar government of Poland was concerned, Stalin won the grudging approval of the Western leaders for his plan to make the Communist-dominated Lublin Poles the nucleus of the future regime. He promised "free and unfettered elections," and the London Poles would be allowed to participate.

No other Allied agreement with Stalin was to generate such anger and pain; for decades European and American conservatives have charged that Roosevelt sold Poland to Stalin for small and sordid coin. The critics decline to attach real significance to the fact that the Red Army totally controlled

Poland and never to indicate precisely who could have dislodged it, or how. In 1945 no detectable sentiment existed in the West for fighting the Soviet Union to ensure Poland's liberty. Under the circumstances, Roosevelt and Churchill simply got the best deal they could for the country, which was not, after all, incorporated into the USSR. It was not they who were to blame for the tragedy but history and geography.

Germany was almost a secondary issue, given the explosiveness of the Polish question. The Allies did however agree on the occupation zones, one of which, at Churchill's insistence, was to go to France. Germany would remain divided indefinitely, and steps taken to ensure that it would never again present a threat to peace. The major Nazi leaders would be tried as war criminals.

The Soviets agreed to enter the war against Japan within weeks of the victory in Europe. In return, they would be granted territory—the southern half of Sakhalin and the Kurile Islands—at Japan's expense. The Allies recognized the Soviet sphere of interest in Manchuria.

In February 1945, the best estimate of the American military establishment was that the war against Japan would go on for about 18 months after the defeat of Germany. Only a few of the generals knew of the frantic attempts to develop the atomic bomb, and those who did were uncertain it would prove the awesomely destructive weapon the scientists claimed. No one could foresee Japan's capitulation in August 1945; American officers calculated the invasion of the home islands would cost many thousands of casualties. The diplomats at Yalta, therefore, were only doing their duty in making a deal with Stalin to bring the Soviet

Churchill, Roosevelt, and Stalin at Yalta, February 3, 1945. Standing behind them are Eden, Stettinius, Molotov, and Harriman. (Department of Defense)

Union into the Far East war and thus help assure a rapid conclusion with as few casualties as possible.

Finally, the three leaders agreed to establish a United Nations. Woodrow Wilson's old dream of international cooperation would at last become a reality. Stalin won the right to have three votes—the USSR, the Ukraine, Byelorussia—in the U.N. That made no sense; the United States might have claimed 48 votes, one for each state in the Union at the time. There is no evidence to suggest, however, that Stalin's two extra votes have altered the course of history.

It seemed odd that the British and Americans were conducting some of the heaviest bombing raids of the war at about the time of the Yalta Conference. Dresden, in particular, suffered an attack so intense as to dwarf all other air raids of the war: about 135,000 people perished in the old German city in the blasts and the flames. (The atomic bombs dropped on Hiroshima and Nagasaki took 114,000 lives.) The raid made little strategic sense. The war in Europe was just about over, and while Dresden did have defense industries there were other targets the Allies could have hit to cripple the German war effort much more severely. The Soviets have repeatedly pointed out that the cities hardest hit in the winter and spring of 1945 were in their intended zone of occupation. In bombing Dresden, Halle, Dessau, and other relatively unimportant targets in the eastern part of Germany, the Allies were brandishing their air arm as a warning to Stalin.

The Allied landings in Normandy in June 1944 created the second front the Soviets had been calling for since 1941. One after another, the Nazi positions crumbled and fell in the West and in the East: France, Belgium, The Netherlands, Romania, Bulgaria, Hungary, and Yugoslavia, where Tito and his Partisans allowed the Red Army to give them a little assistance at the end.

On March 7, 1945, the American First Army crossed the Rhine at Remagen. There was henceforth little organized German defense in the West. A little over a month later American forces reached the Elbe River and linked up with Red Army units on April 25.

Advance parties of the Red Army fought their way into the German capital on April 20; the Battle of Berlin began in earnest on May 1. The last act of the Nazi cycle of death was played out in a week of intense house-to-house fighting. Only the fanatics were left now, the ones who would not dream of trying to conceal their past or their beliefs. The Führer had set the stage for the *Götterdämmerung* but lacked the courage to stay for the finale. He did not want to be put in a cage and exhibited in London and New York, he said. With his wife, Eva Braun, he committed suicide in a bunker beneath the *Reichskanzlei* on April 30.

Roosevelt died on April 12, 1945. Harry Truman, his successor, and Prime Minister Churchill proclaimed the end of the war in Europe on May 8. Stalin waited another day, until the German generals had completed the formalities of surrender, before announcing victory to the Soviet people on May 9.

The Soviet Union entered the Pacific war on August 8, two days after the Americans dropped the atomic bomb on Hiroshima. The Japanese surrendered on August 14, but the USSR had already moved to secure its Yalta concessions in the Far East.

## THE WAR AND THE SOVIET PEOPLE

Approximately 58 million people were killed, or died of causes directly related to the fighting, in World War II. Roughly half were civilians. At least 20 million of the dead were citizens of the Soviet Union, almost one-eighth of the entire population. The Soviet family untouched by tragedy was a rarity. Everyone lost someone; many lost everyone.

In addition to the dead there were the physically and psychologically wounded in such number that no count was possible. No nation in history has ever had so many mutilated veterans as living reminders of its agony. The last of these fragmented human beings will not die until well into the 21st century, and even the death of the last Soviet veteran of World War II sometime around the year 2025 will not close the book of suffering. The great national tragedy is a permanent chapter of Soviet history.

The material damage, which unlike the human could be repaired, was on a monumental scale. West of the Leningrad-Moscow-Stalingrad line destruction was almost total. Cities, towns, and villages lay in ruins. The peasants had lost their homes, barns, and sheds. The invaders had destroyed dams and canals, blown up bridges, clogged waterways, poisoned wells. The USSR lost 31,850 factories and other industrial enterprises, not counting small plants; 1,876 sovhozes; 2,890 machine-tractor stations (MTS); and 98,000 of 200,000 kolhozes, the great majority in the most fertile part of the country. No one who saw European Russia, the Ukraine, or Byelorussia in 1945 could dread Hell.

The Soviet people drew several conclusions from the war, the most important of which was that there must never be another one. Their government expressed this national craving for peace in these terms: no power or combination of powers would be permitted to threaten the security of the USSR. The Soviet Union had proved itself a great power, but the atomic bomb threw the postwar military-political equation into confusion. Poised in the spring and summer of

1945 to dominate Eastern Europe and Northern and Eastern Asia, the USSR, along with the rest of the world, suddenly had to contend with weapons of mass destruction on a scale where "mass" had a hitherto undreamed-of meaning. The development of those weapons would soon make it possible to pack into just one bomb an explosive force greater than that of all the firepower on all fronts in the Second World War. Warfare, diplomacy, and human psychology would never be the same.

The Soviet people learned from the war that suffering is indeed infinite. Even Time, they learned, did not have enough time to heal the wounds of what they would always call the Great Fatherland War.

## SUGGESTED ADDITIONAL READING

**Andreyev, Catherine,** *Vlasov and the Russian Liberation Movement, 1941–1945,* New York: Cambridge University Press, 1987

**Armstrong, John A.,** *Soviet Partisans in World War II,* Madison: University of Wisconsin Press, 1964

**Chuikov, Vasili I.,** *The Beginning of the Road,* London: Macgibbon and Kee, 1963

———, *The Battle for Stalingrad,* New York: Holt, Rinehart & Winston, 1964

———, *The End of the Third Reich,* London: Macgibbon and Kee, 1967

**Churchill, Winston S.,** *The Second World War,* 6 vols., Boston: Houghton Mifflin, 1948–1953

**Erickson, John,** *The Road to Stalingrad,* New York: Harper & Row, 1975

———, *The Road to Berlin,* Boulder, Colo.: Westview Press, 1984

**Inber, Vera,** *Leningrad Diary,* New York: St. Martin's, 1971

**Linz, Susan J., ed.,** *The Impact of World War II on the Soviet Union,* Totowa, N.J.: Rowman and Littlefield, 1985

**Maisky, Ivan,** *Memoirs of a Soviet Ambassador: The War, 1939–1943,* New York: Scribner's, 1968

**Mastny, Vojtech,** *Russia's Road to the Cold War,* New York: Columbia University Press, 1979

**Nekrich, Aleksandr M.,** *"June 22, 1941": Soviet Historians and the German Invasion,* Columbia: University of South Carolina Press, 1968

**Ross, Graham, ed.,** *The Foreign Office and the Kremlin: British Documents on Anglo-Soviet Relations, 1941–1945,* New York: Cambridge University Press, 1984

**Sainsbury, Keith,** *The Turning Point: Roosevelt, Stalin, Churchill, and Chiang Kai-Shek, 1943: The Moscow, Cairo, and Teheran Conferences,* New York: Oxford University Press, 1985

**Salisbury, Harrison E.,** *The 900 Days: The Siege of Leningrad,* New York: Harper & Row, 1969

**Werth, Alexander,** *Russia at War, 1941–1945,* New York: Dutton, 1964

**Wright, Gordon,** *The Ordeal of Total War, 1939–1945,* New York: Harper & Row, 1968

**Zawodny, J.K.,** *Death in the Forest: The Story of the Katyn Forest Massacre,* South Bend, Indiana: University of Notre Dame Press, 1962

————, *Nothing but Honor: The Story of the Warsaw Uprising, 1944,* Stanford, Calif.: Hoover Institution Press, 1978

**Zhukov, Georgi K.,** *The Memoirs of Marshal Zhukov,* New York: Delacorte Press, 1971

# 13

# THE COLD WAR

On August 6, 1945, an American military aircraft dropped history's first atomic bomb on the Japanese city of Hiroshima. Two days later the Soviet Union declared war on Japan and invaded the Japanese puppet state of Manchukuo (Manchuria). A second American nuclear weapon destroyed Nagasaki on August 9; Japan sued for peace the following day.

The formal surrender came on September 2; there would be no invasion of the Japanese home islands. It seemed that the Second World War had at last come to an end.

This was the Western interpretation of events, not Stalin's. In the Soviet view, the capitalist states had fought among themselves for 22 months until June 1941, when one of them, Germany, struck to attain a goal which all held in common: destruction of the world's only socialist state. In attacking the USSR, Stalin believed, Hitler was doing the work of all capitalists. Great Britain and the United States declared themselves allies of the Soviet Union, but in fact, the Communists argued, they had worked for a German victory by refusing for three years to open a second front. Only when the Germans proved unable to crush the USSR did the Western powers jump into the fray with massive forces. And even then, Moscow charged, they did so to establish a base from which to attack the Soviet Union.

Although the Western public had seen the war as a titanic struggle between good and evil, there were many politicians whose publicly expressed admiration for Hitler and Mussolini lent substance to Soviet suspicions. Almost all those politicians detested Stalin and the Soviet Union and several had called for a Western crusade, led if need be by Hitler, to crush the Communists; it was this posture that left the West open to the shock of the 1939 Nazi-Soviet deal. When Hitler attacked the Western democracies, however, there was no choice but to resist him, even if that meant making an alliance with Stalin.

Although Roosevelt believed Stalin a reasonable man who could be persuaded to join the search for a *modus vivendi*, Churchill's views were more typical of Western thinking. The British prime minister saw the wartime alliance with the USSR as at best a disagreeable necessity. He called during the war for an Anglo-American invasion of the "soft underbelly" of Europe at the head of the Adriatic, for a drive into the European heartland to defeat Hitler and deny the Soviets territory west of the Warsaw-Budapest-Bucarest line.

An alliance whose chief architect was after all Adolph Hitler could not survive the defeat of Germany and Japan. A postwar confrontation between Communist East and capitalist West was all but inevitable. The West soon began to speak of a "Cold War," a condition of intense and worsening hostility between two heavily armed camps; it was, many Westerners believed, the opening stage of World War III. The Soviets, on the other hand, saw post-1945 developments as a new phase of the conflict between socialism and capitalism.

## THE POTSDAM CONFERENCE

The "Big Three" leaders—France was not represented—met in the relatively undamaged Berlin suburb of Potsdam on July 17, 1945, to work out a German settlement and refine the Yalta agreements. Some American leaders feared that the untried Truman

Stalin, Truman, and Churchill at Potsdam, July 1945. Visible over Truman's left shoulder is Clement Attlee, Churchill's successor. (Department of Defense)

From left: Stalin, Charles Bohlen, unidentified Soviet officer, Truman, Andrei Gromyko, James F. Byrnes, Molotov. Potsdam, July 1945. (Department of Defense)

would be no match for either Stalin or Churchill. In the midst of the talks the Labour party won the British election of July 26 and Clement Attlee, the Labour leader, immediately came to Potsdam to replace Churchill. That made Western political and military strategists all the more apprehensive; Stalin, they feared, would prevail over his Western counterparts.

The sudden change in the West's leadership made the atomic bomb all the more significant. Midway through the conference Truman informed Stalin and Attlee that the United States had successfully tested a weapon of awesome destructive power. The Soviet dictator seemed strangely indifferent.

Early in 1945 Secretary of War Stimson had told Roosevelt that the Soviets were probably aware of the general nature of the American effort to develop the atomic bomb. Detailed reports from Soviet spies in the United States had reached Stalin before

the Potsdam Conference, and the Soviet leader's noncommital reaction to Truman's announcement indicated that he knew even more than Stimson feared he did. Donald Maclean, a British diplomat whose primary loyalty was to the USSR, had penetrated the Anglo-American Combined Policy Committee on Atomic Matters and relayed information on the American Manhattan Project—development of the atomic bomb—to Moscow.

The Potsdam meeting confirmed the division of Germany into American, British, French, and Soviet occupation zones. The occupation was to be under the control of an Allied Control Council with headquarters in Berlin. The powers of the council were deliberately left vague; each occupying power was free to do as it wished in its own sector. The Allies declared themselves in favor of reunifying Germany after a suitable period of punishment and purge. The Soviets demanded that the German nation should be so reconstructed as never again to be capable of threatening peace in Europe; the British and the French had no quarrel with this. Germany would have to pay about $20 billion in war reparations. Half the sum was to go to the USSR, which was also to receive at least 10 percent of the military industrial equipment of the Western occupation zones, where the bulk of German industry was located.

The Allies pledged to eradicate Nazism and militarism and authorized the trial on charges of crimes against humanity ("war crimes") of the surviving members of the Nazi leadership. Berlin, which lay 150 kilometers inside the Soviet occupation zone, was to be under four-power administration pending a final German settlement. That settlement, the ostensible goal of the Potsdam conferees, was left to a Council of Foreign Ministers, which was to work out peace treaties with Italy and the Balkan states before dealing with Germany.

The Potsdam Conference tacitly established a fifth, Polish, occupation zone. Stalin had proposed that the new Polish-German frontier follow the line of the Oder and Neisse rivers; that meant that the pre-1939 frontier was to be moved far to the west. The Western powers did not formally accept this new frontier but did agree to Polish "administration" of historically German territory *east* of it. They did not raise serious objections to Polish plans to expel about 9 million German citizens from that territory.

Polish administration quickly passed from occupation to outright annexation, Stalin having given Poland some German areas as "compensation" for Polish territories he had seized in the east. The Soviets also took part of old East Prussia, including the city of Königsberg (renamed Kaliningrad), while Poland received the German cities of Danzig and Stettin.

Although the sudden surrender of Japan obviated the need for a military campaign in Asia, it did not prevent the Soviets from occupying or annexing the areas assigned them at Potsdam. The United States did, however, deny Stalin the right to participate in either the occupation of Japan or the determination of that country's future.

The Yalta Conference had established the principle that military and civilian prisoners of war were to be repatriated to their homelands. The Potsdam talks confirmed this decision; the Soviet delegation demanded the acceleration of the process.

The Western Allies had liberated about a million Soviet prisoners of war and civilians employed in German slave-labor enterprises. Another million or so Red Army officers and men in prisoner-of-war camps had gone over to the German side to fight in the "Russian Liberation Army" under the command of General A.A. Vlasov, who had defected to the Germans. Further, roughly 10 million refugees or "displaced persons" from Eastern Europe, including the residents of the Polish "occupation zone" of Germany, were in areas controlled by the West.

There was no question as to the fate of Red Army soldiers who had fought under Vlasov as Wehrmacht auxiliaries; they would have to face Stalin's justice. The civilians, soldiers who stayed in the POW camps, and refugees were another matter. Moscow demanded the return of all save the Germans who fled from the territory now part of Poland. Most of the "displaced persons," especially the Soviet citizens, wanted to remain in the West; the Soviets faced long terms in the Gulag or even execution. In Stalin's view, there were no Soviet prisoners because Red Army soldiers fought to the death. Soviet wounded were often shot to prevent their falling into German hands. Likewise, civilians forcibly dragooned into

German service found no mercy at home after the war: their failure to resist constituted "proof," in Stalin's eyes, of collaboration with the Nazis.

In an action ominously code-named "Keelhaul" the Western Allies forcibly repatriated almost 2 million citizens of the USSR. The Soviets interpreted "citizen" in an aggressive manner to include Estonians, Latvians, Lithuanians, and Poles whose homes were east of the Soviet-Polish frontier fixed in 1945. Very few of these people wished to live under Soviet rule, but the Allies sent them back in order to ensure humane treatment of their own prisoners—about 25,000, mostly British—who had been liberated by the Red Army. Another factor was the necessity of obtaining Stalin's cooperation in the postwar settlement. The forced repatriations, during which hundreds of terrified prisoners were killed in clashes with American and British troops, compounded the horror of war.

Many Soviet and other East European citizens who had collaborated with the Nazis found refuge in the West, where some were recruited to help fight the battles of the Cold War against the USSR. Among them were a number of genuine war criminals who were to escape prosecution for several decades, in many cases forever.

## EASTERN EUROPE

By the time the war in Europe ended the Red Army had gained control of Poland, Czechoslovakia, Hungary, Romania, Bulgaria, and the eastern third of Germany. Soviet troops in Yugoslavia were quickly withdrawn because that country was under the control of an ardent Stalinist, Josip Broz-Tito. Another of Stalin's disciples, Enver Hoxha, was master of Albania. In the Near East, Soviet forces pulled out of the areas of northeastern Turkey they had occupied since late 1941, but the Red Army remained in the northern part of Iran and even established a puppet government.

After the defeat of Nazi Germany the USSR had one overwhelming national goal: ironclad security. Never again, Stalin and his advisers vowed, would Eastern Europe provide a jumping-off point for an invasion of Soviet territory. In a future land war, the first battles would be fought not on the Dnepr but on the Elbe, Danube, or Rhine.

The Soviets did not interpret "security" to involve the incorporation of any East European country into their national territory. The only new areas in Europe physically absorbed into the USSR were some nickel-mining districts in northern Finland, the Carpatho-Ukraine (formerly part of Czechoslovakia), and parts of East Prussia. The "regained" territories included the Baltic states, the eastern part of Poland, Bessarabia, and the Bukovina.

Given postwar realities, Soviet actions were more restrained than might have been expected. Moscow could not permit the reestablishment of independent anticommunist regimes in the strategically important Baltic states. The territory taken from Poland had been disputed between Moscow and Warsaw for centuries and was inhabited not only by Poles but also by Byelorussians, Lithuanians, Ukrainians, Russians, and Jews. About 200,000 Polish Jews, by far the largest group to survive the Holocaust, were natives of the areas seized by the Soviets in September 1939. The Soviets were not willing to relinquish Bessarabia. The Bukovina was taken from Romania without explanation in 1940.

The Western world correctly saw the Communist seizure of power in Eastern Europe as the artificial triumph of parties commanding the allegiance of only a small minority of the population. Westerners erred, however, in viewing the postwar political

**SOVIET TERRITORIAL GAINS IN EUROPE, 1939-1945**

Acquired between 1939-1945

Soviet satellite states

Communist but not Soviet satellites:
Yugoslavia since 1948; Albania
since 1960.

ICELAND

ATLANTIC OCEAN

ATLANTIC

NORWAY

FINLAND

SWEDEN

BALTIC SEA

ESTONIA

Moscow

LATVIA

DENMARK

LITHUANIA

Boundary of USSR
in 1938

IRELAND

BELGIUM

GREAT
BRITAIN

HOLLAND

GERM.
DEM.
REP.

Berlin

EAST PRUSSIA

Warsaw

POLAND

Kiev

Paris

GERM.
FEDERAL
REP.

CZECHOSLOVAKIA

FRANCE

SWITZ.

AUSTRIA

HUNGARY

PORTUGAL

SPAIN

YUGOSLAVIA

RUMANIA

BLACK SEA

BULGARIA

ITALY

ALBANIA

MEDITERRANEAN

GREECE

TURKEY

SEA

Soviet territorial gains in Europe, 1939–1945.

contest in the region as one between totalitarianism and democracy. Democracy had never existed anywhere in Eastern Europe save Czechoslovakia, and even there the Slovak minority had legitimate grievances against the dominant Czechs. Parties paid lip service to democratic principles but proved in the interwar period they would oppress to the point of physically destroying all who opposed them on political, religious, or ethnic grounds. Corrupt politics ran the gamut from military dictatorship to degenerate monarchy. In Croatia, Slovakia, Hungary, Romania, and Bulgaria, there had been a great deal of sympathy for fascism throughout the interwar period and much enthusiastic collaboration with the Nazis during the war.

Nevertheless, the overwhelming majority of East European populations opposed the establishment of Soviet-sponsored Communist regimes. Only in Czechoslovakia, Yugoslavia, and Bulgaria was there some genuine friendship for the USSR in the initial postwar period, and that soon faded.

The political agents who rode into Eastern Europe in the baggage train of the Red Army generally initiated the process of bringing a country under Soviet control by directing the domestic Communist parties, whose ranks had been purged repeatedly on Moscow's orders, to enter coalition governments of "national unity." Those governments held elections in 1946 and 1947.

Western observers were occasionally permitted to monitor the balloting, but this was rare and ineffective. The only real supervising came from the Red Army and Soviet political agents. Nevertheless, nowhere did a Communist party even come close to winning a parliamentary majority.

Confirmed by the elections as a minority party, the Communists nevertheless demanded and received such key ministerial posts as interior (which had control of national police forces), justice, and communications. Noncommunists often held the premiership and the ministry of foreign affairs, but the presence of Soviet occupying forces rendered those offices largely ceremonial.

Once in control of the police, the courts, and mass communications, the Communists isolated and discredited popular noncommunist political figures by any means available. Prewar politicians, Resistance heroes, intellectuals, and professional people were subjected to harassment that often included physical violence. Such people were usually charged with having collaborated with the Nazis or, after 1946, with "Western imperialism."

Having eliminated most noncommunist political figures and other prominent people from public life, a third step frequently involved holding new elections under a bloc system. Each political party was assigned a percentage of seats in parliament based on a complicated formula weighted in favor of urban working-class constituencies and other voter concentrations (poor peasants, civilian bureaucrats, the military) deemed friendly to the Communists. Under this system, the Communists would take a majority of the seats no matter what the size of their vote—which never rose above 34 percent in any uncontrolled election in Europe.

In the now-docile parliaments the Communists proceeded to pass legislation at the pleasure of their Soviet masters. This usually consisted of a series of enabling acts that gave the government, now composed almost exclusively of Communists, carte blanche to carry out its program. Thus, the legislature, like the courts and press, became an arm of the executive power.

This pattern was not universal, but it was typical. By early 1948 every country in Eastern Europe save Yugoslavia lay under Soviet control. And Yugoslavia differed from the puppet states only in that Tito and his associates insisted that they, loyal Stalinists, have charge of their own country.

In the spring of 1947 the United States attempted to meet the Soviet challenge with the "Truman Doctrine." Congress granted the president's request for massive economic and military aid to Greece and Turkey to enable those countries to withstand Communist pressure. Washington accepted the role of policeman in areas deemed vital to American national security and promised to send money, arms, military advisers and even troops to any country threatened by Communists.

The economic aid was still more vital than the military. The Truman Doctrine offered a defense against armed aggression but was useless against economic chaos. American leaders reasoned that the abysmal state of the European economy made communism attractive. Put Europe on its feet, they argued, and the threat will diminish. In June 1947 Secretary of State George C. Marshall proposed that the United States finance Europe's economic recovery with a program of loans, capital investment, grants, and other forms of aid.

A few days later the Soviet delegation walked out of a Paris meeting of foreign ministers of the USSR, Britain, and France called to respond to the tentative American offer. There is evidence that Stalin considered accepting assistance, but when the conditions the Americans would impose became known he rejected them and compelled Czechoslovakia to abandon its announced intention to apply for American aid. Washington insisted on maintaining direct supervision over the use of loan funds.

There is no denying the success of the Marshall Plan. By mid-1951 Western Europe had surpassed 1939 industrial production levels by almost 45 percent. There was virtually full employment, the standard of living was rising, and food rationing had ended everywhere save in Great Britain. The leftward drift in Europe had ceased. Communist strength among French and Italian voters appeared to have peaked at 30–33 percent, much less in other countries.

East and West accused each other of the basest conduct. The Soviets tried to subvert legitimate governments and institutions in the West, while the United States supported resistance in Eastern Europe with money,

propaganda, and night parachute drops of arms, equipment, and Western-trained agents. The Soviet Union assured potential sympathizers that the "world proletariat" marched at their side in every confrontation with "American imperialists."

## GERMANY AND YUGOSLAVIA

Tensions mounted rapidly after March 1946. Stalin responded to Churchill's "Iron Curtain" speech by comparing the former prime minister to Hitler. On July 13, 1949, Pope Pius XII, who had failed to speak out forcefully against Germany's extermination of the Jews, excommunicated all Catholics who voted for Communists or supported them in any way. The same decree denied the sacraments to those who read Marxist or communist literature. The pope's action was the first such mass malediction since the 12th century.

In 1947 the Soviets sought to counter the Truman Doctrine and the proposed Marshall Plan by establishing a Communist Information Bureau, or Cominform, with headquarters in Belgrade. This organization replaced the Comintern, dissolved in 1943 as a wartime good-will gesture. It included representatives from the USSR, its East European puppet states, and the Communist parties of Italy and France. Further, a "Molotov Plan" began to take shape as a structural framework for the integration of the economies of the USSR and its satellites; this was the forerunner of the Council on Mutual Economic Assistance (CMEA, or Comecon), which came into existence in January 1949.

Molotov's scheme merely confirmed Soviet exploitation of Eastern Europe. The Kremlin's view of economic cooperation envisaged the sending of satellite countries' raw materials to the USSR, which would supply manufactured goods to those countries. The Poles explained the system this way: Poland supplies the Soviet Union with coal, and in return the Soviet Union takes Poland's steel. The Soviets set the prices they would pay for the raw materials and those they would charge for manufactured goods, which in fact they frequently could not provide.

Under intense Western pressure the USSR withdrew its forces from northern Iran in the spring of 1946. Until the signing of the Austrian peace treaty in 1955, that represented Moscow's only postwar retreat.

Worsening relations with the USSR dimmed the West's memories of the war more rapidly than anyone could have expected. This process was particularly true in the United States, which had suffered relatively little at German hands and which now assumed the responsibility for defending the West against what most political leaders saw as a grave Soviet menace. Germany was crucial both in that defense and in the psychological-political war. Soviet rule in the eastern third of the country, and Anglo-American-French rule in the west, provided the world with an unobstructed opportunity to view and evaluate the two competing systems.

In the latter part of 1946 the United States formally rejected the various schemes—notably the "Morgenthau Plan" of the American secretary of the treasury—for transforming Germany into an agrarian nation without any war-making potential. That had been the Soviet objective, and American rejection of such a course in favor of rebuilding and rearming Germany exacerbated East-West animosities. Secretary of State James Byrnes, Marshall's predecessor, pledged American support for the rebuilding of Germany and announced the determination of the United States to defend the country against aggression. In December the Americans and British decided to fuse their occupation zones as a first step toward German reunification. France and the Soviet Union were invited to follow suit and bring their sectors into the Anglo-American "Bizonia."

Paris hesitated to cooperate with London and Washington because anti-German feeling, fueled by Communist propaganda, ran high in France. Moscow refused to go along, insisting instead on the $10 billion in reparations promised at Potsdam. It was still the public Soviet position that Germany should be reunited, but Stalin was unwilling to permit free elections in his zone of Germany or anywhere else. The Soviets rightly regarded each step toward unifying the Western sectors as a threat to their rule not only in East Germany but throughout Eastern Europe.

Tensions in Germany were temporarily overshadowed by developments in Yugoslavia, where the Tito regime continued to resist Soviet attempts to make the country a colony. No East European Communist was a more devout Stalinist than Tito, who however saw no contradiction between Yugoslav independence and loyalty to Moscow. In 1947 the Yugoslav Communists purged their ranks of thousands of Stalinists. Moscow protested, but the purge continued as Tito found some top Yugoslav officials plotting to sell the country to Stalin. In March 1948 the Soviets angrily recalled their military and technical advisers.

The quarrel burst into the open on June 28, 1948, when the Cominform expelled the Yugoslav party. The myth of a monolithic Communist bloc lay in ruins.

## BERLIN BLOCKADE

The 1948 Yugoslav crisis, which seemed to portend a Soviet invasion to overthrow Tito, gave way to a new one in Germany. To bring additional pressure to bear on France to stay out of "Bizonia," protest the West's plan to reform the currency in its occupation zones, and force the West out of the old German capital, the Soviet Union manufactured a confrontation in Berlin. Stalin's overriding goal was not to absorb Berlin but to prevent the creation of a unified West German state that would unquestionably be hostile to the USSR.

On June 15, 1948, Soviet authorities closed one of the Autobahns leading from the west into East Germany and Berlin ostensibly for repairs. Within a week, however, all highway, rail, and river communication ceased. Only three 30-kilometer-wide air corridors linked Berlin to West Germany. The Western sectors of the city contained a population of more than 2 million, for whose support about 3,000 tons of supplies in summer, 4,000 in winter, were needed each day.

On June 26, an American C-47 transport aircraft landed at West Berlin's Tempelhof airfield with its maximum load of food, milk, and medicines: three tons. Four days later the first of the 10-ton capacity C-54s landed at Tempelhof; eventually 225 of these planes, plus RAF and French transport craft, were to provide the Berlin Airlift. On July 26, the three air forces landed 3,028 tons of supplies.

The Soviets harassed the flights by "buzzing" the Western planes with fighter aircraft, flashing spotlights to blind the pilots, and raising barrage balloons along the air corridors. They invariably stopped just short of violence. Eventually 39 British, 31 American, and five West German pilots were killed in air accidents, nearly all due to foul weather or pilot error.

The Western Allies were to make more than a quarter million flights. They ferried more than 2.3 million tons of supplies into West Berlin, including hundreds of thousands of tons of coal.

In the first few weeks of the Berlin Blockade the West considered and rejected a plan to send an armored column into East Germany; this would have amounted to an invasion. Truman calculated that the airlift could achieve Allied objectives.

The gamble succeeded. Unable to force the West out of Berlin, the Soviets abandoned the blockade on May 12, 1949, and reopened the surface corridors. The West appeared to have won an impressive victory. Berlin remained under four-power control. France decided to link her occupation zone to "Bizonia," setting the stage for the creation of an independent West German state. The currency reform went forward as planned.

It seemed clear that Stalin had lost face. Only later, when East-West relations deteriorated still further, did some Western political observers suggest that the Soviet dictator too might have gained something from the Berlin crisis: the West apparently would not go to war even when provoked.

There was more than this alleged failure to react properly in Berlin that outraged many anticommunists. The Vietnamese Communists under Hô Chi Minh began a guerrilla war against French colonial rule in 1947. The French resisted fiercely, but a divided public opinion at home sapped military morale and contributed to political instability. As France's position in Southeast Asia deteriorated, the United States stepped in rather tentatively; some in the West again lamented the failure to mount effective opposition. For his part, Stalin provided little but moral support to Hô.

## NATO, CHINA, KOREA

The North Atlantic Treaty Organization came into existence in April 1949, proving the ancient maxim that nothing unites like a common enemy. Scarcely four years after the end of World War II, the United States and 11 of its allies joined in a mutual defense pact. In any future war in Europe, the USSR would face a united West. The Soviets recognized the threat posed by NATO and tried unsuccessfully to block its formation. The Italian and French Communist parties kept those countries in an uproar during the parliamentary debates over the treaty, and Moscow brought intense pressure to bear in several countries in an effort to sabotage the negotiations.

The impasse worsened. The West could not accept Stalin's assurances that he had no territorial ambitions in Europe; no government could afford to repeat the mistakes of the appeasers. On the other hand, Stalin could not believe that NATO was a purely defensive alliance.

In May 1949 the Western occupation zones were fused to form the quasi-independent Federal Republic of Germany. The Soviets protested vehemently, fearing that "West Germany" would become a member of the Western alliance. Stalin continued to call for the reunification and neutralization of the whole German nation. The West, however, insisted on free elections and on renegotiation of the temporary German frontiers established at Potsdam.

The Soviets rejected both demands. The establishment of a West German state with a strong industrial base and an implacably anti-Communist population swollen by the influx of refugees from the Communist East posed a major threat to the USSR. Unable to prevent its creation, the Soviets sought to disrupt it from within and thwart the plans to make it a cornerstone of the Western military alliance. The German Democratic Republic, a puppet state, was created in the Soviet zone in October 1949.

In September 1949 TASS announced that Soviet scientists had successfully tested a nuclear weapon. The American monopoly collapsed; Stalin was well on the way to building the kind of military might he believed necessary to ensure the security of the USSR. The power balance, which had seemed to shift to the West, was again in doubt. The West still had a vastly superior delivery capability in the United States Air Force, and of course the American lead in nuclear weapons remained an enormous advantage. The British were to produce their own atomic bomb in 1952, the French in 1960. But only a concerted, sustained effort could maintain that lead. If the predictions of some Western politicians of an imminent Soviet surge in military might were exaggerated, there was certainly reason to believe that Western superiority would not last forever.

An even greater shock to the West, especially the United States, was the fall of China to the Communists. On October 1, 1949, the People's Republic of China officially came into being. Having defeated the forces of the American favorite, Jiang Jieshi, the Communists of Mao Zedong established a strong central government in Beijing.

The Soviet Union had provided very little aid to Mao. The reconstruction of the USSR had first priority after 1945, and beyond that Stalin, whose record as a China expert was dismal, badly miscalculated the Chinese Communists' chances of taking power. Mao and his deputy, Zhou Enlai, had nothing but contempt for Stalin's China policy but admired him as leader of the Soviet Union. In any event they desperately needed his aid. In February 1950 Mao flew to Moscow to sign a 30-year Treaty of Friendship, Alliance, and Mutual Assistance.

Powerful as they were, the Western democracies, allied in NATO and about to bring West Germany into their circle, felt threatened by the new Sino-Soviet alliance. More than a third of the world was now ruled by Communists, and the Soviet Union had the atomic bomb and the Red Army. An armed clash, most likely in Berlin, seemed inevitable.

Fighting erupted not in Europe but in Korea. On June 25, 1950, Communist North Korea sent its armed forces south into the Western-backed Republic of Korea. There had been fighting along the border for some months as the two halves of the divided nation tested each other. Negotiations for reunification had broken down, and the country plunged into civil war.

The Soviet role in the North Korean decision to attack remains murky. Kim Il Sung, the Communist leader, was capable of acting independently, and Mao's victory had inspired Communists throughout Asia to redouble their efforts to seize power. High-ranking American officials had pronounced Korea beyond the American defense perimeter. In the May 1950 South Korean elections the American puppet, Syngman Rhee, suffered a substantial setback. The time was clearly auspicious for an attack, but whether Stalin inspired it remains unclear.

The North Koreans drove the South Korean forces and their American advisers to the sea; by early September a Communist triumph seemed imminent. Then American, South Korean, and other United Nations forces (the UN had branded North Korea the aggressor) counterattacked and drove the Communists back to the Yalu River, the frontier between Korea and China. That brought hundreds of thousands of Chinese Communist "volunteers" into the conflict, which in the spring of 1951 stabilized into a war of attrition along the 38th parallel.

The Soviets had trained and equipped the North Korean army, but their participation in the war itself was limited. Stalin would not risk any clash between his own forces and those of the United Nations because he could not foresee at what point the United States, on whom the UN effort depended, would employ nuclear weapons to offset Chinese superiority in manpower.

In March 1951 the United States conducted thermonuclear tests at Eniwetak and Bikini in the Pacific; the hydrogen bomb would soon be in the American arsenal. The Soviets called for a cease-fire and armistice negotiations in Korea.

The talks began on July 8, 1951, and continued with many interruptions for two years. An armistice was finally signed in July 1953. The North Koreans and Chinese came to terms after the new American president, Dwight Eisenhower, bluntly informed them that he was prepared to use nuclear weapons in Korea.

It would seem reasonable to assume that Stalin influenced the Communists to make peace. Mao and his lieutenants had repeatedly denounced the United States as a "paper tiger," but Stalin had a healthy respect for the American atomic bomb and knew that Eisenhower was serious in his threat to use it. In December 1952 the Soviet dictator told an American journalist he would welcome a meeting with the president-elect and stood ready to help bring peace to Korea.

The meeting never took place. Stalin died on March 5, 1953.

## THE WEST AND SOVIET SECURITY

Stalin had defined the political and philosophical conflict of the postwar period in terms and categories more pragmatic Westerners found impossible to fathom. He never ceased to denounce Western "imperialists" and "warmongers," threatened to annihilate anyone who opposed him, and insisted that the future belonged to communism. Yet he regularly proclaimed his hope for peaceful cooperation with the West "in spite of the difference of economic systems and ideologies" and declared such cooperation "unconditionally necessary in the interests of general peace."

The Soviet dictator perplexed and sometimes frightened the West, but the confusion was mutual. American leaders tended to threaten nuclear destruction of the USSR rather casually. Their conduct in the Berlin Crisis of 1948–1949 proved that they did not necessarily mean what they said, and *that* made it more difficult for a straightforward leader like Eisenhower to end the crisis in Korea.

Attempts to fix blame for the Cold War persuade only the already convinced and inflict today's politics on yesterday's dilemmas. Both East and West contributed to the tensions that several times threatened to erupt into a Third World War; neither side had a monopoly on virtue or perfidy.

The Soviets made a monumental error in not capitalizing on Western goodwill after World War II. Public opinion in most Western countries was warmly pro-Soviet in 1945; the sufferings and heroic resistance of the Soviet people were universally acknowledged. It is unlikely that any anti-Soviet politician could have survived an election in 1945: Churchill's defeat was due in considerable measure to the electorate's conviction that he could not get along with the Russians.

When the Soviet Union failed to respond to signals that the West was ready to continue the wartime cooperation, and opted instead for a policy of confrontation, Truman had no choice but to follow the advice of those in his administration who urged a harsh policy toward the USSR. Stalin had backed him into a corner.

It is also true, however, that the West all too quickly forgot the enormity of the human damage the war did to the USSR. The West, too, knew the sorrow of the death of young soldiers and of defenseless civilians, but the sheer scale of bloodshed in the Soviet Union loomed so very large: for every Western victim of the war, there were 32 Soviet dead.

The Soviet obsession with security was not negotiable. The formulation of a kind of "Stalin Doctrine" in Eastern Europe was the inevitable result of the suffering, and it reflected the national resolve to build an invincible military and political defense system.

## SUGGESTED ADDITIONAL READING

**Acheson, Dean,** *Present at the Creation*, New York: W.W. Norton, 1969

**Churchill, Winston,** *Triumph and Tragedy*, Boston: Houghton Mifflin, 1953

**Clemens, Diane,** *Yalta*, New York: Oxford University Press, 1970

**Djilas, Milovan,** *Conversations with Stalin*, New York: Harcourt, Brace and World, 1962

**Feis, Herbert,** *Churchill, Roosevelt, Stalin*, Princeton, N.J.: Princeton University Press, 1967

———, *From Trust to Terror*, New York: W.W. Norton, 1970

**Funigiello, Philip J.,** *American-Soviet Trade in the Cold War*, Chapel Hill: University of North Carolina Press, 1988

**Gaddis, John L.,** *Strategies of Containment*, New York: Oxford University Press, 1982

———, *The United States and the Origins of the Cold War*, New York: Columbia University Press, 1972

**Kissinger, Henry,** *Nuclear Weapons and Foreign Policy*, New York: Harper & Row, 1957

**LaFeber, Walter,** *America, Russia, and the Cold War, 1945–1966*, New York: Wiley, 1968

**Loftus, John,** *The Belarus Secret*, New York: Knopf, 1982

**Sayre, Nora,** *Running Time: Films of the Cold War*, New York: Dial Press, 1982

**Simpson, Christopher,** *Blowback: America's Recruitment of Nazis and Its Effect on the Cold War*, New York: Weidenfeld and Nicolson, 1988

**Ulam, Adam,** *The Rivals*, New York: Viking, 1971

**Yergin, Daniel,** *Shattered Peace*, Boston: Houghton Mifflin, 1977

# 14

# THE LATE STALIN YEARS

The Red Army commanders had shaped a brilliant victory. The names of Bagramyan, Chuikov, Konev, Rokossovsky, Tolbukhin, Vasilevsky, Sokolovsky, Vatutin, and Zhukov were now inscribed in the temple of war heroes alongside those of Nevsky and Donskoi, Suvorov and Kutuzov. The prestige of the Red Army eclipsed that of the party and its leader.

That was the trouble: the Communist party had always feared the military. Trotsky had begun the practice of placing "political advisers" throughout the ranks in 1918–1920. Political indoctrination had the same priority as weapons training, and every effort was made to monitor loyalty. The massive purge of 1937 had removed a potential challenge to party leadership. In 1946 Stalin moved to cut the soldiers down to size once

more. In February the Worker-Peasant Red Army, which since its birth had defeated all enemies foreign and domestic, was renamed the Soviet Army. In March Stalin relieved Marshal Zhukov as commander of Soviet occupation forces in Germany and made him head of ground forces. Zhukov fell still further in June 1946 when he became commander of the Odessa-Ural military region.

## FOURTH FIVE-YEAR PLAN

Nine million demobilized Red Army soldiers joined the urban work force, which in 1950 numbered almost 39 million people. In the initial postwar period production inevitably fell. The 1946 gross industrial product was 17 percent less than that of 1945, only 75 percent of 1940 levels; in 1947 the situation began to improve. Coal production was 57 percent higher in 1950 than in 1940, 75 percent above that of 1945. New natural gas pipelines into Leningrad, Moscow, and Kiev made possible the expansion of industry. Hydroelectric power again flowed from the giant Dneproges station in 1947 after capital repairs; in 1950 that station alone produced more electricity annually than prerevolutionary Russia had consumed.

In all, 6,200 major industrial enterprises were established during the plan, and by 1950 there were some 400,000 engineers in the work force. Those engineers undertook to restore, for example, the chemical industry, in which Russia had always lagged far behind the West. In 1937 the total Soviet production of chemicals was about one-tenth the American; by 1950 the gap had been closed to one-sixth.

Considerable progress came in the machine tool industry. Production had fallen to 38,400 units in 1945 compared with 58,400 in 1940. By 1950 the figure stood at 70,600. The early postwar period saw very little innovation in this field, as in most of Soviet industry; Soviet engineers simply copied or adapted foreign models. Lend-Lease had provided American machine tools during the war, and more or less normal trade continued through most of 1946. When the Cold War took hold contracts were cancelled, trade virtually ceased, and the Soviets were left on their own.

Because production was much more important than innovation, continued reliance on old foreign machine tools as a starting point for design and development could be tolerated. In a competitive world undergoing the greatest technological revolution in history, this portended disaster, but as long as Stalin was alive, innovation in any field remained risky. The Gensek had initially opposed research into jet propulsion and rocketry and had been slow to approve a "crash" program to develop atomic energy. There was always the danger he would brand pure research "counterrevolutionary."

The persistent industrial-technological lag behind the West dictated that the USSR continued to give priority to heavy industry. Light (consumer goods) industry accordingly received short shrift from the planners, although in 1946 (and in that year only), because it could reconvert more easily than heavy industry, it actually grew at a faster pace.

The state managed to build or restore 100 million square meters of living space in the cities and to provide 1,119,000 new or restored dwellings in the devastated countryside. This impressive achievement was only a fraction of what was needed.

The new plan aimed at a 27 percent increase over prewar production levels for grain crops and 25 percent for industrial crops, not realistic goals. By 1953, production barely reached 1928 levels (the highest ever), in part because fewer people were engaged in food production. At the beginning of 1946 there were 33 percent fewer collective farmers than there had been in 1940, and the number of able-bodied *men* had declined by 60 percent. Most of the decline was attributable to war deaths and to the return of 9 million demobilized peasant-soldiers not to the farms but to the cities.

The mediocre 1945 harvest yielded 40 percent less than that of 1940. In some important respects this could be blamed on the war. The 1946 disaster in agriculture, however, had purely natural causes. The worst drought in 50 years struck grain-growing districts from the lower Volga to the Romanian frontier.

Once again the Communist party blamed men for nature's caprice. Kolhoz managers and regional party officials were accused of "inept management" and dismissed. This may have had a certain effect on public opinion, but something concrete had to be done. The party sent thousands of urban Communists into the countryside to help with the 1947 planting, released about 2.5 million peasants working in the cities to return to the kolhozes, established a Collective Farm Council, and revised the Collective Farm Statutes. A.A. Andreyev was officially in charge but he reported to Nikita Khrushchev and Georgi Malenkov. Khrushchev, in particular, emerged as an agricultural expert in this period. As a result of the reforms he initiated the number of privately owned cattle reached 30 million in 1949; not since NEP had the figure been anywhere near that. In the same year peasant and other owners held 26.5 million sheep and goats, 7.2 million hogs, about 350 million fowl. Conservative Soviet Marxists attacked this trend and accused Khrushchev of heresy. As long as Stalin was satisfied with the pace of recovery in the countryside, however, Khrushchev was safe.

A second, less successful innovation involved a drastic reduction in the number of collective farms, as these figures indicate:

| 1937 | 1940 | 1950 (Dec.) | 1953 | 1959 | 1962 |
|------|------|-------------|------|------|------|
| 243,500 | 236,900 | 126,000 (approx.) | 93,300 | 54,600 | 40,500 |

Khrushchev assumed that a bigger farm was more efficient. He merged many failing or marginal kolhozes with more successful ones, rewarded good managers and demoted or otherwise punished unsuccessful ones, and shuffled party cadres in the attempt to find the right combinations.

The larger farms, however, produced less. Peasants who had never been happy as members of a collective were still more alienated as cogs in a bigger organization. The mergers broke up teams in which the members, for better or for worse, knew each other and had worked out a *modus operandi*. Crop rotations were changed after the amalgamations; this too had an adverse impact on production. Finally, the state continued to impose an enormous tax burden on the kolhozes in order to finance reconstruction.

The state gouged agriculture to build industry. The farms naturally had to sell their produce in order to earn money to pay taxes, set at a high level. There was only one buyer for agricultural produce, the state, which paid artificially low prices. On the retail market the state kept prices for staples—flour, bread, cabbage, potatoes, milk—low, but meat, dairy products (except milk), fruit, and other items were sold at high markups that constituted a tax on consumers.

The kolhozniks were poorly paid, badly housed, and their medical and educational services inadequate. Already in deep psychological shock because of the loss of so many millions of young men during the war, morale in the countryside plummeted still lower in the difficult postwar years.

By 1950 agricultural production had barely reached prewar levels; the state always hoped for miracles which never materialized. The 1946 drought, the confiscatory tax policy, and low morale kept Soviet agriculture in an inefficient morass from which it seemed incapable of escaping.

## POSTWAR POLITICAL DEVELOPMENTS

Not even their enemies could accuse Soviet Communists of cowardice; the party lost about 3 million members during World War II. Communists regularly volunteered for the most dangerous missions and paid a heavy price. Because of the slaughter, conditions for membership were relaxed early in the war. The party grew from 3.87 million in February 1941 to 5.8 million at the end of the war. More than 75 percent of the July 1945 roster had joined since 1941; between a third and a half were under 35, and three quarters were under 45. The percentage of women in the party increased from 14.9 in 1941 to 19.2 in October 1952.

The membership was young and the leadership was far from old. Excluding Kalinin, who died in 1946, and Stalin, the average age of Politburo members was only 51.7 in June 1945. The same clique was in power, however—the lackies and toadies who had been with Stalin for at least two decades and the newcomers Khrushchev, Malenkov, and (new at least to the innermost circle) Zhdanov. The most ambitious courtier was Zhdanov, who returned to Moscow after the war to resume work as a secretary of the party Central Committee. Quickly determining that only another CC secretary, Georgi Malenkov, stood between him and Stalin, Zhdanov undertook to discredit his rival. He claimed that Malenkov, who had supervised the party and government apparatuses during the war, had neglected ideology.

Early in 1946 Stalin removed Malenkov from the Central Committee Secretariat and authorized Zhdanov to proceed with an ideological housecleaning. By the middle of 1946 Zhdanov controlled the entire ideological network; his position as heir apparent seemed secure. He used his power to put men he trusted into key positions on the party's chief ideological journal, *Bolshevik,* the party newspaper, *Pravda,* and the key Propaganda and Agitation Administration (Agitprop) of the Central Committee, formed in 1938.

In March 1946 the Council of People's Comissars was renamed Council of Minis-

ters. Coming a month after Stalin had done away with the name "Red Army," this jettisoning of another symbol of the revolutionary heritage further indicated Stalin's determination to break with the Leninist past. It would not be long before "Politburo" and "Bolshevik" would have to go too. In the 1946 reorganization, the NKVD, which had been divided into two commissariats in 1943, became the MVD or ministry of internal affairs. The NKGB, as the secret police had been known 1943–1946, now became the MGB or ministry of state security.

## ZHDANOVSHCHINA

Stalin himself initiated the postwar cultural-ideological purge known as *Zhdanovshchina* (Zhdanov time) and directed his chief lackey to pounce on writers and literary journals. The humorist Mikhail Zoshchenko and the poet Anna Akhmatova came under heavy fire as Zhdanov pronounced their works "ideologically harmful" and "steeped in the venom of savage enmity toward Soviet power." The Writers' Union expelled both; they could no longer publish, or earn a living.

Zhdanov accused the film directors Sergei Eisenstein, Vsevolod Pudovkin, Leonid Trauberg, Leonid Lukov, and Grigori Kozintsev of ideological shortcomings and forced Eisenstein to sign a humiliating confession of "error." Stalin preferred such directors as M.E. Chiaureli, in whose *The Vow* (1946) the actor playing the dictator appeared with a halo.

Composers also felt the sting of Stalin's fury, and Zhdanov denounced Shostakovich, Khachaturyan, Prokofiev, and others for "bourgeois decadence," a concept previously unknown in musicology. The Gensek wanted folk music translated into the classical idiom. He declared in 1935 that he wanted music he could hum; his tastes never changed.

Stalin surprised Zhdanov late in 1946 by criticizing G.F. Aleksandrov's *A History of Western European Philosophy*. Aleksandrov, one of Zhdanov's lieutenants, headed Agitprop, supervised the Writers' Union and was the leading authority in philosophy. Stalin attacked Aleksandrov for failing to condemn Western philosophy and for taking the "un-Marxist and anti-Soviet" position that Russian philosophers had profited from the works of Western philosophers.

This was a period of extreme nationalism in the USSR. Stalinists put forward the claim that Russians had invented the radio, the light bulb, the airplane, the steam engine, and so forth. The party denounced everything from the West; Aleksandrov was one of the first condemned for "toadyism toward the West." He had further made the mistake, according to Stalin, of calling Marxism the culmination of Western philosophical thought. In the Gensek's view, Marxism represented the "overcoming" of earlier traditions.

Zhdanov's enemies, notably Beria and Malenkov, now declared that it was *he* who had become ideologically lax. In June 1947, Zhdanov unleashed a scathing assault on his friend Aleksandrov, but it was too late; the conservative ideologue M.A. Suslov replaced Aleksandrov at Agitprop. Suslov's top two deputies, D.T. Shepilov and L.F. Ilichev, were to play major roles as spokesmen for the conservatives. Suslov reigned supreme in the realm of ideology from 1953 until his death in 1982.

The course of the philosophy debate, more extensive than this account indicates, proved that Zhdanov was not invulnerable. A similar debate in economics had even more serious repercussions.

The leading Soviet economist was then Yevgeni Varga, whose 1946 *Changes in the Economy of Capitalism as a Result of the Second World War* became the focal point of a controversy pitting the Zhdanovites against the conservatives. Varga had argued that capitalist governments had acquired a great deal of control over their economies during the war and continued to intervene in them after 1945. Varga implied that the capitalist states, moving in a socialist direction, were less of a threat to the USSR. He also suggested that capitalism might not always suffer periodic crises. These views outraged Soviet conservatives.

In October 1947, Varga lost his job as the director of a major research institute; two months later the economics journal with which he had been associated ceased to exist. N.A. Voznesensky, a Zhdanov protégé promoted to full member of the Politburo in 1947, directed these moves.

Zhdanov died in August 1948 and thus did not witness the end of the economics debate. The following spring, Varga was forced to admit "errors of a cosmopolitan" character, and it seemed that Zhdanov's man had triumphed. But in March 1949, Voznesensky suddenly lost his government and party posts.

## THE "LENINGRAD CASE"

The spectacular reversal in the fortunes of Zhdanov and his men astonished everyone but those who engineered it. The former heir-apparent lost control of Agitprop (Propaganda and Agitation) to Mikhail Suslov, now also secretary for ideology on the Central Committee. Aloof from the Beria-Malenkov faction, Suslov stood still further away from the Zhdanov camp, and his rise spelled Zhdanov's fall.

Zhdanov suffered another setback in the break between Stalin and Yugoslavia's Tito. Along with Malenkov, he had represented the USSR at the founding of the Communist Information Bureau, or Cominform, in September 1947. Although Stalin already regarded Tito with great suspicion, the organization had its headquarters in Belgrade, where the Soviet delegation kept an eye on the Yugoslavs.

The Tito-Stalin quarrel approached the critical stage early in 1948, when delegations from Yugoslavia and Bulgaria came to Moscow. The Bulgarian Communist leader, Georgi Dimitrov, had proposed a merger between his country and Yugoslavia into a Balkan federation; Stalin vigorously opposed the scheme, which had Tito's tentative approval. Tension over this issue arose in Moscow and worsened when the Yugoslav negotiators made it clear that their country would no longer permit Soviet exploitation of its natural resources.

In the midst of the talks the Yugoslav delegates visited Leningrad. Some of them later remarked on the freer atmosphere there, where Zhdanov partisans controlled the party organization.

After the public break with Tito, Stalin accused his erstwhile heir-apparent of having been overly friendly with the Yugoslavs. On June 28, 1948, the Cominform expelled Yugoslavia. Suslov, chief Soviet representative at the meeting, authored the resolution; Malenkov and Zhdanov also attended, and Zhdanov was never seen in public again.

Zhdanov supporters abounded. Scores of high-level officials and hundreds of lesser bureaucrats had tied their careers to his and had carried out the misnamed *Zhdanovshchina*. Their patron's fall from grace left them stranded. Early in 1949 Minister of State Security V.S. Abakumov, a Beria protégé, secretly indicted Zhdanov's chief associates on various trumped-up charges including treason.

Having abolished the death penalty in May 1947, in January 1950 the rubber-stamp Supreme Soviet, acting on Stalin's direct order, restored it for "spies and traitors." With the new law designed expressly for them in place, the principal victims in what became known as the "Leningrad Case" were shot.

In the first of a series of disclosures out of the Kremlin over the past several decades, Khrushchev revealed in 1954 that Beria, Abakumov, and Malenkov had concocted the entire affair. They sold it to Stalin who, as still later revelations indicated, proved an eager buyer.

The most prominent victim, Voznesensky, had won a Stalin Prize in 1948. By early the next year, however, the anti-Zhdanov conspirators had persuaded Stalin of the man's disloyalty. Voznesensky's crime was to have cautiously suggested a modest economic reform. Stalin stripped him of his posts in March 1949; shortly thereafter Beria brought Voznesensky to trial on a charge of mishandling state secrets. Various "leaks" about the absurdity of the case reached high-ranking officials—including Khrushchev—who detested Beria and Malenkov; those officials demanded and won dismissal of the charges.

Voznesensky remained at liberty, worked on a new book, even dined with Stalin in the Kremlin in October 1949. The day after the dinner, the secret police arrested him. Held incommunicado for nearly a year, he was executed without trial on September 30, 1950.

The second chief victim, A.A. Kuznetsov, had been deputy chief of the Leningrad party organization. When Zhdanov went to Moscow in 1946, Kuznetsov went along and became a Central Committee secretary; he also served on the Orgburo, and in his two jobs oversaw the work of the security organs—Beria's special fief. Beria obviously would not willingly tolerate any interference, least of all from Zhdanov's men, but Stalin himself had appointed Kuznetsov. Not until February 1949 did Beria succeed in removing him; Kuznetsov simply disappeared. In the Khrushchev era the world learned he too was shot without a trial.

Aleksei Kosygin, who had held several important Leningrad, RSFSR, and national posts, and later became chairman of the Council of Ministers (premier) in the troika and Brezhnev years, was related to Kuznetsov by marriage. A full member of the Politburo since 1948, he served as both deputy premier and minister of finance. Somehow he survived Kuznetsov's fall.

Partial "rehabilitation" of the innocent victims began in the Khrushchev era and continued, at a greatly reduced pace, even after Khrushchev's fall. Not until the spring of 1988, however, did the Communist party officially reinstate—posthumously, of course—Voznesensky, Kuznetsov, and two dozen other leading Zhdanovites.

## TROFIM LYSENKO

One of the most sinister scientific discussions of modern times took place in August 1948 at the Lenin Agricultural Academy in Moscow. The president of the academy, Trofim Lysenko, brought a decade-long debate over biology and genetics to a head at a meeting of the membership. The controversy had not been conducted in scientific journals or in meetings among genuine scientists, for Lysenko had no standing in reputable circles. It was played out instead in *Literaturnaya gazeta* (Literary Gazette), the voice of the Writers' Union, and in philosophical publications. The Beria-Malenkov faction had taken over this publication, which frequently intervened in matters far removed from belles lettres.

The philosopher B.M. Kedrov, a vigorous opponent of the dogmatists, had published a book on Engels and natural science. This brought him to the attention of party mystagogues, who attacked him for failing to recognize a "Soviet science" distinct from and superior to that of the West.

At a time when Western scientists were on the verge of unlocking the mysteries of DNA, their Soviet counterparts were mired in an absurd dispute over Lamarckism and the "political significance" of the discoveries of the Russian plant breeder Ivan Michurin. Lysenko correctly read the postwar political climate and put forward a "two biologies" position. The Weismannist-Mendelist-Morganist, "bourgeois" variety stood in opposition to "Michurinist, Soviet"—therefore, proletarian—biology. Soviet scientists who believed in the existence of genes, or in the chromosome theory of heredity, were unpatriotic and pro-Western.

At the 1948 Lenin Agricultural Academy meeting, Lysenko delivered his report and waited patiently for his opponents to declare themselves. Most of the real scientists attacked him. Then he sprung his trap, revealing that the party Central Committee had already sided with him. He had Stalin's support; no one could be against him and survive. His opponents capitulated.

In 1948 Lysenko was content to have his opponents dismissed from their positions and denied the right to work in their specialties. There was no blood purge, and only two leading scientists were arrested, but hundreds of professors, senior researchers, and graduate students lost their jobs. Genetics research came to a complete halt and the field collapsed; even the fruit flies used in research were destroyed. The purge also swept through biology, and in related fields such as medicine anti-Lysenkoites were hounded from their jobs. Agricultural institutes endured rigorous ideological inspection.

## THE DEPORTATIONS

The Russians gave Stalin relatively little trouble; his worst problems involved the peoples on the frontiers. The further an ethnic group lived from Moscow, or the more recently it had become a member of the Soviet family, the more problems it seemed to pose. The Gensek was especially exasperated with some of the Turkic, Mongol, and Caucasian minorities.

In the early 1930s several Soviet minorities were resettled far from their homelands, but the most extensive deportations came as World War II was winding down. In November 1943 the entire population of 70,000 of the Karachai Autonomous Region was deported to Kazakhstan and Central Asia because some of the Karachai (a Turkic-speaking people of the northern Caucasus) had collaborated with the Germans. But 9,000 Karachai civilians had been killed in the first five days of the Nazi occupation of their homeland, and at the time of the 1943 deportations virtually all able-bodied adult males were in the Red Army.

At the end of December 1943 the population (about 95,000) of the Kalmyk Autonomous Soviet Socialist Republic (ASSR) in the northeastern Caucasus was deported to Central Asia and Siberia. Some Kalmyks, a Mongol, Buddhist people, had worked for the Germans, but most were loyal to the Soviet state. That did not save them.

The most controversial deportation took place in the Crimea. The Crimean Tatars, a Turkic-Mongol people, had lived on the peninsula since the 13th century. Under the Soviets they had their own ASSR, and they numbered about 250,000 in 1939. In World War II a few Crimean Tatars collaborated with the Germans, some because they hated the Communists, others out of fear. Still others hoped that German flirtation with the pan-Turkic movement would lead to the establishment of an independent Crimean state.

In the Crimea as everywhere in the USSR the overwhelming majority of the population was loyal. Nevertheless, in May 1944 about 200,000 Crimean Tatars were deported to "special settlements" in Central Asia and Kazakhstan and their ASSR was abolished. The Soviet government sent thousands of new settlers, mostly Russians and Ukrainians, into the peninsula, which became part of the RSFSR until February 1954, when it was transferred to the Ukrainian SSR.

The Chechens and Ingush, Caucasian-speaking peoples of the Checheno-Ingush ASSR in the southeastern Caucasus, were deported in 1944; together they numbered about 400,000. The same fate befell most of the 145,000 Kabardinians (Caucasian-speaking) and 38,000 Balkars (Turkic-speaking) of the Kabardino-Balkar ASSR in the south Caucasus.

In 1956 Nikita Khrushchev admitted that none of the deportations were motivated by military considerations. At the time they took place the Germans were in retreat and Soviet lines secure. Khrushchev called the treatment of the Karachai, Balkars, and Kalmyks "crude violations of the basic Leninist principles of the nationality policy of the Soviet Union." Between 1956 and 1967 the government withdrew the charge of treason and collaboration from the deported peoples, most of whom were allowed to return to their homelands. The Volga Germans and Crimean Tatars, however, were denied such permission even in the Gorbachev era.

## LIFE IN THE LATE STALIN ERA

The harvests of 1945 and 1946 were inadequate and shortages continued. Then good weather came in 1947, bringing excellent crops. Food rationing came to an end in December, as did rationing of a variety of other consumer items, most of which, however, remained in short supply. A currency reform the same month exchanged old rubles for new at the rate of 10:1. The reasons given for the reform were superficially plausible: to wipe out the ill-gotten gains of speculators, reduce the amount of money in circulation, and eliminate Nazi counterfeit money. It was indeed desirable to reduce the money supply and curb inflation, but no one could explain how speculators could have flourished under Stalin, and the amount of counterfeit money in circulation was insignificant. The currency reform wiped out the savings of millions of people. To sweeten the bitter pill the government granted price reductions averaging 10 percent on food. The cost of basic foodstuffs was set artificially low as the state subsidized the urban consumer at the expense of the kolhozniks.

The 1947–1950 price reductions appeared to confirm the government's claim that the national income had risen 64 percent between 1940 and 1950, and that productivity under the Fourth Five-Year Plan had increased substantially. Even more dramatic "confirmation" came with the February 18, 1950, decree putting the USSR on the gold standard: the ruble would henceforth be worth 0.22168 grams of pure gold. The exchange rate was fixed at 4.30 to the American dollar, 11.20 to the pound sterling, 0.9147 to the Swiss franc. All this had no meaning outside the realm of propaganda; the ruble did not become a convertible currency.

Except for the steel mills, the Moscow subway, and the secret police, it was difficult to find anything that functioned efficiently. Retail stores were a nightmare, with insufficient supplies of poor-quality merchandise served up by surly clerks; old apartments badly needed repair and new ones were so poorly constructed as to constitute instant slums; the clothing industry turned out garments suitable for storing potatoes; shoes sometimes disintegrated after a few wearings; even in Moscow and Leningrad it was almost impossible to find a laundry. Restaurants provided merely a warm place to eat unappetizing food: a common saying was "We've learned to cook steel but we can't master cabbage soup."

There were few private automobiles. Only high-ranking civilian and military officials and a few privileged people in the arts and the scientific establishment had them. The state began to produce a small Volkswagen-like Pobeda (Victory) after the war; plant managers, kolhoz managers, and other minor functionaries drove it. Middle-level officials drove the ZiM (Molotov Factory), and at the top, the "servants of the people" rode in splendid comfort in the ZiS (Stalin Factory) limousine, styled after American Packards of the 1930s. The masses were encouraged to buy the Penza bicycle.

Consumer goods in general received short shrift under the Fourth Plan and there was no provision for significant change in the Fifth (1951–1955). The Communist party was of course aware of the regime's shortcomings in providing for the material well-being of the citizenry. The overwhelming majority of party members had the same low standard of living as the population at large; only upon promotion to middle-level positions did party officials begin to enjoy the good life. There was little run-of-the-mill venality in Stalin's Russia; even petty thievery was severely punished.

People continued to give themselves or their children exotic names. An Ivan Petrov renamed himself "Cracking Kombinov"; he was probably an oil worker. Parents named girls Elektrifikatsiya (Electrification) and called them "Fika." Some mothers and fathers liked Detektor and Radiola; a few collective farmers preferred Pood (Bushel).

Mass sports began to develop vigorously after the war, and Soviet athletes entered international competition for the first time. In 1950 the Soviet team finished first in the European track and field championships in Brussels. At the 1952 Helsinki Olympic Games, Soviet athletes won 38 gold, 53 silver, and 15 bronze medals. Participation in sport became compulsory in primary and secondary schools, universities, and most institutes. Radio Moscow broadcast calisthenics commands for several minutes each morning and at intervals throughout the day. Some factories made participation in exercise mandatory, but this activity was never popular in industry and in offices—especially those of the party—and shop people ignored it.

The urban population increased from 60.6 million in 1941 to 71.4 million in 1951. To house this increase, the plan provided about 102 million square meters of living space (9.5 m² per person). But because the prewar housing shortage had been so great, and so many dwellings destroyed or damaged in the war, the situation remained desperate. Three generations often lived together in cramped quarters; divorced couples frequently continued to share a room because there was nowhere to go.

A massive construction program in Moscow alleviated the situation there only slightly. Several enormous structures in "Stalin Gothic" (wedding-cake) style went up in the capital. One housed Moscow University, another the ministry of foreign affairs; some were used as apartment houses. The government newspaper *Izvestiya* compared these buildings to those in the United States:

Our tall buildings have nothing in common with foreign skyscrapers. The American skyscraper is the unnatural grimace of a capitalist city, the monstrous expression of hopeless contradictions, the naked symbol of private, animal egoism. On the other hand, the multiple-storied buildings of Moscow are the highest expression of our planned city construction and the free, rational development of our cities.

The people who lived in those tall buildings, like everyone else in the USSR, were subject to laws and regulations that sought to direct every aspect of their lives. To spur population growth, replace wartime losses, and provide the labor force of the future, a July 1944 decree nullified common-law marriages and made divorce more difficult. This was intended to strengthen the family; the state assumed that couples who were merely living together would, as good citizens, comply with the law. In fact, however, many males—both married and unmarried—seized the confusion of the war years and the period right after the war to abandon their families.

Labor was exceedingly scarce, and factory managers often hired workers whose personal documents were open to a variety of interpretations. (The law stipulated that one's entire work record, entered in a special document mandatory for all adults, had to be inspected at each change of jobs.) In 1950 the press discussed the worsening problem of fathers who successfully avoided paying child support—25 percent of the father's wages for the first child, 50 percent for two or more children. As the postwar economy stabilized, and as party and government cracked down on managers who failed to enforce labor regulations, the problem slowly began to abate.

A complicating factor was the tax placed on single adults and childless married couples after the war. The state wanted to encourage marriage and child-bearing; unhappy couples sought divorce. Mothers—almost always granted custody—demanded financial support from ex-husbands who resented child-support payments and tried to avoid them. Many fathers were caught when they presented their children's birth certificates at the workplace to avoid paying the "childless" tax.

In 1943 the state abolished coeducation in primary and secondary schools. This was intended to improve discipline, which had eased during the war; it also reflected the Victorian prudery of Stalinist Russia. The new system was not popular. Ninety-eight percent of the letters to *Literaturnaya gazeta* on the subject in 1950 favored a return to coeducation, which in practice most schools had kept. The schools were terribly overcrowded; most operated two shifts, and except for Moscow, Leningrad, and Kiev, few even tried segregation by sex. Separate education ended in 1954.

Special education for the handicapped, neglected in the first three decades of Soviet rule, improved only slowly after the war, which added several million people to the ranks of the blind, the deaf, the physically mutilated, the psychologically tormented. The government's inability to help the war wounded and the handicapped adequately reflected not a lack of goodwill but rather inexperience and lack of funds. In the RSFSR in 1949 there were only 176 special schools.

Especially tragic was the fate of those who came out of the war with shattered minds. Those who could not cope with life on their own and did not have families were simply warehoused in military hospitals around the country. Psychologically damaged people who lived with their families often proved an unbearable burden.

The state did not make sufficient provision for damaged minds and did not always move quickly to restore shattered bodies. A September 1949 letter to *Pravda* complained that artificial legs did not fit. Many double amputees affixed casters to a small wooden platform on which they propelled themselves by pushing against the ground—a common sight for three decades after the war.

The plight of the handicapped received almost no attention in the media, which had the task of reporting only good news, the sort the state wanted people to read and hear. The media did, however, report the "crimes" of Stalin's victims as a heavy-handed warning to the citizenry.

In 1950, 7,700 newspapers had a combined circulation of more than 33 million. They, like radio and television, did not employ journalists in the Western sense but rather party-state publicists who reported not news but official propaganda.

In the infancy of Soviet television, in May 1950 only Moscow had service to the 7,845 sets in the city, and then only a few hours a day, four days a week. Television came to Leningrad in 1951, Kiev the following year.

By 1963 the number of television stations had grown to 418, and the sets, though expensive, were more reliable and more widely available. The standard Soviet television picture had 625 horizontally scanned lines displayed at 30 frames per second. This made for a sharp, clear image on the screen. (American technicians had prematurely committed themselves to the less satisfactory 525-line system).

## WOMEN IN THE POSTWAR PERIOD

The state only slowly came to the aid of women, upon whom enormous practical—to say nothing of psychological—burdens fell as a result of the death of millions of young men in the war. In 1949 the government proudly revealed that more than 100,000 women in kolhozes were brigade (team) leaders and managers. Behind this statistic, however, lay the brutal truth that many kolhozes were run exclusively by women because the men had not returned from the war. Lack of machinery forced women to perform backbreaking labor.

The same situation existed in urban areas. Female construction gangs and road crews remained a common sight into the 1970s. Women performed heavy labor in the factories, drove trucks, laid bricks, and worked in the mines. Most urban employed women, whether blue- or white-collar, worked the same hours as men, 48 per week. Those who were married had to do housework, shop, and care for the children in their "spare" time; Russian men traditionally shunned these tasks.

By 1949, 700 women had won the title of Hero of Socialist Labor, the highest civilian award. Another 237 had won Stalin Prizes in various fields. About 44 percent of all white-collar workers with a higher education were women; the percentage was much higher among those who had only a secondary education. Women continued to dominate the medical profession at least in numerical terms; about 75–80 percent of general practitioners were women. Men remained in control of prestigious branches of medicine such as surgery, they dominated research institutes, and on the political side of the profession (certification boards, hospital and research administration, the ministry of health) women had limited influence.

This male domination of medical power centers accounts only in part for the failure to address the matter of birth control in an enlightened manner. More significant was the state's desire to increase the population. Women who for any reason did not wish to carry a pregnancy through to term were left to their own devices. Contraception was an area most physicians ignored, as did the state. The population rose slowly after the war, but not at the rate the state desired.

Women's needs in the consumer area were frequently ignored. Dresses were badly cut and the colors drab; it was almost impossible to find an attractive pair of shoes. Underwear of coarse fabric usually came in two sizes, small and extremely large. Sanitary napkins were unknown. Cosmetics were few and of poor quality. After Stalin's death, the black market manufacture and sale of cosmetics became a profitable business.

Of the 1,339 delegates elected to the Supreme Soviet in February 1946, 177 were women. By 1949, 1,700 women were serving in the Supreme Soviets of the constituent republics and autonomous republics; half a million were members of local Soviets. Women deputies had no more power than their male counterparts. Real power lay in the Communist party hierarchy, where women occupied only a few token positions.

A handful of Soviet women married foreigners stationed in the USSR during World War II. After the victory such marriages were still tolerated although the state discouraged them. In February 1947, however, a decree forbade Soviet citizens to marry foreigners, even foreign Communists. Soviet citizens who saw foreigners socially were liable to arrest and deportation to the Gulag under Section 6 of Article 58 of the Criminal Code: Contacts Leading to Suspicion of Espionage.

## "ROOTLESS COSMOPOLITANS" AND THE "DOCTORS' PLOT"

Drawing on the wellsprings of the anti-Semitism that had long flourished in Eastern Europe, Stalin decided that the time had come to turn on the Jews. In the United Nations in 1947/1948 his representatives had backed the creation of Israel, but as the Cold War hardened the general secretary came to see this as a mistake. Many Soviet

Jews were charged with Zionism, which Stalin called treason.

In 1948 the secret police murdered the director (and noted actor) of the Moscow Jewish Theatre, Shlomo Mikhoels (Vovsi), on Stalin's personal order. Beria claimed that he had consorted with enemies of the USSR. During the war, as one of the leaders of the government-sponsored Jewish Anti-Fascist Committee, Mikhoels had visited the United States to raise funds. In 1948 the secret police declared that he had become an agent of the Joint Distribution Committee, a Jewish organization whose mission was to resettle the surviving European Jews after the war. Mikhoels and several other innocent victims won posthumous "rehabilitation" in April 1953.

Early in 1949 the Soviet press attacked an "anti-patriotic group of theatre critics," describing them as "rootless cosmopolitans." This term immediately became a code phrase for Jews in general and Zionists in particular. In August 1952, 24 Jewish poets, writers, actors, and intellectuals were sentenced to 25 years in the Gulag after a secret "trial" convicted them of treason. These talented young men were the flower of Soviet Jewish culture: Itzik Feffer, David Hofshteyn, Leyb Kvitko, Peretz Markish. Their crime was to be Jewish. MGB executioners shot them all in the Lubyanka cellars. In his poem "Day Grows Darker," Kvitko had written,

Let him at least note,
That my heart was bloody young,
That strong, like fear, was my will to live,
Strong and crazed,
Like my final day.

Not content to decimate the Jewish cultural intelligentsia, the Stalinists turned on Jews in the medical profession. According to accounts in the Soviet press in 1988, M.D. Ryumin, deputy head of the ministry of state security, concocted what became known as the "Doctors' Plot."

In the autumn of 1952, Lydia Timashuk, an obscure radiologist in the Kremlin Clinic, accused two superiors of having deliberately misread Zhdanov's electrocardiogram, thus hastening his death. With Zhdanov long dead, the secret police could safely lament his passing—like that of Kirov, Gorky, Ordzhonikidze, and many others—and even use it to settle new accounts.

Unquestionably with the approval of higher authority, Ryumin used Dr. Timashuk's belated testimony to arrest a number of Kremlin Clinic physicians on grounds of having plotted the medical murder of senior officials including Stalin. The spouses of the accused also went to prison, and their children lost their jobs and their standing in party and Komsomol. Seven of the nine who were originally accused were Jewish; the security organs claimed that the Joint Distribution Committee and American intelligence had masterminded the plot.

MGB inquisitioners obtained several "confessions" through torture. In January 1953 Timashuk received the Order of Lenin and a 100,000-ruble cash award that perhaps compensated for the arrest of her own husband, one of the Kremlin physicians.

The USSR broke diplomatic relations with Israel in February 1953. An "anti-Zionist" campaign that clings to life in the late 1980s had begun.

## 19TH PARTY CONGRESS

In an ominous rebuke to Beria, who retained control over the MGB although he technically did not head it, *Pravda* criticized the secret police for not exposing the "Doctors' Plot" earlier. Other top leaders felt Stalin's cold breath: Molotov could not prevent the arrest of his wife on trumped-up spy charges; Kalinin, Andreyev, Budyonny, and Aleksandr Poskrebyshev, chief of Stalin's personal secretariat, were equally powerless in similar situations; Mikoyan saw his son go off to prison. Malenkov suffered a setback in late 1949 when Stalin transferred Khrushchev from Kiev to Moscow and made him a secretary of the Central Committee and leader of the Moscow party organization.

The 19th CPSU Congress, the first in 13 years, met in Moscow in October 1952, a dispirited meeting that reflected anxiety over the anticipated purge. Two-thirds of the delegates were over 40, people who had risen to power over the bodies of the Great Terror's victims; now they too might find their own way to the Gulag.

Stalin had delivered the main report at every Congress since 1924. But this time, at 73 a mere shadow of his former self, he merely sat alone in the first row behind the rostrum, a small, gray-haired old man on whom every terrified eye focused.

Despite his reverses, Malenkov remained the only man at Stalin's right hand in both party and government and thus he gave the main speech outlining the party's accomplishments since the 1939 meeting and its plans for the future. Malenkov pronounced the grain problem solved, the perennial agricultural crisis ended; Stalin alone could have sanctioned such fanciful claims.

The 19th Congress rid the party of most reminders of a Bolshevik heritage Stalin detested because his role in it had been, all things considered, less than heroic. The name All-Union Communist Party (Bolsheviks) now gave way to Communist Party of the Soviet Union (CPSU). Having executed so many members of the old party, Stalin erased the word Bolshevik from the Soviet political lexicon.

Khrushchev revealed new party statutes which *inter alia* renamed the Politburo the Presidium and provided for its fourfold increase to 25 full members and 11 candidates. Newcomers would swamp Stalin's old cronies, who could be made to disappear.

An enlarged Central Committee was to have 125 full members and 111 candidates. The new statutes abolished the Orgburo and transferred its functions to the Central Committee Secretariat, which henceforth became the second most powerful—after the Presidium—party body. The Control Commission, the Rabkrin successor which monitored compliance with party directives and generally acted as a watchdog agency, would report directly to the Central Committee. Party conferences were abolished, and the general secretary was redesignated first secretary.

Stalin spoke only at the last session to welcome the delegates of foreign Communist and worker parties. He offered his opinion that the world bourgeoisie had abandoned the fictions of democratic freedoms and national independence; thus, there now existed just two camps in the world, the socialist and the monopoly-capitalist.

The ex-seminary student had always seen politics and life in general in stark terms. As he neared his end, the forces of darkness loomed ever larger, the one threat with which he could not contend. All his life he had sought isolation; now, we may suppose, he realized that fate had cursed him by granting his wish. He could only lash out at the traitors and take them down with him.

## DEATH OF A GENSEK

On December 21, 1952, Stalin celebrated or at least pondered his 73rd birthday privately. Only a brief mention appeared in the press, nothing like the sickening adulation three years earlier.

Rumors of an impending purge filled the

air as Muscovites speculated on the longevity of Beria, many of whose hirelings in Georgia—his homeland—had fallen from grace earlier in the year. January 1953 saw the arrest of Aleksandr Poskrebyshev, and in February Beria told Molotov of his fear that Stalin would kill them all.

On February 7 the Argentinian ambassador met with Stalin and afterward reported nothing out of the ordinary about the dictator's appearance or manner. Ten days later the Indian envoy found the Gensek sketching wolves. Russian peasants, Stalin said, knew how to deal with wolves: they killed them. The wolves knew this and conducted themselves appropriately.

Three daily shifts of several hundred men each guarded Stalin's *dacha* at Kuntsevo, a Moscow suburb. When the Gensek was alone in his rooms there, no one had the authority to disturb him. Late Sunday evening, March 1, 1953, the chief of the guard called Presidium members to report that the Generalissimo had not rung for his dinner. Several leaders rushed to Kuntsevo and found Stalin unconscious on the floor. The new Kremlin physicians were summoned; they decided to treat the patient at the *dacha* rather than try to move him.

The first public mention of Stalin's illness came on March 4, when TASS announced that the leader had suffered a cerebral hemorrhage. The prognosis was uncertain. The team of 10 physicians led by the minister of public health twice applied leeches to draw blood.

The ministrations were in vain. Although he regained consciousness a couple of times, Stalin was paralyzed and could not speak. According to the official version, he died on March 5 at 9:50 p.m.

All 10 attending physicians—the fate of other Kremlin doctors very much on their minds—signed the death certificate. The Presidium's Secretariat telephoned political and military leaders around the country. Only then, at 4:00 a.m. on March 6, did the second best-known voice in the USSR, that of Radio Moscow's Yuri Levitan, broadcast the news that the dictator was dead.

The party issued a communiqué short on grief. The Presidium insisted on "high political vigilance" in the "irreconcilable struggle against domestic and foreign enemies." The leaders decreed three days of mourning; there had been five for Lenin. State radio played funeral music constantly, interrupting it only to broadcast tributes.

The body was removed to Moscow, embalmed, then taken to the Hall of Columns in Union House. Here Lenin had lain in state 29 years earlier, here his colleagues had been condemned to death on Stalin's orders.

The communiqué announcing Stalin's death had warned against "disorder and panic," but only Beria among the top officials had any plan for controlling crowds and incidentally for positioning himself to seize power. He moved several secret police divisions—including tank units—into striking distance of Red Square.

Thousands of regular police and army troops were no match for the millions of citizens who tried to reach the center of the city. Many people were sobbing uncontrollably; hundreds were trampled to death in the densely packed throngs that stretched 10–15 kilometers in all directions from Union House.

Khrushchev organized the funeral. He had Stalin's body, which would be placed on permanent—until 1961—exhibition in the mausoleum next to Lenin, dressed in a military uniform bedecked with medals, placed on a raised bier surrounded by flowers. An honor guard stood at attention.

On March 9 pallbearers Malenkov, Beria, Molotov, Kaganovich, Voroshilov, Khrushchev, Nikolai Bulganin (appointed to the

Politburo in 1948), and Mikoyan carried the body the few hundred meters to the Lenin Mausoleum. The first three delivered funeral orations; only Molotov betrayed emotion.

Stalin was laid to rest beside the man whose legacy he had claimed nearly three decades earlier. For nearly two of those decades he had wielded more power than anyone in history. No one would ever be able to count his victims. He was the greatest mass murderer of all time, yet even in the Gulag there were prisoners who mourned him, convinced that he had not known of the horrors perpetrated in his name. Stalin took the uncertainty out of life, and millions of people praised him for replacing their many little worries with one big fear.

For a variety of complex historical reasons, Russian society had failed to evolve a constitutional system that could calm the collective fear of chaos, a fear regarded as irrational only by peoples whose own untidy origins have been banished to the outermost corners of the collective memory. In the centuries after the disintegration of the Kievan state, a catastrophe followed by the still greater horror of the Mongol invasion and 250-year occupation, Russia equated salvation with the rule of a powerful prince. None was more powerful, none more terrible, than the Russified Georgian Ossete who held a great nation in thrall for a quarter of a century.

## SUGGESTED ADDITIONAL READING

**Allworth, Edward, ed.,** *Tatars of the Crimea: Their Struggle for Survival*, Durham, N.C.: Duke University Press, 1988

**Conquest, Robert,** *The Nation Killers: The Soviet Deportation of Nationalities*, New York: Macmillan, 1960

**Dunham, Vera S.,** *In Stalin's Time: Middleclass Values in Soviet Fiction*, New York: Cambridge University Press, 1976

**Ehrenburg, Ilya,** *Post-war Years, 1945–1954*, Cleveland: World Publishing Co., 1967

**Graham, Loren R.,** *Science and Philosophy in the Soviet Union*, New York: Knopf, 1972

**Hahn, Werner G.,** *The Fall of Zhdanov and the Defeat of Moderation, 1946–1953*, Ithaca, N.Y.: Cornell University Press, 1982

**Joravsky, David,** *The Lysenko Affair*, Cambridge: Harvard University Press, 1970

**Medvedev, Zhores,** *The Rise and Fall of T.D. Lysenko*, New York: Columbia University Press, 1969

**Nekrich, Aleksandr M.,** *The Punished Peoples*, New York: W.W. Norton, 1978

**Pinkus, Benjamin,** *The Soviet Government and the Jews, 1948–1967*, New York: Cambridge University Press, 1985

**Tucker, Robert C., ed.,** *Stalinism*, New York: W.W. Norton. 1977

# 15

# THE "THAW"

No healthy political organism could grow in Stalin's awesome shadow. After Stalin came nothingness—hence the mediocrity of most of his heirs-apparent.

On March 10, 1953, *Pravda* featured a photograph of Stalin, Mao Zedong, and Malenkov on page one. It was a fake, an old photo altered to crop out other Soviet officials. This crude attempt to place Malenkov on equal footing with the giants of the international Communist movement backfired. Four days later Malenkov "requested" relief from his major party assignments "in order to concentrate on governmental duties." He remained chairman of the Council of Ministers, but Khrushchev replaced him as first secretary of the party. It seemed that a new *troika* was in place: Malenkov in charge of the government,

Beria of security, Khrushchev as party leader.

The emergence of Khrushchev occasioned some surprise because he was known to have sharp differences with several members of the new Presidium. That he nevertheless became party leader, the post from which Lenin and Stalin had derived their power, indicated that he had substantial support in the Central Committee and the party apparatus.

With Malenkov as head of government and Voroshilov as titular head of State, the high-visibility posts remained in the hands of Stalinist party regulars; political cadres around the country were reassured. No one anticipated that Khrushchev would attempt any innovations. The Presidium proclaimed collectivity the "highest principle of party leadership." Few people took this seriously; Stalin had said the same thing in 1924.

The sudden ouster of Malenkov from his party post confused the issue. Khrushchev did not appear to be of dictator caliber. As for Beria: when he failed to mount a coup d'état immediately after Stalin's death he was finished. Molotov deserved the "finest file clerk in Russia" label Lenin pinned on him in 1920; Kaganovich seemed unlikely to step into Stalin's shoes, not least because he was Jewish; Voroshilov richly merited his reputation as a drunken fool; no one considered the other leading members of the Presidium—Mikoyan, Bulganin, Saburov, Pervukhin—anything but run-of-the-mill Stalinist lackeys.

## FIRST STEPS OF THE NEW REGIME

The niggardliness of the "Voroshilov amnesty" of March 27, 1953, marking the changing of the guard reflected the new leaders' devotion to Stalinism: of the 10–12 million people then in prisons and the Gulag, only about 4,000 received their liberty. The amnesty did not extend to political prisoners. The sole well-known "political" among those released, Polina Zhemchuzhina, owed her good fortune to the fact that Vyacheslav Molotov was her husband. Molotov and Beria met her at the railway station on her return to Moscow. Beria gave her a bouquet of flowers and a box of chocolates, and her husband cried.

Price reductions on consumer items had a far greater impact on the Soviet people than the amnesty. On April 1 the state reduced prices for potatoes, cabbage, and fruit by 50 percent; bread, flour, cereals, rice, and legumes dropped 10 percent; meat and meat products, 15 percent. The Council of Ministers also announced cuts in the prices for clothing, shoes, and other consumer goods and declared that Soviet citizens would save 46 billion rubles annually. Unlike previous selective and relatively meaningless price reductions, this one, directed by Malenkov, had substance. Conscious of his tenuous position, Malenkov gambled on a virtually unknown tactic in appealing to public opinion.

Stalin had denied the people any rewards after the war and had continued to emphasize defense spending and the development of heavy industry. His last published work, *Economic Problems of Socialism in the USSR*, had defended this policy; and Stalin had executed the would-be reformer, Voznesensky. Malenkov could hardly go against Stalin's teachings but he could try to carve out a position between Stalinist priorities and those of younger reform-minded Communists who called for improvement in the standard of living. This "middle way" saw him claim that the country could maintain the pace in heavy industry and defense and yet put more consumer goods on the market.

A so-called "steel eater" (priority to heavy industry), Nikita Khrushchev did not at first challenge Malenkov. In the economic sphere, Khrushchev devoted himself to agriculture, the area in which he was allegedly an expert. This price cuts of April 1953 had his support and indeed that of every Presidium member save Molotov.

One of the strongest advocates of courting public opinion was Beria. Keenly aware of his security-organs stigma and unable to seize power by force, he took up Malenkov's economic arguments and attempted to make them his own. Now head of the recombined (March 1953) ministry of internal affairs and state security, he sought to emphasize his non-police functions and reassure party members that Lavrenti Beria was a decent fellow.

The act fooled no one. On April 4 the government branded the "Doctors' Plot" a fabrication, released and reinstated the doctors, and denounced Timashuk for her false testimony. This signalled party cadres that there would be no general purge and constituted a warning to Beria and Malenkov—the anti-Zhdanovites—that other manufactured scandals, certainly including the "Leningrad Case," would come under scrutiny.

## FALL OF BERIA

On April 6 a *Pravda* editorial blamed the "Doctors' Plot" on former Minister of State Security S.D. Ignatyev and his deputy, M.D. Ryumin. These were Stalin's men, not Beria's; Beria may well have breathed a sigh of relief. And he probably convinced himself that this ominous notice in the same issue of the party newspaper did not apply to him:

Nobody will be permitted to violate Soviet law. Every worker, every collective farmer, and every Soviet intellectual can work confidently and in peace, knowing that his civil rights are reliably guarded by Soviet socialist law.

The citizen of the great Soviet state can be confident that his rights, guaranteed by the USSR constitution, will be solemnly preserved and defended by the Soviet government.

Pious assurances of the sanctity of the infamous 1936 "Stalin" Constitution had of course appeared with great regularity over the years. This one, however, published alongside the admission that a recent "conspiracy" had been concocted by the secret police, indicated that a purge of the *purgers* was in the offing. Exposure of the "Doctors' Plot" would not satisfy the party's determination to seek out and punish at least some of those who had tormented its members. The admission that the Kremlin physicians had been framed by the secret police indicated that the party intended to take control of the organization.

Beria applauded the arrest of Ignatyev and Ryumin, confident his own tracks were hidden. He was further lulled into a sense of security by his success in restoring some of his friends to their posts in the Georgian party and secret police bureaucracies.

On June 28, 1953 *Izvestiya* mentioned Beria's name in a routine dispatch that gave no hint of any change in his status. That same evening he was arrested.

The news was not immediately made public. For several days the Presidium waited, evidently fearing that Beria's disappearance might automatically trigger a secret police attempt to free him and install him as dictator. No such attempt materialized.

On July 9 a meeting of about 2,000 key party workers took place in Union House in Moscow. Khrushchev and other officials denounced Beria as an "enemy of the party and the state" and revealed that he had been arrested and relieved of all official functions. The party faithful learned that the deposed minister had acted illegally and arbitrarily; sabotaged the food supply; tried to place his ministry above the party and government; interfered detrimentally in the economy. The Presidium also called Beria a "bourgeois-nationalist deviationist" who had tried to pit nationality against nationality in the USSR and a "bourgeois degenerate and agent of international imperialism." This indictment of a man who had been exceptionally close to Stalin for nearly 15 years was published on July 10.

Several high-ranking officials in Beria's ministry went to prison, as did some of their counterparts in the republics. A five-month investigation uncovered a record of Beria's personal crimes, mostly of a sexual nature, as well as an avalanche of information about the operation of the Gulag system. Khrushchev and other top officials, like the Germans who claimed never to have heard of the SS or the death camps, professed shock. It is not known whether the indictment cited Beria's orchestration of the Katyn atrocity.

The state tried Beria and five of his closest associates on December 17–22 under the Kirov Law—really Stalin's personal decree—of December 1, 1934, that is, without being present or represented by counsel. Marshal I.S. Konev presided. The press reported only that the accused had made use of "strictly forbidden methods of conducting investigations" and had "falsified court proceedings and accused completely innocent persons of state crimes." Communist party complicity was not mentioned. On Christmas Day, 1953, the nation learned that the defendants had been convicted and shot.

## AFTER BERIA

Because the Presidium believed them implicated to some extent in Beria's crimes, the commandant of the Kremlin, the military commandant of Moscow, and the commander-in-chief of the Moscow military district were all dismissed. It was not clear where the purge would end.

One of his most notorious henchmen and a few underlings were gone, but the dead Stalin remained a presence in Soviet politics. His name appeared regularly in the press, which hailed him as the "great continuer of Lenin's cause." On the first anniversary of his death *Pravda* praised his war record and leadership in the purges. No one seemed to have noticed that, six weeks earlier, speaking on the anniversary of *Lenin's* death, Khrushchev had not mentioned Stalin.

In July 1954 M.D. Ryumin was tried and shot for his role in fabricating the "Doctors' Plot." In December 1954 former minister of state security V.S. Abakumov and five of his associates went on trial for fabricating

the "Leningrad Case." Abakumov and three others were convicted and shot; two defendants received sentences of 25 and 15 years.

Testimony in the Abakumov trial implicated only the late Beria among the higher-ups, but Malenkov's role in the affair could not remain hidden for long. The party had repeatedly been decimated by purges, of which the "Leningrad Case" was the last, during the Stalin years. Unfortunately for Malenkov, Stalin had died soon after that episode. The survivors among Zhdanov's friends were free to seek vengeance.

Nikita Khrushchev led the Central Committee faction that successfully argued for putting Ryumin and Abakumov on trial, insisting that the party remove the terrible stain left by Beria. The Malenkov-Molotov "wing," a very loose coalition on this issue, took the opposite line, pleading the shopworn case against washing dirty linen in public. This argument prevailed in the Presidium, but Khrushchev won a majority in the Central Committee.

At the funeral of Andrei Vyshinsky in November 1954, Molotov spoke for party conservatives. Over the corpse of the Soviet chief inquisitioner he said,

His brilliant speeches in defense of Soviet legality and his accusations, which we all remember, against the enemies of the Soviet state, against saboteurs and subversive foreign agents and against traitorous groups of Trotskyites and right-wingers, were a great and unforgettable service to the Soviet people.

Vyshinsky would indeed long be remembered, but not in the way Molotov suggested. The Abakumov trial, the very existence of which constituted an indictment of all that Vyshinsky and Molotov stood for, went forward as Khrushchev and his supporters on the Central Committee had demanded.

## AGRICULTURE AND POLITICS

In the spring of 1953 Khrushchev fought successfully for a change in the way the peasants were taxed. Taxes replaced levies in kind on privately owned cattle and other farm animals, fruit trees, beehives, and so forth, and the state agreed to purchase the products of the private sector at favorable prices. The party thus gave the peasants some incentives, and they responded dramatically. The agricultural situation improved, as did peasant morale.

At a special plenum on agriculture in September 1953 Khrushchev persuaded his Central Committee colleagues to reduce taxes on individual gardens and farm animals still further. The tax on cows and pigs was abolished altogether, and the state encouraged blue- and white-collar workers to keep animals and maintain small gardens where possible. These gardens, and the household plots of the peasants, were limited to 0.25 hectare (0.6 acre), on which the owner could keep a cow, two pigs, a goat, fowl, beehives, etc. This private sector flourished and supplied the cities with fresh vegetables and other products which they otherwise would have had difficulty obtaining. The relaxation of controls on the peasants helped avert a crisis in 1954. The private plots (less than 2 percent of the arable land was involved) alone could not, however, solve the agricultural problems that had plagued the country since the birth of the Soviet regime.

In an attempt to deal with those problems the September plenum injected large sums of money into the countryside. The state raised the prices paid kolhozes for their products, agreed to increase purchases, and cancelled old debts. The income of the average peasant family increased almost 400 percent between 1953 and 1954. This brought the peasants up to the level of the lowest-paid industrial workers for the first time since NEP.

Kolhoz managers used the infusion of funds not only to increase wages but also to provide disguised incentive bonuses. The party did not like this practice but tolerated it. Production rose substantially: meat by 32 percent, milk 61 percent, eggs 44 percent, wool 36 percent. The production of sugarbeets more than doubled. Grain yields increased an average of 7 to 11 centners per hectare.

These achievements enhanced Khrushchev's stature. He was unable, however, to make any headway in establishing "agrotowns," large rural population centers from which the peasants would commute each day into the fields. He had advanced this scheme in 1951 as the logical outcome of his amalgamation of the kolhozes. Malenkov and Beria had opposed him; Stalin had sided with them. There was also a great deal of hostility within the Central Committee and among party committeemen after 1953.

Khrushchev had more success with the development of the "virgin lands" in northern Kazakhstan and the Altai. A December 1953 *Pravda* editorial noted that at least 6 million hectares of arable land in the Altai were used as pasture and for hay. Why, the newspaper asked, should this land not be sown to wheat? Intensive public discussion resulted in the Central Committee's March 5, 1954, "Decree on Virgin and Idle Lands." About 2.3 million hectares would be brought under the plow in 1954, 10.7 million in 1955. By 1958 more than 30 million hectares were sown to grain, principally wheat and corn.

Hundreds of thousands of volunteers went from the old agricultural regions and the cities to develop the new lands. In 1954 almost the entire production of the agricultural implements industry went to the "virgin lands": 50,000 15-horsepower tractors, more than 6,000 trucks, 10,000 mower-threshers, and thousands of other implements were rushed to the area.

The first results were not encouraging. Only about 3 million tons of grain came from the new lands in 1954. The verdict on the scheme, however, was postponed pending more systematic development.

Because the party refused to cut defense spending, the Khrushchev faction's attempt to reform the agricultural sector inevitably had political repercussions. Committing vast sums to revitalize the kolhozes and develop the "virgin lands" made it impossible to provide the consumer goods that Malenkov and his supporters wanted. Khrushchev met this reality squarely and fell back upon the time-tested "hard" line that called for primary attention to defense and heavy industry. Marshal Zhukov and the military supported him, as did Bulganin and Saburov. Taking the opposite tack were Malenkov, Mikoyan, Kosygin, and Minister of Agriculture Ivan Benediktov.

An acrimonious debate in the Presidium and the Central Committee ended with Malenkov's defeat late in 1954 on the eve of the Abakumov trial. The timing suggests that Khrushchev, confident of a majority in the Central Committee, gave Malenkov an ultimatum: accept defeat on the "guns versus butter" issue and resign as premier, or face exposure as architect of the "Leningrad Case."

Malenkov resigned, confessing that he had failed to grasp the rationale behind the party's emphasis on heavy industry and that his attention to party work had left him confused by the complexities of running the government. He accepted blame for the agricultural failures of 1950–1953.

The resignation was not publicly announced until the next regularly scheduled meeting of the Supreme Soviet two months later, in February 1955; the outside world thus received the impression of an orderly transfer of power. Malenkov retained his seat on the Presidium, but he would no longer play a significant role in politics.

Bulganin became premier. A colorless party hack, he had been a member of the Central Committee for 20 years, of the Presidium for six. He had worked with Khrushchev in Moscow in the 1930s and the two men had remained friendly. Khrushchev engineered Bulganin's appointment as premier and placed men loyal to himself in other ministries, notably interior and agriculture. For his support in the conspiracy that toppled Beria, Marshal Zhukov received the ministry of defense.

The governmental changes accompanied an even more important if less publicly visible reorganization of the party apparatus as Khrushchev installed his supporters in key posts and thus consolidated his position. He had become the most powerful man in the USSR without resorting to violence.

Strong as Khrushchev was he was no Stalin, and it appeared in the summer of 1955 that he might lose everything. Weather conditions in the "virgin lands" were miserable; the harvest failed. Malenkov, Kaganovich, Molotov, and others blamed the first secretary for the disaster and argued that the funds and manpower committed to the new lands might better have been applied in the traditional grain-growing districts.

Despite dry conditions in the Ukraine and the Volga Valley, the 1956 harvest was the best in Russian history. The performance of the "virgin lands" was especially good: Kazakhstan alone produced 16 million tons of grain, outstripping the Ukraine. In all, the collective and state farms produced 125 million tons, about half in the eastern part of the country that included the new lands. Khrushchev was saved.

## NEW LOOK IN FOREIGN POLICY

The leaders who succeeded Stalin proclaimed Soviet foreign policy fixed and immutable. In practice they immediately began to alter it. In May 1953 the Soviets abolished the control commission through which they had ruled their sector of Germany and appointed a single high commissioner. This system had earlier proved effective in the Western sectors and had simplified efforts to form an independent West German state. The Soviets and the East German puppet regime instituted a series of reforms, including granting the right to engage in public demonstrations. The new regulations were accompanied, however, by the tightening of labor discipline and a 10 percent rise in production quotas. A disguised form of reparations, the quotas were already high by Soviet standards. On June 16 thousands of East Berlin residents took to the streets to protest harsh new labor rules and to call for a general strike. The following day the Soviet authorities sent tanks against the demonstrators. Wire services flashed photographs around the world of Berliners attacking tanks with rocks and fists.

The East Berlin events helped galvanize the anti-Beria conspiracy in Moscow. Many Central Committee and Presidium members blamed Beria for letting the situation in Germany, where the Soviet secret police was present in force, get out of hand. In 1963 Khrushchev revealed that, on Stalin's death, Beria and Malenkov had urged German Democratic Republic leaders to renounce their socialist policies so as not to offend the West.

The German protests were quelled, but the authorities rescinded the increase in production quotas and made other concessions. They removed travel restrictions between East and West Berlin and on July 11 lifted martial law. The first of the foreign tremors in part traceable to the struggle for power in the Kremlin ended in partial victory for the East Germans. That would have been unthinkable under Stalin, and it foreshadowed further upheavals.

Stalin's major postwar defeat had come at the hands of Marshal Tito, who had defied the USSR and made Yugoslavia a second capital of world communism. The Chinese Communist seizure of power in 1949 added a third, further diluting the Soviet role in the movement. Stalin was infuriated; the last thing he wanted was for strong Communist leaders to come to power. After his death, the world waited to see how new Soviet leaders would deal with Tito and Mao.

The first public indication of a thaw in Soviet-Yugoslav relations came on November 7, 1953, when Soviet newspapers published Tito's congratulatory message on the anniversary of the Bolshevik Revolution. Several months of steady improvement in the diplomatic climate followed. In September 1954 *Pravda* and other Soviet newspapers published extracts from a Tito speech, and in October the Soviet press marked the 10th anniversary of the liberation of Belgrade with a number of interpretive articles. The following January a modest trade agreement was signed.

Stalin had misjudged Tito and the Yugoslavs almost as badly as he had the Chinese Communists in the 1920s. He had backed Jiang Jieshi, and to express his gratitude Jiang had slaughtered every Communist he could find. The Chinese Communists never forgave Stalin, but in 1949 they needed allies.

In December 1949, two months after he seized power, Mao flew to Moscow for talks with Stalin. No longer a guerrilla chieftain living in filthy caves in Shaanxi but leader of a nation of 600 million, Mao had reason to hope he would be treated as an equal. He erred. Behind the public embraces and expressions of respect, the Soviets dealt with him condescendingly, dragging out the negotiations for nine weeks before finally, in February 1950, giving him a mere tip: $60 million in economic assistance annually for five years.

Not only was the amount insultingly small, but China had to agree to a number of minor border rectifications in favor of the USSR and to recognize the independence of Outer Mongolia, a territory formerly subject to China but for two decades a Soviet puppet. Further, Stalin made it clear that he would expect concessions in return for helping develop China's natural resources. Mao later said that getting anything at all out of the Soviet dictator was "like taking meat from the mouth of a tiger."

Mao signed the humiliating agreement; a desperately poor, politically isolated China had no hope of economic aid from any other source. Beyond that, an American-backed invasion by Jiang's forces—now on Taiwan—seemed a strong possibility, and China had to build her defenses. Stalin sent 3,000 military advisers to begin modernizing the People's Liberation Army. The Chinese invested the tiny Soviet credits they had obtained in the armaments industry.

Stalin's demise occasioned no mourning in China. Mao read a statement describing the Soviet leader as the "greatest genius of the present age" who was "known for his ardent love of the Chinese people." That said, it was business as usual.

There was a marked improvement in Soviet-Chinese relations after Stalin's death. In September 1953 the Kremlin agreed to undertake 141 major construction projects in China, providing not only the money but also equipment and technology. The just-ended Korean War had exposed more painfully than ever China's weaknesses, and the new projects would enable the country to emulate the Soviet pattern of development,

building a socialist economy based on heavy industry. Soviet technicians and trainloads of machines and supplies poured into China.

The Soviets had supported the People's Republic of China in the United Nations since October 1949, arguing that the Communists should replace the Nationalist Chinese. Because of the opposition of the United States those efforts were unavailing. At the Geneva Conference on Far Eastern Affairs in April–July 1954, the Soviets again vigorously backed the Communist Chinese, whose delegation leader, Zhou Enlai, was publicly humiliated by Secretary of State John Foster Dulles. The conference formalized the Korean Armistice and reviewed the agreement by which France had abandoned her colonial position in Vietnam.

Stalin had promised to withdraw Soviet occupation forces from Port Arthur, Manchuria, by 1952. Sent as part of the agreement under which the Soviets had entered the war against Japan, the troops had remained ostensibly to protect the Liaodong Peninsula against the possibility of an American invasion during the Korean War. When Khrushchev went to Beijing for the fifth anniversary celebration of the People's Republic, he and Mao announced on October 11, 1954, that Soviet forces would be withdrawn from Port Arthur by the end of May 1955.

Welcoming Khrushchev to Beijing, Mao naturally had no inkling that 17 months later his visitor would begin to dismantle the Stalinist system. Mao offered him a thousand divisions to crush the Americans; Khrushchev retorted that American atomic bombs would incinerate them and asked instead for a million lumberjacks. A deeply offended Mao replied that the Soviets should not look to China as a source of cheap labor.

Khrushchev tried to atone for his blunder with offers of increased military and economic aid calculated to win Mao's support in the impending showdown with Malenkov. Mao accepted the aid but never forgave the insult. When Khrushchev, victorious over Malenkov, began to speak in 1955 of the possibility of "peaceful coexistence" between Communist and capitalist states, Mao abandoned hope of cooperation.

The Khrushchev regime carried its campaign for the relaxation of international tension to the West in 1955. In April the Soviets suddenly agreed to sign a peace treaty with Austria, a step they had resisted for nearly a decade. Only Molotov among the post-Stalin leaders opposed the treaty. Two months later Marshal Zhukov sent a warm message to his former comrades-in-arms in the United States, and in July Khrushchev and Bulganin traveled to Geneva to meet President Eisenhower, Prime Minister Anthony Eden of Great Britain, and Premier Edgar Faure of France. Because of the peculiar nature of the Soviet system, Khrushchev, who held no government post, was merely "attached" to a delegation led by Bulganin.

The Geneva "summit" conference, the first since Potsdam, dealt with German reunification, arms control and disarmament, and European security. The two sides had sparred over the German issue for a decade with no result; hopes for German reunification had plunged in May 1955 when the West German Federal Republic gained its independence and joined NATO. The Soviets responded by creating the Warsaw Pact, a 20-year military alliance with their East European satellites.

East and West had debated arms control since the 1920s. Both sides presented proposals to the United Nations in the spring of 1955, and there was substantial agreement on the size of conventional forces that could be permitted the major powers: 1.5 million each for the United States, the USSR, and

Communist China, and 650,000 each for Britain and France. In the matter of atomic and thermonuclear weapons, however, there was no movement. Both sides professed a horror of nuclear war and insisted that some means of control be found; neither would make concessions. Confident of the huge American lead in nuclear weapons and delivery systems (the B-52 bomber), Eisenhower put forward an "open skies" proposal that would have allowed each side to photograph the other's territory from the air to verify an agreement prohibiting the deployment of new weapons of mass destruction. Existing weapons would remain in place pending further negotiation.

Painfully conscious of their nuclear inferiority, the Soviets would not agree to any treaty that would halt development of new weapons. In rejecting the proposal Khrushchev charged that Eisenhower's "open skies" was a scheme to legalize American spying on Soviet military and industrial capabilities.

Despite the negotiators' failure to make progress on substantive issues, journalists invented a "spirit of Geneva." Khrushchev and Bulganin, with their ill-fitting suits and awkward public manners, seemed far more approachable than Stalin, and they trusted Eisenhower more than they had Truman. They had fought with him against a common enemy and considered him more reasonable than his predecessor. The Soviets and the Americans did agree at Geneva to initiate cultural and commercial contacts. To the extent that these contributed to better understanding the Geneva Conference was not a failure.

Rarely had the world seen such a traveling diplomatic show as Khrushchev and Bulganin staged in 1955. In addition to Belgrade—where they apologized for Stalin's errors—and Geneva they journeyed to India, Burma, and Afghanistan late in the year. John Foster Dulles had informed the leaders of those and other nations that neutralism was "immoral," and the Soviet leaders set out to offer a different interpretation. Prime Minister Jawaharlal Nehru of India and Prime Minister U Nu of Burma had impeccable anti-imperialist credentials which could, Khrushchev and his colleagues realized, be useful to the Kremlin.

In the mid-1950s the United States and its allies continued to maintain an overwhelming military superiority vis-à-vis the Soviet Union and the other Warsaw Pact nations; the Communist seizure of power in China had not significantly altered this imbalance. The post-Stalin Soviet commitment of substantial sums to help the Chinese modernize might lead to the strengthening of the Communist "bloc," but Khrushchev knew what the West did not, namely, that a monolithic bloc did not exist.

The national interests of the Soviet Union and the People's Republic of China were in many areas diametrically opposed. The Chinese historically had detested the Russians as imperialists who had helped dismember the Celestial Kingdom. The Soviets feared an aggressive China with unmatchable manpower reserves. All this made it virtually certain that the fragile alliance of February 1950 would not endure.

India, Burma, Arab lands, Latin American nations, and African territories began to figure prominently in Soviet geopolitical thinking. The peoples of these lands could theoretically be wooed and won through an anti-imperialist, anti-colonialist campaign led by Moscow. As strong as the United States and its allies were, and as powerful as China one day would be, neither would be able to counter a Soviet-led coalition of previously nonaligned nations. The Khrushchev-Bulganin tour of Southeast Asia and Afghanistan in late 1955 marked the beginning of a protracted attempt to establish that coalition.

## HARBINGERS OF "DE-STALINIZATION"

The conduct of foreign policy hinged on the unresolved situation within the Communist party. The party was apprehensive about its future: no one knew how far the regime would pursue the dismantling of the Stalinist system.

The sword which Khrushchev held over Malenkov's head had two edges, and the party leader did not have a sure grip on it. He could at any time reveal what all top party officials knew, namely, that Malenkov had played a major role in the events of 1949–1951 that had swept away so many Zhdanov supporters. The "Doctors' Plot" could be explained away as the criminal scheme of some secret police officials—no one yet dared say it was Stalin's doing—and Beria's crimes as the unholy work of a psychopath, but the purge of the Zhdanovites had been an internal party fight. The decision to try Abakumov had opened Pandora's box.

Fewer references to Stalin appeared in the press in 1955. In part because of the publication lead-time involved for monthly and quarterly journals, the late dictator had figured prominently in them throughout 1953 and well into 1954, but now it was difficult to find references even in the Communist party's house organs *Kommunist* and *Partiinaya Zhizn* (Party Life).

In June 1955 a Supreme Soviet decree confirmed new regulations for the office of public prosecutor. Article 4 stated: "The USSR Prosecutor General and the prosecutors subordinate to him . . . must take prompt measures to eliminate all violations of laws, regardless from whom these violations proceed." This reaffirmed the new spirit of legality proclaimed in April 1953; and other articles carried a warning to those who directed and maintained the forced-labor camps. Article 33 obliged the prosecutor to visit all places of detention regularly for purposes of inspection and required him to halt illegal practices and bring those responsible for them before a court or administrative board. Article 34, if honored, promised to bring about a truly revolutionary change in Soviet society: "The prosecutor is required to free immediately all those unlawfully arrested or detained illegally in places of detention."

There were at least 10 and perhaps as many as 15 million people in the camps. The consequences of releasing them were incalculable. Admitting that not only they but also the millions who had died in the Gulag had been criminally abused by the state would constitute an incredible indictment of Stalin's regime, and of the Communist party.

The Gulag and the Terror could not be blamed on Beria or Yezhov or Dzerzhinsky. The late Gensek himself would have to be brought to account. Would Lenin be next in the dock?

Party leaders recoiled in horror. History offered no precedent for the step that loomed before them, attesting to their own illegitimacy. The Revolution had devoured its young in the 1930s; now history was presenting the bill. All of the older party leaders had been deeply involved in the Terror, and the careers of younger men like Kosygin, Brezhnev, and Suslov had been advanced because of the vacancies it had created.

It was unthinkable that thousands of officials would suddenly ask to be relieved of their posts and indicted. It appeared in the latter half of 1955 that the new regulations for the prosecutor's office would be no more meaningful than the 1936 Constitution; only a small number of people were released from the Gulag. The new leaders seemed content with the modest steps they had taken to punish a few secret police officials and to relax the conditions of life in the post-Stalin USSR.

## THAW

In 1953 Ilya Ehrenburg, a journalist and author of several works of fiction, published a landmark novel entitled *The Thaw*. The plant manager-protagonist is a basically decent fellow who loses his best qualities trying to meet the demands of the Stalinist system. His only real concerns are fulfilling the plan and increasing production, even at the expense of the workers' welfare. He loses touch with normal people and surrounds himself with sycophants, one of whom tries to frame a senior engineer by spreading the rumor that he has a daughter in capitalist Belgium. The manager connives in this plot out of habit rather than conviction; but the scheme backfires when the sympathies of the people favor the innocent engineer. Disgusted by her husband's callous behavior, the manager's wife leaves him; the engineer remains secure in his job; there is change in the air. One minor character, an artist, finally admits to himself that he has wasted his talent painting "socialist realist" works throughout his career. Another artist, who had suffered for insisting on his own standards, is finally recognized and rewarded. The novel ends on a positive, optimistic note; the thaw is coming after the long winter.

This political journalism thinly disguised as fiction had an immediate impact. Reform-minded critics and party officials praised it, while conservatives attacked Ehrenburg for his portrait of Stalinist corruption. Was he advocating "bourgeois" values, placing the individual ahead of the state and the society? Ehrenburg replied that he was merely describing life as he saw it.

Barely six weeks after Stalin's death, Olga Berggolts defended personal expression in lyric poetry; others had been sent to the Gulag for articulating that view. If Berggolts, a minor poet, could get away with this, no one could forsee what giants like Anna Akhmatova and Boris Pasternak might produce. Vera Panova's novel *The Seasons* dealt in part with the negative side of Soviet life and attacked plump party functionaries who lived in luxury. The sharpest assault came in Leonid Sorin's play *The Guests,* which depicted the political and moral corruption of Stalinism as no previous work had dared. In December 1953 the writer and critic Vladimir Pomerantsev's essay "On Sincerity in Literature" assailed the Communist party's attempt to dictate Soviet literature through the Writers' Union.

In the spring of 1954 the party struck back. Aleksei Surkov, mediocre poet, secretary of the Writers' Union, and party member since 1925, lashed out at Pomerantsev and attacked Ehrenburg, Panova, and Sorin. *The Guests,* which had played to shocked, packed houses for months, suddenly closed down. Surkov called for the reimposition of strict party control over literature; by the time his article appeared in *Pravda* in May 1954, that had already taken place. The following December the second All-Union Congress of Writers mounted a vicious attack on Ehrenburg and the others who had sought to escape from the constraints of "socialist realism."

Again it appeared that the party had flirted with a retreat from Stalinism only to be terrified by its own audacity. As the new regulations for the prosecutor's office did not dismantle the Gulag, so the "thaw" of 1953 did not liberate the arts.

## LIFE WITHOUT STALIN

In 1953 a Soviet newspaper reported that a toy rabbit manufactured by the Moscow Haberdashery Cooperative was black, made of coarse material, and had the head of a hippopotamus. Such a toy, the writer noted,

"excites only fear and aversion." *Izvestiya* later declared that a certain doll carriage could also be used to grate cabbage, or perhaps hew logs, and that a poorly constructed metal doll for sale in state stores could easily double as a wolf trap. A cartoon in one of the humor magazines showed a mother warning her child, "Behave or I'll buy you a toy!"

In July 1953 a Moscow newspaper claimed that ordinary working people were buying ZiM automobiles in considerable numbers. This was the vehicle assigned to middle-level officials; honest workers had no hope of buying one. A month later, a *Pravda* reader reported that in March he had ordered spare parts for his bicycle and some film from Mail Order House; he had sent 160 rubles with his order. In July he received the film and 131 rubles' worth of phonograph records. A note informed him that since the bicycle parts were not available, the management had decided he would like records instead. A July 1954 letter to the same newspaper reported that Persian thread (imitation silk) stockings made by Aurora Mills (Riga) and the Leninakan Stocking and Knitwear Mills (Armenia) tore on the second or third wearing. They came in one size, "very large," in an "unpleasant yellow color," and cost 20–25 rubles; nothing else was available.

The revelation of petty inconveniences indicated a cautious willingness to allow examination of a few of the system's shortcomings. More startling was the attention paid to problems of crime, alcoholism, and juvenile delinquency. By 1954 the press was frankly admitting that these phenomena constituted major social problems. A letter to *Literary Gazette* in July stated that "You go into one of these bungs [dives] and all around there is dirt and drunken people rolling on the floor in their own vomit." The writer also charged that many officials were drunkards who could be bribed with vodka.

Early in 1954 *Kommunist* called for a new discussion of the theories of Lysenko, whom it charged with attempting to suppress all criticism. This followed a letter to *Pravda* from a Moscow University biology professor who accused Lysenko of forcing his department to grant a doctoral degree to a candidate who knew nothing of biology or botany. The professor noted that "Academician Lysenko, with his customary sharpness, called all reviewers who had spoken negatively of the dissertation . . . Weismannists." *Pravda* reported that the degree was rescinded after the Communist party investigated; this was one of the first instances in which the party had intervened on the side of scientific truth. In 1955 the *Botanical Journal* revealed that Lysenko's "engendering" of soft wheat into hard was "nothing but the result of hybridization and the subsequent branching out in the descendants of hybrid individuals." Further, Lysenko's claim that a hornbeam tree had "engendered" a hazelnut tree collapsed under investigation.

Lysenko retained considerable authority in the party, if not in scientific circles, and his defenders included powerful people. For the moment, however, it appeared that genuine science was again in vogue.

It began to dawn on increasing numbers of Communist officials that backing such charlatans as Lysenko had cost them dearly. Soviet science and technology lagged far behind that of the West and the gap was widening. The way to improve production and raise labor productivity, Premier Bulganin declared, was to "raise the level of party guidance of industry."

This call for increased Communist supervision characterized the defensive, contradictory nature of many policies of the post-Stalin leadership. There was on one hand frank recognition that the party had not always intervened to good advantage; this was the unmistakable import of the apparent dethroning of Lysenko and the blunt declaration that anti-Semitism had no place in Soviet life. But the party that tacitly acknowledged mistakes often sought to remedy them by increasing CPSU authority, and by allowing errant officials to correct themselves.

While permitting publication of *The Thaw* and the staging—at least briefly—of *The Guests*, the party also commissioned a symphonic poem, "Pavlik Morozov," based on the life of the boy who had betrayed his father during collectivization. The party had allowed publication of some appeals for a free art, yet it condemned vaudeville artist Ruzhena Sikora for singing such "vulgar and even fascist" songs as "Besame mucho." It savagely attacked the "obscene witticisms" of comedians such as Arkady Raikin, whose routines never went beyond mildly suggestive commentary. And the party smiled with satisfaction when a journal of the arts published a stupefying comment to the effect that the "constantly rising culture of Soviet man is setting lofty standards in love."

For all its vacillation and indecision and confusion, the Communist party was changing. Some change was forced on the party by circumstances, some it initiated itself. The leaders patched up some old quarrels, began to speak cautiously of the possibility of an accommodation with the West, did away with some of the shackles on Soviet society. If they did not open the gates of the Gulag, neither did they send many new victims into it. Reform was in the air.

## SUGGESTED ADDITIONAL READING

**Berman, Harold J.,** *Justice in the U.S.S.R.,* New York: Vintage Books, 1963

**Brown, Deming,** *Soviet Russian Literature since Stalin,* New York: Cambridge University Press, 1978

**Crankshaw, Edward,** *Khrushchev's Russia,* Baltimore: Penguin Books, 1959

**Dudintsev, Vladimir,** *Not by Bread Alone,* New York: Dutton, 1957

**Ehrenburg, Ilya,** *The Thaw,* Chicago: H. Regnery Co., 1955

**Leonhard, Wolfgang,** *The Kremlim Since Stalin,* New York: Praeger, 1962

**Rothenberg, Abraham,** *The Heirs of Stalin: Literary Dissidence and the Soviet Regime, 1953–1970,* Ithaca, N.Y.: Cornell University Press, 1972

**Rush, Myron,** *Political Succession in the USSR,* New York: Columbia University Press, 1965

**Swayze, Harold,** *Political Control of Literature in the USSR, 1946–1959,* Cambridge: Harvard University Press, 1962

**Swearer, Howard R.,** *The Politics of Succession in the USSR,* Boston: Little, Brown, 1964

**Vishnevskaya, Galina,** *Galina: A Russian Story,* New York: Harcourt Brace Jovanovich, 1984

# 16

# THE GREAT REFORM
## *Khrushchev and "De-Stalinization"*

It appeared to inveterate Stalinists that their own party would succeed where nearly four decades of anticommunist efforts had failed. Nikita Khrushchev and his allies, they believed, would destroy the Soviet regime. The Stalinists had grudgingly accepted some modest reforms and condemned Beria; that, in their view, was enough. If there had been errors, if Stalin had sometimes acted harshly, there was no need to review all that now. Like Dostoevsky's Grand Inquisitor, they maintained that the party could not survive the dismantling of its myths.

Sensing the distant tremors of reform that preceded the party Congress of 1956, the Stalinists feared a major test of political faith at hand. The principle of party infallibility had not been challenged for decades.

With Stalin gone, no one could be certain whether it would survive a crisis.

## 20TH PARTY CONGRESS

The first post-Stalin Congress convened in Moscow on February 14, 1956. So far as the majority of the 1,349 voting delegates and the foreign Communist guests knew, its main purpose was to approve the Sixth Five-Year Plan covering 1956–1960. That mission was accomplished, unanimously as always, after the delegates had listened to a series of glowing reports on the performance of industry and agriculture. Khrushchev spoke on foreign policy and stressed the Soviet Union's adherence to "peaceful coexistence." Wars were no longer inevitable, he said, but the ideological struggle would continue until the victory of communism.

There were a few hints of the explosion to come. Reporting on the work of the Central Committee, Khrushchev mentioned Stalin only once, noting that he was dead; most people already knew that. The chief ideologist, Suslov, spoke of the "restoration of the norms of party life and principles of party leadership worked out by Lenin and frequently violated prior to the 20th Congress." Still more disturbing to the Stalinists, who had correctly counted him in their ranks, he used a phrase not heard since Marx coined it nearly 80 years earlier: the "cult of the individual," Suslov declared, had flourished for too long.

Anastas Mikoyan, a member of the Presidium and vice-premier, still more bluntly observed, "collective leadership has been [re-]established in our party." The "cult" had existed for "about 20 years" with "an extremely negative effect." Mikoyan attacked Stalin's *Economic Problems of Socialism in the USSR* and condemned the late dictator's disdain for the "treasury of Leninist ideas." These were heretical comments, and Mikoyan spoke Stalin's name. When he went on to claim that Soviet jurisprudence, legislation, and trial procedures had suffered under the dictator, the reactionaries on the Presidium—who had known the purges would be discussed, but not the extent—sensed trouble of enormous dimensions and tried to deflect it. One of their number, Molotov, admitted that the "cult," the instantly established euphemism for Stalin's dictatorship, had not been helpful in conducting foreign policy.

Everyone waited for Khrushchev to speak, but the first secretary did not address this issue during the regularly scheduled sessions, which were to end with the election of party officers. Khrushchev was reelected party leader on February 24. It was his prerogative

to move the adoption of the party's list of candidates for the Central Committee Presidium, but the Congress adjourned before he could do so that day. The motion and the voting were mere formalities; until they took place, however, he was technically the sole leader in office. At this point he struck.

Shortly before midnight on February 24, couriers dashed around Moscow collecting delegates and bringing them back to the Kremlin for a special secret session. Once they were assembled (foreign guests and press excluded), Khrushchev delivered a somber report "On the Cult of Personality and Its Consequences." The worst fears of the Stalinists came true.

He told of the illegal arrest, imprisonment, torture, and execution of thousands of innocent party members, saying nothing of the *millions* of nonparty victims. Stalin himself, the new leader revealed, had signed many orders for these acts, which thus could not be blamed solely on the secret police. Khrushchev also held Stalin responsible for the battlefield reversals of 1941/1942, adding that he had taken credit for all the later victories, belittling the role of the army and the nation at large. Stalin had ordered the mass deportation of whole peoples falsely accused of collaborating with the Germans; "violated the norms of revolutionary legality and ignored all norms of party life"; originated the concept of "enemy of the people"; elevated himself "above party and nation"; caused the senseless conflict with Yugoslavia. Never again could reasonable men call reports of the Great Terror mere anticommunist propaganda. But no one could guarantee that Stalinism would not resurface, and Khrushchev's failure to mention the nonparty victims indicated that the new leadership hoped to limit the consequences of opening the "cult" issue.

The speech lasted four hours; there was no debate. Six years later Khrushchev revealed that party leaders had discussed whether to place the matter of Stalin's crimes on the agenda. Molotov, Kaganovich, Malenkov, and Voroshilov had been "categorically opposed." Molotov not only justified Stalin's actions but predicted that reprisals against innocent persons might unavoidably recur as the party pursued "enemies of the people."

The stunned delegates went back to their hotels for a few hours early in the morning of February 25, then returned to the Kremlin to elect party officers and wind up the Congress. Before the day was over the "secret" speech was the talk of Moscow; within weeks its general outlines were known all over the world. It was published in English that spring; a Polish delegate obtained a transcript and passed it to the West.

Riots erupted in Tbilisi on March 9 as Georgians protested the assault on Stalin. There was violence in many Soviet cities and in some of the Gulag camps in the spring and early summer; both free citizens and convicts seized on the condemnation of Stalin to vent grievances. The Tbilisi riots were apparently the only disturbances in which the mobs defended the late dictator.

The demonstrations were quickly suppressed; security forces had gone on "ready alert" status at the start of the 20th Congress. This was standard procedure, but the alert had a special urgency in 1956. Because of unrest at home and tension abroad, especially in Poland and Hungary, the Central Committee considered it too dangerous to publish Khrushchev's indictment. The document was, however, read aloud at thousands of public meetings.

## "DE-STALINIZATION"

When monthly and quarterly journals attacked the "cult" shortly after the Congress it became clear that a carefully planned campaign was underway. The "secret speech" had signalled the beginning; there would apparently be no turning back. The leading history journal indicated in March that several executed military commanders would soon be cleared of all charges. Beginning the "rehabilitations" with the military was partial repayment for Marshal Zhukov's backing of Khrushchev at the Congress. At the end of March *Pravda* declared that although Stalin had "rendered great services to our party," in the latter part of his life the "cult of the individual and the leadership practices which developed under its influence . . . did much harm." The newspaper went on to disavow both the official party history (*Short Course*) and the official biography of Stalin, and to admit that "many of our films, books, and paintings, especially those dealing with the war, are dedicated chiefly to the praise and glorification of Stalin."

The first public mention in 32 years of Lenin's "testament," in which the founder had urged the removal of Stalin as general secretary, appeared in the Komsomol newspaper on May 18; it was published in full in the party theoretical journal on June 30. The "testament" now assumed a potentially more explosive character than it had had when it was written. It included praise of Bukharin, Trotsky, and other early party leaders whom Stalin had liquidated. Stalin's mistreatment of Lenin's wife would not be revealed until 1964.

In June 1956 the Soviet press published the Central Committee resolution "On Overcoming the Cult of the Individual and Its Consequences." Written by Suslov, the resolution indicated that the party would limit criticism. Complaining that Western political circles were exploiting the revelation of Stalin's crimes, the resolution paid tribute to the Gensek's services and seemed to retreat, calling his less commendable acts mere mistakes. The party insisted that its "Leninist core" had remained intact during the Stalin years.

Addressing the question of party responsibility, the resolution declared that it would have been impossible to remove the dictator "under the conditions then prevailing," not least because the Soviet people would not have supported anyone who spoke or acted against him. Finally, the document advanced the claim that party leaders had simply "not known" the full extent of the abuses until the arrest of Beria. The CPSU leadership was composed exclusively of Stalinists until March 1953, but now of Stalin's former admirers only Molotov, Kaganovich, Malenkov, and Voroshilov could be found.

The liberation of innocent people (all of them, not just Communists) from the Gulag constituted the most urgent task facing the party after the Congress. The cautious, mostly unpublicized "rehabilitations" of 1953–1955 had resulted in the liberation of a mere handful of Communists, and even the "secret speech" had implied that reviews of questionable legal proceedings would in the beginning affect only party members. "De-Stalinization," however, generated its own logic and momentum.

In the spring and summer of 1956 the leadership bowed to enormous public pressure and began to free nonparty prisoners en masse, about 8 million by the end of 1957. A year later only a relative handful of "politicals" remained in the camps.

The state gave special treatment to former Soviet POWs whom Stalin had sent into the Gulag after the war. Marshal Zhukov announced that military personnel who had died in the Gulag—of whatever cause—had in effect fallen on the battlefield; their widows and orphans would receive monetary "compensation," preferential treatment for housing and jobs, and the widows, lifetime pensions. The state exonerated Soviet citizens coerced into working for

the Germans and restored them to full citizenship. With the tragic exception of the Crimean Tatars, the minority peoples brutally uprooted as "collaborators" returned to their homes, cleared of all charges.

The return of millions of innocent victims of Stalin's terror had an enormous impact on Soviet society. Broken in body and spirit, some returnees simply lived out their days quietly, but their very presence affected the community deeply. Diehard Stalinists, refusing to hold the Gensek responsible for their misery, found their fellow citizens no longer afraid to debate his rule. And millions of liberated *zeks* demanded the restoration of their honor, punishment of those who had taken it and their freedom from them, and ironclad assurances against a repetition.

The leadership could not meet these demands and remain in office. Accountability for Stalin-era crimes would sooner rather than later come to rest at the doorsteps of those who had served in high posts and survived: *Khrushchev himself*—both in the Ukraine and in the Moscow party organization—had been part of the terror apparatus, and blood was on his hands. The reformist regime tried and shot one of Beria's cronies and several of his subordinates in April 1956 and quietly removed an unknown number of Gulag and secret police functionaries from their jobs. That was as far as Khrushchev and his allies would go.

## FURTHER REFORMS

This did not mean the end of the reforms. Local, regional, and even republic courts had been little more than moribund appendages of the power-mad center in the Stalin era. In an attempt to break the grotesque centralization of judicial powers, in June

1956 the government simply abolished the All-Union (i.e., federal) ministry of justice, transferring its functions to the ministries of the constituent republics.

Justice by administrative fiat came to an end, at least on paper, in a revised Code of Criminal Procedure. Article 7 specified that "No person may be considered guilty of having committed a crime and subjected to criminal punishment save by the sentence of a court." While not a writ of habeas corpus, this proviso would, if honored, constitute a major step forward from Stalinism. In April 1956 a legal journal assailed the Stalinist theory of evidence, according to which a confession constituted proof of guilt. In April 1957 police and prosecutor were forbidden to trick suspects into incriminating themselves.

In 1962 the chief prosecutor declared that his office was strictly observing the new Criminal Code, specifically the prohibition against nonjudicial arrest and punishment. The same year, however, a Moscow prosecutor publicly reasserted the validity of Vyshinsky's contention that anyone bound over to a court for trial was guilty. The court's sole function, in this reading of legal principles, was to determine the "objectivity" of police conclusions. In practice this interpretation prevailed in all "political" cases, the number of which was however only a fraction of what it had been under Stalin. No longer were masses of citizens accused of "anti-Soviet" behavior; but those accused were invariably found guilty.

The public welcomed Khrushchev's assurance that the secret police would no longer be allowed to run amok. But even though some shuffling of personnel took place, by and large even the most notorious of the interrogators, guards, and administrators merely retired on comfortable pensions. Ivan Serov, a loyal Beria aide who had become head of the KGB in 1954, continued in office.

Serov had won his post and now retained it because he knew where skeletons were buried, including some connected with Khrushchev's prewar service in the Ukraine. He had also earned a reputation for his brutal supervision of the wartime deportations, and because he was vulnerable he was obliged to cooperate with Khrushchev in dismantling the Gulag. By December 1958 the population of the Archipelago had dwindled to about a million, almost all common criminals. The acronym "Gulag" disappeared from the official lexicon; no one could erase it from history.

After completing this work, Serov was transferred to military intelligence. Aleksandr Shelepin, a career party bureaucrat, succeeded him at the helm of the KGB; the CPSU thus regained control of the secret police. In 1963 Khrushchev stripped a number of present and former high-ranking KGB officials, including Serov, of the medals Stalin had given them in 1944 for their role in the deportations.

Only a few days after Serov's ouster as head of the KGB, new laws were passed (December 25, 1958) providing safeguards against extrajudicial punishment and curbing the powers of the secret police. Six months later, the Supreme Court directed courts to deemphasize punishment in favor of reeducation and preventive measures and to work for the eradication of the social causes of criminal behavior.

Dealing with Stalin in the schools and in the writing and teaching of history posed a special problem. *Kommunist* admitted in April 1956 that the official Soviet encyclopedia was replete with errors on Soviet history; the leading history journal confessed in August that the story of the Russian invention of the airplane had been a hoax; military journals disclosed that Stalin's role in the Civil War had been falsified and that he had committed numerous costly errors as commander-in-chief in the war against Germany.

It was impossible to revise textbooks before the start of the 1956–1957 school year, and yet, because Stalin had been the supreme authority in all fields of knowledge, something had to be done. Late in August 1956 *Pravda* provided some vague guidance: "The teacher, while giving credit to J.V. Stalin's merits and showing his role as organizer and theoretician, must at the same time throw light on the very grave errors he committed." The party thus invited the teachers to become political analysts, a role that until 1953 had led many people to their doom. Only when a new party history was published in 1959 could teachers relax.

The Khrushchev reforms embraced all aspects of Soviet life. The legal liability of workers leaving the workplace without permission ended with an April 1956 decree. A September 1957 order stipulated an end to the practice of naming places, enterprises, and organizations for living persons; all such existing names were to be changed. Not until 1961, however, did Stalingrad become Volgograd, and efforts to style the great conflict there the "Battle on the Volga" proved unsuccessful. Stalin Prizes again became Lenin Prizes, as they had been prior to 1935. In 1958 the press admitted there had been no grounds for calling Shostakovich and other composers—and by extension, writers and artists—"anti-popular" and "formalist." Such evaluations, *Pravda* confessed, "reflected J.V. Stalin's subjective approach to certain works of art."

## "REHABILITATIONS"

The revelation of Stalin's crimes made it imperative for the CPSU to exonerate thousands of persecuted members. This was an exceedingly delicate matter. Would the party be obliged to accept Bukharin, Zinoviev, Kamenev, and Trotsky back into the ranks of its revered heroes? Even anti-Stalinist Communists shuddered. The regime declared that there would be no review of the judicial proceedings against, let alone rehabilitation of, Trotsky and the three chief defendants in the purge trials.

Public exonerations of lesser fry began in *Pravda* while the 20th Congress was still in session: the newspaper published an article praising the Hungarian revolutionary Bela Kun but did not mention his execution on Stalin's orders in 1937. The same issue disavowed the 1938 dissolution—really a super-purge—of the Polish Communist party, which, according to NKVD reports at the time, "enemy agents" had infiltrated. Moscow now claimed that "this accusation rested on materials falsified by subsequently exposed provocateurs." Those "provocateurs" had acted on Stalin's orders, but *Pravda* did not report that.

Over the next several years, the press revealed names of many prominent Communists now cleared of charges that had sent them to the executioners in the period 1936–1952. Courts and prosecutors exonerated thousands of party members—people who had helped construct the system that devoured them, and for whom the masses understandably had little sympathy—posthumously. Not until the *glasnost* era of the late 1980s, however, did the CPSU complete the rehabilitation of its slain comrades by reinstating them in its ranks, and not until Gorbachev became leader did the party pay serious attention to the millions of Stalin's victims who had *not* been in those ranks.

As early as October 1955 the party secretly cleared General Yan Gamarnik of all charges, and in January 1957 the state prosecutor rescinded—also in secret—the June 11, 1937, guilty verdicts against Gamarnik's fellow officers Tukhachevsky, Kork, Yakir,

Uborevich, Eideman, V.P. Primakov, and B.M. Feldman. A.I. Yegorov and V.K. Blücher also won posthumous acquittal. Once again, however, the Soviet Communists made a more or less complete *public* statement of the full legal and party rehabilitation of the military commanders only in 1988.

The 1956 anticommunist, anti-Soviet violence in Poland and Hungary gave the Khrushchev regime an excuse to suppress the news of the review of the "repressions." The process continued, however, limited to CPSU members and a few prominent nonparty people. The great mass of *zeks* simply returned to the factories and collective farms, in a sense on parole.

Complete rehabilitation had to follow established judicial procedure: cross-examination of witnesses, presentation of documentary evidence, and so on. That took time, and such cases inundated the courts; more often than not it took years to reach a decision. Hundreds of thousands, perhaps millions, of illegally imprisoned people simply declined to bother, trusting the new regime to keep its word not to abuse the innocent.

## THE "ANTI-PARTY GROUP"

Thousands of CPSU and secret police officials had a keen personal interest in halting the revelations about the Stalin era. Many others, devout Communists not involved in the Terror, felt threatened by any challenge to their faith. Returning *zeks* were filing innumerable petitions demanding the arrest and trial of their tormentors, most of whom remained at their posts even after the 20th Congress; affidavits attesting to the criminal acts of the accused accompanied the demands. The regime could sidetrack petitions from obscure citizens indefinitely, but

Khrushchev's own brief against Stalin had set an irreversible precedent. Something would have to be done to calm the country.

Conservatives argued that *everyone* had been a Stalinist while the Gensek lived; Khrushchev's hands were as bloody as anyone's. Many Communists resigned their posts to wait out the storm. The pseudoscientist Lysenko was the most prominent example. He left the Agricultural Academy chairmanship in April 1956, only to regain his political influence the following year. A few officials involved in the arrest and imprisonment of innocent people killed themselves when threatened with exposure. This was the path of Aleksandr Fadeyev, secretary-general of the Writers' Union. Finally, some Stalinists decided that only the removal of Khrushchev could restore sanity and order to party affairs.

Various plots to kill the first secretary failed, but a political maneuver aimed at deposing him almost succeeded. In June 1957, while Khrushchev and Bulganin were on a state visit to Finland, the Stalinists struck. Summoned to a meeting of the Presidium the day after his return, Khrushchev was voted out of office. He was supported only by Suslov and Mikoyan among the full members; with his own vote, that meant that his faction numbered three against eight— Molotov, Kaganovich, Malenkov, Voroshilov, Bulganin, Pervukhin, Kirichenko, Saburov. Among the six candidate members, Khrushchev had the support of all save Shepilov, but of the five who backed him only Marshal Zhukov was in a position to be of immediate service.

Khrushchev demanded that the entire Central Committee, which alone could legally elect or depose a first secretary, be summoned to Moscow. The conspirators had taken steps to prevent CC members from learning of events in Moscow until presented with a *fait accompli*. Premier

Bulganin had posted his own bodyguards inside the Kremlin and at Committee headquarters on Old Square; the conspirators planned to arrest Khrushchev if he refused to submit.

At this point the first secretary called in his debts. He had retained Ivan Serov as chairman of the KGB despite his link to Beria; Serov now supported him. The conspirators could not use the KGB to arrest Khrushchev or prevent the convening of the Central Committee. Further, Khrushchev had rescued Marshal Zhukov from oblivion; Zhukov now repaid the favor and arranged for military aircraft to fly Central Committee members to Moscow. Finally, Frol Kozlov, whom Khrushchev had installed as head of the Leningrad province party organization, rushed to support his patron, as did Leonid Brezhnev, a candidate member of the Presidium who had strong ties to the Ukrainian party organization.

By June 21 more than 300 top party leaders, including nearly all 133 full members of the Central Committee, had assembled in Moscow. Neither Bulganin's bodyguard nor any other agency available to the conspirators could prevent the convoking of a plenary session.

That session took place June 22–29, 1957. According to the published account there was no time limit on speeches, and Molotov, Kaganovich, and Malenkov each spoke twice. Khrushchev's opponents denounced "de-Stalinization" and rejected the decision of the 20th Congress to expose Stalin and rehabilitate his victims. They assailed the "virgin lands" scheme and called for reversal of plans to enlarge the powers of union republics. Molotov bitterly attacked "peaceful coexistence," normalization of relations with Japan, reconciliation with Yugoslavia, the peace treaty with Austria, and "summit" conferences. He and his associates demanded an end to the prosecutions—few though they were—of officials involved in the Terror. The Molotov group demanded restoration of the *Short Course*, the grotesque "history" which exalted Stalin and denigrated Lenin, as an authoritative guide to the past.

Khrushchev defended his policies vigorously; speaker after speaker supported him. No one save the conspirators wanted a return to Stalinism. Molotov's prediction that the day would come again when the innocent would "inevitably and unavoidably" be imprisoned along with the guilty in the fight against "imperialist agents and class enemies" sent a chill through the meeting.

The anti-Khrushchev faction had mustered eight votes in the Presidium, but the number fell to four in the plenary session of the Central Committee. Voroshilov broke down and cried admitting his mistakes; he had learned to love his job as titular head of state and wanted to keep it. Pervukhin and Saburov, short on political acumen but aware of the difference between four and 300, recanted with slightly more dignity. Bulganin backed off in an attempt to remain premier.

Only Molotov, Malenkov, Kaganovich, and Shepilov were left in what became known as the "anti-party group." *Pravda* had referred to the first three more colorfully in 1956 as "sycophants and hallelujah-shouters." The plenary session now heard an account of their crimes. Malenkov had assisted Yezhov in the purge in Byelorussia in 1936 and with Beria had fabricated the "Leningrad Case." Kaganovich had conducted bloody purges in the Ukraine and the North Caucasus. Molotov liked to write on secret police lists of candidates for the Gulag, "arrest, convict, shoot." A few years later the party would learn that he had once had several innocent people arrested as "terrorists" when his car skidded on an icy road.

The session expelled Molotov, Kaganovich, and Malenkov from the Presidium and the Central Committee, expelled Shepilov from the CC, and dismissed him as a candidate member of the Presidium. These relatively lenient measures indicated both Khrushchev's own shaky hold on power and the determination of the Committee not to resort to terror. It was content to strip the "anti-party group" of their posts and give them humiliating assignments. Molotov became ambassador to Mongolia. Malenkov was sent to manage the Ust-Kamenogorsk hydroelectric plant in Kazakhstan. Kaganovich became manager of a Sverdlovsk cement plant. Shepilov, who had briefly been minister of foreign affairs (June 1956–May 1957), went to the Academy of Sciences as a junior specialist in political science.

In order to give the country and the outside world the impression of a stable political order, three Presidium members—including Bulganin—who had voted against Khrushchev were permitted to remain on that body for a brief period. Bulganin retained the premiership for nine months, then was downgraded to the post of chairman of the State Bank. A few months later, allegedly because he had failed in that job, he received an assignment as director of the economic council of the backwater town of Stavropol. Voroshilov held on to the presidency until May 1960, when Brezhnev replaced him. One of Khrushchev's opponents on the Presidium, Pervukhin, was demoted to candidate member, and another, Saburov, was removed altogether.

The June session elected a new Presidium and increased the membership from 11 to 15. Among the new full members were Marshal Zhukov and Leonid Brezhnev. Khrushchev's allies Aleksei Kosygin and Andrei Kirilenko were among the eight new candidate members.

## 22ND PARTY CONGRESS

The defeat of the "anti-party group" did not give Khrushchev a free hand to run the party. The fact that several of his opponents retained their posts—however temporarily—after the June Plenum of the Central Committee indicated that the Committee wished to demonstrate control over the first secretary.

The Central Committee was determined to keep a check on the party leader, and it was still more cautious where the military commanders were concerned. In October 1957 the Presidium expelled Marshal Zhukov from its ranks and dismissed him as minister of defense. The party press charged that Zhukov had attempted to exaggerate his role in the war and had neglected ideological work in the armed forces. Professional officers did resent interference in military affairs, and Zhukov had tried to lessen CPSU meddling. After his fall the party instituted (January 1958) a 50-hour ideological training program for officers.

Khrushchev at Lenin Stadium, Moscow, 1958. (Thomas T. Hammond)

The extent to which this program improved military efficiency and morale is open to question; but the party reasserted control of the armed forces.

The CPSU also accused Zhukov of "bonapartism" and of attempting to create his own "cult of personality" as a step toward seizing political power. It is impossible to say with certainty that Zhukov never harbored political ambitions, but nothing in his record substantiates that charge. There is, however, a mountain of evidence attesting to the Communist party's fear of a military coup d'état. The party feared the military, and it seemed that the best way to neutralize the threat was to pin an unflattering label on its leader. Zhukov disappeared for a second and final time into obscure retirement.

The charge of exaggerating his role in World War II was more properly directed against Stalin. Throughout the Khrushchev era the late generalissimo was frequently taken to task for his failure to prepare the nation for the war and for his mistakes in the early campaigns. *Pravda* repeated the accusations and attacked Stalin's other errors in marking the 80th anniversary of his birth in December 1959. The same article, however, praised him as an "outstanding theoretician and propagandist of Marxism-Leninism." This ambivalent approach reflected the continuing debate in party circles.

A militant "hard" line reminiscent of the Stalin era returned in October 1958 when the Khrushchev regime savagely attacked Boris Pasternak, awarded that year's Nobel prize for literature by a Swedish Academy bent as much on fueling anti-Soviet propaganda as honoring Pasternak. Although he had published little except translations in the Stalin years, Pasternak had been in the front rank of Soviet poets for a generation. In 1956 the censors, urged on by pathetically untalented wordsmiths who controlled the Writers' Union, rejected Pasternak's first and only novel, *Dr. Zhivago*. Published abroad to great acclaim in 1957, the circumstances of its birth constituted an indictment of Soviet repression.

This gave Soviet conservatives their opportunity. At their prompting, Khrushchev and A.N. Shelepin, then head of the KGB, led a savage, indeed quite literally an obscene campaign against the defenseless writer. Rejecting the appeals of unscrupulous organizations and individuals—who cared nothing for him—to come to the West, Pasternak endured public humiliation, renounced the prize, begged Khrushchev not to force him to leave the country . . . and was left to die in such peace as he could find less than two years later.

Increasingly on the defensive at home and abroad, Khrushchev did not retreat from his reform program but he varied its pace. In 1961, when his popularity was at a low ebb, he summoned the 22nd Party Congress; the 21st, in 1959, had been devoted largely to economic matters.

Nearly 4,400 voting delegates, the most ever, assembled in Moscow for the Congress October 17–31, their ostensible mission to approve a new party program. Khrushchev defended his policies, vilifying the "anti-party group" and revealing new details of the participation of its members in Stalin's crimes. He had succeeded in replacing Voroshilov with Brezhnev in May 1960, and at the 22nd Congress he told the delegates of Voroshilov's complicity in mass murders. He reviled Molotov and Kaganovich, describing hideous scenes in Stalin's office when they co-signed orders condemning hundreds of thousands of innocent people to death. Stalin signed in red ink, Molotov in black, Kaganovich and Voroshilov in blue. The first secretary heaped scorn on his former traveling companion, ex-Prime Minister Bulganin, and made public more details of Malenkov's cooperation with Beria in the "Leningrad Case."

Khrushchev hinted at the possible involvement of Stalin in Kirov's murder:

Great efforts are still needed to find out who was really to blame for . . . [Kirov's] death. The more deeply we study the materials connected with . . . the case, the more questions arise. . . . A thorough enquiry is now being conducted into the circumstances of this complicated matter.

This could only mean that Kamenev and Zinoviev, shot for inspiring the murder, had been innocent. That left the secret police as the only possible assassins, and in December 1934 the NKVD could not have planned and carried out the murder without Stalin's approval. Before the Kirov case could be cleared up publicly, however, Khrushchev was deposed. His immediate successors shut the books on the matter.

More rehabilitations were announced at the Congress and Khrushchev proposed that the party erect a monument to Stalin's victims. Other speakers, however, insisted that people who had "deserved" their punishment should not be rehabilitated or reinstated in the party. The head of the party Control Commission, N.M. Shvernik, indicated that the judicial review of questionable convictions was proceeding slowly and that fewer than a quarter of those applying for reinstatement had been accepted back into the party.

By decision of the Congress, Stalin's body was removed from the Lenin-Stalin Mausoleum, which now became simply the Lenin Mausoleum. The late tyrant was buried under 10 meters of concrete in the small cemetery for party and state heroes at the foot of the Kremlin's east wall.

Khrushchev assured the Congress that the "cult" was safely buried along with the man who had created it. Having listened to speeches praising him lavishly, he noted that

a certain special emphasis is placed on me personally, and my role in carrying out major party and Government measures is underlined. I understand the kind feelings which guide these comments. Allow me, however, to emphasize vehemently that everything said about me should be said about the Central Committee of our Leninist party and about the Presidium of the Central Committee. (*Stormy, prolonged applause* [note in official transcript].) Not one measure, not one responsible pronouncement, has been carried out upon anyone's personal directive; they have all been the result of collective deliberation and collective decision. (*Stormy applause.*)

This was disingenuous. Khrushchev was certainly no Stalin, but he dominated the Presidium and the Central Committee and generally had his way in CPSU councils. At a time when most party officials were ready to back off from "de-Stalinization," he chose the 22nd Congress as an occasion to wash still more extremely dirty party linen in public. He did so, moreover, with the ideological quarrel with the Chinese, Albanian, and Romanian parties growing more vitriolic and with the CPSU beset by all manner of other difficulties.

Yet Khrushchev's power was precarious. Behind his back party members began to quote the Russian proverb: "When the Devil grows old, he becomes a monk." Had the first secretary acknowledged his own past, resigned his post, and become manager of an obscure collective farm somewhere in the south, his fellow citizens would have recognized a syndrome often encountered in Russian history and in Dostoevsky's novels: guilt, repentance, atonement, salvation. Khrushchev, however, repented Stalin's sins, not his own, and grew ever more fond of power.

Nevertheless, the atheist Khrushchev, educated and taught Holy Writ by Russian Orthodox priests (he admitted in 1960 that he had been a "model pupil"), did make one final attempt to atone. In 1962 he personally authorized publication of Aleksandr Solzhenitsyn's powerful novel about the Gulag system, *One Day in the Life of Ivan Denisovich.* That book, and Khrushchev's own "secret speech," changed history by changing the way history looked at Stalin.

## SUGGESTED ADDITIONAL READING

**Breslauer, George W.,** *Khrushchev and Brezhnev as Leaders,* Boston: George Allen and Unwin, 1982

**Khrushchev, Nikita S.,** *The Crimes of the Stalin Era,* New York: New Leader, 1962

**Kopelev, Lev,** *To Be Preserved Forever,* Philadelphia: Lippincott, 1977

**Linden, Carl A.,** *Khrushchev and the Soviet Leadership,* Baltimore: The Johns Hopkins University Press, 1966

**McCauley, Martin, ed.,** *Khrushchev and Khrushchevism,* Bloomington: Indiana University Press, 1987

**Orlova, Raisa,** *Memoirs,* New York: Random House, 1983

**Potichnyj, Peter J., ed.,** *The Soviet Union: Party and Society,* Cambridge, England: Cambridge University Press, 1988

**Schatz, Marshall S.,** *Soviet Dissent in Historical Perspective,* Cambridge, England: Cambridge University Press, 1980

**Solzhenitsyn, Aleksandr I.,** *One Day in the Life of Ivan Denisovich,* New York: Dutton, 1971

**Tatu, Michel,** *Power in the Kremlin: From Khrushchev to Kosygin,* New York: Viking, 1969

**Wolfe, Bertram,** *Khrushchev and Stalin's Ghost,* New York: Praeger, 1957

# 17

# REFORM ERA FOREIGN POLICY

A domestic upheaval on the scale of "de-Stalinization" inevitably had sweeping ramifications abroad. As Molotov had warned, foreign enemies used the revelations of the 20th Congress as a stick with which to beat the USSR and communism; friends in Europe and Asia looked on in astonishment as the CPSU shook its own foundations. Petty Soviet minions in Poland, Hungary, East Germany, and elsewhere waited anxiously for the dust to settle in Moscow, where their own fortunes were determined. In Beijing, Chairman Mao listened silently as Marshal Zhu Deh, head of the Chinese delegation to the 20th Congress, reported on the events in Moscow. Seeing himself as China's Stalin, a stern, powerful leader confronting the colossal task of modernizing a backward nation, Mao could only regard Soviet devel-opments apprehensively. For a few months he would go along with the Khrushchev regime, speaking of the inadvisability of exaggerating the role of any individual. In mid-1957, however, he would decide that an attack on Stalin constituted an attack on him.

## TURMOIL IN POLAND

On June 28–29, 1956, thousands of workers from the Zipso Locomotive Factory in Poznan, where an international trade fair was in progress, marched through the streets carrying banners reading BREAD AND FREEDOM and RUSSIANS GO HOME. This would have embarrassed the regime and the Soviets at any time, but during the fair, which brought several thousand foreigners to Poznan, it was humiliating. The authorities sent in police; riots ensued, and in two days of violence 53 people died. The Polish government had however managed to avoid calling in the army, which was under the command of Polish-born Soviet Marshal Konstantin Rokossovsky.

The Polish Army was considered unreliable. Rokossovsky had contingency plans to use Soviet troops stationed in Poland, plus reinforcements from East Germany, in the event of serious disorders. Warsaw hoped to avoid that.

On October 19, a few days after a court sentenced the alleged ringleaders of the Poznan riots to prison, Khrushchev and Mikoyan, accompanied by the unrepentant Stalinists Molotov and Kaganovich, flew to Warsaw for discussions with the new Polish party leader, Wladyslaw Gomulka. Because the situation in Hungary was likewise threatening to get out of control, it was imperative to reach some sort of accommodation or crush Poland quickly. Gomulka insisted that the Soviets accelerate the repatriation of Polish citizens from the Gulag, regularize the stationing of Soviet troops in Poland by statute, and give Poland a fair price for the coal it supplied to the USSR. He also wanted a share of German reparations payments.

The negotiators reached a compromise. The Soviets accepted the appointment of Gomulka as head of the Polish Communist party. Rokossovsky resigned his Polish posts (as minister of defense and vice-chairman of the Council of Ministers) and returned to Moscow. An agreement guaranteeing equality in relations between the two states was concluded in mid-November, and on December 17 a treaty regulating the presence of Soviet troops on Polish soil was signed.

## HUNGARIAN REVOLT

Spurred on by Secretary of State Dulles's rhetoric, American officials had encouraged the Hungarians to launch an uprising. The exhortations were broadcast over CIA-controlled Radio Free Europe, staffed by East European émigrés, and the Voice of America, an arm of the State Department. Launched from West Germany and Italy, millions of balloons containing propaganda leaflets and instructions on waging guerrilla warfare were carried into Hungary on wind currents. Secret agents, mostly émigrés trained by the CIA, parachuted into the country with instructions to make contact with people known to be hostile to the regime, foment discontent, and commit sabotage. Most of them were caught and shot.

These activities had been going on for years but intensified in the wake of Khrushchev's "secret speech." Hungarian Stalinists interpreted that speech correctly and began tidying up their affairs. Late in March 1956 they announced the posthumous rehabilitation of a former foreign minister arrested and shot in 1949 on trumped-up charges of "Titoism." Hungarians who had been imprisoned in the Soviet Gulag began to return home. Censorship eased slightly, and more food appeared in the markets. In July Ernö Gerö replaced Stalinist Mátyás Rákosi as leader of the party; Gerö was no improvement but he was a change. The propaganda barrage from the West continued without interruption.

In Budapest the Petöfi literary circle became the center of a spontaneous reform movement. Hundreds of intellectuals, journalists, professional people, students, and workers participated. In mid-July *Pravda* took note, claiming that through the Petöfi Circle "certain elements which oppose the policy of the . . . [Communist] party and which have succumbed to the external influence of imperialist circles have tried . . . to spread their anti-party views." The Soviet newspaper warned Hungarians to remember Poznan, where 53 people had died protesting Communist rule.

Imre Nagy, who had served nearly two years as prime minister before being ousted in April 1955 as insufficiently Stalinist, returned to head the government on October 24. The same day, anti-Soviet riots erupted in Budapest; Soviet forces moved against the demonstrators with tanks and infantry. On October 25 the Communist party's Central Committee, after consulting with Soviet Ambassador Yuri Andropov, appointed János Kádár to succeed Gerö.

At this juncture fate intervened in the form of Middle Eastern politics. The UN voted on October 28 to discuss the Hungarian situation, but the next day Israeli forces attacked Egyptian positions in the Sinai Desert and drove rapidly toward the Suez Canal, recently nationalized by Egypt's Nasser. Britain and France rejected an American proposal (supported by the USSR) for an Israeli-Egyptian cease-fire and issued an ultimatum to both sides to stop fighting and permit Anglo-French occupation of strategic points along the waterway. On October 31 the British and French bombed Cairo and the Canal. Israel continued to attack Egyptian positions in concert with France and Britain. Only on November 6, bowing to intense pressure from the United States, did the British government accept a cease-fire; Israel and France followed suit. Eisenhower was reelected the same day.

The West was thus distracted in a week that proved decisive for Hungary. Even had there been the will to intervene on the side of the Hungarian rebels, it would have been impossible because of the Suez crisis. That tragic affair, and the added complication of the American election, allowed the Soviets to move without interference in Hungary.

On October 27 Nagy and Kádár appealed for order and promised to negotiate the withdrawal of Soviet military forces, the chief goal of most noncommunist Hungarians. The Soviets began to pull their troops out; columns of tanks and infantry moved eastward. Nagy promised free elections, an end to one-party dictatorship, and took leaders of a previously outlawed peasant party into his cabinet. The head of the Roman Catholic Church in Hungary, Josef Cardinal Mindszenty, still in the American embassy after seeking asylum in February 1949, hailed the Soviet withdrawal as the beginning of the end of Communist rule.

The Soviet move was only a feint, a tactical move to regroup. Nagy summoned Ambassador Andropov on November 1 to question him about the ominous Soviet buildup in the eastern part of the country. Andropov promised that there would be no invasion. Determined to force the Kremlin's hand, Nagy declared that Hungary was withdrawing from the Warsaw Pact. He informed Andropov on the afternoon of November 2 that his nation would henceforward be neutral in world politics.

The Soviet Army struck on November 4. After 10 days of fighting, the peace of the tank and the bayonet again enveloped Hungary. Kádár became leader of the new Hungarian regime. Unswervingly loyal to Moscow even though he had been imprisoned and tortured by the Stalinists, Kádár supervised the brutal pacification of his country.

Imre Nagy had received assurances from Kádár and Andropov of safe conduct out of the country; he was arrested on November 22 as he left the Yugoslav embassy. Nagy and the military leader of the uprising, Pal Maléter, were executed at a Soviet base in Romania after a secret trial in June 1958.

## CHINA

Russia had been resolving problems in Eastern Europe by force for almost two centuries; the events of 1956 were wholly in keeping with that tradition. China was another matter.

In his public remarks at the 20th Congress, Khrushchev had carefully praised the Chinese and Yugoslav Communists, knowing that their reaction to the impending disclosure of Stalin's crimes would be crucial. Soon after the Congress, Mikoyan and an Uzbek official were despatched to Beijing to explain the "secret speech."

Beyond the tensions that arose from "de-Stalinization" there were fundamental political differences between China and the post-Stalin USSR. The Soviets had a horror of nuclear war, while the Chinese leaders jeered that they were not afraid of the American "paper tiger." The Soviets spoke ever more seriously of "peaceful coexistence," while the Chinese, who had laid down the principles of this policy in 1954, rapidly moved away from that posture and called for "uninterrupted revolutions" to topple capitalism and imperialism. Moscow accused Beijing of flirting with Trotsky's "permanent revolution." When the Soviets began to normalize relations with Japan, China attacked this trafficking with a "Yankee puppet." Moscow reversed itself in the mid-1950s and announced that it would work with the "national bourgeoisie"—for example in India. The Chinese condemned this "capitulation" and declared they would deal only with Communists and the masses.

Zhou Enlai came to Moscow in January 1957 to try to iron out the differences; his mission failed. Mao himself headed a delegation to the festivities marking the 40th anniversary of the Bolshevik Revolution later the same year, but his discussions with Khrushchev likewise produced no compromise.

The Chinese already suspected that the Soviet leader's attacks on "Talmudists and pedants" and "pedantic quotation-lovers" in the CPSU were in part directed at them. And when the first secretary jibed that it would be "absurd to comb Marx and Engels for instructions on what to do about deliveries of farm products by collective farmers" he was referring to a common Chinese practice, one that in the 1960s assumed vast dimensions in Mao's Cultural Revolution.

Khrushchev and Suslov went to Beijing in September 1959 for the 10th anniversary of the Communist seizure of power and were treated coldly. By 1960 relations had deteriorated to the point where only a change of leadership on one side or the other could bring about a rapprochement.

## FROM SPUTNIK TO BERLIN

In August 1957 Khrushchev's position at home and abroad seemed to become stronger with the world's first successful test flight of an intercontinental ballistic missile, or ICBM. No radar or other early warning system, no amount of air or sea power, could guarantee any nation against attack. A new era in international relations had begun.

Less than two months later the Soviets put the first artificial satellite, "Sputnik" (Companion), into orbit around the earth. Radio signals from the 83.6-kilogram device left no doubt as to the success of Moscow's space program. Sputnik gave further testimony to both the capabilities of Soviet science and the vulnerability of the United States.

Two days after the launching of Sputnik the Soviets successfully tested a powerful new hydrogen bomb. Soviet sabre rattling, however, far from cowing the United States into seeking an accord, produced an American response in the form of about 30 thermonuclear tests in the Marshall Islands in the spring and summer of 1958.

The most serious confrontation in this period occurred in Berlin, a city marked by decennial crises. Shut out of the Middle East by an American show of force in Lebanon in the summer of 1958 and increasingly concerned over the Chinese surge in Asia and Africa, the Khrushchev regime announced on November 18, 1958, that the USSR would expel the Western powers from West Berlin. A few days later Khrushchev issued an ultimatum: the West would leave within six months or face a showdown, presumably nuclear. Reflecting the long-simmering Soviet bitterness over the rearming of West Germany, forbidden by the Potsdam Conference, and over the August 1956 banning of the Communist party in West Germany, the first secretary declared that West Berlin would become a free city. That could only mean incorporation into the East German puppet state.

The Western powers rejected the ultimatum. Soviet Foreign Minister Andrei Gromyko (in office since February 1957) escalated the crisis on Christmas Day 1958 when he told the Supreme Soviet "there is a growing threat that Berlin may become a second Sarajevo."

In January 1959 the Soviet Union presented a draft German peace treaty to the West. Since 1945 the four powers had not been able to agree on a treaty and the West had come to regard the absence of one as an advantage. The German question remained unsettled; that meant that the East German regime still had merely provisional status as a Soviet occupation zone. Determined to force recognition of that regime, the Soviets submitted a document which would have legalized it. The West, however, had never accepted the Oder-Neisse line as the *de jure* border between East Germany and Poland and was in no mood to do so in 1959.

The West rejected the Soviet draft but agreed to continue negotiations. Khrushchev indulged in more bluster, warning of a new Berlin blockade, then agreed in March that East and West Germany could continue to exist side by side. He pledged the Soviet Union would not resolve the German question by force. Once again the first secretary had ranted and threatened, only to back down. This was to cost him considerable support in Moscow, not to mention Beijing.

Khrushchev withdrew his ultimatum because he and President Eisenhower agreed in the spring of 1959 to exchange state visits in an attempt to improve the international climate. It was typical of Khrushchev's diplomacy that the Soviets landed a rocket—their second—on the moon on the eve of his departure for Washington. The space feat heralded a September 15–27 tour that produced little substance. Only in the last three days, when the two leaders met privately outside Washington, did any real accord develop, and then they merely agreed to continue talking about Berlin and other matters and to expand the cultural, educational, scientific, and sports exchanges negotiated in 1958.

The press featured photographs of the smiling leaders and promptly created a "spirit of Camp David" that had as little in common with reality as the 1955 "spirit of Geneva." Nevertheless, the tension that had entered an acute phase in October–November 1956 did seem to ease a little, and prospects for a calmer exchange of views improved.

## U-2

The Soviets sought to take advantage of the new attitude in Washington to reach an accord on Berlin and perhaps on arms control before the November 1960 U.S. elections. A conference of American, Soviet, British, and French leaders was planned for May in Paris. On May 1, however, Soviet rockets shot down an American U-2 high-altitude reconnaissance aircraft near Sverdlovsk, 2,000 kilometers from the nearest frontier.

The meeting was now doomed. The four leaders arrived in the French capital on schedule, but Khrushchev announced that he would not negotiate until the United States apologized, promised to halt the U-2 flights, and punished those responsible. Eisenhower responded on May 16 that there would be no more flights as long as he remained in the White House, but he declined to apologize. The conference thus concluded before it began and Khrushchev announced that the president's planned visit to the Soviet Union would be postponed indefinitely. The Soviets had won a major propaganda victory.

Seeking to pursue his political advantage, Khrushchev came to New York in September to participate in the 1960 session of the UN General Assembly. Several other Communist leaders came along to support him: Castro, Novotny, Kádár, Gomulka, Zhivkov, and Mehmet Shehu of Albania. Also on hand were Tito, Nehru, Macmillan, Nkrumah of Ghana, and Eisenhower.

The conclave threatened to turn into a circus. When a speaker irritated him the first secretary took off his shoe and pounded it on his desk. Khrushchev and Castro harangued crowds from the balcony of the Hotel Theresa in Harlem and engaged in debates with journalists, spectators, police guards, passers-by—anyone who wanted to match wits. The New York *Journal-American* urged "all patriotic Americans" to switch off their television sets when Khrushchev was interviewed. In this atmosphere it was impossible for the General Assembly to make any head-

Khrushchev and Eisenhower at Andrews Air Force Base near Washington, September 1959. (Department of Defense)

way discussing the most pressing item on the agenda, disarmament.

## KHRUSHCHEV, KENNEDY, BERLIN

Following the U-2 incident and the collapse of the Paris conference, Khrushchev pronounced the Monroe Doctrine a dead letter and warned that the Soviet Union would use its rockets should the United States try to overthrow the Castro regime. In part because the United States reacted so vehemently to Castro's nationalization of foreign—chiefly American, including Mafia—private property, the Soviets and Cubans had drawn ever closer after Castro came to power in January 1959. In the 1960 presidential campaign Richard Nixon counselled patience and moderation in dealing with Cuba, while John Kennedy spoke of "liberating" the island. On January 3, 1961, in one of his last official acts, Eisenhower severed diplomatic relations with Cuba.

Eisenhower had earlier approved plans for an invasion of Cuba by anti-Castro Cuban émigrés trained, equipped, and financed by the CIA. President Kennedy gave the signal for the operation to commence, and on April 17, 1961, the émigrés attacked the beach at the Bay of Pigs. The invasion was a disaster; within three days Castro's forces had captured or killed all the attackers. Following Eisenhower's precedent in the U-2 incident, Kennedy accepted responsibility.

The tragic farce was followed by theatre of another sort: Khrushchev and Kennedy met in Vienna on June 3–4, 1961. The grandiosity of the agenda—Germany, disarmament, a test-ban treaty, Southeast Asia—indicated that both saw the meeting as a public relations stunt. The first secretary and the new American president simply took each other's measure. There was no accord save an insincere pledge to support a peaceful, independent Laos and respect its neutrality. The June 1961 "summit" constituted an argument against the casual holding of such meetings.

The encounter nevertheless had important consequences. Khrushchev declared on June 15 that the Soviet Union would sign a peace treaty with East Germany by the end of 1961 whether or not the Western Allies and West Germany participated. He revived his demand that West Berlin be made a free city and warned that, after the conclusion of the Soviet-East German treaty, the Allies would have to deal with the East Germans.

The conflict escalated on August 13, when the East Germans closed the border between East and West Berlin. Two days later they began constructing a wall between the two sectors of the city. Within a few weeks the human hemorrhage, which had cost East Germany several million citizens since 1945, was stanched. The Berlin Wall, eventually extended along the entire East-West frontier in Germany, became a symbol of Communist terror and failure in Eastern Europe.

The East Germans and their Soviet masters were content to stop the outflow of people and did not press the 1961 crisis further. Khrushchev did not sign a treaty with East Germany, Berlin did not become a "free city." The Soviets waited a year to abolish the office of Soviet Commandant in East Berlin; this theoretically obliged the Allied Commandant in West Berlin to deal with East German authorities, but in practice that did not happen.

Khrushchev continued to bluster, telling the West German chancellor in December 1962 that "if the war to which your present political course is leading is unleashed, the Federal Republic of Germany will burn up like tinder in the very first hours of that war." By this time, however, he had become the boy who cried "Wolf!"

In June 1964 a subdued first secretary, his foreign policy in disarray, signed a treaty of friendship and mutual aid with the East German regime of Walter Ulbricht, perhaps Moscow's most faithful henchman. The limited, basically insignificant accord, his last statement on the issue, provided eloquent testimony to Khrushchev's failure to resolve the German problem.

## SINO-INDIAN DISPUTE

From 1957 on, Khrushchev regularly proposed an international "summit" conference to include India but not China. He argued that the American refusal to deal with China constituted an insurmountable barrier, and that it was better to accept half a loaf. The Chinese Communists bitterly resented this attitude, and to embarrass Khrushchev they embarked on a strange adventure in India.

China and India had shared a common frontier since 1950, when Chinese forces occupied Tibet. The mountainous, remote border was quiet for nine years. In August 1959, however, China suddenly moved into the Northeast Frontier Agency territory, also claimed by India. Khrushchev was to visit the United States three weeks later.

The invasion left the Soviets in an impossible situation. Supporting the Chinese would cost them the friendship of the nonaligned nations. Backing India would alienate China and her ally, Albania, possibly North Korea, and the Indonesian and other Communist parties sympathetic to Beijing. The Khrushchev regime adopted a neutral position and called for negotiations. This did not please the Indians, who saw themselves as victims of unprovoked aggression. It outraged the Chinese, who insisted that *they* had been attacked—no one believed this—and further that it was the USSR's duty to come to the aid of a fraternal socialist country no matter what the circumstances.

A TASS statement on September 9, 1959, stressed Moscow's desire for friendly relations with both countries but criticized states which sought to "obstruct the relaxation of the international tensions and to complicate the situation on the eve of the exchange of visits [Khrushchev to the United States, Eisenhower to the USSR]." This was the first public attack on China.

Khrushchev had stumbled into the Chinese trap, although there was probably no way he could have avoided it. Beijing accused him of being more interested in having a glass of beer at the White House than in the emancipation of oppressed peoples. One of the two main Chinese goals in the Indian adventure was at least partially achieved: Beijing's claim to lead the militant wing of the international Communist movement was now firmly established if not universally recognized. A cornered first secretary had no choice but to pursue the logical consequences of his policy and cut off supplies of weapons, spare parts, aircraft, and fuel to China.

The other Chinese goal in India remained elusive: as opposed to neutralism as John Foster Dulles, Mao had hoped to discredit "nonalignment" and compromise Nehru. The Indian leader, as Beijing suspected, secretly requested American aid. Hard evidence of Nehru's "sell-out" to capitalism, however, did not materialize, and with few exceptions the leaders of the other nonaligned nations supported him against the Chinese.

Mao's reaction to the Soviet declaration of neutrality, which amounted to siding with Nehru, provoked Khrushchev to redouble his efforts to woo India. In September 1959 Moscow extended a 1.5 billion ruble credit to New Delhi, and the following February Khrushchev went ahead with his scheduled visit to the country. Still trying to straddle both sides of the fence, he persuaded Nehru to invite Zhou Enlai to New Delhi for talks on the border dispute.

The Sino-Indian border remained quiet for more than three years after the 1959 Chinese invasion. Then suddenly, on October 20, 1962, the People's Liberation Army attacked at several points along the line separating it from the Indian Army. The Indians were routed; the Chinese drove southward against only token resistance.

A desperate Nehru turned to the Soviet Union, only to find Kremlin officials speaking on October 25 of India's "imperialist legacy" as the reason why Moscow would now support China. Stunned, the Indians could only watch in horror as their defeated soldiers stumbled out of the Himalayas and down into the valleys. But on November 2 a *Pravda* editorial announced Moscow's support of . . . India. The Soviets would supply weapons, including MiG-21 fighter aircraft.

This bewildering about-face neither calmed Indian fears nor slowed the Chinese advance. Nehru asked for American aid on November 19; two days later President Kennedy ordered transport aircraft to India.

At this point the Chinese announced a unilateral cease-fire. Beijing declared that it would withdraw its forces behind the lines that had existed in the Northeast Frontier Agency as of November 7, 1959. The retreat indeed took place, and by mid-January 1963 Chinese forces had abandoned the areas seized in the autumn 1962 fighting.

The Himalayan conflict in October–November 1962 was only superficially a dispute between China and India. The Chinese forced the crisis not to seize Indian territory but once again to humiliate the Soviet leader. They could not have chosen a better time: in October 1962 the Soviet Union was locked in a confrontation with the United States.

## CUBAN MISSILE CRISIS

On August 31, 1962, Senator Kenneth Keating charged that the USSR was installing offensive missiles aimed at the United States in Cuba. The Kennedy Administration issued a prompt denial. On September 1 a TASS statement warned that an attack on Cuba would mean war with the Soviet Union. Soviet weapons on the island, the agency declared, were "intended solely for defensive purposes," to prevent another Bay of Pigs operation. In fact, the missiles were deployed in a "soft"—easily targeted—configuration; this made them feasible only for first-strike use.

TASS did not mention that Castro's deputy, Ernesto "Ché" Guevara, was then in Moscow working out final details of emplacing Soviet nuclear-tipped rockets in Cuba. Construction of the launch sites had been under way for some time; the missiles were to be aimed at targets on the American East Coast. Had this plan succeeded, the number of Soviet nuclear systems able to strike the United States would have increased substantially.

As late as October 14, 1962, Kennedy's national security adviser declared that there were no offensive missiles on Cuba. That same day, photos taken on a U-2 reconnaissance flight showed four launch sites for medium-range missiles nearing completion and two others under construction. Soviet personnel were also preparing to assemble Il-28 medium-range "Beagle" bombers which had been shipped to the island in crates.

When Foreign Minister Gromyko met Kennedy at the White House on October 18 and again insisted that only defensive weapons were on Cuba, the President concluded that the Soviet Union wanted a showdown. Kennedy did not tell Gromyko what he knew; but he set procedures in motion to prepare a response.

In a somber televised speech on October 22, Kennedy reported the presence in Cuba of Soviet missiles capable of hitting targets in the United States. He declared that the United States would not tolerate aggression anywhere, least of all in the Western Hemisphere. He announced a naval "quarantine" of Cuba. This amounted to a blockade involving the risk of an incident on the high seas that would tip the crisis over the brink of war. Kennedy warned the Soviets that the United States would consider a missile launched from Cuba against any nation in the hemisphere as "an attack by the Soviet Union upon the United States," and he called upon Khrushchev to "halt and eliminate this clandestine, reckless, and provocative threat to world peace and to stable relations between our two nations."

After Kennedy's speech there could be no doubt that the world was on the verge of a nuclear conflict. The American advantage was overwhelming: nearly 1,000 American intercontinental delivery systems against 10 Soviet operational ICBMs and about 200 long-range bombers in the Soviet arsenal. Had war come, the United States would have taken some severe blows, but it would have inflicted far greater destruction on the USSR.

For more than 48 hours the world awaited Moscow's response. Capitulation would make Khrushchev's position virtually untenable at home and in the Communist camp at large, but he had the alternative of caving in or going to war. He quickly determined that Kennedy was not bluffing. American forces around the globe went on ready alert and the Pentagon radioed missile-carrying Polaris submarines an uncoded message ordering them to "put into play" their objectives.

On October 24 the 18 Soviet-bloc freighters bound for Cuba with military cargo halted dead in the water; Khrushchev would not try to run the blockade. Four days later Soviet technicians began dismantling the missiles already in place and preparing them for shipment, presumably back to the Soviet Union. Construction of new launch sites ceased.

It was later revealed that Washington and Moscow had worked out a compromise. In response to a Soviet plea to allow Khrushchev to save face, Kennedy agreed to pledge that, on demonstration of Soviet readiness to capitulate, he would not invade Cuba. Further, on October 26 the president's brother, Robert Kennedy, informed Soviet Ambassador Anatoli Dobrynin that after the resolution of the crisis the United States would remove its missiles aimed at the USSR from Turkey; this pledge was soon extended to cover missiles based in Italy. This was not a *quid pro quo* for the withdrawal of Soviet missiles from Cuba. The weapons in Turkey and Italy were outmoded and vulnerable, and the United States had planned for some time to substitute Polaris submarines.

The crisis passed. In failing to specify which offensive weapons the Soviets could not deploy on Cuba, American officials neglected to pursue the advantage gained when Khrushchev capitulated. Kennedy had merely said missiles then on the island had to be removed. This oversight left the door open. Eight years later, when the Soviets began constructing a submarine base on Cuba, American officials searched for records of Kennedy's 1962 understanding— or presumed understanding—with Khrushchev. They found nothing.

Twenty-seven years later, the world learned just how close its brush with nuclear catastrophe had been. At a January 1989 Moscow conference of advisers to Kennedy, Khrushchev, and Castro, the Soviets reported that half their 42 missiles on the island in 1962 had been operational and could have been launched within four or five hours. Not without reason, Castro feared an American invasion and spent the night of October 26, 1962, in a bunker at the Soviet embassy. According to one report he urged Moscow to attack, and Khrushchev's son said in 1989 that the Cuban dictator sent his father a cable saying he and his comrades "were prepared to die" in defense of the island.

## THE SOVIETS AND NUCLEAR WEAPONS

The chief lesson Khrushchev and Kennedy drew from their horrifying confrontation was that they would prefer to avoid another. They agreed on various safety measures, including an emergency communication link and better access to top officials for ambassadors. In February 1963 the Soviets presented a draft nonaggression treaty; the West rejected it as a meaningless gesture. The first secretary and the president, however, both deeply sobered, resolved to reach an agreement on nuclear weapons.

The Soviet Union detonated its first atomic bomb in August 1949, its first U-235 weapon in 1951. The United States introduced tactical nuclear weapons into Europe in 1952, thus virtually ensuring that any violent Soviet-NATO clash would witness their use. NATO maintained that the substantial Soviet superiority in conventional forces necessitated deployment of atomic hardware. The Soviet Army and Air Force received atomic and thermonuclear weapons in 1953.

The period 1953–1960 saw the Soviets develop an arsenal of atomic and thermonuclear weapons and build various delivery systems for them, chiefly rockets. As the nuclear stockpile grew, Khrushchev reduced conventional forces, alienating the professional military establishment. The number of men in uniform, 5.763 million in 1950, fell to 3.623 million by 1960.

In the spring of 1957 the Kremlin called for the banning of all tests of nuclear and thermonuclear weapons. The proposal was not taken seriously, but Khrushchev repeated it in December 1957 shortly after renewing his "absolute weapon" boast, and this time there was—as Western intelligence soon learned—reason to believe him. The USSR was ready to suspend tests, the first secretary announced, as of January 1, 1958.

This proposal was generated in part by Moscow's reaction to a November 1957 disaster: a military reactor producing plutonium for atomic bombs had exploded in the Ural Mountains. The area around the town of Kyshtym, between Sverdlovsk and Chelyabinsk, had long been dangerously polluted because of incredibly careless waste disposal procedures at the plant. Radioactive waste stored in liquid form in dry lakes seeped into ground water and thence into the Techa River, a tributary of the Ob. Further, water contaminated in cooling the reactor was simply pumped into a holding pond, and from there directly into the Techa. Gas containing radioactive particles was expelled through a smokestack, subjecting a wide area to deadly "rain" of nitric acid and radioactive iodine-131.

Kyshtym and its environs had thus been bombarded with high levels of radioactivity for about a decade when the November 1957 catastrophe struck. The explosion at the reactor was apparently chemical rather than nuclear, the product of careless storage in close proximity of a combustible combination of chemicals. There was considerable loss of life, and thousands of people suffered exposure to enormous doses of radioactivity. Plant and animal life was destroyed over an area of at least 100 and perhaps as many as 1,000 square kilometers. The entire area was cordoned off; dams were constructed to halt the spread of water-borne contamination. The inhabitants of some 30 villages, which disappeared from subsequent editions of Soviet maps, were resettled elsewhere, leaving everything but the clothes—burned as soon as possible—on their backs in the disaster area.

*Pravda* later noted that the "harmful effects of thermonuclear tests on living organisms are well known in the Soviet Union." Nothing about the events in the Urals in November 1957, however, appeared in the popular press; only through scientific journals did some segments of the Soviet public learn what had happened.

The Kyshtym tragedy, the world's first nuclear catastrophe of such dimensions, played a role in the March 31, 1958, Soviet decision to suspend nuclear testing. Khrushchev called on the United States and Great Britain, then the only other nuclear powers, to halt their own tests.

The United States continued to test after the Soviet suspension, as did Britain. On October 31, 1958, however, both Western nations declared that they would halt tests for one year while negotiations to limit nuclear arms went forward; three-power talks had begun in Geneva earlier the same month.

Polish Foreign Minister Adam Rapacki had proposed creation of a nuclear-free zone in Central Europe in October 1957. Under his plan, unquestionably born in Moscow, no atomic or thermonuclear weapons would be permitted in either of the two German states, Poland, or Czechoslovakia, an area with a combined population of more than 100 million. The West rejected the "Rapacki Plan" as a Communist maneuver to secure withdrawal of American nuclear weapons from West Germany—an acknowledged Kremlin goal—and perpetuate division of the German state.

The West also rejected Khrushchev's 1959 call for a nuclear-free zone in the Pacific Basin. The Soviet leader was however speaking not to Washington but to Beijing. The Chinese were trying to develop their own nuclear capability, which would primarily threaten the USSR. Khrushchev's proposal was ignored in the United States and derided in China.

In August 1961, at the height of the year's Berlin crisis, the Soviet government announced its intention to resume thermonuclear testing. The "aggressive actions of the imperialists," *Pravda* declared, necessitated this step, which was accompanied by a decree extending military service "until the signing of a peace treaty with Germany." On September 5, 1961, Kennedy ordered the resumption of "safe" tests, those which allegedly produced little or no radioactive fallout. At the end of October the UN General Assembly formally asked the Soviets not to detonate a 50-megaton hydrogen bomb; the Kremlin ignored the request and exploded the device in the Arctic.

Secret negotiations for a test-ban treaty began early in 1963 and continued for several months. Averell Harriman, who had once served as American ambassador to the Soviet Union, went to Moscow in July to direct the final stages of the bargaining. On August 5, 1963, the United States, Great Britain, and the Soviet Union signed a limited nuclear test-ban treaty barring tests in space, the atmosphere and under water. Underground tests were not affected.

The treaty went into effect in October 1963. Within a year more than 100 nations had signed it; China and France refused. Described at the time as a major step forward in bringing the nuclear arms race under control, the accord had a more modest impact. It reduced radioactive fallout and helped prepare the ground for the Outer Space Treaty of 1967, the Non-

Proliferation Treaty of 1970, and the Strategic Arms Limitation (SALT) I pact of 1972.

## MOSCOW AND THE KENNEDY ASSASSINATION

The Soviet leaders were apparently as stunned as the rest of the world by the assassination of President Kennedy on November 22, 1963, barely six weeks after the test-ban treaty went into effect. A kind of bond had developed between Khrushchev and Kennedy after the near-catastrophe in the Caribbean, a recognition that they were united by a common desire to avoid annihilation.

It quickly developed that the alleged assassin was an American citizen who had once defected to the USSR, Lee Harvey Oswald. Returning to the United States, he developed an affinity for Castro's Cuba. Anticipating charges of Soviet-Cuban involvement in the affair, the Kremlin took the unprecedented step of conveying what it claimed was the complete KGB file on Oswald to the American authorities. No Soviet link to Oswald after his departure from the USSR was established, and the Warren Commission which investigated the matter concluded that the assassin was a deranged fanatic who had acted alone.

The possibility of a Cuban link was also dismissed, but this was a much stickier wicket. It would be revealed in the 1970s that, after Castro came to power in January 1959, the CIA had concocted a number of plots to assassinate him, going so far as to negotiate a murder contract with the crime syndicate, the Mafia. Several CIA-sponsored attempts on Castro's life failed.

Critics of the Warren Commission denounced its report for failing to refute the claim of some Americans that the Kennedy assassination was Castro's retaliation for the CIA's attempts on his own life. And if Castro was involved, the critics argued, his Kremlin masters had surely been consulted at every stage of the plot and had approved it.

The question of Soviet-Cuban involvement has never been laid to rest. It is unlikely that any security agency involved, or the Mafia, will soon release its unsanitized files.

## THE THIRD WORLD

When Egypt's Nasser flirted with Communists at home and abroad he brought down on himself the wrath of John Foster Dulles. In July 1956 the United States, obediently followed by Anthony Eden's government in Britain, withdrew its offer to help finance the construction of the Aswan high dam on the Nile. The Suez crisis of 1956 deepened the rift between Egypt and the West despite the fact that the United States had forced the Israeli-Franco-British alliance to halt its aggression against Nasser.

Preoccupied with events in Poland and Hungary and the stresses of "de-Stalinization," the Soviets were slow to step into the breach. In the autumn of 1956, however, Moscow pledged unequivocal support for Egypt and took up that country's cause in the UN, although it was not until Nasser visited the Soviet Union in April–May 1958 that the two governments began to cooperate closely. Nasser opened negotiations with the Soviets for a loan to finance construction of the dam. In October 1958 the Kremlin announced that it would lend Egypt—known as the United Arab Republic during the 1958–1961 union with Syria—$100 million toward construction; that sum would later be substantially augmented. Design work was completed in July 1959, and

Nasser turned the first shovel of earth in January 1960.

Ignoring the warnings of some officials, Moscow misjudged Nasser badly. The majority opinion in Soviet governmental circles considered the Egyptian leader an essentially weak, malleable politician who could be bent Moscow's way. In reality Nasser was exactly what he claimed to be, a devout Muslim and an Arab nationalist. He would traffic with Communists only when it suited his purposes.

In January 1961 the Egyptian police arrested 200 leading Communists, and Cairo warned the Kremlin to cease interfering in Egyptian politics. So far as the Egyptians were concerned, construction of the dam, which involved the influx of several thousand Soviet technicians, was strictly a business deal requiring no political concessions, least of all any ideological cozying up to the atheists from the USSR. Relations between the two countries deteriorated, and Anwar Sadat, then chairman of the UAR National Assembly, went to Moscow in May to explain to Khrushchev that only Communists suspected of plotting to overthrow the regime had been arrested.

Nikita Khrushchev visited Egypt in May 1964 to join Nasser in celebrating completion of the first stage of the dam. When he fell from power a few months later, one of the charges against him was that he had given so much to and received so little from the Egyptian leader.

Elsewhere in the Middle East the Soviets sought to subvert the bilateral defense agreements which the United States concluded in 1959 with Iran, Pakistan, and Turkey. Equally to their distaste was the 1955 defensive alliance between Iraq and Turkey (Baghdad Pact), to which Britain, Pakistan, and Iran adhered. The Baghdad Pact, renamed Central Treaty Organization (CENTO) after Iraq's March 1959 withdrawal, constituted a *cordon sanitaire* to thwart a Soviet move toward the Persian Gulf, around which lay the world's richest oil-producing area. Further adding to Soviet problems in the region, American nuclear-tipped missiles in Turkey were pointed at the USSR until their removal in 1962–1963, and the U-2 flights over European Russia originated from airfields in Pakistan.

Soviet apprehensions did not lessen when the shah of Iran settled an oil-revenues dispute with the West in August 1954 and took his country into the anti-Soviet alliance of Middle Eastern and Western nations. In 1955–1956 the USSR and Iran resurveyed their 2,000-kilometer frontier, one of the most heavily guarded in the world. The tension between the two countries did not ease when in 1959 the shah unilaterally abrogated the 1921 Irano-Soviet agreement permitting the movement of Soviet troops into Iran in the event that military forces constituting a threat to the Soviet Union entered that country. Moscow did not recognize the shah's action.

In East and Southeast Asia the Soviet Union frequently used domestic Communist forces to achieve its political goals. After the July 1954 division of Vietnam into a Communist North and a noncommunist South, the Soviets naturally backed the North and stepped up military and economic aid. The Soviet effort in Vietnam was however dwarfed by that of Beijing: in July 1955 China granted the Hanoi regime of Hô Chi Minh $338 million in aid. When the United States increased its own assistance to the South Vietnamese regime in the early 1960s, the Soviets again expanded their aid to the Viet Cong (South Vietnamese Communists) and to Hanoi, which sponsored, trained, equipped, and maintained them.

The Vietnamese conflict escalated dramatically in 1964, a presidential election year in the United States, and the Americans became deeply enmeshed. The Soviets adopted a holding pattern, keeping up the flow of aid to the Viet Cong and Hanoi and remaining aloof from the fighting. Beijing periodically halted the transhipment of Soviet supplies by rail across China.

The ancient enmity between China and the peoples of Southeast Asia went back at least 1,000 years and stemmed from both cultural differences and Chinese attempts to dominate the area. The Soviets thus had only to call Hanoi's attention to Chinese obstructionism. The Moscow-trained Hô Chi Minh was like Nasser in that he took help from the Devil when he had to, but he never wavered in his preference for Moscow over Beijing.

The Soviet Union fostered Communist and Communist-dominated insurrectionary movements elsewhere in Southeast Asia. Most important were those in the Philippines, Malaya (Malaysia), Burma, Cambodia, and Laos. Sizable American and British aid programs helped defeat the Communists in the first three countries, but Cambodia and Laos long remained unstable.

In the largest, wealthiest, and strategically most important nation in the region, Indonesia, a strong man, Sukarno, led the postwar struggle against the Dutch colonial regime. A nationalist with a visceral hatred of colonialism, Sukarno believed he could manipulate the large Indonesian Communist party (PKI) to his own ends and deal with the Soviet Union without compromising his newly independent country.

In April 1955 Sukarno was a sponsor of the conference of 29 Asian and African states that took place at Bandung, Indonesia. The final communiqué denounced "colonialism in all its forms"—omitting, however, to list the Soviet variety. The Soviet Union was one of the behind-the-scenes organizers of the Bandung Conference, which also approved the "five principles of coexis-

tence" first enunciated by Zhou Enlai and Nehru in April 1954 but later repudiated by Beijing.

Sukarno took Moscow's side in the Sino-Soviet dispute, and his imposition of severe restrictions on the millions of Indonesian Chinese late in 1959 provided one of the first clues to the depth of that quarrel. Indonesia acted as a Soviet surrogate in Southeast Asia in other ways, notably by repeatedly launching guerrilla raids against the new Federation of Malaysia, which included Sarawak and North Borneo, both claimed by Jakarta. The PKI, many of whose members were Indonesian Chinese, was loyal to Mao. Overestimating his own political sagacity, Sukarno believed that he could tack between Moscow, Beijing, and the PKI with impunity, playing each off against the other to his own advantage. When the Sino-Soviet conflict reached the stage of open hostilities, his efforts came undone.

In 1965, a year after the ouster of Khrushchev, Sukarno's patron, the PKI attempted to seize power through an armed coup d'état. The action was ruthlessly put down by the Indonesian Army which slaughtered about 300,000 Communists. After the 1927/1928 events in China it was the largest massacre of party members in the history of the international Communist movement.

Khrushchev's protégé stood accused by the army of complicity in the PKI putsch. Sukarno was forced to yield most of his powers in March 1966.

The Soviet Union courted leaders in Black Africa, among them Kwame Nkrumah of Ghana, Sékou Touré of Guinea, and Patrice Lumumba of the Congo Republic. Its unswerving anti-colonialist policy won the Soviet Union some friends in Africa, and foreign aid likewise purchased a certain amount of unstable affection. The Soviets had little experience on the Dark Continent, however, and they underestimated the ability of Western nations to learn from their mistakes and come to terms with new realities. Further, the persistent Soviet refusal to bring any sort of serious pressure to bear on the racist Republic of South Africa, a major, semi-clandestine Soviet trading partner, hurt Moscow's image in Africa, as did the racism which Black African students encountered in the USSR.

The Soviet Union had not paid much attention to Latin America before the Castro revolution of 1959. When the United States failed to move decisively against the quasi-Communist regime on its doorstep, the Soviets plunged into the Caribbean Basin. Soviet aid, amounting in the 1960s to $1 million a day, kept Castro afloat, neutralized the American economic boycott, and left something over for Cuban mischief-making.

Castro's principal aide, Ernesto "Ché" Guevara, became a Soviet favorite. Through Guevara, Moscow began to organize a network of revolutionary underground organizations throughout Latin America. In some areas skeleton forces were already in place and needed only an infusion of guns, money and hope; elsewhere, Guevara and the people he trained had to build organizations from the ground up. The Soviets did not spare the purse. The Cuban cadres were well-financed, and huge amounts of arms flowed into the region through Havana. Thousands of Latin American youths were trained in guerrilla warfare tactics at special camps in Cuba, Czechoslovakia, and the Soviet Union.

The great crisis of October 1962 momentarily brought the increasingly aggressive Soviet-Cuban revolutionary mission to a halt. The activity resumed in 1963, however, and the pace was to quicken after 1964.

## KHRUSHCHEV'S FOREIGN POLICY: A SUMMARY

Khrushchev was a bold innovator, as audacious as Stalin had been prudent. He subdued the Hungarians by force and the Poles by a few concessions and the threat of force. He undertook a foreign aid campaign that matched that of the United States.

Soviet philanthropy was designed to serve the political interests of the USSR, but the billions spent in the Third World ultimately purchased relatively little goodwill. One cannot conceive of Egyptian peasants praising Moscow as they irrigate their fields with water from Aswan high dam, but to the extent that those peasants were more productive, prosperous, and presumably happier, Soviet aid was not in vain, at least not from the standpoint of the Egyptians. The Soviets helped raise the standard of living of millions of people around the world at enormous cost to themselves. As a percentage of gross national product, Soviet foreign aid greatly exceeded the American figure.

A Soviet population whose own standard of living remained among the lowest in Europe deeply resented the expenditure of vast sums on foreign aid. More significantly, given the nature of the Soviet political system, many high-ranking officials began to question the largesse. Nasser's harsh treatment of Egyptian Communists, Sukarno's inability to turn the PKI away from its pro-Beijing orientation, and the failure of Communist parties to make significant headway in Black Africa led some Soviet leaders to undertake their own cost-benefit analysis of foreign aid and conclude that the Soviet Union simply was not getting an adequate political return for its investment. The experience of Castro's Cuba seemed an exception until those leaders faced the realities of the $1 million per day needed to shore up that regime, and of course the 1962 crisis accentuated the vulnerability of the USSR's most distant client state.

The reappraisal of Soviet foreign policy began after the Cuban missile crisis. A subdued first secretary undertook no substantial new gambles; the sums allocated for foreign aid declined. It would appear that a majority of the leadership reached the conclusion that, because the dams and steel mills and factories and refineries built with Soviet aid had not noticeably altered the East-West balance of power, Soviet foreign policy should in the future concentrate not on stabilizing the Third World but on *destabilizing* it. Moscow abandoned the policy of collaborating with the "national bourgeoisie" and moved closer to the Chinese position, which called for working with Communist revolutionaries to overthrow existing regimes, even freely elected, reasonably progressive and "popular" regimes. This amounted to a revival of the Comintern's "united front" policy of the 1920s.

Soviet leaders disenchanted with Khrushchev insisted that the USSR needed Ché Guevaras more than construction engineers. The Third World revoluntionaries, indoctrinated, trained, and equipped by the Soviets, would destroy the old society, smash the last vestiges of Western colonialism and imperialism, and bring their countries into the Communist fold. Khrushchev had spoken with increasing frequency of "wars of national liberation" but did relatively little to encourage them, concentrating instead upon showy, costly construction projects. It was far cheaper and more to the benefit of the Soviet Union, his critics believed, to supply AK-47 assault rifles and ammunition to Communist guerrillas than to build a road or construct a factory.

In the end, Khrushchev proved an inept manager of revolution. His colleagues on the Presidium could not tolerate his incompetence.

## SUGGESTED ADDITIONAL READING

**Allison, Graham T.,** *Essence of Decision: Explaining the Cuban Missile Crisis,* Boston: Little, Brown, 1971

**Blight, James G., and David A. Welch,** *On the Brink: Americans and Soviets Reexamine the Cuban Missile Crisis,* New York: Hill and Wang, 1989

**Bromke, Adam, ed.,** *The Communist States at the Crossroads between Moscow and Peking,* New York: Praeger, 1965

**Chayes, Abram,** *The Cuban Missile Crisis,* New York: Oxford University Press, 1974

**Clemens, Walter C., Jr.,** *The Arms Race and Sino-Soviet Relations,* Stanford, Calif.: Hoover Institution Press, 1968

**Dinerstein, Herbert S.,** *The Making of a Missile Crisis: October 1962,* Baltimore: The Johns Hopkins University Press, 1976

**Ellison, Herbert J., ed.,** *The Sino-Soviet Conflict,* Seattle: University of Washington Press, 1982

**Khrushchev, Nikita S.,** *On Peaceful Coexistence,* Moscow: Foreign Languages Publishing House, 1961

**McDougall, Walter A.,** *The Heavens and the Earth: A Political History of the Space Age,* New York: Basic Books, 1985

**Medvedev, Zhores,** *Nuclear Disaster in the Urals,* New York: W.W. Norton, 1979

**Miller, R. F., and F. Féhér, eds.,** *Khrushchev and the Communist World,* Totowa, N.J.: Rowman and Littlefield, 1984

**Porter, Bruce D.,** *The Soviet Union in Third World Conflicts,* Cambridge, England: Cambridge University Press, 1984

**Ulam, Adam,** *Expansion and Coexistence,* New York: Praeger, 1968

**Zagoria, Donald S.,** *The Sino-Soviet Conflict, 1956–1961,* Princeton, N.J.: Princeton University Press, 1962

**Zinner, Paul E.,** *Revolution in Hungary,* New York: Columbia University Press, 1962

# 18

# INTERNAL AFFAIRS IN THE REFORM ERA

## POLITICAL DEVELOPMENTS

The U-2 crisis produced dramatic changes in the Soviet leadership: a Central Committee plenary session on May 4 elevated the Khrushchev loyalists Aleksei Kosygin, Nikolai Podgorny, and Dmitri Polyansky to the party Presidium and removed A.I. Kirichenko from that body. On May 7 Leonid Brezhnev succeeded Kliment Voroshilov, last of the Stalin cronies still in high office, as chairman of the Supreme Soviet Presidium.

Khrushchev now had a team composed in part of people whose careers he had made and in part of old-line party officials. On the 14-member party Presidium, seven members (Brezhnev, Kosygin, Podgorny, Polyansky, Kozlov, Furtseva, and Mukhitdinov)

owed their positions to the first secretary, who thus had a majority. Khrushchev believed that he could also count on the support of Anastas Mikoyan, an economic expert with no personal political ambitions. N.M. Shvernik, 72, and O.V. Kuusinen, 78, were party hacks interested in little but a comfortable ride on life's last journey. Two younger bureaucrats, A.B. Aristov and N.G. Ignatov, did as they were told.

The final member of the Presidium, the conservative ideologist Suslov, had helped propel Khrushchev into the party leadership and sided with him against the Stalinists in 1957. Suslov had become the political conscience of the party; his support was crucial to anyone who wanted to be first among the leaders. As long as he backed Khrushchev, all but the most rigid Stalinists could rest assured that the CPSU was on a true Leninist course.

The Khrushchev team was of uneven caliber. Kosygin, a competent economic manager, supplanted Mikoyan in this area and took his ideological cues from Suslov. Brezhnev was a gregarious individual remarkable more for his personal charm—rare among Communist leaders—than his intellect, a skillful politician who also deferred to Suslov on ideology. Podgorny headed the Ukrainian party organization. N.A. Mukhitdinov, the first non-Caucasian to sit on the Presidium, led the Uzbek branch. Yekaterina Furtseva had long served in the Moscow party organization, as had her husband, diplomat Nikolai Firyubin. Mukhitdinov, Furtseva, Aristov, and Ignatov, however, lost their Presidium seats at the 22nd Congress.

A key Khrushchev appointee was Frol Kozlov, head of the party in Leningrad province and a major figure in the 1957 defeat of the Stalinists. Kozlov, who had ambitions to higher office, subsequently broke with his mentor.

In 1961 the Khrushchev faction pushed through more "de-Stalinization" at the 22nd Congress. This was the last time the faction held together on a major issue, and it did so only with difficulty.

Party conservatives were distressed by the split within the international Communist camp, which burst into the open at the 22nd Congress when Khrushchev denounced Albanian Stalinism. Representing the Chinese party, Zhou Enlai vigorously defended the Tirana regime. In the middle of the Congress Zhou abruptly left Moscow. In a demonstration of his hostility toward Khrushchev, Mao went to the Beijing airport to greet Zhou on his return.

Fundamentalist Communists were further disturbed by the Khrushchev faction's declaration that, "because the construction of socialism has been completed, the dicta-

torship of the proletariat has fulfilled its historical mission." The Soviet state, the Central Committee report and the new party program declared, was a "state of the whole people"—workers, peasants, and people's intelligentsia; this adumbrated the granting of full civil rights to the peasants beginning in 1974. Abandoning the concept of "dictatorship of the proletariat" struck many Stalinists as anathema.

Many middle-of-the-road party members disapproved of Khrushchev's unqualified prediction that "this generation of Soviet people will live under communism." This smacked of his May 1957 boast that the USSR would overtake the United States in several categories of agricultural production by 1960 and recalled his taunting Americans in 1959 that their grandchildren would live under communism.

A 1961 innovation in party rules adopted at Khrushchev's demand alienated party cadres. Article 35 called for the replacement at each regular election of at least a quarter of the membership of the Central Committee and its Presidium; at least a third of the republic Central Committees and regional party committees; and at least half the town and district party committees and half the officers of all cells. There was an escape clause permitting the exemption from this turnover of "experienced party workers of special merit," i.e., Khrushchev and his friends. The first secretary's stated motive in seeking to bring new blood and vigor into the party bureaucracy had much to commend it, but his enemies believed he was preparing a purge. Career officials became apprehensive and many supporters broke with him on this issue.

The 22nd Congress marked Khrushchev's last major triumph; thereafter he seemed to lose his political touch and occasionally—as in the Cuban missile affair—his grip on reality. One of his advisers, Fyodor Burlatsky, revealed in 1988 that the first secretary's enemies slyly persuaded him to adopt a crackpot scheme that called for the division "on the production principle" of district and province party committees into independent industrial and agricultural sectors. Khrushchev pushed this bizarre plan through a November 1962 Central Committee plenum; the result, Burlatsky wrote, "undermined his authority among party leaders once and for all."

Chaos ensued as the party obediently tried to follow orders. Within a month of Khrushchev's fall in 1964, *Pravda* pronounced the caper a failure.

## TROUBLES IN AGRICULTURE

Agricultural production, which had seemed on an upward curve after the 1956 harvest, began to decline again. The 1957 harvest was a poor one and 1958's not much better. Yields of the "virgin lands" fell precipitately as natural nutrients in the soil declined and were not replaced by chemical fertilizers. Further, the shelter-belt forestation program, designed to protect steppe topsoil from wind erosion, proved a dismal failure, not least because the seedlings were planted in Lysenkian "clusters." By planting several together, Lysenko declared, only the fittest would survive. The plowing of vast territories unprotected by forests inevitably produced disaster: 1.5 million hectares were ruined in Pavlodar province alone in 1962, and in 1963 severe windstorms blew millions of tons of topsoil away.

The party searched for scapegoats. Unwilling to blame Lysenko, it also declined to admit that nature could defeat Communists. Moscow refused to face the fact that the "virgin lands" lie in an area where the May–July probability of drought is 20–40 percent. Khrushchev gave a supernatural explanation for the troubles in March 1961, pointing out that the name of the region's chief town, Akmolinsk, means "White Grave" in Kazakh. He proposed renaming it "Tselinograd," Russian for "Virgin Land City."

Akmolinsk was renamed; the harvests did not improve. In 1962 Kazakhstan fell about 35 percent short of fulfilling its grain quotas and likewise failed to fulfill the plan for meat, milk, and wool. The new lands did not emerge as the salvation of Soviet agriculture; in European Russia the annual grain production per capita in 1961–1964 was lower than in 1913.

In 1956 the party reexamined the role of machine-tractor stations (MTS) and began to switch them to a cost-accounting basis. Established in 1928, the MTSs were state-owned and -operated machinery pools serving the kolhozes, which had paid a high tax for the use of the machinery before 1956. In 1957 there were about 7,900 MTSs, each serving an average of 6 or 7 kolhozes; the sovhozes had their own implements.

The move to cost-accounting was necessary, CPSU spokesmen said, because the financing of the stations bore no relation to crop and livestock yields. That was true; but what the party really wanted was to abolish them altogether by having the kolhozes buy their own machinery. Before the war the average MTS had serviced 30–35 kolhozes. The postwar amalgamation of the farms, however, created huge agricultural enterprises. In 1958 the average Ukrainian kolhoz had 3,000 hectares of land, 600 head of cattle, 200 milk cows, 500 pigs, and 640 sheep (privately owned animals not included). Organizations this size and larger—there were 20,000-hectare kolhozes in Kazakhstan—clearly needed their own machinery and repair shops. Beyond that, Khrushchev admitted that the cost of MTS services had been pegged artificially high. Because the stations had outlived their usefulness, party leaders decided to abolish them rather than reform the price structure.

Fearing that self-contained and even self-sufficient kolhozes might generate delusions of independence that could have political implications, conservatives opposed abolition of the MTSs. Khrushchev prevailed, however, and in 1958 the enterprises were liquidated. Their property, worth 32 billion rubles, was sold to the kolhozes, which had already amortized 18 billion of this sum. Thus the compulsory deliveries and payments in kind for MTS work came to an end. The former MTS became a repair and technical service station or RTS which performed capital repairs on agricultural machinery on a realistic cost-plus basis.

Abolition of the MTSs did not solve the agricultural problem. The situation did not improve after the 1958 reorganization of many kolhozes into sovhozes, nor with the reform of the sovhoz wage system in 1961–1962, nor with the introduction of a minimum wage for kolhozniks—whose income previously came only from profits of the farm—in 1967–1970. Even in the best of years, Soviet agriculture remained barely capable of meeting the country's needs. More than any other factor, the constant meddling of Communist politicians who knew nothing about agriculture brought about this dismal state of affairs, but natural phenomena also played a certain role. The drought of 1963 obliged the state to buy 12 million tons of grain on the world market— bitter medicine for a first secretary who had sworn to overtake the United States in food production.

## SEVEN-YEAR PLAN

The Sixth Five-Year Plan of 1956–1960 called for an increase in industrial production of about 65 percent, and at the 22nd Congress the Central Committee claimed that the actual growth figure for 1955–1961 stood at an astonishing 80 percent. Although exaggerated, the boast came closer to reality than most Soviet statistics: Vasily Selyunin and Grigori Khanin wrote in 1987 that the 1950s represent "the most successful period in [Soviet] economic history." Labor productivity rose 62 percent, return on assets increased 17 percent, and material-intensiveness declined by a healthy 5 percent. After the twelvefold increase of 1928–1950, retail prices fell and wholesale prices stabilized during the first half of the 1950s, while in the last five years prices rose very little.

Khrushchev attributed the success to the reforms he pushed through a reluctant Central Committee in 1957, when the party scrapped the existing plan for a new Seven-Year Plan. In many important respects the 1957 reorganization of the economic administration was the largest peacetime social upheaval since the abandoning of NEP.

The reorganization involved the creation of 105 economic regions, among them 70 in the RSFSR, 11 in the Ukraine. Leningrad, with 600 very large enterprises employing about a million people and producing 50 billion rubles worth of goods annually, constituted one region, as did the entire Uzbek republic, the Byelorussian republic, and so on. Each economic region would be under the control of a regional economic council, or *sovnarhoz*, empowered to deal with problems of supply, production, and marketing. Only large enterprises would come under the purview of the *sovnarhozes;* smaller ones remained responsible to the appropriate ministry of the republic. Under the law of May 10, 1957, all Union industrial ministries save those directly involved in defense and nuclear power were abolished, their powers divided between the national Gosplan, republic Gosplans, and the *sovnarhozes.*

The boundaries of the new economic regions coincided with those of provinces or groups of provinces. The party boss in the province, or the senior boss in a group of provinces, acquired substantial economic powers because the *sovnarhozes* reported directly to him.

The aim of the reform was decentralization. When industry was under national control each ministry, seeking to fulfill its assignment, tried to produce materials and components in its own plants. Sometimes that meant going a considerable distance for items which could have been purchased locally from plants belonging to another *competing* ministry. Yet another problem in attempting to fulfill the plan was the constant striving to do so rapidly; this led ministries to encourage production of expensive items in order to meet the plan "in gross," that is, in terms of the ruble value of output. Further, as Khrushchev pointed out, officials were often "afraid of specialization and extensive cooperation because these involved a certain break in the established forms of production organization."

The 1957 reorganization failed as pressures which had induced the ministries to try to become self-sufficient influenced the *sovnarhozes* in the same way. Research and development remained under control of Union committees for particular branches of industry, thus creating a "rupture in the research-production cycle" and vitiating the decentralizing effort.

The decentralization of management had been accompanied by a new emphasis on the *centralization* of planning. There were at the time about 200,000 "state industrial enterprises" and more than 100,000 construction sites. Coordinating the activity of them all was like playing chess on a board with 300,000 squares. Computers would have helped, but they were either not available or, when available, unequal to the demands

placed on them. The Soviet Union began to feel the effects of its lag in computer technology and automation.

In January 1959 the CPSU admitted that Soviet labor in heavy industry was only half as productive as its American counterpart. There were a number of factors involved here, among them lack of incentives. Soviet steelworkers were paid much less than those in the United States, and the party could no longer summon up the specter of imminent war to produce a 1930s-like enthusiasm for work and sacrifice. Soviet production was still using prewar technology, while the Americans, West Germans, and Japanese had rebuilt all or a substantial part of their industrial plants.

Still another problem which stunted growth was the lag in the chemical industry. The Soviets invested 11.5 billion rubles in that area during the Seven-Year Plan; this produced a 240 percent increase in production—an average annual growth rate of 13.6 percent. That was impressive but below the Japanese figure. Worse, the output of plastics increased by only 300 percent against the 700 percent called for, and that of synthetic fibers by only 250 percent against a projected 1,200 to 1,300 percent.

In 1961 the party admitted that the reorganization simply was not working. The *sovnarhozes* aped the inefficient practices of the ministries; the gap between planning and capabilities did not appreciably narrow; labor productivity had slowed its growth rate. Early in 1961 the 105 economic regions were reduced to 17, dramatic evidence of "creeping recentralization." More evidence came in March 1963 with the creation of the Supreme Council of the National Economy, a super-agency charged to supervise and coordinate the work of Gosplan, the *sovnarhozes*, the state construction agency (Gosstroi), and all production committees.

In 1962 the party began an experiment

with the profit motive. Encouraged by the authorities, economist Yevsei Liberman of Harkov University argued that the way to make enterprises efficient was to make them profitable, giving labor and management a share in those profits. Many Communists must have shuddered when they read Liberman's article in the September 9, 1962, edition of *Pravda;* one could hardly imagine a more unlikely proposal in the pages of Lenin's newspaper.

The government had announced a plan to reduce taxes in 1960 only to be forced to postpone it until 1962, when it was again postponed, this time indefinitely. A monetary reform in January 1961 exchanged 10 old rubles for one new one. The attendant publicity did not distract the public's attention from price increases of up to 50 percent on meat, butter, eggs, and other consumer items. These increases did not reduce demand sufficiently to bring it more in line with decreasing production; and on June 1, 1962, the state announced still higher prices for meat and butter.

The 1962 price hikes produced serious unrest in Leningrad, Odessa, Krivoi Rog, and other industrial centers, but the authorities were able to contain the various sitdown strikes and demonstrations. In Novocherkassk, however, an industrial town of 104,000 near the mouth of the Don River, violence erupted; officials had made the mistake of announcing a 30 percent wage cut at a major factory the same day the increase in food prices was made public. The factory manager told protesting workers to put jam on their bread instead of meat. The men immediately went on strike and several hundred others from nearby plants joined them. The strikers held meetings at the locomotive factory—where the movement began—all day on June 1. That night about 30 were arrested.

The next morning several hundred people marched on CPSU headquarters; thousands of spectators flocked into the square where the building was located. According to some reports, troops of the local garrison refused an order to open fire. Non-Russian soldiers were brought in; firing over the heads of the crowd, they shot some small boys out of their perches in trees. The crowd surged forward, and the troops fired directly into it: 70 or 80 people were killed, more than half with dum-dum bullets.

Mikoyan and Kozlov flew to the city and took charge. On June 3 they announced over local radio that the "enemy provocateurs" who had organized the events of June 1–2 would be severely punished. Mikoyan declared that the agitators had used dum-dum bullets, which were not Soviet Army issue. A trial was held and nine men were sentenced to be shot, two women to 15 years in prison.

The tragedy at Novocherkassk and demonstrations elsewhere frightened the party, which promptly stocked stores in affected cities with food. Neither that nor longer range solutions in the form of capitalist-style incentives, or the new super-agency in charge of planning, brought the economy out of the doldrums. The vested interests of party bureaucrats and industrial managers triumphed over every attempt to rationalize the Soviet economy. Recentralization gathered momentum and by 1964 the 1957 reforms were but a distant memory; the party abolished the *sovnarhozes* shortly after Khrushchev's fall.

## LIFE IN THE KHRUSHCHEV ERA

For all the shortcomings of the economic reforms, the standard of living did improve between 1957 and 1964. Residents of the showcase cities—visited by millions of Soviet and foreign tourists annually—Moscow, Leningrad, and Kiev were better housed, fed, and clothed than at any time in Soviet history. The three urban agglomerations dazzled visitors, although not always in the way the party intended. New housing was often poorly constructed; food shops had adequate supplies of bread, potatoes, and cabbage but were frequently out of meat, vegetables, and fruit; clothing remained drab and poorly tailored.

Cities were far better supplied than small towns and villages, but no matter where one found them consumer goods continued to be of inferior quality. *Pravda* admitted in May 1956 that Soviet radio tubes, for example, lasted only 800–1,000 hours, whereas British tubes were designed to serve 10,000 hours. In 1963 the inspection service of the RSFSR's ministry of trade tested 12.6 million manufactured items and found fully half defective. A large Moscow shoe store inspected 672,000 pairs in 1959 and rejected 50,000.

The problem was not only quality but availability. Visitors to the Black Sea port of Novorossiisk in late 1961 assumed that it was a local custom for men to wear beards. *Izvestiya* investigated and found that there were no razor blades in the city of 100,000. The same situation prevailed in Lvov (450,000), Tbilisi (770,000), and elsewhere.

Another index of the quality of urban life was the shortage of telephones. In 1957 there were only 5,000 in Harkov, a city of more than a million. Saratov (620,000) had only 3,800, and Stalingrad (from 1961 Volgograd), with a population of 600,000, had only 1,300. The tiny minority who did have telephones had to go to a central office each month to pay their bills; there was no system for payment by mail.

An extensive black market made up for some of the shortages, and a network of influence-peddling helped those who became part of it to cope with the problems of daily life. White-collar crime flourished and fortunes were made. Entrepreneurs from the Caucasus and Central Asia would fly to Moscow or another large city with fresh fruit, vegetables, or even flowers, set up shop on a street corner, and make a substantial sum within a very short time. The police generally did not interfere. Likewise, the free market, through which peasants disposed of food grown on their private plots, operated with official sanction. The free market provided by far the larger portion of the fresh fruit and vegetables consumed in cities.

The Seven-Year Plan called for construction of more than 205 million square meters of housing space. Although there was considerable improvement in the housing situation, the goal remained elusive. By 1965 the number of people living in communal apartments in the most favored city, Moscow, had dropped to perhaps 3 million of a total 6.5 million. Khrushchev had initially favored prefabricated, five-story apartment houses, which were cheap and easily assembled. Block after block of the ugly, inefficient buildings were constructed until experts pointed out that, at the 1950s rate of construction, the suburbs of Moscow and Leningrad, 600 kilometers apart, would merge before the end of the 20th century. Gosstroi then switched over to more efficient high-rise apartment buildings.

To lower construction costs the party ordered reduction of ceiling heights from the standard 3.2 meters to 2.7 or even 2.3 meters. The average area of a one-family apartment (still a luxury) was reduced from $41.6 \text{ m}^2$ to $28.3 \text{ m}^2$. Prefabricated units were used whenever possible, and lighter-weight materials introduced; the new dwellings weighed about 278 tons per 100 square meters as against 315 tons in prewar buildings. New apartments were smaller, more oppressive, and noisier. So desperate was the housing shortage, however, that citizens overlooked these shortcomings and rejoiced when they finally obtained an apartment. The urban population had increased from 60.4 million in 1939 to more than 100 million in 1959; people could not afford to be choosy.

Housing woes continued to exacerbate social problems. According to the 1959 census the divorce rate was 8.5 percent (compared to 26.3 percent in the United States), but the figures did not tell the whole story. The rate was always low in the countryside but considerably higher in the cities; in Moscow and Leningrad it roughly matched the American figure. Furthermore, so difficult was it to find housing that couples who would otherwise have divorced often remained together in misery.

Overcrowding likewise played a role in child and wife abuse and the abandoning of families by fathers. These problems were discussed with increasing frankness in the press, and malefactors were often subjected to stern penalties including imprisonment.

Alcoholism and alcohol abuse continued to be major social problems despite periodic governmental campaigns. The situation was complicated by the fact that in the 1950s and 1960s the turnover (sales) tax on alcoholic beverages accounted for 10–12 percent of all state revenues. The planners paid little attention to the hidden costs; in 1982 the overall cost of alcohol abuse was approximately 5–7 percent of the Soviet national income.

The left hand not knowing what the right was doing, the authorities attacked the problem with public awareness campaigns, shorter hours for the sale of alcohol, higher prices, and other tactics. So-called sobering-up stations were established in Moscow and other cities; there was no fine, but there was a fee for the service, and the police informed the culprit's workplace of his actions. There

was an increasing willingness to recognize alcoholism as a disease and to treat it accordingly. In May 1956, for example, reporting the suicide of the head of the Writers' Union, Aleksandr Fadeyev, the press noted that he had long suffered from the "severe and chronic ailment" of alcoholism.

In 1958 Khrushchev announced the state's readiness to pass a law limiting customers in bars and restaurants to one drink. No such law was ever enacted. In 1960 the RSFSR ministry of trade issued an order establishing a limit of 100 grams—three ounces—of spirits per customer; it was never enforced.

Drugs such as hashish, opium, and cocaine had long been in use among a tiny percentage of the population, and the problem seemed to grow worse in the late 1950s. Dealers known in the argot as "bankers" bought a "plan"—about a kilo—of hashish in Soviet Central Asia or Afghanistan and brought it to European Russia. A hashish cigarette sold for 25 kopecks in 1963. Cocaine ("marafet") from overseas entered the country through the ports of Odessa and Leningrad, as did opium. Marijuana, indigenous to Central Asia, grows wild in many parts of the Soviet Union. Smoked for centuries in steppe villages, it did not constitute a problem until the 1960s. Partly because of the publicity the Soviet press gave to drug abuse in the West, marijuana became increasingly fashionable in student and artist circles in the cities.

The state continued the Stalinist practice of intruding into the private lives of citizens even in trivial matters. In February 1957 the Komsomol newspaper asked rhetorically,

Who is not familiar with these utterly repulsive young men with their ultra-modish jackets, their ultra-tight and ultra-short trousers and their eccentric neckties in all colors of the rainbow, with an air of self-satisfied stupidity on their faces? Or with the even more disgusting girls, with their coiffures 'à la garçon'—pitiful bristles of cropped hair—and their shoes that remind one of caterpillar tractors?

The newspaper was referring to the "stilyagi" (modish ones), young people who—the puritans charged—adored everything foreign, shunned work, and in general did not behave like disciplined citizens of a socialist society.

It was not only the hair styles and the clothes that outraged conservatives. The music growing numbers of young people preferred generated apoplectic outbursts such as this one from Foreign Minister Shepilov: "All these 'boogie-woogies' and 'rock-and-rolls' [sic] sound like the wild orgies of cavemen." As a music critic Shepilov presumably remained in favor, but he was fired as foreign minister a month later for his association with the "anti-party group." Attacks on "vulgar"—no one could define the term—popular music appeared with increasing frequency in the press.

The party deputized the Komsomol to act as morals police; the zealots and prigs gladly assumed such functions. Komsomol "music patrols" began in 1960. Members went around to restaurants—many of which had live orchestras—and checked on the music; if they heard any Western music from the mid-1930s or later, they stopped it, summoning the police if necessary. Because there were no laws against music, the police had to charge people with such vague offenses as "outrage against public morals" or "disturbing the peace." The patrols posted signs in restaurants and clubs: DANCING "IN THE STYLE" IS FORBIDDEN. Komsomol deacons alone knew what this meant.

Occasionally some petty crime was unearthed. In 1960 a policeman reported the corruption of the young by dealers in "rocks and bones"—recordings of forbidden music on X-ray film.

Cultural and political fundamentalists believed that music, hair styles, and clothing constituted a statement of political opposition. To some extent this was true, but it was almost impossible to do anything about it without sealing off the country. Modern communications had made the USSR another outpost of the "global village."

## EDUCATION

Despite the highly publicized successes of Soviet science and technology in the 1957–1964 period, the educational system had a number of serious problems. The 1959 census revealed virtually universal literacy among the population, but only about 30 percent of primary school graduates went on to obtain a secondary education, and only seven percent of secondary school graduates continued their education in universities and university-level institutes. (In the United States both percentages were about double.)

Economic factors were partially responsible. The work force was too small and the state encouraged people to enter it early. Further, wages were so low that it was important for every family member to become a wage-earner as soon as possible. Beyond that, the overcrowding which led schools in the large cities to operate double and even triple shifts influenced some pupils to drop out because the teachers had too little time for individual counseling. The overcrowding also helped foster a lack of discipline. For a variety of complex reasons of which the troubled educational system was part, juvenile delinquency increased in this period.

The first post-Stalin reforms were timid. Sex-segregated education was ended in 1954. The following year saw the introduction of a slightly modified curriculum:

|  | GRADE | | | | | | | | | |
|---|---|---|---|---|---|---|---|---|---|---|
|  | (Hours per week per subject) | | | | | | | | | |
| *1955–1956 School Year* | *1* | *2* | *3* | *4* | *5* | *6* | *7* | *8* | *9* | *10* |
| Russian lang., lit. | 13 | 13 | 13 | 9 | 9 | 8 | 6 | 6/5* | 4 | 4 |
| Mathematics | 6 | 6 | 6 | 6 | 6 | 6 | 6 | 6 | 6 | 6 |
| History | — | — | — | 2 | 2 | 2 | 2 | 4 | 4 | 4 |
| USSR Constitution | — | — | — | — | — | — | — | — | — | 1 |
| Geography | — | — | — | 2 | 3 | 2 | 2 | 2/3 | 3 | — |
| Biology | — | — | — | 2 | 2 | 2 | 3 | 2 | 1 | — |
| Physics | — | — | — | — | — | 2 | 3 | 3 | 4 | 5/4 |
| Astronomy | — | — | — | — | — | — | — | — | — | 1 |
| Chemistry | — | — | — | — | — | — | 2 | 2 | 3 | 3/4 |
| Psychology | — | — | — | — | — | — | — | — | — | 1 |
| Foreign languages | — | — | — | — | 4 | 4 | 3 | 3 | 3 | 3 |
| Physical education | 2 | 2 | 2 | 2 | 2 | 2 | 2 | 2 | 2 | 2 |
| Drawing | 1 | 1 | 1 | 1 | 1 | 1 | — | — | — | — |
| Mechanical Drawing | — | — | — | — | — | — | 1 | 1 | 1 | 1 |
| Singing | 1 | 1 | 1 | 1 | 1 | 1 | — | — | — | — |
| Practical work | 1 | 1 | 1 | 1 | 2 | 2 | 2 | — | — | — |
| Practicum | — | — | — | — | — | — | — | 2 | 2 | 2 |
| TOTAL | 24 | 24 | 24 | 26 | 32 | 32 | 32 | 33 | 33 | 33 |

*Six hours first semester, five hours second semester

This course of study did not differ greatly from the one it replaced. The emphasis on mathematics, science, and foreign languages, however, caught the attention of the Western world after the 1957 launch of Sputnik, the first in a long series of impressive technological feats. Soviet pupils were generally better educated in mathematics and science than their American counterparts; in the social sciences and the humanities the situation was reversed.

There remained some shortcomings, even in the sciences. Most universities and institutes failed to anticipate the development of polymer chemistry; as late as 1962 few graduating chemists had any idea what a polymer compound was. Further, Lysenko regained a position of great authority in the agricultural sciences, biology, and botany. In December 1958 he told the Central Committee that Western scientists who claimed the "double helix" of DNA was the key to heredity did not know what they were talking about.

The most controversial Khrushchev reform, surprisingly enough to those who believed the USSR a classless society, involved an attempt to democratize the educational system. At the 13th Komsomol Congress in April 1958 the first secretary denounced the "shameful situation" in which unqualified children of party officials and other influential poeple could obtain a higher education, while qualified offspring of workers, peasants, and others without *blat* ("pull") often could not. This syndrome was reflected in the privileged classes' contempt for work and the skill with which they avoided doing any. In 1958 only 5 percent of first-year university students had worked in factories or on collective farms.

The law of December 25, 1958, provided for the reorganization of the school system over a five-year period beginning the following September. There were to be eight rather than seven years of compulsory schooling at the primary level; secondary schooling remained three years. Admission to secondary schools, universities, and institutes would be determined by merit, with trade unions and the Komsomol involved in the process to ensure fairness. Individuals with two years of work experience were to receive preference for admission except in the case of talented students in mathematics and the natural and physical sciences. A system of advanced technical-vocational schools enabled young workers to continue their education while holding down production jobs.

In theory, all secondary school students were to work two years at a trade. As part of a "from the asphalt to the land" scheme, all agricultural institutes were to be moved from the cities to rural areas and admission to them restricted to those who pledged to make careers in agricultural *production* (rather than administration). In June 1959 higher education became the responsibility of the republics.

Forty years after the Revolution, these reforms did help. By 1963, 80 percent of the places in higher education went to students with production experience, only 20 percent to those coming straight from school.

Bureaucrats and others in favored positions were enraged by Khrushchev's assault on their privileges, the more so because he took handsome care of his own family and friends. They were especially incensed by his attempt to block them from purchasing places for their children in the universities. For a few years it was difficult to bribe those who administered entrance examinations or sat on admissions boards, but gradually corrupt practices returned. The "Communist bourgeoisie" hated the first secretary for making their offspring work in factories and on collective farms. Both children and parents tried to circumvent this rule, which was rescinded shortly after Khrushchev's fall.

## WOMEN

Khrushchev frequently bragged of women's equality in the Soviet Union, and he appointed Yekaterina Furtseva to be the first woman to sit on the party Presidium and hold ministerial rank. Furtseva pointed out in 1960 that 27 percent of the deputies to the Supreme Soviet were women, as were 47 percent of the urban work force and 45 percent of the industrial workers. There were more than 1,000 women on the faculty of Moscow University, Furtseva boasted; she did not add that most were laboratory assistants and language instructors. About 1.845 million Soviet women had graduated from universities and advanced institutes since the Revolution.

The devastating impact of the war continued to reverberate throughout Soviet society. Especially difficult was the lot of Soviet women. The following figures are from the January 1959 census:

Number of Men and Women in Various Age Groups As Of January 15, 1959 (in thousands)

| Age 1959 | (Age 1941) | Men | Women |
|----------|------------|------|-------|
| 0–24 | (2–6) | 10,056 | 10,287 |
| 25–29 | (7–11) | 8,917 | 9,273 |
| 30–34 | (12–16) | 8,611 | 10,388 |
| 35–39 | (17–21) | 4,528 | 7,062 |
| 40–44 | (22–26) | 3,998 | 6,410 |
| 45–49 | (27–31) | 4,706 | 7,558 |
| 50–54 | (32–36) | 4,010 | 6,437 |
| 55–59 | (37–41) | 2,906 | 5,793 |
| 60–69 | (42–51) | 4,099 | 7,637 |
| 70 and over | (52 and over) | 2,541 | 5,431 |

Almost 15 million women between the ages of 30 and 59 had no husbands. Many older women were war widows; most younger ones probably remained unmarried not by choice but simply because there were not enough men. The psychological trauma that tormented two generations could not be measured.

In Muslim Central Asia ancient customs kept women in a state of quasi-servitude. In the Kirgiz and Turkmen republics, for example, girls as young as 12 were frequently abducted for the purpose of marriage. In the eyes of the law, this constitued kidnapping and rape. Local officials normally made no arrests; instead they tried to reconcile custom and law by solemnizing the affair with a Komsomol wedding. In the Turkmen republic some parents still gave their underage daughters in marriage. Often "bride money" was due the parents, who retained custody of the girl until it was paid. Bigamy and polygamy were still encountered in Central Asia and the Caucasus. Most of the native populations lived in villages and small towns where European customs had had little impact. They preserved the old ways, lived by the Koran, and many of their practices, the state charged, constituted "offenses against the personal freedom and dignity of women."

## ARTISTS AND INTELLECTUALS

Party conservatives did not like Ehrenburg's *The Thaw*, which suggested the end of the long Stalinist winter, and were outraged by Vladimir Dudintsev's *Not By Bread Alone* (1956), an attack on the Stalinist bureaucracy. Khrushchev called the novel "slanderous." In 1958 the editor of the *Literary Gazette*, Vsevolod Kochetov, published an "answer" to Dudintsev in the form of a novel entitled *The Yershov Brothers*. Without literary merit, the work embodied a "primitive and savage attack on the liberal intellectuals who perpetrated the rebellion against Party controls in literature."

With the Pasternak affair behind him, Khrushchev could afford to strike a generous pose. In a speech to the Third Congress of Soviet Writers in the spring of 1959 he rehabilitated several authors who had been on what amounted to probation and allowed that even Dudintsev "was never our enemy." He also repeated the party's demand that literature serve party goals.

Denied access to state publishing houses, writers who refused to conform normally had only the option of silence. In the late 1950s, however, some courageous individuals revived the tradition, which dated back to the late 18th century, of *samizdat*, or self-publishing. This in turn led to *tamizdat*, or publishing abroad, and *magnitizdat*, or tape-recording. Two of the best-known *samizdat* writers in the Khrushchev era were Andrei Sinyavsky, who wrote as "Abram Tertz," and Yuli Daniel, who took the pen name "Nikolai Arzhak." For nine years the KGB hunted the two mysterious writers, even using computers to analyze their styles. Finally, in September 1965, the men were arrested and charged with slandering the state. They were tried in February 1966 by what amounted to a kangaroo court. Sinyavsky received the maximum sentence of seven years at hard labor; Daniel five years.

This savage farce 16 months after the fall of Khrushchev marked the first time in Soviet history that anyone had been tried for what he or she had written. Other writers had been accused of various crimes and hounded by the state, and some who had angered the authorities had simply disappeared into the Gulag. Not even under Stalin, however, had anyone been forced to stand in the dock and answer for the alleged political content of literary works.

In the second half of 1962, it briefly appeared that the party might again relax its control over the arts. In October *Pravda* published Yevgeny Yevtushenko's poem "The Heirs of Stalin," which begged the party to redouble the guard at the late dictator's grave. In November the publication of Solzhenitsyn's *One Day in the Life of*

*Ivan Denisovich,* an indictment of the whole Stalinist system, caused an immediate and sustained sensation. In the same month Viktor Nekrasov published *Both Sides of the Ocean,* one of the first nonpolitical accounts of travel in the West to appear in the USSR.

Hopes for a new "thaw" quickly faded. Salieri-like, the Soviet "socialist realist" art establishment plotted the destruction of talented young artists who refused to conform to Communist party dictates and tricked them into bringing some of their most daring—in the Soviet context—works to the December 1962 exhibit titled "Thirty Years of Moscow Art." Khrushchev and several other high officials attended; not one knew anything about art.

Conducting the tour, the "socialist realist" hacks attacked the "severe" style of the post-Impressionist canvases and drew the leaders' attention to the favorable comments on them in the Western press. Egged on by his fellow conservatives, especially Suslov and Andropov, Khrushchev savagely attacked the artists as "pederasts." Three months later, to the accompaniment of organized chants for the poet's head, he shook his fist and hurled threats at Andrei Voznesensky at a public meeting with writers and intellectuals.

Conservatives rejoiced and stepped up their attacks on nonconformist artists and writers. They began a campaign against Solzhenitsyn that was to culminate in his expulsion from the USSR in 1974. He was denied a Lenin Prize in 1963 but did publish two short stories that year.

As in the West, conservatives sanctioned violence and condemned sex. CPSU watchdogs assailed "naturalistic scenes of intimacy" in such films as *The Forty-First* (1956) and *Quiet Flows the Don* (in three parts, 1957/1958). Puritans saw no political value in fleeting glimpses of unclad women in these and a few other postwar works. More to their liking were the dozens of straightfor-

ward war films, but even those began to change in the Khrushchev era. M.K. Kalatozov's *The Cranes Are Flying* (1957) depicted the civilian population in wartime. Moreover, there were no heroic Communists in the film; some characters actually had flaws and were the more believable for them. The film won the Gold Palm award at the Cannes Film Festival. Another war film set in the rear, Grigori Chukrai's *Ballad of a Soldier* (1959), made a party-pleasing point about patriotism but also included a decidedly apolitical love story.

More evidence of a new approach in cinematography came in 1962 with the restoration of cuts Stalin had ordered 36 years earlier in Eisenstein's classic *October;* the Gensek had excised many scenes depicting Lenin. In the same year *Izvestiya* admitted that "the Stalin cult had a ruinous effect upon our motion pictures."

In December 1962 the party demanded changes in Dmitri Shostakovich's Thirteenth Symphony, in which Yevtushenko's poem "Babi Yar" constitutes a choral interlude. The poem lamented the absence of a monument to the World War II massacre in Kiev and suggested that anti-Semitism lurked in the background. Party officials denied this and insisted the poem be altered. Yevtushenko agreed to add four lines pointing out that Russians and Ukrainians perished alongside Jews at Babi Yar.

The première of the symphony took place on schedule on December 18. The Moscow intelligentsia had learned of the pressure on composer and poet; the concert became an occasion for expressing solidarity. The performance was a huge success. The prolonged ovation for Shostakovich and Yevtushenko embodied a certain defiance of the regime—and the Communist party proved capable of tolerating it.

It would be misleading to leave the impression that the 22 months after Khrushchev's emergence as an art critic were a period of unrelieved oppression in the arts. Shostakovich's new symphony, after all, made its debut on schedule, and the altered lines of the poem did not dilute Yevtushenko's expression of outrage at the party's failure to honor the martyrs of Babi Yar. Further, the opera which had very nearly led Shostakovich to his doom in 1936, when Stalin expressed distaste for *Lady Macbeth of Mtsensk,* was restaged in 1963. Retitled *Katerina Izmailova,* it was substantially the same work. Shostakovich had completed his Fourth Symphony in 1936 but because he feared Stalin's reaction, it was first performed, to critical and public acclaim, in 1961.

The off-again, on-again campaign to suppress nonconformist art and literature confused everyone in the party and further alienated the Stalinists, to whom one poet with an unfettered pen was more dangerous than an enemy army. Khrushchev's vacillation would not alone have tipped the scales against him but it did add another arrow to his opponents' quiver. Communists too prudent to take a stand on political issues without an unequivocal signal from Moscow were not reluctant to express themselves on art and literature. Many party members resolutely condemned writers and artists who did not depict Soviet life in the brightest and most flattering colors.

## FALL OF KHRUSHCHEV

There was no one issue on which opposition to Khrushchev focused; his long string of errors and bad judgment had slowly swelled the ranks of his enemies. Cuba, China, Berlin and Germany, Albania, and India were the scenes of some of his foreign policy debacles. He had made a mess of agriculture, his special field. Vested interests in and outside the party resented his assault on their privileges, the more so because he constantly increased his own. The CPSU bureaucracy was outraged by his attempt to introduce the principle of systematic renewal of party officers. The professional military establishment condemned his reduction of conventional forces at a time when the USSR was still vastly inferior to the United States in missiles and bombers. The average citizen held him in contempt for failing to keep grandiose promises.

In April 1964 the Soviet press celebrated the first secretary's 70th birthday with an orgy of congratulations: *Pravda* devoted 11 pages to the occasion over six days. Most speeches were embarrassingly effusive, but Leonid Brezhnev was more restrained: "The Soviet people will always be grateful to you for the fact that . . . you demonstrated courageous initiative in unmasking the Stalin cult of the individual. . . ." The speeches of Suslov and Kosygin were likewise fairly muted, but the general chorus sang a song of adulation. Many Communists wondered whether a new "cult" had materialized.

In the summer of 1964, Khrushchev sent his son-in-law, who had no foreign-policy qualifications, on a diplomatic mission to West Germany. In September, he sent an insultingly low-ranking delegation to the Beijing celebrations marking the 15th anniversary of Mao's victory. Uneasy about the quarrel with China, Soviet party leaders considered this the last straw.

Early in 1989 the man who then headed the Ukrainian party organization and sat on the Presidium, Pyotr Shelest, revealed that an anti-Khrushchev conspiracy took shape around Leonid Brezhnev and Aleksandr Shelepin. The plotters assured themselves of the support of KGB chief Vladimir Semichastny and other key security officials, then approached Suslov and stunned him with the news. Suslov managed to overcome his misgivings, as did Shelest himself and the rest of the Presidium.

While Khrushchev vactioned on the Black Sea under the watchful eye of Mikoyan, his opponents struck. They summoned the full members of the Central Committee to Moscow, where Suslov read an indictment of the first secretary. Only two or three people spoke in defense of Khrushchev, who was then summoned back to Moscow.

On October 14, 1964, a special plenary session of the Central Committee ousted Khrushchev as first secretary. Confronted with the unanimous opposition of his colleagues, the ousted party leader also resigned his post as chairman of the Council of Ministers. Leonid Brezhnev succeeded him in the party post, Aleksei Kosygin in the government.

The Soviet press merely noted that Khrushchev had asked to be relieved of his posts on the grounds of advancing age and deteriorating health. Members of the Presidium flew to cities around the country to brief officials on the changes in Moscow. If support for the former first secretary existed, it remained well hidden.

Khrushchev became simply another retired official with a decent apartment in Moscow and the use of a state *dacha*. He and his family were allowed to use the Kremlin clinic, the special stores, and a chauffered limousine. He also had a KGB bodyguard whose duty it was to protect him and also to ensure that he did not have any contact with political dissidents, journalists, or foreigners.

Nikita Sergeevich Khrushchev died on September 11, 1971; the party denied him burial in the Kremlin wall, which was reserved for Soviet heroes. He was buried instead in the cemetery of Novodevichy Convent in Moscow, not far from the grave of Stalin's second wife. No ranking Soviet official attended; the party Central Committee sent a large wreath. A year later, Ernest Neizvestny, one of the artists who had felt his wrath in 1962, sculpted a monument in black and white stone that dramatically captured the bifurcated character and career of the late first secretary.

Before he died, Khrushchev apologized to Andrei Voznesensky for treating him so brutally in 1963. But he could not make amends to Boris Pasternak, much less to the people he had sent to their graves in the 1930s as Stalin's faithful henchman.

## KHRUSHCHEV IN RETROSPECT

A few days after cashiering Khrushchev, the new rulers explained their actions in *Partiinaya zhizn* (Party Life). They charged him with "crudeness, shouting . . . [and] a tone of offensive superiority." They condemned his "bombastic phrases and braggadocio, overhasty conclusions and harebrained schemes divorced from reality," and went on to say that

Even the most authoritative person cannot be permitted to escape the control of the guiding collective, the party organization, or get the idea that he knows everything and can do eveything, that he has no need for the knowledge and experience of his comrades.

The first Soviet leader to admit publicly that power had corrupted Stalin, Khrushchev did not recognize the same process in himself. To the end he saw himself as a democratically elected leader whose power derived from a party consensus. The burgeoning "cult" so visible at the time of his 70th birthday was only partly of his own making; to a considerable extent the aging leader acquiesced in the schemes of his entourage.

While Khrushchev was in the Kremlin, the Soviet Union moved sharply and in some respects decisively away from Stalinism. The Gulag was dismantled, and by and large citizens had no reason, after the 20th Congress, to fear arbitrary arrest and imprisonment. The KGB came under party control, a less sinister if still immensely powerful organization. The standard of living improved significantly. Intellectual and cultural life flourished as it had not done since the days of NEP. All told, Khrushchev's were the most sweeping reforms since 1917.

But Russia has historically held her great reformers in high regard only if they were simultaneously tyrants, and that crown never sat well on the reforming first secretary's head. His policies won wide approval, but Khrushchev himself was never a genuinely popular leader. When the Soviet public learned of his fall a joke began to circulate almost immediately to the effect that he had won a gold medal at the 1964 Olympics for "falling from an unprecedented height."

He had indeed become something of a comic character, and that contributed mightily to his downfall. Stalin had been remote, aloof, mysterious. Khrushchev, by contrast, was extremely approachable. He met Soviet and Western journalists frequently in both formal and spontaneous interviews. He was accessible and frequently displayed emotion. He had a sense of humor and told jokes. Stalin spoke, and nations trembled. People laughed with—and sometimes at—Khrushchev even as they nervously waited to see whether he meant his threats.

Leonid Brezhnev was to emerge as the most powerful member of the new group of rulers, and during the 18 years of his tenure

in office there was almost no mention of Khrushchev in the Soviet press. Like so many victims of Stalin's wrath, the former first secretary became a "nonperson." Within a few weeks after Brezhnev's own death in November 1982, however, the party began to rehabilitate Khrushchev and praise his role in the Battle of Stalingrad, the first step in a gradual reassessment of the man who had toppled the idol that was Stalin.

## SUGGESTED ADDITIONAL READING

**Azrael, Jeremy R.,** *Managerial Power and Soviet Politics,* Cambridge: Harvard University Press, 1966

**Dodge, Norton T.,** *Women in the Soviet Economy,* Baltimore: The Johns Hopkins University Press, 1966

**Hough, Jerry F.,** *The Soviet Prefects,* Cambridge: Harvard University Press, 1969

**Johnson, Priscilla, ed.,** *Khrushchev and the Arts,* Cambridge: MIT Press, 1965

**Kellen, Konrad,** *Khrushchev,* New York: Praeger, 1961

**Khrushchev, Nikita S.,** *The Great Mission of Literature and Art,* Moscow: Progress Publishers, 1964

**McCauley, Martin,** *Khrushchev and the Development of Soviet Agriculture,* New York: Holmes and Meier, 1976

**Medvedev, Roy,** *Khrushchev,* Garden City, N.Y.: Anchor Press/Doubleday, 1984

——**, and Zhores Medvedev,** *Khrushchev, the Years in Power,* New York: Columbia University Press, 1976

**Pinkus, Benjamin,** *The Soviet Government and the Jews, 1948–1967,* New York: Cambridge University Press, 1985

# 19

# RULE OF THE TROIKA, 1964–1971

The men who came to power in October 1964 claimed to be acting in the spirit of the 20th Party Congress. They announced the return of "Leninist collective leadership" and there seemed some reason to take them at their word; one of their first acts was to establish the principle that the same individual could not simultaneously hold the offices of party first secretary and chairman of the Council of Ministers. They offered no timetable for the triumph of communism, hurled no threats.

The transfer of power took place with a minimum of dislocation. Khrushchev went into ignominious but comfortable and secure retirement; his name was not mentioned in the press.

The new leaders had declined to support Khrushchev's "radicalized anti-Stalinism" at the 1961 22nd Congress and had repeatedly clashed with him on this and other issues in the ensuing three years. They refused to put Molotov, Kaganovich, and Malenkov on trial or to indict hundreds of thousands of lesser figures involved in Stalin's crimes and insisted on pardoning Voroshilov altogether. They thwarted plans to build a monument to the victims of the terror and slowed the pace of the "rehabilitations." Unable to prevent publication of *One Day in the Life of Ivan Denisovich*, they denied Solzhenitsyn a Lenin Prize. Finally, they overthrew the architect of "de-Stalinization" himself. Would they now direct a return to the Stalinist order?

Such a "Thermidorean" course of action seemed unlikely. The leaders of the party's conservative and now dominant wing demanded a halt to the assault on Stalinism but did not shoot Khrushchev or anyone else, reopen the Gulag, or try to effect a wholesale reversal of the post-1953 reforms. They renounced terror as a political weapon. The leaders insisted that theirs was a truly collective leadership; the party approved the change of command and direction. The nation at large, granted only token participation in the management of public affairs, seemed as indifferent to the birth of the new regime as to the death of the old.

## COLLECTIVE LEADERSHIP

At the center of the tough new regime were Suslov, Kosygin, and Brezhnev, all close Khrushchev associates remarkable for the uniformity of their political and personal profiles. All were Russian, born into worker or peasant families early in the 20th century. They were between eight and twelve years younger than Khrushchev—too old to constitute a new generation, too young to have any coherent memory of stable tsarism in peacetime. They were the first Soviet leaders whose political consciousness was formed under Communist rule. In October 1917 Suslov was 14, Kosygin 13, Brezhnev 10.

Brezhnev was not the intellectual equal of either Suslov or Kosygin but, the more ambitious politician, he became party first secretary. He had served in the Russian, Ukrainian, Kazakh, and Moldavian republics in important party posts and successfully completed a number of assignments in industry and agriculture. He served as a political commissar during the war, emerging with the rank of major general. Later he supervised the reconstruction of the devastated Ukrainian industrial centers of Zaporozhe and Dnepropetrovsk. At the 19th Party Congress he won an appointment to the Central Committee Secretariat, where he served with Stalin, Malenkov, Suslov, Khrushchev, and

Leonid Brezhnev. (CPSU photo)

five others. Having also become a candidate member of the Presidium, he seemed destined to join the inner circle.

For a time after Stalin's death, however, it appeared that Brezhnev would become a casualty of party infighting. He was demoted to a relatively insignificant defense ministry post, possibly because he was closely identified with Malenkov's rival, Khrushchev. As Khrushchev outmaneuvered the other contenders for power, however, his protégés again thrived; Brezhnev went to Kazakhstan in 1954 to supervise the Virgin Lands project. After presiding over the spectacular 1956 harvest he returned to Moscow and a job as a Central Committee secretary. Firmly in Khrushchev's camp—as were Suslov and Kosygin—in the clash with the "anti-party group," he became a full member of the Presidium.

Brezhnev's new duties made him responsible for heavy industry, defense, and the space program; as early as 1958 there was talk in the party of him eventually becoming first secretary. The anti-Khrushchev faction, however, sidetracked him in the shakeup that followed the May 1960 U-2 incident. Frol Kozlov, who coveted Khrushchev's job, won the unofficial but powerful post of "second secretary," while Brezhnev was shunted over to the chairmanship of the Supreme Soviet Presidium. Although that position carried only ceremonial responsibilities, Brezhnev made more of it than any of his predecessors. In his 1960–1964 tenure in office—he would resume the post in 1977—he traveled widely and established his credentials in foreign policy. He had already made a solid record in heavy industry, defense, and agriculture; this new expertise consolidated his standing. In June 1963 he returned to the Secretariat. Kozlov having been felled by a stroke that removed him from active politics, Brezhnev again became the unofficial heir apparent. In the summer of 1964 he relinquished the "presidency" to concentrate on party responsibilities, the most important—if not publicly acknowledged—of which was preparation of Khrushchev's ouster.

In the early years of *troika* rule Brezhnev's duties involved party work. He did speak out on foreign affairs and economic policy but only as party leader; Kosygin articulated official Soviet policy. Kosygin traveled widely, directed the attempts to contain the quarrel with China, went to the United Nations to present the Soviet view on developments in the Middle East and Southeast Asia. He bore responsibility for the initiation of a major economic reform. In ideological matters Suslov held unchallenged sway.

There was thus no first among equals on the *troika*, which had come to power on a wave of hostility toward one-man rule. It appeared that the party had at last decided to heed Lenin's warning not to permit too much power to reside in the office of general—or first—secretary.

## RESTORATION OF STABILITY

The new leaders abolished the division of party organizations, local Soviets, Komsomol, and trade unions into industrial and agricultural sections. In November 1964 they reunited the provincial industrial and rural party organizations into single entities and reestablished the rural district party committees (*raikoms*). They abolished the separate industrial and agricultural bureaus of Union and republican Central Committees.

The 1961 party statute requiring regular rotation of officials came under attack. Turnover of cell secretaries had doubled since the enactment of that statute, sapping morale and creating instability. The same situation affected party bureaucrats up the ladder through the republic level.

Sounding the cry of "Leninist respect for cadres!" the leadership simply ignored the 1961 rotation rule, then abolished it at the 23rd Congress in 1966. More than three-quarters of the RSFSR regional first secretaries in mid-1965 had held the same job three years earlier. Only 10 percent had been rotated out; the others had been promoted, transferred, pensioned on schedule, or died. The same situation existed in the other republics. Party officials who carried out their responsibilities satisfactorily could now assume job security, and even those who got into trouble were rarely disciplined.

All this bred contentment and loyalty. The cadres rejoiced that the men in the Kremlin understood their problems—and there quickly appeared the smug sense of inviolability that leads to stagnation or worse. When the press attacked bureaucrats who worried more about careers than responsibilities, it was usually the critics, not the bureaucrats, who were rebuked.

## FATE OF THE REFORMS

There were indications that the *troika* would continue some post-Stalin reforms: within days of Khrushchev's ouster the press attacked Trofim Lysenko with a campaign all the more significant because it repeated the arguments of a maverick geneticist and political liberal, Zhores Medvedev, whose exposé had been circulating in *samizdat* for months. By the middle of November the press was speaking of a Lysenko "cult." Agricultural journals revealed that farm production *declined* wherever Lysenko's theories were applied.

In February 1965 Lysenko lost his job as director of the Genetics Institute. In May *Izvestiya* published an article on Gregor Mendel by the late N.I. Vavilov, perhaps Lysenko's most distinguished victim. *Pravda* carried a laudatory article on Mendel in June; the following month the appearance of the scientific journal *Genetics* completed the rehabilitation of the science. By 1966 ten new laboratories were functioning within the Institute of Biological Problems, where previously all research had had to bear the imprimatur of "Lysenkoism." The ultimate sanction came in October 1968, when Academician B.M. Kedrov argued in *Pravda* that Lenin himself approved of genetics.

Another positive signal came with the ending of the antireligion campaign of 1959–1964. The state certainly had not made its peace with religion, but it no longer deemed it necessary to pursue a war against it. It became rare for Komsomol and KGB thugs to break up religious services, the destruction of ancient churches ceased, and there were minor improvements in the working conditions of the clergy.

In 1968 four Muslim minorities expelled from their homes in Georgia 20 years earlier as "unreliable" were permitted to return. That left about 500,000 Crimean Tatars, several thousand Koreans transported by the Japanese to Sakhalin Island before 1945, and an indeterminate number of border peoples languishing in indefinite exile.

The reestablishment in September 1970 of the Union ministry of justice, abolished in 1956 as part of "de-Stalinization," seemed to some observers a further sign of liberalization under *troika* rule. The reconstituted ministry was to ensure the strict observance of "socialist legality" but had a limited mandate, charged with overseeing and coordinating the work of the republic courts, correcting technical mistakes in court practice, and analyzing court statistics. It did not have the right to protest court decisions; appeals could be directed only to a higher court. The ministry undertook to create a new Collection of Laws in Effect.

Laws regulating marriage and family were liberalized between October 1965 and December 1968. Restrictive wartime rules ended and unwed mothers won the right to sue to establish paternity. The legal concept of illegitimacy was abolished, divorce became easier, and new regulations defined the responsibility of children for the care of aged parents.

The divorce rate rose. Before the end of 1968 the press was suggesting reinstitution of the old Russian custom of posting wedding banns six months before the intended marriage to help end the plague of three-day marriages.

The new regime's record with regard to literature and the arts was mixed. The harsh punishment meted out to Sinyavsky and Daniel early in 1966 on the eve of the 23rd

Congress to mollify the Stalinists proved to be exceptional, in no small measure because many writers were frightened into silence. Books and articles critical of the shortcomings of Soviet society—but not of the party—continued to appear, as did works dealing with the Gulag. The number of titles dropped, editions were smaller, works more heavily censored, but they were published.

For the first time in 40 years the state had to deal with "those who think differently," or dissidents. After the 20th Congress, some citizens had begun to speak out in favor of transforming the paper liberties of the 1936 Constitution into reality; in particular they demanded the right of free speech. In the USSR the voicing of the demand embodied exercise of the right.

In the beginning the authorities treated the dissidents relatively gently. The KGB and the police warned them to cease their activities, threatened them with dismissal from their jobs, and occasionally beat them up. In the Soviet context this amounted to great restraint. The government could afford to proceed in this manner because the few people involved posed no threat, and their very existence demonstrated the state's tolerance. Until Aleksandr Solzhenitsyn and Andrei Sakharov won worldwide recognition as opponents of the Kremlin's policies, the dissidents were a minor irritant and were treated accordingly.

Some individuals who voiced dissent in an unacceptable manner—for example, by speaking to the foreign press—suffered harsh punishment. They were arrested, tried, convicted of "anti-Soviet activity," and sent to forced-labor camps. Others—including Zhores Medvedev—were lodged in psychiatric hospitals, diagnosed by unscrupulous KGB psychiatrists as suffering from "sluggish schizophrenia" or "reformist delusions," and treated with heavy doses of mind-altering drugs. Only a handful of people were so treated, but their suffering kept the threat of violence hovering over every Soviet citizen.

The public rehabilitation of Stalin's victims continued, but at a substantially reduced rate. There was never any thought of exonerating Trotsky, Kamenev, or Zinoviev, but in 1961 Bukharin's widow and son launched a sustained campaign to clear his name. Joining them were several Old Bolsheviks, among them Elena Stasova, one of Lenin's associates. The regime began an investigation, but opposition from party conservatives stalled the process and the case was still pending when the *troika* came to power. Only in 1977 did the family learn the party's decision: the criminal charges remained valid. That could only mean that the purges themselves were still considered legitimate.

## 23RD PARTY CONGRESS

On the surface the reformist elements seemed to hold their own in the first year and a half of *troika* rule, but powerful currents flowed in the opposite direction. In the spring of 1965 *Pravda* suggested the reevaluation of certain historical figures who had suffered from one-sided treatment. The trial balloon went nowhere and indeed generated sharp attacks on Stalin's wartime leadership and on some of his henchmen, notably the sinister prosecutor, Vyshinsky. And about this time General Serov, wartime supervisor of the deportations and later (1954–1958) head of the KGB, was dismissed from all his posts and forced to return his medals.

The Stalinists proved tenacious. In January 1966 three historians declared in *Pravda* that the term "cult of personality" was incorrect and un-Marxist, conveniently overlooking the fact that Marx had coined it. The obvious implication was that at least some of the criticism levelled against Stalin was wrong. A few days later a kangaroo court tormented Sinyavsky and Daniel, proving that the "Boss's" spirit lived. Newspapers around the country applauded the sentences and complained about the denigration of Stalin. Mikhail Sholokhov lamented the absence of the "revolutionary justice" of the 1920s that would have sent Sinyavsky and Daniel to a firing squad. This from the winner of the 1965 Nobel Prize for Literature—awarded by a Swedish Academy intent on placating the Kremlin for its earlier selection of Boris Pasternak.

Signs that the impending 23rd Congress would effect at least a partial rehabilitation of Stalin led a group of 25 leading Soviet citizens to send a letter of protest—one of thousands—to the leadership. Any whitewashing of the discredited past, the letter warned, would shatter the bond of trust that had been restored between party and people. Among the signers were physicists Pyotr Kapitsa, Igor Tamm, and Andrei Sakharov, writer Konstantin Paustovsky, prima ballerina Maya Plisetskaya, film director Mikhail Romm, and diplomat Ivan Maisky.

The party conceded a minor victory to the reformers. The Congress convened on schedule on March 29, 1966, and did not discuss Stalin. The proceedings were marred only by the embarrassing absence of a guest delegation from Communist China, where Stalin was still officially revered.

First Secretary Brezhnev gave the major report outlining foreign and domestic developments since the last Congress. Only toward the end of his remarks did he refer obliquely to Stalin in proposing to rename the party Presidium the Politburo; that would merely restore nomenclature in use before 1952, when Stalin himself had changed it. The delegates roared approval; the Politburo had led them through the difficult and glorious years, most of them

under the Gensek. They welcomed its return.

Between 1922 and 1952 the Politburo had had a general, not a first, secretary. The 23rd Congress restored the old title. First Secretary Brezhnev, who stood to gain most from the change, did not propose it; it was buried in a list of 10 changes in the statutes routinely approved on the last day. No doubt caution led the *troika* collectively and Brezhnev personally to resort to such stealth. There could of course be only one Gensek, and Russia would forever live in his shadow.

Like Brezhnev, Prime Minister Kosygin did not speak Stalin's name, but his comments on the economic achievements of 1929–1941 obviously constituted homage to the man who had supervised it all. The only public mention of the late dictator came from the leader of the Moscow city party organization. Speaking first in response to Brezhnev's report, N.G. Yegorychev signalled the party's decision to accept the *fait accompli* of previous "de-Stalinization" while bringing the actual process to an end. No one, he declared, could use the "scarecrow of so-called 'Stalinism' " to discredit the party. He insisted that the "personality cult"—the term having been rehabilitated—and other abuses were now safely buried, and that the general line of the 20th Congress continued to guide the party. But it was impossible, he declared, simply to cross out the history of those years when so much was achieved at such cost.

There were other triumphs for the conservatives. The mass murderer and alcoholic Kliment Voroshilov, expelled from the Central Committee in 1961, was restored to that body. Aleksandr Tvardovsky, liberal editor of *Novy mir* and the man who had discovered and published Solzhenitsyn, lost his seat, as did Khrushchev's son-in-law, Aleksei Adzhubei.

After the Congress the great debate continued. Some Communists called for the restoration of Stalin to his place in the mausoleum beside Lenin; others were willing to settle for an heroic statue on his grave beneath the Kremlin wall; some tried to revive Khrushchev's project to build a monument to the victims of the Terror; not a few suggested that "rehabilitations" had already gone too far.

By 1969, the suppression of the "Prague Spring"* behind them, the conservatives—not all of whom were Stalinists—had gained the upper hand. Articles and books defended the generalissimo's war record; a February article in *Kommunist* indicated that a full-fledged rehabilitation was well under way. The following month, however, a serious border clash with the Chinese took place in the Far East, and a number of Soviet soldiers died. The times were suddenly inauspicious for public resurrection of the memory of the man who had inspired Mao Zedong.

In December 1969 Stalinist and conservative elements regained the offensive with a lavish funeral tribute—in which Molotov emerged from disgrace to participate—to Voroshilov. If that mediocrity merited such praise, the party seemed certain to use the occasion of the 90th anniversary of the Gensek's birth a few days later to proclaim his complete vindication. A long article replete with fulsome accolades was prepared and set in type; *Pravda* was to publish it on December 21, Stalin's birthday. Other newspapers in the USSR and the foreign Communist press were scheduled to reprint the piece the following day.

The reformers counterattacked, joined by several foreign parties. The Soviet leadership reconsidered, then cancelled the article. Someone forgot to call the editor of the

---

*See Chapter 21.

Mongolian party newspaper in Ulan Bator, eight hours ahead of Moscow time. On December 22 the article rehabilitating Stalin appeared in *Unen* with the notation that it was reprinted from *Pravda* of December 21.

The article *Pravda* did carry disappointed the Stalinists. It simply reviewed the dictator's career, praising him as an "outstanding theoretician and organizer" and as principal architect of the World War II victory. It also noted that Stalin had frequently claimed credit for the accomplishments of the Soviet people as a whole, had come to believe in his own infallibility, and had violated legal norms and sent innocent people to their deaths. His "mistakes and perversions" had done "harm" but had only temporarily sidetracked Soviet society's march toward communism.

In January 1970 a revised party history both criticized Stalin and admitted the existence of the Terror instead of euphemistically referring to mere "repressions." In June a gray granite bust, promised in the original birthday article, suddenly materialized over Stalin's grave without public ceremony. The greatest "rehabilitation" of all took a giant step forward.

## THE ABORTIVE ECONOMIC REFORM

The notion that political expertise or at least success is translatable into economic wisdom is as much a pillar of Soviet thinking as the western belief that financial success is synonymous with political sagacity and moral virtue. In the USSR, three successive crises of enormous dimensions had indeed seen the commissars perform economic miracles. The industrialization of the 1930s, the war economy, and the postwar reconstruction represented unparalleled triumphs.

What might be called the Thirty Years'

Crisis, however, had come to an end. The country had industrialized and had emerged from the war victorious and able to rebuild. Now it was time to modernize, automate, introduce innovations. Heroic measures were as anachronistic in the economy as cavalry charges on the battlefield. Having built physically the largest—if not the most productive—industrial base of any nation, the population was demanding some rewards. Modern communications and the attendant penetration of foreign influence were exerting powerful pressures.

In June 1965 a prominent economist, Abel Aganbegyan, informed a group of Leningrad editors that, in the preceding six-year period, the growth rate of the economy as a whole had declined by a factor of approximately three. Spelling out the reasons for this dismal state of affairs, Aganbegyan pointed first to the Soviet industrial structure, which he called "the worst and most backward of all the industrially developed countries." So badly organized and equipped was mining, for example, that it normally cost the state more to extract a ton of raw materials than could be earned by selling it abroad. The lumbering industry wasted fully half the timber it processed and made only one-third as much use as the American industry, one-eighth as much as the Swedish, of the remaining half. Frequent, often wholly artificial shortages further distorted the economy. Some industries stockpiled huge, unnecessary reserves. Wages increased, heightening demand, but still the goods remained in warehouses. Inflationary price increases failed to halt the process.

Aganbegyan revealed that unemployment, which officially did not exist, affected about 8 percent of the work force. In small and medium-sized cities the rate averaged 20–30 percent. He did not mention underemployment, also a serious problem. Several million citizens worked for a pittance at menial, often meaningless jobs—for example, as doorkeepers.

The defense industry, which employed 30 to 40 percent of the 100 million working people, constituted an enormous drain on the economy. The country had of course to be defended; but the attempt to keep pace with and even outstrip the United States guaranteed a debased standard of living.

The factor of decline of the growth rate in agriculture, Aganbegyan noted, was eight. Agricultural production in 1961–1965 was substantially below that of the preceding five-year period, and the disastrous 1963 harvest obliged the state to import about 12 million tons of grain. There was another crop failure in 1965, and again it was necessary to turn to foreign suppliers.

Long after the need for "superindustrialization" had passed, the state continued to gouge agriculture to finance heavy industry and defense. Collective farmers produced a 22-billion ruble net income and were forced to yield fully half of it to the state through taxes and the "scissors" effect—high industrial prices, low agricultural prices. In 1965 a kolhoznik could earn only 1.50 rubles a day on the collective farm, 3.50 on his private plot. He *had* to work on the farm, but clearly he had little incentive to make that farm productive and profitable.

Like the Stalinist planners of the late 1920s and early 1930s, the post-Khrushchev leaders remained convinced that big meant better. They constructed buildings Andrea Lee has described as "like American vegetables—all size and no taste," and they increased the size of already unwieldy and unproductive farms still further. Of the 95,000 collective farms that existed in June 1945, only 20,000 remained in 1987. Quadrupling the size of the farms quintupled their problems, and the country remained hungry.

The party blamed "subjectivism," that is,

Khrushchev's schemes, for the slowdown, but also admitted that there had been errors in planning. The problem went deeper. Until about 1940, Soviet economists had argued that the bourgeois concept of value had no meaning in a socialist society; they called prices and money bourgeois indexes of bourgeois value, relics of capitalism that would soon disappear. Then party theoreticians decided that the concept of value was after all appropriate to socialism, but "in a changed form." No one could say precisely what that form was. After the war, Stalin advanced some bizarre theories in his *Economic Problems of Socialism in the USSR*, setting Soviet economics back still further.

A September 1965 Central Committee plenum called for reform. Rejecting the advice of economists who argued that the rationalization of planning through the increased use of computers would solve the country's economic problems, the plenum opted for a complex scheme that sought to blend decentralized economic decision making with a more centralized administrative structure. Plant managers were to assume greater responsibility for establishing and fulfilling local plans, or rather the local shares of the national plan. That represented a startling departure from the norm; planners and bureaucrats in Moscow had always treated managers as obedient executors of their orders.

Prime Minister Kosygin revamped the organizational framework of the economy and switched from a regional to a ministerial system. He abolished the *sovnarhozes,* which gave way to industrial ministries and state committees organized along pre-1957 lines, with this difference: the new bodies could not simply dictate but had to negotiate and consult with the managers of enterprises as partners in the decision-making process.

Party conservatives—especially Brezhnev and Suslov—were stunned when the reform-

ers announced that sales and profits would henceforward be the chief indicators of plant performance. Until 1965 gross output had always been the main criterion; the very idea of profits was anathema. Emphasis on mere output, however, had naturally led managers to produce as much as possible with little regard for quality or even deliverability. The plan had been fulfilled, even overfulfilled; but no one profitted, least of all the state. This had the further effect of discouraging innovation; managers stuck with what they knew they could do.

Although the 1965 reform owed a substantial debt to Bukharinist economic thinking, the Communist party insisted that Kosygin and his colleagues were reviving the theories of Yevsei Liberman, whose 1962 *Pravda* article, "Plan, Profit, Bonus," had created a sensation. Liberman's insistence that incentives would make industry more efficient had won few supporters in the party bureaucracy. Kosygin, however, persuaded the Central Committee plenum to measure factory efficiency by only seven success indicators—as opposed to several dozen—of which the most important were sales and profits.

Enterprises retained some of the profits to establish three funds: one for bonuses for workers and management, one for social and cultural facilities and housing construction, and one for reinvestment and development. The enterprise would have considerable latitude in disposing of the first two, but the central authorities retained veto power over the reinvestment fund.

The 1965 reform fostered the consolidation of factories. Small and medium-sized plants producing the same goods in a given locale united under one management, where possible under one roof. Large factories began to merge with some of their satellite suppliers. This tendency accelerated after a September 1968 decree provided for a closer link between research-design and production.

The innovations encountered great opposition from party conservatives, Gosplan, bureaucrats, and from managers terrified by the prospect of having to shoulder real responsibility for plant performance. Party ideologues were bitter. Three years after the 23rd Congress made economic incentives official CPSU policy, an economist told a newspaper that "party conscience does not allow me to vote for profits." But the Moscow party boss reminded the Congress that socialism's watchword was "from each according to his ability, to each according to his work." Incentives were necessary until the achievement of communism.

Speakers at the 23rd Congress bragged of Soviet economic achievements but acknowledged glaring shortcomings. Brezhnev reported that the Seven-Year Plan's output targets for coal, machinery, chemicals, and consumer goods had not been met. The chairman of Gosplan, N.I. Baibakov, spoke of the "extremely slow assimilation" of new assets and indicated an especially critical situation in ferrous metals and chemicals. Baibakov also admitted the existence of sizable cost overruns, a problem usually associated with contracts awarded by the state in *capitalist* countries. Brezhnev and others assailed bureaucrats and managers for the low shift index at most new plants and indeed at many old ones. Idle factories produced no goods and turned no profits, yet managers, citing inability to find workers, usually refused to introduce a shift system that would keep them operating 16 or 24 hours a day.

The shift index problem pinpointed a disturbing phenomenon that had been lurking in the background for nearly four decades: the USSR was beginning to experience a labor shortage. Moreover, the failure to automate and modernize rapidly enough

to compensate for the shortage was exacerbating the situation. Technological advances were not keeping pace with the relative decline in the size of the labor force, and it was becoming increasingly difficult to substitute capital for labor. One Thirty Years' Crisis had ended. Another loomed menacingly not on the horizon but at the front door.

The 1965 reform did not pursue its initiatives to their logical conclusion and consequently had little success. According to unquestionably inflated official figures, the economy expanded at an average annual rate of 5.2 percent during the eighth Five-Year Plan of 1966–1970. Cost accounting was extended to include a 6 percent charge on capital, but there were exceptions for projects in remote areas and many defense plants. Labor productivity rose only slightly. The chemical industry, machine building, ferrous metals, and coal all failed to meet output targets. At the 24th Congress in 1971 Brezhnev bragged one minute about the increased per capita consumption of meat and other food items, then admitted that the farms had not met the goals set for them and that at times there had been "interruptions in trade." What he meant was that it was frequently impossible to find butter, unprocessed meat, fish, or fresh fruit and vegetables outside Moscow, Leningrad, and Kiev—and even those three favored cities frequently experienced shortages.

Only vodka remained in not only plentiful but disastrously bountiful supply. In February 1988 Mikhail Gorbachev revealed that the *troika* and Brezhnev regimes actually *increased* the already substantial production of distilled spirits in order to swell the state's coffers . . . and the wallets of the corrupt officials who plundered the national wealth in the "era of stagnation."

The new attention to sales and profits made prices critically important, but the existing structure did not correspond to economic realities. The years of denying "bourgeois" laws and concepts came back to haunt Soviet planners struggling to determine fair market value. A revised industrial wholesale price index went into effect on July 1, 1967; it represented a major step forward but did not go far enough. Competition for some undervalued goods produced artificial shortages. Some goods in great demand were priced so high as to make it virtually impossible to buy them; this generated production bottlenecks as factories shut down for lack of supplies.

The attempt to decentralize economic decision making while simultaneously recentralizing administration was doomed to failure. Nor was this the only problem. The reformers declined to introduce genuine market mechanisms even as they were insisting that factories become profitable. Real competition would have threatened central planning, the "main guarantor of defense industry supply priority." This was—and is—a crucial area not only in terms of national security. Brezhnev noted in 1971 that 42 percent of the defense industry's total output went into the civilian sector—civil aircraft, merchant ships, consumer durables, etc. Whether capitalist or socialist, no nation can permit defense to be at the mercy of the market, but the peculiar Soviet system made it virtually impossible to incorporate market mechanisms even for the civilian sector into the 1965 reform.

Finally, the bonus system threatened to worsen the already significant problems generated by wage differentials. Worker resentment of the "Stakhanovites," the superachievers, had created tensions since the mid-1930s. If now there were to arise a privileged new group of exceptionally productive and innovative workers, technicians, managers, and research-development specialists, there might also come into existence

class conflicts not seen since the days of NEP.

## COMMUNISM AND COMPUTERS

No party Congress could do anything about the labor shortage. Demographers, sociologists, legal experts, other specialists and party officials were devoting considerable if largely uncoordinated attention to the matter, but while there was growing concern there was no general sense of urgency. Most people who dealt with the problem on a professional basis simply assumed that the automation of industry and the further mechanization of agriculture would suffice to compensate for the shrinkage of the labor pool.

The mechanization and chemicalization of agriculture was itself not a simple task. To a much greater extent than in agriculture, however, the automation of industry and concomitant rationalization of planning and management depended on the application of computer technology. In this area the Soviet Union lagged behind the West and Japan. Only in the mid-1960s did the party finally heed warnings of scientists and engineers and jump into the field with a crash program to catch up.

The Soviet Union was behind in computer technology and the application of that technology for two reasons: (1) Stalinist ideology put major restraints on the field until 1956, and (2) after 1956 the Soviet approach to computers did not give enough room to decentralized market-driven forces. In the Stalin years cybernetics was denounced as "un-Marxist"; this set the development of computers back several years. The first cybernetics seminar was held in the USSR in 1956; two years later the Academy of Sciences established a special Scientific Council to supervise the field. Still the party hesitated, and as late as 1961 its official program devoted only one paragraph to automation.

The ideological brake eased dramatically after 1956, however, and by the early 1960s the state tried to introduce computers into the defense complex and the economy in general. That was precisely the problem: the political authorities attempted to force computers on potential users, few of whom wanted them. Abel Aganbegyan reported in 1965 that the Central Statistical Board (!) did not have a single electronic computer and no plans to obtain one. Accustomed to commanding, the leadership was unfamiliar with the art of persuading, and the attempt to create a market miscarried. The introduction of computers was a painfully slow process that even by the late 1980s showed meager results.

There was of course another side to this. Planners, managers, and even military leaders resisted computers for fear the machines would be used to tighten central control. Such individuals had a vested interest in preserving the inefficient system the Communist party had created. The introduction of data-processing equipment threatened the sinecures from which the holders had for decades attacked the problem of plan-fulfillment with a variety of extralegal and illegal measures. Beyond that, creative accounting performed on old-fashioned adding machines and even abacuses enabled managers to tell Moscow what Moscow wanted to hear.

In March 1966 a party-state decree detailed responsibility for developing automated management systems and for the utilization of computers in planning. The ministries, Gosplan, the Central Statistical Board, the Academy of Sciences, the State Committee on Science and Technology, and the State Committee on Standards all shared authority. The bewildering division

of power created confusion and waste. Worse still was the failure to establish clear responsibility for organizing a nationwide computer network; both Gosplan and the Central Statistical Board claimed that right. The dispute was resolved only in 1971 with the creation of the Statewide Automated System (OGAS).

At the 23rd Congress Brezhnev referred several times to the necessity of making the most effective use of the achievements of science and technology; he meant automation and computers. This did not, however, constitute a major theme of the Congress, and most delegates probably regarded his words as the usual obeisance of a materialistic political party to science. The resolution approving the Central Committee's report directed industrial ministries to introduce new technology as rapidly as possible but listed computers last among the priority areas.

Senior party officials, military leaders, scientists, economic planners, and managers conferred for more than two years to plan for the computer age. A key September 1968 decree called for the establishment of four types of research-development and production complexes aimed at creating new processes, developing new products, improving production methods and work organization, and providing research institutes for large industrial enterprises.

Computers were obviously at the heart of this new program. During the eighth Five-Year Plan the output of the computer industry grew 480 percent in value terms, and the record was almost as good in the ninth Plan of 1971–1975. But more than anything else these figures reflected the late start. By 1970 there were about 5,000 computers in the USSR, or 20 per million of population. In the United States there were 344 computers per million in 1970; in Japan the figure was 96 and in Great Britain 91. Moreover, the most powerful Soviet computer of 1970 operated at only one-sixth the level of the most advanced American machine. Substantially more than half the American, Japanese, and British computers were third-generation, while that year there was not a single Soviet-manufactured third-generation machine; 23 percent of all Soviet computers were first-generation. Even in late 1975 second-generation computers comprised 83 percent of all Soviet machines.

This technological backwardness could not be overcome simply by building new machines. The technology advanced in gigantic, unpredictable leaps; research and development assumed crucial importance. And because the West and Japan were not standing still, the Soviet political, military, and scientific establishments considered it essential to obtain Western and Japanese machines and knowledge by any means possible. Legal, questionable, and blatantly illegal deals brought many electronic items to the USSR. Despite an American embargo the Soviets managed to obtain about 40 second- and third-generation IBM computers before the Nixon administration tightened controls in the early 1970s. Unscrupulous entrepreneurs, espionage agents, and even some naive Western scientists kept up the flow of technology to the Soviet Union.

By the mid-1980s it had become clear that the Western nations and Japan could not keep all their computer technology out of Communist hands. In 1984 the Coordinating Committee for Multilateral Export Controls (Cocom), which represented Japan and all NATO countries save Spain and Iceland, recommended abandoning efforts to prevent the sale of microcomputers to the USSR and other Communist countries in favor of concentration on preventing transfer of super-sophisticated technology with military applicability. The United States,

which had advocated strict controls, bowed to Cocom and instituted relaxed rules on January 1, 1985. The Soviet Union immediately began negotiating to buy large numbers of personal computers.

Computer education was at the heart of the new educational program adopted in April 1984, and a year later the new Gorbachev Politburo decreed that such training would begin in the 1985–1986 school year in the last two grades of secondary school. More than 8 million students would be involved. If the program were to go forward, the USSR would be obliged to purchase tens of thousands of microcomputers, primarily from the United States and Japan.

## SUGGESTED ADDITIONAL READING

**Amann, Ronald, Julian Cooper, and R.W. Davies, eds.,** *The Technological Level of Soviet Industry,* New Haven, Conn.: Yale University Press, 1977

**Brown, Archie, and Michael Kaiser,** *The Soviet Union Since the Fall of Khrushchev,* London: Macmillan, 1975

**Cave, Martin,** *Computers and Economic Planning: The Soviet Experience,* New York: Cambridge University Press, 1980

**Cohen, Stephen F., ed.,** *An End to Silence: Uncensored Opinion in the Soviet Union from Roy Medvedev's Underground Political Diary,* New York: W.W. Norton, 1982

**Dornberg, John,** *Brezhnev,* New York: Basic Books, 1974

**Hahn, Werner G.,** *The Politics of Soviet Agriculture, 1960–1970,* Baltimore: The Johns Hopkins University Press, 1972

**Hayward, Max,** *On Trial: The Soviet State vs. "Abram Tertz" and "Nikolai Arzhak,"* New York: Harper & Row, 1967

**Lee, Andrea,** *Russian Journal,* New York: Random House, 1981

Litvinov, Pavel, and Peter Reddaway, eds., *The Trial of the Four,* New York: Viking, 1972

Marchenko, Anatoli, *My Testimony,* New York: E.P. Dutton, 1970

Matthews, Mervyn, *Privilege in the Soviet Union: A Study of Elite Life-Styles under Communism,* Boston: Allen & Unwin, 1978

Reddaway, Peter, ed., *Uncensored Russia,* New York: American Heritage Press, 1972

Rothenberg, Abraham, *The Heirs of Stalin,* Ithaca, N.Y.: Cornell University Press, 1972

Tatu, Michel, *Power in the Kremlin,* New York: Viking, 1970

# 20

# THE BREZHNEV ERA, 1971–1982

The concatenation of events in the half-dozen years after the ouster of Khrushchev favored Leonid Brezhnev. He took care of his friends, of whom he had many, seeing to their careers and personal welfare, winking at foibles great and small, taking care of families, remembering birthdays and other special occasions. Adept at resolving quarrels and reconciling conflicts, he dealt severely with challenges to party authority. He gave the KGB considerable latitude to deal with dissent but did establish limits. In all political cases there was to be a formal accusation and a public trial—at which spectators, however, were usually, but not always, KGB employees. There were to be no mass arrests, no executions on political grounds, no new Gulag—in other words, no Stalinist terror. Nevertheless, the Brezhnev regime

sanctioned the secret police tactic, which dated from the reign of Nicholas I, of incarcerating dissidents in psychiatric hospitals on monstrously absurd charges.

Brezhnev engineered the May 1967 appointment of Yuri Andropov, a party regular without previous secret police experience, to head the KGB. The move was evidently calculated in part to counter the possibility that the security organs might support their former chief, the ambitious Stalinist A.N. Shelepin, in a power struggle.

## 24TH CONGRESS

A new "cult" bearing some superficial resemblance to Stalin's sprang into view at the 24th Party Congress of March-April 1971.

The spectacularly corrupt Azerbaijani party leader and Brezhnev protégé Geidar Aliyev declared that "In all the work . . . [of] the Central Committee, an enormous role belongs to Leonid Ilyich Brezhnev . . . who has won universal affection and respect for his tireless activity and constant solicitude for the people's welfare."

Brezhnev was able to put together a solid Politburo majority at this Congress. A "core" consisting of himself, Suslov, Kosygin, Podgorny, and Kirilenko had been a minority on the 11-member body, but the Congress enlarged it to 15 and approved the appointment of four new full members, all of whom were the general secretary's men: V.V. Grishin, F.D. Kulakov, D.A. Kunayev, V.V. Shcherbitsky. The Congress also increased the size of the Central Committee from 195 full members to 241. Among the new members was Mikhail Gorbachev.

The general—or first—secretary always read the Central Committee's report, the longest and most comprehensive; this held true at the 24th Congress. Brezhnev, however, not only spoke far longer than anyone else but scheduled Kosygin's speech on the economy a full week after his own and intruded into Kosygin's territory with extensive comments on economic matters. Further, he said more about foreign policy and defense than the ministers responsible, Gromyko and Grechko.

Brezhnev stressed the need for "relaxation of tensions" (détente) with the West. He proclaimed the USSR's innocence in the quarrel with China and proposed an all-European conference to discuss collective security.

Pronouncing the party healthy, Brezhnev reported that membership had doubled in 14 years, in which period the staff was trimmed by 20 percent. He could not, however, claim that the party was being proletarianized; only 40.1 percent of the members were workers. The CPSU had been good to Leonid Brezhnev; he would repay it. About 81 percent of full members of the Central Committee were reelected with his blessing.

To spur innovation, improve efficiency, and achieve economies of scale, the Brezhnev regime supported the territorial production association movement. An outgrowth of both the *sovnarhoz* experiment and elements of the abortive 1965 reform, the creation of conglomerate enterprises represented yet another attempt to restructure Soviet industry. Several enterprises in a given industry and territory amalgamated into a production association; the lesser ones became subordinates of the most important—usually the largest—of their number. Directors of the chief enterprise exercised a limited number of functions previously reserved for the appropriate Union ministry in Moscow. The consolidation of all or as many as possible stages of the production of a given commodity would, Brezhnev maintained, characterize "developed [mature] socialism."

A latecomer to the computer age, the USSR would have to automate factories, even whole industries. The general secretary stressed this theme and emphasized the crucial link between scientific-technological developments and progress in the economic and social spheres.

Kosygin echoed Brezhnev's ideas and called for automation of industry. Automated management systems had already been introduced on a partial basis at Gosplan and one or two other Union agencies. The forthcoming Ninth Five-Year Plan would see the introduction of "at least" 1,600 more such systems. Failure to take these steps earlier, Kosygin declared, had resulted in the economy's unsatisfactory performance during the Eighth Plan.

A systems approach in management would be coupled with "continuous planning," that is, constant review from birth of creative idea to series production. The introduction of modern technology, Kosygin maintained, would make it possible to raise the standard of living substantially during the Ninth Plan, but labor would have to do its part by increasing output. Once again, automation would be crucial. The premier predicted that by switching machine-tool production to digital programmed control, labor productivity would increase by 200–300 percent.

If that prediction proved accurate it would be nothing short of a miracle. Abel Aganbegyan had revealed in 1965 that, although the Soviet Union had about the same number of machine tools as the United States (2 million), only half were operational at any given time. The others were either "not in use or in repair." Capacity was underutilized, and crews assigned to out-of-service machines contributed nothing to the national economy.

If the Soviet Union could not keep the nonautomated sector working at more than 50 percent of capacity it was unlikely to do much better after automation, at least initially. The problem of user resistance to computers had by no means been overcome and there was some evidence that it was worsening. Beyond that, by the time the cumbersome state machinery had actually managed to automate a factory or group of factories, it was quite likely that the computers installed would be outdated. Brezhnev's "developed socialism" simply was not geared to the rapid assimilation of new technology. Bureaucratic inefficiency and inertia, coupled with the labor force's insistence on working strictly according to established procedure and rules, tended to stifle innovation. Managers began to speak of the "dehumanizing" effects of automation and hint of unemployment.

Spelling out targets for the Ninth Five-Year Plan of 1971–1975, Kosygin stressed that this would be the first plan to provide for a faster growth rate in the consumer sector than in the producer. At last the Soviet people were to be rewarded for their sacrifices. The standard of living would rise dramatically through a combination of greater production efficiency, scientific and technological innovations, and a rise in labor productivity.

## ECONOMIC DECLINE

The new plan was ambitious not so much in terms of goals as of assumptions. In percentage terms the targets for production and real income differed little from those authorities *claimed* had been achieved in the 1966–1970 period; this indicated that the actual results had been less impressive. The one realistic projection of the new plan was that the total nonagricultural labor force would increase by 13 percent against 19 percent in the preceding plan, the industrial labor force by only 6.5 percent against 15 percent. The relative decline in the labor pool meant that the planners banked heavily on a dramatic increase in labor productivity and on achieving enormous economies in raw materials and energy. The Soviet economy had never performed that way and it was exceedingly doubtful that it would do so now, computers or no computers.

The assumptions were all the more unrealistic in view of the fact that the new plan increased pressures on resources and managers. As always, the safest course of action was to defer to Moscow on all issues, even the most trivial, and as usual Moscow was willing to shoulder the burden. Gone was the modest freedom Kosygin had tried to extend to local managers and engineers. The massive centrifugal force of centralization again proved impossible to resist.

The planners also made the risky assumption that détente would continue to thrive. The introduction of new technology depended to a great extent on the uninterrupted flow of machines and expertise from the West, and in this area Soviet options were limited. There were already signs that opposition in the United States Senate might succeed in reversing that policy, or at least in forcing Nixon to attach strict conditions to it. If that happened, the Ninth Plan's timetable would be thrown off schedule.

Determined to solve forever one of their most vexing economic problems, Soviet leaders planned to increase the already huge investment in agriculture. The agricultural sector had taken an average of 23 percent of the total gross fixed capital investment in the latter half of the 1960s, and by 1973 its share reached 26.5 percent and continued climbing.

Midway through the Ninth Plan conservative economists and party ideologues who had defeated the 1965 reform stepped up their attacks on the attempt to modernize. In the journal *The Planned Economy*, they assailed the Western-style econometrics practiced at the Central Economics-Mathematical Institute, founded in 1963. They denounced as "bourgeois" such innovations as systems analysis, economic forecasting, and decentralized decision making. The critics tended to be older economists who were to some extent simply unable to adjust to new thinking. Part of the opposition, however, had a strong ideological quotient. Many Communists had never been able to come to terms with attempts to revise and modernize Marxism-Leninism, let alone with the radical departures of the 1965 reform, and they rejoiced as the leadership abandoned that venture.

These people opposed the assignment of priority to the consumer sector. Was this another bit of Khrushchevism, they asked, a sign that the millennium was here? Had the capitalists folded their tents? Until the whole world was Communist, the conservatives insisted, the Soviet economy must continue to emphasize heavy industry, to produce the steel that made the country strong.

The Ninth Plan did not meet its goals, partly due to what a Western scholar called the "longer-term retardatory trends in the Soviet economy" and partly because of nature's caprice. According to customarily inflated official figures the total national income rose by 28 percent during 1970–1975 for an average annual growth rate of 5.1 percent. The plan had called for 38.6 and 6.7 percent, respectively. Measured against 1966–1970 performance, agricultural production rose 13 percent in average-annual gross value terms instead of the projected 21.7 percent. Total industrial production was 43 percent higher in 1975 than in 1970, or 7.4 percent annually; the target figures were 47 and 8.0 percent, respectively. Production of consumer goods rose 37 percent (6.5 percent annually) instead of the planned 48.6 and 8.2 percent; thus heavy industry continued to enjoy priority.

Western experts estimated the average annual growth rate of the national economy closer to 4 percent than the claimed 5.1 percent. Abel Aganbegyan indicated in 1965 that CIA estimates had been "absolutely accurate." Moreover, industrial output cannot have reached the published levels, which represented a 97 percent fulfillment of goals.

There were two major crop failures during the period. The first, in 1972, was overcome in part through the purchase of 30 million tons of grain abroad, chiefly from the United States. The poor harvest of that year was only a foretaste of what was to come three years later, when it became necessary to obtain even greater amounts of grain from foreign suppliers.

The purchases ate into Soviet gold reserves, but the dramatic rise in oil and natural gas prices after 1973 temporarily softened the blow. An energy exporter, the USSR experienced a highly favorable balance of trade in the mid-1970s, but history has shown nothing so clearly as the cyclical nature of the world economy. That situation would not last, nor would Soviet reserves and domestic requirements permit the continued unlimited sale of hydrocarbons abroad.

The drought and resulting crop failure of 1975 were the worst since the early 1930s: Soviet farms failed to meet the revised target of 215.7 million tons of grain by 76 million tons. This time imports could not take up all the slack, for Soviet ports were physically capable of handling fewer than 40 million tons *per year*. Soviet consumers, including the collective farmers who needed seed and fodder, could only tighten their belts. An American economist described the 1975 disaster as "possibly the largest single blow suffered by the Soviet economy since the German invasion of 1941."

There were innumerable "ripple" effects from the 1975 crop failure. It was necessary to dip into reserve stocks—never large—to provide for human consumption, and that meant inadequate fodder. That in turn led to the premature slaughter of many animals, including breeding stock. There was a temporary glut, high sales, and then inevitable scarcity. Moreover, the slaughter of breeding stock obviously made it more difficult to rebuild the herds; the meat shortage would be a protracted one. Finally, the slaughter reduced the organic fertilizer available, increasing pressures on producers and transporters of chemical fertilizers.

Soviet consumers were obliged to endure shortages and lower their expectations. The standard of living, which had been improving at a modest rate, began to decline despite several wage increases for broad categories of workers. By 1976 the average wage for all workers had reached 145.80 rubles per month: 126.80 for farm workers, 162.20 for industrial workers. The average family spent less than 40 rubles a month for rent and utilities, perhaps 10 for transportation. Medical care was of course "free" in the sense that it involved negligible direct cost. Before the 1975 crop failure the average family spent 40–50 percent of its income on food despite massive state subsidies for bread, milk, and a few other items. Crop failures raised prices; the state had to intervene to fight inflation and limit political damage.

## 25TH CONGRESS

In April 1973 Brezhnev reorganized the Politburo. He ousted Voronov and Shelest—who also lost their government posts—and promoted four men on whom he could rely. Minister of Defense Grechko became a full member, as did Foreign Minister Gromyko and the KGB chief, Andropov. Grigori Romanov, the Leningrad party boss famous in the inner circle for high living, became a candidate member. The changes brought the number of full members to 16, the number of candidate members to seven.

Substantial opposition to détente necessitated the changes. Brezhnev counted on the promotion of the chiefs of the armed forces, secret police, and foreign ministry to shore up his personal position and party support for his foreign policy.

After the 1973 reorganization, Brezhnev's team seemed to function smoothly for two years. Then, in 1975, the general secretary unceremoniously ousted the trade union chief, Aleksandr Shelepin. Having served both Stalin and Khrushchev, Shelepin had played a role in deposing the latter and in the aftermath won a seat on the Presidium. But the Brezhnev people suspected him of wanting the top job, or at least the directorship of the KGB, a position he had held 1958–1961; neither Brezhnev nor Andropov could tolerate rivals.

The 25th Party Congress convened on February 23, 1976, with 4,998 delegates representing 15,694 members. Brezhnev opened the meeting with a lengthy speech defending détente. He again criticized China, blaming Beijing for the split. He reprimanded the French and Italian Communist parties for seeking independence from Soviet tutelage.

Brezhnev criticized the poor performance of the economy, singling out the "Group B" (consumer goods) sector for special reprimand. He blamed officials at the ministerial level for the dismal record, rebuking them for their insistence on regarding the production of consumer goods as "something secondary and ancillary." That was for public consumption; he made no promises to shift emphasis away from "Group A" (heavy industry). If Soviet consumers were to enjoy a higher standard of living, they would have to rely on improved efficiency and quality rather than a reorientation of state priorities. Brezhnev said little about the production associations, but declared that a restructuring of the economy could no longer be postponed. Guidelines for the new plan called for development of existing associations and formation of new complexes "with common communications, engineering facilities, and ancillary plants."

Offering the party a scapegoat for the 1975 farm disaster, Brezhnev ousted Minister of Agriculture Polyansky from the Politburo. The party secretary in charge of agriculture, Fyodor Kulakov, escaped without a public reprimand, but events were to prove that his standing with the general secretary had been compromised. Brezhnev pointed out that 213 billion of the 320 billion rubles allocated to agriculture since 1917 were invested during the Eighth and Ninth Five-Year Plans.

Obliged for political and ideological reasons to emphasize the positive, Kosygin called the Ninth Plan a success despite the enormous problems in agriculture and the continuing problems of inefficiency, lagging labor productivity, and the unsatisfactory quality of many goods. About 18 percent of all industrial enterprises, he noted, failed to meet their profit plans in 1975. Kosygin boasted of Soviet self-sufficiency in energy—no other major industrial nation could make such a claim—but in the same breath referred to a decline in proven oil reserves. In the future the USSR would have to rely more on hydroelectric power, nuclear energy, and coal.

Spelling out the goals of the Tenth Five-Year Plan, the premier called for a 24 to 28 percent increase in the national income to be achieved by an increase in "Group A" industrial production of 38–42 percent, in "Group B" of 30–32 percent. The "steeleaters" had prevailed. Wages were to increase 16–28 percent for industrial and clerical workers, 24–27 percent for collective farmers. The automation of industry and the mechanization and chemicalization of agriculture were to proceed at a quickened pace. Above all, Kosygin warned, managers, workers, engineers, scientists, and researchers had to improve efficiency and quality.

At its first plenary meeting, held while the 25th Congress was still in session, the new Central Committee ousted Polyansky from the Politburo and promoted two candidate members, Grigori Romanov and Dmitri Ustinov, to full membership. This brought the number of full members back up to 16. The inner circle of Brezhnev, Suslov, Kosygin, Grechko and Gromyko had an average age of 71; the entire Politburo averaged 66. The average age of the six alternate members was nearly 60, with Geidar Aliyev the youngest at 52.

The implications disturbed some party

members although no one dared speak publicly on the subject. A new generation of potential leaders who had come to political maturity after 1953 waited to assume command, but no one was being groomed for leadership. The old guard born between 1902 and 1918 clung tenaciously to power, growing ever more rigid, resisting new ideas and new people, fighting innovation, demanding order above all. The untidy but normal infighting that occurs in all political organizations was distorted after 1971; party business tended to stagnate. The consequences of the "stability of cadres" were becoming painfully obvious.

Brezhnev boasted to the 25th Congress that he had put "an end . . . to the unjustified reshuffling and frequent replacements of cadres." He had, but he was blind to the ossification of those cadres into a mass of sinecure-holders whose overriding goal was to brake the healthy trends in Soviet society. Between 1964 and 1976, 78 percent of the regional party bureaus in European Russia either kept the same leader or saw her or him replaced only once. This contrasts with the 33 percent "stability index" under Khrushchev.

## THE POLITICS OF 1976–1977

In May 1976 Brezhnev was promoted from four-star general to marshal of the Soviet Union, becoming the first politician since Stalin to hold that rank; Khrushchev had been content with three stars. At about the same time it was revealed that he was president of the Defense Council, the existence of which had previously been kept secret. A bust of the general secretary was unveiled in his home town to the accompaniment of nationwide publicity. In December 1976 *Pravda* devoted one or two pages to Brezhnev each day December 11–18, then on the 19th gave him six of the total eight pages in celebration of his 70th birthday. He was awarded his fifth Order of Lenin and his second Gold Medal Hero of the Soviet Union.

Brezhnev loyalists continued to flourish. Dmitri Ustinov became defense minister upon Marshal Grechko's death in April 1976 and was promoted to the rank of marshal, although—like Brezhnev—he was not a professional military man. Yuri Andropov of the KGB and N.A. Shchelokov, minister of internal affairs, became generals of the army in September. The three promotions testified to the strength of his political machine and to Brezhnev's control over the military establishment.

More evidence of the general secretary's power came in September 1976 with the appointment of Nikolai A. Tikhonov, 71, as first deputy prime minister and thus heir apparent to the ailing Kosygin. Like a substantial number of key officials, Tikhonov had served in various posts in Dnepropetrovsk, where Brezhnev was born and began his political career. An American scholar pointed out in 1976 that, of 185 officials from 25 regions who were promoted to high office outside their home regions, 24 transfers came from Dnepropetrovsk; no other region had more than 15. Beyond that, 11 Central Committee members came from Dnepropetrovsk, more than twice as many as the next best-represented area, Harkov. One of Brezhnev's closest personal and political associates, Andrei Kirilenko, spent considerable time in party work in Dnepropetrovsk, as did Shcherbitsky and Shchelokov. Two of Andropov's deputies at the KGB rumored to be Brezhnev's personal watchdogs, Viktor Chebrikov and Georgi Tsinev, had similar backgrounds.

The Tikhonov appointment coincided with rumors of the impending ouster of Podgorny from the leadership. In May 1977 a Central Committee plenum dropped the 74-year-old Ukrainian from the Politburo without explanation; three weeks later the Supreme Soviet dismissed him as chairman of its Presidium and immediately elected Brezhnev in his place. The party general secretary thus became chief of state; he was the first Soviet politician to hold both posts simultaneously.

Brezhnev's assumption of the "presidency" for the second time was designed, he declared in his first speech in office, to demonstrate the primacy of the Communist party in Soviet political life. That had not been in doubt since 1920.

It was awkward for Brezhnev, in a formal sense merely the head of a political party, to deal with foreign heads of state. Moreover, all Soviet-bloc countries save Hungary and Poland were ruled by men who held the top position in both party and state. At a time when Moscow's domination of the satellites was increasingly in jeopardy, Brezhnev's technically inferior rank amounted to an unnecessary irritant. Too, the logic of the "cult" dictated that Brezhnev should have the post of chief of state, the last prize his fellow oligarchs could offer him.

There was nothing subtle about the timing. Four days after taking office, Brezhnev paid a state visit to France and was greeted with full honors, including the 101-gun salute his new rank demanded.

## NEW CONSTITUTION

There was another factor in the 1977 maneuvers. In 1959 a conference of legal experts had proposed sweeping changes in the 1936 constitution, ostensibly to bring it into line with the development of socialism. In reality the document was hateful to the "de-Stalinizers": it had, after all, provided legal sanction for the whole Stalinist system. In 1962 Khrushchev became chairman of a Constitutional Commission. Brezhnev replaced him in November 1964.

As he consolidated his power Brezhnev took an ever greater interest in the project. He frequently referred to the Commission's work and in 1973 declared publicly that a document would be submitted to a nation-wide referendum, an unheard-of procedure in the USSR. When the text of his speech was published, his reference to a referendum had been deleted.

The draft was published June 4, 1977, 12 days before Brezhnev replaced Podgorny as chief of state. It was much like the old Constitution but there were some changes. One had a bearing on the 1977 politicking: for the first time there was to be a "vice-presidency." A first deputy chairman of the Supreme Soviet Presidium would fulfill routine ceremonial duties previously entrusted to the chairman, who would be free for the grander task of negotiating with foreign leaders. Brezhnev of course wanted the chairmanship for himself and apparently offered the lesser post to Podgorny, who declined.

Submitted to nationwide discussion—but not a referendum—over the summer, the new Constitution spelled out the party's role: "The Communist Pary of the Soviet Union is the leading and guiding force of Soviet society, the nucleus of its political system and of [all] state and public organizations. The CPSU exists for the people and serves the people" (Art. 6). The equality of citizens and their basic civil and human rights were spelled out (Art. 50) as in the earlier document, but in more specific form. The second paragraph of Art. 39, however, declared that "The exercise of rights and liberties by citizens must not injure the interests of society and the state or the rights of other citizens." This caution constituted the *ultima ratio:* according to Art. 6, the

Communist party was to be the sole judge of injury to the state or the rights of others.

Art. 4 recognized each citizen's right to own a dwelling and a farm. An innovative Chapter 4 (Arts. 28–30) on foreign policy reflected the Kremlin's attempt to prove compliance with the Final Act of the Helsinki Conference. It emphasized the peace-loving nature of the Soviet state, called for "general and complete disarmament," and specifically forbade war propaganda.

Presenting the slightly revised document to the Supreme Soviet for ratification in October 1977, Brezhnev indicated that the party had been stung by foreign criticism. He named half a dozen Western newspapers critical of the constitution and hurled a challenge. Did the West wish to boast of guaranteeing the "right" to unemployment, inadequate medical care and neglect of the elderly, racial discrimination, crime, the propagandizing of sociopathic values? He declared that none of these phenomena were present in the USSR. Brezhnev had perhaps nicked Western democracies where they were vulnerable, but it was an odd defense.

Like its predecessors of 1918, 1924, and 1936, the new Constitution reflected the antidemocratic nature and values of the ruling party. It made no pretense of seeking political or social equilibrium and did not recognize even the theoretical possibility of error on the part of the Communist party. It did not sanction political or ideological compromise and provided no curb on the powers of the party. Only the party truly had rights; the guarantee of freedom of speech meant freedom to agree with the party.

The "Brezhnev Constitution" was unanimously approved, as until 1988 was all business, by the Supreme Soviet in time for the 60th anniversary of the Bolshevik Revolution in November 1977. The republics and autonomous republics also adopted new constitutions at this time. It is unlikely that Lenin, Stalin, or Khrushchev would have objected to a single word in any of them.

## DECLINE OF THE BREZHNEV MACHINE

The new Constitution had little impact on the life of the Soviet people. Party and government spokesmen argued that the orderly transition from one constitutional order to another proved the genius of the framers. In reality it demonstrated the irrelevance of a constitution in a one-party state.

Veteran diplomat V. V. Kuznetsov, negotiator of SALT I and a former ambassador to China, became the country's first deputy chairman of the Supreme Soviet Presidium or vice president. Never an insider, Kuznetsov, 76, would perform the routine state duties that bored Brezhnev and taxed his health, which was beginning to fail noticeably.

Several personnel changes during 1977–1980 seemed to indicate the leadership's inability to agree upon a succession policy. Brezhnev promoted one of his closest friends, Konstantin Chernenko, to candidate member status—along with Kuznetsov—on the Politburo in October 1977 and to full member a year later. There was little doubt that he was Brezhnev's personal choice as the next general secretary.

Having suffered a cerebral hemorrhage in 1976 and a massive heart attack in 1979, Kosygin relinquished his party and government posts in October 1980. Tikhonov succeeded him as prime minister, and Kosygin's seat on the Politburo went to Mikhail Gorbachev, 49, party secretary in charge of agriculture since Kulakov's death in 1978.

The coalition that had ruled for 16 years collapsed. Suslov remained officially in charge of ideology, but his own health deteriorated rapidly. For all practical purposes Leonid Brezhnev stood alone, in the ever-tightening grip of Alzheimer's disease. Politics shifted backstage as he became a mere figurehead.

Kosygin died on December 18, 1980. The party did not immediately publish the news; Brezhnev's entourage did not want to spoil his birthday the next day. The fading general secretary received the Order of the October Revolution, long reserved for highest-level party mediocrities, and obscenely lavish tributes from his cronies. Not until December 21 did the Communists see fit to inform the world that Aleksei Kosygin, a decent, self-effacing bureaucrat who never meshed with the Brezhnev machine, had died.

## LAST POST: 26TH CONGRESS

No potential candidate for leadership had a clear party mandate; Chernenko, Kirilenko, and Andropov propped up the general secretary like El Cid and kept him in office pending some shift that would enable one of them to assert primacy without generating an intraparty fight. By the time the 26th Party Congress convened on Army-Navy Day (February 23), 1981, however, it had become impossible to conceal Brezhnev's infirmities. The television cameras kept a respectful distance, and the state network broadcast only the opening and closing sections of his unusually short speech, but the pictures mercilessly revealed the general secretary trapped in the decrepit old age that is the special dread of people grown too fond of power.

The nation waited for vigorous new leadership. The economy desperately needed a revolutionary overhaul; nationalist unrest in Estonia, Azerbaijan, Kirgizia, and elsewhere pulled on the resources and patience of the center; a hopeless war in Afghanistan demoralized the army in the field and the civilians at home. In the wake of the Decem-

ber 1979 invasion of Afghanistan, Soviet relations with the West and China plunged to their lowest level since the Cuban missile crisis of 1962. The fading old man in the Kremlin could do nothing about any of this.

Thus the 26th Congress unfolded in splendidly Brezhnevist fashion: nothing much happened. Save for a wistful call for a meeting with the new American president, Ronald Reagan, Brezhnev's abbreviated remarks lacked substance. The general secretary's speechwriters—almost certainly under Andropov's supervision—had him defend Soviet foreign policy vis-à-vis Poland and Afghanistan, but with those exceptions the speech struck a generally conciliatory note. Lurking in the background was nostalgia for the heady days when he and President Nixon had met regularly in an attempt to lay the foundation for an era of harmony and cooperation. Brezhnev blamed the collapse of détente and nearly 60 percent drop in the value of bilateral trade in 1980 on the United States. Soviet foreign policy had remained consistent, he declared, and dialogue could resume at any time so long as it did not touch on the closed subjects of Poland and Afghanistan.

His public remarks seemed to indicate that Brezhnev was little disturbed by the sluggishness of the Soviet economy. He bragged of an enormous increase in labor productivity, announced that the territorial production complexes were functioning satisfactorily, and spoke of the "truly revolutionary possibilities" created by the development and introduction of microcomputers and industrial robots. Nevertheless, he could hardly ignore the stagnation in industry or the monumental problems of Soviet agriculture. He called for more discipline, better leadership, and an end to the widespread practice of adjusting plan targets downward. He warned again of the decline in energy reserves and spoke more bluntly than ever of the economic consequences of an increasingly severe labor shortage.

The 11th Five-Year Plan of 1981–1985 would place a greater strain than ever on both human and material resources, but the party had no coherent program to deal with what was manifestly a worsening crisis. Unable for ideological reasons to initiate the decisive decentralization that alone seemed to offer a way out of the morass, the party continued to employ half-measures, tinker with the planning mechanism, exhort managers and workers to perform more efficiently.

It was of course the party's duty to direct the reinvigoration of the economy that Brezhnev and Prime Minister Tikhonov demanded, but how a party that refused to rejuvenate its own leading organs would accomplish that remained a mystery. For the first time in post-Revolution history there was no change in the composition of the Politburo. The new Central Committee (increased in size from 287 full members to 319) elected at the 26th Congress included 231 holdovers—80 percent—from 1976 and seven members who had come into office after that year. Of the 81 newcomers, approximately 38 had been candidate members. Among these newcomers were at least five KGB officials, including three known to be part of the growing Andropov machine: Viktor Chebrikov, Georgi Tsinev, and Semyon Tsvigun. There were also nine generals on the new Committee, which dropped such former high-ranking officials as Podgorny, Polyansky, K.T. Mazurov, and V.V. Matskevich. Only eight women were elected, along with about a dozen genuine workers.

## THE ARTS

As often happens under repressive, corrupt regimes, the arts enjoyed an underground renaissance in the Brezhnev era. Artists and writers protested the shortcomings of Soviet life. Outstanding films came out of studios in Russia, Armenia, Georgia, Lithuania, Uzbekistan, and other republics; with very few exceptions the party forbade their release.

Inextricably linked to factories and therefore cities, communism had always detested the village; both Khrushchev and his immediate successors predicted the total urbanization of the nation by the turn of the 21st century. Several writers lamented the death of the village and warned of the loss of such a "spiritual gold mine." The term came from a member of the unofficial "rural school" of writers, Fyodor Abramov, whose moral strictures might have carried more weight had he not been a *Smersh* ("Death to Spies") executioner during World War II. The trend took hold in the 1950s and quickly won wide respect as writers with greater talent than the bloodstained Abramov published stories and books with rural settings that featured heroic peasant—almost always noncommunist—characters; Vladimir Soloukhin and Yefim Dorosh were two of the best such writers.

Communists belatedly realized that the idealization of the village evoked doubts about their values and tried too late to suppress the "rural school." Soloukhin wrote of the beauty and simplicity of rural life in central Russia; Valentin Rasputin and Sergei Zalygin of Siberia; Chingiz Aitmatov of Kirgizia and Kazakhstan; Fazil Iskander of Abkhazia. These and other writers made the hacks who controlled the Writers' Union uncomfortable because, like talented people everywhere, they tended to be nonconformists. In the mid-1970s only half—the talentless half—of the Union's 2,000 members belonged to the party.

In 1979 the Writers' Union expressed "heartfelt thanks" to Leonid Brezhnev, whose recently published memoirs had had "an enormous influence on all types and genres of literature"; real writers relished the perverse humor. The general secretary's entourage had arranged for him to win a Lenin Prize for the hopelessly banal, ghost-written memoirs.

The Writers' Union expelled one of Russia's greatest literary talents of the 20th century, Aleksandr Solzhenitsyn, from its ranks in 1969. Protected from imprisonment or worse by his international fame, Solzhenitsyn lived precariously after winning the Nobel Prize for Literature in 1970. Officially silenced, his influence as a writer waned but he retained a measure of moral authority. After his monumental history of the Gulag began to appear in the West the government denounced him as a traitor, never addressing the central question: was his account true? The Brezhnev regime expelled Solzhenitsyn from the USSR in 1974.

Solzhenitsyn was to be followed into exile by scores of poets, writers, and other artists. The flight resembled the exodus from Germany after the Nazis seized power and it robbed the USSR of some of its finest talent: Mstislav Rostropovich, Galina Vishnevskaya, Mikhail Baryshnikov, Natalia Makarova, Maksim Shostakovich, Yuri Lyubimov, Joseph Brodsky, Vasily Aksyonov, Lev Kopelev, Georgi Vladimov, Vladimir Voinovich, Ernest Neizvestny, Andrei Tarkovsky, Viktor Korchnoi, Boris Spassky, and many others. Some went willingly; others were literally thrown out of the country.

But many of the writers who remained managed to retain their integrity in the difficult conditions. Notable among those who did was Yuri Trifonov, who in *The House on the Embankment* and other works succeeded in conveying the central message of the intellectuals' protest: only through a thorough, honest examination of the Stalin era could the country cleanse itself and move forward. The Kirgiz dramatists Chin-giz Aitmatov and Kaltai Mukhamedzhanov pursued this theme in *The Ascent of Mount Fuji*. Yuri Lyubimov, director of Moscow's avant-garde Taganka Theatre, staged Bulgakov's *The Master and Margarita* in 1977, faithfully preserving the author's condemnation of the ultra-authoritarian state.

The Taganka under Lyubimov was the home of the truly daring, but another theatre startled audiences in 1977 with a production of Vasili Shukshin's *And in the Morning They Awakened*, which dealt with the problem of alcohol abuse. Aleksandr Gelman's *We, The Undersigned* presented the "fixers" who wormed their way around production bottlenecks and moral dilemmas in a sympathetic light. Viktor Rozov's *Nest of Wood Grouse* attacked pompous, insensitive bureaucrats and expressed sympathy for young idealists impatient with the shortcomings of Soviet society. Lyubimov was forced into remaining abroad in 1984 (he had gone to London to stage a play) by, as he wrote, "stupid little men" who had done more damage to Russian culture than any foreign enemy.

In 1979 nearly two dozen writers and poets collaborated on a *samizdat* venture called *Metropol*. Vasili Aksyonov, Fazil Iskander, and three lesser-known writers served as editors. Bella Akhmadulina and Andrei Voznesensky, both prominent poets, contributed works, as did Vladimir Vysotsky. The collaborators insisted that *Metropol*, of which only 10 copies were produced, was strictly nonpolitical: the goal was simply to demand the right of free artistic expression.

The Communist party obviously could not agree. It denounced the poems dealing with the Gulag, the stories of corruption, the fictional accounts of sexual adventures, the nude drawings. *Metropol*, the authorities declared, was "pornography of the soul." The Writers' Union expelled two young contributors (who were later briefly reinstated) and warned the others to cease their attempts to evade censorship.

The watchdogs were no less zealous in other fields. In September 1974 the Moscow authorities used bulldozers to break up an unauthorized outdoor exhibition of "non-conformist" art. When photographs of the episode appeared in newspapers around the world, the Kremlin fired a couple of officials and in effect apologized by permitting a similar exhibition later in an obscure hall. The works shown, however, were about as avant-garde as Impressionism; more modern schools remained proscribed.

Conservatism continued to reign in classical music, where the Lysenko-like head of the Composers' Union, Tikhon Khrennikov, sought to freeze the clock in 1893—the year of Tchaikovsky's death. Orchestras did perform the works of Dmitri Shostakovich, but only rarely did such avant-garde composers as Edison Denisov, Aleksandr Knaifel, and Alfred Schnitke have the opportunity to present their music to Soviet audiences. Schnitke's *Latin Requiem Mass* did enjoy a great triumph at its Moscow première in the spring of 1980, several years after it was first heard in Budapest. Soviet audiences in general, however, became aware of Schnitke's genius chiefly through his many film scores. Knaifel and Denisov worked only rarely in that medium.

Most of the 150–175 films made annually in the *troika* and Brezhnev eras had little to commend them. The party continued to commission quasi-documentary feature films such as *Lenin in Poland, Lenin in Paris, Lenin Manuscripts, Conversation with Comrade Lenin,* and *The Living Lenin,* none of which left much doubt about the subject matter. Other heavy-handed propaganda exercises such as *Our March, Banner over the World,* and *The Internationale* likewise mesmerized Communists and stupefied everyone else.

Films about World War II remained popular in cinemas and on television, but there were signs that the genre was beginning to pall. *Ordinary Fascism* had 479 showings to 118,000 people in Gorky in 1967; in the same year the American *Some Like It Hot* had 1,037 showings to 268,000 viewers. The diminishing interest in war films was another manifestation of the aging of the population.

An outstanding young director was Andrei Tarkovsky, whose first film, *My Name Is Ivan* (1962), was a rather conventional portrayal of a young boy orphaned in the Second World War. Its success, however, freed Tarkovsky to make the brilliant *Andrei Rublev* (1966) about the great icon painter who died in 1430. The harshly realistic film showed human beings rather than symbols of the class struggle. Party watchdogs did not like it and withdrew it from general circulation. Tarkovsky's science-fiction *Solaris* (1972) proved too arcane to be popular, as did the stream-of-consciousness *The Mirror* (1975). His *Stalker* (1980) had not been released by early 1989. In the summer of 1984, citing frustration over impossible working conditions in the USSR, Tarkovsky found asylum in the West.

An immensely popular actor, director, and writer was Vasili Shukshin, a practitioner of "village" prose who translated several of his own stories into successful films. *The Guelder-rose* (1974) was the story of a criminal who, after completing a prison term, tries to rehabilitate himself by moving from the corrupt city to the countryside, only to be hunted down and killed by his old gang. The portrayal of unsavory party officials, bored workers unable to stay awake during political lectures, and religious peasants electrified Soviet audiences. Shortly before his premature death Shukshin appeared in Gleb Panfilov's *I Want to Speak* (1976), which dealt with mindless bureaucrats, the painful

Stalinist legacy, and spoiled youth. The Soviet authorities tolerated these films but really preferred such banal comedies as *The Quiet Bride* (1979) and *Moscow Does Not Believe in Tears* (1980).

## DISSIDENTS

In most modern societies the cultural avant-garde is heavily populated by people from marginal or even outcast groups and by individuals whose personal histories are often irregular and sometimes embarrassing. The broad middle classes in the West and Japan have generally followed in the wake of such groups in the areas of popular music, dance, dress, and "lifestyle," but the men who control the Soviet Union have never made their peace with such groups and have tried to keep the population from imitating them. Cultural innovation has always been unacceptable to Soviet leaders, and the slightest hint of political deviation has invariably triggered a brutal response.

The regime's failure instantly to demolish the dissident movement which took on identifiable outlines in the mid-1960s reflected the progress made since Stalin's death. The state dealt harshly with the *samizdat* writers Sinyavsky and Daniel, but both were eventually allowed to emigrate. Several individuals who publicly protested the invasion of Czechoslovakia likewise suffered under the blows of the KGB but survived and ultimately left the country. Solzhenitsyn was silenced, harassed unmercifully, and finally expelled, escaping the fate of Mandelstam and other writers consumed by the Gulag in Stalin's time.

In an unprecedented development thousands of Jewish citizens were permitted to go to Israel and the West before the collapse of détente virtually closed the borders again. A group of citizens who demanded the right to monitor Soviet compliance with the human rights provisions of the Helsinki Final Act drew world attention to the Kremlin's hypocrisy. Several members were imprisoned, some were accused of having CIA connections, all were silenced. They had, however, been heard, and like the 19th-century Decembrists and other revolutionaries, they would not be forgotten.

Andrei Sakharov, the nuclear physicist who became the most articulate and respected critic of the regime, was exiled to Gorky on the Volga. Cut off from the outside world, his fate became a source of concern around the world—and thus a major dilemma for the Kremlin.

There was little cohesion among the dissidents, no agreement on goals. Solzhenitsyn's conservative Russian nationalism and devotion to the Russian Orthodox Church appealed to some oppositionists but by no means all. Sakharov sometimes seemed remote and aloof. The Moscow and Leningrad intellectuals in the shapeless movement frequently squabbled among themselves. The KGB penetrated most groups—and the ranks of the émigrés and defectors.

The dissidents were few in number, and the public, which knew little of them, remained indifferent, even hostile. The state's rough suppression of the movement seemed yet another grossly excessive application of force, but the authorities knew better than anyone that—as the Bolsheviks had proved in 1917—numbers do not always reflect the strength of ideas. Unwilling to take chances, the Kremlin moved against the dissidents and in the process created martyrs—never the practice of confident, secure regimes.

## END OF THE BREZHNEV ERA

Leonid Brezhnev had brought political stability, and he had presided over the rise of the country to an unprecedented position of strength and prestige. But now, old and feeble, he could not comprehend the cost of his victories, let alone make arrangements to pay it. It was time to leave; but the Soviet system had no provision for dealing with an infirm leader.

The last 20 months of Brezhnev's life blended into a bizarre collage of intrigue and scandal. Never able to translate his party popularity into a real following among the public, the general secretary became the butt of increasingly pointed criticism which spread to areas where it could only have appeared with the sanction of high-level officials. In December 1981 the play *Thus We Will Win* opened in Moscow. Set in October 1922, at one point the actor playing Lenin speaks emphatically of the need to curb the general secretary's power.

The December 1981 issue of the Leningrad literary journal *Avrora* (Aurora) was dedicated to Brezhnev on his 75th birthday. On page 75 was a brief, savage satire dedicated to an unnamed "wonderful writer" who had astonished everyone by remaining alive long after he ought to have died. The narrator exclaims that his daughter, who loves a joke, delighted him one day with the news that this writer had died, only to disappoint him when she confessed the news was false. The writer would probably die soon, however; everyone had been waiting so long for the event. A couple of years earlier Brezhnev had won a Lenin Prize for his memoirs and collected works.

Suslov died at the age of 79 on January 25, 1982. Ardent Stalinist, mastermind of Khrushchev's rise to power and chief architect of his fall, Suslov had groomed Brezhnev for leadership and had been the Kremlin's Richelieu since 1957. For more than three decades he was the ideological conscience of the party. His death allowed the floodgates of scandal to open.

Four days after Suslov's demise the official in charge of the passport office was arrested and charged with selling exit visas. On the same day an individual connected with the Moscow Circus was arrested on charges of illegal financial dealings. It had long been an open secret that the Brezhnev machine was both riddled with corruption and disinclined to do anything about it; "stability of cadres" extended to the covering-up of malfeasance. The arrest of the passport official indicated that the carefree days were over. The circus individual was a close personal friend of Brezhnev's daughter.

It would soon be revealed that the death in January—six days before Suslov's—of a KGB official, Semyon Tsvigun, had been a suicide, and that Tsvigun had clashed with Suslov over the arrest of people close to the Brezhnev family. Suslov opposed the arrests and prevailed. Presumably because he believed his career ruined, Tsvigun killed himself. It suddenly became clear why Suslov and Brezhnev had not signed Tsvigun's obituary, which *was* signed by Andropov and all top KGB officials.

In March a Suslov protégé, Aleksei Shibayev, was ousted as head of the central trade union organization. Fourteen months later he would be reprimanded for illegal financial dealings. In July 1982 an old Brezhnev friend who was in charge of the Krasnodar party organization was forced out of office; after Brezhnev's death he would be arrested on charges of corruption.

The leader of the anticorruption drive was Yuri Andropov, who was to succeed Brezhnev in the Kremlin. Long considered a possible contender for the general secretaryship but generally ruled out because of his lengthy tenure as head of the KGB, Andropov began the political maneuvers that would result in victory over his rivals in April 1982. In that month he gave the main speech on the anniversary of Lenin's birth, which he had done in 1976 when Brezhnev was indisposed. But with the general secretary now obviously unable to continue in office much longer, the fact that he was chosen to give one of the most important speeches of the year took on new significance. The following month Andropov was appointed to the Central Committee Secretariat with unspecified responsibilities. Two days later he resigned his KGB post and was replaced by his deputy, Vitaly K. Fedorchuk, who continued the investigation of shady practices among high officials.

As the play *Thus We Will Win,* the *Avrora* piece, the arrests, and other developments indicated, Andropov and his top KGB aides could barely contain their impatience for Brezhnev to die; none of this could have transpired without their sanction. Television—always under strict KGB control—showed a tired, indifferent, disoriented Brezhnev at Suslov's funeral and two weeks later zeroed in on his uncontrollable weeping at another burial. Until this, Soviet television had never, ever shown leaders in any but the most favorable light.

Brezhnev suffered a slight stroke in March 1982 but seemed to revive during his usual prolonged summer vacation. In September, however, the KGB planted rumors—eagerly snapped up by the Western press—of Brezhnev's impending resignation. Out of public view in October, Brezhnev stood atop the Lenin Mausoleum on November 7 to review the parade marking the anniversary of the Bolshevik Revolution.

During the evening of November 10, 1982, Soviet television and radio suddenly and without explanation interrupted regular programming to broadcast classical music. At 11 o'clock the next morning the party announced that its leader had suffered a fatal heart attack the previous evening.

The Communist party buried Leonid Brezhnev with the unsurpassed pomp and circumstance of Russian funerals, renamed

a city on the Volga in his honor, and proceeded to forget him. Four years later Mikhail Gorbachev would personally direct a sustained, public assault on the entire Brezhnev legacy.

The ex-head of the KGB, Yuri Andropov, installed himself as general secretary and president, cracked down on economic corruption—except when it involved friends such as Politburo members Grishin, Romanov, Kunayev, Aliyev, and others—and solidified KGB control of every phase of Soviet life. The myth of Andropov's "liberalism" reflected a remarkably successful KGB disinformation campaign.

Andropov attacked the economic rather than the political legacy of his predecessor. Brezhnev had enjoyed greater uncoerced popularity inside the party than any leader since Lenin, and the 18 years when he had served as part of the *troika* with Kosygin and Suslov and then ruled as first among equals had seen unprecedented social and political stability. Brezhnev avoided the confrontations of the Khrushchev period and the bloody terror of Stalinism. Under Andropov's direction, Brezhnevist terror employed prisons, psychiatric hospitals, social ostracism, and economic sanctions to achieve domestic tranquillity. Where Khrushchev limited himself to verbal assaults on artists and poets, the Brezhnev regime expressed its disapproval by sending bulldozers to level unofficial outdoor art exhibits. As Gorbachev said in November 1987, "the process of restoring justice . . . [begun by the 20th and 22nd Congresses] was actually suspended in the mid-1960s."

The year of Brezhnev's death saw the Soviet economic growth rate reach its lowest postwar level; the year before that witnessed the smallest grain harvest in 20 years. The Brezhnev machine had left the economy in shambles. Were it not for the high world market price for oil, and the "totally unjustified increase in the sale of alcoholic beverages," the state treasury would have collapsed. Speaking on February 18, 1988, Gorbachev declared,

If we remove the influence of these factors from the economic growth indices, the result is that we had no increase in the absolute growth of the national income over almost four five-year plans, and it even began to *decrease* [emphasis added] in the early 1980s. That is the real picture, comrades!

The bureaucrats tried to hide the disaster they had made behind statistics. In February 1987, however, the sociologist Tatiana Zaslavskaya pointed out in *Pravda* that "Among developed countries, we rank among the last in the level of social statistics . . ." Selyunin and Khanin reported a few months later that the 1976–1983 period saw only a nine percent increase in physical-unit output but—because of inflation and price-juggling—a 75 percent increase in ruble-value output. The government and party reported only the latter, essentially meaningless figures.

Even in the *troika*-Brezhnev "years of stagnation," however, the standard of living of the poorest stratum of the *working* population improved, although retirees on small, fixed pensions continued to subsist on next to nothing. The kolhoz peasantry finally won access to the state pension system and other social security benefits; they also received the internal passports necessary for unrestricted movement around the USSR.

During the *troika*-Brezhnev epoch, the Soviet Union moved from inferiority to parity with its great rival, the United States. Russian-Soviet humiliation at foreign hands had ended. Brezhnev, Kosygin, Suslov, Ustinov, and the generals and admirals bequeathed the nation something that had eluded all the tsars, Lenin, and Stalin. As the bills came due, however, it fell to the next generation to reexamine the bequest.

## SUGGESTED ADDITIONAL READING

**Aksyonov, Vasily, ed.,** *Metropol,* New York: W.W. Norton, 1983

**Amann, Ronald, and Julian Cooper, eds.,** *Industrial Innovation in the Soviet Union,* New Haven, Conn.: Yale University Press, 1982

**Barron, John,** *KGB,* New York: Reader's Digest/ Dutton, 1974

**Berliner, Joseph,** *Soviet Industry from Stalin to Gorbachev,* Ithaca, N.Y.: Cornell University Press, 1987

**Binyon, Michael,** *Life in Russia,* New York: Pantheon, 1983

**Desai, Padma, ed.,** *Marxism, Central Planning, and the Soviet Economy,* Cambridge: MIT Press, 1983

**Dunlop, John B.,** *The Faces of Contemporary Russian Nationalism,* Princeton, N.J.: Princeton University Press, 1984

**Feshbach, Murray,** *The Soviet Union: Population Trends and Dilemmas,* Washington: Population Reference Bureau, 1982

**Fireside, Harvey,** *Soviet Psychoprisons,* New York: W.W. Norton, 1979

**Freedman, Robert O., ed.,** *Soviet Jewry in the Decisive Decade, 1971–1980,* Durham, N.C.: Duke University Press, 1985

**Friedgut, Theodore H.,** *Political Participation in the USSR,* Princeton, N.J.: Princeton University Press, 1979

**Grancelli, Bruno,** *Soviet Management and Labor Relations,* Winchester, Mass.: Allen & Unwin, 1987

**Hansson, Carola, and Karen Liden, eds.,** *Moscow Women,* New York: Pantheon, 1983

**Hoffmann, Erik P., and Robbin F. Laird,** *The Politics of Economic Modernization in the Soviet Union,* Ithaca, N.Y.: Cornell University Press, 1985

**Holland, Barbara, ed.,** *Soviet Sisterhood,* Bloomington: Indiana University Press, 1985

**Jones, Ellen,** *The Red Army and Society: A Sociology of the Soviet Military,* Winchester, Mass.: Allen & Unwin, 1986

**Kerblay, Basile,** *Modern Soviet Society,* New York: Pantheon, 1983

**Knight, Amy,** *The KGB: Police and Politics in the Soviet Union,* Winchester, Mass.: Allen & Unwin, 1988

**Lapidus, Gail W.,** *Women in Soviet Society,* Berkeley and Los Angeles: University of California Press, 1978

**Littlejohn, Gary,** *A Sociology of the Soviet Union,* London: Macmillan, 1984

**Matthews, Mervyn,** *Poverty in the Soviet Union,* New York: Cambridge University Press, 1987

**Millar, James R., ed.,** *Politics, Work, and Daily Life in the USSR: A Survey of Former Soviet Citizens,* New York: Cambridge University Press, 1987

**Pipes, Richard,** *Survival Is Not Enough,* New York: Simon & Schuster, 1984

**Ratushinskaya, Irina,** *Grey Is the Color of Hope,* New York: Knopf, 1988

**Starr, S. Frederick,** *Red and Hot: The Fate of Jazz in the Soviet Union, 1971–1980,* New York: Oxford University Press, 1983

**Tucker, Robert C.,** *Political Culture and Leadership in Soviet Russia,* New York: W.W. Norton, 1987

# 21

# FOREIGN POLICY, 1964–1985

The stupendous expansion of Soviet military power began under Khrushchev; his successors drove the program forward. The Kremlin maintained that the buildup was designed solely for defense, a claim that mirrored the West's justification of its own huge arsenal. The Soviets wanted to achieve a warmaking capability roughly equal to that of the West and China *combined;* there could be no assurance that they would not face their two adversaries simultaneously.

## THE EAST EUROPEAN EMPIRE

In the tradition of medieval Russian churchmen who proclaimed Moscow the "third and final Rome" after the fall of Rome and Constantinople (New Rome) to infidels, the Soviets claimed to be sole leaders of the world Communist movement. The ideological purity of that movement, second in importance only to Soviet national security, took on new significance after the 1948 defection of Yugoslavia. That shook Moscow's claim to leadership; the departure of China and Albania destroyed it.

Romanian Communist leaders seized the opportunity provided by the Moscow-Beijing quarrel to edge away from Soviet domination. They boldly attempted to mediate between the two Communist giants in 1964, launching a foreign policy that became increasingly independent. Soviet leaders tolerated this because they approved the harsh Stalinist domestic policies of the Romanian Communists.

The Communist party of Bulgaria, Moscow's ideal satellite, tried to make that country a mere appendage of the USSR. The Bulgarian writer Georgi Markov, who paid with his life for denouncing the Communists' sale of the country, charged that party leaders poured the "Soviet chemicals of ruthless demoralization and moral corruption" onto Bulgarian soil. Bordering two NATO nations, Greece and Turkey, Bulgaria served as a singularly valuable Soviet satellite.

In the middle of the post–World War II border zone between East and West, Hungary's value as a Soviet ally disappeared in the wake of the terrible repression— masterminded on the scene by the "liberal" Yuri Andropov—of the 1956 revolution. Three years after that heroic episode, the Hungarian Communists who had cooperated in the Soviet slaughter of their countrymen began to experiment with economic liberalization. They carefully labelled their innovations "socialist" and proclaimed fealty to Marxism-Leninism. In 1968 the regime installed a "new economic mechanism" designed by young Western-oriented economists also influenced by the Lenin-Bukharin NEP. The disastrous Soviet-style command economy gave way to a decentralized market system.

The Czechoslovaks did not master the Hungarian method of soothing the Soviets with Marxist-Leninist lullabies while actually doing whatever seemed best for Czechoslovakia, and their failure doomed the democratic socialist regime that flashed through the Czechoslovak firmament briefly in 1968. Not until late 1967 did Moscow, realizing that the Prague Stalinists had outlived their usefulness, sanction a change in the Czechoslovak party leadership. A group of forward-looking young Communists came to power in 1968 and initiated sweeping reforms: they democratized the party, abolished censorship, curbed the secret police, began the

investigation of past abuses of power, declared they could accept a multiparty system. Led by Alexander Dubček, the reformers proclaimed loyalty to the USSR and insisted they would leave Communist dominance intact.

The reformers operated in the glare of worldwide publicity; their "socialism with a human face" won widespread sympathy in both East and West. Their protests of submission to Moscow did not reassure the men in charge there; reform in Czechoslovakia might well inspire imitation. The Kremlin found itself on the defensive as the "Prague spring" gave way to summer.

In what came to be called the "Brezhnev Doctrine," the USSR proclaimed its right to intervene militarily in any Warsaw Pact country if "internal and external forces hostile to socialism" threatened to push that country "toward restoration of a capitalist regime." That had not happened in Czechoslovakia. The new "doctrine," like the one bearing President Monroe's name, merely justified a great power's hegemony.

Ignoring world—including Communist— public opinion, the USSR invaded Czechoslovakia on August 20, 1968, with the assistance of other Warsaw Pact forces. Resistance ceased within a week. The Brezhnev-Suslov-Kosygin forces, now including the savage new KGB chief, Andropov, resumed the postwar process of incorporating Czechoslovakia into their empire.

Brutal Soviet hypocrisy next surfaced in Poland: the "Mother Country of All Workers"—the USSR—demanded the destruction of a free labor movement. Weakened by the anti-Soviet riots of 1968 and the economic catastrophe it had created, the Gomulka regime slunk out of office in 1970. Under Edward Gierek, its successor promised reform and modernization, to finance which it borrowed heavily abroad. Poland's debt to Western banks leaped from $1.1 billion in January 1971 to $22.3 billion in December 1982 as Gierek tried to make a new industrial revolution. He seemed successful in 1971–1975; the net material product (roughly, GNP minus services) grew at an average annual rate of more than 9 percent, much better than the Soviet performance and only slightly behind that of Romania.

After 1975 the inevitable consequences of living beyond its means on borrowed funds caught up with Poland. Very little of those funds had been used rationally; party bosses squandered billions on projects designed chiefly to reward cronies and extend fiefdoms. The growth rate fell below 3 percent in 1976–1980; industrial production dropped almost 25 percent 1979–1982.

A sharp increase in meat prices in July 1980 touched off a wave of strikes and demonstrations that continued for nearly 18 months. Unofficial labor organizations arose all over the country; at a September meeting they merged into a single national industrial trade union, Solidarity.

In a decision without precedent in the Soviet bloc, a Warsaw court conferred legitimacy on Solidarity in October. The Kremlin immediately summoned Polish party officials to Moscow to warn of possible intervention. The situation seemed to stabilize briefly, but strikes resumed in February 1981; *Pravda* accused Solidarity of receiving CIA funds. A tumultuous summer was capped by a Solidarity Congress in Gdansk at which leaders boldly called for the formation of free trade unions and free elections throughout the Soviet empire. When Soviet fleet exercises just offshore failed to intimidate the meeting, the Kremlin again demanded the Polish Communists take action. General Wojciech Jaruszelski, already prime minister and minister of defense, became party first secretary and prepared for a showdown.

Solidarity and its charismatic leader, Lech Walesa, clearly posed a major threat to the Communist domination of Poland and to the Soviet hold on Eastern Europe. The Brezhnev regime, however, displayed a forbearance unique in the annals of Russo-Polish conflict. The Kremlin anticipated the international outcry that would attend an invasion; it would be all the more fierce because of the election of a Polish pope in 1978. Too, the Soviets were bogged down in a costly, confusing war in Afghanistan, which dictated caution in committing forces elsewhere.

Moscow's patience was not, however, unlimited; General Jaruszelski stepped up the pressure. On December 12, 1981, trade union leaders proposed the establishment of a provisional, noncommunist regime and the holding of free elections. The following day Jaruszelski proclaimed martial law. Solidarity was outlawed; its leaders, and thousands of workers, intellectuals, and students, were arrested.

Though spared the horrors of invasion, Poland was morally shattered. Once again her identity, so thoroughly rooted in Western civilization, threatened to disappear in the East. Nevertheless the reprisals, severe though they were, involved little bloodshed and in some respects were milder than those visited on Czechoslovakia in 1968. Some Solidarity leaders admitted that Jaruszelski was far from the worst of Poland's Communists.*

Soviet efforts to build a strong economic empire in Eastern Europe proved unsuccessful. In 1949 Stalin created the Council for Mutual Economic Assistance (CMEA, or Comecon) and gave it the task of putting a

---

*In April 1989, faced with economic catastrophe, the Jaruszelski regime reached a compromise with Lech Walesa and agreed to the restoration of Solidarity as a legal organization.

gloss on Soviet colonialism in the area. Toward the end of the 1950s, however, the East European countries ceased to be profitable to Moscow. That, and the upheavals of 1956, led to renegotiation of the one-sided trade agreements. Reciprocal trade among CMEA countries (the East European satellites plus Cuba, Mongolia, the USSR, and Vietnam) increased enormously. When the price of Soviet oil and natural gas soared in the 1970s, the East European members went heavily into debt to Moscow.

To deal with that debt and defuse potential social unrest, the Kremlin reversed normal imperialist procedure and began to send cheap raw materials to Eastern Europe and to import inferior manufactured goods from that region. This hidden subsidy, estimated at $1.6 billion in 1973, increased to $20 billion in 1981 but did not offset the increase in Soviet energy prices. And not only were the East European countries in debt to Moscow: between 1970 and 1984 their collective debt to the West increased from $6.0 billion to $55 billion.

## MOSCOW AND BEIJING

When the *troika* failed to patch up relations with China it became clear that the dispute hinged less on ideology than on leadership of the world Communist movement; that would not be settled overnight. Still less amenable to quick solution was a dispute involving huge tracts of land in the Far East and Central Asia seized by tsarist Russia in the 19th and early 20th centuries. Lenin denounced the treaties through which the tsars had taken these areas, but neither he nor his successors saw fit to renegotiate them even after the Chinese Communists came to power in 1949. In the beginning Mao did not press the matter.

Beijing was however determined to settle ancient scores, and Russia was no less guilty than Western powers of abusing China. The Chinese Communists did not demand return of 1.5 million square kilometers they claimed had been stolen by the tsars. They *did* insist on Moscow's acknowledgement that the treaties had been imposed on China by force, and they demanded adjustment of the border. Beijing also maintained that Mongolia, a Soviet satellite, belonged within China's sphere of influence.

The Soviets declared that they bore no more responsibility for the sins of the tsars than Mao for those of the emperors. The treaties were simply part of history. The Mongolian People's Republic, the Kremlin insisted, was an independent nation.

The Soviet and Mongolian frontiers with China stretch more than 7,500 kilometers. In 1962 bands of Chinese soldiers and civilians crossed the border at various points seeking to "absorb" tiny sections of territory. More incursions took place in the next two years; on several occasions minor scuffles with Soviet border guards produced casualties.

The Soviets proposed talks, and topographic maps were exchanged in Khabarovsk in 1964. Chinese maps showed hundreds of border rectifications in Beijing's favor, some moving the line 150 kilometers into the USSR. Moscow declared that the Chinese claims had "no juridical foundation whatsoever ... and do not coincide with lines fixed by ... treaties." The talks collapsed.

The situation continued to deteriorate. That, plus new developments in China's warmaking potential, affected the military provisions of the 1966 Soviet-Mongolian treaty. Moscow's forces had long been stationed in Mongolia, but now the Kremlin despatched more ground troops, tanks, and antiaircraft batteries, some equipped with tactical nuclear weapons. Soviet bases were now only 600 kilometers from Beijing. As Soviet intelligence knew, the Chinese were about to test a rocket with a nuclear warhead.

From May 1966 Mao's Cultural Revolution exacerbated the already tense relations between Beijing and Moscow. When Soviet police in Moscow broke up a demonstration by Chinese students in Red Square in January 1967, Red Guards in Beijing besieged the Soviet embassy and forced a humiliating evacuation of diplomatic dependents. The Chinese press called the USSR "a most reactionary and savage fascist dictatorship."

Violent border clashes erupted in March 1969 on Damyansky (Zhenbao) Island in the Ussuri River about 400 kilometers north of Vladivostok; more than 800 Chinese and 60 Soviet soldiers were killed. Talk of war erupted in both countries. The Kremlin accused Beijing of obtaining arms from West Germany and called Mao a "traitor to communism." Soviet newspapers reported American charges that China was selling 8,000 tons of opium annually to earn hard currency. Brezhnev attacked China at the June 1969 International Conference of Communist and Workers' Parties in Moscow, but opposition from the Romanian, Italian, and other delegations kept criticism of the Chinese to a minimum in the final communiqué.

In late summer 1969 a KGB journalist declared that China was not exempt from the imperatives of the "Brezhnev Doctrine" and that Moscow's readiness to destroy the Chinese nuclear weapons center in Xinjiang Province was "common knowledge." *Pravda* warned that Beijing was risking nuclear war. General V.F. Tolbuko, a rocket specialist, took command of the Soviet Far Eastern Military District. Nuclear missiles deployed against Western Europe were shifted from the western USSR to Central Asia and the Far East.

Kosygin and Zhou Enlai met in Beijing in September 1969 following Hô Chi Minh's funeral in Hanoi and agreed to negotiate the border dispute and other issues. High-level delegations began talks the following month; ambassadors were again exchanged. At precisely this time, however, an ominous cloud appeared on the horizon of Soviet-Chinese relations: rapprochement between China and the United States.

The situation did not improve after Mao's death in September 1976. The two sides had still failed to agree on an agenda for the border talks. Moscow rejected the Chinese demand that it withdraw its military forces from the disputed border areas. In the broader sphere, China rejected Soviet proposals for a nonaggression pact, and in April 1979, shortly after reestablishing full diplomatic relations with the United States, Beijing announced it would not renew the 1950 Sino-Soviet Treaty of Friendship, Alliance, and Mutual Assistance when it expired in 1980.

From 1978 on China repeatedly called the Soviet Union the greatest threat to world peace and sought a grand alliance with the United States, Japan, Western Europe, and some Third World countries to halt Soviet aggression and imperialism. When China invaded a Soviet ally, Vietnam, in February 1979, the Kremlin could not muster world opinion to condemn the attack. The Soviet invasion of Afghanistan later the same year found China and the United States united in opposition.

The Soviets counted on President Reagan's long-standing hostility toward Communist China to cool Washington-Beijing ties. Brezhnev regularly reminded the Chinese that the USSR had always supported their claim to Taiwan, and he offered increased trade and aid. Mongolia agreed in the spring of 1982 to discuss the surveying of its border with China. Wary of such gestures, Beijing repeated its conditions for better relations with Moscow: pullback of the Soviet-Mongolian forces along the frontiers, withdrawal of Soviet forces from Afghanistan, cessation of Soviet support for Vietnam's intervention in Cambodia.

Brezhnev rejected these stipulations, as did his two immediate successors, Andropov and Chernenko. Tempers remained at dangerously high levels.

## THE MIDDLE EAST

In the Middle East the USSR and the United States confronted each other chiefly through unpredictable surrogates. To make matters worse, neither power had a coherent policy for dealing with Arab nationalism, Muslim religious fundamentalism, or ancient conflicts between peoples and religions.

The decisive Israeli victory in the 1967 Middle East War alarmed and humiliated the Kremlin as much as the Arab capitals. Soviet arms proved inferior, Arab troops trained by Soviet advisers performed badly, and the disaster could not be blamed on Khrushchev. There was no choice but to start again. Arms deliveries to Egypt, Syria, and Iraq increased and new teams of advisers were sent to rebuild Arab armies.

Egypt's expulsion of 20,000 Soviet military specialists in 1972 slowed but did not halt the reconstruction. The Arabs gave a much better account of themselves in the 1973 October War, not least because the new military hardware Moscow had sent proved a match for Israeli tanks and aircraft. The Kremlin thus recovered much of its prestige. The Communist party, however, remained outlawed or severely restricted in most Arab states.

Syria proved a no less difficult friend than Egypt. When the Baath (Renaissance) party—closely affiliated with similar parties elsewhere in the Arab world—came to power in 1966, Syria began to make common cause with the USSR in Middle Eastern politics. After the expulsion of its advisers from Egypt, Moscow began to build up Syria as a counterweight to Israel. But the Syrians suffered greater losses than the Egyptians in the 1973 war, especially in tanks. The Soviets had to step in with new tanks, a larger military advisory group, MiG-23 fighters, and surface-to-air missiles.

Disapproving of Syrian participation in the Arab League's intervention in Lebanon, the Kremlin withheld arms deliveries briefly in 1976, only to resume them when United States shipments to Israel upset the military balance in the area. Syria broke with the Soviet-backed leader of the Palestinian Liberation Organization, Yasir Arafat, and over strenuous Kremlin objections sided with Iran in its war with Iraq which began in September 1980.

## THE PERSIAN GULF

Napoleon had urged the Russians to look south, toward the Persian Gulf and the Indian Ocean, to satisfy their expansionist impulses. That would keep them out of the Mediterranean, where France claimed hegemony, and it would bring them into conflict with the British. The tsars sometimes followed his advice, pushing the Empire's frontiers to the south but also to the west. In mid-20th century, however, a powerful Germany stood in the way of further advance in the west, and Russia's Communist rulers were anxious to avoid conflict there. Agreeing in principle to adhere to a Four-Power Pact with Germany, Italy, and Japan, in November 1940 Moscow stated as one of its conditions "that the area south of Batum and Baku in the general direction of the Persian Gulf is recognized as the center of the aspirations of the Soviet Union."

The immediate Soviet objective in 1940 was Iran. The 1921 treaty between that country and Lenin's regime specified the action to be taken should Iran itself be threatened or a third country seek to use it as a base for aggression against Russia: "If the Persian Government, having been alerted by the Russian Soviet Government, is not itself able to avert the danger, the Russian Soviet Government will have the right to send its forces into the territory of Persia in order, in the interests of self-defense, to take the necessary military measures." Stalin cited the 1921 agreement to justify keeping his troops in northern Iran until May 1946; and the USSR on several occasions refused to accept Iran's unilateral renunciation of the treaty clause sanctioning Soviet intervention.

When the British withdrew from the Persian Gulf in the late 1960s, Shah Muhammed Reza Pahlavi, with the backing of London and Washington, assumed the role of policeman of the area. Suspicious of Pahlavi's megalomania, the Arab states nevertheless welcomed his efforts to eradicate Communist influence. The shah armed Iran with enormous quantities of expensive Western weapons, to pay for which—having obtained American consent—he raised the price of his oil.

The shah's action helped precipitate the energy crisis of 1973–1974. As world oil prices leaped the Persian Gulf became the object of intensified Western and Soviet attention. Kosygin warned in November 1973 that the USSR, the world's largest oil producer, faced a shortage and might have to increase imports from the Middle East and Persian Gulf well above the 6 million tons (2 percent of consumption) of 1972.

Despite their differences the Soviet Union and Iran had reasonably good relations in the 1960s and 1970s. Iranian natural gas went to the USSR through a jointly operated pipeline and small quantities of Iranian oil fueled Soviet factories and military installations in Central Asia and the Caucasus. The two governments sometimes cooperated in attempts to bring the Kurdish nomads who roamed freely across frontiers under control.

The shah fell early in 1979 to the Shiite Muslim fundamentalists of the Ayatollah Ruollah Khomeini. The Soviets relished the discomfort of the United States, which lost its staunchest client in the region and suffered the further humiliation of having many of its diplomatic personnel held hostage for more than a year. One of the new regime's most passionate slogans, however, was "Neither East nor West!" The Ayatollah's unquestionably sincere denunciation of the American "devil" was motivated in part by a desire to keep the USSR at bay by convincing it of Iran's implacable hostility toward the United States.

Concern about the effect of the Iranian revolution in particular and the Islamic revival in general on the 50 million Soviet citizens of Muslim heritage played a significant role in the Kremlin's decision to invade Afghanistan in December 1979. The world wondered whether Iran would suffer the same fate; Soviet radio broadcasts from Baku regularly hinted at such a possibility. The Kremlin likewise made no secret of its interest in the 3 million Azeri Turks in northwest Iran. There were 5 million Azeris in the Azerbaijani SSR, and the USSR had briefly established an "independent" Azeri state in Iran after World War II. In the war between Iran and Iraq the Soviets outraged the Iranian fundamentalists, who saw the conflict as a *jihad* or holy war, by adopting a neutral stance.

Moscow proved to have as little understanding of the Khomeini revolution as did Washington. It groomed the Tudeh (Communist) party to inherit that revolution, seeing in Khomeini a mere Kerensky. But Khomeini outlawed the party, expelled a number of Soviet diplomats early in 1983, and stepped up support of the anti-Soviet guerrillas in Afghanistan.

The Soviet Union learned it would have to deal with Iran as patiently as it did with Iraq, a fiercely anticommunist country with perhaps the most volatile political tradition in the Arab world. There were more Communists in Iraq than in any other Arab nation, but after a right-wing military coup d'état in 1963 all known party members were imprisoned and many executed. There was a shift back to the left a few years later, however, and although the ban on the Communist party remained in effect the new regime sought better relations with the USSR. Moscow sent technicians and marketing experts and helped construct a modern naval base near the head of the Persian Gulf. Partly in exchange for docking facilities, the Soviets sent large quantities of arms, making the Iraqi army the best-equipped in the region.

Soviet policies appeared to backfire in September 1980 when war erupted between Iraq and Iran. For all its Khrushchevian adventurism the Kremlin did not want war in an area where American, West European, Japanese, South African, and Israeli interests coincided. In the late 1970s about 70 percent of Western Europe's oil passed through the gulf and the Strait of Hormuz, as did 90 percent of Japan's, almost all of South Africa's and Israel's. United States imports had declined after the fall of the shah, but every post-1945 president had warned that Washington would resist any attempt to block the gulf.

The Soviet Union declared its neutrality in the Iran-Iraq war, suspended arms deliveries to Iraq, and tried unsuccessfully to mediate. Only when President Saddam Hussein threatened to mend Iraq's relations with the United States—broken off after the 1967 Middle East War—did the Kremlin resume weapons shipments.

Moscow registered one of its rare long-term successes in the Arab world in Yemen, with which it established cordial relations in 1955. Both Britain and Egypt opposed Communist influence in the Arabian Peninsula, however, and tried to halt its spread. But Nasser had to withdraw his troops after the 1967 war with Israel, and Britain ended its police mission east of Suez at about the same time. These developments enabled the USSR to intervene militarily in the 1967 Yemeni civil war on the Communist side. In the partition which followed the conflict, the extreme left-wing Southern Yemen regime allied itself closely with the Soviet Union, which thus gained the use of the port of Aden and a British-built airfield. The Yemeni-controlled island of Socotra near the entrance to the Gulf of Aden was also at the disposal of the Soviet military.

## AFGHANISTAN

After World War II the sleepy feudal monarchy of Afghanistan was drawn into Persian Gulf politics because it shared frontiers with the Soviet Union and Iran, into South and East Asian politics because it had a common border with China and Pakistan. The Soviets built roads and tunnels in the high mountains; the Chinese built the Karakorum Highway from Xinjiang through Afghanistan to Pakistan; the United States spent huge sums on various major construction projects.

Under the monarchy, Western influence appeared to hold sway over the government and the tiny intelligentsia. With the ouster of King Muhammad Zahir Shah and the proclamation of a republic in 1973, however, Afghanistan became unstable. The People's Democratic party (Communist) came to power in an April 1978 coup d'état and a few months later signed a 20-year Treaty of

Friendship, Good-Neighborliness, and Co-operation with the Kremlin. Moscow sent economic aid; Soviet civilian and military advisers were given free run of the country.

Russia had never been popular with the people of Afghanistan and the formation of a Communist regime in Kabul did not alter that. In the spring of 1979 more than 200 Soviet advisers were killed in riots in Herat. Attacks on Soviet personnel became so common that many took to wearing ersatz "cowboy" garb in an attempt to pass as Americans.

Events elsewhere had an impact upon Afghanistan. The Soviets feared U.S. military intervention in Iran after the seizure of its embassy in Tehran in November 1979. The following month, the NATO Council approved an American plan to install nuclear missiles in Western Europe, and the United States Senate appeared ready to block the SALT II treaty. Also in 1979, China established full diplomatic relations with the United States, announced its intention to terminate the 1950 treaty with the USSR, and went to war against a Soviet ally, Vietnam.

To complicate matters for the Kremlin, three charismatic national leaders on the southern and southwestern flanks of the USSR had recently fallen: Sheik Mujibur Ali Rahman of Bangladesh in 1975, Zulfikar Ali Bhutto of Pakistan in 1977, and the shah of Iran in January 1979. Sternly anticommunist military rulers came to power in Bangladesh and Pakistan, and Muslim fundamentalists took control in Iran. Bangladesh and Pakistan both had close ties to China. Iran under Khomeini promised to create great mischief throughout the Islamic world, including the USSR.

The available evidence indicates that, because of the deteriorating political situation in South Asia, Moscow decided at the end of the summer of 1979 to send troops to Afghanistan to crush the anticommunist

guerrillas and strengthen its military posture near the Persian Gulf. The Kremlin's timetable collapsed, however, when puppet President N.M. Taraki was killed in September in a clash with his chief rival, Hafizullah Amin. An unstable journalist-politician, Amin became president despite Soviet suspicions that he had become too cozy with the CIA during a period of study in the United States. He launched a bloody campaign against the guerrillas.

Declaring there was nothing unusual about the buildup of troops and materiel on its frontiers with Afghanistan, the Kremlin likewise denied reports of displeasure with Amin. On Christmas Eve, 1979, the Soviet Army began airlifting four divisions into airports near Kabul. With the aid of some Afghan units, Soviet forces staged a coup d'état on December 26–27 in which Amin was killed. It would appear that he refused to yield his office to a pliant Soviet creature, Babrak Karmal, installed as president following the coup.

The invasion force that rapidly swelled to more than 110,000 troops took control of the cities and key points around the country. Kabul radio broadcast appeals for calm and praised Soviet "fraternal assistance."

The outside world condemned the invasion, first of its kind in peacetime beyond the frontiers of Moscow's satellites since Lenin tried to bolshevize Poland in 1920. In the United States, the Carter administration withdrew the SALT II treaty from Senate consideration, pulled out of the 1980 Moscow Olympic Games, and suspended shipments of grain beyond those specified in earlier agreements. The Soviet harvest of 1979 had fallen far short of goals, and Carter's Soviet experts, ignorant of the history of the siege of Leningrad, tried to use food as a weapon.

Ominously, from not only the Soviet viewpoint but also New Delhi's, the United States lifted its ban on military aid to Pakistan. China and several Arab nations increased their military aid to the Islamabad regime. After some hesitation, the Ayatollah Khomeini denounced the invasion and promised aid to the Afghan guerrillas.

A broad, diverse coalition took shape as the United States, China, Pakistan, Egypt, Saudi Arabia, some of the smaller Arab states, and several Muslim nations rallied to the anti-Soviet cause in Afghanistan. Even the cautious Japanese sent sophisticated communications equipment through third parties. No nation, however, sent troops. The material aid, though pathetically small in the beginning and hardly generous until the mid-1980s, did enable the fight against the invaders to continue.

Split into four major factions and innumerable smaller ones, the Afghan guerrillas found their lack of unity almost as great an enemy as the Soviet forces. Nevertheless, they never controlled less than three-quarters of the countryside. They killed about 2,000 Soviet soldiers each year and lost several times that number of their own. Civilian casualties were astronomical, and more than a quarter of the prewar population of about 15 million sought to escape Soviet terror bombing by fleeing to Pakistan.

The Soviet press did not comment on a tragic record set on November 13, 1983. As of that date, the Soviet Army had fought one day longer in Afghanistan than in World War II, and there was no end in sight. The political situation remained as unstable as the war itself, the Karmal regime the prisoner of its dependence on Moscow. So long as Soviet forces remained the guerrillas could not win; neither would they be defeated.

Their political goals eluded them, but the Soviets achieved some strategic objectives. Construction of a bridge across the Amu

Darya at Termez in Uzbekistan began in December 1979 with a suddenness that indicated the invasion and occupation had been long in the planning; work was completed early in 1982. Soviet forces occupied the strategic Wakhan corridor, a narrow, extremely mountainous finger of Afghanistan surrounded by Soviet, Chinese, and Pakistani territory. The Kremlin soon announced "border adjustments" in its own favor in that corridor. In the west the Soviets built a military airport at Shindand, 900 kilometers from the Strait of Hormuz.

The threat on the Soviet southern flank neither excused the antipersonnel mines scattered indiscriminately around Afghanistan to take heavy civilian casualties nor explained the use of poison gas, napalm, helicopter gunships, tanks, and heavy artillery against villagers equipped until 1985 with vintage rifles and little else. Using the cruel logic of great-power politics, however, the Soviet Union, fighting just across its own southern frontier, called offense "defense," and destruction—"liberation."

Until 1986 the Kremlin did not have to contend with an informed public opinion. But it could not bury thousands of Soviet soldiers in secret, hide the wounded and disabled, or suppress the bitter antiwar songs—many composed by soldiers—of the younger generation. Forever inundated by state propaganda concerning the glories of Soviet arms in World War II, the public interpreted the official silence correctly: the leaders had embarked on a policy of genocide in Afghanistan and did not care how many Soviet soldiers died in enforcing it.

## AFRICA

The Soviet Union appeared to win a major diplomatic victory in 1974 when it persuaded Somalia to become the first Black

African nation to sign a treaty of friendship and cooperation. Arms and aid flowed into the desperately poor country on the Horn of Africa and Soviet crews built naval and air installations. Already ensconced in Southern Yemen, with considerable influence in Djibouti and in the breakaway Ethiopian province of Eritrea, the Soviet Union was thus in a position to dominate the Gulf of Aden and the Strait of Bab al Mandab. Thus it could easily choke off the flow of Persian Gulf oil to the West. Hoping to solidify its position and counterpose a Marxist federation to the anti-Soviet alliance of Egypt and the Sudan, in March 1977 the Kremlin despatched Fidel Castro to the region to reconcile two potential members.

The centuries-old enmity between Muslim Somalia and Christian Ethiopia had not evaporated when Marxists seized power in both countries and did not fade under the impact of Castro's charm. Shortly after the Cuban leader's visit to the Gulf of Aden, however, the military regime in Addis Ababa broke with the United States and asked the USSR for military and economic assistance. Gambling that they could hold Somalia's allegiance, the Soviets promised $500 million worth of arms to Ethiopia; this brought them into the conflict between the two countries.

Somalia invaded Ogaden, an Ethiopian province inhabited by Somali tribespeople, in July 1977. When Moscow sided with the Ethiopians, Somalia broke relations and turned to the West for help.

With the aid of 10,000 Cuban troops and Cuban pilots flying Soviet aircraft, Ethiopia drove the enemy forces out of Ogaden early in 1978. They halted at the frontier, enabling Cubans and Soviets to fulfill their promises to limit intervention to the defense of Ethiopian territory.

The "loss" of Somalia was offset by gains in Ethiopia. The southern approaches to the Suez Canal, which had reopened in June 1975 after an eight-year shutdown, remained under Soviet surveillance and potential domination. One major goal in Africa had been achieved.

Another objective was to establish a measure of control over African strategic minerals. Neither Ethiopia nor Somalia had any significant such resources, but other nations with which the USSR was deeply involved did. The establishing of close ties with the Addis Ababa regime appeared to provide an ideal base from which the Soviets could, in time of crisis, threaten the flow of those resources to NATO countries.

The Soviets and Cubans intervened in the 1975–1976 civil war in Angola and large numbers remained in the country as military advisers and technicians. Angola became a base from which Soviet influence percolated throughout West Africa. Moscow also had good relations with Nigeria, which permitted Soviet ships to use its ports. Guinea served as a Soviet military staging area. In Zimbabwe the Soviet Union and Cuba backed Joshua Nkomo's guerrilla faction, which was eventually defeated by a rival group with Chinese backing. A Marxist party ruled in Mozambique. In North Africa the erratic Libyan dictator, Colonel Qaddafi, welcomed Soviet arms and served Soviet interests by backing terrorists in the Middle East and Europe. By early 1984 Soviet or Cuban military and technical advisers were serving in 14 African nations, and Moscow had treaties of friendship with Angola, Mozambique, Ethiopia, and Congo.

And yet the Soviet position that had seemed so strong in the spring of 1978 appeared far less impressive a few years later. Only a half-dozen of Africa's 50 countries espoused Marxism-Leninism as their official ideology. Soviet influence remained roughly as great as that of the United States but was eclipsed in North Africa by that of

Libya, in West and Central Africa and Madagascar by that of France, and the Republic of South Africa remained the dominant power in the south.

## INDIA

The most substantial Soviet triumph in the Third World came not in Africa but in India, which had benefited from massive Kremlin aid since the 1950s. The Soviets cemented their friendship by consistently supporting India against Pakistan and backing her—after some early confusion—in the border dispute with China. When India defeated Pakistan in the December 1971 war, Soviet prestige soared throughout the Third World.

The ties between Moscow and New Delhi were mutually beneficial. The Kremlin gained a friend who served as a bulwark against China and regularly supported Soviet interests in the United Nations and around the world. The Indians received billions of rubles in economic aid, using them to build a solid industrial base. Paradoxically, the very success of this industrialization, in which the United States and other nations also participated, threatened to weaken India's ties to her chief benefactor. The USSR could supply factories, heavy machinery, oil, and arms, but it had relatively little to contribute to the building of a post-industrial economy. India increasingly turned to the West and Japan for technology.

## LATIN AMERICA

Some of the same factors that facilitated Soviet penetration of India also applied to Latin America, where communism's best allies were poverty, disease, ignorance, corruption, economic imperialism, and despair.

The success of the Castro revolution in Cuba vitiated the Monroe Doctrine and cleared the way for expansion of Communist activity in the Western Hemisphere. The USSR delegated the direction of revolutionary insurgencies to Castro, however, and filtered subsidies to Communist parties through Havana.

The Soviets did not mastermind every guerrilla insurgency and land reform movement in Latin America, but fear of Soviet machinations led the United States to topple a democratically elected government in Guatemala in 1954. When J. Edgar Hoover discovered 53 Communists in the Dominican Republic in 1965, President Johnson sent in 20,000 American troops. Moscow did have some influence—less than Washington believed—on the Socialist regime of Salvador Allende, elected president of Chile in 1970 despite massive American support of a pliant conservative rival. An erratic reformer unquestionably naive about the real aims of his Chilean Communist allies and their Moscow masters, Allende died in the 1973 *coup* that brought an American-sponsored fascist dictator, Augusto Pinochet, to power.

In the 1980s the USSR provided extensive economic and suspiciously large military aid to the leftist Sandinista regime in Nicaragua, which had come to power after overthrowing another American puppet, Anastasio Somoza. Through Cuba, the Kremlin supported a left-wing insurgency in El Salvador against the landed oligarchy and its quasi-military "death squads."

All this activity in Latin America reflected a Soviet decision to step up pressure on a United States that had lost some of its enthusiasm for foreign misadventures after the Vietnam disaster. The Soviets calculated each move carefully, however, apparently never entertaining any thought of sending troops to the Western Hemisphere.

## THE WEST

Khrushchev's successors compiled an uneven record in dealing with Eastern Europe, China, and the Third World, but on the whole managed their relations with the West cleverly: obliging the West to recognize the USSR as a military equal stands as the greatest political triumph in Soviet history. Another major goal was achieved when 35 heads of state signed the Final Act of the Conference on Security and Cooperation in Europe (CSCE, or Helsinki Conference) in Helsinki on August 1, 1975. The signatories promised to respect each other as equals, refrain from using force to settle disputes, and recognize each other's territorial integrity. This legitimized the postwar division of Europe and sanctioned the creation of the Soviet empire.

A "second basket" of agreements pledged the nations of Europe, the United States, and Canada, to expand cooperation in trade, scientific and technological exchanges, protection of the environment, and tourism. The "third basket" promised an increase in human contacts, including an increase in the exchange of information, improved working conditions for foreign correspondents, extension of cultural and educational exchanges, and reunification of families.

The Soviet Union touted the security provisions of the Final Act as a great victory, found nothing controversial in the "second basket," almost totally ignored the provisions for improved human contacts. The Helsinki Conference, which became a permanent institution, gave the Soviets what they wanted, the West a lesson in the art of interpreting agreements.

The Western allies and especially the United States found it difficult to accept the loss of the military superiority they had enjoyed since 1945. Relations began to sour in the late 1970s, and when a new adminis-tration came to power in Washington in 1981 pledging to restore Western supremacy, political observers in both countries began to speak of a new Cold War.

Soviet policy toward the West was grounded in the belief that socialism was winning the great struggle with capitalism. By the 1970s more than half the world's people lived under mixed capitalist-socialist, socialist, or communist regimes. Socialist governments succeeded right-wing dictatorships in Spain and Portugal, France elected a Socialist president, Italy's first Socialist prime minister took office in 1983. Colonialism had died, and Soviet ideologists declared capitalism in deep, protracted crisis.

Persistent attacks on an allegedly moribund system indicated Kremlin strategists knew the opponent remained strong. In the post–World War II world, capitalism had made a spectacular comeback in the Federal Republic of Germany (West Germany); nowhere did the Soviet Union press so hard to reverse the tide.

The original Soviet goal in defeated Germany, permanent demilitarization, proved elusive. Moscow settled for partition, a solution far from disagreeable to the nations of Western Europe. The Soviets claimed the right to do as they wished in their zone of occupation but contested the West's right to unify its three zones into an independent state. Unable to prevent that, Moscow also failed to prevent the Federal Republic from joining NATO. The USSR did, however, draw a nonnegotiable line: nuclear weapons in West German hands would mean war.

American strategists wanted to equip the West German Bundeswehr with tactical nuclear weapons, but the opposition of Western—including West German—public opinion, and of France's de Gaulle and other political figures, thwarted such plans. The Soviets thus "won" on this issue. Former Nazis served in the Bundeswehr, however, and thousands of Hitler's civilian officials were posted throughout the West German bureaucracy, even the judiciary. A small but ominous neo-Nazi movement won headlines in the 1960s. The Soviets, overlooking the presence of many ex-Nazis in the East German bureaucracy, notably in the secret police, vigorously protested these developments in the Federal Republic.

The coming to power of the Social Democrats in October 1969 led to a reconciliation not only between Bonn and Moscow but also between the two German states. The new government promptly signed the Non-Proliferation Treaty, formally renouncing nuclear weapons. A relieved Soviet Union began negotiations with West German representatives on December 8 and signed a treaty in August 1970. The Bonn regime accepted the Oder-Neisse line as the permanent frontier between East Germany and Poland and thus abandoned any claim to German territory lost as a result of World War II.

The defusing of tensions in Central Europe continued. In October 1971 a Quadripartite Agreement on Berlin regulated access to the divided city within a divided nation and codified the four occupying powers' understanding of West Berlin's relationship to the Federal Republic. The two German states established virtually complete diplomatic relations in May 1973, exchanging representatives rather than ambassadors, and in September 1974 the United States formally recognized the German Democratic Republic.

West Germany became a major Soviet trading partner. In 1977 annual bilateral trade reached a value of $5 billion and stabilized around that figure. The largest deal involved a Bonn contract for Soviet natural gas over a 25-year period. West German firms supplied much of the equipment for the construction of a pipeline from Siberia.

The Soviet-West German rapprochement helped Poland avoid Czechoslovakia's fate. The Christian Democratic regime in Bonn had imperfectly disguised its support of the 1968 Czechoslovak reformers, increasing Soviet paranoia and contributing in some measure in the decision to invade. In 1980–1981 the Social Democratic government, despite its sympathy for Solidarity, scrupulously avoided meddling in the explosive situation in Poland. The Bonn authorities even persuaded the Dresdner Bank of West Germany to arrange a $675 million loan to Warsaw in 1980 to ease the economic crisis.

After the deaths of dictators in Spain and Portugal the USSR established diplomatic relations with those countries. Communists entered the cabinet in France in 1981. Britain expelled more than 100 Soviet diplomatic personnel for espionage in 1971 but four years later granted Moscow $2.39 billion in low-interest credits for the purchase of British goods. European interests financed and helped construct a huge automotive plant at Naberezhnye Chelny after Washington denied the Ford Motor Company permission to participate. France and Italy joined West Germany in making long-term contracts for Soviet natural gas, and all three countries, plus Britain and Japan, defied the United States and supplied pipeline equipment to the USSR.

The Kremlin often had better relations with "bourgeois" governments in Western Europe than with national Communist parties. The leaders of the Spanish and Italian parties, Santiago Carillo and Enrico Berlinguer (who died in 1984), were in the vanguard of a "Eurocommunist" movement that saw several West European parties declare independence from Moscow. They frequently opposed the Soviets on major issues—for example, the invasion of Afghanistan—and rejected Soviet attempts to dictate their political strategy.

Unable to seal all the cracks in its own far-flung empire, the USSR was adept at exploiting differences within the capitalist camp. When American firms withdrew under pressure from Washington, Japan participated heavily in the development of a number of gigantic projects in Siberia and helped the Soviets develop an oil find off Sakhalin Island. Argentina and Canada gladly filled huge orders for grain when political developments curtailed deliveries from the United States. Moscow cooperated with the racist government of South Africa in a number of lucrative trade deals.

East-West trade developed in spurts, notably in 1973–1976 when the value of Soviet imports from the industrialized countries increased 101 percent. The USSR imported $3 billion worth of goods from the West in 1970, $26 billion in 1980. In June 1983, however, the total Soviet hard-currency debt to the West stood at more than $28.7 billion. For 40 months following the invasion of Afghanistan the West did not grant any substantial loans to Moscow. Then, in May 1984, an international consortium led by Dresdner Bank agreed to lend $250 million; no United States bank participated.

The USSR normally received preferential treatment from Western bankers. However inefficient, the country's huge economy could absorb reasonable debts, and after 1973 its hard-currency reserves increased dramatically as the price of oil and gold—the USSR is the leading producer of both—soared. The Soviets also managed their debt carefully, keeping the ratio of debt service to current earnings at about 16 percent in the early 1980s.

American businessmen were no less eager than their counterparts abroad to participate in the lucrative Soviet market, but shifting political winds in Washington made it difficult to establish a stable Soviet-American trade, especially in the area of grain sales.

In June 1972 President Nixon announced the largest grain transaction in history. The Soviet Union would purchase a minimum of $750 million worth of American wheat, corn, and soybeans over three years. In reality, the Kremlin purchased much more. The following spring Brezhnev predicted a long-term Soviet need for American grain and asked for an expansion of trade. He proposed a 30- or 40-year pact permitting the USSR to buy millions of tons of grain annually, to be paid for with increased Soviet exports to the United States of raw materials, oil, and certain specialized equipment.

Stung by the domestic outcry over the 1972 deal, Washington was wary of such lengthy commitments, and in any event Nixon fell before a new agreement could be negotiated. In October 1975 President Ford signed a five-year pact which *obligated* the Soviets to buy 6 million tons of wheat or corn annually and *permitted* them to buy up to 8 million tons without advance notice. The agreement seemed certain to help solve the perennial Soviet agricultural crisis, and it was of enormous benefit to American farmers and grain companies. From 1976, when it took effect, through 1979, the United States accounted for 70 percent of the Soviet grain trade.

To punish the USSR for its invasion of Afghanistan, President Carter embargoed all but the minimum sales required by the 1975 agreement. He could not, however, halt sales by Canada, Argentina, or West European countries. The 1980 harvest was good around the world; the Soviets easily found other sources. The American share of the Soviet market fell to 20 percent. President Reagan, drawing a distinction between technology—sales of which his administration sought to restrict—and grain, lifted the embargo in 1981.

The 1972 grain deal represented a by-product of Nixonian détente. Moscow had braced itself for confrontation when Nixon came to the presidency, but there ensued a period of cordiality and cooperation.

Nixon and Kissinger widened the Vietnam War—sanctioning the near-total destruction of defenseless Cambodia—even as they attempted to negotiate the American defeat, supported Pakistan against a Soviet friend, India, and initiated rapprochement with Beijing. That the Kremlin maintained normal, even warm relations with the United States through all this reflected the unprincipled cynicism that reigned in both Moscow and Washington.

The most dramatic, if not necessarily most meaningful, fruit of détente, the 1972 Anti-ABM Treaty, brought SALT I to a conclusion. The following year, Soviet leaders expressed relief when the disgraced Nixon's successor, Gerald Ford, announced his retention of Henry Kissinger. The Soviets had made great gains against the United States in the Nixon-Kissinger years; with the inexperienced Ford in charge, they anticipated still more. Brezhnev and Ford appeared to sustain the friendly momentum of those years when, at their November 1974 meeting in Vladivostok, they outlined a new agreement to regulate the nuclear arms race. Developments on the American political scene, however, threatened the proposed agreement and clouded relations in general.

The Soviets were clearly anxious to trade, and some American politicians demanded that the administration extract concessions in the area of human rights, notably the right of Soviet citizens to emigrate. Passed over the objections of Ford and Kissinger, the Jackson-Vanik Amendment to the 1974 Trade Act linked most-favored-nation status and special trade credits for the USSR to the emigration of Jews and other citizens. Protesting interference in its internal affairs, the Kremlin refused to give any public assurances on emigration. Trade continued

to increase despite the new tensions, but emigration remained at low levels until 1979. In that year the Soviets signalled their satisfaction over the conclusion of the SALT II treaty and new grain agreements by permitting a record number of citizens (51,320) to leave. Because of the events in Afghanistan and other issues, however, trade declined after 1979 and by 1983 emigration had virtually ceased.

Soviet-American contacts continued to grow despite the Carter administration's attempt to inject a confrontational Christian morality into international affairs; not since Alexander I of Russia sponsored the Holy Alliance had the world seen anything quite like this. The Kremlin was first astonished, then outraged. The Brezhnev regime denounced Carter's criticism of Soviet violations of human rights and repeatedly threatened to break off arms control talks. Negotiations and contacts, however, went forward; the SALT II agreement was signed in 1979 and trade continued at levels far above those of a decade earlier. Sophisticated American computers and other "high-tech" items went to the USSR in increasing quantities, sometimes through third countries when Washington attempted to impose restrictions. The United States imported small quantities of such strategic commodities as enriched uranium, titanium, manganese, and oil from the Soviet Union.

The Soviets did not like Carter but managed to deal with him. The 1979 NATO decision to deploy American nuclear missiles in Europe, however, ensured that no American president would be able to maintain anything more than formally correct relations with Moscow. The 1980 election of Ronald Reagan was followed by the unraveling of many of the ties that had been established between the two countries since 1969. Themselves proponents of an all-embracing ideology, the Soviet leaders could not adjust to the most ideological American president of the century. Accustomed to denouncing the West and the United States in particular with reckless abandon, and to predicting the imminent collapse of capitalism, the Soviets were outraged when Reagan referred to their "evil empire" and declared that the revolutionary overthrow of the Soviet regime loomed in the not-too-distant future.

## TWO DECADES OF SOVIET DIPLOMACY

Soviet leaders expressed contempt for Presidents Carter and Reagan and succeeded in convincing the Soviet public that the United States bore the responsibility for the rise in international tensions. Perplexed when their own threatening words and actions strengthened the resolve of the West to resist the extension of Soviet power and influence, the men in the Kremlin capitalized on the threats coming out of Washington to rally their own people and prepare them for the possibility of enormous sacrifices. In the spring of 1984 Radio Moscow began playing patriotic popular songs associated with the 1939–1941 period.

The USSR championed revolutionary change everywhere save in its own empire. The West tended to resist change everywhere *except* in the Soviet empire. Neither side could compromise. Each probed constantly for weaknesses, and the wonder was not that there were serious clashes but that those clashes invariably took place through surrogates on at least one side and did not lead to war between the two superpowers.

Approving change and seeking to profit from it are not the same as causing it; the Soviet Union frequently received blame for events over which it had little control. Developments in the Middle East and the Persian Gulf moved at a pace far beyond the capabilities of strategic planners in either Moscow or Washington. Volatile black Africa gave the USSR more defeats than victories. No Soviet leader dared count such dictators as Colonel Qaddafi as friends. The problems of Latin America antedated the Soviets and Fidel Castro by generations. Nothing could justify the blatant aggression in Afghanistan, yet even there the Kremlin confronted genuine dilemmas.

The little wars went on, wars in which most of the victims were strangers to the inhabitants of Leningrad and New York, but always the great question was, Will there be war between the superpowers? Despite the tensions and scares of the post-1945 period there seemed to be little danger that either side would deliberately launch an attack. The real threat was war by accident, or war concocted by the machinations of terrorists or client states, especially in the Middle East.

## SUGGESTED ADDITIONAL READING

**Anwar, Raja,** *The Tragedy of Afghanistan,* New York: Verso, 1988

**Bloomfield, Lincoln P.,** *Khrushchev and the Arms Race,* Cambridge: MIT Press, 1966

**Bradsher, Henry S.,** *Afghanistan and the Soviet Union,* Durham, N.C.: Duke University Press, 1983

**Edmonds, Robin,** *Soviet Foreign Policy 1962–1973,* London: Oxford University Press, 1975

———, *Soviet Foreign Policy: The Brezhnev Years,* New York: Oxford University Press, 1983

**Garthoff, Raymond L.,** *Détente and Confrontation: American-Soviet Relations from Nixon to Reagan,* Washington: Brookings Institution, 1985

**Gervasi, Tom,** *The Myth of Soviet Military Supremacy,* New York: Harper & Row, 1986

**Haykal, Muhammed,** *The Sphinx and the Commissar,* New York: Harper & Row, 1978

**Hersh, Seymour M.,** *The Price of Power: Kissinger in the Nixon White House,* New York: Summit Books, 1983

**Holloway, David,** *The Soviet Union and the Arms Race,* New Haven, Conn.: Yale University Press, 1983

**Kissinger, H.A.,** *White House Years,* Boston: Little, Brown, 1979

**Markov, Georgi,** *The Truth That Killed,* New York: Ticknor and Fields, 1984

**McGwire, Michael,** *Military Objectives in Soviet Foreign Policy,* Washington: Brookings Institution, 1987

**Porter, Bruce D.,** *The Soviet Union in Third World Conflicts,* Cambridge, England: Cambridge University Press, 1984

**Sakharov, Andrei D.,** *My Country and the World,* New York: Knopf, 1975

**Stevenson, Richard W.,** *The Rise and Fall of Détente,* Urbana and Chicago: University of Illinois Press, 1985

**Terry, Sarah M., ed.,** *Soviet Policy in Eastern Europe,* New Haven, Conn.: Yale University Press, 1984

**Valenta, Jiri,** *Soviet Intervention in Czechoslovakia, 1968,* Baltimore: Johns Hopkins University Press, 1979

**Wozniuk, Vladimir,** *From Crisis to Crisis: Soviet-Polish Relations in the 1970s,* Ames: Iowa State University Press, 1987

# 22

# INTERREGNUM

Where was the Soviet Union to turn after Brezhnev? No constitutional or traditional mechanism for the transfer of power existed. Brezhnev had created a kind of vice-presidency, but the "presidency" itself—chairmanship of the Supreme Soviet Presidium—had a largely ceremonial character. For nearly 60 years real power had reposed in the office of party general secretary; and only the Central Committee can elect or depose the holder of that office. In practice the Politburo makes a recommendation to the Committee, which so far as the public knows has always unanimously endorsed its choice. There is no statutory mechanism for dealing with a deadlocked Politburo or Central Committee.

## ANDROPOV

Within 48 hours of Brezhnev's demise, a docile Central Committee endorsed the Politburo's recommendation of its own most powerful member, Yuri Andropov, for the post of general secretary. He would soon add the chairmanship of both Supreme Soviet and Defense Council to his portfolio.

Andropov's character was carved from the same stone that produced Dostoevsky's austere, coldly rational Grand Inquisitor; the French ambassador compared him to a computer. The KGB had launched a disinformation campaign about its chief in 1980, coincidentally with his assumption of all Leonid Brezhnev's domestic decision-making functions. The drive lifted Andropov out of the Lubyanka's designed obscurity to make him an instant friend of democratic reforms and free thought in general, a patron of the arts. One of his admirers, the historian Roy Medvedev, wrote that Andropov was "an outwardly urbane and civilized leader, a man of intellectual interests . . . fond of painting and music, fluent in English, German, and Hungarian . . . a good conversationalist." This bizarre public-relations offensive continued in a hagiographic film commissioned by Andropov but only released after his death.

In the mid-1970s, as the "Dnepropetrovsk mafia's" rampant corruption became a nationwide scandal and Brezhnev himself sank into senility, the morale of the young generation of party and government officials, including economic managers, plant directors, and the intellectual and scientific establishment, fell alarmingly. Only military commanders approved Brezhnev-era economic priorities. Many mid-level civilian bureaucrats, including Mikhail Gorbachev, owed their careers wholly or in part to Yuri Andropov and looked to him to reverse the slide of the nation's economic fortunes and restore its moral fiber.

Hope for reform quickly faded for all but those who welcomed KGB control of the country. Gravely ill when he assumed power, Andropov proved incapable of initiating new directions.

Wrongheaded economic theories and a gargantuan military buildup had distorted the economy catastrophically. As Vasily Selyunin wrote early in 1988,

truly tectonic shifts toward manufacture of producer goods . . . have put us in a paradoxical situation where accelerated rates of development and more rapid growth in national income have little effect on the standard of living. More and more the economy works for itself, rather than for man.

Another economist, noting the USSR's long-standing supremacy in most branches of heavy industry, called in question the need for stupendous quantities of steel and heavy machinery:

What good is it [Otto Latsis asked] that we produce 6.5 times more tractors than the United States? Or 16 times more grain-harvesting combines? You can't eat tractors and combines . . . despite our abundance of combines, we harvest only two-thirds as much grain [as the USA].

Soviet planners and managers clung to gross-output indices as reliable indicators of economic health, but decades of "the more, the better" produced an indigestible glut.

Selyunin called attention to the fact that in 1928, the last year of NEP, 60.5 percent of all Soviet output went into consumer goods. By 1985, long after the nation had industrialized and recovered from World War II, the figure had fallen to 25.2 percent; the Soviet Union supported a space-age military machine on the back of a Third-World civilian economy. Rockets carrying humans soared into space, but the nation could not feed, clothe, or house itself properly, let alone provide high-quality disposable-income items common in all developed countries.

Andropov would be remembered not for genuine reforms—none materialized—but for the KGB sweeps that struck the large cities at the outset of his regime. In search of people taking unauthorized time off work to attend to personal business, squads swooped down on that fixture of Soviet life, long lines of consumers. The KGB and the police (militia) barged into restaurants, cinemas, parks, public baths, sports arenas, barber shops, beauty parlors, and department stores in search of shirkers. The raids extended even to innocent pedestrians, who were forced to produce internal passports and explain their business.

Ominous and humiliating though the

raids were, the most sinister method of dealing with corruption and economic crisis resurrected a tactic employed in the 1930s. In thousands of factories, mines, workshops, offices, schools, and even ships at sea, "black boxes" for complaints and denunciations suddenly materialized as citizens were invited to report anonymously to the KGB. In the Stalin tradition, the state did not announce the results of this campaign.

Andropov admirers pointed to a shake-up in party and government as evidence of his even-handed reformist zeal. In his less than 15 months as general secretary, he replaced about one-fourth of the 150 *oblast* (administrative district) chiefs and removed 19 of 84 members of the Council of Ministers. Hardly revolutionary, the turnover involved officials whose average age was 67.3 years.

Cut from the same cloth as Andropov's liberal mask, a selective, well-publicized "crackdown" on corruption chiefly involved the settling of various accounts. Within a month of coming to power Andropov ousted N.A. Shchelokov—another old Brezhnev friend—as minister of the interior and replaced him with Vitaly Fedorchuk, Andropov's hand-picked successor at the KGB. Notorious for bribe-taking during Shchelokov's 16-year reign, the regular police—a national service under the interior ministry—had earned the people's contempt. Fedorchuk began an investigation which continued under his successor, Viktor Chebrikov. Hundreds of high-ranking police officials, including Brezhnev's son-in-law, ultimately went to prison.

Andropov cracked down severely on nonconformist artists, dissidents, members of religious sects who strayed outside narrow state-defined corridors, and Soviet citizens who sought to emigrate. During his KGB years he had directed the persecution and expulsion from the country of Aleksandr Solzhenitsyn as well as the exiling of Andrei Sakharov to Gorky and Yuri Orlov to Siberia; the imprisonment and torture of Anatoli Marchenko and other political prisoners; the severe harassment of Christian believers and clergy; the jailing and exile of Ida Nudel, Iosif Begun, Anatoli Shcharansky, and other Jewish activists.

Of the Jews allowed to emigrate in the 1970s, the majority came from the Caucasus and Central Asia and had no higher education or special skills. Many had to be urged to file for permission to leave. Andropov's KGB directed the severe restrictions placed on most educated Jews and other citizens who wished to emigrate, and from 1980 to February 1984 emigration almost totally ceased.

## FOREIGN POLICY

Andropov increased the pace and savagery of hostilities in Afghanistan. He ordered the terror-bombing of villages in rebel-controlled areas and the indiscriminate strewing of millions of camouflaged antipersonnel mines over the landscape.

Relations with the United States deteriorated to the lowest level in 30 years. In September 1983, the Soviet Union shot down an unarmed Korean Air Lines passenger aircraft with the loss of 269 Korean and American lives. Moscow's uncoordinated but brutally aggressive handling of the incident itself and the aftermath obscured legitimate, still-unanswered questions about the possibility of KAL 007 having had an intelligence mission. In part as a riposte, the United States mounted a military action of sorts the following month, invading Grenada to overthrow a leftist regime to which the USSR was providing assistance not normally associated with the needs of a tiny, desperately poor "nation" in the Windward Islands.

Also in the autumn of 1983, in belated response to the threat of nuclear-tipped Soviet rockets aimed at Western Europe, the United States deployed cruise missiles—which could strike targets in the USSR—in four NATO countries. Andropov immediately broke off bilateral talks aimed at reducing the numbers of these weapons and also of long-range (strategic) missiles. Far from pulling Soviet rockets back, he transferred some from the Asiatic part of the country to Byelorussia.

Warning of a "runaway race" in nuclear arms, Andropov did much to speed it up. President Reagan was also spending money on the military at an unprecedented rate. The verbal exchanges between Moscow and Washington grew ever more heated, and hopes for the revival of "détente" faded.

To the special regret of Soviet conservatives, who longed for the 1950s, when Moscow and Beijing constituted a more or less united Communist front, relations with China did not improve under Andropov's brief stewardship. The two parties made no progress on border issues or trade disputes; and Moscow's invasion of Afghanistan and support for the Vietnamese incursion into Cambodia exacerbated the tensions of the 1960s and 1970s.

In the Warsaw Pact nations, unyielding neo-Stalinist leaders held back pressures for reform which the Kremlin had smashed with military force in Hungary in 1956, Andropov playing a promotion-winning role in the crushing of liberty. As the new KGB chief he had helped plan the 1968 invasion of Czechoslovakia, and he directed the rebuilding of Prague's ferocious secret police. Moscow employed threats rather than troops against Poland in 1980–1981, a time when, as *de facto* Soviet leader, Andropov dictated the mutilation of Solidarity.

Andropov's KGB may or may not—the evidence remains unclear—have master-minded the 1981 attempt on the life of Pope John Paul II, but its moral responsibility for the heinous October 1984 murder of Father Jerzy Popieluszko, a strong supporter of Solidarity, is beyond dispute. The Polish security agents who actually beat the courageous priest to death admitted in open court that they acted on orders "from a very high level." Precisely how "high" may never be known; but the Warsaw regime's policies vis-à-vis Solidarity bore a "Made in Moscow" stamp and dated from the time Andropov supplanted Brezhnev as the Soviet strongman.

Roy Medvedev and others argued that the new general secretary's failure to undertake a thorough overhaul of Soviet foreign policy stemmed from lack of time and the pressure of President Reagan's uncompromising hostility toward the USSR. Such a defense comes to grief on the fact of Andropov's major role in Kremlin policy-making after Khrushchev; the 15 months of his *de jure* rule witnessed the logical continuation of those policies.

In the summer of 1983, the general secretary disappeared from public view; for 176 days the state drifted. Andropov died from kidney failure early in February 1984, and Roy Medvedev claimed that "for many years most of our people will recall . . . [his] death with regret." That seems unlikely. The best that can be said for Andropov is that he did not revive Stalin's terror.

## CHERNENKO

The Communist party buried Andropov between Dzerzhinsky and Kalinin near the Kremlin wall. A few hours earlier, its Central Committee had followed the recommendation of the Politburo in electing Konstantin Chernenko to succeed him.

Born in Siberia in 1911, Chernenko claimed the nationality of his Russian mother rather than that of his father, a Ukrainian. According to his official biography, he worked as a hired laborer for kulaks during the NEP period, became an officer in the Komsomol, and served in the secret police Border Guards on the frontier with China in the early 1930s. He joined the Communist party in 1931.

Unlike his predecessors, Chernenko did not serve in the military during the Second World War, which he sat out first as a minor party official in Siberia, later as a student at the Higher School for Party Organizers in Moscow. When he became general secretary that proved an embarrassment; in April 1984 the party began a campaign to inflate his Border Guards duty into an heroic saga. In December it published glowing reviews of a documentary film that highlighted that episode, a film which no one but a few party faithful ever saw.

Chernenko became a soldier in the "Dnepropetrovsk mafia" in 1950, when he did party work in the Moldavian republic as one of Brezhnev's subordinates. Transferred to Moscow in 1956, Brezhnev brought Chernenko along; the two men's careers advanced in tandem. Chernenko became head of the General Department of the party Central Committee shortly after Brezhnev supplanted Khrushchev as general secretary.

As Brezhnev's health declined the press regularly published photographs showing Chernenko at his side lighting his cigarette, steadying him by the elbow, showing him where to sign. Modestly educated and inarticulate, having no political constituency, Chernenko had evidently peaked as Brezhnev's alter ego. In time of crisis the Politburo rejected him in favor of Andropov.

But that was November 1982. In February 1984 no candidate for the general secretaryship was strong enough to unseat the Brezhnevists; protracted debate over the six months of Andropov's terminal illness had produced no agreement. When Chernenko was named head of the Andropov funeral commission it appeared he would become general secretary, but for the three days prior to the announcement the USSR apparently had no leader at all.

Chernenko suffered from ailments of his own; a British physician-politician who met him after his predecessor's funeral detected signs of emphysema. Later it would be revealed that Chernenko, like Brezhnev a lifelong heavy smoker and rather more than social drinker, also suffered from heart disease and cirrhosis of the liver. At times he appeared as disoriented as Brezhnev in his later years; at Andropov's funeral Andrei Gromyko—his voice picked up by a microphone—admonished the new general secretary not to take off his hat.

The Brezhnevist old guard, of which Andropov for all his power had never been a member, emerged victorious from what would be its last real campaign. Clinging to biological and political life, it included Chernenko himself, Grishin, Kunayev, Solomentsev, Tikhonov, and Ustinov. Although an outsider, the Ukrainian leader Shcherbitsky cooperated on major issues. Andrei Gromyko, at 75 the old guard's coeval, had survived as foreign minister since 1957 largely because he did *not* attach himself to any particular faction; so long as Brezhnevists were in control he carried out their orders.

The average age of the old guard was nearly 72. That was 10 years beyond the life expectancy of the average Soviet male, and these politicians were not renowned for their healthful lifestyles. They resisted turning over control of party and state to either of the two younger contenders, Gorbachev, 53, or Romanov, 61.

His remarkable comeback constituted the most impressive accomplishment of Chernenko's few months as general secretary. Following the pattern established by Brezhnev and maintained by Andropov, he became head of state in April 1984.

With the new general secretary manifestly a mere caretaker, Gromyko now had free rein in foreign affairs. Nearing the end of a career noted for caution, he undertook no serious initiatives to repair relations with China, repeatedly denied seeking a face-saving way out of Afghanistan, did nothing to dampen world tensions. Nearly a year passed before Moscow tacitly acknowledged that the emplacement of American nuclear-tipped, medium-range missiles in Western Europe had thwarted the Brezhnev-Ustinov-Andropov attempt to tilt the balance of power on the Continent. In January 1985 the Soviet Union agreed to resume arms negotiations with the United States.

Military policy now came under the sole control of Defense Minister Ustinov, who was determined to push ahead blindly in Afghanistan. Hardly the man to recommend military cutbacks no matter what the state of the economy, Ustinov suffered a stroke in September 1984 and died three months later.

Chernenko's time seemed oddly out of joint: a contemporary Moscow joke had conductors on public transportation calling out, "Next stop Chernenko—transfer from Brezhnev to Andropov!" No matter what the actual chronology, Chernenko, not Andropov, represented continuation of the Brezhnev era. Reform would have to await his death.

A man of the past whom historical accident had elevated beyond his capabilities, Chernenko had no discernible vision of the Soviet future. Confronted with a problem, like Brezhnev he either denied its existence or prescribed further party intervention. Foreign policy consisted of building more rockets and tanks. To deal with the glut of steel, the USSR produced still more steel. If Soviet kolhozes and sovhozes could not feed the country, the state would create new farms out of prairies and reclaimed swamps and run them in exactly the same inefficient way. If artists and writers and intellectuals clamored for freedom, the party would crack down even harder. If some comrades illegally built lucrative fiefdoms, what mattered was their loyalty to the party.

Chernenko paid lip service to Andropov's program to reduce the swollen state bureaucracy but cancelled his predecessor's plans to trim *party* officialdom by 20 percent. The "stability of cadres" slogan under which the Brezhnev-Suslov-Kosygin *troika* had come to power remained as valid as ever; Communist party privileges remained unassailable.

The enquiry into the monumental interior ministry scandal proceeded, and not long after it stripped him of his military rank in November 1984, Shchelokov committed suicide. By that time, however, the Chernenko deathwatch had become a round-the-clock matter; under the direction of Mikhail Gorbachev, the Secretariat conducted almost all state and party business. Unpublicized investigations of corruption in Kazakhstan and Uzbekistan continued, and in connection with the latter republic's scandals, Yuri Churbanov, Brezhnev's son-in-law, finally lost his job as first deputy minister of the interior early in 1985.

Frequently out of public view for long periods, Chernenko died on March 10, 1985. Three changes of the guard in 28 months had finally broken the old guard's back. The Central Committee chose the dynamic young Andropov protégé, Mikhail Gorbachev, to lead the country out of the stagnation of the Brezhnev years.

## SUGGESTED ADDITIONAL READING

**Ash, Timothy,** *The Polish Revolution: Solidarity,* New York: Vintage Books, 1985

**Beichman, Arnold, and Mikhail Bernstam,** *Andropov,* New York: Stein and Day, 1983

**Cracraft, James, ed.,** *The Soviet Union Today,* Chicago: Bulletin of the Atomic Scientists, 1983

**Doder, Dusko,** *Shadows and Whispers: Power Politics Inside the Kremlin from Brezhnev to Gorbachev,* New York: Penguin, 1988

**McCauley, Martin, ed.,** *The Soviet Union after Brezhnev,* New York: Holmes and Meier, 1983

**Nagorski, Andrew,** *Reluctant Farewell,* New York: Holt, Rinehart and Winston, 1985

**Shipler, David K.,** *Russia,* New York: Times Books, 1984

**Walker, Martin,** *The Waking Giant: Gorbachev's Russia,* New York: Pantheon Books, 1986

# 23

# RELUCTANT REVOLUTION
## Gorbachev, Glasnost, and Perestroika

A strange Soviet scenario: Uninhibited political debate, public criticism of Politburo members and calls for their resignations; protest marches and anti-government demonstrations. Frank discussion in the mass media of high crime rates, drug addiction, prostitution, AIDS, teenage suicide. Documentary television films on Gulag horrors, interviews with survivors; official acknowledgment of the "repression," that is, *slaughter,* of more than 10 million peasants during collectivization. Freedom of worship a reality; official apologies for the persecution of religion; reopening of long-closed churches, mosques, synagogues. Demands for autonomy and even independence for minority peoples; reform leader's opponents sanction massacre of demonstrators in Tbilisi. Humiliating end to a war of genocide in Afghanistan; rapprochement with Washington and—more cautiously—Beijing; major arms reductions. Near-unanimous admission of the failure of communism.

Meanwhile, no improvement in the standard of living: food more scarce than in 30 years, long lines even for staples, rationing even in Moscow. Inadequate health care; average life expectancy of males below that of some Third-World countries; 90 percent of all first pregnancies terminated by legal abortion.

But steel in abundance, millions on millions of unneeded, rusting, low-grade, expensive tons of steel.

These monumental paradoxes confronted the 285 million people of the Soviet Union in the spring of 1989. Politically and spiritually freer than at any time since the

1920s, they remained in the stifling clutch of an inefficient, carnivorous socioeconomic machine built and fueled with their blood and treasure over six decades by the Communist party. Popular patience with the new regime, now nearly four years in office, eroded daily.

## THE TRANSITION

Shortly before midnight on March 11, 1985, the CPSU's Central Committee announced that Mikhail Sergeevich Gorbachev, 54, would succeed Konstantin Chernenko, dead barely four hours, as general secretary. With the publication of Andrei Gromyko's nominating speech, the world learned that Gorbachev had actually governed the country much of the time during Chernenko's frequent, prolonged illnesses.

Three years later, one of the new leaders, Yegor Ligachev, inadvertently revealed that the selection of Gorbachev had not been unanimous, the unprecedented swiftness of the announcement and months of *de facto* Gorbachev governance notwithstanding. Only the determined support of Gromyko, party disciplinarian Mikhail Solomentsev, and KGB chief Viktor Chebrikov had swung the vote. These three men represented elements in the party which did not fully share Gorbachev's enthusiasm for change but accepted the need for vigorous leadership.

## GORBACHEV'S BACKGROUND

Born into a Russian family in the village of Privolnoye in the Stavropol region of the North Caucasus on March 2, 1931, Mikhail Gorbachev grew up knowing the land and politics; his father and grandfather were peasant Communists. The grandfather

The new general secretary of the CPSU, Mikhail Gorbachev (right), with Foreign Minister Gromyko (center) and Premier Tikhonov on the day of Konstantin Chernenko's funeral, March 13, 1985. (AP/Wide World Photos)

chaired one of the first collective farms established in the area; the father worked as a combine operator. Mikhail attended local schools from 1938 on and evidently was not evacuated during the 1942–1943 German occupation. The Gorbachev family suffered along with the rest of the Soviet people during the war; Mikhail's mother revealed after her son came to power that at one point he could not attend school because he had no shoes.

Like the mothers of Stalin and Khrushchev, Mariya Panteleyevna Gorbacheva had her son baptized, and she raised him in the Russian Orthodox Church—during the Stalinist terror. Young Mikhail formally renounced religion when he entered the Komsomol. When he became Communist party general secretary forty years later, however, he removed most of the restrictions on the Russian, Georgian, and Armenian Churches, eased many of the restrictions on Catholics and Lutherans in the Baltic States, and after a brief, unsuccessful assault on Islam, extended his policy of toleration to that faith. In 1988 the state participated actively and all things considered positively in the celebration of the millenium of Christianity in Russia and the Ukraine.

Working alongside his father on the kolhoz after World War II, Mikhail Gorbachev won the Order of the Red Banner of Labor at the unusually early age of 18. That, an unblemished Komsomol record, and the silver medal—second in his class—on graduation from high school gained him admission to the country's most prestigious institution of higher learning, Moscow State University. Opting to study law instead of another love, mathematics and physics, Gorbachev read not only Marx, Engels, Lenin, and Stalin, but also St. Thomas Aquinas, Hobbes, Locke, and Machiavelli; he was one of the few students at the university to take Latin. In 1954 he married a sociology student, Raisa Titorenko.

According to Zdenek Mlynar, a classmate who later became a high official in the 1967–1968 reform regime in Czechoslovakia, Gorbachev expressed private doubts about Stalin and Stalinism while still at the university and in later years spoke of the need for political and economic decentralization. These assertions have not been confirmed. At the 19th CPSU Conference, however, Gorbachev used a phrase—startling even in the relaxed 1988 Soviet context—made famous by Mlynar's colleague Alexander Dubček, "socialism with a human face." His early association with cultured Europeans like Mlynar may help explain his quoting Hillel in asking Soviet writers and editors in 1986, "If not we, who? If not now, when?"

Unmistakable markers of conformity, however, overshadow the faint and perhaps misleading signs of liberal views in the young Gorbachev. He joined the party in 1952 and served as a Komsomol organizer at Moscow University. Evidence of the state's absolute trust in a faithful son came in the 1960s, when Gorbachev was permitted not only to travel abroad with a couple of official delegations but even to drive through France and Italy with his wife.

After earning his law degree, Gorbachev returned to his native Stavropol region and local politics, a move that was to weigh heavily in his favor. He worked his way up through the ranks slowly but surely enough to be named a delegate to Khrushchev's second "de-Stalinizing" Party Congress, the 22nd in 1961. According to Mlynar, he applauded Khrushchev's ouster and continued to do so even after coming to power and condemning Brezhnev's rule. In 1970 he became first secretary of the regional party organization—that is, member of the Communist elite.

A giant boost came in 1971 when Gorbachev became a full member of the national party Central Committee without having served the customary probationary period. In the absence of any particularly noteworthy achievements on his part, such a promotion can only have reflected a record of perfect obedience to the party and the patronage of highly placed individuals: Fyodor Kulakov (party secretary for agriculture), Yuri Andropov, and Mikhail Suslov. All three began their careers in the Stavropol area, regularly vacationed at nearby resorts, and maintained the kind of sentimental interest in local party affairs that Brezhnev did in Dnepropetrovsk.

When Kulakov died suddenly in 1978, the leadership appointed Gorbachev to take his place on the Central Committee Secretariat. Although he did not initiate it, Gorbachev became identified with the "Ipatovsky method" of harvesting grain through the use of massive squads of combines, a method that enjoyed success in some regions; *Pravda* published an interview with the young official on page one. Recalling the "from the asphalt to the land" campaign, he began the gradual transfer of responsibility for agriculture from the bloated Moscow bureaucracy to regional bodies and reintroduced a cooperative brigade system on some kolhozes. Given charge of a block of arable land or a herd of animals, a brigade received income based solely on performance. Incentives reappeared in scattered areas of the countryside, as did flickers of the ancient, organic tie between peasants and land.

In those few areas—including the Stavropol region—where the reforms enjoyed the support not only of the local bureaucracy and peasantry but also nature, increased yields resulted. Nationally, however, poor weather, mismanagement, and waste saw harvests decline from a record 237 million metric tons in 1978 to 179 million in 1979, a

disastrous 158 million in 1981. In 1983, Gorbachev's last year in charge of agriculture, the farms produced 192 million metric tons of grain.

Only the protection of Yuri Andropov accounts for the party's failure to make Gorbachev the scapegoat for these failures. The young man from Stavropol became a candidate member of the Politburo in 1979, full member a year later.

Much of the time between November 1982 and February 1984 saw Gorbachev act as grand vizier to the new general secretary, Andropov. He retained authority for agriculture for most of that period, took over the ideological portfolio on the Secretariat, and spearheaded experiments to loosen the chains on industry, a job that normally would have gone to Romanov. He also played a major role in the attempt to eradicate Brezhnev-era corruption; curiously, the KGB excesses of that campaign did not stick to him in the public mind. Gorbachev was in short to Andropov as Andropov himself had been to Brezhnev, the indispensable aide to a dying man, the major and frequently only link between general secretary and party.

Andropov clearly hoped that Gorbachev or another reform-minded leader would succeed him, but the absence of both mechanism and tradition frustrated his wishes; no Soviet leader has ever been able to handpick his successor. Thus in February 1984 the moribund Brezhnev machine revived sufficiently to deny any of Andropov's protégés—Gorbachev, Ligachev, Chebrikov—the general secretaryship but lacked the strength to remove Gorbachev as second in command. Neither Romanov, the boorish former Leningrad boss now in charge of industry and defense, nor Viktor Grishin, the drudge who had long run the Moscow party, could muster more than one vote for their ambitions. The ambitious Geidar Aliyev's graft, nepotism, and other misdeeds caught up with him in 1987; he lost his seat on the Politburo.

## GORBACHEV IN POWER

The perfunctory obsequies for Chernenko disposed of, Gorbachev moved quickly to implement the one great weapon in his arsenal that set him apart from all potential rivals, a platform. The new regime capsulated that platform as *glasnost* (openness, candor) and *perestroika* (restructuring of society and economy). Prior to the spring of 1985 these words had embodied no more ideological significance than *soviet* (council) had in 1905, but now they became part of not merely the Soviet but also the international political vocabulary almost overnight. That phenomenon, wholly beyond the control of any political movement much less any individual, indicated startling new departures in the USSR.

Sounding a call for "revolutionary" changes in all aspects of Soviet life at an April 1985 Central Committee plenum, Gorbachev and his allies refused to back away from terminology no one in authority in the Soviet Union ever dared take lightly. In a July 1986 speech the new leader said of the term *perestroika*, "I would equate it with the word 'revolution.' "

The Gorbachevites—some from the broad ranks of the Establishment, others from the academic and intellectual fringe— frankly acknowledged the failures of the Soviet system, which they promised to overhaul thoroughly. Domestic opponents, chiefly in the 18-million-strong bureaucracy, bitterly condemned this "abandonment of socialism." The Gorbachev people responded with the exhortation "More socialism!" even as they began dismantling what had *passed* for socialism since 1928. In

a June 1988 speech, the new general secretary responded to his critics:

> In all spheres of life, including the spiritual, we must overcome a very basic factor, alienation, which unfortunately occurs when socialism is deformed by authoritarian-bureaucratic distortions. Alienation, bureaucratism, and formalism can be overcome only along lines of democratization and openness . . . of a moral cleansing of our society.

One who would describe Stalinism as a mere "authoritarian-bureaucratic distortion" might complain that the Nazis "misbehaved" in Russia during the war; and "formalism" is devoid of political meaning. Nevertheless, in breaking with the Soviet past, Gorbachev sought to align the USSR with the mainstream of European democratic socialism.

## POLITICAL DEVELOPMENTS

In a few brief months in 1917, the moderate-center and then extreme left wings of a civil society born barely half a century earlier in the ashes of serfdom overthrew a thousand-year-old sociopolitical system. After a savage civil war, that society reemerged and prospered for nearly eight years, only to fall to a barbaric despotism that did not begin to recede until the despot's death in 1953. The retreat accelerated in 1956, and there emerged what Moshe Lewin has called a "civil society recovering." That recovery slowed to a crawl after 1964.

By the time Gorbachev came to power, the dreaded step from which the Communist Party had recoiled in 1956 and 1961, that of attesting to its own illegitimacy,* had become unavoidable. None of the myths the party touted as its history could rescue it now;

---

*See above, Chapter 16.

everyone knew too much about Soviet-style communism to believe in it. Nothing could salvage an economic system that had produced near-ruin. No mere reform could atone for the indiscriminate slaughter of the Soviet people. The country *needed* revolution, a frontal assault not only on Stalinism—the easy part—but also on the Leninism that had nourished the soil in which Stalinism grew.

Gorbachev inherited an under-strength Politburo of 10 members, of whom only he did not owe his promotion to Brezhnev. Even after he filled three of the four (or six, if the 16-member body of a decade earlier be the standard) vacancies in April 1985, the Brezhnev old guard maintained its majority. The promotion of Ligachev (party secretary in charge of personnel and ideology), Chebrikov of the KGB, and Nikolai Ryzhkov (party secretary in charge of the economy in general), strengthened the reformist wing but did not license it to make a revolution.

Between April 1985 and October 1988 the new general secretary slowly put together a Politburo majority, albeit a far from mechanically obedient one, leaving in power only two Brezhnev-era members, the seemingly immovable Ukrainian party boss Vladimir Shcherbitsky and Vitaly Vorotnikov, premier and then president of the RSFSR. Gorbachev forced the jackleg politicians Romanov and Grishin into ignominious retirement. The sinister Kunayev—who like Geidar Aliyev had retained his seat on the Central Committee even after dismissal from the Politburo—conveniently died before the state was forced to decide whether to indict him. Andrei Gromyko lost control of the foreign ministry to Eduard Shevardnadze, a close Gorbachev ally and in early 1989 the only non-Slav—he is a Georgian—on the Politburo.

The September-October 1988 extraordinary Central Committee plenum left Ligachev and Chebrikov, who had acted as a brake on Gorbachev, on the Politburo. In a demonstration of the general secretary's growing might, however, it assigned Ligachev the thankless task of running agriculture and removed Chebrikov as head of the KGB. Chebrikov did however take command of a new Central Committee commission on legal affairs and thus retained considerable influence in security matters and ideology.

Gorbachev had shown strength and even decency in making Gromyko titular head of state in July 1985; the deliberate break with recent precedent gave the former foreign minister an honorable transition into retirement. In 1988 the general secretary demonstrated naked political power in taking the office *away* from Gromyko and assuming it himself. According to constitutional reforms scheduled to take effect in 1989, a revamped presidency will have broad authority in legislation, foreign policy, defense, and in the economic and social arena.

The special November 1988 Supreme Soviet session that approved this change also endorsed creation of a 2,250-member Congress of People's Deputies, which is to choose the president by secret ballot and to which the president will be responsible. Meeting up to eight months a year in spring and fall sessions, the Congress is to elect from its own ranks a restructured 422-member Supreme Soviet that will review legislative and administrative acts during biannual sessions of 2 to 3 days each. The president, members of Congress and the Supreme Soviet, and all other state officials can serve a maximum of two 5-year terms.

For the first time since the balloting for the ill-fated Constituent Assembly in November 1917, Soviet voters went to the polls on March 26, 1989, in a reasonably free election. Theirs still the only legal party, the Communists won 87 percent of the seats in the new

Congress; but non-party candidates such as Arkady Murashev—whose platform called for a multiparty democracy—and maverick Communists like Boris Yeltsin scored impressive victories. Andrei Sakharov won a seat despite fierce Communist opposition in the Academy of Sciences. Many entrenched Communist functionaries lost their bids for seats: the mayor of Moscow; the Leningrad party chief (and candidate member of the Politburo), who received only 15 percent of the votes; the mayor of Leningrad; the Kiev party chief; the mayor of Kiev; the premier of Lithuania; the president of Lithuania; several high-ranking military officers. Twenty percent of the regional party secretaries failed to win seats, as did 30 percent of other high-ranking Communists. The independent Lithuanian political movement, Sajudis, won three-quarters of the republic's

(Map by Larry Fogel, *The Washington Post*)

seats in the Congress, while the independent Popular Front won 25 of Latvia's 29 seats. Many victorious Communists won in districts where officials illegally kept non-communists off the ballot.

Flawed and heavily weighted in favor of Communists, the March 1989 elections nevertheless represented a monumentally important step forward. Reforms along these lines promised to remake the political system in the rough image of some Western systems, perhaps a cross between the Fifth Republic in France, with its strong presidency, and modern Mexico, essentially a one-party democracy with a legal opposition.

Russia has looked westward before. Peter the Great, and to a lesser extent his father, Tsar Aleksei, sought to modernize the country with Western technology even as they tightened the grip of autocracy and serfdom. From the 17th century on, some of the intellectuals urged the nation to reject or sharply modify the old Muscovite order, based on Byzantine-Mongol tradition, and follow the lead of the freer West. Alexander I and his "kitchen cabinet" discussed and ultimately rejected an attempt to introduce a British-style constitutional monarchy. Conservative keepers of official ideology—including the Russian Orthodox Church—and the 19th-century Slavophiles denounced all attempts to imitate foreign ways and demanded that Russia remain true to her Byzantine-oriental heritage. The opposition to *glasnost-perestroika* followed the tradition of these anti-Westernizers.

In everything from political reforms to economic restructuring to social customs and public relations, Gorbachev and his people looked westward, but the West offered no examples of the throwing-off of a despotism quite like Stalin's. China, however, did.

Deng Xiaoping's *gaige*, the rough equivalent of *perestroika*, began in 1978—

coincidentally a fateful year for Mikhail Gorbachev, who cannot have failed to pay close attention to developments in China. As a first step, Deng emancipated the peasantry from nearly three decades of ruthless Maoist exploitation. The peasants could keep and with relatively minor restrictions sell on the open market all they produced above state quotas, which were set at reasonable levels.

As in Russia under NEP, relative—if unevenly distributed—prosperity quickly returned to the countryside; the cities were well supplied with food. The Beijing reformers could then cautiously initiate political and social reforms, secure in the support of the massive—80 percent of the population—rural rear and reasonably confident that well-fed city dwellers would at least give their programs a fair hearing. They could also begin the costly modernization of industry.

*Gaige* had its share of problems. Some rural areas did not share at all in the new prosperity; the bureaucracy—three times the size of the Soviet—fought to retain its privileges; central planners continued to interfere; and the Chinese Communist party remained divided on the question of reform in general.

Only dictators like Mao and Stalin can deal summarily with bureaucratic resistance and political disagreement. Deng had to move slowly, but his pacification of the peasant sector at least partially neutralized the greatest single weapon of his opponents—urban discontent.

## GORBACHEV AND THE ECONOMY

A conservative party bureaucracy barely three decades in power did its best to thwart Deng Xiaoping's reforms; in early 1989 the jury is still out. Mikhail Gorbachev faced a party-state apparatus in place more than twice as long and pampered outrageously by the corrupt central leadership since 1964. Beyond that, he could do nothing about adverse weather and bore no responsibility for the low price of Soviet oil on the world market, the cost of cleaning up after the 1986 nuclear catastrophe at Chernobyl and the 1988 earthquake in Armenia. The staggering loss of revenue—37 billion rubles 1984–1987—from the anti-alcohol abuse campaign was indeed his doing; less measurable were the savings and enhanced profits that theoretically should have resulted.

The attempt to revolutionize the Soviet economy proceeded in stages. This was the program:

(1) The Soviet people, conditioned to regard socialism as a system that guaranteed easy jobs, had to learn to work in order to improve their standard of living and enable their country to compete in the world market. They would have to accept some unemployment as the price of modernization; a Gorbachev adviser, Leonid Abalkin, declared that 15–20 million jobs would be cut from the industrial and agricultural work force by the year 2000. Affected workers would shift to the service sector or become unemployed.

(2) Enterprises had to become profitable; socialism did not subsidize failure. The Kremlin acknowledged that such subsidies had long contributed to massive deficits, the size of which it understated. Aleksei Kosygin had recognized this problem two decades earlier; *perestroika* now revived many of his proposals, which party-industrial bureaucracies—by sheer inaction—had sabotaged with help from a Brezhnev innocent of any understanding of economics. By January 1988 Gorbachev's "self-financing" (i.e., survival dependent on profitability) system embraced enterprises that produced 60 percent of total industrial output.

(3) Declaring that an economy could no more be half planned than a woman half pregnant, the Gorbachevites sought to emasculate the power of Gosplan, the state planning agency, and to abolish most of the 800-plus ministries and ministry-level agencies—national, repub-

lic, and local—that oversee production. A shrunken Gosplan and the few ministries that survived would simply provide guidelines and advice along the lines of Western "think tanks." The 1987 Law on Enterprises specified that factories, plants, and companies would no longer have to organize their operations according to a plan handed down from Moscow. Such a plan would henceforward be merely a general guide, a statement of priorities. Enterprises would deal with each other on a "wholesale trade" basis and conclude contracts based on negotiated rather than state-set prices.

A major flaw threatened to compromise this impressive decentralization: Enterprises were legally obligated to give priority to state orders, the vast majority. Abel Aganbegyan, a leading architect of *perestroika*, predicted the decline of state orders from two-thirds of all orders in 1988 to one-fourth by the turn of the century; Abalkin, Gavril Popov, and other experts did not share this optimism. The agencies issuing the orders manipulated them in their own interests, and many of the forces that had defeated Kosygin loomed before Gorbachev.

(4) Economic *perestroika* depended heavily on a revolutionary change in the price structure. Over the decades, Gosplan bureaucrats had established prices for more than 24 million different items; in the Gorbachev era they continued to set more than 200,000 per year. The bureaucrats could quote the price of anything but knew the real cost of nothing. *Perestroika* economists estimated that the retail price of bread covered only about 7 percent of the cost of production; the monumental subsidy made it so cheap that many kolhozes and sovhozes illegally fed bread to livestock instead of grain or fodder. The state last raised the price of bread in 1954, meat in 1962. Rents have remained stable since 1928.

The Moscow price-setters had no idea what such a basic commodity as money cost. In 1989 there were more than 3,000 different, secret exchange rates for the ruble—which is nonconvertible—against foreign currencies. The one published rate, for tourists and petty transactions, pegged the ruble at three to five times its real internal purchasing power.

The state intended to deregulate most

retail prices beginning in 1990. Early in 1989, however, Gorbachev and his advisers quietly shelved plans to do so, fearing both outraged public opinion and runaway inflation. But precisely how long price changes could be avoided remained uncertain. In the absence of such a major step, there seemed little possibility of an economic recovery.

(5) The state will reorganize its financial institutions and restore credit markets. Instead of turning to ministries for funds, enterprises will apply for loans at branches of the State Bank. The branches will have sole discretion to grant the loans and sole responsibility for their soundness.

Of secondary economic importance are joint ventures with foreign firms, which may own up to 49 percent of such projects. Likewise, some individual business—far less than in China—is permitted, e.g., plumbers, carpenters, electricians, shoemakers, drivers, tailors, and so on. Small groups are permitted to establish cooperative restaurants and other undertakings. Most notably, the state is encouraging the development of family farms as autonomous satellites of state farms, from which they are to receive—for a fee—seed, implements, fertilizer, and technical advice.

For a variety of reasons, by the spring of 1989 *perestroika* had registered only modest success. First, the Gorbachevites had not overcome the opposition of Communists who saw the collectivization of agriculture as one of their finest accomplishments. Therefore, *perestroika* reversed Chinese procedure and sought to eliminate central planning, decentralize and modernize the outmoded industrial base, *before* liberating agriculture; this was going from the complex to the relatively simple. The Soviet work force, which might have responded to incentives programs, concentrated its attention on bare shelves and long queues at food stores and sidewalk stalls.

Second, Gorbachev had through spring 1989 proved unable to reform the bureaucracy. As the economist Nikolai Shmelyov put it:

. . . there are three million bureaucrats in our Ministry of Agriculture. Think of it. These people know nothing except how to carry their briefcases. All . . . these bureaucrats are afraid of losing their jobs, and they are anathema to a healthy economy.

Shmelyov pointed out that "[r]esistance to the perestroika reforms no longer comes from the top levels of our bureaucratic pyramids." By early 1989 Gorbachev had replaced more than two-thirds of all ministers, more than three-fifths of all provincial party first secretaries, three-quarters of all first secretaries of city and district party committees. Resistance came from the lowest—thus broadest—levels of the "pyramid."

Third, Russia had no pool of individuals trained in modern management techniques; numerous high-level delegations observed American business school training but produced only a glut of position papers. Soviet managers excelled above all in executing—or giving the appearance of so doing—orders from Moscow. With gross output long the sole index of success or failure, they had no interest in anything else; they were not risk-takers or modernizers. They asked their respective ministries for the largest possible budgets and work force, the longest possible time to fulfill contracts, the lowest possible quotas. They feared computerization and cost accounting like the plague. If *perestroika* succeeded, they were doomed as a species.

## THE THIRD DEATH OF STALIN*

Social *perestroika* proceeded no more smoothly than economic. Mikhail Gorbachev had been in power 21 months when Anatoli Marchenko died in the Gulag. Conflicting

---

*The phrase comes from Elena Joly, *La troisième mort de Staline*, Arles: Editions Actes Sud, 1989

official versions of the autopsy lent weight to the widespread suspicion that the cause of death was yet another savage beating, the last of many administered to a man who spent 20 years in the camps simply for daring to protest. The release of Andrei Sakharov, Yuri Orlov, Anatoli Shcharansky, Iosif Begun—all but a small handful of political prisoners and detainees—could not conceal the deaths in the Gulag of more prisoners in Gorbachev's first two years than during the entire Brezhnev era. Those lonely, tragic deaths—Marchenko's was one of the few to which the world paid attention—must be factored into any evaluation of *glasnost*.

In 1988 a Soviet historian announced that the twelfth and last volume of a general history of the USSR could not be published because, with an honest look at the past now permitted, it would negate everything in the previous eleven. In the 60th anniversary year of the Russian Revolutions of 1917 Gorbachev declared, "There should be no forgotten names or blanks either in history or in literature." This and similar invitations opened the floodgates; Yegor Ligachev and conservative scholars attempted to slow the process. Remembering the collapse of previous thaws and the persecution of those who had boldly ventured forth into them, some historians and writers held back. In June 1988 the government cancelled end-of-the-year school examinations in history throughout the country.

In the wake of an unremitting assault on Stalin's rule that went far beyond Khrushchev's "de-Stalinization," by January 1989 the Supreme Soviet and the courts had overturned the convictions of all defendants in the "show trials" of the 1930s. Over vigorous conservative opposition the Communist party posthumously reinstated many—most notably Nikolai Bukharin—in its ranks. Kamenev, Zinoviev, Radek, Rykov, and thousands of lesser-known victims of the "troikas" and "special boards" of 1934–1953 were exonerated.

Yuli Daniel lived to see publication of some of his poems and even one of the stories for which he spent five years in the Gulag. He died late in December 1988. Andrei Sinyavsky, who had gone to prison with him and was later allowed to emigrate, received a visa to attend the funeral; not accidentally, the Soviet embassy in Paris issued it too late. But Sinyavsky did finally return to visit his friend's grave in Moscow's Vagankovskoye Cemetery, where Sergei Yesenin, Vladimir Vysotsky, and some of the Decembrist rebels of 1825 also lie.*

After 60 years as archfiend, even Trotsky won quasirespectability. A September 1988 *Pravda* article maintained that he "was not an enemy of the revolution or of socialism . . . [but rather] of Stalin." Moreover, "[t]he source of his tragedy," the writer continued, "lay not so much in his struggle with Stalinism as in his struggle with Stalin for power." In its first issue of 1989, *Literaturnaya gazeta* informed Soviet readers of Stalin's responsibility for the assassination of Trotsky. Not in doubt elsewhere, this had never been officially acknowledged in the USSR.

Responding to pent-up public demand and the prodding of editors such as Vitaly Korotich of *Ogonyok* and Sergei Zalygin of *Novy Mir,* the state published long-banned works of Bulgakov, Zamyatin, Akhmatova, Mandelstam, Nikolai Gumilyov, Vladislav Khodasevich, and other writers anathema to the Stalinists. An essay and a novel by Vladimir Nabokov appeared, as did poems of Joseph Brodsky. The Writers' Union posthumously reinstated Boris Pasternak; *Dr. Zhivago* was published in Moscow. Anatoli Rybakov's *Children of the Arbat,* set during the Terror and suppressed for two decades, saw the light of day in 1987.

After what he described as "several deep discussions" with Gorbachev about Solzhenitsyn, in April 1989 Sergei Zalygin announced that *Novi Mir* (New World) would publish long excerpts from *The Gulag Archipelago* later in the year. If Zalygin succeeded, publication of Solzhenitsyn's monument to the victims of Lenin and Stalin would deal yet another heavy blow to the Stalinist wing of the party.

In the cinema, the Georgian director Tenghiz Abuladze's powerful, surrealistic anti-Stalin trilogy of *Supplication, Tree of Desire,* and *Repentance* won the 1988 Lenin Prize, the Soviet "Oscar." The Latvian director Juris Podnieks provided a startlingly frank look into the problems of Soviet youth in *Is It Easy to Be Young?* The youthful team of director Vasili Pichul and screenwriter Mariya Khmelik gave audiences an honest, unvarnished depiction of Soviet anomie in the brilliant *Little Vera.* A first-class drama, this and other films helped change the bland face of the Soviet cinema, as did changes in the leadership of the Union of Cinematographers. Aleksandr Askoldov's *The Comissar,* a tale of Soviet anti-Semitism and Nazism made in 1968 but never released in the USSR, went on a triumphal tour of the United States. In the spring of 1988 Vladimir Khotinenko's *Mirror for a Hero* lauded the heroism of the older generation, which it portrayed as victim rather than accomplice of Stalinism.

*Glasnost* and social *perestroika* had strict limits. Speaking of Stalin's crimes on the 60th anniversary of the October Revolution, Gorbachev callously referred to mere "thousands" of the "illegally repressed." To appease party conservatives, he regularly paid tribute to Stalin's "contributions" to the building of that very perversion of socialism which he—Gorbachev—had denounced, and to the defense of the country during the war.

---

*On Daniel and Sinyavsky, see above, Chapter 18.

The new regime did not permit any serious reevaluation of World War II, which so traumatized previous Soviet generations. On the crucial issue of one of the most monumental single NKVD atrocities, late in 1988 *Izvestiya* announced the Kremlin's plans to erect a memorial at Katyn, where "Polish officers . . . [and] Soviet prisoners were shot by the fascists in 1943." The new respect for history thus did not extend to Katyn; and no one could foresee whether it would embrace the Kirov murder despite the regime's promise to reopen the more than 100 volumes of evidence collected by Khrushchev and buried by Brezhnev.

In the spring of 1988 Vasili Selyunin and the historian Nikolai Popov published articles critical not only of Stalin but also of Feliks Dzerzhinsky, founder of the secret police, and Lenin himself. The oblique and cautious assault on Lenin seemed intended as a trial balloon, although *any* mention of the founding father in anything other than reverent tones was indeed unprecedented. Both writers implicated Lenin in the supercentralization of power in the hands of the party leadership, and Selyunin boldly laid blame for the Gulag at Lenin's doorstep.

The "good" Lenin of the NEP did not have enough time, Popov and Selyunin argued, to complete his work, which Stalin perverted. This harmonized with the general line of Gorbachev and his chief ideological adviser, Aleksandr Yakovlev, who attempted to use the rehabilitation and glorification of Nikolai Bukharin—politely ignoring the man's darker side—to push the analogy between *glasnost-perestroika* and Lenin's New Economic Policy. The mild, delicately phrased criticism of the "war communism" of Lenin seemed the limit of what the new regime would permit. Gorbachev presided over what Elena Joly has called the "third death of Stalin," but he would not sanction, much less officiate at, any rites for Lenin.

## NATIONAL MINORITIES

Nationalism, far from the least of the passions *glasnost* unleashed, burst into the open in 1986. A nation of 130 different ethnic groups, of which only two are ethnically and linguistically directly related to the Russians, suddenly raised scores of non-Russian voices to express a multitude of sometimes conflicting aspirations.

Until the end of World War II, the nationality question did not have a high priority because the Soviets claimed it did not exist. The Ukrainians had suffered severe penalties for their prolonged resistance to Muscovite-Soviet rule, the Kazakhs paid a collosal price in blood for opposing collectivization, and the Muslim peoples of Kazakhstan, Central Asia, and the Caucasus suffered religious and cultural persecution. As we have seen, Stalin deported hundreds of thousands of ethnic minorities for allegedly cooperating with the Nazis. Through all this, the Communists portrayed the USSR as the very model of a large, happy family of nations.

In the Khrushchev era, the state permitted most of the "punished peoples" to return to their homes. For the most part the return took place peacefully, but in 1958 riots in the Chechen-Ingush ASSR (Autonomous Soviet Socialist Republic) took a number of lives as Georgians, Dagestanis, Avars, and others who had taken over the homes and farms of the Chechen and Ingush resisted eviction.

In 1967 the Kremlin "rehabilitated" the Crimean Tatars but did not restore their homeland to them. Now simply in the way of Moscow's plans for the Crimea, which had been incorporated first into the RSFSR and then into the Ukrainian republic, the Crimean Tatars continued to pay for the crimes of Stalin, Voroshilov, Serov, and Suslov. Peaceful demonstrations that called for the restoration of Crimean Tatar property and civil rights took place in Moscow in 1987 and early 1988; the police and KGB quickly disrupted them. In June 1988 a special commission chaired by Gromyko reported that "no grounds" existed for the restoration of a Crimean Tatar autonomous republic. The population of the peninsula had tripled since the war, the cities were now overwhelmingly Russian and Ukrainian, settlers of those nationaliites had established themselves on the farms, spas catering to Russian trade-unionists dotted the landscape, and—the report did not mention this—party bosses had luxurious villas set in huge parks. There was no room for the people—descendants of Genghis Khan—who had for five centuries called the Crimea home.

Under Khrushchev and Brezhnev, the Communist party tried to make good on its promise—or threat—to create a new, purely "Soviet" nationality. What that meant in practice was the forcing of a Russian culture stripped of its essentials—religion and unfettered artistic creativity—on the other 129 nationalities. The party struck especially hard at the Ukrainians: their institutions of higher learning could not conduct classes in the Ukrainian language, the Ukrainian Catholic Church was outlawed, and in 1975 Kiev firemen were not permitted to extinguish a fire of suspicious origin that destroyed a major part of an ancient Ukrainian library and archive. Pyotr Shelest, Ukrainian party boss under Brezhnev, and his successor, Vladimir Shcherbitsky, slavishly did Moscow's bidding to the point of speaking Russian rather than Ukrainian in public appearances.

Smaller nationalities also felt the heavy hand of Russian overlordship. Russian settlers flooded Kazakhstan and other republics, diluting the native populations with their presence and threatening the survival of native cultures. Russians moved to the major cities of all republics in great numbers. Few learned the native language. Russians had their own schools, and federal-level official business in all republics was transacted in Russian.

The odd troupe of native dancers allowed to tour the USSR and even foreign countries could not hide the Kremlin's long-range designs, which in truth it openly proclaimed: Sooner rather than later, a hybrid *homo sovieticus* would come into being. That was the plan. When the first liberating breezes of *glasnost* swept across the country, however, many nationalities regained their identities.

The Turkic Kazakhs rose up en masse when in December 1986 the Politburo dismissed the aged, corrupt Dinmukhammed Kunayev as leader of the Kazakh branch of the Communist party. Riots erupted in Alma Ata and elsewhere in Kazakhstan over the appointment of Gennadi Kolbin, an ethnic Russian, as the new leader. Grievances that had accumulated for more than half a century burst into the open: the million deaths—a greater percentage than in any other area—during collectivization; the suppression of the Kazakh language and culture; the influx of Russians that gave them a plurality—40.8 percent to 36 percent Kazakhs—in the republic; the burial of Kazakh soldiers who fell in Afghanistan in military cemeteries rather than in Muslim sacred ground.

The government put down the riots, which it had shown on television and publicly blamed on "youth from a degenerate class," but it tacitly acknowledged that the uprising had deep-seated roots. Within days of taking office, Kolbin had Alma-Ata's food

(Map by Larry Fogel, *The Washington Post*)

stores fully stocked; under Kunayev, one-third of the city's supplies had been reserved for the elite. Kolbin ordered that a Kazakh-Russian dictionary begun in the late 1950s be published and pledged to improve the teaching of the Kazakh language in schools; non-Kazakh officials and residents were encourged to learn the language. The exposure and punishment of Kunayev-era corruption intensified.

The most important lesson of the Alma-Ata disorders was not lost on the Kremlin: Gorbachev quietly brought his anti-Islam campaign to a halt. The war in Afghanistan could not be won by any means, least of all by alienating still further 50 million Soviet Muslims.

In regions where long-standing ethno-religious disputes existed, it had long been Communist policy to divide and rule, at times by gerrymandering the borders of republics and smaller administrative districts. Just eight years after the first 20th-century holocaust saw the Turks of Turkey massacre 1.5 million Armenians, in 1923 the Kremlin deliberately assigned an Armenian region, Nagorno-Karabakh, to the Azerbaijani republic. The Azerbaijanis are a Turkic people—in the main Shiite Muslims, while the Armenians are Christian.

Armenians had long lobbied unsuccessfully for the return of Nagorno-Karabakh; in 1988 the dispute erupted. Not only in Nagorno-Karabakh but also in Baku and Yerevan, riots that dwarfed events in Alma Ata resulted in more than 100 deaths and uncounted injuries. The Soviet mass media again covered the developments and in so doing shattered forever the myth of the "great friendship" between the country's many nationalities. A second governmental commission studied the problem briefly and recommended that Nagorno-Karabakh, despite its nearly 80 percent Armenian majority, should remain part of the Azerbaijani republic.

Any other decision would almost certainly have produced a violent reaction in Azerbaijan and other Muslim republics. Party leaders in both Azerbaijan and Armenia lost their jobs for failing to keep ethnic tensions in check.

In neighboring Georgia, scene of frequent violent outbursts of nationalism rarely reported until the age of *glasnost,* massive demonstrations erupted in April 1989 as Georgians demanded greater independence from Moscow. Paradoxically, the riots were ignited earlier in the month in the Abkhazian ASSR (Autonomous Soviet Socialist Republic), a part of Georgia: the Abkhazians, a Caucasian people quite distinct from the Georgians ethnically and linguistically, began clamoring for their own independence. Georgian officials and the public refused even to discuss the matter; but the challenge inflamed nationalist passions.

The largest manifestation occurred on

## ARMENIA

**Total population:** 3,037,259
**Armenians:** 2,724,975
**Azerbaijanis:** 160,841
**Russians:** 70,336

## AZERBAIJAN

**Total population:** 6,026,515
**Armenians:** 475,486
**Azerbaijanis:** 4,708,832
**Russians:** 475,255

## NAGORNO-KARABAKH

**Total population:** 162,181
**Armenians:** 123,076
**Azerbaijanis:** 37,264
**Russians:** 1,265

SOURCE: Soviet Census, 1979

(Map by Brad Wye, *The Washington Post*)

April 14, the eleventh anniversary of the restoration of Georgian as the official language of the republic; the Brezhnev regime had attempted and failed to stifle Georgian nationalism by substituting Russian. The language victory inspired many Georgians to distance themselves still further from Moscow and the Russians. The generally permissive atmosphere of the Gorbachev era, coupled with the threat—which the Tbilisi crowds vastly exaggerated—from Abkhazia, led to the events of April 14.

In a scene ominously reminiscent of St. Petersburg's 1905 "Bloody Sunday," Georgian Communist party leaders overreacted to the peaceful demonstration and called out troops untrained in crowd control. The Soviet Army used sharpened shovels, hardwood cudgels, tear gas, and—incredibly—poison gas against the demonstrators, whose ranks included thousands of women, children, and elderly people. About 40 deaths resulted, and several hundred serious injuries. Foreign Minister Shevardnadze, a Georgian, flew to Tbilisi to direct the restoration of order. Accepting responsibility, the head of the party, the premier, and the president of the republic resigned.

The new Georgian republic Communist party chief revealed the use of poison gas. For nearly three weeks, however, the Army refused to disclose the chemical composition of the gas; physicians had to treat the surviving victims by trial and error. The blood in Tbilisi's streets mingled with that of Nagorno-Karabakh, Alma Ata, Baku, Yerevan, Yakutsk, Vilnius, and other Soviet cities.

Far to the north, in the smallest but most productive and literate republic, Estonia, *glasnost* permitted the blossoming of yet another nationalist movement with major implications for the federal structure of the state. Unfurling the forbidden blue-black-white flag of independent—from 1918 to

1940—Estonia, the Finnic Estonian people established the People's Front. The organization proclaimed independence from the Communist party and indeed did not permit Communist officials to occupy leadership posts. The Front demanded an end to Moscow's control of more than 90 percent of Estonian industry. Tired of its colonial status, Estonia would be in the vanguard of the "self-financing" movement and would control its own industries, selling their output to Moscow—for hard currency. The Estonians also demanded establishment of their own language as the republic's official tongue, restrictions on immigration, especially of Russians, and the right to veto All-Union laws. The People's Front stopped just short of calling for complete independence, but in November 1988 the Estonian Communist party leadership itself declared the "supremacy of the Estonian Supreme Court's laws over the laws of the USSR."

The Kremlin quickly rejected both the Estonian claims and the more modest demands they spawned in Latvia and Lithuania. The Gorbachev regime would allow the display of flags, formation of quasi-political popular fronts, free debate in republican parliaments, and reaffirmation of national cultures, but it would not tolerate secessionist movements—a right guaranteed on paper since 1918 to all constituent republics of the union.

The events described here constituted only a fraction of the nationality problems that confronted the Kremlin, but such conflicts did not threaten *glasnost* in the way some foreign observers suggested. As Andrew Ezergailis has pointed out,*

National[ist]s can be bought off; their movements can be split, as Lenin so successfully demonstrated during the civil war, and Stalin even more success-

_____
*New York Times Magazine, April 23, 1989

fully thereafter. Nationalists can be satisfied by a variety of political forms—constitutionalism, dictatorship or even tyranny. Only democracy is contagious and international; it ripples across frontiers and ethnic boundaries. The threat of the republics, if it is a threat, is that they will network with each other and with the liberation movement in Moscow and Leningrad.

## FOREIGN AFFAIRS

The urgent need to restructure the Soviet economy stemmed not only from the system's internal contradictions but also from various elements of a foreign policy predicated on military strength and a view of capitalism a hundred years out of date. At the cost of nearly bankrupting the nation and a miserably low standard of living, the USSR had achieved nuclear parity with the United States and its allies and had built a military machine that was on paper a match for the West and China together. The crushing burden of military spending, which some experts estimated at as much as 25 percent of gross national product, had succeeded in making the Soviet Union poorer, but not more secure.

Few people outside the Soviet defense establishment would argue with such an assessment, which taken in isolation, however, begs the question. A mere reduction in expenditures on conventional arms—cutbacks in nuclear weapons bring relatively little savings—without a reappraisal of the theoretical basis of its foreign policy could not solve the fundamental dilemmas that faced the Kremlin toward the end of the 20th century. In their first four years in power, the architects of *glasnost* and *perestroika* appeared determined to reduce defense expenditures and cautiously inclined to reexamine the premises that have guided Soviet foreign policy since World War II.

The Soviet Union agreed to a humiliating

withdrawal from Afghanistan because it had no choice. A public opinion unleashed by *glasnost* overwhelmingly opposed the conflict, which had sapped the blood and morale of the nation while depleting the state treasury. Not only that: with American surface-to-air missiles in the hands of the Afghan guerrillas, the war that was never winnable was lost. The Soviet Army could hold Kabul and a few fortified outposts, but nothing else. After the United States agreed to stop supplying weapons to the guerrillas, Soviet troops began a withdrawal that was completed by early 1989.

By coincidence, Soviet-American negotiations aimed at reducing the numbers of short- and intermediate-range nuclear weapons in Europe began the day after Gorbachev became general secretary. The new regime revamped its delegation and issued new instructions. At last there were men in the Kremlin who understood that the United States would accept nothing less than the famous "zero option": no Soviet nuclear missiles aimed at Western Europe, and removal of all such American weapons based in Western Europe and aimed at the USSR. A treaty embodying this agreement was signed at the third meeting between Gorbachev and President Reagan in Washington in December 1987.

The first of those meetings had taken

New York, December 1988. (The New York Times/Paul Hosefros)

place two years earlier in Geneva, the second in Reykjavik in October 1986; the final "summit" saw Reagan go to Moscow in May–June 1988. Despite the agreement on the shorter-range missiles, fundamental disagreements remained. The American side insisted on its right to proceed with research and development of the Strategic Defense Initiative's "space shield," a futuristic construct the Soviets insisted would violate a 1972 treaty. If the Afghanistan war and the Soviet-Cuban intervention in Angola appeared to be winding down, other regional conflicts remained in Cambodia, Nicaragua, the Middle East, and elsewhere. The Soviets continued to finance a North Korean military build-up that went far beyond any legitimate defense needs.

But Soviet thinking was changing. Like General de Gaulle, Gorbachev frequently spoke in terms of a Europe "from the Atlantic to the Urals." Attempting to demonstrate his country's wish to play a peaceful role in the European community, in December 1988 Gorbachev spoke before the United Nations and announced the impending withdrawal of 50,000 troops and 5,000 tanks from bases in Eastern Europe as part of an overall plan to reduce the Soviet Army by 500,000 men and 10,000 tanks over two years.

Western analysts differed on the significance of these proposals, although most argued that the Soviets would retain overwhelming conventional-force superiority in Europe. Such an argument missed at least one major point: the Soviets enjoyed a superiority because West European nations refused to bear anything remotely resembling a fair share of the costs of maintaining NATO. Beyond that, Gorbachev and his people realized that, with American short- and medium-range nuclear missiles leaving Europe, the Continent no longer posed any serious threat to Soviet security; a NATO inferior in con-

ventional weapons could hardly mount an invasion *à la* Napoleon or Hitler. Needing Europe—for technology and loans to finance *perestroika*—far more than it needed him, Gorbachev appeared to appreciate the symmetry of simultaneous rapprochement with the Americans and reintegration—for the first time since 1917—into the European continent.

The great unknown in Soviet foreign affairs remained China. A modest warming trend in Moscow-Beijing relations developed in 1987–1988, and a "summit" meeting was scheduled for May 1989. Soviet military cutbacks were no less welcome in China than in the West; between them, the two countries spent enormous sums each year to guard their common border, sums more profitably employed on *perestroika* and *gaige*.

As he prepared to negotiate with new American and Chinese leaders, Gorbachev found himself in a favorable position. He had played a major role in reducing world tensions: he had ended the Afghan war, which in January 1989 he called a "sin"; he and Ronald Reagan had signed the most important arms control agreement in a quarter of a century; he had made a highly publicized pledge to reduce both conventional and nuclear arms; he held out an olive branch to China. All this won the Soviet leader enormous popularity in the West; Gorbachev had at least for a time deprived the United States and its allies of an enemy.

## THE GORBACHEV REVOLUTION

Early in his administration, Mikhail Gorbachev called for the revival of the country's 52,000 Soviets, which he proposed to develop into administrative instruments of democracy as he understood the term. He clearly had in mind the bodies that had come into existence spontaneously in 1917. The suddenly liberated peoples of the Russian Empire had voiced their aspirations through those Soviets, which were however quickly submerged beneath the onrushing tide of bureaucratic despotism set in motion by the Communist party.

The restoration of the Soviets in their original form had not taken place by the spring of 1989, and indeed it seemed unlikely that institutions peculiar to 1917–1918 could be replicated at the end of the 20th century. Whatever the fate of Gorbachev's revolution, however, the *perverted* Soviet period of 1918–1985 had clearly come to an end. As Gorbachev completed his first four years in power, no reasonable individual could doubt his commitment to a revolution as authentic as it was invented. His enemies charged him with digging the grave of "socialism," their euphemism for the Stalinism he was indeed trying to bury.

Whether Gorbachev would lead his country to a uniquely Soviet democratic socialism remained to be seen. The dynamic general secretary appeared more firmly wedded to one-party rule than to socialism, and even those who wished him well remembered that it was *Stalin* who called in 1929 for "decisive victories" in "socialist *perestroika* (reconstruction)."*

Change never lacks enemies, but come what will in the Soviet Union, Gorbachev has made an indelible mark on his times. As he entered his fifth year in power, he seemed close to completing what Nikita Khrushchev—now restored to a place of honor in the Soviet pantheon—had begun: He gave the Soviet people back their history, and thus hope for the future.

---

*Stalin, *Sochineniia* (Works), vol. 12, Moscow: Gospolitizdat, 1949, p. 118.

## SUGGESTED ADDITIONAL READING

**Aganbegyan, Abel G.,** *The Economic Challenge of Perestroika,* Bloomington: Indiana University Press, 1988

———, ed., *Perestroika,* New York: Scribner's, 1989

**Akiner, Shirin,** *Islamic Peoples of the Soviet Union,* London: Kegan Paul International, 1983

**Bennigsen, Alexandre, and S. Enders Wimbush,** *Muslims of the Soviet Empire,* Bloomington: Indiana University Press, 1986

**Buss, Gerald,** *The Bear's Hug: Christian Belief and the Soviet State, 1917–1986,* Grand Rapids, Mich.: Wm.B. Eerdmans, 1987

**Ellis, Jane,** *The Russian Orthodox Church,* Bloomington: Indiana University Press, 1986

**Friedberg, Maurice, and Heyward Isham, eds.,** *Soviet Society under Gorbachev,* Armonk, N.Y.: M.E. Sharpe, 1987

**Goldfarb, Jeffrey C.,** *Beyond Glasnost: The Post-Totalitarian Mind,* Chicago: University of Chicago Press, 1989

**Gorbachev, Mikhail S.,** *Perestroika,* New York: Harper & Row, 1987

**Goricheva, Tatiana,** *Talking About God Is Dangerous,* New York: Crossroad Publishing Co., 1987

**Hewett, Ed A.,** *Reforming the Soviet Economy,* Washington: Brookings Institution, 1988

**Karkins, Rasma,** *Ethnic Relations in the U.S.S.R.,* Winchester, Mass.: Allen & Unwin, 1988

**Kozlov, Viktor,** *The Peoples of the Soviet Union,* Bloomington: Indiana University Press, 1988

**Lefever, Ernest W., and Robert D. Vander Lugt, eds.,** *Perestroika: How New Is Gorbachev's New Thinking?,* Washington: Ethics and Public Policy Center, 1989

**Lewin, Moshe,** *The Gorbachev Phenomenon,* Berkeley: University of California Press, 1988

**Lubin, Nancy,** *Labour and Nationality in Soviet Central Asia,* Princeton, N.J.: Princeton University Press, 1985

**Sherr, Alan B.,** *The Other Side of Arms Control: Soviet Objectives in the Gorbachev Era,* Boston: Unwin Hyman, 1988

**Subtelny, Orest,** *Ukraine: A History,* Toronto: University of Toronto Press, 1988

**Suny, Ronald G.,** *The Making of the Georgian Nation,* Bloomington: Indiana University Press, 1988

**Wixman, Ronald,** *The Peoples of the USSR: An Ethnographic Handbook,* Armonk, N.Y.: M.E. Sharpe, 1984

# INDEX